REDESCRIBING PAUL
AND THE CORINTHIANS

SBL

Society of Biblical Literature

Early Christianity and Its Literature

Series Editor
Gail R. O'Day

Editorial Board
Warren Carter
Beverly Roberts Gaventa
Judith M. Lieu
Joseph Verheyden
Sze-kar Wan

Number 5

REDESCRIBING PAUL AND THE CORINTHIANS

REDESCRIBING PAUL
AND THE CORINTHIANS

Edited by

Ron Cameron

and

Merrill P. Miller

Society of Biblical Literature
Atlanta

REDESCRIBING PAUL
AND THE CORINTHIANS

Copyright © 2011 by the Society of Biblical Literature

All rights reserved. No part of this work may be reproduced or transmitted in any form or by any means, electronic or mechanical, including photocopying and recording, or by means of any information storage or retrieval system, except as may be expressly permitted by the 1976 Copyright Act or in writing from the publisher. Requests for permission should be addressed in writing to the Rights and Permissions Office, Society of Biblical Literature, 825 Houston Mill Road, Atlanta, GA 30329 USA.

Library of Congress Cataloging-in-Publication Data

Redescribing Paul and the Corinthians / Ron Cameron, Merrill P. Miller, editors.
    p. cm. — (Early Christianity and its literature ; no. 5)
    Includes bibliographical references and index.
    ISBN 978-1-58983-528-3 (paper binding : alk. paper) — ISBN 978-1-58983-529-0 (electronic format : alk. paper)
    1. Bible. N.T. Corinthians, 1st—Criticism, interpretation, etc. 2. Corinth (Greece)—Church history. I. Cameron, Ron. II. Miller, Merrill P. III. Society of Biblical Literature.
    BS2675.52.R43 2010
    227'.206—dc22
                      2010042833

18 17 16 15 14 13 12 11   5 4 3 2 1

Printed on acid-free, recycled paper conforming to
ANSI/NISO Z39.48–1992 (R1997) and ISO 9706:1994
standards for paper permanence.

Dedicated to

Yaffa Frenkel Miller
(August 9, 1946–September 1, 2010)

In loving memory

Contents

Abbreviations.. ix

Introducing Paul and the Corinthians
   Ron Cameron and Merrill P. Miller 1

Re: Corinthians
   Jonathan Z. Smith 17

Rereading the Christ Myth: Paul's Gospel and
the Christ Cult Question
   Burton L. Mack 35

Bringing Paul and the Corinthians Together? A Rejoinder
and Some Proposals on Redescription and Theory
   William E. Arnal 75

Kinds of Myth, Meals, and Power: Paul and the Corinthians
   Stanley K. Stowers 105

Paul's "Apocalypticism" and the Jesus Associations at Thessalonica
and Corinth
   Richard S. Ascough... 151

Greco-Roman *Thiasoi*, the *Ekklēsia* at Corinth,
and Conflict Management
   John S. Kloppenborg... 187

Does Pauline Christianity Resemble a Hellenistic Philosophy?
   Stanley K. Stowers 219

Redescribing Paul and the Corinthians
   Ron Cameron and Merrill P. Miller 245

Selected Bibliography 303

Index of Ancient Texts. 309

Select Index of Modern Authors 319

Index of Subjects 321

Contributors. 325

Abbreviations

Primary Sources

Apost. Const.	*Apostolic Constitutions*
Appian	
Hist. rom.	*Historia romana* / *Roman History*
Aristotle	
Eth. nic.	*Ethica nichomachea* / *Nicomachean Ethics*
CIG	*Corpus inscriptionum graecarum.* Edited by A. Boeckh et al. 4 vols. Berlin: Ex Officina Academica, 1828–77.
CIJ	*Corpus inscriptionum judaicarum.* Edited by Jean Baptiste Frey. Vatican City: Pontificio istituto di archeologia Cristiana, 1936–.
CIL	*Corpus inscriptionum latinarum.* Berlin: Reimer, 1862–.
1 Clem.	*1 Clement*
Did.	*Didache*
Did. Apost.	*Didascalia apostolorum*
Epictetus	
Diatr.	*Diatribae* (*Dissertationes*)
Epiphanius	
Pan.	*Panarion* (*Adversus haereses*) / *Refutation of All Heresies*
Eusebius	
Hist. eccl.	*Historia ecclesiastica* / *Ecclesiastical History*
Herodotus	
Hist.	*Historiae* / *Histories*
Hippocrates	
Morb. sacr.	*De morbo sacro* / *The Sacred Disease*
IG	*Inscriptiones graecae.* Berlin: Reimer, 1873–; Berlin: de Gruyter, 1895–.
ILS	*Inscriptiones latinae selectae.* Edited by Hermann Dessau. Berlin: Weidmann, 1892–1916.
Josephus	
Ag. Ap.	*Contra Apionem* / *Against Apion*
Ant.	*Antiquitates judaicae* / *Jewish Antiquities*
War	*Bellum judaicum* / *Jewish War*

Justin
  1 Apol.   *First Apology*
KJV   King James Version
Lucian
  Peregr.   *De morte Peregrini / The Passing of Peregrinus*
LXX   Septuagint
MAMA   *Monumenta Asiae Minoris antique.* Manchester: Manchester University Press; London: Longmans, Green, 1928–93.
NRSV   New Revised Standard Version
Origen
  Cels.   *Contra Celsum / Against Celsus*
Pausanias
  Descr.   *Graeciae descriptio / Description of Greece*
Petronius
  Satyr.   *Satyricon*
Philo
  Gig.   *De gigantibus / On Giants*
  Hypoth.   *Hypothetica / Hypothetica*
  Legat.   *Legatio ad Gaium / On the Embassy to Gaius*
  Mos.   *De vita Mosis / On the Life of Moses*
  Prob.   *Quod omnis probus liber sit / That Every Good Person Is Free*
  Sacr.   *De sacrificiis Abelis et Caini / On the Sacrifices of Cain and Abel*
  Virt.   *De virtutibus / On the Virtues*
Pindar
  Nem.   *Nemeonikai / Nemean Odes*
Plato
  Pol.   *Politicus / Statesman*
Pliny the Elder
  Nat.   *Naturalis historia / Natural History*
Pliny the Younger
  Ep.   *Epistulae*
Plutarch
  Def. orac. *De defectu oraculorum*
  Stoic. abs. *Stoicos absurdiora poetis dicere*
RSV   Revised Standard Version
SEG   *Supplementum epigraphicum graecum.* Amsterdam: Gieben, 1923–.
Seneca
  Ep.   *Epistulae morales*
  Herc. fur. *Hercules furens*
  Prov.   *De providentia*
SIG   *Sylloge inscriptionum graecarum.* Edited by Wilhelm Dittenberger. 3rd ed. 4 vols. Leipzig: Hirzel, 1915–24.

Strabo
   Geogr.   *Geographica / Geography*
Tertullian
   Apol.   *Apologeticus / Apology*
Theophrastus
   Caus. plant.   *De causis plantarum*
   Hist. plant.   *Historia plantarum*

Secondary Sources

AB	Anchor Bible
ABD	*Anchor Bible Dictionary*. Edited by David Noel Freedman. 6 vols. New York: Doubleday, 1992.
AGJU	Arbeiten zur Geschichte des antiken Judentums und des Urchristentums
AJA	*American Journal of Archaeology*
AJP	*American Journal of Philology*
ANRW	*Aufstieg und Niedergang der römischen Welt: Geschichte und Kultur Roms im Spiegel der neueren Forschung*. Edited by H. Temporini and W. Haase. Berlin: de Gruyter, 1972–.
ASOR	American Schools of Oriental Research
BCH	*Bulletin de correspondance hellénique*
BCSSR	*Bulletin: Council of Societies for the Study of Religion*
BibInt	Biblical Interpretation
BJS	Brown Judaic Studies
BTB	*Biblical Theology Bulletin*
ByzF	*Byzantinische Forschungen*
BZNW	Beihefte zur Zeitschrift für die neutestamentliche Wissenschaft
CahRB	Cahiers de la Revue biblique
CBET	Contributions to Biblical Exegesis and Theology
CBQ	*Catholic Biblical Quarterly*
CP	*Classical Philology*
CSHJ	Chicago Studies in the History of Judaism
EPRO	Etudes préliminaires aux religions orientales dans l'empire romain
ER	*The Encyclopedia of Religion*. Edited by Mircea Eliade. 16 vols. New York: Macmillan, 1987.
FF	Foundations and Facets
FRLANT	Forschungen zur Religion und Literatur des Alten und Neuen Testaments
GCS	Die griechische christliche Schriftsteller der ersten [drei] Jahrhunderte
GNS	Good News Studies

GR	*Greece and Rome*
HDR	Harvard Dissertations in Religion
HNT	Handbuch zum Neuen Testament
HNTC	Harper's New Testament Commentaries
HO	Handbuch der Orientalistik
HR	*History of Religions*
HSM	Harvard Semitic Monographs
HTR	*Harvard Theological Review*
HTS	Harvard Theological Studies
HUT	Hermeneutische Untersuchungen zur Theologie
JAC	Jahrbuch für Antike und Christentum
JBL	*Journal of Biblical Literature*
JECS	*Journal of Early Christian Studies*
JJS	*Journal of Jewish Studies*
JR	*Journal of Religion*
JRH	*Journal of Religious History*
JRS	*Journal of Roman Studies*
JSJ	*Journal for the Study of Judaism in the Persian, Hellenistic, and Roman Periods*
JSNT	*Journal for the Study of the New Testament*
JSNTSup	Journal for the Study of the New Testament Supplement Series
JTSA	*Journal of Theology for Southern Africa*
KEK	Kritisch-exegetischer Kommentar über das Neue Testament (Meyer-Kommentar)
LCL	Loeb Classical Library
LSJ	Liddell, H. G., R. Scott, H. S. Jones. *A Greek-English Lexicon*. 9th ed. with revised supplement. Oxford: Oxford University Press, 1996.
MTSR	*Method and Theory in the Study of Religion*
NewDocs	*New Documents Illustrating Early Christianity*. Edited by G. H. R. Horsley and S. Llewelyn. North Ryde, N.S.W.: Ancient History Documentary Research Center, Macquarie University, 1981–.
NIGTC	New International Greek Testament Commentary
NovT	*Novum Testamentum*
NovTSup	Novum Testamentum Supplements
NPNF	*Nicene and Post-Nicene Fathers*
NTAbh	Neutestamentliche Abhandlungen
NTOA	Novum Testamentum et Orbis Antiquus
NTS	*New Testament Studies*
OCD	*Oxford Classical Dictionary*. Edited by S. Hornblower and A. Spawforth. 3rd ed. Oxford: Oxford University Press, 1996.

OTP	*Old Testament Pseudepigrapha.* Edited by James H. Charlesworth. 2 vols. Garden City, N.Y.: Doubleday, 1983.
PW	Pauly, A. F. *Paulys Realencyclopädie der classischen Altertumswissenschaft.* Edited by G. Wissowa. 49 vols. Munich: A. Druckenmüller, 1980.
RB	*Revue biblique*
RGG	*Religion in Geschichte und Gegenwart*
SBL	Society of Biblical Literature
SBLDS	Society of Biblical Literature Dissertation Series
SBLSP	Society of Biblical Literature Seminar Papers
SBLSymS	Society of Biblical Literature Symposium Series
SBS	Stuttgarter Bibelstudien
SemeiaSt	Semeia Studies
SJLA	Studies in Judaism in Late Antiquity
SNTSMS	Society for New Testament Studies Monograph Series
SP	Sacra pagina
StPB	Studia post-biblica
TSAJ	Texte und Studien zum antiken Judentum
TU	Texte und Untersuchungen
TynBul	*Tyndale Bulletin*
USQR	*Union Seminary Quarterly Review*
UUA	Uppsala Universitetsårskrift
WUNT	Wissenschaftliche Untersuchungen zum Neuen Testament
ZNW	*Zeitschrift für die neutestamentliche Wissenschaft und die Kunde der älteren Kirche*
ZPE	*Zeitschrift für Papyrologie und Epigraphik*
ZWT	*Zeitschrift für wissenschaftliche Theologie*

Introducing Paul and the Corinthians

Ron Cameron and Merrill P. Miller

This is the second of a proposed three-volume set of studies by members of the Society of Biblical Literature's Seminar on Ancient Myths and Modern Theories of Christian Origins, concerned with redescribing the beginnings of Christianity as religion.[1] *Redescription* is a form of explanation that privileges difference and involves comparison and translation, category formation and rectification, definition and theory. The writers of the papers in this volume have proposed explanations of the following issues central to Paul and the Corinthians: (1) the relationship between Paul and the recipients of 1 Corinthians; (2) the place of Paul's Christ myth for his gospel; (3) the reasons for a disinterest in and the rejection of Paul's gospel, and/or for the reception and attraction of his gospel; and (4) the disjunction between Paul's collective representation of the Corinthians in 1 Corinthians and the Corinthians' own engagement with Paul in mythmaking and social formation, including differentiated responses to his gospel and mutual (mis)translation and (mis)appropriation of the other's discourse and practices. Some explanations of these matters stand in tension, though they do not have to be seen as mutually exclusive proposals. They converge in a set of working assumptions adopted by the seminar.[2]

Redescription

We need to specify how the work of the seminar and the papers in this volume relate to the history of scholarship on Paul and the Corinthians and constitute a set

---

1. The generative problem for a project of redescription, its objectives, rationale, theoretical foundations, primary strategies, working procedures, principal findings, and achievements are discussed in detail in our first volume, as part of a redescription of (1) the Jesus schools of the Sayings Gospel Q and the *Gospel of Thomas*, (2) a possible Jesus school in Jerusalem, and (3) a pre-Pauline *christos* association (Ron Cameron and Merrill P. Miller, eds., *Redescribing Christian Origins* [SBLSymS 28; Atlanta: Society of Biblical Literature; Leiden and Boston: Brill, 2004]).

2. See below, 4–5.

1

for the redescription of the site. The relationship between Paul and the Corinthians was already seen in antiquity as one characterized by disjunction (*1 Clem.* 47). This perception has also set the agenda of modern scholarship on Paul's Corinthian correspondence. The different reasons for the disjunction that have been proposed constitute the history of scholarship since Ferdinand Christian Baur.[3] The proposals include the competing missions of Peter and Paul, the influence of mystery religions and an overrealized eschatology, pneumatic enthusiasm especially associated with Gnosticism, social stratification, political rivalries, philosophical influences and rhetorical sophistication, conventions of friendship, and factionalism associated with patronage.[4] While the reasons given for the disjunction have changed, the picture has largely remained the same:

> The shift in focus from religious or theological ideas to social and political ones nonetheless results in a picture with a familiar structure: rather than focus on Gnostic tendencies or realised eschatology as the Corinthian error that Paul strives to correct, now it is the secular practices of the wealthy or the prevalent imperial ideology that represent[s] the Corinthian failings and the target of Paul's critique. In either case, Paul is the guardian of theological, social, or political correctness in face of the Corinthians' obduracy and error.[5]

---

3. For the most recent critical discussion and exemplification of the history of scholarship with an emphasis on recovering the situation and ethos of the church of Corinth, see Edward Adams and David G. Horrell, eds., *Christianity at Corinth: The Quest for the Pauline Church* (Louisville: Westminster John Knox, 2004). The volume includes a critical survey of scholarship by the editors, followed by eighteen extracts from the history of modern scholarship, beginning with Ferdinand Christian Baur, and concluding with four methodological reflections.

4. See the overview of the different phases, changing trends, and bibliography in David G. Horrell and Edward Adams, "The Scholarly Quest for Paul's Church at Corinth: A Critical Survey," in Adams and Horrell, *Christianity at Corinth*, 13–40. Sociohistorical and social-scientific perspectives have tended to dominate the scholarly agenda on Paul and the Corinthians since the early 1970s (26–34). Among the key issues and debates on the current scholarly scene, Horrell and Adams name in particular (1) the relative weight given to different sources and the particular use of these sources, archaeological and literary, elite and popular; (2) questions of theory and method, sociohistorical approaches versus the more model-oriented approaches of social anthropology, and the necessity of grappling with the social ontology governing different theoretical frameworks; (3) reflexivity concerning the subject position, interests, and ideologies influencing historical reconstruction; and (4) the awareness of multiple contexts impinging on any historical situation and recognition of the entailments and partiality of any reconstruction of an ancient context (40–43; see also the four concluding essays of methodological reflections).

5. Ibid., 33, adding: "In . . . feminist approaches to the Corinthian correspondence, however, we meet a strand of modern scholarship in which the tendency to favour Paul and to criticise the Corinthians has been questioned and, sometimes, firmly reversed" (33–34). See, among others, Elisabeth Schüssler Fiorenza, "Rhetorical Situation and Historical Reconstruction in 1 Corinthians," *NTS* 33 (1987): 386–403; Antoinette Clark Wire, *The Corinthian Women Prophets: A Reconstruction through Paul's Rhetoric* (Minneapolis: Fortress, 1990); Elizabeth A. Castelli, *Imitating Paul: A Discourse of Power* (Literary Currents in Biblical Interpretation; Louisville: Westminster John Knox, 1991).

The present set of papers takes its place within the recent shift in this history, but with an important difference concerning the picture that emerges. We suggest that there is a still more fundamental assumption underlying this pattern of relationship, the assumption that the Corinthians to whom Paul addresses his letters constitute collectively an *ekklēsia* of Christ, at least since the time that Paul first preached to them "Christ crucified," as he says, and won converts to his gospel (1 Cor 2:2; cf. 1:17, 23).[6] This collective identity is a given; it does not have to be argued and defended.[7] How else, it is assumed, can one explain that, despite what

---

6. See Stanley K. Stowers, "Kinds of Myth, Meals, and Power: Paul and the Corinthians," 108 (in this volume): "The idea of a community is the idea of a highly integrated social group based on a common ethos, practices, and beliefs. Paul preached the gospel, people converted, and Paul welded them into a community. With this assumption, Paul's words in 1 Cor 1:10 become the basis for asking the question, How did the Corinthian community become divided? What false doctrine from inside the community, or infiltrating from the outside, corrupted the community or seduced a portion of it?"

7. We have tried to formulate this unexamined assumption carefully. The emphasis falls both on Paul's role in establishing group formation by preaching "Christ crucified" and on the whole idea of the existence of a Corinthian collective that can be identified without question as an *ekklēsia* of Christ before Paul left Corinth. In this formulation, we are taking into account the position of those who have questioned Paul's self-representation of his authority as sole founder ("father," 1 Cor 4:15) of the *ekklēsia* of Corinth, as well as the more common avoidance today of projecting a later established Christian church on the Corinthian situation: "One must not assume that the Corinthians conceived of themselves as 'Christians' in the way that later believers did, given a period of institutional and doctrinal development" (Horrell and Adams, "Scholarly Quest for Paul's Church at Corinth," 1 n. 1). As Margaret Y. MacDonald notes, "It is interesting to examine to what extent the Corinthian church has sometimes been seen as a reflection of 'Christianity' with a separate and distinct identity that can be permeated by influences from the outside. There is great variation with respect to whether the Corinthian correspondence is seen largely as a reflection of life in the *ekklesia* or whether it is located much more broadly within the social-religious-political framework of the Roman world" ("The Shifting Centre: Ideology and the Interpretation of 1 Corinthians," in Adams and Horrell, *Christianity at Corinth*, 276). Similarly, there is today an increased sensitivity to plural identities and affiliations, membership in the *ekklēsia* of Christ being only one—and, perhaps for most who participate, not the most important one. Thus, C. K. Robertson, developing a thesis of overlapping networks, acknowledges that the church was hardly the only group with which the Corinthians could, and wanted to, identify: "Many members remained firmly entrenched in the relational networks in which they previously existed." Paul's departure was the catalyst for giving priority to the claims and roles of their other, preexisting networks rather than to those of the Christian *ekklēsia* (*Conflict in Corinth: Redefining the System* [Studies in Biblical Literature 42; New York: Lang, 2001], 97). And in an influential essay comparing the different relationships of Thessalonian Christians and Corinthian Christians to their respective city environments, John M. G. Barclay writes concerning the Corinthians: "The church [of Corinth] is not a cohesive community but a club, whose meetings provide important moments of spiritual insight and exaltation, but do not have global implications of moral or social change. The Corinthians could gladly participate in this church as one segment of their lives. But the segment, however important, is not the whole and not the centre.... Once again, then, we have an example of the mutual reinforcement of social experience and theological perspective, which this time involves a major realignment of Paul's apocalyptic symbols. When the first Corinthians became Christians, they did not experience hostility, nor was their apostle hounded out of town. And the more firmly the church got established in conditions of social harmony, the more implausible the apocalyptic content of Paul's message became, with its strong implications of social dislocation" ("Thessalonica and Corinth: Social Contrasts in Pauline Christianity," *JSNT* 47

Paul describes as quarrels and factions, he never questions the identity of those he addresses as people who are in Christ, nor distinguishes among the Corinthians in this regard (1 Cor 1:4–7; 11:2; 12:12–13, 27; 15:22–23)? How else can one explain what appear to be Paul's claims and exercise of authority among the Corinthians (1 Cor 3:10–11; 4:15, 18–21; 5:3–5; 11:16; 12:28; 14:37–38; 15:1–2; 16:1–4; and the many instructions he gives throughout the letters)? How else can one account for a long and rather extensive set of exchanges between Paul and the Corinthians (1 Cor 1:11; 2:2; 3:1; 5:9; 7:1; 11:18; 16:5–7, 10–11; 2 Cor 1:15–16, 23; 2:1; 7:6–8; 8:6, 16; 12:14; 13:1–3)? It is this last question, in particular, that elicited sustained debate among members of the seminar. The papers by William E. Arnal and Stanley K. Stowers ("Kinds of Myth, Meals, and Power: Paul and the Corinthians") are extensively rewritten versions of the papers presented at our consultation and seminar and are intended, in part, as critical responses to the papers of Jonathan Z. Smith and Burton L. Mack.

The working assumptions of the seminar on this site require emphasis, since they depart significantly from the usual scholarly assumptions. (1) The collective identity of those to whom Paul writes was never assumed merely on the basis of Paul's representation of the Corinthians or of his own practices. Whether some Corinthians could be characterized as Pauline "Christians" was a matter of debate and, as one can see from the papers in this volume, a question of definition and nuance, requiring the adoption of positions that had to be argued and defended.[8] (2) Corinthian attraction to Paul's gospel was not taken as self-evident. Indeed, it was viewed as a problem that might be amenable to different solutions.[9] (3) What, in fact, was Paul's gospel? The papers in this volume that address the issue have concluded that it cannot be the death and resurrection of Christ, certainly not in any exclusive way that would not require taking account of other Pauline myths.[10]

[1992]: 71). While we do not wish to dismiss or ignore these more plausible perspectives, they continue to presuppose without debate Corinthian social formation as an *ekklēsia* of Christ and assume Paul's gospel as the catalyst (or, at least, the primary catalyst) in this social formation.

8. E.g., Stowers states, "In my view, two things are very clear from the evidence of the Corinthian letters: first, Paul very much wanted the people to whom he wrote to be a community, and he held a theory saying that God had miraculously made them into a community 'in Christ'; second, the Corinthians never did sociologically form a community and only partly and differentially shared Paul's interests and formation" ("Kinds of Myth," 109).

9. Thus, Stowers's "solution" ("Kinds of Myth") is related differentially to a recognition of Paul as a producer and distributor of specialized knowledge. In contrast, William E. Arnal's "solution" ("Bringing Paul and the Corinthians Together? A Rejoinder and Some Proposals on Redescription and Theory") is related, also differentially, to a multiethnic mix and conditions of dislocation from homelands with their attendant processes of deracination.

10. The papers in this volume by Arnal, Burton L. Mack ("Rereading the Christ Myth: Paul's Gospel and the Christ Cult Question"), and Stowers ("Kinds of Myth") highlight the importance of Paul's Abraham myth and his Spirit myth. All of these papers, along with Jonathan Z. Smith's ("Re: Corinthians"), agree that discourse associated with spirits/Spirit was likely to have been a source of mutual interest, a contributing factor to sustaining communication between Paul and the Corinthians.

(4) Instead of focusing on what pertained or happened after Paul left Corinth, we thought that the problems and issues identified in Paul's letters were just as likely to tell us something about who the Corinthians were before Paul got to Corinth and, therefore, how we might imagine their initial response to Paul.[11] In sum, these working assumptions, which have elicited argument and debate in the course of the seminar's work, have contributed to the conclusions attested in the papers as a set, that Paul as founder and community builder, the Corinthians as converts to the Christ myth and ritual, and the *ekklēsia* of Corinth as a singular, bounded, collective identity must all be questioned; and though not necessarily dismissed, they must be explained and appropriately qualified, if they are to hold any conviction.[12]

---

11. We have already referred to an increased appreciation among scholars concerning the effect of continuing outside influences on relations within the *ekklēsia* of Corinth, though there is a wide range of views about the nature of these influences. In general, they are understood as bundles of practices, associations, networks, and interactions constitutive of affiliations and identity formations continuing after the Corinthians formed an *ekklēsia* of Christ in response to Paul's activity (and, perhaps, to the activity of other apostles and teachers as well). But this recognition never seems to call for questioning whether these prior affiliations and identity formations may have occasioned, in the first place, resistance to the formation of Christ-identified groups. One need not conclude from such questioning that Paul's activity would have met with no interest by Corinthian groups already in existence, nor that Paul could not have had extensive contact with individuals and households affiliated with such groups. None of the papers in this volume actually argues that Paul's teaching would have met with no interest or positive response from any Corinthians. On the other hand, the place where efforts in the interest of boundary formation for an *ekklēsia* of Christ can be found in abundance is in the letters of Paul.

12. On Paul's intrusion in Thessalonica on a previously existing professional association, see Richard S. Ascough, "The Thessalonian Christian Community as a Professional Voluntary Association," *JBL* 119 (2000): 311–28. Ascough proposes that Paul's preaching led the association to exchange its patron deity. Arnal has developed Ascough's proposal but modified some of the dynamics, suggesting that Paul's intervention led initially to the formation of a subgroup. He applies a model to Corinth drawn from a contemporary film, *The Fight Club*, arguing that it is a more plausible way to understand the dynamics of Paul's intrusion on an existing group in Corinth and, at the same time, to account for the data of the Corinthian correspondence ("Paul and the Corinthians," 83–89 [in this volume]). Arnal's striking observation about Romans should also be noted: "If we wish to test the hypothesis that Paul (habitually?) addresses himself to already constituted non-'Christian' groups, Romans would probably be the best place to start" (94 n. 44). John S. Kloppenborg's statement regarding responsibility for the formation and organization of associations is also pertinent, though he is not necessarily questioning the identity of these associations as groups devoted to Christ: "Much of the conceptual apparatus employed in the description of Pauline communities derives either from Acts, according to which Pauline groups are offshoots of synagogues, or from Paul's own rhetoric, according to which Paul 'founded' churches and claimed responsibility for their organization and orientation. This is to confuse rhetorical statement and its persuasive goals with a description of Pauline communities" ("Critical Histories and Theories of Religion: A Response to Burton Mack and Ron Cameron," *MTSR* 8 [1996]: 282–83, cited more fully in Richard S. Ascough, "Paul's 'Apocalypticism' and the Jesus Associations at Thessalonica and Corinth," 173 [in this volume]). On the relation of Paul's Christ myth to Corinthian social formation, Smith has concluded: "This experiment in redescription suggests that a Christ myth, as represented by Paul in the course of his intrusion on the Corinthians, would have been uninteresting to some Corinthians; and that a spirit myth, as they appear to have understood it, might have been interesting to some Corinthians in that it was 'good to

Double Disjunction

Following the sessions of the second year of the seminar, the steering committee decided to turn to Paul and the Corinthians as the next site for redescription. It was already clear at the time of the decision that the seminar would be engaged with a "double disjunction": Paul and the Corinthians, on the one hand, and Paul and the Jesus-*christos* associations, our hypothetical site in the work just completed, on the other.[13] With respect to the latter disjunction, the still influential Germanic tradition of a pre-Pauline Hellenistic Christ cult had already been called into question as the site of the introduction and usage of the term *christos*:

> In our redescriptions of a possible Jesus school in Jerusalem and of the Jesus-*christos* association, both "Jerusalem" and "Christ" turn out to be pre-Pauline, diaspora issues and constructions, not what has been imagined as either "the kerygma of the earliest Church" or "the Hellenistic Church aside from Paul." All this is the consequence of our having begun to extend the reconstructed Jesus movements into the pre-Pauline sphere.[14]

But crucial matters pertaining to this disjunction remained unexplored. The social context and significance of the Christ myth and ritual, as they appear in Paul's explicit references to "traditions" in 1 Cor 11 and 15, had not been located. While the paper by Mack in this volume treats issues bearing on the Paul–Corinthian disjunction, the primary assignment and goal of his paper were to locate the form, social context, and logic of the "traditions" that Paul cites in 1 Corinthians.

---

think'" ("Re: Corinthians," 34 [in this volume], quoting Claude Lévi-Strauss, *Totemism* [trans. Rodney Needham; Boston: Beacon, 1963], 89). On the assumed singularity and centrality of the Christ myth for Paul's gospel, Mack has stated: "It might be good to question the single myth, single *kērygma* assumption," and continues, following Stowers, "Paul did not get the idea of a mission to the Gentiles from the Christ myth" ("Rereading the Christ Myth," 59; cf. 38 [in this volume], citing Stanley K. Stowers, *A Rereading of Romans: Justice, Jews, and Gentiles* [New Haven: Yale University Press, 1994], 71, 307; cf. 167, 171, 225, 229). And Stowers has questioned the contemporary Christian imagination of Pauline communities because it is grounded in conditions that could not have obtained in Paul's time: "In fact, it takes a massive cultural-institutional structure, say with something like bishops, textually oriented religious education, the massive production and religious use of texts, and so on, in order to reproduce religions that focus on intellectual practices and doctrines of need and salvation. Greek and Roman religion and the religion of the Judean temple were not such religions. It is unlikely that Paul's formation and interests substantially overlapped with those of most of the Corinthians" ("Kinds of Myth," 108–9).

13. See Ron Cameron, "Agenda for the Annual Meeting, Discussion, and Reflections," in Cameron and Miller, *Redescribing Christian Origins*, 419: "The notion of a *christos* association belongs to a redefinition of 'pre-Pauline' as something that looks like, and has links with, the Jesus movements, which is not the conventional scholarly understanding of 'pre-Pauline Hellenistic Christianity.'"

14. Ibid., citing Rudolf Bultmann, *Theology of the New Testament* (trans. Kendrick Grobel; 2 vols.; London: SCM, 1952–55), 1:33, 63.

Mack's thesis, "that both the 'Christ myth' and the 'ritual meal' text can be traced to mythmaking within the Jesus schools at some point where the thought of Jesus as a martyr for their cause was entertained,"[15] draws on earlier work of the seminar.[16] The thesis entails a significant revision of his chapter on the "Congregations of the Christ" in *A Myth of Innocence*, where Mack had located the Christ myth and ritual traditions of 1 Cor 11 and 15 in the Hellenistic Christ cult.[17] Moreover, by arguing that the social logic of the martyr myth as an enhancement of the status of Jesus and as a myth of origins is entirely plausible in the context of Jesus schools and Jesus-*christos* associations, Mack has made a signal contribution to the larger project of the seminar to redraw the map of Christian beginnings. But we would like to point out, especially, the way in which his study addresses several significant issues that were on the table and debated, but hardly resolved, in *Redescribing Christian Origins*.[18]

Mack's paper is the only one in this volume that treats the second disjunction to which we have been referring. This fact relates to a concern among some members of the seminar that we should not return to the construction of hypothetical sites to "risk crash-landing our conceptual craft on hardly visible . . . runways," as Willi Braun put it,[19] runways that are constructed largely on the basis of deducing social locations, situations, and interests from the social logic of mythic texts. The issue was not whether our work had made a major contribution to the problematization of the dominant paradigm of Christian origins. On that project goal, there was general agreement about the work of the seminar.[20] Nor was it primarily a question of whether such reconstructions were possible and could be made more plausible than attempts to reduce myths to their supposedly historical core of unique events and numinous experiences. Rather, there were three more fundamental concerns that surfaced. First, that sites should be selected on the basis of the prospects for sharpening our conceptual instruments and testing our categories of mythmaking and social formation. Second, that we should resist giving

---

15. Mack, "Rereading the Christ Myth," 37.
16. Mack has indicated this in the introduction to his paper (ibid., 35–38). See Merrill P. Miller, "The Problem of the Origins of a Messianic Conception of Jesus," in Cameron and Miller, *Redescribing Christian Origins*, 301–35; and, in the same volume, Miller, "The Anointed Jesus," 375–415; Burton L. Mack, "Why *Christos*? The Social Reasons," 365–74; and Christopher R. Matthews, "From Messiahs to Christ: The Pre-Pauline Christ Cult in Scholarship," 349–63.
17. Burton L. Mack, *A Myth of Innocence: Mark and Christian Origins* (Philadelphia: Fortress, 1988; repr., Minneapolis: Fortress, 2006), 98–123.
18. In what follows, see in particular Burton L. Mack, "Backbay Jazz and Blues," in Cameron and Miller, *Redescribing Christian Origins*, 421–31; and, in the same volume, Willi Braun, "Smoke Signals from the North: A Reply to Burton Mack's 'Backbay Jazz and Blues,'" 433–42; and William E. Arnal and Willi Braun, "Social Formation and Mythmaking: Theses on Key Terms," 459–67.
19. Braun, "Smoke Signals from the North," 436.
20. See Ron Cameron and Merrill P. Miller, "Conclusion: Redescribing Christian Origins," in Cameron and Miller, *Redescribing Christian Origins*, 505–6.

even the suspicion that we were engaged in the construction of an alternative narrative paradigm that required the same sequencing of sites found in the canonical narrative. Third, that we should give analytical priority to social contexts over discursive formations, including mythmaking, because the focus on mythmaking has the consequence, even if unintended, of making a linear sequence of ideas the primary cause in accounting for Christian beginnings.[21]

These concerns are largely responsible for the focus of this volume on Paul and the Corinthians, not on pre-Pauline "traditions." Here, at last, was a site not only of Paul's Christ-*kyrios* myth but also one where we could draw on more detailed social data than we had encountered before. Nevertheless, it still seemed crucial to include in the work of the seminar on this site a redescription of the texts Paul presents as traditions. As was argued at the time, we should not leave unexplained, in our terms, the very texts that have served as the primary evidence of the historical foundations of the Christian religion, in the view of most New Testament scholars.[22] Mack's paper also underlines the importance of the concerns that made the Corinthian site attractive in the first place and has put to rest, we think, any suspicion about "connecting all the dots on the 'Christian' map"[23] by establishing a linear sequence of myths as a generative cause. On the contrary. Not only has Mack shown that an earlier martyr myth cannot account for Paul's Christ myth; he also argues that Paul's gospel does not account for Corinthian social formation or contribute much to it. While the latter is a point of dispute among the authors in this volume, it does instantiate what we had concluded in *Redescribing Christian Origins*: there is no simple nexus or mechanism that links mythmaking and social formation.[24] If turning to a site that was "visible" has tested our categories, it has confirmed that their relationship is messier than we had initially imagined. Precisely where more social data are available and analytical priority is given to reconstructing a social situation, we see what appear to be the gaps between the agents' discourses and practices in a given setting, the mutual but also conflicting interests, and the fluidity of social formations.

Among the matters taken into account are not only different kinds of social formations but how we imagine social formation taking place, whether we are

---

21. Braun, "Smoke Signals from the North," 435–42; Arnal and Braun, "Social Formation and Mythmaking," 462–67.

22. Mack, "Backbay Jazz and Blues," 428; idem, "Rereading the Christ Myth," 35–36. See Ron Cameron and Merrill P. Miller, "Issues and Commentary," in Cameron and Miller, *Redescribing Christian Origins*, 448; and, in the same volume, Cameron and Miller, "Conclusion," 500–501, 515–16.

23. Braun, "Smoke Signals from the North," 440.

24. Cameron and Miller, "Conclusion," 513–15. On the issue of the analytical priority of material conditions and social situations to discursive formations, or of deducing social interests and situations from mythmaking, Jonathan Z. Smith advised that "the challenge, here, will be to avoid formulations which see the one as the dependent variable of the other, or which see the one as congruent to the other," adding: "Such formulations introduce insufficient difference" ("*Dayyeinu*," in Cameron and Miller, *Redescribing Christian Origins*, 486).

thinking of Jesus schools, Jesus-*christos* associations, or Pauline churches. If people are always already socially constituted by family, status, gender, city and region, ethnicity, a wide range of networks and associations, and the like, it is more plausible to imagine social formation in the name of Jesus or Christ as various kinds of interventions in other already existing groups, than to imagine these formations as arising *de novo* as a secure set of boundary markers, or as responses to a cultural deposit cultivated in earlier Jesus groups. The principal contribution of Mack's paper to our double disjunction site is to have thoroughly problematized the notion of a pre-Pauline Christ cult and the historical work generated by that notion. In the Bultmannian tradition, it has served as a bridge between Jesus and Paul, making it possible to ring the changes without giving up the primitive Christian church as a historical datum, the unique "eschatological community" at the foundations of the Christian religion.[25] At the same time, Mack's paper reflects a different and more provocative use of the temporal expression "pre-Pauline," referring to already existing group formations among the Corinthians prior to Paul's initial contact and preaching. This notion of "pre-Pauline" is a matter that all the papers in this volume have taken into account as a necessary consideration in constructing a social situation, albeit with different emphases and without unanimity as to whether, or in what way, it is appropriate to think of the Corinthians to whom Paul writes as a Pauline *ekklēsia*.

Another commonality to be found in the papers of this volume is the attention given to procedures of comparison. All of the papers have a comparative focus and have taken account of, and explicitly referred to, the theoretical program of analogical comparison in the work of Smith in order to establish aspectual features of similarity and difference with various kinds of associations and schools, situating the Corinthians to whom Paul writes in the environment of Roman Corinth and in the wider eastern Mediterranean world of the early Roman Principate. In our earlier volume, Smith had referred to the seminar's successful defamiliarization of the gospel paradigm by means of a "radical alteration of the habitual terms of description."[26] He called this procedure a "first sense" of redescription. And he pointed to a "second sense" of redescription that depended on stronger comparative investigations, and noted a certain wariness in the seminar to take up the task of rectifying middle-range conceptualizations and categories in light of a comparative study of the data.[27]

---

25. See Cameron and Miller, "Issues and Commentary," 445–46.
26. Smith, "*Dayyeinu*," 484; see Cameron and Miller, "Conclusion," 497–516.
27. Smith, "*Dayyeinu*," 484–85 with n. 4, adding: "I have in mind here our discussions of categories such as 'schools' or 'associations' in which, at times, the overarching question appeared to be that of the degree of fit/no fit between the model and the early Christian data, rather than the possibility of rectifying the model in the light of the data.... I should note that so limiting the question has, in the past, served as a stratagem for maintaining Christian uniqueness" (485 n. 5). Replacing the dominant theological vocabulary with terms more appropriate for a social and anthropological description of Christian

In his paper in this volume, Smith has not attempted to rectify the categories that have become habitual in the history of reception of Paul's letters to the Corinthians.[28] However, by adopting a strategy of comparing exempla from radically different times and places, Smith not only avoids the interference of genealogical comparisons; he is also required to cross a far greater range of difference, allowing him to take cognitive advantage of the mutual distortion to propose more "surprising" similarities, which have more striking consequences for a redescription of the data.[29] The other papers in this volume, for the most part, draw analogical comparisons from the practices and discourses of different peoples and of different types of associations and schools documented in the world of Paul and the Corinthians.[30] These comparisons, while perhaps less capable of surprising perspectives on the data, certainly have a bearing on judgments of difference in the drawing of comparisons from more distant exempla. Smith's contemporary exemplum is situated in a colonial world featuring Christian missions among its colonial enterprises and registering a high volume of intercultural exchange. That the world of Paul and the Corinthians is also colonial and featured intercultural exchange is obvious. But that does not settle the issue of situating Paul in relation to the Corinthians, or in relation to Roman colonial enterprises, even though the papers are in agreement—and the agreement is significant—that Paul's presence

---

beginnings in their Greco-Roman context, as we did in our earlier volume, does not by itself yield an explanation of the phenomena under consideration, if the meanings of the terms are not examined but taken as self-evident. For an expanded generalization of the term "association" achieved by comparing it with other loci of religious practices and institutions in antiquity, see Jonathan Z. Smith, "Here, There, and Anywhere," in *Prayer, Magic, and the Stars in the Ancient and Late Antique World* (ed. Scott Noegel et al.; Magic in History Series; University Park: Pennsylvania State University Press, 2003), 21–36; repr. in idem, *Relating Religion: Essays in the Study of Religion* (Chicago: University of Chicago Press, 2004), 323–39. Associations flourished in the Greco-Roman world by reproducing and transforming features of domestic religious practices ("here") and religious practices of temple and state ("there") in locations "anywhere" in response to changes in social and cultural conditions in the Greco-Roman world.

28. Smith, "Re: Corinthians," 34 n. 50.

29. Compare Jonathan Z. Smith's statement regarding the requirement of difference in the relationship of models and data: "Indeed, the cognitive power of any translation, model, map, or redescription ... is ... a result of its difference from the phenomena in question and not its congruence" ("Bible and Religion," *BCSSR* 29/4 [2000]: 91; repr. in *Relating Religion*, 208, cited more fully in idem, "Dayyeinu," 484 n. 3). As Smith has persistently argued, "Both explanations and interpretations are occasioned by surprise. It is the particular subject matter that provides the scholar with an occasion for surprise. Surprise, whether in the natural or the human sciences, is always reduced by bringing the unknown into relations to the known. The process by which this is accomplished, in both the natural and the human sciences, is translation: the proposal that the second-order conceptual language appropriate to one domain (the known/the familiar) may translate the second-order conceptual language appropriate to another domain (the unknown/the unfamiliar)" ("A Twice-told Tale: The History of the History of Religions' History," *Numen* 48 [2001]: 143–44; repr. in *Relating Religion*, 370–71).

30. We note that Arnal has also drawn on contemporary exempla in his references to the myth of Hainuwele and to the contemporary film *The Fight Club* ("Paul and the Corinthians," 100–101, 85; cf. 89).

and preaching are appropriately described as "intrusive" on people of different geographical and ethnic origins who were already "getting together." For example, in relation to the colonial authority and culture, Stowers points out that "Christian missionaries and teachers in New Guinea, even when they were natives bringing domesticated forms of the religion, carried the background authority of an enormously powerful imperial culture from the West that exerted both attraction and repulsion. Paul, the Diaspora Judean, carried no such background authority. The Corinthian reception of Paul [thus] needs explanation."[31] On intercultural exchange, Arnal maintains that cultural differences, and the translations and misunderstandings arising from them, are less significant in determining the relationship between Paul and the Corinthians than are the conditions that pertain across the world of the early Roman Principate, which create a similar situational incongruity for both Paul and the Corinthians.[32] The questions broached by Arnal at the end of his paper could also be construed as a Pauline intrusion on the central institutions of the Roman Empire.[33]

Paul's Apocalypticism, Conflict Management, and "Mind Goods"

Recent scholarship has pointed to significant differences of constituency, group formation and organization, and local circumstances among Pauline churches.[34] Such differences seem especially pronounced in the case of Thessalonica and Corinth.[35] Richard S. Ascough has written elsewhere about the particular constituency and circumstances of group formation of the *ekklēsia* of Thessalonica.[36] In contrast, his paper in this volume finds an underlying concern common to Paul's addressees in both cities. The interest of the seminar in Paul's response to a question about the dead in 1 Thess 4:13–18 initially arose from a suggestion that Paul might be responding to a similar concern among the Corinthians in 1 Cor 15. Taking his bearings from Smith's observation that "Paul's most extensive discussions of the resurrection of the dead—in 1 Thessalonians and 1 Corinthians, the earliest treatments of the topic in Christian literature—are *both* triggered by questions concerning the status of dead members of the community,"[37] and from Mack's

---

31. Stowers, "Kinds of Myth," 116.
32. Arnal, "Paul and the Corinthians."
33. Ibid., 103–4.
34. See, e.g., Richard S. Ascough, *What Are They Saying about the Formation of Pauline Churches?* (New York: Paulist, 1998).
35. See especially Barclay, "Thessalonica and Corinth."
36. Ascough, "The Thessalonian Christian Community as a Professional Voluntary Association." In this article, Ascough makes a case for seeing the Thessalonians as an already existing association of handworkers when they turned to "a living and true God" *collectively*, thus accounting for their reputation among other *ekklēsiai* in Macedonia and Achaia (1 Thess 1:8–9).
37. Jonathan Z. Smith, *Drudgery Divine: On the Comparison of Early Christianities and the Reli-*

recognition in 1 Thessalonians that "the question was not really about 'personal salvation' either of the living or of the dead . . . [but] about belonging,"[38] Ascough has undertaken to survey the evidence of burial, memorials, and cults of the dead in the context of kinship and of associations in Greco-Roman cities, in order to show the central role of death rituals for establishing collective identity and group cohesion.[39] With these matters in view, he explores the intelligibility and relevance of Paul's apocalyptic discourse in 1 Thess 4:13–18. Building on his findings, he turns to 1 Corinthians and concludes his study with a proposed trajectory of social formation and mythmaking, starting from a pre-Pauline memorial foundation and hero myth and moving to a specifically Pauline memorial meal and a developing Pauline apocalyptic myth. Both the memorial meal and the mythmaking are viewed as responses to concerns for the status of the dead.[40]

The papers by Stowers ("Does Pauline Christianity Resemble a Hellenistic Philosophy?") and John S. Kloppenborg compare Paul and the Corinthians with

---

gions of Late Antiquity (Jordan Lectures in Comparative Religion 14; London: School of Oriental and African Studies, University of London; Chicago: University of Chicago Press, 1990), 131 n. 33 (emphasis original).

38. Burton L. Mack, *Who Wrote the New Testament? The Making of the Christian Myth* (San Francisco: HarperSanFrancisco, 1995), 110; cf. Ascough, "Paul's 'Apocalypticism,'" 151–52.

39. Ascough, "Paul's 'Apocalypticism,'" 155–72. The paper concentrates on 1 Thessalonians because the inscriptional evidence from Macedonia for associations is more abundant and better preserved than what is available from Corinth (152). Indeed, "there is much literary and documentary evidence for burial practices in the Greco-Roman world, but very little that can be related specifically to Corinth" (Mary E. Hoskins Walbank, "Unquiet Graves: Burial Practices of the Roman Corinthians," in *Urban Religion in Roman Corinth: Interdisciplinary Approaches* [ed. Daniel N. Schowalter and Steven J. Friesen; HTS 53; Cambridge, Mass.: Harvard Divinity School, 2005], 249). For a systematic account of what has thus far been published in many scattered publications of the funerary remains of the Roman Corinthia, see Joseph Lee Rife, "Death, Ritual, and Memory in Greek Society during the Early and Middle Roman Empire" (2 vols.; Ph.D. diss., University of Michigan, 1999), 1:199–332. Regarding the epigraphic evidence, Rife states that the tombs of the Corinthia "were the product of descent groups, with the male head of the family most often, but sometimes a female, clearly identified as the person responsible" (1:257), adding: "The epigraphic and archaeological record of the Roman Corinthia offers no evidence for corporations owning or operating tombs, like the burial clubs . . . of Roman Italy" (1:257 n. 177). On this last point, however, we call attention to the continuing research being conducted by Walbank and Kathleen W. Slane in an area northeast of the ancient city. Walbank reports on skeletal remains in one of the cists of a chamber tomb that show very dissimilar genetic traits in seven individuals buried there. She suggests that these individuals may have belonged to a trade association or burial club. Nearby in the same chamber is a grave in which the dead had similar genetic traits, indicative of family ties (Walbank, "Unquiet Graves," 267–68).

40. Ascough organizes his study following the operational procedures of Jonathan Z. Smith ("The 'End' of Comparison: Redescription and Rectification," in *A Magic Still Dwells: Comparative Religion in the Postmodern Age* [ed. Kimberley C. Patton and Benjamin C. Ray; Berkeley and Los Angeles: University of California Press, 2000], 239), as summarized by Burton L. Mack ("On Redescribing Christian Origins," *MTSR* 8 [1996]: 256–59; repr. in idem, *The Christian Myth: Origins, Logic, and Legacy* [New York: Continuum, 2001], 70–74), for comparative analysis capable of achieving a redescription of the data and the rectification of categories.

philosophies and associations, respectively. Both papers are exercises in analogical comparison and comment on appropriate procedures and goals for their comparative projects. Both reject any simple identification of Pauline "churches" with particular models that have been suggested—households, associations, mysteries, philosophical schools, synagogues—finding more appropriate and useful the comparison of particular features and associative practices of these group formations.[41] And while focused on the features and practices of different models, both authors acknowledge the value of the particular features being compared in the work of the other.[42]

For Stowers, "Paul's social formations resembled those of Hellenistic philosophers because they were productive of 'mind goods' in a way that subordinated other goods."[43] By contrast,

> the typical sacrificial religion of the Greco-Roman world was closely intertwined with economic production and made no sense apart from that production. This holds true of associations, the Judean temple, and the religious practices of dispersed Judean communities. The ideal economic production in this Mediterranean religion is the fruit of the land, but artisanal, trade, and other sorts of economic production were also included in the structuration effected by the linking of shared practices.[44]

---

41. John S. Kloppenborg, "Greco-Roman *Thiasoi*, the *Ekklēsia* at Corinth, and Conflict Management," 189 (in this volume): "Preliminary analysis of the available models makes it unlikely that any one will commend itself fully.... Hence, rather than engaging in rhetorical overstatement and claiming, for example, that the Corinthian *ekklēsia* was a *philosophia*, or was a cult association, it is far more useful to compare particular aspects of Christian, Jewish, and pagan associative practices" (emphasis original). Compare Stanley K. Stowers, "Does Pauline Christianity Resemble a Hellenistic Philosophy?" 229 (in this volume): "I do not think that Pauline Christianity was a philosophy, and differences are as important as similarities.... [T]he similarities with the philosophies are not exclusive of similarities with other social formations." Stowers also makes a point of distinguishing "Pauline Christianity" from the Corinthians themselves: "[I]t is important to remind ourselves that we have only Paul's representation of these groups. I am skeptical about inferring much concerning the Pauline groups themselves and thus will focus on Paul's conceptions in the letters" (221–22). With respect to this latter distinction, we simply note that Stowers's other paper ("Kinds of Myth") in this volume is more directly responsive to the definition of the site for a redescription that clearly includes the Corinthians themselves.

42. Kloppenborg, "Greco-Roman *Thiasoi*," 190 n. 5: "Stowers argues that similarities between Pauline Christianity at Corinth and philosophies are stronger than with Judean communities (synagogues) or voluntary associations.... This type of comparison helpfully illumines an important aspect of Pauline Christianity, but obviously does not pretend to provide a comprehensive account of its associative practices." Compare Stowers, "Pauline Christianity," 229 (cf. 219–21 with nn. 3, 7): "I do, in fact, think that it is worth comparing the Christian groups to Judean communities and to so-called voluntary associations. Similarities do exist but ... overall I judge differences to be greater than the similarities. Comparison is thus a complex, multitaxonomic activity."

43. Stowers, "Pauline Christianity," 241.

44. Ibid., 238.

Regarding the oddity of the Pauline "household," Stowers notes that "the ancient household was the locus for almost all of the economic production in Greco-Roman antiquity.... [But] the economic engine is missing from the Pauline household. The only labor and goods that he values are those related to his teaching, assembly building, and leading activities."[45] For Kloppenborg,

> What makes the study of *collegia* particularly interesting is, first, that the available documentation discloses much more about social conflict than what remains of the other types of associations and, second, that various forms of conflict appear to have been endemic in *collegia* and that many *collegia* developed mechanisms by which to manage conflict, both internal and external.[46]

Summarizing his findings from the data of *collegia*, Kloppenborg concludes:

> Thus, associations both cultivated a degree of rivalry and had to devise means by which such rivalry could be limited and contained. Fines for disorderly conduct at meals, injunctions prohibiting members from taking other members to court, and the insistence on settling all disputes among members within the association—all served as means by which an association sought to prevent internal conflict from reaching divisive proportions.[47]

This volume concludes with an essay by the editors, seeking to bring the papers into further conversation. We have engaged the papers in order to present our own explanatory proposals for the redescription of Paul and the Corinthians and to assess the seminar's work on this site as a contribution to the project of redescribing Christian origins. In order to achieve this goal, we have highlighted agreements and important matters of consensus among the papers, while analyzing and evaluating positions where the paper writers have offered different judgments and arguments on related issues, including, in particular, the generative problematic for the redescription of the site, the subject positions of the Corinthians to whom Paul is writing, the place of Paul's Christ myth for his gospel, the significance of Paul's apocalyptic persuasions and discourse, especially in relation to practices of burial, memorial, and cults of the dead, and strategies of comparison in proposing analogues to features of Paul's discourse and practice in 1 Corinthians. And even though the seminar has not focused on issues particular to Paul's correspondence in 2 Corinthians, some of those issues were clearly in view as members of the seminar formulated proposals for a redescription of the site.

The purpose of the Seminar on Ancient Myths and Modern Theories of Christian Origins is to contribute both historiographically to a redescription of

---

45. Ibid., 240, 241.
46. Kloppenborg, "Greco-Roman *Thiasoi*," 205.
47. Ibid., 214.

Christian beginnings and imaginatively to the construction of a general theory of religion. As an effort to relate mythmaking and social formation, our work demonstrates that the relationship is complex, first, because mythmaking and social formation are already intertwined from both sides of the encounter between Paul and the Corinthians and, second, because this double set of systems is reproduced and transformed in the course of the encounter. Thus, though mythmaking and social formation are linked, the implication is that the one is not simply a reflection, or the cause, of the other. This means that we cannot always infer social formations from the evidence of mythmaking, as though there were some simple way to specify the nexus that links them. It also means that a site for redescription does not have to constitute a single social formation, as though it consisted in some firmly bounded corporate entity. The larger import for redescribing Christian origins is that the existence of Jesus- or Christ-centered myths and other literary forms does not necessarily presuppose Jesus- or Christ-centered collective identities or bounded groups as their formative social contexts. The picture of the Corinthians as a Christ-identified religious community and of Paul as a founder and builder of religious commmunities is as dependent on Paul's own mythmaking, and on contemporary scholarly desires, as the view of Paul as the innovator of a program of social and political reform. What Paul achieved at Corinth was not the establishment of an alternative community founded on the Christ myth and unified through Paul's moral and ritual instructions, but the attraction of a certain cadre of followers.

Re: Corinthians

Jonathan Z. Smith

> But capitalization does not convert a muscular twitch into a god.
> — Peter Buck [Te Rangi Hiroa], *The Coming of the Maori*[1]

> There is something strange about the Corinthians, to be sure. They fantasized about themselves and their achievements, as Paul himself did. We must wonder, however, if some of their strangeness is not due to the way in which Paul presents them.
> — Robert M. Grant, *Paul in the Roman World*[2]

I

If Burton L. Mack is correct in his understanding of the cunning of Mark, then surely Mark's Gospel is one of the most contaminating texts for the understanding of early Christianities. How much more so 1 Corinthians! This text, especially—although not limited to—those aspects that have been traditionally viewed as resonating with Luke's Pentecost narrative, has contaminated the general field of the study of religion well beyond any limitation to Christian data. It has affected not only scholarly constructions such as charismatic movements, "ecstatic religions," and models of both archaic and contemporary cult associations but also native religious self-representations. Indeed, in the latter case, at times in a sort of feedback

---

This is a slightly revised version of a paper that was prepared for the Ancient Myths and Modern Theories of Christian Origins Seminar, presented at the annual meeting of the Society of Biblical Literature, held in Denver in November 2001, and first published in Jonathan Z. Smith, *Relating Religion: Essays in the Study of Religion* (Chicago: University of Chicago Press, 2004), 340–61. It is reprinted here with permission.

1. Peter Buck [Te Rangi Hiroa], *The Coming of the Maori* (2nd ed.; Wellington: Whitcombe and Tombs, 1950), 532.

2. Robert M. Grant, *Paul in the Roman World: The Conflict at Corinth* (Louisville: Westminster John Knox, 2001), 44.

loop, 1 Corinthians has influenced anthropological data and theories which then have been used by New Testament scholars to interpret early Christian data.[3]

First Corinthians has also been used more than any other New Testament text (with the possible exception of Luke's composition of the Areopagus speech) for direct Christian (missionary) interpretation of the religions of other folk—most especially their rituals. The so-called Chinese Rites Controversy is, perhaps, the classic example,[4] but a more commonplace instance would be the twenty years of

---

3. This is by no means a singular contamination. For example, one needs to use extreme caution in evaluating the Christian influence on "native apocalyptic" traditions, which are then redeployed, on the basis of ethnographic reports and anthropological theories, to interpret both Jewish and Christian apocalypticisms. See, e.g., Jonathan Z. Smith, "Too Much Kingdom, Too Little Community," *Zygon* 13 (1978): 123–30.

Early examples of such feedback often gave rise to secondary mythologies, such as the presence of Native American versions of biblical stories, which had been received from missionaries but which were taken to be indigenous "originals." (See, already, Stith Thompson, *European Tales among the North American Indians: A Study in the Migration of Folk-Tales* [Colorado College Publication Language Series 2/34; Colorado Springs: Colorado College, 1919].) The alleged parallels were then deployed as proof that the Native Americans were the "lost tribes" of Israel.

Edward B. Tylor's 1892 article remains, to the best of my knowledge, the first responsible discussion of the question of Christian contamination of "native tradition" ("On the Limits of Savage Religion," *Journal of the Anthropological Institute of Great Britain and Ireland* 21 [1892]: 283–99). See, further, Jonathan Z. Smith, "The Unknown God: Myth in History," in idem, *Imagining Religion: From Babylon to Jonestown* (CSHJ; Chicago: University of Chicago Press, 1982), 66–89, 145–56.

4. The Chinese Rites Controversy was a seventeenth- and eighteenth-century Catholic argument over the degree of "accommodation" with Chinese ritual practice by recent Roman Catholic converts, part of a wider, chiefly Jesuit, missionary strategy that was first experimented with in Japan in the mid-sixteenth century and later applied to India and China. Not at all irrelevant to issues raised later in this paper, the controversy concerned participation by Chinese Christians in domestic rituals honoring the ancestral dead, as well as in public and state rituals honoring Confucius. The controversy was sparked by Matteo Ricci's position that these were civil and social rituals and, therefore, not idolatrous. (See Johannes Bettray, *Die Akkommodationsmethode des P. Matteo Ricci S.I. in China* [Analecta Gregoriana 76; Rome: Universitas Gregoriana, 1955].) Ricci's position was reenforced by a decree of the emperor, K'ang Hsi. (See the widely read pro-accommodation treatise by Charles Le Gobien, the procurator in Paris of the Chinese Mission, *Histoire de l'edit de l'empereur de la Chine, en faveur de la religion chrestienne: avec un eclaircissement sur les honneurs que les Chinois rendent à Confucius et aux morts* [Paris: Anisson, 1698].) The question was debated until prohibited by Benedict XIV in the bull *Ex quo singulari* (1742).

Just short of two centuries later, Ricci's position on China was reaffirmed by Pius XII. The 1939 reversal began with pressure by Japanese Christians concerning their participation in state Shinto rituals for the emperor, defined by the state as a civil, and not a religious, act. At the request of then Commander (later Admiral) Yamamoto, Louis Bréhier and Pierre Batiffol prepared a brief, seventy-three-page monograph, *Les Survivances du culte impérial romain: A propos des rites shintoïstes* (Paris: Picard, 1920), defending the participation by indicating the accommodation with imperial cult practices and themes in Roman Christianity. While this work was surely not a direct cause of the reversal, it played a role in a subsequent series of diplomatic exchanges and conferences that led to the relaxation of the prohibition against participation, first for Manchuria (1935), then Japan (1936), then China (1939,

Dutch Calvinist missionary debate (1914–34), as summarized by Webb Keane,[5] over native sacrificial practice in West Sumba (Indonesia), an island separated on the east by the Savu Sea from its better-known neighbor, Timor. The question was the native practice of commensalism with respect to meat resulting from sacrifice, a central index of Sumbanese sociality. "To demand of converts that they withdraw from this commensuality is to threaten their participation in society altogether."[6] The issue was joined with the publication of a latitudinarian article by D. K.

---

reconfirmed in 1941)—and, later, citing these precedents, with Catholic Vietnamese being permitted to "honor" ancestors (1964). See Jean Guennou, "Les Missions catholiques," in *Histoire des religions* (ed. Henri-Charles Puech; 2 vols.; Encyclopédie de la Pléiade; Paris: Gallimard, 1970–72), 2:1167–71.

For the seventeenth- and eighteenth-century controversy, François Bontinck, *La Lutte autour de la liturgie chinoise aux XVIIe et XVIIIe siècles* (Publications de l'Université Lovanium de Léopoldville 11; Louvain: Éditions Nauwelaerts; Paris: Béatrice-Nauwelaerts, 1962), remains the most important account. From a wider perspective, see the fascinating study by D. E. Mungello, *Curious Land: Jesuit Accommodation and the Origins of Sinology* (Studia Leibnitiana Supplementa 25; Stuttgart: Steiner, 1985; repr., Honolulu: University of Hawaii Press, 1989). See also the judicious summaries in one of the great historiographical achievements of our time, Donald F. Lach and Edwin J. Van Kley, *Asia in the Making of Europe* (3 vols. in 9 parts; Chicago: University of Chicago Press, 1965–93), 3/1:260–69, 385–86, 423–24, 429–30; 3/4:1674–80, et passim. Many of the relevant documents are translated in Antonio Sisto Rosso, *Apostolic Legations to China of the Eighteenth Century* ([South Pasadena, Calif.: Perkins,] 1948). The richest guide to the voluminous controversy literature remains Robert Streit and Johannes Dindinger, eds., *Bibliotheca missionum* (30 vols.; Aachen: Franziskus Xavierus Missions-verein Zentrale), vol. 5, *Asiatische Missionsliteratur 1600–1699* (1929), 803–961; vol. 7, *Chinesische Missionsliteratur 1700–1799* (1931), 1–44. See also Henri Cordier, ed., *Bibliotheca Sinica: Dictionnaire bibliographique des ouvrages relatifs à l'empire chinois* (2nd ed.; 5 vols.; Paris: Librairie orientale et américaine, 1904–24), 2:869–926, 1279–94.

We still await a definitive study of the effect of the Rites Controversy on seventeenth- and eighteenth-century European theories of religion as part of a wider preoccupation with Chinese philosophy and religious practice. (See the effective summary in Paul Hazard, *The European Mind [1680–1715]* [trans. J. Lewis May; Cleveland: World, 1963], 20–24.) A major source for these theories was the pro-accommodation work by Louis Le Comte (sometimes, Le Compte), *Nouveaux mémoires sur l'état présent de la Chine* (vols. 1–2, Paris: Anisson, 1696; 3rd ed., Amsterdam: Desbordes and Schelte, 1698; vol. 3, Paris: Anisson, 1698; 3rd ed., 1702), which was rapidly translated into English (1697, reprinted at least four times by 1738), Dutch (1697), and German (1699). Le Comte's work was condemned by the faculty of the Sorbonne (1700)—partly under pressure from a powerful French Catholic secret society, the Compagnie du Saint Sacrement. For the influences of the Rites Controversy on some strands of European religious and philosophical thought, see Virgile Pinot, *La Chine et la formation de l'esprit philosophique en France (1640–1740)* (Paris: Geuthner, 1932; repr., Geneva: Slatkine, 1971); and D. P. Walker, *The Ancient Theology: Studies in Christian Platonism from the Fifteenth to the Eighteenth Century* (London: Duckworth, 1972), 194–230.

5. For the Sumbanese materials, see Webb Keane, "Materialism, Missionaries, and Modern Subjects in Colonial Indonesia," in *Conversion to Modernities: The Globalization of Christianity* (ed. Peter van der Veer; Zones of Religion; New York: Routledge, 1996), 137–70. In presenting the historical narrative, Keane is largely dependent on Th. van den End, ed., *Gereformeerde Zending op Sumba: Een Bronnenpublicatie* (Alphen aan den Rijn: Raad voor de Zending der Ned. Herv. Kerk, de Zending der Gereformeerde kerken in Nederland en de Gereformeerde Zendingsbond in de Ned. Herv. Kerk., 1987), which I have not seen.

6. Keane, "Materialism," 149.

Wielenga in 1914, whose title, "On the Eating of Flesh Offered to Idols,"[7] displays its Corinthian genealogy; and the issue was officially resolved by the prohibition of eating such meat proclaimed by a Special Assembly of Missionaries in 1934:

> A Christian, through the accepting and eating of meat brought to the house (that comes) from animals slain according to pagan *adat* [custom], of which he knows the source, has objective communion with the worship of the devil. Moreover, the accepting and eating of [such] meat . . . is (a) unworthy of the Christian, (b) dangerous for the Christian and the young Christian congregation, (c) contrary to the commandment of brotherly love. Also on the ground of all these considerations, the accepting and eating of such flesh is in conflict with God's Word, for which reason . . . our Christians must hate and eschew such a thing from the heart.[8]

What official documents fail to indicate is the sort of commonplace, commonsense resolutions in practice of such a social dilemma that can, at times, be captured by an observer's ethnographic report. For example, as the number of individuals following the traditional Sumbanese practice declined over the years, owing largely to successful missionizations, the sacrificial rituals became increasingly dependent on native Christian support. Hence, since the 1980s, "one pig" would "often [be] omitted from the offering prayers" so it could "be fed to the Christian visitors."[9] That is to say, a "legal fiction" was created that one pig was slaughtered in an ordinary act, in contradistinction to its fellows, which were ritually slain. Alternatively, from the Christian side, a notion of "functional equivalence"[10] could be invoked. Rather than meat being brought home as gifts for the traditional spirits, it could be "transposed" as being brought home to be distributed as "support for the poor";[11] rather than a piece of meat cut from the shoulder of the victim being presented to the headman, a different cut of meat could be offered "on the grounds that the shoulder cut was pagan, but the substitute gift still bore the *secular* display of deference."[12]

While a reception history of 1 Corinthians deserves attention, both in terms of theories of religion and in terms of Christian praxis with respect to other religions, I turn now to the task at hand and attempt a redescription of the Corinthian situation in relation to a set of data from Papua New Guinea.

---

7. Wielenga's article is briefly summarized in Keane, "Materialism," 147–48.
8. Keane, "Materialism," 152.
9. Ibid., 153.
10. Ibid., 160.
11. Ibid., 156.
12. Ibid., 160 (emphasis original).

II

Papua New Guinea was, in the 1960s and '70s, an important site for theorizing about religion in terms of data from indigenous "cargo cults"—an interest that has largely disappeared among students of religion.[13] Later, in the 1980s and '90s, it became a site for important anthropological theorizing about sexuality—materials that have not, by and large, been taken up by students of religion.[14] Most recently, Papua New Guinea, along with Melanesia, has been the site of important discussions of a widespread "new" religious pattern: a concomitant increase, within the same locale, in both native Christianities, especially Pentecostalisms (whether independent of or affiliated with North American churches), and nativistic movements (that is to say, the invention of new traditionalisms). One important point of intersection between these two "new" religious forms has been healing, often spirit-healing. These matters are just beginning to find a place in the agenda of scholars of religion.[15]

---

13. One of the earliest attempts to relate "cargo cults" to the wider phenomenon of nativistic movements is the classic work by the Italian Marxist scholar Vittorio Lanternari, *Movimenti religiosi di libertà e di salvezza dei popoli oppressi* (Milan: Feltrinelli, 1960); ET: *The Religions of the Oppressed: A Study of Modern Messianic Cults* (trans. Lisa Sergio; New York: Knopf, 1963). See, in general, the bibliographies by Ida Leeson, *Bibliography of Cargo Cults and Other Nativistic Movements in the South Pacific* (South Pacific Commission Technical Paper 30; London: South Pacific Commission, 1952); and Weston La Barre, "Materials for a History of Studies of Crisis Cults: A Bibliographic Essay," *Current Anthropology* 12 (1971): 3–44. For an important, detailed ethnography of a New Guinea Highlands movement that resulted in the formation of an independent church, see Patrick F. Gesch, *Initiative and Initiation: A Cargo Cult-Type Movement in the Sepik Against Its Background in Traditional Village Religion* (Studia Instituti Anthropos 33; St. Augustin, Germany: Anthropos-Institut, 1985). For reviews of the history of cargo cult research, see Friedrich Steinbauer, *Melanesian Cargo Cults: New Salvation Movements in the South Pacific* (trans. Max Wohlwill; Santa Lucia, Queensland: University of Queensland Press, 1979); and Lamont Lindstrom, *Cargo Cult: Strange Stories of Desire from Melanesia and Beyond* (South Sea Books; Honolulu: University of Hawaii Press, 1993).

14. Gilbert H. Herdt has been central to this discussion, both in his own works and through edited volumes. Among the latter, see especially idem, ed., *Rituals of Manhood: Male Initiation in Papua New Guinea* (Berkeley and Los Angeles: University of California Press, 1982); idem, ed., *Ritualized Homosexuality in Melanesia* (Berkeley and Los Angeles: University of California Press, 1984). See, further, idem and Fitz John P. Poole, "'Sexual Antagonism': The Intellectual History of a Concept in New Guinea Anthropology," *Social Analysis* 12 (1982): 3–28. For a corrective to some of the interests reflected in these works, see Gilbert Herdt, ed., *Third Sex, Third Gender: Beyond Sexual Dimorphism in Culture and History* (New York: Zone Books, 1994); and Nancy C. Lutkehaus and Paul B. Roscoe, eds., *Gender Rituals: Female Initiation in Melanesia* (New York: Routledge, 1995).

15. With respect to Papua New Guinea and Melanesia, see, among others, the following special issues of journals: Roger M. Keesing and Robert Tonkinson, eds., "Reinventing Traditional Culture: The Politics of Kastom in Island Melanesia," *Mankind* 13 (1982): 297–399; Margaret Jolly and Nicholas Thomas, eds., "The Politics of Tradition in the Pacific," *Oceania* 62 (1992): 241–354; Andrew Lattas, ed., "Alienating Mirrors: Christianity, Cargo Cults and Colonialism in Melanesia," *Oceania* 63 (1992): 1–93; and Richard Feinberg and Laura Zimmer-Tamakoshi, eds., "Special Issue on Politics of Culture in the Pacific Islands," *Ethnology* 34 (1995): 89–153, 155–224. For a useful overview of new Melanesian spirit-

The particular group under discussion is the Atbalmin (or Nalumin),[16] comprising some three thousand individuals, clustered in settlements of some thirty to forty folk. They inhabit the Telefolmin area in the Star (or Sterren) mountain range, part of the continuous mountain chain, running from northwest to southeast, that divides the world's second-largest island. On a contemporary map, their settlements are sited at the border between the nominally Christian independent Papua New Guinea and the Muslim state Indonesian territory of Irian Jaya (or Irian Burat, or West New Guinea, or West Papua). It is a region that as late as 1969 could be described in the *Encyclopaedia Britannica* as "still little known."[17] While there was some European exploration after 1910, there was no direct contact until government officials of the Australian Trust Territory made periodic visits after 1950. In the same period, a station of the Australian Baptist Missionary Society was established. Following independence in 1975, a small airport was constructed, along with copper mines, a health clinic, and a primary school. The Christian mission made little progress until this period (1976-79), when, using native "pastors"

---

ist movements, see Manfred Ernst, *Winds of Change: Rapidly Growing Religious Groups in the Pacific Islands* (Suva, Fiji: Pacific Conference of Churches, 1994).

    I should note that despite criticisms of the term, I retain "nativism" to indicate, largely, the creation of new traditionalisms in the context of social and cultural change. (For this reason, I would classify many so-called fundamentalisms as nativistic movements.) Note William E. Arnal's creative use of the nativistic model in the concluding pages of *Jesus and the Village Scribes: Galilean Conflicts and the Setting of Q* (Minneapolis: Fortress, 2001), esp. 199-203, 257. I accept the current criticisms of the closely related term "revitalization movements" as bearing a pejorative sense. While prescinding from the Weberian schema of magic/rational, Ralph Linton's classic article, "Nativistic Movements," *American Anthropologist* NS 45 (1943): 230-40, remains one of the most formally correct efforts at taxonomy in the anthropological literature. For the critique of the term, see *The HarperCollins Dictionary of Religion* (ed. Jonathan Z. Smith; San Francisco: HarperSanFrancisco, 1995), 763, s.v. "nativistic movements"; cf. Carole A. Myscofski, "New Religions," *HarperCollins Dictionary of Religion*, 771-72.

    16. I rely, here, on Eytan Bercovitch, "The Altar of Sin: Social Multiplicity and Christian Conversion among a New Guinea People," in *Religion and Cultural Studies* (ed. Susan L. Mizruchi; Princeton: Princeton University Press, 2001), 211-35; cf. idem, "Mortal Insights: Victim and Witch in Nalumin Imagination," in *The Religious Imagination in New Guinea* (ed. Gilbert Herdt and Michele Stephen; New Brunswick, N.J.: Rutgers University Press, 1989), 122-59; idem, "The Agent in the Gift: Hidden Exchange in Inner New Guinea," *Cultural Anthropology* 9 (1994): 498-536. Bercovitch conducted his fieldwork during the periods August 1981-March 1982 and November 1982-December 1985. To my knowledge, the only guide to tribal groups related or adjacent to the Atbalmin remains the physical anthropological study by K. H. Rieckmann, Olga Kooptzoff, and R. J. Walsh, "Blood Groups and Haemoglobin Values in the Telefolmin Area, New Guinea," *Oceania* 31 (1961): 296-304. See also Terence E. Hays, "Mountain-Ok Bibliography," in *Children of Afek: Tradition and Change among the Mountain-Ok of Central New Guinea* (ed. Barry Craig and David Hyndman; Oceania Monographs 40; Sydney, N.S.W.: University of Sydney Press, 1990), 169-97. For the geography, see the excellent frontispiece map in Fredrik Barth's classic comparative study of the region, *Cosmologies in the Making: A Generative Approach to Cultural Variation in Inner New Guinea* (Cambridge Studies in Social Anthropology 64; Cambridge: Cambridge University Press, 1987), xii. Barth's work may be used with caution as parallel comparative cultural material for the region.

    17. *Encyclopaedia Britannica*, 14th ed., s.v. "New Guinea" (16:341).

from the neighboring, and linguistically related, Urapmin and Tifalmin tribes, the majority of Atbalmin converted, "see[ing] themselves as part of a much larger Christian community that encompassed Europeans as well as Melanesians." Unlike the successive colonial administrations, Christian conversion required abandoning their indigenous religion. Clearly, indigenous religion was so intercalated into the fabric of everyday Atbalmin social and material relations that such abandonment was, practically speaking, impossible. From kinship with its structure of ancestral myths and requirements of exchange relations, to place-names, to ritual roles for household implements and utensils, indigenous religion defined quotidian life. Beyond this "background," cult sites, particularly those associated with the ancestors, such as men's houses and temples, which focused on ritual performances and the transmission of traditional wisdom, were "foregrounded" concentrations of the old traditions that continued post-conversion.[18] While the ethnographer I am following here unfortunately gives little detailed account of these traditions, and Fredrik Barth's important study of the region makes plain the significant variations among these geographically proximate and linguistically related groups that prevent secure inference from the practices of neighboring tribes, the overall Atbalmin pattern is similar enough to allow reporting Jack Goody's generalization concerning one aspect of Barth's work:

> Since knowledge is held largely in the minds of men ... the older are inevitably at once the most experienced, and the most privileged communicators, as well as the most likely to die, taking their knowledge with them to the world of the ancestors. The dead must therefore know more than the living; the forefathers are also the forebearers, the carriers of "tradition." And it is in the cult of the ancestors that the dead reveal some of their superior, more comprehensive, knowledge.[19]

For the Atbalmin, it was the Christian language of "sin" that gave voice to this tension between indigenous and Christian.[20] "The Atbalmin found in Christianity a source of both desires and fears; a new way of living but also a disturbing ongoing critique of their lives, individually and collectively."[21]

This tense new identity negotiating relations between indigenous/Christian was complicated, within a very few years, by the appearance of two "new" religious movements that occurred almost simultaneously.[22]

The first was a Christian "revival" (in English-based Tok Pisin pidgin, *rebaibel*) movement that had as its apparent catalyst a powerful wind that struck an Atbalmin settlement on March 21, 1985, building as well on a general Christian

---

18. Bercovitch, "Altar of Sin," 214, 215.
19. Jack Goody, foreword, in Barth, *Cosmologies in the Making*, xi.
20. Bercovitch, "Altar of Sin," 211, 217–18, et passim.
21. Ibid., 213.
22. Ibid., 213, 221.

enthusiasm during the previous months (September 1984–February 1985) brought about by the return to the community and the renewed baptizing activities of James, one of the native "pastors" responsible for their first conversions:[23]

> This wind ... [was] widely understood to be the work of the Holy Spirit.... [A] number of women became possessed.... Over the next two days, women in other settlements became possessed by what they and others believed to be the Holy Spirit. In their possessed state, the women emphasized that Christ was about to return and that people had to prepare themselves.... "Finally," a number of people told me, "we will have our own Revival!" In saying this, they were drawing on their knowledge of another Christian religious movement known as the Rebaibel ... that had taken place in 1977–78 among people who lived east of the Atbalmin. It had involved widespread possession by the Holy Spirit, most often by women, and destruction of many existing temples of the indigenous religion. Many Atbalmin had been disappointed when the movement had failed to enter their own area. Now, people felt they had another chance.... On March 25, I awoke to find people ridding the settlement of things they linked with indigenous ways.... A young man told me, "If we give up all the non-Christian ways and only go to church, they say God will send his spirit—the Holy Spirit, a new life—into all of us and heat us up." The next day, on March 26, ... [at an] intense Sunday service at the church at Okbil ... [t]here was a great emphasis on disclosing and ending forever the kinds of routine concealment of non-Christian practices and beliefs that had been occurring.... [A] woman ... suddenly became possessed and began beating the floor and yelling for people to rid their house of evil. A few days later, the same possessed woman began to urge people to destroy the crucial temple at Bomtem. She said she was willing to enter it first herself to exorcize Satan.[24]

---

23. Ibid., 222; cf. 216.
24. Ibid., 222–23. For this earlier movment, Bercovitch (232 n.14) refers to the article by Dan Jorgensen, the dean of Telefolmin studies, "Life on the Fringe: History and Society in Telefolmin," in *The Inland Situation* (vol. 1 of *The Plight of Peripheral People in Papua New Guinea*; ed. Robert Gordon; Occasional Paper 7; Cambridge, Mass.: Cultural Survival, Inc., 1981), 59–79; as well as to an unpublished dissertation by Robert Conrad Brumbaugh, "A Secret Cult in the West Sepik Highlands" (Ph.D. diss., State University of New York at Stonybrook, 1980), which I have not seen.

I should stress that "Holy Spirit" is an imported term, derived from the English within Tok Pisin, the "pidgin" lingua franca of Papua New Guinea. See Don Kulick, *Language Shift and Cultural Reproduction: Socialization, Self, and Syncretism in a Papua New Guinean Village* (Studies in the Social and Cultural Foundations of Language 14; Cambridge: Cambridge University Press, 1992), for an important meditation on the cultural implications of the shift from indigenous languages to Tok Pisin; see also John W. M. Verhaar, ed., *Melanesian Pidgin and Tok Pisin: Proceedings of the First International Conference on Pidgins and Creoles in Melanesia* (Studies in Language Companion Series 20; Amsterdam: Benjamins, 1990), for the current state of research. (As an aside, recall the most important single study on translation in relation to conversion, Vicente L. Rafael's instant classic, *Contracting Colonialism: Translation and Christian Conversion in Tagalog Society under Early Spanish Rule* [Ithaca, N.Y.: Cornell University Press, 1988; repr., Durham, N.C.: Duke University Press, 1993].)

The temple was, in fact, never destroyed. It stands—a structure of wood and vine—at the highest point of the settlement.[25]

The second religious movement was a nativistic one spurred, in the early 1980s, by the arrival of West Papuan refugees from conflicts in Irian Jaya with the Indonesian government who settled in villages close by the Atbalmin. Related to the larger Free Papua movement (the Organisasi Papua Merdeka):

> The leaders of these refugees sought to unite all Melanesians against outside forces, a category that included not only Indonesians but also Christians and the existing Papua New Guinea government (which was seen to serve outside interests). They emphasized the need to reject new influences and return to ancestral Melanesian social and religious practices. They also said that they had special ties to the dead ancestors themselves, who would ensure their victory.[26]

This general agendum took a more specifically cargo cult–like form just a few days after the Christian revivalist episodes. On April 5, 1985, an Atbalmin returned from a visit to one of these refugee settlements. He announced that

> ancestors were on their way back bringing the wealth and power that had been promised. "They [the West Papuans] say we will clap our hands," he reported, "and the Europeans will cry out once and will trade positions with us. They will carry things for us, they will work for us for money. We will look after them and pay them." The Atbalmin who remained Christians after the return of the ancestors would not get any benefits and might perhaps be killed.[27]

Neither one of these two, apparently oppositional movements canceled the other out. "For a period of several months, from April to June, both were active

---

With respect to the proximate dead and the ancestors as well as to spirit-beings, "spirit" (lowercase) may be a reasonable rough translation. Communication with the ancestors occurs both through dreams and through male and/or female initiations and transmits "wisdom." (For connotations of "wisdom," see, e.g., Fitz John Porter Poole's discussion of this theme with respect to the neighboring Bimin-Kuskusmin, "Wisdom and Practice: The Mythic Making of Sacred History among the Bimin-Kuskusmin of Papua New Guinea," in *Discourse and Practice* [ed. Frank Reynolds and David Tracy; SUNY Series, Toward a Comparative Philosophy of Religions; Albany: State University of New York Press, 1992], 13–50.) Communication with the dead occurs through spirit mediums, often in song, or, in the case of individuals, in dreams. "Spirit possession" is not an accurate omnibus term for these diverse native indigenous religious contexts and activities—see Raymond Firth's widely cited distinctions between Melanesian "spirit possession, spirit mediumship and shamanism" (*Tikopia Ritual and Belief* [Boston: Beacon, 1967], 296)—though it may well be apropos in some native Christian religious contexts.

25. Bercovitch, "Altar of Sin," 216.
26. Ibid., 215.
27. Ibid., 223–24.

in the [same] area at the same time."²⁸ By December 1985, both "new" religious movements had declined,²⁹ though not without affecting the post-1976 situation: "What was indigenous in Atbalmin Christianity in the early to middle 1980s was ... not so much how they were Christian but how they were both Christian and non-Christian at the same time."³⁰

In this abstract, I have largely prescinded from Eytan Bercovitch's analytical framework, which emphasizes the creativity of multiplicity. In the service of this viewpoint, he maps the Atbalmin world in terms of "landscapes," which may serve us as a summary of his ethnographic report:

> Despite their conversion to Christianity, people commonly seemed to situate themselves in an indigenous landscape of settlements, territories, and descent groups constituted from a long history of indigenous social and religious relations. Sacred narratives of the indigenous religion explained many features of this visible world, such as physical or social differences between people and the existence of prominent natural landscapes. At other times, people showed their knowledge of a landscape defined by the government and business. It was marked by a profound difference in wealth and power between New Guineans and Europeans, and by a hierarchy of places beginning with the nearest government outpost and leading up through the provincial government capital at Vanimo, larger cities, the national capital at Moresby, and finally the place of Europeans.... The West Papuans had contributed another landscape. It had its center far away in the lowlands of Irian Jaya, where the place of the dead was located.... The last landscape was provided by Christianity. It encompassed an even vaster world, including Christians as well as all pagans, Satan (and a host of devils) as well as God and Jesus, and Hell and Heaven as well as the visible world.³¹

One last comment. Based on Bercovitch's ethnography, it is the Christian myth of the Holy Spirit, and not the Christ myth, that seems of greatest interest to the Atbalmin. It is the Spirit that appears associated with particular acts ("sins"), which are named in public confession.³² The Pauline sense of "Sin" as a

---

28. Ibid., 224.
29. Ibid., 230.
30. Ibid., 228.
31. Ibid., 219.
32. I would give much to know if confession was also a part of indigenous Atbalmin tradition. Neither Bercovitch nor any ethnography I am familiar with for neighboring tribes notes its occurrence. It does occur elsewhere in New Guinea, for example, in the Madang District hinterlands (see the material cited in n. 45 below). To this brief mention must be added Kenelm Burridge's work on the Tangu of the Bogia region of the Madang District. In all of his work, especially in his *Tangu Traditions: A Study of the Way of Life, Mythology, and Developing Experience of a New Guinea People* (Oxford: Clarendon, 1969), Burridge emphasizes the centrality of confession in a variety of social and religious contexts (495, s.v. "confession"). Compare his odd generalization on traditional Melanesians, who tend "to be prudish, obsessional, suspicious, and much given to wrestling with their consciences" (idem, *New Heaven, New Earth: A Study of Millenarian Activities* [Pavilion Series; Oxford: Blackwell, 1969], 40).

cosmic power that defines a view of human nature and, therefore, entails some sort of Christ myth with both cosmic and anthropological implications does not seem to be present. There appears to be some native Christian Christ mythology in the formulations concerning "the sending of the Spirit," at times associated with the "return of Christ," which would eliminate "sin" as the tension between native and Christian practices by an erasure of indigenous practices.[33] It is impossible to judge the degree to which the "sending" or the "return," or both, are homologized to the quite different indigenous concept of a return of the ancestors, a concept reinterpreted in the cargo cults.[34] (For ways in which the Christ myth is interpreted in coastal Papua New Guinea, see the materials quoted in n. 45 below.)

III

As I have understood the term, *redescription*, at the level of data, is neither a procedure of substitution nor of synonymy; it is the result of comparison across difference, taking cognitive advantage of the resultant mutual distortion. (For this reason, among others, I have preferred analogical comparisons, such as the Atbalmin to the Corinthians, over homological ones.) Redescriptions, at the level of data, are in the service of a second, more generic revisionary enterprise: redescribing the categories employed in the study of religion.[35]

In the cases at hand, I should like to focus on two different fields. The first encompasses the social situation; the second, various mythic formations. One might, in a quite commonsense fashion, suppose the first to be relevant to the attraction of the second.

Two major elements stand out in which the New Guinea materials make more plausible our imagination of some early Christian social formations. The first is the ability of a small, relatively homogeneous community[36] to absorb a stunning series

---

33. Bercovitch, "Altar of Sin," 223.

34. The theme of the return of the ancestors bearing goods is an element in indigenous religions of the region, reconfigured in cargo cults. See the literature cited in Jonathan Z. Smith, "A Pearl of Great Price and a Cargo of Yams: A Study in Situational Incongruity," *HR* 16 (1976): 16 n. 46; repr. in *Imagining Religion*, 161 n. 46.

35. See, further, my remarks on *redescription* in Jonathan Z. Smith, "*Dayyeinu*," in *Redescribing Christian Origins* (ed. Ron Cameron and Merrill P. Miller; SBLSymS 28; Atlanta: Society of Biblical Literature; Leiden and Boston: Brill, 2004), 483–87.

36. I use the term "relative homogeneity" to reflect on the fact that, among folk who live in small-scale societies with traditional kinship systems, while ethnically identical, kinship serves both to manufacture difference and to overcome that difference. I have generalized this as culture being "constituted by the double process of both making differences and relativizing those very same distinctions. One of our fundamental social projects appears to be our collective capacity to think of, and to think away, the differences we create" (Jonathan Z. Smith, "Differential Equations: On Constructing the Other," in *Relating Religion*, 242). Compare the cuisine analogy in idem, "Sacred Persistence: Towards a Redescription of Canon," in *Approaches to Ancient Judaism: Theory and Practice* (ed. William Scott Green; BJS 1; Missoula, Mont.: Scholars Press, 1978), 14–16, 28; repr. in *Imagining Religion*,

of situational changes within a brief span of time through strategies of incorporation and resistance. In the case of the Atbalmin, we might list, in rough chronological order, first contact with Europeans; European presence; Christian missionization (both Australian and, more successfully, by neighboring native Christians); the adoption of non-native language (Tok Pisin) to denote central elements of this new religion; European alteration of the landscape (especially the copper mines); intrusion of ethnically distinct natives (the West Papuans); a disastrous storm; and the destruction or interruption of some traditional sacra.[37] The West Papuans, with whom the Atbalmin interacted, having experienced the intrusion of foreign governments and Europeans at home, now, within the same time frame, underwent displacement from their land and their honored dead. The second element is the capacity of a small, relatively homogeneous community to experiment, simultaneously, with multiple modes of religion. (Bercovitch described four.) The Atbalmin have exhibited, within their social and religious history, the dialectical relations of processes of reproduction and transformation that constitute, with particular clarity, what Marshall Sahlins has termed "structures of conjuncture."[38]

As a generalization, all of this makes more plausible the presumption of the coexistence of multiple experiments by early "Christian" communities as well as their localism. It alerts us to the presence of sorts of changes not necessarily captured by the historical record. The small, relatively homogeneous communities of the Atbalmin resemble more closely our imagination of the Galilean villages associated with the Sayings Gospel Q and the Jesus traditions. However, in a locale such as Corinth, the clear presence of face-to-face communications networks and the relative prominence of "households" suggest the existence of analogous communities within the larger urban landscape that served as the primary sites of earliest Christian experimentations. This suggests the possibility of thinking of Paul (and

---

39–41, 141. In "Differential Equations," 242–45, 250, I explored this "fundamental social project" in terms of the Hua people who live on the slopes of Mount Michael in the Eastern Highlands province of Papua New Guinea.

37. Note that such a series of events is capable of being addressed through more dramatic mythic and ritual means. See, e.g., the Bimin-Kuskusmin response to first contact (Poole, "Wisdom and Practice," 29–31, 42–44 n. 8); alteration of the environment, in this case, taking oil samples (ibid., 31–38); and destruction of sacra (idem, "The Reason of Myth and the Rationality of History: The Logic of the Mythic in Bimin-Kuskusmin 'Modes of Thought,'" in *Religion and Practical Reason: New Essays in the Comparative Philosophy of Religions* [ed. Frank E. Reynolds and David Tracy; SUNY Series, Toward a Comparative Philosophy of Religions; Albany: State University of New York Press, 1994], 263–326, esp. 284–306).

38. See Marshall Sahlins, *Historical Metaphors and Mythical Realities: Structure in the Early History of the Sandwich Islands Kingdom* (Association for Social Anthropology in Oceania 1; Ann Arbor: University of Michigan Press, 1981). For a later, more general statement, employing a different vocabulary, see idem, "Goodbye to *Tristes Tropes*: Ethnography in the Context of Modern World History," *University of Chicago Record* 27/3 (February 4, 1993): 2–7; repr., with a considerable number of revisions, in *Journal of Modern History* 65 (1993): 1–25; repr. in *Culture in Practice: Selected Essays* (New York: Zone Books, 2000), 471–500.

others) as intrusive on the native religious formations of the Corinthians addressed in 1 Corinthians, analogous, to some degree, to intrusions on the Atbalmin.

We would expect (and therefore may find less surprising or interesting) more diversity and historical complexity in pluralistic urban settings, especially those coastal cities engaged in translocal commerce. This has been a historical truism for circum-Mediterranean settlements; it holds as well for the Papua New Guinea coast, as any number of ethnographies that focus on so-called syncretism would indicate. (See the coastal Ngaing example, n. 45 below.) Corinth has been taken as a "usual" exemplar of such pluralisms. Yet there is more. The Corinthians are the result of a relatively recent displacement and re-placement: the resettlement of Corinth (44 B.C.E.), involving the movement of non-Roman populations of freed slaves from Greece, Syria, Judea, and Egypt.[39] In this respect they bear some situational analogy to the West Papuan refugees.

Informed by this analogy, I would propose, as an initial move, deploying the West Papuans' interest in ancestors and the land of the dead in order to interrupt the usual lexical chain that moves from "Spirit" (*pneuma*) and "Holy Spirit" in the New Testament to *rûaḥ* in the Hebrew Bible with, more recently, a crucial detour to Qumran, before rushing on to invoke the dominant paradigm in New Testament scholarship of Easter/Pentecost. If careful, the usual semasiological litany pauses briefly to note some aberrations (F. W. Horn terms them "unique uses of *pneuma*")[40] such as *pneuma* meaning "ghost" in Luke 24:37, 39, or *pneumata* as referring to the (righteous) "dead" in Heb 12:23. (Depending on how the scholar decides the undecidable "spirits in prison," 1 Pet 3:19 may be cited as a parallel to the plural usage in Hebrews.) I would like to suggest, on the basis of our ethnographic comparative example, that, for some Corinthians with whom Paul interacts, such usages, linking spirit(s) with the dead, are by no means aberrant but rather constitute the norm.

If this be maintained, a different genealogy for "spirit" in Corinth suggests itself: one that begins in the Hebrew Bible with the scattered, polemic references to *ʾôb* or the word pair *ʾôb* and *yiddĕʿōnî* (more frequently, the plural *ʾôbôt wĕyiddĕʿōnîm*), with newer translations, such as the RSV and the NRSV, rendering *ʾôb* as "medium."[41] While Bernhard W. Anderson, in *The Oxford Annotated Bible*

---

39. I presume the summary of Corinthian data in Jerome Murphy-O'Connor, *St. Paul's Corinth: Texts and Archaeology* (GNS 6; Wilmington, Del.: Glazier, 1983), as updated in idem, "Corinth," *ABD* 1:1134–39. At our meeting in Nashville in 2000, John S. Kloppenborg drew the seminar's attention to the possible significance of the resettlement of Corinth.

40. F. W. Horn, "Holy Spirit," *ABD* 3:266.

41. The translation history of the terminology is revealing. Both the Greek and the Latin shift the force of the term to the performer. The Vulgate employs the generic *magus*; the LXX, the rare word *engastrimythos* in the majority of cases. In the latter, the implication of fraud ("ventriloquist") has shifted to "medium" as in the parallel *engastrimantis* (compare the 9th ed. of LSJ [467a] with the 1968 Supplement [46b]). I know of only one scholar, the always interesting if often eccentric comparative philologist Richard Broxton Onians, who, in an addendum, has attempted an explanation of the term

to the RSV (1962), glosses *ʾôb* as "necromancy" (*ad* Lev 19:31), Jacob Milgrom, in *The HarperCollins Study Bible* to the NRSV (1993), glosses the term as "mediums, or [consulting] 'ancestral spirits'" (*ad* Lev 19:31; cf. 20:5–6, 27). Our Papua New Guinea materials would strongly support the latter reading, requiring us to delete the sanitary pips.

What has brought about this revisionary understanding of the biblical term, that *ʾôbôt* means "ancestral spirits" or "spirits of the dead," is a set of studies of comparative Near Eastern materials effectively summarized by Joseph Tropper.[42]

Analogous notions of oracular relations to the ancestors and the more proximate dead, in the context of a set of cultic relations and responsibilities to the dead, are thus found in Papua New Guinea, Israel, and the ancient Near East and are likewise present in each of the culture areas from which the resettled population of Corinth was derived. While such relations are often seen as problematic from the perspective of temple-based religion, they are an essential component of domestic religion. Drawing on my previous work on this theme[43] and influenced by the Papua New Guinea materials, we might imagine two different sorts of essentially familial practices obtaining for some groups in Corinth. (I separate here what may, in fact, be joined in practice.) One would focus on cultic relations with the spirit(s) of the now dislocated ancestors left behind in the homeland. Such relations would include attempts to obtain oracular esoteric wisdom. Another would focus on cultic relations with the more immediate dead, now buried in Corinth, and would include a range of activities from memorial meals with the dead to oracles guiding present behavior, including moral guidance. I see nothing that would have prevented both sorts of honored dead being referred to as *pneumata* (analogous to the honored dead being termed *ʾĕlōhîm* in 1 Sam 28:13; cf., less unambiguously, Isa 8:19; Mic 3:7; also 2 Sam 14:16)[44] or, collectively, as *pneuma*.

---

as a proper translation reflecting an Israelitic and Greek conception of a spirit in the belly (*The Origins of European Thought about the Body, the Mind, the Soul, the World, Time, and Fate* [Cambridge: Cambridge University Press, 1951], 480–505, esp. 488–90 with nn.). The KJV translates "familiar spirit," keeping the magical/demonic sense, but shifting away from the performer. More recent scholarship has translated *ʾôb* more directly as "spirit of the dead" or the "deified spirit of the ancestors," while rendering the associated term *yiddĕʿōnî* as "all-knowing," an "epithet of the deceased ancestors or a designation of the dead in general" (J. Tropper, "Wizard," in *Dictionary of Deities and Demons in the Bible [DDD]* [ed. Karel van der Toorn et al.; Leiden: Brill, 1995], 1706).

42. J. Tropper, "Spirit of the Dead," in *Dictionary of Deities and Demons in the Bible*, 1524–30; cf. idem, "Wizard," 1705–7.

43. See especially Jonathan Z. Smith, "Here, There, and Anywhere," in *Prayer, Magic, and the Stars in the Ancient and Late Antique World* (ed. Scott Noegel et al.; Magic in History Series; University Park: Pennsylvania State University Press, 2003), 21–36; repr. in *Relating Religion*, 323–39.

44. See the important treatment of (spirits of) the dead as *ʾĕlōhîm* in Theodore J. Lewis, *Cults of the Dead in Ancient Israel and Ugarit* (HSM 39; Atlanta: Scholars Press, 1989), 49–52, 115–17, 178–79, et passim; cf. idem, "The Ancestral Estate (נַחֲלַת אֱלֹהִים) in 2 Samuel 14:16," *JBL* 110 (1991): 597–612, esp. 602–3.

It would be my suggestion that Paul has misconstrued these relations, understanding the variety of cultic activities with respect to the spirit(s) of the dead as being related to his already formed notion of the (holy) spirit (1 Thess 1:6; etc.) as well as to his already formed notion of tripartite anthropology (1 Thess 5:23). This is the same sort of mistranslation the Atbalmin Christians and Revivalists employed with their specifically Christian Tok Pisin term "Holy Spirit," and their recasting of spirit-possession relations to the ancestors in the specifically Christian vocabulary of "possessed by the Holy Spirit."

Thus, I think, Paul would have understood one thing, some groups of Corinthians another, when *pneuma* is associated with *gnōsis*; when Paul claims to have authority for guiding present behavior because he "has the spirit of God" (1 Cor 7:40) or when he himself can be present "in spirit" (1 Cor 5:3–4) at the occasion of a communal moral dilemma; when they meet together for a meal for/with the dead (the celebratory meal of 1 Cor 11:20–21, which seems both traditional and non-Christian), to which a Lord's supper has apparently been added; or when they are concerned about baptism for the dead (1 Cor 15:29).

The imagination of such an understanding among some Corinthians requires another sort of redescription, at the level of the data, with respect to our scholarly imagination of the "divisions" at Corinth (the strong/weak, the spiritists, let alone claims for the presence of proto-Gnostics). What I have been terming, with deliberate vagueness, "some Corinthians," does not map a group (or groups) that accord(s) with the topography of "parties" provided by those fragments conventionally identified as "slogans" quoted by Paul from his opponents. However, I am not prepared, in this paper, to offer a counterproposal.

One consequence of this hesitation is that I have made no mention of "speaking in tongues." I suspect that Paul himself is straining to understand the phenomenon that he encounters in Corinth as suggested by his (surprising?) appeal to the Delphic model of ecstatic speech interpreted by a prophet. Paul may well have misunderstood the practice. I am tempted to suggest that if the communication is with the spirits of the ancestral dead, and if the Corinthians are, at most, second-generation immigrants to Corinth, then perhaps the ancestral spirits are being addressed in their native, homeland language. Such language is frequently maintained for ceremonial and religious purposes by second-generation immigrants. If this be the case, Paul has taken "xenoglossia" (the *lalein heterais glōssais* of Acts 2:4) to be "glossolalia."

I raise these matters as having relevance to my assigned topic: Paul's Christ myth at Corinth. If what I have redescribed is at all plausible, then Paul is implausible. Perhaps this is why, except for formulae (e.g., the repeated "Christ crucified"), the myth is rarely elaborated in 1 Corinthians. It appears to play a role chiefly in those instances where Paul is palpably in difficulty: his shift on "idols" from being meaningless to meaningful (1 Cor 10:14–30); the polemic against Corinthian meal practice (1 Cor 11:23–26), where his strongest argument, finally, is not mythmaking but rather the threat of supernatural sanction (1 Cor 11:31-32); and the discourse on resurrection (1 Cor 15).

It is this last issue that makes clear why a Christ myth would be, strictly speaking, meaningless to some Corinthian groups.[45] If Christ, having died, is no longer

---

45. In the coastal regions of Papua New Guinea, which have a long history of being missionized by Christians, there is some focus on translating some understanding of the Christ myth into native idiom and practice. Take, for example, the Ngaing linguistic groups inhabiting the Madang region on the Rai Coast, first contacted by Europeans in 1871 and missionized since at least 1885—a date that may be extended back to 1847-55. Indigenous religion focused on male ceremonies "honouring the spirits of the dead" (Peter Lawrence, *Road Belong Cargo: A Study of the Cargo Movement in the Southern Madang District, New Guinea* [Manchester: Manchester University Press, 1964], 13, 17-18, et passim). For a more complete account, see idem, "The Ngaing of the Rai Coast," in *Gods, Ghosts and Men in Melanesia: Some Religions of Australian New Guinea and the New Hebrides* (ed. P. Lawrence and M. J. Meggitt; Melbourne: Oxford University Press, 1965), 198-223, esp. 206-12; repr. in *Cultures of the Pacific: Selected Readings* (ed. Thomas G. Harding and Ben J. Wallace; New York: Free Press; London: Collier-Macmillan, 1970), 285-303, 456-58, esp. 292-96.

There was a short-lived Madang cargo movement (1956-61), led by Lagit, an indigenous, former Christian catechist from a Catholic mission who killed a man in front of assembled villagers by slitting his throat. The incident was prearranged, we are told, as the victim went voluntarily to his death. Lagit's explanation, in the ethnographer's paraphrase, was that "it was necessary for a native to make the same sacrifice as Jesus Christ had made for Europeans before the native standard of living could be raised" (Lawrence, *Road Belong Cargo*, 267).

A more complicated case of translation, in both ritual and narrative idiom, ultimately involving the sequence of the Synoptic passion narrative, is from another Ngaing-speaking group "located in the hinterland of the Rai Coast," whose name has been concealed by the ethnographer, Wolfgang Kempf, in "Ritual, Power and Colonial Domination: Male Initiation among the Ngaing of Papua New Guinea," in *Syncretism/Anti-Syncretism: The Politics of Religious Synthesis* (ed. Charles Stewart and Rosalind Shaw; European Association of Social Anthropologists; New York: Routledge, 1994), 108-26.

For this group, traditional male initiation involves, above all, the display to the initiates of secret objects related to the ancestors that are usually kept hidden in water. After a last meal with his family as an uninitiated male, the novice went into seclusion for a three-week period, during which he was shown the sacra and was governed by a wide-ranging set of prohibitions. He then emerged and his new status was publicly recognized.

In the early 1950s, circumcision was introduced to one village in the region as a hygenic practice by a native medical orderly. It subsequently became linked with initiation as a ritual practice, as well as with the characteristic Melanesian male rationale for penile bloodletting: removal of the dark, female blood from the bright male blood so that one's body is healthy and shining. (Kempf presumes some cultural interaction with Austronesian coastal traditions that, unlike the Ngaing peoples but like some Papua New Guinea Highland tribes, practice a variety of forms of penile bloodletting.) Here, on the basis of an interchange of native traditions, a new ritual was inserted into the traditional initiatory sequence: immediately after the novice's farewell meal and before the first display of sacra. Following a public confession, usually stressing sexual misconduct, the circumcision commenced, discarding the first, dark blood and saving the subsequent bright blood. This was bound together with a bundle of bullroarers (one of the sacra to be displayed).

For indigenous Christians who practice these initiatory rituals, translation was required of this new ritual into their understanding of Christian idiom, informed by a sentiment widely held

dead, then this violates the fundamental presupposition that the ancestors and the dead remain dead, even though they are thoroughly interactive with their living descendants in an extended family comprising the living and the dead. For the ancestral dead, it is the fact of their death, not its mode and significance (e.g., topoi of martyrdom, sacrifice, enthronement), that establishes and sustains their power.[46]

The problematic, for both the West Papuans and the Corinthians here imagined, is not death but rather distance. To take the West Papuan refugee immigrants at their word, there is a problem because their "center" is "far away in the lowlands of Irian Jaya, where the place of the dead [is] located."[47]

Some Corinthians may have understood Paul as providing them, in the figure of Christ, with a more proximate and mobile ancestor for their new, non-ethnic "Christian" *ethnos*.[48] Certainly, celestial figures often have a mobile advantage over

---

in cargo cults, that the European missionaries have reversed or concealed the true meaning of Scripture from the natives. To present the ethnographer's summary of this native Christian translation: "Jesus' baptism by John the Baptist at the River Jordan has come to be associated with displaying the traditional gourd instruments. John is considered to be Jesus' classificatory mother's brother and, as such, is held to have initiated him into the domain of the secret gourd instruments which . . . are associated with water. The . . . men know too that Jesus was circumcised. The young men particularly interpret the crucifixion of Jesus as his ritual circumcision. The Last Supper is . . . compared with the last meal eaten by the . . . candidates the evening before their circumcision. Judas is not considered as a betrayer but as Jesus' classificatory mother's brother. He led him to Pontius Pilate who . . . was [understood as] a member of an oppositional patriclan and thus responsible for the circumcision. Pilate is believed to have questioned Jesus thoroughly on his premarital affairs but could not establish that Jesus had "sinned." This cross-examination is the equivalent of the confession conducted before circumcision. . . . Then the crucifixion took place, this being nothing but Jesus' circumcision. The three days after Jesus' death are interpreted as his three weeks of seclusion. Finally, the resurrection is identified with the public presentation of the initiates at the close of the circumcision rites" (Kempf, "Ritual, Power and Colonial Domination," 113). Note that basic elements of the Christ myth (in its narrative form) are here refused. Congruent with my discussion above, death is not death, nor is resurrection a resurrection.

46. I have explored some of these themes elsewhere, especially in Jonathan Z. Smith, *Drudgery Divine: On the Comparison of Early Christianities and the Religions of Late Antiquity* (Jordan Lectures in Comparative Religion 14; London: School of Oriental and African Studies, University of London; Chicago: University of Chicago Press, 1990), 109–14, 120–43.

47. Bercovitch, "Altar of Sin," 219.

48. I have been influenced here by the observations of Stanley K. Stowers in his important contribution ("On Construing Meals, Myths and Power in the World of Paul") to our Consultation on Ancient Myths and Modern Theories of Christian Origins, held in New Orleans in 1996. I draw particular attention to three of Stowers's remarks with respect to the meal at Corinth, which have been incorporated into his paper "Kinds of Myth, Meals, and Power: Paul and the Corinthians," 136, 137, 138 (in this volume): "[T]he signals and expectations suggested by the Lord's supper might be read as confusing and contradictory in the context of the codes of eating in Greco-Roman culture. . . . Instead of the community being constituted and tested by eating meat, it exists by eating bread that is a symbol of an absent body that points both to the significance of giving up that body and to the loyalty of the social body toward that symbol. . . . [W]here is the body in the Lord's supper? It is present in its absence. The bread of human art is the reminder of a body that occupies no place." Compare Burton

chthonic ones, who are more readily bound to a place. Perhaps some Corinthians found support for a new sort of ancestor in Paul's first/last Adam language in 1 Cor 15 (esp. v. 45), but this is vitiated by its context as part of a defense of resurrection, unless it was previously heard in another context. Perhaps some Corinthians found support for a new sort of ancestor in the complex set of registers played by Paul on *sōma*, with the body of Christ understood in a corporate sense (1 Cor 12:12–14, 27) as a new collective ancestor. (Compare the term that used to be popular with respect to Israel, "corporate personality.") This new ancestor continues to be experienced in a traditional way, in a meal (1 Cor 10:17).

However, none of this will do without a major effort in non-Pauline mythmaking by some Corinthians. For the continuing present liveliness of the ancestors and the dead is predicated on their continuing status as dead. This effort at mythmaking would need to be coupled with their apparent ritual experimentation on new modes of relations to the dead, such as that suggested by 1 Cor 15:29.

One might go on to redescribe other themes in 1 Corinthians as a result of the Papua New Guinea comparison. For example, "sin" as a term for expressing the tension between traditional indigenous and native Christian behavior, especially in matters of sexual conduct, kinship, eating, and "idolatry"—to list topics the Atbalmin have in common with the Corinthians.[49] Or, one might explore the attraction of the promise of participation in an enlarged Christian landscape for a relatively small group, as described for the Atbalmin, and as suggested in 1 Corinthians with its multiple references to an extended Christian "family," present in other locales but bound together by a communications network of letters, travels, and gifts.

I shall let matters rest at this point. This experiment in redescription suggests that a Christ myth, as represented by Paul in the course of his intrusion on the Corinthians, would have been uninteresting to some Corinthians; and that a spirit myth, as they appear to have understood it, might have been interesting to some Corinthians in that it was "good to think." The Corinthian situation may well be defined as the efforts at translations between these understandings and misunderstandings.[50]

L. Mack's remark concerning "Christ the first father of a non-ethnic genealogy," in his response to Stowers's paper at the same consultation.

49. The issue of eating meat sacrificed to idols at Corinth would receive an assist from the interpretative framework that Keane brings to his Sumbanese example ("Materialism," 137–70).

50. In this paper, I have not followed redescription at the level of data with an attempt at the rectification of generic scholarly categories within the study of religion, nor within the study of early Christianities. As indicated above, a prime candidate for rectification would be the broad, somewhat diffuse category of "enthusiasm," one of a set of terms of Christian pedigree (e.g., "charismatic") that have frequently been applied to nativistic social and religious phenomena. In the history of scholarship, in both the study of religion and the study of early Christianities, 1 Corinthians has served as the canonical example for these categories.

Rereading the Christ Myth: Paul's Gospel and the Christ Cult Question

Burton L. Mack

Introduction

I have been asked to revisit my chapter on the "Congregations of the Christ" in *A Myth of Innocence*,[1] a reconstruction that came up for review and critique in our final sessions of the seminar, on Mark, in Atlanta (2003). In that chapter I had used the term "Christ cult" and had in mind what the (Bultmannian-)German tradition of scholarship called "pre-Pauline Hellenistic Christianity." My intention was to explain the rhetorical and social logics of the "Christ myth" and the "ritual meal" as evidence for an early "community" from which the Jesus movements and the Markan milieu markedly differed. It is that assumption that now needs to be addressed. Nor is it the first time in the history of our seminar that the notion of a pre-Pauline "Christ cult" has caused problems. After our sessions in Boston (1999) on the Jesus movements, we had planned to redescribe the "pre-Pauline Christ cult" before going on to Paul and the Corinthians. However, at the end of the Boston sessions we decided that the notion of a pre-Pauline, Hellenistic Christ cult was too problematic to tackle at the time. Not only was the notion itself loaded with questionable historical and theological assumptions; the texts traditionally used to document such a community were also difficult to isolate from Paul's letters and place in a non-Pauline social setting. We decided instead to move directly to Paul's correspondence with the Corinthians, where a social situation was more in evidence. This left the question of a Christ cult unaddressed, a question that has continued to simmer and haunt us throughout the seminar's project.[2]

---

1. Burton L. Mack, *A Myth of Innocence: Mark and Christian Origins* (Philadelphia: Fortress, 1988; repr., Minneapolis: Fortress, 2006), 98–123; cf. idem, *Who Wrote the New Testament? The Making of the Christian Myth* (San Francisco: HarperSanFrancisco, 1995), 75–96.
2. See Burton L. Mack, "Backbay Jazz and Blues," in *Redescribing Christian Origins* (ed. Ron Cameron and Merrill P. Miller; SBLSymS 28; Atlanta: Society of Biblical Literature; Leiden and Boston: Brill, 2004), 421–31.

There are several reasons for taking up this question again, now at the end of the project. One is that our work on Paul and the Corinthians made it quite clear that we were dealing with a "double disjunction." One disjunction was that between Paul's address to the Corinthians and the language and practices of the Corinthians themselves. It was this disjunction that took most of our attention, and we were able to make a significant advance on our understanding of the conceptual (i.e., mythic) and social issues involved. The other disjunction was that between Paul's address to the Corinthians, on the one hand, and the "traditions" he said he had "received" which grounded his "gospel," on the other. We did note that Paul had himself elaborated on these "traditions" in ways that made it difficult to determine their pre-Pauline formulations. In addition, Jonathan Z. Smith noted that "the [Christ] myth is rarely elaborated in 1 Corinthians,"[3] this despite Paul's claim to have known "nothing among [the Corinthians] except Jesus Christ, and him crucified" (1 Cor 2:2). This means that the texts Paul recited for the traditions he had received were left largely unexplored. The texts he cited as "traditions" were those of the "Christ myth" (1 Cor 15:3–5) and the "ritual meal" (1 Cor 11:23–25). These texts turn out to be the major loci for the customary Christian and scholarly imagination of the earliest Christian "communities" or congregations of the Christ. Not only has Paul's construction upon these texts been taken to reconstruct the beliefs and practices of the earliest Christian communities, but the resulting picture has then been used to position and interpret the Jesus materials and the Gospel of Mark, and especially the "passion narratives," as evidence for the way in which Christianity began. Thus, the dominant paradigm of Christian origins has been to imagine it anachronistically by lumping together the diverse data of the New Testament as a whole and taking it as a coherent collection of accounts that document the origins of a single group formation with its practices and persuasions. Since the project of the seminar has been to offer an alternative to this picture of Christian origins, the failure to include a closer look at each of these texts, pivotal for the customary imagination, points to a bit of unfinished business.

It is not that the seminar's work has not made progress in its project of redescription, or that many of its findings are not directly related to a revision of the way in which the Christ myth and meal texts have usually been read. Merrill P. Miller's papers on the term *christos* in Hebrew literature and the New Testament showed that the "Christ myth" was not a myth of "the Christ" understood as "Messiah" at all.[4] The papers on the "Jerusalem church" by Miller, Dennis E. Smith, and Christopher R. Matthews problematized Paul's account in Galatians of the "pillars" there and the "gospel" he discussed with them.[5] As for the meal text in 1 Cor

---

3. Jonathan Z. Smith, "Re: Corinthians," 31 (in this volume).

4. Merrill P. Miller, "The Problem of the Origins of a Messianic Conception of Jesus," in Cameron and Miller, *Redescribing Christian Origins*, 301–35; and, in the same volume, idem, "The Anointed Jesus," 375–415.

5. Merrill P. Miller, "Antioch, Paul, and Jerusalem: Diaspora Myths of Origins in the Home-

11, the text traditionally taken as primary evidence for an early Christian ritual of mythic reenactment, Stanley K. Stowers's paper given at our consultation in New Orleans (1996)[6] and the papers by Stowers, Jonathan Z. Smith, and Richard S. Ascough on Paul and the Corinthians in Nashville (2000) and Denver (2001)[7] did not support the customary reading. Instead, we were able to account for the Corinthians' practices and Paul's instructions to them solely in terms of issues raised by the different conceptual and social models underlying the discussions between and among them. Nevertheless, the question of a "Christ cult" and the ways in which these crucial texts have usually been read to document the beliefs, practices, interests, and social formations of early Christian communities have not been forthrightly addressed by the seminar. That, I take it, is the assignment given to me.

I propose making a set of exegetical observations on the texts in order to reposition them away from the dominant paradigm and onto the seminar's emerging "map" of Christian beginnings. The thesis will be that both the "Christ myth" and the "ritual meal" text can be traced to mythmaking within the Jesus schools at some point where the thought of Jesus as a martyr for their cause was entertained. Ever since Miller's work on the emergence of the term *christos* in the Jesus schools (and my elaboration of that possibility in "Why *Christos*? The Social Reasons," also for the sessions in Boston),[8] as well as in our discussions of Mark and his martyrology in the traditions of the Jesus schools, this location of a Jesus martyr myth has been touched upon several times by the seminar, even if only tangentially. I shall assume this work as essentially correct and need not rehearse the reasons for coming to this hypothesis. However, since there were several narrative patterns available for "noble death" traditions at the time, and since there are different rationales and logics expressed by the several martyrological texts in the New Testament, I shall want to take note of the various ways in which these martyr myths may have been formulated, developed, and may have functioned within Jesus schools and *christos* associations. I can do this in the course of exploring the possible rationales implicit in features of the Pauline texts when read as martyr myths. I plan to

---

land," in Cameron and Miller, *Redescribing Christian Origins*, 177–235; and, in the same volume, Dennis E. Smith, "What Do We Really Know about the Jerusalem Church? Christian Origins in Jerusalem according to Acts and Paul," 237–52; and Christopher R. Matthews, "Acts and the History of the Earliest Jerusalem Church," 159–75.

6. Stanley K. Stowers, "On Construing Meals, Myths and Power in the World of Paul" (paper presented at the annual meeting of the Society of Biblical Literature, New Orleans, Louisiana, November 1996), now incorporated, in part, in idem, "Kinds of Myth, Meals, and Power: Paul and the Corinthians" (in this volume).

7. Stanley K. Stowers, "Does Pauline Christianity Resemble a Hellenistic Philosophy?" (in this volume); Smith, "Re: Corinthians"; Richard S. Ascough, "Paul's 'Apocalypticism' and the Jesus Associations at Thessalonica and Corinth" (in this volume).

8. Burton L. Mack, "Why *Christos*? The Social Reasons," in Cameron and Miller, *Redescribing Christian Origins*, 365–74.

use the term "Christ myth" for the text as we have it in Paul, and the terms "Jesus myth" and "*christos* myth" for earlier variants within the Jesus schools and *christos* associations hypothesized. All three variants can be called martyr myths. The point will be to offer an alternative to the customary readings that have taken these texts as evidence for a "Christ cult," that is, a religious community that formed soon after the "Christ event" (i.e., the "death and resurrection" of Jesus understood as that event that changed the course of history and inaugurated the new Christian time) and that gathered for prayers, rituals, and instructions on the model of later Christian churches. It is, as a matter of fact, this penchant for seeing later forms of Christian practice already established at the beginning of Christian history that has determined the way in which these texts have always been read. After discussing each of these texts, I will then want to say something about Paul's own interest in and manipulation of the martyr myth in relation to his own "gospel," the formulation of which Stowers has seen in Gal 3:8, that is, the promise to Abraham that the Gentiles would be justified.[9] Finally, it will be necessary to describe the new "landscape" of "*christos* associations" that has emerged to take the place of the older notion of "Christ cult."

I. The Christ Myth: 1 Corinthians 15:3-5

Paul calls this text a "tradition" that he had "received" and "passed on" to the Corinthians. But where does the text end, given the fact that Paul adds himself to the list of those apostles to whom Christ appeared after his being raised, and how can this be a "tradition" when elsewhere (Gal 1:11-12) he says that he did not receive his gospel from a human source? The critical reader need not stumble over Paul's attempts to enhance his authority as a tradent of a teaching in need of rationalization, or his inconsistencies of argumentation. These moves can be understood as rhetorical swerves in the interest of particular argumentations, a common feature of Paul's style. But if this is so, what exactly about the text is "traditional," that is, not Paul's construal? And where might any of its non- or pre-Pauline elements be located among the Jesus or *christos* associations plausibly imagined on the basis of data available to us from the Jesus schools? Thus, the task facing us is to account for the more obvious Pauline elaborations (in light of the larger textual context of his writings and the thrust of his argumentation in which this text occurs), reconstruct from the textual unit the "traditions" he elaborated, and explain their logic as myths in the service of some social formations. At this point I need to mention my reconstruction of the text and rather extensive discussion of it in *A Myth of Innocence*.[10] Some of that discussion is still appropriate for our present purposes despite the revisions that now need to be made. When writing that chapter, I saw

---

9. Stanley K. Stowers, *A Rereading of Romans: Justice, Jews, and Gentiles* (New Haven: Yale University Press, 1994), 71, 307; cf. 167, 171, 225, 229.

10. Mack, *Myth of Innocence*, 103-13; cf. idem, *Who Wrote the New Testament?* 79-87.

the textual unit as a thoughtful composition created by scribal activity within the "Christ cult," a composition that imagined Jesus' death with the general pattern of a "noble death" in mind. But the evidence for "scribal activity" is no longer sufficient for locating my reconstruction in the pre-Pauline *christos* associations, much less Jesus traditions. A closer reading of the composition will show that the several components have different logics, that the several logics do not complement one another, and that taken together they do not describe a conventional martyrdom nor fit what we can imagine for the social formations and mythmakings of a Jesus or *christos* association. Thus, Paul's hand may well have added more to this "tradition" than the inclusion of himself in the list of those to whom Jesus appeared. The revisions will therefore have to be critical considerations regarding the "cause" for which Jesus died, the assertion of a burial, the purpose of the statement that "he was raised," and other oddities of the formulation including the "appearances." These matters are not clear in the formulations of the textual unit as it stands or as I reconstructed it, and thus require renewed attempts to place the several statements in social contexts with larger sets of interests and persuasions to provide their significance.

A. *The Term* Christ

The first revision will have to be some caution with the use of the term "Christ." In *A Myth of Innocence,* I suggested that Jesus had come to be imagined as the "king" of the "kingdom" basic to his teachings in the course of the mythmaking that resulted in the "Christ myth." It is obvious that I was thinking of the term "Christ" as a royal figure of expectation, that is, the "Messiah." Miller's work on the question of "How Jesus Became Christ: Probing a Thesis" presented a critique of my suggestion.[11] He argued that the combination of a martyr myth with the term "Christ," if taken as a reference to a royal figure of expectation, made no sense at all and called for further study. Then, in his work on the term *māšîaḥ/christos* for the seminar, both in "The Anointed Jesus" and in his paper on "The Problem of the Origins of a Messianic Conception of Jesus," Miller succeeded in reconstructing a history of the uses of the term *māšîaḥ/christos* from the Hebrew literature of the time (where it was used as an ascriptive adjective for several social roles and *not* as a noun or title for a royal figure of future expectation, i.e., "the Messiah"), through Paul's use of it as a name or byname (*cognomen*) for Jesus (where the point was not to assert that Jesus was or is "the Messiah," a concept not yet in view), to end with its occurrence in Mark and Luke-Acts as a titular substantive, that is, "the Messiah." It was this titular use and its development into second-century Christian usage that turned a non-titular, non-"messianic" term into the concept of "the Messiah." Note that this took place at the end of the history of the term's uses. In

---

11. Merrill P. Miller, "How Jesus Became Christ: Probing a Thesis," *Continuum* 2/2–3 (1993): 243–70.

the early Jesus movements, where the term does not appear in any of the extant literature and thus cannot be documented as an original designation of or ascription for Jesus, Miller nonetheless hypothesized a social situation in which the term must have been used to enhance the authority of Jesus as a teacher and to claim legitimacy for his "school" (my term) by linking both to the epic mythology of "Israel." The reasons for thinking that the term must have been used at some point in this way within the Jesus movements are twofold. One is that Paul's usage of the term as a name (or cognomen) can hardly be understood except as derived from an earlier ascriptive use in some Jesus schools. The other reason is that the use of the term as the title for an eschatological role (i.e., "the Christ," "the Messiah") in Mark, Luke-Acts, and subsequent early Christian literature must have taken place in the course of creating a *bios* for Jesus the founder-teacher, for whom the ascriptive *christos* would already have been in use. Note, however, that in Mark the apocalyptic and/or eschatological frame is required in order to take *christos* as a title and substantive for a "messianic" social role, but that the linkage between this role for "the Christ" and the apocalyptic frame is held together only loosely in the larger story line. A "messianic" mythology was apparently not yet fully developed, but only in the making.

What all this means is that the logic of the martyr myth in 1 Cor 15:3–5 cannot be explained as the imagination of an originary event of significance in the eschatological appearance of "the Messiah" as usually assumed. The concept of the royal Messiah as a figure of future expectation had not yet been imagined (i.e., invented). And if we see that the enhancement of Jesus' role and authority by means of the ascriptive *christos* is similar to other ways of ascribing authority to him in the Jesus schools, a martyr myth could have been imagined for the "anointed Jesus" as easily as for any of the other enhancements of his importance as founder-teacher of a Jesus "school" in the process of forming an "association." But there is nothing about such an ascription that calls for or complements the logic of a martyrdom. Thus, if this text is to be seen as a martyr myth imagined for Jesus, its logic will have to be determined from the statements made in the text about the figure, not from the term "Christ" or derived from any "Christ cult" imagined on the Pauline model. The term *christos* is used in the text as a cognomen for Jesus, just as throughout Paul's letters. Since Paul uses the term *christos* as if it were common coin in the circles with which he was in contact, *christos* may have been the "name" attached to some form of the myth in its pre-Pauline or non-Pauline context. However, even with this observation in view, what Paul says elsewhere about Christ, or makes of this myth, has to be set aside if we want to understand the composition and logic of the text in a non-Pauline setting.

B. The Cause

A second revision of my earlier reading has to do with the "cause" for which Jesus died as expressed in the phrase "for our sins." It was the phrase "died for" that caught my attention the first time around, for it clearly indicates derivation from the tradition of martyrologies pervasive during the Greco-Roman age. In keeping with that derivation, I took the term "for" (ὑπέρ with the genitive) as referring to the "cause" for which a martyr died, examples being the city, the laws, the teachings, and so forth, all of which were understood to be defended by the martyr while under attack by the "tyrant." Since this setting and scenario were definitive for the traditional martyrology, and since a social logic was integral to this definition, I thought that the martyr myth for Jesus must have worked the same way. The "cause," I thought, must have been the "congregations of the Christ" on the Pauline model, in which a mix of Jew and Gentile required "justification." In his work on this text in *Jesus' Death as Saving Event*, Sam K. Williams had focused primarily on Rom 3:21–26,[12] where the language of "justification" does occur, to argue that the purpose of Jesus' death in the logic of martyrdom was exactly for the "justification" of Gentiles. Since the notion of Gentiles as "sinners" seemed to be standard in Jewish parlance of the time, the point of the myth did seem to be the justification of a Jesus-*christos* association of Jews and Gentiles as a legitimate heir to the history and epic of Israel. It did not occur to me at the time that this reading did not distinguish between Pauline and pre-Pauline conceptions of early "Christian" congregations. It actually allowed the traditional assumption to stay in place, namely, that the picture painted by Paul was somehow definitional for all early Christian "communities," and could be pressed back to the very beginnings.

Upon closer reading, of course, a few problems popped up, but none that called the basic rationale into question at the time. One problem was that the cause for which all other martyrs died was already known and in place as a social-cultural construct worth dying for. The cause for which Jesus died, however, was (in my interpretation) a social formation yet to come. I regarded this as an intellectual twist and challenge for the Jesus people wanting to use a martyr myth in order to imagine the approval of Israel's God for the association they had become. Another problem was that the emphasis on "our sins" was surely an odd formulation if intended as a description of the community in need of justifying a Jew–Gentile mix. A third problem was that dying "for" sins hardly made sense as the "cause" for which a martyr would die, especially attributed to Jesus, in whose teachings and schools the topic of sins and what to do about them never surfaced as issues. So what now can be said about this text in light of all the seminar's work on the redescription of Christian beginnings?

Well, the first thing to say is that the social group responsible for the martyr myth need not have been a mix of Jews and Gentiles troubled about their legitimacy by reason of the mix. Given our reconstructions of the Jesus schools and the association of Mark's milieu, both the "mission" to the Gentiles and the Jew–Gentile issue turn out to be Pauline concerns. We know, of course, that the

---

12. Sam K. Williams, *Jesus' Death as Saving Event: The Background and Origin of a Concept* (HDR 2; Missoula, Mont.: Scholars Press, 1975).

question of Gentile participation in the social life and institutions of Judeans was widely discussed at the time. But as an issue of fundamental importance for association with Jesus people, it appears not to have played a role as far as we have been able to tell, judging from the Jesus school materials available to us as data. Note, as well, that the notion of "justification" had to be added to the logic of the myth from Rom 3:21–26, a concern and formulation that are clearly Pauline and not indicated or called for by anything in the logic of the martyr myth or the Christ myth text. So that construction of the "cause" for which the martyr died looks now to be Pauline, both in the sense that Paul apparently construed the myth that way, and in the sense that a scholarly reading of the text solely in the context of Paul's letters has to be called "Pauline" as well.

But what, then, about "sins" as the "cause" for which Jesus died, and especially the fact that the sins were "ours"? We need not parry the classic Christian doctrine of sin and salvation, of course, nor should we worry about Paul's use of the term in Romans, where Christian exegetes have always found evidence for the beginnings of such a doctrine. Stowers has demonstrated that Paul's concept and language of sin(s) agree with its use and meaning in the Greco-Roman world at large, where the context is what he calls "Decline of Civilization Narratives."[13] The term should then be understood as a description of the state of the world or the condition of the peoples ("Gentiles" in Pauline parlance) in general when compared with social and cultural ideals imagined for the "primitive" or "ideal" past of civilization. And the state of the world so observed had to do with social practices and thinking held to be "failures" against that ideal standard. In no case should a moralistic psychology be used to define the term. It registered a social notion, and it was this social notion as I understood it in *A Myth of Innocence* that let me imagine the "cause" related to the "justification" of "Gentiles." Nevertheless, even if we read the phrase "for our sins" in the light of this usage, it puts considerable pressure on the notion that Jesus, if thought of on the model of other martyrs, died for an obvious "cause." "Our sins" is difficult to imagine as a "cause" worth dying for, and this makes the formulation problematic. As a shorthand social description, it is also odd. And the identity of the speakers (the "we" behind the "our") is exceptionally unclear, especially if coming from a mixed group if the problem addressed by the myth stemmed from Jewish concerns about the mix, and in which the authors then come to speech as if they were Gentiles (i.e., "sinners"). So while the phrase "died for" clearly resembles the formula found in traditional martyrologies, the formulation of "our sins" as the "cause" does not seem to work on that model. Can we nevertheless make some sense of it?

We might want to stop here for a moment and remind ourselves of the long-standing difficulties scholars have had with this text. The issue of translation quickly focuses on the two connotations of the term ὑπέρ with the genitive. In

---

13. Stowers, *Rereading of Romans*, 85, 382, s.v. "sin."

the martyrological tradition, the term is used in the sense of "for," "in defense of." But since this does not seem to work in the case of the present text, the nuance of "because of" or "on account of" has sometimes been tried. It may be helpful at this point to note that ἀποθνῄσκειν ("to die") also served as the passive for ἀποκτείνειν ("to kill"), and thus could be translated "was killed" or "put to death." In combination with ὑπέρ, then, both connotations of the "cause" are possible, whether "in defense of" or "on account of." It was the completion of the phrase with the genitive, as well as the known character of the martyr and the circumstances of the scenario imagined, that determined both the way in which a martyr's resolve and the tyrant's reasons were construed. Because the scenario is missing in this case, no translation has been completely satisfactory, even with the addition of a few provisos. All attempts have resulted in curious statements that require a lively mental gymnastic in order to work out the complicated relations among martyrological nuances, historical scenarios, and social consequences to any sort of satisfaction. It might be helpful, of course, to consider that construing a martyr's death for Jesus may actually have been a radical and mind-stretching thought for a Jesus school. There is little evidence in the Jesus traditions of lore about his death, much less about a martyr's death, until we get to Paul and Mark, whose views are clearly the result of mythmaking. Imagining a martyr's death for Jesus would therefore have been much less plausible a claim for a Jesus association to make about their founder-figure than for an Antioch synagogue to imagine the Maccabees as martyrs. What we have in our text is not a death "for the law," as in their case, or for some other "cause" for which a martyr may have died, but "for (or because of) our sins." There is, however, a more plausible "cause" for which a martyr's death for Jesus may have been entertained within a Jesus association, and that would have been "for his teachings" or "for the kingdom." Some such reference to what the Jesus schools understood Jesus to represent could have significantly positioned him, his teachings, and an association in his name in their differences from other Judean associations or synagogues in respect to customary codes of behavior and self-identification. The teachings and social formation of a Jesus association as "cause" would at least fit the logic of a traditional Greek martyrology, and the thought of the founder-teacher as a martyr would certainly have registered a claim worth making. I do not make this suggestion in the interest of imagining a plausible scenario for a historical crucifixion. As we know, attempts to find the motivation for a crucifixion in the teachings of Jesus have never been convincing in any case. But as mythmaking in the interest of a claim on the part of a Jesus-*christos* association to represent a legitimate school of teachings, it would not have been more difficult to entertain the notion of the teachings as the cause, than it would have been to think the thought of a martyr's death of Jesus at all.

Suppose we imagine a Jesus association in Antioch in conversation with a synagogue, or even as a subgroup within a Judean Diaspora synagogue, and think of it as a group in a network of associations of the kind responsible for both Paul's animosity and then his "conversion." We can easily reconstruct a plausible situation in which Jesus people, both Judeans and Gentiles, were interested both in the Diaspora synagogue and in the teachings of Jesus; the teachings of Jesus about the kingdom of God were under discussion within both the Jesus associations and the Diaspora synagogues; debates were also going on about torah, the Hasmoneans, the Romans, and the current state of the world; and intellectuals were rewriting the Scriptures, reconfiguring the epic, and writing martyrologies for the Maccabees (an odd preoccupation for Diaspora Judeans?). What if the Jesus people found themselves wanting (or pressed) to give an account of themselves as staying true to the traditions of Israel, and thought to stake out their claim upon the epic of Israel in a succinct and pointed statement? They could do it by suggesting that their founder-teacher, possibly already being thought of as a teacher "anointed" by God, certainly as a folk hero with impeccable credentials as "wisdom's child," died true to his teachings (without naming the tyrant!) and was "taken up" by God. This reading makes it possible to emphasize the main function of a martyrology, namely, to demonstrate the character and integrity of the martyr without having to be more precise about the cause. In the case of teachers who were killed for their teachings, Socrates being the prime example, it was this demonstration of the teacher's character that mattered most. Staying true to one's teachings was the standard test both of character and of the "truth" of the teachings. Thus, to think of Jesus staying true in the face of the threat of death would have validated his teachings as the association had come to understand them. It is even probable that an association in the name of the "anointed Jesus" had made the connection between the kingdom of God in his teachings and their own social formation. Since statements about the kingdom of God in the extant Jesus traditions are the only indication of a concept used to name the *ethē*-in-the-making of these Jesus schools, such a concept may well have been available to name the *ethos* of an "anointed Jesus" association. If this is plausible, it would mean that such an association could have seen itself included in the "cause" for which Jesus had died. The main difference between the loosely knit groupings of peoples interested in pursuing the "teachings of Jesus," as we have had them in mind, and the formation of a Jesus association that had come to think of itself by reference to the kingdom of God, would be the result of the normal processes of social formation itself, that is, regular meetings, recognition of "members," taking meals together, distribution of responsibilities, producing simple rules of etiquette, discussing common interests, and so on. It would have been enough for such a group to imagine a martyr's death for Jesus by saying, "He died for (our) kingdom." And if the Jesus in mind was the "anointed Jesus," the God of their kingdom was also the God of Israel. Thus, the various enhancements of the importance of Jesus in the Jesus traditions, including the thought of dying as a martyr for his teachings on the kingdom, had much less to do with the veneration of a divine being than with desires for clarity and claims regarding teachings, social identity, social relations, and legitimacy.

What, then, about the text as we have it? Might we not be suspicious of the phrase "for our sins"? Sins were not at issue in the Jesus traditions, as far as we can tell. It was Paul who used the term to name the problem that had to be solved in order to "justify" the Gentiles in the eyes of Israel's God. What if it was Paul who substituted the phrase "for our sins"? We would then have before us the result of an important shift in mythmaking from the Jesus-*christos* associations to Paul. Paul was certainly capable of putting his own construction upon the "traditions" he had received. And he apparently found a way to compress and resignify the Jesus martyr myth in the interest of his own, expanded worldview. He did this with his "Christ crucified" formulation, a much more graphic depiction of martyrdom than what we have imagined for the Jesus associations. And notice that the reduction of the "died for" to "crucified" implicates the Romans as the "tyrants," thus coming close to an altogether different "cause" for the death than the Jesus associations would have needed or dared imagine. But did Paul do that in order to suggest that the crucifixion was a political event of conflict between the Romans and the followers of Jesus? Not at all. In Paul's mind, the crucifixion was a dramatic event of world-historical significance that marked the end of the old order and the inauguration of his mission to the Gentiles, a mission that described a new aeon in the grand plan of Israel's God. As we will see later in this essay, it was Paul's mission to the Gentiles that determined his construction upon the Jesus myth as he formulated his own gospel. The substitution of "for our sins" for "the kingdom of God" as the "cause" in the Christ myth fits that agenda.

C. That He Was Raised

This is the text traditionally used to document "the resurrection" of Jesus as an event and belief for his disciples and the first Christians. But the term "resurrection" has been used for such a wide range of images and truncated scenarios contained within the literature of the pre-Constantine period that it has become not much more than an empty cipher for an unimaginable moment. Even if we take it as a startling and daring thought expressed here for the first time in order to provide a sequel to a martyr's death and burial, and an event of transformation making the appearances possible, it is difficult to imagine how it could have been accepted by those to whom it was addressed. It is true that a postmortem transformation or life in another realm was sometimes suggested as a sequel to a noble death. But to be "raised" after having been "buried" is much more graphic than the usual euphemistic depictions. It is in fact unusual and, together with the statement that "he appeared," which makes matters much worse, it violates both Jewish and Hellenistic sensibilities of the time which would have found the report offensive if not shocking. The dead were not supposed to get up, move about, and appear. So the (social) logic of this statement is as difficult to understand as the formulation of the "cause" for the death. What, then, might the sense of the statement have been "that he was raised"?

Suppose we accept the reasons given above for a Jesus association to have claimed a noble death for Jesus as its founder-teacher. If so, the statement "that he was raised" might be thought to have functioned as a "proof" that his was a noble death, that is, that God thereby demonstrated his approval of Jesus and his teachings. There may not have been anything in the statement of the "cause" that would have demonstrated that, especially if Jesus and his teachings were known to be troublesome in the eyes of others and those imagined to have killed him. So something may have had to be added that could make it clear that Jesus' teachings were right and worthy of a noble death. This, in any case, is how I construed the logic of "the resurrection" component in *A Myth of Innocence*. One would think, however, that a statement of divine validation would have to be immediately clear in the common coin of customary images and activities of the divine. This is not the case with the statement "that he was raised." It is the combination with "was buried" and "appeared" that demonstrated the "proof" as I imagined it necessary. But it is exactly this combination that produced the offensiveness of the image in relation both to customary cults and concepts of the dead, and to acceptable martyrological sequels. The more acceptable notion was that a pious and virtuous person could be "taken up" by God, that is, "translated" to a transcendent and divine world.[14] But to imagine that a person had been killed and buried, then raised from the dead and seen—that would have created confusion and consternation. That would have been shocking. Even in the Hellenistic romances, the thought of encountering the ghost of a person dead and buried was frightening and resulted in flight from a tomb. This means that the statements that he was "buried . . . raised . . . and appeared" are curiously inappropriate for a martyr myth. The customary depiction of a martyrdom hardly needed such a sequel. And the translation of a virtuous person by being "taken up" by God hardly needed a noble death as occasion. Perhaps we need to take a closer look at the term ἐγείρειν.

It may help to note that the term ἐγείρειν did not automatically mean "resurrect (from the dead)." It meant "awaken" or "rouse" from any state of inactivity, such as sleeping, sickness, or emotional doldrums. And it does not appear to have been a usual term for "translation" to a transcendent state after death. Instead, forms of the terms μετατιθέναι, μετάστασις, and ἀνιστάναι were used. It is, however, the case that ἐγείρειν could be used for "the resurrection of the dead" (collectively) in the context of an apocalyptic eschatology. Might it be that the use of this term in the Christ myth was intended to evoke apocalyptic imagery? If so, it would have made little sense as a sequel to a martyr myth for Jesus as a founder-teacher of a Jesus-*christos* association. But what about Paul? The first thing to notice is that Paul did use the term ἐγείρειν in 1 Cor 15:52 to describe the transformation of the dead at the eschaton. The change, he said, would be from a perishable body to an immortal and imperishable (spiritual) body. And earlier in the chapter he had argued *from* this concept of a general resurrection of the dead at the end of history *to* the claim that Christ had been raised: "If there is no resurrection (ἀνάστασις)

---

14. See, e.g., Gen 5:24 LXX (Enoch); Heb 11:5–6 (Enoch); Philo, *Mos.* 1.158–59 (Moses); *Mos.* 2.288–91 (Moses); *Sacr.* 8–10 (Moses); *Gig.* 47–57 (Moses); *Virt.* 73–79 (Moses); Wis 3:1–9 (the "righteous one").

of the dead, then Christ has not been raised" (ἐγήγερται, 1 Cor 15:13). Miller has alerted me to the important ch. 5 in Byron R. McCane's *Roll Back the Stone*.[15] McCane makes the point that apocalyptic images of death and resurrection are quite different from funereal images of death and afterlife, and that each belonged to a different social context. The funereal images were cultivated by (extended) families on particular occasions in proximity to the tombs of their special dead, while apocalyptic images were cultivated within groups "in which ideas of final judgment were vibrant."[16] If we put these observations together with Jonathan Z. Smith's discussion of the difference between earlier "Christ-traditions" and Paul's "thoroughly utopian understanding,"[17] the conclusion is that it was Paul who construed a (locative) *christos* martyr myth in an apocalyptic (utopian) sense. As he said, "Christ has been raised from the dead, the first fruits of those who have died" (1 Cor 15:20).

This does leave us with the question of whether, in the pre-Pauline Jesus-*christos* martyr myth, some other noneschatological sequel to the death was added. If so, it could have been "that he was taken up," using some form of the more customary terms for a transposition into a transcendent order. Such a statement would have supported the social logic of such a martyr myth and would not have been shocking. For us to imagine such would also help build a bridge to Paul's Christ myth by noting how easily a change could have been made toward the apocalyptic nuance merely by substituting ἐγείρειν for a term of transposition such as μετατιθέναι or ἀναλαμβάνειν.

D. *That He Was Buried*

This component of the Christ myth has seldom been seen as problematic, thinking that the mention of a burial would have been natural as a sequel to any death, and important as a sequel to a martyr's death for those concerned about proper rites for a person regarded as special despite a martyrdom. And yet, making a point of such was not usual in martyrological narratives and seems strange in this case, given the fact that early Jesus people and Christians did not seem to know anything about the location of a tomb for Jesus. As a matter of fact, the later stories about an "empty tomb" confirm this lack of evidence for a burial and register very troubled attempts to balance the desire to think that Jesus was properly buried, the knowledge that the location of his tomb was not really known, and lore about his disappearance and/or μετάθεσις. But if reasons for the mention of burial in a

---

15. Byron R. McCane, *Roll Back the Stone: Death and Burial in the World of Jesus* (Harrisburg, Pa.: Trinity Press International, 2003).

16. Ibid., 128.

17. Jonathan Z. Smith, *Drudgery Divine: On the Comparison of Early Christianities and the Religions of Late Antiquity* (Jordan Lectures in Comparative Religion 14; London: School of Oriental and African Studies, University of London; Chicago: University of Chicago Press, 1990), 141.

Jesus martyr myth cannot be found, in Paul's construction of the Christ myth the reason is clear. "Burial" complements "raised," if in fact the notion of being raised was meant to evoke eschatological imagery. According to this reading, Christ was "raised *from the dead*," that is, "the first fruits" of an apocalyptically conceived general "resurrection of the dead." If so, we have another Pauline construal on our hands, one that changed rather dramatically a founder-figure's death for his teachings into an eschatological event of world-historical and divine cosmic finality.

E. *That He Appeared (Was Seen)*

The standard argument for the "reality" of the resurrection of Jesus is to point to the appearances listed in this text, as if they were the way in which the fact of the resurrection was first "experienced." And it is this text that is called upon to document the sequence, for it goes on to list those to whom Jesus appeared, starting with Peter and ending with Paul. It should be obvious that Paul's hand has been busy at this point. He was personally interested in the "appearances," for these were used to validate his own commission. That his need for authorization was obsessive is documented throughout his writings. And here he calls himself "one untimely born," in order to include himself in the list of "apostles." It is not surprising that Peter is first in line, for it was Peter (in Jerusalem, of all places!) to whom Paul said he resorted after his conversion in order to compare "gospels" (Gal 1:15). It is important to note that the only "gospels" compared in this report had to do with the Gentile question, and that nothing was said about Peter or Paul "seeing" the "resurrected" Christ. So Paul took advantage of the Christ myth in order to substantiate his own authority as an "apostle" to the "Gentiles." But the problem in this case is not merely whether Paul's own interest can be detected in the statement "that he appeared." The problem is to account for the notion itself and ask about its logical link to the first three statements of the Christ myth. Reports of appearances usually occurred in the genre of (dream) visions in which deities were encountered, usually to answer questions from or to give instructions to a devotee. Thus, the statement that Christ "appeared" assumes some kind of apotheosis or divinization already in place, a transformation of a kind that does not automatically follow either from a martyrdom or from a proleptically imagined eschatological resurrection. And when such an appearance was joined to a narrative description of a crucifixion and its sequels, as in the later Gospels, it is clear that the very idea was problematic for the authors and had to be rationalized by forced argumentations. That is because "appearances" cannot be a firsthand witness of Jesus' "resurrection from the dead" at all, but of encounters with a divinized Jesus at some later time. This means that the "reports" of appearances, supposing that Paul was not the only one to lay claim to such, must have belonged to a mythic tradition other than that of a martyrology. This does not explain the concept of appearances per se, or help us with the question of where among the Jesus traditions reports of appearances may have occurred, but it does deny their automatic link to a martyr myth, and it does begin to explain how and why Paul included such in his Christ myth.

Unfortunately for this line of reasoning, however, reports of "appearances" are not in evidence even for those Jesus traditions in which some form of continuing "presence" was imagined, such as in the voice of the Q tradition or the *egō eimi* of the *Gospel of Thomas*. And paying attention to the voice of the teacher, or meditating on the *egō* of the "living Jesus," was not limited to an "apostle's" special experience. Thus, the only textual data for "appearances" are linked to the notion of "apostle" and serve the function of claims to authorization, that is, claims to privileged encounter and thus to special revelation or instruction not immediately available to others. That, of course, is the purpose of Paul's reference to such a "tradition" as part of his Christ myth. But note that it does not follow from any other statement in the Christ myth, much less as a conclusion to a condensed scenario in which all the statements could be imagined to have happened in fitting sequence. That, of course, is the way in which the traditional Christian imagination has pictured the event, reading the Christ myth as a shorthand script for the narrative Gospels and the Gospels as the way to understand the Christ myth as "historical." It is this traditional imagination which, even when recognized as mythic—that is, as not "historical"—has nevertheless influenced the critical analyses we have undertaken. At every point, the departure has been from the traditional ways of reading the text, and the struggle has been to problematize the traditional reading. This amounts to being snookered by an unexamined assumption about the composition and intention of the myth, namely, by continuing to work with the text on the traditional model of an account of a death and "resurrection," whether as a martyrdom or a divinely sanctioned "sacrifice." Luckily, however, and quite by surprise, the analysis has been close and critical enough to have discovered that the four major statements do not derive from a narrative imagination interested in any kind of "historical" logic, whether as lore or as myth of origin. The four statements simply do not fit together as a connected narrative that would have been recognized as a meaningful martyr myth for any of the Jesus schools, Jesus associations, or *christos* associations we have had in mind. It actually flies in the face of the normal ways of imagining a meaningful, mythic end for a Jesus enhanced as wisdom's child, God's *christos* teacher for the times, prophet like Moses, miracle man, or even folk hero.

What then? Well, by now it should be obvious. The Christ myth has to be a "Pauline" construction in the interest of interpreting a *christos* martyr myth away from its function as a myth of legitimation and/or memorial for a Jesus-*christos* association, and turning it instead into a myth of cosmic transformation, epic redirection, and apocalyptic inauguration. Whatever the "traditions" may have been upon which he built, it is clear that the current formulations cannot have been "original" to those traditions. And although it has been possible to reconstruct and imagine plausible a Jesus (*christos*) martyr myth as that presupposed by the Christ myth, it is clear that the Christ myth violated the logics of setting and function for such a martyr myth in order to imagine an entirely different set of consequences from a drastically revised event, reset in "cosmic-historical" terms. And so, the conclusion must be that Paul took advantage of a *christos* myth to anchor his apocalyptically driven "mission" to the Gentiles, and to substantiate his own authority as an "apostle" to the "Gentiles."

I have used the word "shocking" to describe the impression given by Paul's Christ myth if read in keeping with normal sensibilities associated with funereal practices. However, it now appears that the shift to a cosmic-apocalyptic setting may have been obvious enough to have overcome such a shock. That is because the conception of the death is no longer martyrological and funereal, but dramatic and eschatological. It was probably not possible for Paul's audiences or readers to check him out on the Christ myth as "tradition" in any case, even if they knew about a martyr myth for Jesus with which they could make comparisons. That is because the extravagance of the cosmic-apocalyptic mythology that gave the Christ myth its Pauline significance far overshadowed the shocking aspects of the Christ myth if taken as a martyr myth. Even the notion of dying "for our sins" could now make sense if and when the crucifixion was seen as the inauguration of an apocalyptic battle for the final chapter in God's plans for Israel. The "resurrection" (from the dead, i.e., after being "buried") would have supported such a thought. And the "appearances" need not have been linked to or derived from any particular mythology of martyrdom or postmortem translation, but instead may have been the way Paul found to connect traditions of "prophetic" and "visionary" authorization to the apocalyptic "message" he saw in the "crucifixion" of Jesus. He used the proclamation (*kērygma*) of "Christ crucified" (in the language of death-resurrection) regularly as a metaphor for conversion, justification, baptism, the transition of the epochs from law to gospel, dealing with hardships in his mimetic "ministry" as an apostle to the Gentiles, and the transformation of the Christian after death in order to inhabit the spiritual kingdom of God. That's quite a bit of application. And he may well have preferred to cite it in its compressed form as "Christ crucified," leaving the full form for full argumentations regarding apostleship and appearances, what to think about those who have died, eschatological scenarios, the resurrection of the dead, and the transformation of Christians into spiritual bodies at the end of time as in 1 Cor 15. One might say that, in such a circumstance, the shocking aspects of the Christ myth would be overridden by the more extravagant cosmic scenarios.

This means that Paul's constructions upon a *christos* myth should not be used to ask about its social logic in the Jesus associations where it was generated. There is no need to think of a "resurrection from the dead" (after being buried), or appearances of a "resurrected" Jesus, whether to an apostle or to an association, in order to make sense of the Jesus myth. A *christos* martyr myth, though daring in and of itself, is understandable as the way in which a Jesus association could have claimed legitimacy in conversation and debate with other schools of Jewish thought in the Diaspora. Thus, it was the teachings of Jesus, whether as a philosophy, an ethical guide, a social vision, or an epic rehearsal, that provided the association with its mythologies and ideologies, not the desire for communication with the divine mediated by appearances of a divinized Jesus.

II. The Meal Text: 1 Corinthians 11:23–25

We come now to the crucial text used by scholars to document the earliest Christian communities as congregations of the Christ. The popular picture of the "Last supper" has been taken from the narrative Gospels, of course. But when in the course of New Testament studies the Gospels turned out to be much later in time than Paul, it was this text in 1 Cor 11 that scholars used to support the thought that the "Last supper" actually happened (or that having such an image in mind was fundamental for the meal rituals of the early churches). And, as with the Christ myth text, Paul also presents this meal text as a "tradition" that he received. Scholars have taken these two references to a pre-Pauline tradition very seriously as evidence for pre-Pauline Hellenistic Christianity, but then read both in the light of Paul's constructions upon them and in the light of the Gospels' "passion narrative." So we are left with the same kind of task in this case that we faced with the Christ myth text, namely, the task of isolating the pre-Pauline features of the cited "tradition" from the Pauline constructions upon them. Keeping in mind the seminar papers mentioned above on this text and Paul's "instructions" to (and debate with) the Corinthians about their meal and other matters, we actually have not one but five pictures of a group meal to parse: (1) the Corinthians' association meal; (2) the "Lord's meal" according to Paul; (3) the text Paul cites that depicts the meal; (4) the customary pattern of the symposium meal; and (5) the customary pattern of the funerary/memorial meal. I can assume the work of Stowers on the funerary meal (θυσία)[18] and that of Dennis Smith on the symposium,[19] as well as the discussions of the seminar on Paul and the Corinthians (1996, 2001). These studies and discussions indicate that the Corinthians were already in the practice of meeting together before Paul came along, that some kind of meal was part of the practice, and that Paul wanted to change that practice in order to align it with his conception of an *ekklēsia* in the name of Jesus Christ. I shall need therefore to make several points about these views on the practice of common meals before asking about the function of the meal text that Paul cites as "tradition."

---

18. Stanley K. Stowers, "Greeks Who Sacrifice and Those Who Do Not: Toward an Anthropology of Greek Religion," in *The Social World of the First Christians: Essays in Honor of Wayne A. Meeks* (ed. L. Michael White and O. Larry Yarbrough; Minneapolis: Fortress, 1995), 293–333; idem, "Elusive Coherence: Ritual and Rhetoric in 1 Corinthians 10–11," in *Reimagining Christian Origins: A Colloquium Honoring Burton L. Mack* (ed. Elizabeth A. Castelli and Hal Taussig; Valley Forge, Pa.: Trinity Press International, 1996), 68–83; idem, "Kinds of Myth."
19. Dennis E. Smith, *From Symposium to Eucharist: The Banquet in the Early Christian World* (Minneapolis: Fortress, 2003).

A. The Corinthians' Meal

The Corinthians were apparently meeting together as an association of non-native persons in the recently repopulated city of Corinth. There are indications that this association was not homogeneous and that they were actively exploring issues of social practice that had been raised by the resettlement of Corinth as a Roman colony, and especially by their own displacements from other homelands where the ancestral patterns of life were more understandable. Stowers found that characteristic markers from two types of Greek meal traditions were mixed and confused in the Pauline descriptions of the Corinthians' meals, one type of which was the θυσία, which has often been translated as a "sacrifice." Dennis Smith has pointed to features of both the common association pattern and the symposium, and Jonathan Z. Smith has noticed the many "translations" of older practices and mythologies in evidence as Paul and the Corinthians debated "the spirit myth." It seems clear that the Corinthian "association" was not "Christian," at least not according to Pauline definitions, and that many of the issues Paul raised with them about their group meetings and meal practices, practices that he found objectionable, were not problems in their own eyes. It was Paul who took issue with them over matters of meats, rankings, factions, and the boisterousness of what appears to have been a feast or symposium atmosphere after dinner. That the Corinthians had bothered to give him a hearing at all can only be understood as their reception of a traveling teacher/philosopher, with something of interest to say about "wisdom," "spirits," group identities, and meals in memory of ancestors. According to Paul, all of his instructions along these lines were derived from his message of "Christ crucified." But it seems that the Corinthians received him just as they would have entertained others and debated some of his ideas without having to assent to his gospel. That Paul chose to engage them on issues of the meal as memorial, the group as a single "body," and the right way to think about "the spirit" indicates that the Corinthians may have been at work on "translating" modes of remembering and relating to their ancestors now that they no longer had access to their tombs and the proper performance of their festivals in the districts from which they had come. It was Paul who wanted to relate his gospel of "Christ crucified (and resurrected)" to these interests of the Corinthians and find ways to urge their persuasion.

B. The Lord's Meal according to Paul

Paul calls the tradition he cites the "Lord's meal," but it is clear that the picture he presents and the instruction he gives are his own. The text he cites is actually set forth mainly as an authorization for his instructions overall and occurs in the course of an extended argumentation addressed to the Corinthians in which the Lord's meal is presented as a contrast and correction to their own meal and meeting practices, giving rise to many ancillary issues in need of clarification. Moreover, Paul's instruction to them continues through the next four or five chapters and works with themes derived from his citation of the meal text and his construction upon it. Since we want to isolate the tradition represented by this text, it means that we need to be clear about Paul's construction upon it.

The first thing to notice is that the term "Lord" belongs to Paul's vocabulary of references both to God and to Jesus as sovereign figures presiding over the cosmos, the realm of the spirit, and the end of history. It reflects Paul's own mythology and is remarkably inappropriate as the title and role attributed to the figure presiding over the meal "on the night he was handed over." The thought of Jesus as Lord presiding over a memorial meal as an instruction for his followers on the night before his death does not easily follow from a martyr myth. That, however, is exactly the way the picture looks as Paul presents it. As in the case of the Christ myth, we need not try to smooth all of the seams in Paul's infelicitous merging of arguments. Working out a consistent characterization for Jesus throughout all of the realms and roles Paul had in mind for him was not Paul's project. Some authorization "from the Lord" "from the beginning" was what mattered at this point. The meal text could be used to authorize his instructions to the Corinthians about "meals and community," but it was not the meal text that grounded the instructions. It was the Christ myth in its more developed form of the "Christ crucified" language and application in Paul.

The second thing to notice is that Paul's instructions to the Corinthians do not treat the text as a script for reenactment. The transition from the Lord's meal to the Corinthians' meals is made by referring to bread and cup, of course, symbols in the "tradition" that I shall have to discuss in the next section. For the moment, however, it is important to note that these symbols are items that marked important moments in any common meal. As such, they are used by Paul matter-of-factly in reference to the Corinthians' common meal, which he says takes place "as often as" or "whenever" they "come together to eat." His interest in the "tradition" is not to describe a "liturgy" called for by the Lord's meal, but to authorize his instructions to the Corinthians about their own common meals in accordance with his notions of how an association should behave and think about itself if focused on the Christ myth. What Paul makes of these terms ("bread," "cup") is directly related to his own elaborate gospel of the death and resurrection of Jesus Christ in its cosmic-apocalyptic context. Thus, the elaborations about calling to mind the death of Christ, proclaiming the "Lord's death until he comes," "discerning the body," eating and drinking in an unworthy manner in the present that will make one "liable" for the "body and blood of the Lord" in the future, and so forth. Then the topics change in the next paragraphs to include "spiritual gifts," the (corporate) "body of Christ," ranking leadership roles, the *agapē* ideal, rules for coming to speech during the meeting of the association, proof for the spiritual resurrection of the believer, and the victory of the spiritual kingdom (of God) at the eschaton. The topics change but the subject remains the same. It is the death of Christ as symbol for the ethos and ethics of Paul's concept of *ekklēsia*, that is, an eschatological congregation on the model of "Israel" as a holy people prepared for the final judgment. Paul wanted the Corinthians to take the Christ myth seriously in his own elaborations of it as a theology of history and judgment. He wanted them to think and behave accordingly. It is not at all clear that Paul thought that the Lord's meal scenario called for mimetic behavior of any kind, much less its replication by a "worshiping community" as customarily assumed. As gross as the meal text is on its own, it stays at the level of origin myth even in the context of Paul's horrendous extensions and applications of its symbolisms.

C. The Tradition

As with the Christ myth, the tradition Paul cites for the Lord's meal is a small, highly crafted literary unit manifesting the signs of intellectual labor. Even in this compact and truncated scenario, most of the marks characteristic of a martyrology are there: "handed over," "body," "blood," "for you," and memorial. There is also more than just a touch of the epic anchor ("covenant") required to make sure the "cause" aligns the purpose of the death "for you" with the proper mythic and cultural traditions for thinking of Jesus and his followers as belonging to "Israel." This means that the meal text is closely related to the *christos* martyr myth. Both appear to be applications of a Jesus martyr myth to questions of concern within a network of Jesus associations, at about the same time and for the same reasons. If we compare the meal text to the martyr myth text, however, there are some new wrinkles to be noticed in the meal text that create additional oddities. The first new wrinkle is that Jesus comes to speech in an instruction to his followers at one of their meals on using their meals to remember his death. That the martyr comes to speech on the occasion of his martyrdom is not new to the traditional Hellenistic pattern, as the examples in 4 Maccabees show. But it is odd to have the martyr address only his followers at a regular meal meeting on the very night of his being handed over without any indication of who the tyrant may be or that he is waiting in the wings. We know, of course, that even as the death of Jesus received more and more extensive embellishment in the Pauline tradition, the major focus was on the "faithfulness" of Jesus and his "validation" by God. There was really no room in this mythology for any (earthly) tyrant, because that would have introduced another set of considerations and motivations sure to ruin the mythic system at work (as a purely ethical-divine event). But that does not relieve the oddness of Jesus coming to speech about his imminent death at a common meal on the model of the meetings of the Jesus associations. The problem is not primarily that Jesus speaks from an imperious position of foreknowledge and that the instructions function as self-authorization. That is exactly the way in which the figure of Jesus and his teachings were enhanced by degrees from the beginning within the Jesus schools and their several traditions. So the offensiveness of this scene is not related to its inappropriateness for a teacher of divine wisdom. It is that Jesus links the primary symbols of the association meal with the major symbols for a martyr's death. It is that link that at first creates consternation.

There is, however, a way to explain this move. The martyr myth focused on the validation of Jesus as *christos* and his teachings, but without express mention of a *christos* association as part of the "cause." The meal text expressly includes a scene that reflects the social formation of a Jesus association as the "cause" for which Jesus (will) die(s). The faces around the table are mercifully not painted in. But the meal practice easily reminds one of the social formation of an association, and the problem of prolepsis is overcome by the phrase "as often as." The problem of a "cause" not yet in place is therefore overcome, and the normal practice of meeting for meals is visualized as definitive from the very beginning. Thus, there is a two-way exchange of symbols at the level of discernment or imagination. Imagining the first time a scribe suggested a consideration of the story, the exchange of symbols might have looked like this: "Well, we are a kingdom association, aren't we? And we do have meals at our meetings just as any other association does. And we do already mention Jesus as our founder-teacher and patron when we break bread and pour the wine, just as any association would do. So, now that we have been talking about Jesus having died 'for the kingdom,' I guess it might be okay to imagine him telling us that our meal markers should remind us of the reasons for his death." This, of course, means that neither the meal markers, already in place, nor the symbolic equivalents suggested by the story work without the other. But together they form a tightly knit myth of origins. And coming from Jesus the teacher, now portrayed as a martyr for the very cause of the social formation they were wanting to authenticate, the instructions to "Remember who you are" and "Take the meal marker occasions to mention me" are very tight and workable.

We have to assume, of course, that coming to agreements on the symbolic equivalencies must have generated considerable discussion and taken some time to settle into their single reference formulations. That is because there really is no single reference equivalency that automatically comes to mind with either set. No matter whether one starts with the meal markers or the martyrological symbols, bread and cup do not easily call to mind body and blood, and body and blood do not readily call to mind bread and cup. I have therefore taken another look at what I wrote about this problem in *A Myth of Innocence*,[20] and find that I can still refer to it as relevant to the present discussion. I noted that each of the terms in both sets did indeed have a wide range of connotations in what might be called the basic concepts and languages referring to "life" and "living." I also noted that scholars had frequently expended effort in trying to find just that correlation intended, without having come to any satisfactory conclusions. To take the body–bread correlation as an example, there really is no overlap of connotation that creates an immediately plausible and striking symbolic. What we have simply is a juxtaposition of two sets of basic symbols at a concisely condensed narrative and social setting. I therefore switched from the usual assumption about symbolic equivalency

---

20. Mack, *Myth of Innocence*, 114–20; cf. idem, *Who Wrote the New Testament?* 87–91.

based on a single reference, single connotation meaning of a term, and did some sleuthing on the "this is" formula used to link the sets. What I discovered was that this formula was used in Philo's commentaries and elsewhere simply to stipulate an allegorical or symbolic correlation even if there was little or no association of ideas from which to argue. The phrase "this is" simply meant that, "For the purpose of developing our textual reading and allegorical theme, we are going to take this term from the Scripture to refer to this term in our allegory." More than that, the antecedent of "this," always in reference to something in the text, but frequently left purposefully unclear and in need of further detailing, could end up referring to a cluster of features from elsewhere in the text or allegory that were brought to the term and its equivalent symbol in the course of their elaboration. I returned to the meal text and saw a whole new set of possible referents for each term. The "this is" and the "do this" began to overlap and swim around within both the story itself and my imagination of an association at meal. Bread, breaking of the bread, meal marker moment, distribution, someone calling the meeting of the kingdom association to order, a mention of the patron teacher-martyr, a cup poured out for the founder-teacher—all of that was packed into the two condensed sets of equivalencies. I should admit that I was grateful at this point for the prayers of thanksgiving in *Did.* 9–10, for they clearly documented the practice and development of treating the meal markers of a Jesus association as memorial moments, but without any reference to the body and blood of a martyr's death. The cup reminded these Jesus people of the "holy vine of David," and the "broken bread" reminded them that just as something "was scattered upon the mountains and was gathered together to become one, so may your *ekklēsia* be gathered together from the ends of the earth into your kingdom" (*Did.* 9.4).

This means that 1 Cor 11 does not document a "ritual meal" for a "Christ cult" as I mistakenly imagined in *A Myth of Innocence*, by accepting uncritically the notion of the "pre-Pauline Hellenistic Christ cult," as the dominant paradigm had it. There is no suggestion of mimetic replication of "the Lord's supper," no indication that the Jesus in the picture was expected to be present (symbolically or "spiritually") when the association met for meals, no script for ritual reenactment. There is only a myth of origins that grounds an association practice already in place and suggests that the major markers of the common meal as process (taking bread, drinking wine) could be used as "reminders" for the martyr's death of Jesus their founder-teacher and patron. The text is important because the martyr myth (1 Cor 15:3–5) was mainly focused on the integrity and validation of their teacher and folk hero. Only the meal text clearly turned the "purpose" of the death from what the teacher stood for at the time into what might be imagined for his teachings and followers after his death, namely, the social formation of the Jesus schools and associations. One might want to see the martyrological symbolism of the bread and cup as too heavy for a common meal without some ritualization of the myth. But that would be to continue viewing the text as it has functioned for later Christian ritualization, cultivating the sensibilities associated with the ritual of the "Lord's supper" in the context of Christian worship. The ritualization of the common meal was quite customary for Greek associations when "remembering" their patron hero. And as we know, there was a range of patron types from patronyms through various configurations of divine men and heroes, to including even the deities. But the point would be that the meal markers ritualized the meal, not the myth. The meal markers merely became the occasion for the momentary recognition, via recognizable gestures and pronouncements, of an association's patron and namesake.

And so, wresting ourselves free from the long tradition of Christian cultivation of this symbolism and text, what may we take this meal text to have been about in the context of a Jesus-*christos* association? Simply that a Jesus association had found a way to announce its identity by recalling its patron at the proper meal marker moments. The meal text does not suggest a ritual whether in memorial for the (historical) Jesus who died, or to celebrate the continuing spiritual presence of Jesus as "the Lord." Neither the bread moment nor the wine moment need be thought of as fraught with anything like pensive veneration. As a matter of fact, this positioning of Jesus as the link between the epic of Israel and the history of the association is achieved with such a combination of evocation and imprecision that stopping to meditate at either of these meal moments would have caused confusion. As far as we can tell, the meal markers of an association were rather pro forma practices, not occasions for religious experiences with their patron deities. Thus, the meal text at hand is a myth of origins. It is the product of mythmaking in the interest of a social formation. It documents the mythmaking and social interests of the Jesus schools/associations at a particular juncture of situational incongruity when their practices and orientation to the teachings of Jesus were not enough to claim legitimacy in the larger scheme of things.

The thought may still persist, however, that it is not enough to work out the social logic of these texts when generated in the Jesus associations. Now they are found in the Pauline correspondence, and the jump to Paul, who does not appear to have been interested in the teachings of Jesus, is too great. Don't the texts shift attention away from the teachings to the teacher, and don't the transformations of the teacher overshadow the martyrology? What Paul understood these "traditions" to be also has to be figured in, and how they were used in his congregations of the Christ has to be explained. Even if a pre-Pauline Jesus association generated these martyr myths, didn't they soon become the myth and ritual texts of the churches Paul established by his preaching of Christ crucified?

Well, in order to answer this we will have to have a look at Paul's own gospel and then rephrase the questions we might want to ask about the "congregations of the Christ." But before leaving the text at hand I want to suggest that, even with a full-blown mythology of Jesus Christ as Lord, a mythology clearly in view as Paul interprets the meal tradition, he does not portray it as a ritual text of the kind imagined by the dominant paradigm for the "Christ cult." In fact he ruins any chance of taking it that way when he tries to link the meal text to the Corinthians' meals and gain from it an argument for his charge that their meal is "not the Lord's meal." Not only is it clear that the "Lord" in view is now the cosmic sovereign, but the symbols are turned into a kind of poison to test the "worthiness" of the partaker, lest he or she become answerable (ἔνοχος ἔσται) for "the body and blood of the Lord." Goodness. This is the kind of logic used to kill witches under the ruse of questing for the truth, namely, if they are not witches and are telling the truth, the poison will not hurt them. We can safely say, I think, that the Corinthians were not overly impressed or unsettled by Paul's threat of judgment. But to note his many appeals to aspects of his Christ crucified gospel at this point and in the subsequent chapters, and to see them as his attempts to use the meal tradition against the Corinthians' practice, should be a sufficient warning against taking the entire set of pericopes (1 Cor 11:17–34) as documentation for a ritual meal known to Paul in which "discerning the body" of the Lord was the point of piety, prayers, reenactments, and meditation. It is Paul's reading of the text as a myth of origins and his rhetorical elaborations of it as mythological argumentations that are to be noticed.

III. Paul's Gospel

Our effort to reconstruct the "traditions" from which Paul claimed to have learned about the Christ myth and the Lord's meal has actually been quite successful. We have been able to imagine a Jesus-*christos* association entertaining a martyr myth as a way to position itself as legitimate heir to the promise of the epic of Israel. We might want to see this development as a kind of bridge between the Jesus schools and their teachings, on the one hand, and the Pauline depictions of *ekklēsiai* in the name of Jesus Christ the Lord, on the other. However, since in the process we had to dismantle both the Christ myth and the Lord's meal texts, accounting for much of them as Pauline construals, it is time now to ask whether Paul's construals can be accounted for as further "developments" of the *christos* myths and associations. Having already noticed that Paul's Christ myth, though drawing upon a *christos* martyr myth, drastically changed its language, logic, frame of reference, and function, the questions that now surface for consideration have to do with Paul's own gospel. It is customary in scholarly circles to take Paul at his word when he claimed that his mission was based on a single proclamation (*kērygma*), namely, "Christ crucified." Thus, the scholarly efforts to make sense of Paul's many applications of the Christ myth, including his own authorization as an apostle, links to the epic past, the present cosmic sovereignty of Jesus Christ the Lord, an apocalyptic eschatology where judgment would soon be rendered, the justification of Gentiles as children of Abraham, the spirit of the Lord effective for conversions, new births, baptisms, and new powers to be found in the assemblies of the new family of God. To be sure, Paul's use of the death–resurrection metaphor is pervasive and was used by him in applications ranging from the radical nature of personal conversions to the transformations of the Christian after death in order to inhabit the spiritual kingdom of God. And yet, since the mechanisms by which these applications were made in Paul's mind, and presumably accepted and understood by some of those addressed, have always been most problematic to modern scholars and thus debated without end, it might be good to question the single myth, single *kērygma* assumption. It does not take much analysis to see that what Paul made of the martyr myth had little to do with what the Jesus associations thought important about Jesus, and little to do with the logic of a martyr myth, but much to do with Paul's own "mission to the Gentiles."

That being the case, it might be best to think of Paul working with several myths, not just one. We have already mentioned (1) Stowers's suggestion that Paul's gospel was based on the "promise to Abraham" as cited in Gal 3:8. It has also become obvious that (2) it was the apocalyptic frame of reference that reset the martyr myth in cosmic and eschatological perspective. And, in the light of Jonathan Z. Smith's redescription of the Corinthian situation, we can now add yet another mythology to the list, namely, (3) that of the "spirit" or "spirits" under debate in Corinth. That gives us three very important mythologies to add to the Christ myth, mythologies with which Paul was working and with which the Christ myth became integrally entangled. It will not be possible to do a thorough analysis of the many ways in which Paul tried to weave these myths together in the interest of his Gentile mission. But something can be said about his interests in each one. And something has to be said about each one in order to come back to the question with which we began, the question, namely, about the "Christ cult."

A. The Promise to Abraham

Paul did not get the idea of a mission to the Gentiles from the Christ myth, and Stowers is right to see Gal 3:8 as the clue to Paul's gospel, a message for the Gentiles. We know, of course, that the culture, history, and institutions of the Judeans of the time were attractive to Gentiles and that the term "Gentiles" referred to other Semitic peoples as well as Greeks and other non-Judean nations. And the question of how to regard, treat, and invite Gentiles to take part in Judean associations, especially in the Diaspora, was lively. All we have to do is recognize that Paul was a Jew much interested in this question, and that he thought he had found a way to use the Jesus-*christos* associations and their martyr myth to invite and enable Gentiles to become "Israel" without having strictly to become Jews. How and why he came to think that are questions that have never really been asked, much less answered, for all we have in his writings are arguments for his mission drawn from the many myths he had put together as his rationalization for the conviction. But one of the myths must have been rooted in a Jewish conviction and tradition that did not seem to require explanation. It was the promise to Abraham that all the nations would be blessed in him. One can easily read the entire Pauline correspondence from this point of view and find that it works out quite nicely. But it does mean that his gospel had at least two major points of departure, not one, and that the promise to Abraham about blessing all the nations was the more important of the two. The problem that scholars have had trying to explain everything in Paul's program from the "Christ crucified" gospel he claims was basic, is that it will not work, that most of his program was rooted in the other gospel: "Just as Abraham 'believed God, and it was reckoned to him as righteousness,' so, you see, those who believe are the descendants of Abraham. And the scripture, foreseeing that God would justify the Gentiles by faith, declared the gospel beforehand to Abraham, saying, 'All the Gentiles shall be blessed in you.' For this reason, those who believe are blessed with Abraham who believed" (Gal 3:6–9 NRSV; cf. Gen 12:2–3; 15:6; 18:18).

Caroline Johnson Hodge, Stowers's student, has provided the exegetical study to demonstrate this thesis.[21] In this study it becomes clear that Paul's "mission to the Gentiles" was his passion, and that he construed every issue and every solution in terms of this mission. The major concept in play during the time and in Paul's design was that of "patrilineal descent and the construction of identities" (ch. 1). The major task for Paul was "reconstructing Gentile origins" in order to bridge the difference between "Jews and non-Jews [on] Paul's ethnic map" (chs. 2–3). And the strategy he worked out was what Johnson Hodge calls "aggregative ethnic strategies" (chs. 3–8). In course, the notion of fictive kinship and the possibility of reconstructing Gentile origins by means of "aggregative ethnic strategies" are found to be thoroughly possible and plausible within the common discourses of the time. And of course the patrilineal descent for Paul had to be from Abraham. But instead of moving directly from the promise to Abraham to the status of Gentiles in Diaspora synagogues, Paul inserted the figure of Christ as the mechanism by which the promise became a message. The Pauline scholar will do tailspins reading this monograph. All of the terms customarily thought to be Pauline coins derived from the meaning of the *kērygma* (i.e., the Christ crucified gospel) are instead found to be the product of very clever moves in the interstices between the Christ myth and the scriptural accounts of the promise to Abraham. As for the meaning of the Christ myth and the languages supposedly derived from it, moves similar to those mentioned above have to be in mind. But the reader will be astounded at how many of these constructions, thought to derive from the *kērygma*, were actually taken from Paul's reading of the Scriptures in relation to the promise to Abraham or were coined in order to implicate both the promise to Abraham and the Christ myth at the same time. Thus, "righteousness," "justification," "faith," "adoption," "promise," "blessing," "birth," "new life," "father," "family," "incorporation," "sins," "redemption," "sacrifice," "law vs. gospel," "heirs," and so forth, are all products of Paul's clever attempt to merge the two myths into his single gospel for the Gentiles.

---

21. Caroline Johnson Hodge, *If Sons, Then Heirs: A Study of Kinship and Ethnicity in the Letters of Paul* (New York: Oxford University Press, 2007).

B. *The Apocalyptic Myth*

As for the elaborate mythology of Christ as cosmic sovereign and eschatological judge, it might be understood as an expansion upon the Christ myth in the interest of encompassing all peoples and their histories with this "timely" manifestation of the intervention of God and his plan for the ending of history. But it cannot be imagined as "derived from" the martyr myth, for the theological, conceptual, and social-historical interests that pop up in its applications are not at all the same as those that attend the martyr myth. The trick here would be to isolate the situational incongruities that called for such embellishments, and as far as our textual data let us see, there is really only one set of incongruities in view. It was Paul's intellectual problem of trying to work out a comprehensive mythology for his "mission to the Gentiles." That the cosmic sovereign bears little relation to the Jesus of the martyr myth did not seem to matter. The event of "Christ crucified and raised" had become the point in recent history where God or God's son touched down for a moment to let those open to a revelation of its significance know that the human situation that pertained since "times past" had changed, that now was the time for the Gentiles also to be blessed by the God of Israel. This does not make sense as an elaboration of the martyr myth at all. But if we assume that Paul's "conversion" was an encounter with a *christos* association of the kind we have imagined, there may have been a few features of its social formation and mythmaking that commended themselves to his apocalyptic mentality and vision for Israel. One seems to have been the Jesus talk about the kingdom of God. Another may well have been the ideal that the martyrdom was "for the kingdom." Yet another could have been the emergence of the Jesus movements in a time of social and political change and uncertainty, the very set of circumstances that invited a range of apocalyptic imaginations. Finally, what if the *christos* associations were composed of a mix of peoples? Such a mix need not have been a burning issue for these associations, but it certainly could have been for Paul. It is even thinkable that both his animosity and his conversion might be explained in terms of attitudes and views taken with respect to this feature of the *christos* associations. Paul, at any rate, seems to have found a couple of hooks of this type to link the *christos* persuasion with his apocalyptic mythology. But putting the *christos* martyr myth together with the apocalyptic myth drastically changed the martyr myth, as we have seen. However, once the notion of an eschatological take on the "resurrection" was conceived, a range of sequels became thinkable that the *christos* martyr myth would not have allowed. The "resurrection" could now be imagined to make possible an apotheosis, appearances, ascension, enthronement, and cosmic sovereignty. Each of these mythic notions seems to have played a role at some time or other in subsequent applications of the Christ myth to various social and intellectual challenges. But none was selected and detailed as pivotal in relation to the large conglomeration of mythologies with which Paul was working, and none was used to explain how and why a crucifixion revealed an eschatology. A clue to the fact that Paul's mythmaking process was only under way is the confusion in reference for terms like "Lord," and the confusion in roles for terms like "Christ," "Lord," and "Son of God." The divine agent Paul had in mind throughout was not so much the Christ of the Christ myth, but the God of the Christ myth, namely, the God of Abraham, Israel, the nations, and the end of history, the one who raised Jesus from the dead and gave to Paul his credentials.

And so, because Paul construed Christ's death and resurrection as an event of cosmic restructuring and apocalyptic inauguration, resulting in the role of Christ as Lord, it was Paul's apocalyptic mentality that drove his mythmaking. It was certainly not his interest in the Jesus movements, the teachings of Jesus, or the *christos* associations per se with their martyr myth of a founder-teacher. And it was this apocalyptic persuasion, not the Christ myth, that informed the ways in which he understood the legacy and promise of "Israel"; the state of the world on its way to final judgment; the threat to the traditions of the fathers that he saw in the Jesus movements; his precipitous conversion, intellectual about-face, and tumble into the *christos* associations; his obsession with thoughts of the sovereignty, power, and agency of God; and his vision of a universal kingdom of God calling for a mission to the Gentiles and the restoration of Israel. It seems safe to say that both the Abraham myth and the apocalyptic myth were deeply rooted in the Jewish intellectual life of the times, and that Paul took both of them more or less for granted. What he found of interest in the *christos* associations was a social formation and mythic rationale that, with a little repositioning in response to the Roman times, could bring together his Abraham myth and his apocalyptic myth in such a way as to imagine the turn of the aeons in the grand plan of Israel's God, and so commission as urgent his own mission to the Gentiles. The question is whether and how it could have made sense to "Gentiles."

C. *The Spirit Myth Debate*

In his paper on Paul and the Corinthians for our sessions in Denver, Jonathan Z. Smith remarked on the lack of elaboration of the Christ crucified message in the Corinthian correspondence,[22] the very message that Paul said was all he wanted them to know and all he had known when "preaching" to them. That observation can now be explained. There was little in the Christ myth that Paul could draw upon, except the way in which he used it to insert the language of "Lord" and the threat of judgment into his argumentations about shaping up as a people preparing for the judgment. And in Paul's view, there was much shaping up to do. The Corinthians were only beginners (babes, immature, not able to digest the full diet) in grasping the wisdom of God revealed in the Scriptures and in the Christ myth. Sexual mores show that they had not grasped the importance of being a holy people

---

22. Smith, "Re: Corinthians," 31.

in the eyes of Israel's God. They had apparently spurned (or been unimpressed by) the threat of judgment at the end of history, thinking that they need not wait for the eschaton in order to enjoy the benefits of the spirit(s). Their meals were not the Lord's meal, and some even said, "There is no resurrection." At our sessions we therefore wondered what the common topic may have been that kept them talking to one another. It seemed to have had something to do with "spirit," "meals," and "festivals." Even the issue about eating meats pointed to θυσίαι and so began to figure into the discussions and debate about what the meeting of an association should be about. Smith thought that the basic impasse had to do with differences of view about "spirit myths." His hunch was that the Corinthians were concerned about the spirits of their ancestors, and that the issue for them was (or perhaps had been) how to practice their traditional festivals at a distance from their home districts. This hunch drew upon his reading of the text as a whole, Stowers's paper on the meal text presented at our consultation in New Orleans ("On Construing Meals, Myths and Power in the World of Paul"), Smith's own reconstruction of the recently repopulated Roman colony at Corinth, and his comparison with the Atbalmin and West Papuans of Papua New Guinea. The result was a redescription of the Corinthian "association," no longer a "church" converted by Paul's preaching of "Christ crucified," but a grouping of displaced peoples working on the "translations" called for by separations from their homelands.

Since the issues under discussion with the Corinthians seemed to be about "spirit(s)" (spirits of ancestors, human spirits, divine spirits, spirits of powers in the world and cosmic orders), and especially about the spirits of the special dead, I have tried to figure out what Paul's own "spirit myth" might have looked like. It is a difficult assignment, because Paul's references to "spirit" do not spell out a connected mythology in the way that the apocalypticized Christ myth and the Abraham myth do. But it is clear that the range of functions is even greater than with the Abraham myth (which serves to ground collective group identities) and the Christ myth (which grounds the message of great changes occurring in history, cosmos, and divine plans for the eschaton). Paul's spirit myth grounds the connectivity of a tripartite anthropology with a transcendent God. In keeping with Hellenistic anthropologies and cosmologies, spirit could refer both to the essence of a person (beyond body [or flesh] and mind) and to a person's "influence" on others outside the body. Thus, as an ontologized abstract, the Spirit of God could bridge the distances and differences between the absolute sovereign and human groups via mediators such as Christ and Paul. Paul himself claimed not only to have the "mind of Christ" but access to the spirit (of God, the Lord, and Christ) as well. Thus, his own spirit is portrayed as charged with divine power, and his message can mediate the transfer of life-giving spirit to believers. The Corinthians have apparently been slow in accepting Paul's picture of the necessity of Christ's resurrection in order to be in touch with Christ's spirit, and how it made possible the various forms of mediation of the divine spirit of Israel's God for the reconstruction of "ethnic identity" offered to them. Their hesitation seems to start with consternation about the power and presence of Paul's own spirit by virtue of his apostleship. That is because they were already able to communicate with the spirits of their ancestors at what must have been θυσίαι-at-a-distance from their home districts. They may well have wanted to compare notes with a traveling teacher talking about the spirit of a martyred folk hero at a distance from his tomb, and about how Gentiles were really heirs of Abraham now that God had made that clear at the end of history. The problem was how to get all of the spirits with which both were dealing together, then sorted out and "discerned" so that everyone knew what to do, say, and think when getting together as a "new" social formation. It is clear that Paul's message and sense of presence were not helping.

It may well be that Paul had run into a situation in which the question of ancestral spirits and the appropriate ways to stay in touch with them had surfaced as the major issues for debate—and it may be that he was not prepared for that. Neither the Abraham myth nor the Christ myth could help much with questions about ancestral spirits and memorials. In the letter to the Galatians, Paul made the attempt to link Christ with Abraham as his "seed," thus forging a genealogy in which Gentiles "in Christ" could be understood as "children of Abraham." But in Corinth, this line of mythmaking was apparently not enough to satisfy the questions being raised. It was the issue of the spirit available in Christ that needed explication. Paul, however, seems to have taken the concept of spirit for granted, and he was not at all clear about how the resurrection could be imagined to have made the divine spirit more available. As we have seen, the topic of resurrection and spirit is not expressly in focus until it surfaces in 1 Cor 15, where it is the notion of resurrection from the dead that Paul uses to argue both for the reality of the resurrection of Christ and that Christ became a "life-giving spirit" (1 Cor 15:45). Throughout the letter, of course, Paul struggled with the "translation" of the Christ myth (often not expressly mentioned) into the languages of *ethos*, spirit, and spirituality. But these translations are extremely belabored and mark a problematic relation between Paul's *kērygma* and the concepts of spirit, whether of Christ, the Lord, God, the cosmos, or of ancestors. It has often been taken for granted by New Testament scholars that the concept of the "outpouring of the (divine) spirit" in Paul was directly related to and imagined as the result of the resurrection (and transformation) of the crucified Christ. In Corinth, however, no automatic correlation was made, even supposing that some had been willing to consider the Christ myth and ask about its consequences. Even Paul had to stretch in ch. 15 to make any connection, and then it was purely on the basis of an eschatological imagination.

What, then, might we say about the terms of this debate and why Paul was hard pressed to persuade some people of his message? In the first place, two fundamentally different frames of reference were at odds when thinking about the dead and their memorials. The Corinthians were working with standard, age-old funereal conceptions of memorials for their special dead as ancestors. Paul was proposing a proleptically eschatological crucifixion and resurrection as an image of transformation. Paul wanted the Corinthians to accept a new identity, whether "in Christ," or as "children of Abraham," or as "Israel," that is, belonging to the "family of (Israel's) God." Even if the Corinthians may have been interested in "belonging to Israel," some apparently balked at the acceptance of the Christ myth as the means. And it apparently was not clear, even to those who may have been willing to entertain the Christ myth, how it might affect their relation to their own recent and special dead, how they were to live differently in the world, and why the new spirits (of Christ and the Lord) wanted to cancel out their relations with (and "knowledge" of) the old familiar ones. Since both the Corinthians and Paul were meeting in a Diaspora situation, it may have been that they thought they had much in common. And since Paul appeared as a teacher from afar, the Corinthians may have received him just as they would have any wandering philosopher. But the Corinthians and Paul were apparently working with different sets of assumptions about religious practices. In his paper "Here, There, and Anywhere,"[23] Jonathan Z. Smith has worked out a typology of practices in relation to their locations, whether domestic ("here" at home), centralized (at the "there" of the temple and city that centered a district), or in the associations that emerge during the Hellenistic period (the "anywhere"). The Corinthians were apparently working with the problems of "translating" their homeland "domestic" cults in a place away from home. Paul was working with the "translation" of a "polis-based" cult in a city of the Diaspora. Features of each of these two types of ancient religious practice could be dislodged in the Hellenistic period and translated in the practice of religion "anywhere," that is, within an association. But the concerns, practices, "spirits," deities, social models, and social notions were still quite different. In the case of Paul's Christ, there was no tomb, whether "here" or "there," to provide the "locative" anchor for re-placement in the "anywhere" of the present social system. And his Christ was not a likely candidate for representing or substituting for patriarchal ancestors. The world Paul imagined and offered with his mythologies was "utopian," that is, "elsewhere." And so, there should be no surprise that some Corinthians said, "There is no resurrection," and that Paul was greatly exercised to argue that there was. But his argument must have been in vain. He with his resurrected, heavenly Christ, and they with their dead and properly buried ancestors were simply talking past one another when debating about the spirits of the dead.

IV. The Question of the "Christ Cult"

Well, we have carefully analyzed the two texts traditionally regarded as evidence and documentation for the earliest Christian "community." No Christ cult there.

---

23. Jonathan Z. Smith, "Here, There, and Anywhere," in *Prayer, Magic, and the Stars in the Ancient and Late Antique World* (ed. Scott Noegel et al.; Magic in History Series; University Park: Pennsylvania State University Press, 2003), 21–36; repr. in idem, *Relating Religion: Essays in the Study of Religion* (Chicago: University of Chicago Press, 2004), 323–39.

We have retrieved the basic core of each text, a martyr myth and a myth of origin for a Jesus-*christos* association. No Christ cult there. We have put each of them back into the hands of Paul to observe the changes he must have made to the original myths and to ask about his own description and assessment of their meanings. No Christ cult there. We have then explored the way in which Paul turned the Christ myth into a message for his mission and brought it into play with several other large-scale myths to support his concept of *ekklēsia* as a new congregation of "Israel." No Christ cult there. If these observations are correct, it means that the term "Christ cult" is a misnomer both as a concept for a "pre-Pauline Hellenistic Christianity" and as the definition for the "churches" of the Pauline mission to the Gentiles. In *A Myth of Innocence*, I used the term "Christ cult" as a corollary to the term "Christ myth" in keeping with the (Bultmannian-)German tradition of charting the "development" of Christian beginnings from Jesus through "the earliest Church," the "Hellenistic Church aside from Paul," to the Pauline "churches." I had substituted the "Jesus movements" for "the earliest Church" in order to revise our understanding of the Jesus traditions in relation to which the Gospel of Mark could be reinterpreted. This I could contrast with the "Hellenistic Church aside from Paul" and the Pauline churches where, according to Rudolf Bultmann, "Jesus was called 'Lord' Κύριος and was cultically worshiped."[24] Bultmann did not devote a special section of his theology to the topics of "cult" or "worship," but in his descriptions of the early "Church" he rather offhandedly mentioned all of the characteristics and practices I listed in my footnote on the "Christ cult" in *A Myth of Innocence*.[25] Naturally, Bultmann's attention was taken primarily by the purported evidence for baptism and "the sacrament of the 'Lord's Supper' as celebrated in the Pauline or Hellenistic congregations, whose liturgy we know from Mark and Paul."[26] It was this description of the "Hellenistic Church" as a cult and worshiping community that I inadvertently allowed to stand without critical assessment when I used the term "Christ cult." I will now have to retract the use of the term in keeping with the seminar's redescription of Christian origins.

Smith has helped me see that the use of the term "cult" in New Testament scholarship has traveled a tortuous path through many polemical and apologetic discourses in the attempt to describe Christianity, and especially early Christianity, as a "religion." In course, the terms "religion," "cult," "ritual," and "sect" all suffered significant shifts in reference, most of which resulted in negative connotations, leaving the terms "church," "Christianity," "liturgy," "worship," and "belief" for the most part untouched as positive concepts and accepted definitions. The use of the terms "ritual" and "cult" in the description of Christianity seems to have entered scholarly discourse both as an attempt to wear the mantle of the academy

---

24. Rudolf Bultmann, *Theology of the New Testament* (trans. Kendrick Grobel; 2 vols.; London: SCM, 1952–55), 1:51.
25. Mack, *Myth of Innocence*, 100 n. 2; cf. idem, *Who Wrote the New Testament?* 75–76.
26. Bultmann, *Theology of the New Testament*, 1:57.

(and thus appear *wissenschaftlich* and "objective"), but also with a Protestant's eye on Roman Catholicism (and thus subtly polemical). In this context, "cult" lost its technical meaning as a system of rituals practiced regularly by a group and came to be used popularly for a group itself engaged in a particular practice of devotion or veneration. Thus, there have been references to the "cult of saints," the "cult of candles," the "veneration of the Virgin," and "deviant cults" when viewed in relation to larger, more encompassing and traditional "religions."

The special problem for New Testament scholars has been the comparison of early Christian formations with other religions of late antiquity, on the one hand, and with the later formations of Christianity, on the other. Since Christianity has been regarded as unique, incomparable, and definitional for the study of religion, and since the desire to see its later formations implicitly taking shape at the beginning has determined the interest in New Testament studies, the terminology used to describe early Christian phenomena has always been problematic. Smith's *Drudgery Divine* has traced the history of this problem for us and noted the exaggerated interest in the alleged "mystery religions," a helpful comparison for some reasons, but one too close for comfort for others. In the process, descriptions both of the mysteries and of early Christian groups were necessarily skewed, as his study makes clear. Bultmann called the "mystery religions" *cults* and used them to enhance and partially explain early Christian "worship" of the crucified and resurrected Messiah. This interest in the "similarities" between early Christianity and the religions of late antiquity was typical of the history of religions school, and one might think that Bultmann was also interested in early Christianity as a Hellenistic "religion." But of course, the important difference from the "mysteries" was that Jesus was the Messiah and the Messiah had been crucified and resurrected, whereupon the disciples got together and formed an "eschatological Congregation." Curiously, Bultmann did use the term "cult" for early Christian rituals without negative nuance (avoiding, I think, a consistent use of the even more troubling terminology of *ritual* in keeping with the Protestant aversion to Catholic Christianities), because early Christian rituals were, as he sometimes said, "appropriate expression[s]" of the "eschatological Congregation."[27] It was the "eschatological Congregation" that defined the "Church" for Bultmann, and this "Church" was there from the very beginning, from the turn of the aeons that took place in the death and resurrection of Jesus the Christ. This church then "developed" (rather quickly, it seems) forms of preaching, worship, and cultic expressions (i.e., "rituals") "appropriate" for "participation" in that founding event and new collective consciousness. It does not require a close reading of Bultmann's *Theology* to see that the language of *cult* was subsumed by the language of the "Church," which allowed the familiar languages of "liturgy," "sacrament," "preaching," and "worship" to be used. And what was true of Bultmann's imagination of

---

27. Ibid.

the "early Church" was true for an entire chapter of German New Testament scholarship. They all thought that the "Christ event" was the "hinge of history" and that the only appropriate response to the resurrection of the Christ was the Christian faith and the formation of the church. All New Testament data were organized by that imagination. Martin Dibelius, for instance, thought that the pronouncement stories in Mark had first been sermon illustrations in the early church.[28]

The work of the seminar has made it impossible to continue the use of these terminologies and the description of Christian beginnings that they imply. Although the term "cult" may still be of descriptive value generally for a system of rituals practiced by a group, it can no longer be used to refer to a "pre-Pauline Christ cult," given the data at our disposal. One reason for dispensing with the use of the term "Christ cult" is that I used it to name a group in contrast to the "Jesus schools/associations." A group is not a "cult" except in popular parlance. A second reason is that, despite the Protestant scholarly tradition of using Paul to imagine a pair of "cultic expressions" from the beginning, namely, baptism and the "Lord's supper" (both understood to be grounded in Paul's proclamation of "Christ crucified"), we just do not have evidence for the Christ myth working that way or for any system of rituals that constituted a regular sequence of practices of any first-century group. A third reason is that the term easily shifts in connotation from "ritual practices" to "veneration," and we have not been able to document any "veneration" (presumably of Jesus as a divine figure and presence) in our redescription of the *christos* associations, or in the logics of the "Christ myth" and "supper text," or in our investigations of Paul and the Corinthians. So the term is suspect when used in the interest of imagining the "earliest Christian congregations" on the model of later forms of Christian liturgy. Nor is it precise enough as a technical term of description or definition to guard against that anachronism in the interest of comparison with other religions of late antiquity.

I know that this does not do justice to a long list of unanswered questions that still need to be asked about Christian origins. After all, the term "Christ cult," though not seriously questioned until now, has held the place on this map for all of those "churches" traditionally imagined to be visible through the windows of the Pauline corpus, and we have only now called it into question. That is because the distinction between "Jesus movements" and "Christ cult" has been extremely important for the large-scale map of Christian beginnings that we have been sketching for the first century. This has allowed us to read a number of texts differently and to imagine several groupings of Jesus people and schools of thought without having to assume that they were "Christians." But now that we have paid a visit to the "church" at Corinth and decided to revisit two of the major texts for the

---

28. Vernon K. Robbins, "Chreia and Pronouncement Story in Synoptic Stories," in Burton L. Mack and Vernon K. Robbins, *Patterns of Persuasion in the Gospels* (FF; Sonoma, Calif.: Polebridge, 1989), 3–6, citing Martin Dibelius, *From Tradition to Gospel* (trans. Bertram Lee Woolf; New York: Scribner, [1934]), 37–69; cf. 26.

"pre-Pauline Hellenistic Christ cult," only to discover that the term "Christ cult" is no longer helpful, we are left with many other texts, traditions, practices, interests, and phenomena from the first century for which we now have no names. The "liturgical materials" I included in the list of features that described the "Christ cult" in *A Myth of Innocence*[29] still need to be redescribed and explained. As an example, the "hymn" in Phil 2:6–11 acclaims the (earthly, human) "humiliation" of Jesus Christ, who was "in the form of God," and the (heavenly, divine) "exaltation" to become Jesus Christ the Lord, before whom "every knee should bow." This text appears to be working with a "son of God" mythology, a "royal" mimetic model (of a king "taking the form of a slave" to circulate among his people incognito), and a social-political vision of universal sovereignty and scope. It does not easily fit with or appear to be an elaboration of Paul's mythology in the interest of forming a "holy people" in preparation for the judgment, nor from the *christos* associations where a locative myth and mentality prevailed. And yet, someone or some group was apparently thinking big, and thought how grand it would be to imagine the importance of Jesus *christos* on the imperial model of sovereignty and the cosmic model of divine power. How such a group came to such an imagination, and how they must have understood themselves in relation to the real Roman world are not at all clear. Paul picked the poem up for citation, focused on the willing reversals of honor–shame–honor status on the part of a royal figure, and used it to call for a similar attitude and behavior on the part of individual Christians in their relations to and service for one another. This does fit with Paul's application of the crucifixion–resurrection myth to every human moment of encounter and change, turning such into events fraught with consequences interpreted by a death–life metaphor. But still, the poem is hardly Pauline, for it draws upon a kingship myth in which the son of God must first experience enslavement as a human being before being exalted to the throne of his father. There is nothing extraordinary about the myth itself, for it was known by others in application to the king-tyrant contrast. But it cannot be explained as a simple elaboration of the Christ myth, for the divinity of the son of God is given from the beginning, and the social model is that of universal obedience to the newly installed king. Even if one thought that the image may have been nurtured by thinking about Paul's apocalyptic image of the kingdom of God, the shift toward interest in political supremacy needs to be explained. What group, in what tradition of the Jesus-*christos* associations, would have or could have found such a myth appropriate? And what kinds of activities, celebrations, and discussions might be imagined? With such a myth, one might ask, was Jesus the teacher or *christos* the martyr no longer in the picture? (Scholars have noted that it must have been Paul who added the line about "even death on a cross.") Thus, there is much remaining to redescribe.

Paul does give the impression of people converted to his gospel forming congregations in the name of Jesus Christ the Lord. And it is, of course, that picture,

---

29. Mack, *Myth of Innocence*, 100 n. 2.

spread out through Asia Minor and Greece, if not also allowed to influence the traditional imaginations of the "churches" at Jerusalem and Rome, that was held in place by the term "Christ cult." But now that we have taken a close look at the way Paul's gospel was put together and the trouble he had persuading the Corinthians to accept it, we cannot just assume that all of these "churches" were converts to Paul's gospel. Suppose we extrapolate a bit from our project of redescription running from the Jesus movements to Paul at Corinth. We could then begin to imagine the terrain once held by the terms "Jesus movement" and "Christ cult" as a diverse set of sites in the wake of early interests in the teachings of Jesus and their spread and cultivation. The work of the seminar has made it possible to imagine "associations" forming to cultivate different collections of these teachings and to explore their applications to a range of intellectual, social-ethical, and cultural identity questions. We have noted the many directions in which mythmaking occurred in the interest of placing both the teachings and the teacher in legitimate and distinctive relation to other respected and important traditions of teachings current at the time. We have debated both the question of authorship and authority on the part of "creative" intellectuals as mythmakers, as well as the corollary question of social interests that must have contributed to the formation of groups that produced, supported, considered, and accepted such ideas. And in course we have encountered again and again the shift in focus created by the phenomenon of mythmaking from the teachings to the teacher. We have not gone back to explore all of the ways in which the figure of Jesus as a founder-teacher was "enhanced" within the Jesus schools and movements. Nor have we made precise the mechanisms at work when changes in myths and shifts in the forms and circumstances of associations took place. But we know that there was no single line of "development" from the teacher Jesus to a specific mythology and a particular social formation that can be called a Christian church by the end of the first century. This means that we have made some progress in our project of redescribing Christian beginnings. But of course, now that we have imagined a *christos* association forming in the interest of a Jesus-teacher group, and a Pauline take on the *christos* myth and association to inaugurate a mission to the Gentiles, it should be possible to imagine many other instances of social experimentation and mythmaking in the wake of the Jesus-*christos* phenomenon. There would be differences depending on the social situation, the people and their own traditions, the multicultural climate, the political circumstances, the way in which the representation of a Jesus teaching or mythology came to them, the current interests and issues under consideration, local cults and practices, and the way in which their several social and intellectual worlds impinged on them.

Our work on the Corinthian site can be used as a case in point, and perhaps as an example of the kinds of pictures still to be painted of many other sites. The association at Corinth has always been viewed as a congregation formed by conversion to Paul's gospel of "Christ crucified," meeting to worship their Lord Jesus Christ and receive his spirit as the manifestation of authentic, personal devotion and faith, working out the social relational and ethical questions that the new faith implied, and engaging Paul in serious theological discussions. Our redescription does not support this picture. That is because we were able to reconstruct the Corinthians' situation, their own traditions, their responses to Paul's approach, and the current interests and issues under debate among them. The association had formed before Paul came along. They were busy with their own questions and debates about doing domestic religion at a distance from home. They disagreed among themselves on what to make of Paul's message. There was no common agreement to become a community of "believers" in Paul's gospel. Some apparently found themselves interested in Paul's gospel, interested enough to give Paul the impression that they were being persuaded, and interested enough to keep talking to Paul and asking questions. But the questions they asked allow us to see that there was much else going on among them than working at the task of shaping up as an *ekklēsia* to fit Paul's vision. So even though Paul wrote to them as if they were an association "in Christ," it was possible for us to see a much more complex process of social and intellectual activity under way.

I would like to conclude by offering a few observations on the importance of Smith's paper, "Re: Corinthians," for our redescription. As you will recall, his reading of the text of 1 Corinthians was enough to surmise that the issue under debate had to do with cults of the dead and memorial meals. We all knew something of the importance of these practices for the several cultures of the time, and Smith knew from his ethnographical studies how important they were for many other peoples. He then took note of John S. Kloppenborg's point about the recent colonization of Corinth by the Romans, and Stowers's study of the Corinthians' meal in the light of Greek θυσίαι and memorials. Noting that Paul was a "missionary" who arrived from another land and culture, he found a comparable situation in Papua New Guinea where the Atbalmin, West Papuans, and other indigenous peoples "absorb[ed] a stunning series of situational changes within a brief span of time through strategies of incorporation and resistance."[30] The situational changes could be described as a complex interweaving of newly expanded European colonial administration, a Christian mission, relocated peoples, intermingling of religious and quotidian practices both indigenous and new, shifting relations to lands and special places, and ancestor cults. The languages, conceptions, experiences, behaviors, and social affects of dealing with the "spirit(s)" became the coin for negotiating the differences between the indigenous ancestor cults and the Christian mission. Drawing upon his "Here, There, and Anywhere" typology, a comparison of the two situations began to clarify Paul's problem with the Corinthians. From Eytan Bercovitch's description of the situation of the Atbalmin,[31]

---

30. Smith, "Re: Corinthians," 27–28; cf. 29 n. 39, 33–34 n. 48.
31. Eytan Bercovitch, "The Altar of Sin: Social Multiplicity and Christian Conversion among a New Guinea People," in *Religion and Cultural Studies* (ed. Susan L. Mizruchi; Princeton: Princeton University Press, 2001), 211–35.

Smith helped us see the consequences of living in several worlds ("landscapes") at the same time, that even though the Atbalmin had been converted and understood themselves as Christian, they were in fact both Christian and not Christian at the same time. Applied to the Corinthian situation, then, we were able to imagine a much more lively conversation about Paul's gospel than he himself lets us see. I suspect that would also be true for other sites where traveling teachers with something to say about Jesus and what his teachings and transformations might mean for understanding and living in the world showed up and gained a hearing. We already know that there were many ways of forming groups, many reasons for doing so, many "landscapes" in view, and many different situations and circumstances in which talk about Jesus (*christos*) must have taken place. We can no longer think of a single myth, calling for a single response, creating a single community, supporting a new religion of enclaves and devotion to (the Son of) God in isolation from the rest of the world.

Conclusions

So it looks as if the mythologies under review work quite well to supply social logics to associations in the schools of Jesus. A martyr myth gives you many benefits. You have a myth of origin that can provide an imaginary anchor to the beginnings of your association, can then be used to analyze and discuss the many factors that impinge on your social formation, or that can be manipulated in order to address newly encountered contemporary circumstances. This could have been very attractive in the various situations of displacement and the breakup of different levels of social cohesion experienced by many at the time. Questions about links and loyalties to families, locales, districts, cities, nations, temple-states, and so on, could all be negotiated in imagination by manipulating such an origin myth. The "truth" of his (or your) teachings, philosophy, ideology, worldview, etc., could be confirmed, and the integrity of the teacher's character would be demonstrated. You would have a champion to whom you could point, one who could take his place among the teachers of the world and the powers that be. A "subtle" advance in standing would also occur whereby your man would now have to be seen as having a greater importance and more pure character than the powers that be. There could be, in fact, an implicit condemnation of the "tyrants" involved, should you want actually to name some. Mark, for instance, found it quite easy to use irony as a vehicle for disclosing the ineptitude of the (Roman-Judean) "tyrants" in the face of the power of the teachings of the teacher, because the kingdom he represented was "hidden" from them. Thus, a martyrology seems to have been used in many ways to let an association of people in the schools of Jesus take their place with confidence in the larger ecumene.

As associations, such groups must have met together on a regular basis and taken common meals together. It would have been natural for such an association to have remarked on its collective identity as a school in the tradition of the teachings of Jesus when meeting to eat together. In keeping with what we know about associations in general of the time, these remarks would probably have been made at the "breaking of bread" and when wine was distributed. The term "ritual" has been used for this practice, and it is understandable, given a martyr myth of the founder-teacher of the association, that these meal markers may well have taken on symbolic reference to that myth. If we use this observation to imagine how the rituals of some *christos* associations may have been formalized and elaborated, for instance, by creating prayers of thanksgiving as we know some did, another set of questions about the circumstances, interests, and consequences for social formation and identity could be engaged to help us better describe what might be called the social mood or *esprit* that may be imagined. But the caution remains, namely, that we be clear about the social climate or atmosphere of such ritual occasions in keeping with customary association practices and interests of the time and not let them take on the aura of later forms of Christian ritual and worship. Neither Graydon F. Snyder's *Ante Pacem* nor Henry Bettenson's *Documents of the Christian Church*[32] lets us imagine rituals of the first four hundred years on the model of later medieval worship and pieties. We must be done with the traditional and pervasive picture of early Christian associations as Paul's "Christ cult," where, as has customarily been imagined, Christians met to give thanks for the sacrifice of Christ and the salvation from the wrath to come that it made possible. Such an ambience does not follow from the social logic of the martyr myths we have to explain or the rituals we are allowed to imagine. Thus, I hope to have problematized the standard imagination of the "Christ cult" in light of the seminar's project of redescription. And the term itself I hope to have made questionable as a reference to the practices and interests of the early Jesus-*christos*- and Christ associations known to Paul.

---

32. Graydon F. Snyder, *Ante Pacem: Archaeological Evidence of Church Life before Constantine* (Macon, Ga.: Mercer University Press, 1985); Henry Bettenson, ed., *Documents of the Christian Church* (ed. Chris Maunder; 3rd ed.; Oxford: Oxford University Press, 1999).

Bringing Paul and the Corinthians Together?
A Rejoinder and Some Proposals
on Redescription and Theory

William E. Arnal

I. Introduction: The Redescriptive Effort

Paul is a mystery—in many ways, more of a mystery than are the other fragments and figments of ancient "Christianity" that we possess and that this seminar has attempted to redescribe. In Paul's case, the standard myth of Christian origins typically inflates his importance while attenuating his distinctiveness. In doing so, it makes him less of a mystery, domesticates him by fitting him into the same narrative sequence as Jesus, Peter, the prophets, and the apostles. This myth in its more elaborated versions actually provides a theory of social attraction and repulsion, offering a genuine explanation—and an ethnic and social one, at that—not merely for the sources of Paul's own ideas but, in addition, for the reasons anyone would listen to these ideas in the first place, and even why others would fail to be moved by them. According to this theory, Paul's converts heard and responded to his gospel because it allowed them, finally, to be what they had always wanted and needed to be: beloved people of the one true God. The Jews, by contrast, jealous of their privileged position, rejected the message out of a selfish desire to retain their unique status as the people of God at the expense of the salvation of the whole human race, while unrepentant "pagans" rejected the gospel out of economic interests (see, e.g., Acts 16:18–19; 19:24–29; etc.) or other base motives.[1]

---

1. I observe parenthetically that, like many Christian myths (e.g., "the story" [singular] of Christmas), this explanation and account may derive not so much from the actual texts in question as from a selective and conflationary reading of them. That is, I am hardly arguing or assuming here that all of these notions are drawn from or promoted in Acts, but rather that fragments from Acts, the Pastorals, Paul's own letters, and a variety of other texts and developing Christian theology were drawn together into this synthetic but very effective portrait, which was (and is) then used as the lens through which to read the primary texts (Acts, the canonical letters attributed to Paul) from which it is supposedly derived.

This explanation (or various facets thereof)— as a direct result, I would claim, of its genuine explanatory potential and broad ability to render quite diverse data intelligible—has been invoked ever since it was first cobbled together, and continues to appear, in slightly modified forms, in even the most recent scholarship on Paul.[2] The minute we reject this narrative—and this rejection is a, perhaps *the*, fundamental goal of this seminar—Paul starts to make less sense, both because we have lost the key explanatory framework through which he has always been made sense of, and because the reliable data for Paul himself (the seven New Testament letters of generally undisputed authorship)[3] provide a great deal (rather too much, in fact) of scattered data but no historical or sociological framework, and little ideological framework, for understanding that data. The letters are, as letters, ancillary to other types of contacts and assumptions which they take for granted and about which they fail to provide direct information. The Christian Paul, read through Acts and theological extrapolations therefrom, is a sensible object; but Paul the Greco-Roman Jew who interacted with a variety of associations and left us seven letters is, generally speaking, not. When we render him in terms genuinely independent of the mythic paradigm of the heroic founder of Christian churches and missionary of the Christian gospel inherited from those who were apostles before him (the latter a claim and characterization that Paul himself repudiates in Gal 1:17), Paul becomes "implausible."[4] Conversely, when we endeavor to render

---

2. For example, John Dominic Crossan and Jonathan L. Reed argue that (alleged) Jewish opposition to Paul's message and activity stemmed from the fact that Paul was stealing away Gentile hangers-on and potential benefactors from the synagogue (*In Search of Paul: How Jesus's Apostle Opposed Rome's Empire with God's Kingdom. A New Vision of Paul's Words and World* [San Francisco: HarperSanFrancisco, 2004], 39–40; cf. Gerd Theissen, "Social Stratification in the Corinthian Community: A Contribution to the Sociology of Early Hellenistic Christianity," in idem, *The Social Setting of Pauline Christianity: Essays on Corinth* [ed. and trans. John H. Schütz; Philadelphia: Fortress, 1982], 104). Such an explanation makes logical sense, but is utterly in step with the age-old (and distinctively Lukan) notion of Jewish "jealousy" at the success of the Christian mission.

3. The so-called Dutch radicals have reopened the question of authorship even with respect to the *Hauptbriefe*. See, e.g., the overview in Hermann Detering, "The Dutch Radical Approach to the Pauline Epistles," *Journal of Higher Criticism* 3/2 (1996): 163–93. It seems to me, however, that too many of the arguments adduced for the redacted or inauthentic character of the Pauline corpus rely on too schematic a view of Christian origins, in which it is known, essentially in advance, that certain concepts did not originate until a particular time. As a result of such a schematic perspective, the presence within the Pauline corpus of, say, disputes about faith versus the law is regarded as too theologically developed for the first century and as not securely attested until the time of Justin (so Detering). The problem with this sort of reasoning is that it makes the actual texts that attest to such concerns (i.e., Paul's letters) dependent for their interpretation on an already established view of ancient Christian history. But our views of ancient Christian history are actually dependent on these texts themselves. The argument assumes what it sets out to prove. Nonetheless, I do not think the proposals of the "Dutch radicals" can be summarily dismissed, either. The redaction of the Pauline corpus remains an unsolved problem.

4. See Jonathan Z. Smith, "Re: Corinthians," 31 (in this volume): "If what I have redescribed is at all plausible, then Paul is implausible."

Paul in genuinely plausible terms, and make that plausibility our central goal, the mythic Paul of the Christian story returns—albeit often disguised or in unfamiliar garb—to rattle chains in our attic.

Of course, the agenda of this seminar is, precisely, to do both of these things: (1) to challenge and provide alternatives to traditional pictures of Christian origins; and (2) to explore the nexus between "mythmaking" and "social interests" among the ancient Jesus people. It is on the assumption that this double focus constitutes our agenda that my comments are based, and, more pointedly, my objections to, criticisms of, and/or emendations of the proposals put forward by the other contributions to the seminar that appear in this volume, particularly those of Burton L. Mack.[5] That is to say, it seems to me that it is the very success of Mack's work, in particular, in redescribing Paul that has created something of a conundrum for comprehending Paul, both with respect to his relations with the people who preserved his letters (one assumes, the people to whom he was writing), and with respect to the fundamental sensibility of Paul's ideas in an ancient context, specifically, in an urban Greco-Roman context.

Mack's paper for this volume, "Rereading the Christ Myth: Paul's Gospel and the Christ Cult Question," represents a dramatic step forward for our redescription of Paul in this seminar and indeed, in my view, a major step forward for scholarly discourse on Paul in general. Mack's discussion gives us some purchase on how Paul's ideas—his "gospel"—might (and can) be understood apart from a conception of "Christianity" so developed as to appear medieval. While the contributions of Stanley K. Stowers and Richard S. Ascough to this volume largely provide us with appropriate ancient ways of understanding Paul's activity and the social formations of the groups with whom he interacted,[6] and while Jonathan Z.

---

5. Burton L. Mack, "Rereading the Christ Myth: Paul's Gospel and the Christ Cult Question" (in this volume). The following comments are primarily a rejoinder to this paper.

6. For Ascough, see now Richard S. Ascough, "A Question of Death: Paul's Community-Building Language in 1 Thessalonians 4:13–18," *JBL* 123 (2004): 509–30; idem, "Paul's 'Apocalypticism' and the Jesus Associations at Thessalonica and Corinth" (in this volume). Stanley K. Stowers's paper ("Does Pauline Christianity Resemble a Hellenistic Philosophy?" [in this volume]) focuses on finding a model or analogue for Pauline activity (and groups) in the philosophical schools of antiquity; Ascough, in the "voluntary associations." Stowers's other paper ("Kinds of Myth, Meals, and Power: Paul and the Corinthians" [in this volume]) stresses the extent to which various practices are not under the intentional control of those who engage in them. The various observations and arguments of Stowers and Ascough are thoroughly valid and, to my mind, correct the tendency in Mack's paper to focus on intentional intellectual production (i.e., "mythmaking") at the expense of the real circumstances (that is, my understanding of "social formation") that constrain that activity and within which that activity takes place (see further below on this imbalance; the effort to relate Paul's intellectual activity somehow to his social circumstances and those of his auditors is the inspiration behind nearly all of my comments about Mack's paper, especially my demurrals). On the other hand, by focusing more exclusively on the nature of Pauline groups and Pauline practice, these pieces do not thoroughly engage Mack's efforts to reconstruct the genesis of the Pauline myth. I note, of course, that this is not due to a lack of interest in the topic: Stowers's immense contribution to the study of Paul (*A Rereading of*

Smith ("Re: Corinthians") attempts—boldly—to reconstruct the mythic assumptions of the group Paul is addressing in 1 Corinthians, Mack deals more precisely with that central enigma that is Paul, and the genesis, development, and deployment of his central myth, an understanding of which must be achieved if we are indeed to provide a genuine redescription of Christian origins. Paul emerges in Mack's paper as, precisely, an ancient, and in a way that is more successful, I think, than many other efforts at taking seriously the content of Paul's "proclamation." Representations of Paul in ancient garb abound, of course, but almost always at the cost of either ignoring the content of his "gospel" or allowing that content to stand in its too-developed, retrospective, appallingly Christian form.[7] But in this volume Mack has finally managed to bring together a genuinely ancient Greco-Roman Paul with a convincing description of the content of his myth. Whatever quibbles I have with Mack's characterization of the Pauline myth (on which, see below), his successfully having offered such a redescription provides a template for any and all subsequent efforts to understand Paul in a reasonable way. Moreover, Mack's discussion makes it clear both that "deconstructing" Paul's place in the first century is categorically necessary for cleaning up our historical understanding of subsequent moments in the "Christian" myth (e.g., the Gospel of Mark), and that a discussion of Paul's ideological forebears in the Jesus/*christos* associations is useful, not so much as a self-sufficient intellectual lineage, but as a demonstration of the absence of anything like "Christianity" both among Paul's forebears, and in Paul himself.

The core of Mack's paper is the positing of a "double disjunction" at the heart of 1 Corinthians, that is, an assertion of ideological discontinuity on both (temporal) sides of Paul's activity: a discontinuity, on the one hand, between Paul's version of the *euangelion* and the "traditions" imagined to serve as sources of his message (especially those explicitly cited as sources in 1 Cor 11:23–25; 15:3–5), and, on the other hand, an ideological discontinuity between Paul's gospel and the beliefs, assumptions, and practices of the groups he addresses in Corinth. Thus, instead of a linear model involving the communication of an idea (or ideal) from one context

---

Romans: Justice, Jews, and Gentiles [New Haven: Yale University Press, 1994]) is precisely an exegesis of the letter to the Romans.

7. In the first category, the work that gives us a genuinely ancient Paul, I am especially including material that compares Paul's *ekklēsiai* to voluntary associations of various sorts, so providing an ancient analogue for Pauline groups, but not so much a description or ancient contextualization of Paul's ideology, that is, his "gospel" (especially useful now is Philip A. Harland, *Associations, Synagogues, and Congregations: Claiming a Place in Ancient Mediterranean Society* [Minneapolis: Fortress, 2003]). In the second category falls nearly all "traditional" scholarship on Paul, devoted to an exegesis of his various epistolary pronouncements, but doing so in terms of highly developed Christian theological categories. Again, I am quite self-consciously excepting Stowers's work from this broad critique, as I think it very effectively gives us a Pauline proclamation that is genuinely comprehensible in an ancient context (I am thinking especially of his *Rereading of Romans*), as well as a number of other rhetorically oriented studies. I am still unconvinced, however, that these types of studies have effectively linked the core content of Paul's *euangelion* or *kērygma* to an identifiable social formation.

to another (that is, the communication of the gospel message from the "primitive, Palestinian church" to the "Hellenistic churches" of "the Diaspora," and thence to Paul and Paul's "converts"), we now have mythic conceptions being deliberately modified in the service of distinctively Pauline agenda—in both cases, by Paul's creative "misunderstanding" of his interlocutors, whether those from whom he "receives" "the gospel" or those to whom he "transmits" it. Mack's description of and explanation for the first of these two disjunctions are the more convincing and consequential: by examining the Pauline modifications to the logic of the "traditions" in 1 Cor 11:23–25 (the supper tradition) and 15:3–5 (the resurrection appearance tradition), Mack puts paid, I think, to any notion of a *Paul-like* pre-Pauline "Christ cult," with which Paul's own ideology is in smooth continuity. Rather, pre-Pauline (or better, now, thanks to Mack: simply non-Pauline) traditions concerned with Jesus as sage, as martyr, as vindicated and risen one assumed into heaven, and as presider over a communal meal are transformed by Paul into dense ciphers for cosmic transformations, leading to the juncture of the nations with Israel's epic history and grounding Paul's own authority for his Gentile mission. Such transformations have been made, according to Mack, through subtle modifications of wording and contextualization: for example, with the resurrection tradition alone, the Pauline specification that Jesus "was crucified" (as opposed simply to "died"), that the cause for which he died was "our sins" (rather than "the kingdom"), the specification that he "was buried" (which Mack sees as invoking apocalyptic imagery), and the use of ἐγείρειν to describe the resurrection (rather than an original ἀναλαμβάνειν or μετατιθέναι, denoting assumption and vindication).

The disjunction hereby identified is extremely important at the theoretical level: it tends to confirm Smith's insistence (citing Marshall Sahlins) that cultural production is dialectical and mutually transformative when different groups encounter one another (and so, also, that misunderstanding and misrecognition are as common and important as is accurate communication),[8] and (citing Claude Lévi-Strauss) that cultural production is a form of bricolage, the deliberate emendation and use of "found" cultural artifacts to address new intellectual problems.[9] And it accords well with Willi Braun's and my insistence that ideas do not unfold in linear fashion of their own accord.[10] Paul, now, is understood not as a purveyor

---

8. Smith, "Re: Corinthians," 28.
9. See, e.g., Jonathan Z. Smith, "Differential Equations: On Constructing the Other," in *Relating Religion: Essays in the Study of Religion* (Chicago: University of Chicago Press, 2004), 246: "As Lévi-Strauss, among others, has convincingly demonstrated, when we confront difference we do not encounter irrationality or bad faith but rather the very essence of thought. Meaning is made possible by difference. Yet thought seeks to bring together what thought necessarily takes apart by means of a dynamic process of disassemblage and reassemblage, which results in an object no longer natural but rather social, no longer factual but rather intellectual. Relations are discovered and reconstituted through projects of differentiation."
10. William E. Arnal and Willi Braun, "Social Formation and Mythmaking: Theses on Key

of ideas whose content he has received from others and passes along, but as a *bricoleur*, who uses mythic content, forms, and fragments as he encounters them, to construct novel notions that address his own problems, issues, and circumstances. The disjunction described by Mack is equally important at the historical level, the level of redescription, for it demolishes any basis for concluding that Paul's "gospel" predates Paul himself, thus providing room for a completely fresh reconsideration of Paul's antecedents (which Mack has, in fact, offered here) and a serious caution against reading distinctively Pauline notions into later texts, such as the Gospel of Mark. And the disjunction here reconstructed is extremely convincing exegetically: I find myself giving unqualified assent to Mack's proposals for Pauline conceptual emendations to the supper and resurrection appearance traditions, as well as to some aspects of Mack's construal of Paul's deliberate "misunderstanding" of Corinthian meal practices.

Also persuasive are some of Mack's characterizations of the social situation among the Corinthians addressed by Paul, drawing on work by Smith and Stowers, especially as composed of ethnically uprooted and ethnically mixed folks. What is missing here, however, and what must be stressed, is that *this characterization applies to Paul too*—it is even implicit in his being a Jew with a Roman name, as Corinth itself is a Greek city refounded as a Roman colony. Paul's circumstances almost perfectly mirror those of his Corinthian interlocutors. This observation hints at my greatest reservation with the work of the seminar on Corinth so far. Mack and Smith have constructed what is, in my view, too great a disjunction between Paul and the folks to whom he is writing.[11] There is a double disjunction as Mack's paper describes it, but it is the first disjunction—that between Paul and the tradents he draws from—that is most sensibly described and explained. The disjunction between Paul and his interlocutors in Corinth, on the other hand, is, in my view, much exaggerated, both by Mack and by Smith, and raises some serious conceptual problems for the project of this seminar. The first problem is that if our goal is redescription, the characterization of the disjunction between Paul and the Corinthians returns us to a much older scholarly chestnut in which the obvious frictions between Paul and his interlocutors as attested in the Corinthian correspondence are put down to "misunderstanding." This has always been a rather foolish construct—Paul, we are told, came preaching a gospel of "liberty" from the law or from death or from some other ethereal notion, and the minute he was gone the Corinthians "misunderstood" this gospel as license to engage in drunken orgies and commit incest.[12] This bizarre "misunderstanding" is often put

---

Terms," in *Redescribing Christian Origins* (ed. Ron Cameron and Merrill P. Miller; SBLSymS 28; Atlanta: Society of Biblical Literature; Leiden and Boston: Brill, 2004), 459–67.

11. See further below for more extended discussion of this problem.

12. Such a claim is a mainstay of New Testament introductions. Representative is Stephen L. Harris, *The New Testament: A Student's Introduction* (Mountain View, Calif.: Mayfield, 1988), 214, 216: "In reading Paul's letters to Corinth, remember that he is struggling to communicate his vision of union

down to the Corinthians' being Gentiles (who, we assume, have a proclivity for orgies and incest); otherwise, we must conclude that these people were uniquely stupid, or that Paul was a phenomenally bad teacher. The virtue of Smith's proposal, especially—that Paul "misunderstood" the Corinthian associations' ancestrally oriented meal practices and "xenoglossia" as oriented toward *the* Spirit—is that it both reverses this scenario and makes Paul out to be the source of the misunderstanding, as well as acknowledging the creative or productive nature of the misconstrual. But Smith's proposal founders, I think, on the same rocks as the traditional view: we are required to assume an extended communicative incompetence among members of the same (urban, Greco-Roman) culture, and among people and groups whose social circumstances appear to be more or less identical. To stress Paul's difference from his Corinthian interlocutors on the grounds that he is an alienated Jewish foreigner while they are alienated foreigners of different derivation is of course to reify the old Jew–Gentile split, another mainstay in the ancient myth of Christian origins. In any case, I fear that this reconstruction of a sharp disjunction between Paul and his interlocutors feels right for us and has an intuitive attraction, precisely because it is such a familiar story, such a close fit with that massively rich and explanatory myth of the "rise of Christianity" that I recounted in my opening paragraph. The second conceptual problem comes when we attempt to move from this redescription to explanation, for we are left with a Paul who is disconnected, unique, insensible, largely incomprehensible in any but self-referential terms, a Paul who speaks only in idiolect (almost literally so, in Smith's reconstruction). Paul's agenda appears to be shared with few others, and so we are left without any way to understand the preservation of Paul's letters, the later influence of Pauline-style ideology, Pauline *ekklēsiai*, and, especially damaging for our project, without any way to understand the attraction of Paul's project, since, by this reconstruction, nobody was attracted to it. If this is so, then Corinth is a uniquely bad site for our inquiries. I want to stress that I am not saying here that the disjunction posited by Mack and Smith is not there: I am convinced that they are correct in describing a Paul who creatively (and deliberately?) "misunderstands" the extant practices of a Corinthian association in order to attempt to swerve those practices in a direction more congenial to his *euangelion*. My reservations concern the assumption and argument that this remodeling could have held no attraction for the group in question.

In any case, the characterization of ethnicity as the core issue in the Corinthian association being addressed by Paul—as developed by Stowers, Smith, and

---

with Christ to an infant church that has apparently only begun to grasp the basic principles of Christian life.... Paul's doctrine of freedom from Torah restraints is easily abused by those who interpret it as an excuse to ignore all ethical principles. As a result of the Corinthians' misuse of Christian freedom, Paul finds it necessary to impose limits on believers' individual liberty." The examples could easily be multiplied.

in Mack's paper being linked carefully to the topics Paul treats in 1 Corinthians[13]—may help us solve these problems and help us get at the heart of what Paul was really up to, how and why he latched on to Jesus as a mechanism for his agenda, and why anyone would have found this attractive. Especially notable is Mack's comment:

> [W]hat if the *christos* associations were composed of a mix of peoples? Such a mix need not have been a burning issue for these associations, but it certainly could have been for Paul. It is even thinkable that *both his animosity and his conversion* might be explained in terms of attitudes and views taken with respect to this feature of the *christos* associations.[14]

This statement describes a nexus among the interests of various different groups with which we are concerned, a continuity of interests from the *christos* associations through Paul to the Corinthian associations, thus laying the groundwork for a productive conversation among these entities, a conversation that 1 Corinthians itself indicates was indeed taking place. We thus need not, with Mack, assume that Paul was only given a hearing because such an association as is addressed in 1 Corinthians would have unproblematically given ear to various marketplace philosophers, Paul no distinctively important figure among them. Rather, this group is clearly engaged with a cluster of figures apparently related to the *christos* associations and seems to be engaged in a process of sorting out which of them (if any) is most appealing.[15] The shared interests in ethnic mixing provide a reasonable basis for mutual communication and influence, and thus give us no reason to think, a priori, that Paul's message would have been distinctively unintelligible.

---

13. One should note, once again, that precisely these kinds of issues have also been shown to be typical of Paul's own concerns, especially by Stowers and his students. See, e.g., Caroline Johnson Hodge, *If Sons, Then Heirs: A Study of Kinship and Ethnicity in the Letters of Paul* (New York: Oxford University Press, 2007); cf. Pamela Eisenbaum, "Paul as the New Abraham," in *Paul and Politics: Ekklesia, Israel, Imperium, Interpretation. Essays in Honor of Krister Stendahl* (ed. Richard A. Horsley; Harrisburg, Pa.: Trinity Press International, 2000), 130–45.

14. Mack, "Rereading the Christ Myth," 61 (emphasis added). Note, however, that we still need to account for why an unproblematic practice for these associations would have interested Paul so much. It will be the answer to this question that establishes continuity between Paul and his predecessors, however tenuous.

15. I am thinking here of 1 Cor 1:12–13: "Each one of you says, 'I belong to Paul,' or 'I belong to Apollos,' or 'I belong to Cephas,' or 'I belong to Christ.' Is Christ divided?" I am assuming that Paul is here (probably selectively) referring to Jesus/*christos*-associated people, although this certainly cannot be taken for granted. But I take "Cephas" here to refer to the Cephas of Gal 1:18, that is, Peter (or in this case, representatives thereof?), and "Apollos" to refer to the Apollos of 1 Cor 16:12, who is blandly assumed to be in continued contact with Paul and is described as "the brother." (Interestingly, Acts 18:24–25 shows ambivalence regarding the status of Apollos as a "Christian.") Moreover, Paul's argument against this factionalism is predicated on all named parties being connected to Jesus somehow: "Is Christ divided?"

Likewise, Mack's paper very nicely brings together the centrality of the Abraham myth for Paul, various issues of problematic and contested lineage, the import of Paul's reconfiguration of Israel by means of this myth, and the way that Paul the *bricoleur* combines essentially distinct idea clusters (especially the combination of Abraham as promise to the nations/Gentiles with Christ crucified and risen/vindicated). Again I note that this description meshes extraordinarily well, in my view, with Braun's and my thesis that new social constellations are not the product of a linear unfolding of ideas. To put it more directly, Paul's use of the Christ myth is opportunistic, offered to solve a very particular problem that is a function of Paul and his context, not a function of intellectual conundrums created by earlier Jesus people. It remains, however, to identify more precisely what this problem, this situational incongruity, might have been, and how it might plausibly have meshed with the interests and concerns of the Corinthian association. All of this, I think, sets the stage not only for a more thorough and genuinely redescriptive exposition of Paul, but also for a more thorough exposition of him as an ancient Jew, rather than as an honorary Saint Augustine.[16]

II. The Workings of Social Formations and the Corinthian *Ekklēsiai*

Agreements, however, are much less interesting than disagreements, reservations, and extrapolations, and I would not bother to write a paper whose sole purpose was to say "me too" or "amen," even to Mack. I will instead concentrate, in what follows, on (1) indicating what I think are some of the problems with his paper; and (2) developing an account of Paul in a slightly different direction, primarily influenced by the general direction of Mack's paper, but also reflecting my departures from or problems with his reconstruction.

I should note, first, that I continue to have some troubles with Mack's expressions of how social formation works, not so much in the abstract (though surely we could exchange, and have, divergent ideas at that level, too),[17] but in terms of the very concrete representations Mack makes of Paul's agenda and development.

---

16. The qualifications at the end of Mack's paper should also be stressed, because they bring into view not only areas for further work, but additionally show a consciousness of some of the data that his reconstruction cannot explain, and that it therefore stumbles on. These include the "Christ hymn" in Philippians (which not only represents an ideological schema not currently accounted for but also indicates the extent to which Paul's "gospel" was able to absorb foreign elements, which ought to give us some pause in reconstructing Paul's agenda in terms of logical extrapolations), and especially the awareness that we cannot simply dismiss Paul's claims to have "founded" various *ekklēsiai*—this latter being, I think, among the most significant potential lacunae in the paper.

17. Still representative is Arnal and Braun, "Social Formation and Mythmaking." See also William E. Arnal, "Why Q Failed: From Ideological Project to Group Formation," in Cameron and Miller, *Redescribing Christian Origins*, 67–87; cf. Burton L. Mack, "Social Formation," in *Guide to the Study of Religion* (ed. Willi Braun and Russell T. McCutcheon; London: Cassell, 2000), 283–96.

Taking Smith's perspective on the intellectualism of "religious" language rather too far, I think, Mack exaggerates the intellectual dimension of Paul's motivations and mental production, a problem I had also with his work on the Sayings Gospel Q (and for the same reasons, that is, slightly different theories of social formation with slightly differing emphases on intellectual motivations).[18] It is not, of course, that Paul is not an intellectual. He clearly is, by any definition of the term. But a social explanation is in order for why Paul finds certain problems, issues, and situational incongruities to be pressing. That mere intellectual contradiction is insufficient in itself to create a situational incongruity for Paul is evident, among other things, from the fact that Paul himself manufactures such contradictions throughout and among his letters, willy-nilly, without apparently being bothered by it. To say "people were (or Paul was) thinking about *x*" (apocalypticism, Jewish identity, etc.) is never to my mind a sufficient explanation for anything, but is rather among the data in need of explanation. We might quite correctly assert, for instance, that people in Corinth were thinking about ethnic identity—but this is not occurring in a vacuum, or because such thoughts are "in the air";[19] such thinking is occurring precisely because these people are in concrete circumstances that make such thoughts pressing.[20] The incongruity is, precisely, a situational incongruity, and that situation must always be elaborated. The question then arises, What is Paul's situational incongruity? Might not this mesh, rather than conflict, with that of his converts? We should not repeat the traditional mistake of separating Jewish identity from other forms of ethnic identification: if Paul is thinking about being a Jew, and the Corinthians are thinking about their ethnic uprootedness, both parties are actually thinking about similar topics. I would like to propose a slightly different model of social formation to apply here, one that, I think, takes more seriously the mutual influence of groups on each other, the flexible nature of group dynamics and identities, and therefore one that I have a hunch would work best with Paul's recruitment activities,[21] in many ways dispensing with the traditional

---

18. See the (rather too polemical) discussion in Arnal, "Why Q Failed."

19. Conversely, see the characterization of intellectual ferment in Mack, "Rereading the Christ Myth," 43–44: "We can easily reconstruct a plausible situation in which Jesus people, both Judeans and Gentiles, *were interested* both in the Diaspora synagogue and in the teachings of Jesus; the teachings of Jesus about the kingdom of God *were under discussion* within both the Jesus associations and the Diaspora synagogues; debates *were also going on* about torah, the Hasmoneans, the Romans, and the current state of the world; and intellectuals *were rewriting* the Scriptures" (emphasis added). What I am stressing here is the vague character of the description of intellectual production in this description: it seems to happen more or less of its own accord.

20. So, notably, Smith, "Re: Corinthians," 27–29, who stresses the concrete circumstances that made relations with the ancestors problematic and dictated therefore that they be of critical interest to the preexisting association.

21. As reconceived, in various ways, by Richard S. Ascough ("The Thessalonian Christian Community as a Professional Voluntary Association," *JBL* 119 [2000]: 311–28), Smith ("Re: Corinthians"), and Mack ("Rereading the Christ Myth"), all of whom float variations of the important

understanding of his "mission" while nonetheless taking seriously what he says about his *ekklēsiai*.[22] I am drawing here from an example both modern and fictional, but which, I think, has important applicability to Paul (if not broad theoretical applicability): the 1999 movie *The Fight Club*, which offers a very nice and quite realistic example of the dynamics of group formation. The movie begins with (1) a socially contextualized individual who happens to feel alienated from that context; (2) he then begins to haunt already constituted groups that help, partially, to compensate for this alienation; (3) other like-minded individuals using these groups the same way gravitate to him and form something of a faction within the existing group; (4) this faction eventually breaks away from the group to pursue more effectively its own purposes; (5) the new group propagates and formalizes (albeit, in the movie, rather more rapidly than I would find realistic for the propagation and formalization of the Pauline *ekklēsiai*).[23]

Near the end of his article "The Thessalonian Christian Community as a Professional Voluntary Association," Ascough drops a hint that suggests to me that this *Fight Club* model would work very nicely for Paul. Ascough invites us to imagine a Thessalonian trade association of artisans with, as would be usual, a patron deity, but whose main function is collegial and whose real social basis is common occupation. Paul, a traveling tinker himself (providing a real social foundation for both his travels and contacts without needing to invoke the Christian notion of "mission"), attends meetings of this club when he is in town simply by virtue of occupational affinity, his being another artisan. Paul manages, then, to redirect this already extant club from the worship of its original patron deity to that of Christ/Yahweh. This is where Ascough stops,[24] but I would suggest some further specifics. We might imagine the opportunity for Paul to replace this club's patron as a "situational incongruity" of precisely the non-momentous sort that Smith is so fond of: one can easily visualize a meeting place for this association with a statue of its patron deity displayed more or less prominently; at a meeting it is noticed that this statue has become damaged or contaminated in some trivial way (chipped, broken, fallen, or perhaps profaned by vermin), or, alternatively, that

---

hypothesis that Paul's activity to a large degree consisted of attempting to seize control of or redirect already extant associations.

22. "Taking seriously" does not mean "accepting at face value," but it does mean accounting in some way for these Pauline claims.

23. Smith ("Re: Corinthians," 31) states: "What I have been terming, with deliberate vagueness, 'some Corinthians,' does not map a group (or groups) that accord(s) with the topography of 'parties' provided by those fragments conventionally identified as 'slogans' quoted by Paul from his opponents. However, I am not prepared, in this paper, to offer a counterproposal." I believe that Smith implies here something similar to the pattern just described, an informal movement among porous group boundaries themselves in a state of flux.

24. At least in this particular article (Ascough, "Thessalonian Christian Community," 324). See now Richard S. Ascough, *Paul's Macedonian Associations: The Social Context of Philippians and 1 Thessalonians* (WUNT 2/161; Tübingen: Mohr Siebeck, 2003).

this divine patron has failed to deliver expected goods.[25] Paul would hardly need more than this to launch into a disquisition on dead and false idols (cf. 1 Thess 1:9: "you turned to God from idols, to serve a living and true God"), and how the group might adopt a better patron. Paul's own motives for joining a group such as this might not accord with the main intentions of the group (i.e., occupational commonality, shared meals, etc.), but be overdetermined by Paul's own particular issues and alienations (which I assume to be mainly ethnic in character, on which see further below). And so, he is in fact using this group to gain something—a sense of belonging, identification, kinship—that eludes him in the other aspects of his ordinary life (e.g., the synagogue) and which he genuinely does gain from the group, but which is not really the group's intent to provide.[26] So we can imagine the membership of this trade association giving Paul a hearing as he puts his case for a new patron; but we must also imagine some of them finding his case discomfiting because Paul's proposed deity is being presented as functioning in ways that the original patron did not (e.g., saving them from the "wrath to come," joining them to "Israel," etc.). By contrast, those who share some of Paul's alienations, problems, and interests (and these need not be Jews) might be stimulated by his descriptions of the "salvations" proceeding from such a patron, and thus form a more and more distinctive subgroup within this association at the instigation of Paul's agitating, a subgroup that eventually breaks off on its own. In this way we are able to imagine a group that Paul really has introduced to the gospel—as per his claims—and so has "founded" as an *ekklēsia*. Yet at the same time that we take seriously this characterization from Paul, we can also recognize that the group as a group was not founded by Paul at all, and so we can go on thinking in terms of new *ekklēsiai* without having to adopt the view (especially as it appears in Acts) that Paul's supposed public or synagogal proclamation of his gospel was itself the sufficient and necessary cause of these new(ish) social formations. What remains to be identified, however, are the types of alienation or situational incongruities that Paul himself was attempting to address through his association with this club, and which those who were attracted to his new patron felt such a patron could address.

This imaginative reconstruction may now be transported to Corinth and applied to some of the problems with Mack's reconstruction. Mack, following Smith, has stressed far too much the disjunction between Paul and his Corinthian interlocutors (but in my view has stressed the disjunction between Paul and his "precursors" to exactly the right degree). Shortly after our seminar's second

---

25. See, e.g., Richard S. Ascough, "Greco-Roman Religions in Sardis and Smyrna," in *Religious Rivalries and the Struggle for Success in Sardis and Smyrna* (ed. Richard S. Ascough; Studies in Christianity and Judaism 14; Waterloo, Ont.: Wilfrid Laurier University Press, 2005), 41: "After the earthquake of 17 CE [in Sardis], the temple of Artemis lay in ruins for over fifty years, presumably because these gods were viewed as having failed to protect the city."

26. People do this all the time: I use academic institutions, for example, for social purposes, among other things, which though not illegitimate are clearly not what they are there for.

sessions on Corinth, held in Denver in 2001, a member of the seminar noted that while our description of a "double disjunction" may work as long as we restrict ourselves to the evidence of 1 Corinthians alone, a consideration of 2 Corinthians badly undermines several of our conclusions or assumptions, insofar as its multiple letter fragments[27] imply, both in terms of their bare existence and in terms of their content,[28] a much stronger link between Paul and Corinth than the seminar's hypotheses might suggest. This objection may actually be extended to 1 Corinthians itself. Especially important here is the work of John Coolidge Hurd, Jr., *The Origin of I Corinthians*.[29] While his overall hypothesis may not be wholly convincing, especially in light of the seminar's redescription of Paul's "precursors," a point that he emphasizes and which cannot be ignored is that 1 Corinthians is quite clearly a node in an extended train of prior correspondence, even if one leaves aside the copious additional contacts, visits, travels, and correspondence attested or implied by 2 Corinthians. This prior communication attested in 1 Corinthians alone includes: (1) a letter that Paul has already written to Corinth (1 Cor 5:9); (2) a letter that they have written to him (1 Cor 7:1); and (3) gossip that he has heard about them (1 Cor 1:11). That the issues addressed seriatim from 1 Cor 7 on can generally be associated with the concerns over ethnicity or identity that Smith has identified as driving the Corinthian association is surely significant; but it is just as significant that all of these issues have apparently been addressed to Paul by the Corinthians themselves, to which assertions and/or inquiries 1 Corinthians is itself a response. The picture that emerges from these observations is one in which the Corinthians and Paul are having an ongoing conversation about identity issues (including ones linked to becoming or being "Israel," and the implications thereof). And this in turn might cause us to think twice about claims that Paul's ideas are unintelligible to the Corinthians, or that they are talking past each other, or that Paul's mythmaking is taking place at a kind of intellectual remove from the Corinthians. In short, the observation of the extent and character of Paul's extended correspondence with Corinth calls into question any notion of an extreme disjunction between the two parties. In addition to this we must also be able to account for Paul's numerous claims and assumptions throughout his letters to have actually established (whatever this may mean) *ekklēsiai* that are "in Christ" (recognizing, of course, the rhetorical use of such claims), composed at least in

---

27. See, e.g., Harris, *Student's Introduction*, 220–22; Burton L. Mack, *Who Wrote the New Testament? The Making of the Christian Myth* (San Francisco: HarperSanFrancisco, 1995), 127; Norman Perrin and Dennis C. Duling, *The New Testament: An Introduction. Proclamation and Parenesis, Myth and History* (2nd ed.; New York: Harcourt Brace Jovanovich, 1982), 130–31; Calvin J. Roetzel, *The Letters of Paul: Conversations in Context* (4th ed.; Louisville: Westminster John Knox, 1998), 94–95; and many others for reconstructions of the original constituent letter fragments behind canonical 2 Corinthians.

28. Particularly with the evidence they give for repeated extraepistolary contacts between Paul (or his fellows) and the recipients.

29. John Coolidge Hurd, Jr., *The Origin of I Corinthians* (London: SPCK, 1965).

part of people he has baptized,[30] and who apparently provide him with various types of assistance (e.g., Phil 2:25-26) and contribute to collections of funds (e.g., 2 Cor 8:2-4; cf. Rom 15:25-27). In driving too sharp a wedge between Paul and his Corinthian interlocutors, too, we run the risk of describing a Paul who is incomprehensible and, thus, unique and inexplicable. This is a perennial difficulty with Mack's reconstruction of Paul's thought processes: having (appropriately) detached them from a pre-Pauline source, they now appear as too idiosyncratic, and thus essentially decontextualized. This is a difficulty I also find with Smith's characterization of Paul in *Drudgery Divine*: his "utopian" category appears to have only a single developed member (Paul), and is more or less used as a "miscellaneous" designation for "not locative."[31]

In the case of Corinth, we also seem to have a faction, a subgrouping of the (original?) group, that is closely associated with Paul. This is attested both by Paul's own statement to this effect (1 Cor 1:12) and by his assertion that he personally baptized some of these people, but not most of them (1 Cor 1:14-16). We need not view Apollos as a subordinate of Paul, or even as discernibly "Christian" (in the Pauline sense, or in any sense), to recognize nonetheless the existence of a

---

30. Particularly notable here is 1 Cor 1:14-16, an acknowledgment of Paul's having baptized some of his addressees in the Corinthian association, and an acknowledgment that runs counter to his own argumentative line, where he is founding a point upon not having baptized any of his auditors. There also appears to be a "Paul faction" (1 Cor 1:12; 3:4) to which he might properly lay claim. I am of course leaving aside Paul's clever and evidently self-conscious choice of metaphorical wording in describing his role in the *ekklēsia* as that of the one who plants (as opposed to the one who waters) and the one who lays the foundation (as opposed to the one who builds upon it) in 1 Cor 3:5-15.

31. Jonathan Z. Smith, *Drudgery Divine: On the Comparison of Early Christianities and the Religions of Late Antiquity* (Jordan Lectures in Comparative Religion 14; London: School of Oriental and African Studies, University of London; Chicago: University of Chicago Press, 1990). These remarks may be unfair to Smith's intent, or to the complexity of his schema in the book, but at the very least I can say that I find the "utopian" orientation of Paul as described in the book to be underexplained and not especially well accounted for. A slightly modified spin appears to be placed on this typology in idem, "Here, There, and Anywhere," in *Prayer, Magic, and the Stars in the Ancient and Late Antique World* (ed. Scott Noegel et al.; Magic in History Series; University Park: Pennsylvania State University Press, 2003), 21-36; repr. in *Relating Religion*, 323-39, which proposes a topography in terms of three spatial categories to sort out domestic religions of the home space ("here"), state religions of the temple ("there"), and itinerant and nonlocalized religious practices such as are embodied in ancient "magic" ("anywhere," i.e., location unspecified). Smith here interestingly (and convincingly) argues that the religions of "anywhere" were becoming more and more prominent in the Roman period; he further argues that such religions represent a displacement of the national/state religious imagery and practice (sacrifice, temple, etc.) to the domestic sphere of the home, a claim that makes excellent sense in light of the Roman imperial disruption of native politics. Smith is careful to note, however, that this typology does not correspond to the locative/utopian distinction (23 with n. 9; repr. in *Relating Religion*, 325, 335 n.9), and so appears to rule out an equivalence between utopian religion (whose only significant representative seems to remain Paul) and the religions of "anywhere" (which are much better attested in antiquity and much better explained by Smith). If I have made too much of Smith's caution here, I would be delighted to admit the mistake and construe Paul as a proponent of the religions of "anywhere," making him, I would think, much more comprehensible.

Pauline faction among the original—preexisting—group of ethnically confused association members in Corinth. So for some of the Corinthians, I submit, Paul's ideas have struck a chord, and we need to know why. The scenario would resemble that presented in *The Fight Club*: Paul has been drawn to a group for his own reasons, attempts to make his idiosyncratic interests more prominent within the group, and succeeds in doing so among some members of the group and not others, producing—and here we have direct evidence from 1 Corinthians itself—factions, one or more of which may eventually persist through time and preserve the very letters that constitute our data (whose preservation and eventual collection are, themselves, data implying that Paul did make some inroads with this association). This is not to imply, of course, that there are no disjunctions between Paul and anyone in Corinth. We can indeed assume that significant disjunctions exist between Paul's agenda and ideas, on the one hand, and the bulk of the original group, which has remained unpersuaded by his "gospel."[32] And we can assume that various less-fundamental disjunctions persist even between Paul and those who have essentially become convinced by his message—otherwise the tone of the letter or, for that matter, its content would be utterly unintelligible. But if we are trying to understand what has happened with the Pauline *ekklēsiai*, we cannot be too dismissive of the potential agreements between Paul and his fellows, if only because this directs our attention away from the potential intelligibility and attractiveness of Paul's ideas.

III. The Logic of the Pauline Myth

My speculations about the constitutive processes of the Pauline *ekklēsiai* allow us to avoid the problem of unintelligibility while retaining the important insight that a preexisting ethnic situation had generated a preexisting ethnically focused group, into which Paul intervened. We can imagine a group constituted by its ethnically mixed and uprooted constitution and attractive to Paul because of that fact. The circumstances of empire, and Corinth in particular, have thrown together a group of people at a remove from their ancestral lands and customs, and pressed by issues of identity in consequence of this.[33] Meanwhile, Paul himself is a Jew

---

32. I want to stress that I honestly cannot even guess whether this larger group as a whole is being addressed in 1 Corinthians, or if the "Pauline" faction has already established its own distinctive identity, which Paul is attempting to shape and preserve.

33. A matter to which we have, rather unaccountably, given insufficient consideration is that of slavery, especially in light of the attention the seminar has given to questions of ethnicity, ancestry, and metaphoric access to the homeland from afar. In the case of slaves, who may constitute some of Paul's projected auditors in 1 Corinthians (see, problematically, 1 Cor 7:21; much less problematic is the discussion of Onesimus in Paul's letter to Philemon, which indicates, on the one hand, that Paul does regard slaves as worthy members of his *ekklēsiai*, but which, on the other, does not indicate the presence of any such slaves in Corinth), we are dealing with people who have been violently, materially, and obviously deracinated from their ancestral context (in perhaps every respect). If Corinthian

living in a non-Jewish land, with a non-Jewish name,[34] speaking Greek, and trying to figure out what his identity as an Israelite means and how that identity works. In short, his situational incongruity is the same one that marked any number of Jewish reform, sectarian, and revitalization movements of the time: the question of how a deity with his temple in the capital city and his cultus dedicated to preserving the sociocosmic order exemplified and sustained by his chosen kings can be worshiped in a world in which all of these fundamental presuppositions are no longer operative—basically, the meaning of the national deity of a nation that no longer existed as such—and what all of this means for the issue of identity, for being an Israelite under these circumstances. That Paul was concerned with such questions is indicated by his self-identification as a Pharisee in Phil 3:5 (and so showing an interest in efforts of the time to define national identity in terms somewhat divorced from the existence of an independent temple state). Moreover, this Pharisaic orientation, together with Paul's "ethical" obsessions, his assertions of blamelessness under the law (Phil 3:6), of the necessity of the circumcised to obey the tenets of the law (Gal 5:3), and his extended and direct considerations of the topic of righteousness (e.g., Gal 3:6–14; Rom 1:16–4:25; etc.),[35] all indicate that he very closely associated the meaning of Israelite identity with the practice of righteousness. To be Israel is to be righteous: that is how this identity is defined, that is what it means.

This generates a more precise problem for Paul, a situational incongruity of a sharper sort. Relying on Stowers's reading of Romans, particularly his focus on righteousness, ethnicity, and collective identities as considerations driving Paul's comments in Romans and, perhaps, his gospel as a whole[36]—though departing from it in some specifics—where Stowers may see Paul in Rom 2:17–24 as engaging with an imaginary nomistic missionary, I see the rhetorical address as much more general: Paul is showing concern here for how it is that Israel, which has the law, could ever behave unrighteously. In short, Israel's collective identity as God's people, as those who have the law, is called into question by its failure to be consistently righteous at this collective level. Paul is not being autobiographical here and/or offering an anguished discourse on the inability of any given individual

---

colonists face the problem of interrupted contact with the ancestral graves or spirits, how much more so do slaves, who may not, in some instances, even have ancestors or an *ethnos*. While one might claim that Paul's offer of inclusion in the Israelite *ethnos* by virtue of a creative redescription of its boundaries might not appeal to persons more interested in reviving contact with overseas touchstones, it may indeed have spoken quite poignantly to those lacking ancestors altogether.

34. Note that if we dismiss Acts' (in my view, completely spurious) claim that Paul was a Roman citizen, slavery in Paul's own background could constitute another explanation for his Roman name.

35. Note also Paul's invocation of the Deuteronomistic motif in Phil 2:15: "children of God without blemish *in the midst of a crooked and perverse generation*," a line that would have been perfectly at home in the Sayings Gospel Q.

36. Stowers, *Rereading of Romans*.

to live up to the law,[37] nor is Paul characterizing the Jewish people as a whole as wicked and fallen from God.[38] The problem for Paul, rather, is that anyone who is part of God's Israel, who has the law, who is circumcised and so shares in the promise to Abraham, could fail to be righteous. That this sort of issue was an issue among Jews in Roman antiquity—especially in historical and political circumstances that seemed to undermine traditional interpretations of God's promises to the Jews—is attested, for example, in *4 Ezra* 3:35–36: "[W]hat nation has kept your commandments so well? You may indeed find individual men who have kept your commandments, but nations you will not find."[39] What we see here, quite clearly, is a strong interest in the status of obedience to God in national terms, explicitly over against individual obedience, and a linking of such questions to the fate of the nation. One thus need not take Rom 2:21–23 as a characterization of the entire Jewish people as thieves, adulterers, and temple robbers, nor must one think that Paul is characterizing those who teach the law as such, nor even need one regard him as creating a crassly self-serving straw man. The difficulty for Paul is created by any Jew who steals, or commits adultery, or robs a temple; let any of these things happen even once, and the equation of righteousness with the identity of Israel becomes problematic.[40] Israel must be a holy people; that they are not so (by Paul's exacting standards) is why "the name of God is blasphemed among the Gentiles because of you" (Rom 2:24, speaking rhetorically to *any* unrighteous Jew), and God's judgment is itself manifested in the very situational incongruity that motivates this line of thought in the first place: Israel's status as a scattered and dominated people.[41]

---

37. A traditional, Protestant reading, one that is too modern, too individualistic, and contradicted by some of Paul's own statements, and one that has by now been put paid to, it is to be hoped, especially by Krister Stendahl, *Final Account: Paul's Letter to the Romans* (Minneapolis: Fortress, 1995).

38. A traditional anti-Jewish reading, and also one that is contradicted by Paul's own statements, especially in Rom 11:1–32.

39. B. M. Metzger, trans., "The Fourth Book of Ezra," *OTP* 1:529. The Latin reads: aut quae gens sic observavit mandata tua? Homines quidem per nomina invenies servasse mandata tua, gentes autem non invenies (A. Frederik J. Klijn, *Der lateinische Text der Apokalypse des Esra* [TU 131; Berlin: Akademie-Verlag, 1983], 28). I wish to thank Eduard Iricinschi for drawing this particular passage to my attention.

40. This also solves the problem noted by E. P. Sanders (*Paul and Palestinian Judaism: A Comparison of Patterns of Religion* [Philadelphia: Fortress, 1977], 474–75), that Paul's characterization of universal sinfulness in Rom 1:18–2:29 is unconvincing and exaggerated. If we think of collectives instead of individuals, Paul's point seems to be simply that "sin" is humanly pervasive, that the sorts of behaviors he enumerates occur at all—not that they are practiced by everyone.

41. In speaking this way about Paul's views of Israel, I run the risk of a retrograde move, against the recent work of Stowers (especially his *Rereading of Romans*), Lloyd Gaston (*Paul and the Torah* [Vancouver: University of British Columbia Press, 1987]), and John G. Gager (*Reinventing Paul* [New York: Oxford University Press, 2000]), all of whom emphasize that we should not adopt the traditional view of Paul's rejecting or turning his back on Israel and its traditional claims to inherit God's promise, as such notions would be uncharacteristic of a first-century Jew. I should note, on the one hand, that I am unimpressed with this line of argument, insofar as we can be pretty certain that

Faced with such a problem—as well as the more pervasive social circumstances working at odds with the meaningfulness of traditional understandings of Jewish identity—Paul latches on to the figure of Jesus as a potential solution, a device for radically reconfiguring "Jewish" identity in such a way that addresses both the general (social) and specific (intellectual) problems just outlined. In agreement with Mack, it was precisely the mixed character of the Jesus groups with which Paul was familiar that accounts for both Paul's initial aversion to these groups and his excitement at their potential for solving his problems. Paul sees in this mixture both an affront to his threatened Israelite identity and, subsequently, a way of creating a new identity that preserves the righteousness of Israel (and the salience of membership in it). He does this, as Mack argues, by combining at least two formerly distinct mythological clusters: (1) that Christ died in obedience to God's will and so was vindicated (somehow) for his righteousness and faith; and (2) that Abraham serves as the collective representation of Israel (and the promises of God to Israel) by virtue of his righteousness and faith. This allows Paul essentially to replace Abraham with Christ as the collective representation of a righteous Israel (a replacement he justifies, badly, by drawing a lineage between Abraham and Christ, as per Gal 3:16). That Paul does think in such terms, that is, in terms of mythic persons standing in for collective identities (especially via the vehicle of ancestral relations), is reflected not only in Paul's linkage of Christ to Abraham in Gal 3:16 but also in his discussion of Adam versus Christ in Rom 5:12–17. This reconstruction already sets aside the standard view of Paul's agenda by making the whole issue of his tale of "Christ crucified" not the substance or motive of Paul's work, but a lever that he uses to accomplish his real agenda, a mission to the Gentiles and, thereby, a reconstitution of Israel in terms that both avoid the sharp intellectual incongruity of the unrighteousness of God's people, and solve for practical purposes the problem of a national identity for people—various ethnically mixed Jews and Gentiles living in nonancestral cities—who have no nation.[42]

The question then becomes—given the seminar's strong interests in intellectual lineages, which I have become convinced are important at least in this case (though without giving up the theoretical point that such lineages are not in themselves

---

Paul was not a typical first-century Jew, and insofar as such arguments both stereotype the intellectual possibilities inherent in Judaism (ignoring, e.g., the pervasive deployment of Deuteronomistic polemic among Jews) and also assume that we can reconstruct the ideas of individuals from what we know about general intellectual trends—both ideas that I have criticized roundly in William E. Arnal, *The Symbolic Jesus: Historical Scholarship, Judaism and the Construction of Contemporary Identity* (Religion in Culture: Studies in Social Contest and Construction; London: Equinox, 2005). At the same time, I want to stress that I am actually not here departing from Stowers's and Gaston's correct insight that Paul is not "abandoning" Israel but is rather primarily involved in the task of rendering its boundaries differently. So I would not wish to have my comments here misunderstood as a claim that Paul regards Israel as "wicked" and hence has turned his back on the "Jewish religion."

42. The question of the identity of Israel is intellectually the more basic, but the question of the inclusion of Gentiles is sociologically the more basic.

explanatory)—how, and why, Jesus? What was it about the form of Jesus-talk with which Paul became familiar that allowed and suggested this (new) role for Jesus as ethnic progenitor of a reconfigured *ethnos*? And what does this imply about Paul's use of a "Christ myth," both in terms of the centrality (or lack thereof) of that myth in the formulation and execution of Paul's agenda (specifically, his "mission to the Gentiles/nations"), and in terms of Paul's creation, modification, and understanding of that myth? This is really the central question, from the perspective of the seminar's agenda, and it is a question whose answer hinges greatly on Mack's analysis of 1 Cor 15:3–5. For now, I think the crux of the matter rests with the conception that God had directly vindicated Jesus. This is a commonplace enough notion for a martyr, and so we hardly need imagine any earth-shattering *novum* to account for it prior to Paul. For Paul himself, however, struggling, as it were, with the "antivindication" of Israel's scattered existence, as a result of its identity-confounding lack of perfect righteousness, such an action on God's part assumes enormous consequentiality. For it provides precisely what has been lacking: a sure sign of God's approval for righteousness.[43] Paul has, in essence, fused two independent mythic considerations: the cluster of martyrological ideas inherited from Jesus/*christos* people before him, and the cluster of ideas associated with the righteousness/faithfulness of Abraham as the ethnic progenitor of Israel, as well as (incidentally, at this point, but with huge consequence for Paul's self-conception) the one through whom the nations (Gentiles) will be blessed. The result is a huge weight being put on the rather commonplace notion that "some guy" (Jesus, in this case) died for a noble cause and was vindicated. By combining this rather prosaic idea with the larger problem of Israel's identity, function in the world (in theory as per God's promise versus in fact as per Israel's status in the Roman Empire—a situational incongruity), and the need for divine rectification (whether apocalyptic, judgmental, sociohistorical, or the like), the idea of Jesus' death and vindication suddenly assumes cosmic importance. Thus, Paul (apparently) places these concepts at the center of his *kērygma*—but in fact they are logically secondary to the much more pressing issue of ethnic identity and place in the world, and achieve their "central" import only by virtue of their provision of an answer to such "cosmic" questions. In short, the unexceptional death and "resurrection" (vindication, assumption) of a martyr as a warrant for group identity become transformed as a result of Paul's insight that the warrant for group identity can apply to the problem of Israel's place in the world, as well as to the relationship of God to the Gentiles. As such, suddenly Jesus' death is an act of obedience on par, as an etiological founding gesture, with Abraham's call by God; and his "resurrection," an act of divine intervention as consequential as God's "gift" of the land of Canaan to his people. All that has really changed is the formulation of the question to which Jesus' death and vindication

---

43. Or "faithfulness." I am in fact assuming that the two terms' function is nearly synonymous in Paul's writing, an assumption that will, of course, need to be tested at some point.

are applied as an answer; when the question shifts from the quotidian to the cosmic, so too does the "salvific" import of the martyrdom. That Paul would make such a shift seems natural enough, if we assume, as Mack argues, that Paul already found striking (whether negatively or positively) the ethnically promiscuous nature of the Jesus clubs he had already encountered (a response not actually shared by such groups themselves, Mack notes, for the simple reason that their problems were not Paul's, and Paul's not theirs).

Some aspects of Mack's reconstruction of the Pauline intervention into the "tradition" behind 1 Cor 15:3–5 support such a scenario. His exceptionally well-grounded claim that the "cause" for which the martyr dies in Paul's rendering, that is, "for our sins," only makes sense as a Pauline embellishment is certainly correct, as is his view of this addition as a warrant for Paul's Gentile mission. But there is more to it than that. As Paul represents it, Jesus died for "our" sins, not "your" (i.e., the Gentiles') sins. And, some commentators to the contrary, while Paul's extended comments on the law[44] and his own sense of mission do seem to

---

44. An issue that I think runs the risk of being overblown, particularly in traditional presentations. Paul's explicit and extended discussions of the law, especially as understood in some sort of opposition to whatever Paul's message is, are really restricted to Galatians and Romans. This is part of the reason that the sequence of Galatians is important. If one places Galatians between 2 Corinthians (or rather, the majority of the various letters that make up 2 Corinthians) and Romans, as I do, this places Romans and Galatians side by side chronologically, which in turn rather relativizes the import of their shared themes. Obviously, if Galatians is an early letter (which I do not think it is) and Romans is late (which I do think it is), then Paul's strong interest in opposing the law to his gospel spans the range of his "mission." But if both were written one after the other, that interest emerges as a momentary concern, and thus one better linked to concrete circumstances than to a general characterization of Paul's gospel. In the case of Galatians, this emphasis on the law is actually secondary to the immediate problem of circumcision (i.e., that Paul's auditors have been getting circumcised in spite of having "received the spirit"), which would obviously constitute a fundamental challenge to Paul's agenda as I have described it here (i.e., as having to do with a reconstitution of Israel apart from explicit ethnic markers). In the case of Romans, the situation strikes me as much more puzzling. Scholarly confidence in our habitual assumptions aside, we really have no clue as to the addressees of this letter. Paul indicates that he has never visited this group. Moreover, recent scholarship recognizes that Paul's general comments on the law, Judaism, and the like are to be contextualized mainly in terms of his mission to the Gentiles, and so takes the assertions of Romans as likewise directed to Gentiles (as is implied also by Paul himself in Rom 1:13). But then who is this group of Gentiles sitting in Rome whom Paul has never seen and whom he describes both as "God's beloved" and, at the same time, as people from whom he might "reap a harvest" and to whom he intends to "proclaim the gospel"? Note that Paul never describes these people as constituting an *ekklēsia* and, in fact, never even uses the word in this, his longest letter (I am assuming that Rom 16, where *ekklēsia* does occur a few times [vv. 1, 4, 5, 16, 23], is a fragment from another letter, as indicated by various manuscript problems and by the presence of a concluding benediction to Romans in 15:33). Likewise, Paul entirely avoids the word cluster associated with crucifixion: "cross" never occurs in this letter, "crucify" only at 6:6, perhaps indicating a reluctance on Paul's part to risk alienating these strangers (who in Paul's view do not constitute an *ekklēsia*) with provocative innovations of his own. If we wish to test the hypothesis that Paul (habitually?) addresses himself to already constituted non-"Christian" groups, Romans would probably be the best place to start.

be focused on Gentiles more or less exclusively, his sense of who requires the "free gift of righteousness" (Rom 5:17) seems to be quite general, and to include himself and other Jews: "I have already charged that all men, both Jews and Greeks, are under the power of sin" (Rom 3:9). Likewise: "There will be tribulation and distress for every human being who does evil, the Jew first and also the Greek, but glory and honor and peace for everyone who does good, the Jew first and also the Greek" (Rom 2:9–10). In short, while Paul's own task is the Gentile mission, the span of his concern embraces the question of Israel's righteousness and salvation as well. Paul's mission may be understood by him preeminently as a mission to the Gentiles, but this activity all takes place in the conceptual shadow of the mythic and epic Israel.

On the other hand, Mack's explanations for Paul's modification of the "resurrection tradition" by assumption/vindication language with the apocalyptic imagery of ἐγείρειν rely too much, I think, on Paul's prior and thorough commitment to apocalyptic beliefs, including those revolving around a general resurrection of the dead.[45] As Mack notes, Paul argues from a general resurrection to the resurrection of Jesus in 1 Cor 15:13, but offers precisely the opposite argumentative sequence in 1 Thess 4:13–14: "We do not want you to be uninformed, brothers, about those who have fallen asleep, so that you may not grieve as others do who have no hope. For since we believe that Jesus died and rose again, even so, through Jesus, God will bring with him those who have died." Also problematic, in my view, is Mack's association of a thoroughgoing apocalypticism on Paul's part with Smith's characterization of Paul as "utopian."[46] One of the important claims made in Smith's *Drudgery Divine* is that apocalypticism is essentially "locative" in its orientation;[47] Smith is careful not to make an equation of apocalypticism with utopianism, and for very good reasons: his explanation for the driving force behind apocalypticism in his paper on "Wisdom and Apocalyptic" is firmly locative.[48] This really means that if we accept Smith's characterization of Paul's ideology as utopian, we cannot describe Paul's mythic transformations in terms of rendering the locative *christos* myth into an apocalyptic and hence utopian direction. This

---

45. Mack, "Rereading the Christ Myth," 45–47. However, Mack's additional claim (ibid., 44–45), that Paul has also modified this tradition by substituting "was crucified" for "died" or "was killed," thereby implicitly identifying the tyrant at whose instigation Jesus died, is extremely provocative and in my view likely to be correct (although there are some logical problems here: we must assume that Paul accurately added a secondary detail to the tradition that happened to be true; or that the tradition that Jesus was crucified originated with Paul; or, most plausibly, that this detail was widely known but not exploited theologically).

46. Ibid., 47, citing Smith, *Drudgery Divine*, 141.

47. Smith, *Drudgery Divine*, 137.

48. Jonathan Z. Smith, "Wisdom and Apocalyptic," in *Religious Syncretism in Antiquity: Essays in Conversation with Geo Widengren* (ed. Birger A. Pearson; Series on Formative Contemporary Thinkers 1; Missoula, Mont.: Scholars Press, 1975), 131–56; repr. in *Map Is Not Territory: Studies in the History of Religions* (SJLA 23; Leiden: Brill, 1978; repr., Chicago: University of Chicago Press, 1993), 67–87.

may sound like a pedantic quibble, but it has some significant implications that are of great interest to me: if one strongly associates apocalypticism with a locative framework and insists on describing Paul as "utopian" (whatever that means), this may call into question just how apocalyptic he really was. In general, I think that the apocalypticism of Paul and its salience for understanding his project have been greatly exaggerated, both in standard scholarship and in Mack's redescription of Paul.[49] While there are apocalyptic aspects to Paul's ideas, and while he certainly uses apocalyptic motifs opportunistically when he gets into trouble, there is too much in Paul's thought that ill accords with an apocalyptic framework, or that does not require it, for me to be comfortable with viewing apocalypticism as the overarching framework of his thought.[50] Paul's utopianism, and his familiarity with and use of apocalyptic tropes deployed in a nonlocative fashion, should rather lead us, if we are seeking to understand his thought typologically, to the construct of Gnosticism over that of apocalypticism.[51]

---

49. Representative is Gager (*Reinventing Paul*, 75), who asserts that fundamental distortion of Paul's thought occurs, among other things, "when we ignore the intense eschatological framework of Paul's thought and action."

50. See, e.g., Sanders, *Paul and Palestinian Judaism*, 543: "The similarity between Paul's view and apocalypticism is general rather than detailed. Paul did not, as has been observed, calculate the times and seasons, he did not couch his predictions of the end in visions involving beasts, and he observed none of the literary conventions of apocalyptic literature. Since the conventions of apocalypticism had so little influence on him, the hypothesis might be put forward that before his conversion and call Paul was not especially apocalyptically oriented. This is one more reason for not supposing that Paul began with a set apocalyptic view and fitted Christ into it." Of course, Sanders is taking it for granted here that the most ancient forms of "Christianity" that preceded Paul were motivated by an "expectation of the parousia," and therefore that apocalyptic elements in Paul's thought are derived therefrom, a view that in my opinion cannot be sustained. Nonetheless, I think Sanders's description of the limitations of apocalyptic tropes in Paul is quite accurate, and I regard his conclusion that Paul did not begin with an apocalyptic framework and fit Christ into it to be essentially correct as well.

51. Since I am quite thoroughly convinced by the arguments of Michael Allen Williams (*Rethinking "Gnosticism": An Argument for Dismantling a Dubious Category* [Princeton: Princeton University Press, 1996]) and Karen L. King (*What Is Gnosticism?* [Cambridge, Mass.: Belknap Press of Harvard University Press, 2003]), that the normal application of the term "Gnosticism" is to a heterogeneous body of texts that have little in common, and that there is no unified ancient "Gnosticism" at all, I must specify precisely what I mean by describing Paul this way. In fact, I think that similar criticisms may be applied to "apocalypticism," such that it too becomes an incoherent and misleading label. Here, at least (unlike with "Gnosticism," which describes materials encompassing a huge range of literary genres), we certainly have a real literary genre; but the extension of the genre of apocalypse to an ideology marked by adherence to the themes normally purveyed by this literary genre—as is implied by the problematic terms "apocalyptic" and "apocalypticism"—is probably about as legitimate as would be such constructs as "epicism" or "epistolism." However, Smith's careful specification of the social circumstances underlying, precisely, the production of the (real) apocalyptic genre (i.e., the apocalypse) and the ideological impulses leading to a radicalization and interiorization of this genre's claims, which Smith refers to, respectively, as the "apocalyptic situation" (the wrong king is on the throne) and the "gnostic situation" (the wrong god in is heaven) ("Wisdom and Apocalyptic," 137, 144, 146–47, 148–49; repr. in *Map Is Not Territory*, 72, 77, 79, 81; idem, "A Pearl of Great Price and a Cargo of Yams: A Study in Situational Incongruity," *HR* 16 [1976]: 7–8; repr. in *Imagining Religion: From*

An alternative, not quite so apocalyptic explanation for Paul's use of the language of burial in his "resurrection tradition" in 1 Cor 15:3–5 is that this alteration may be more a function of Paul's interests in baptism than an invocation of a full-blown apocalyptic schema. The only other place in the (genuine) Pauline corpus where one can find the term "bury" or "entomb" is in Rom 6:3–4, where precisely the same cluster of ideas as in 1 Cor 15:3–5 (death, burial, resurrection) is linked to baptism: "Do you not know that all of us who have been baptized into Christ Jesus were baptized into his death? Therefore we have been buried with him by baptism into death, so that, just as Christ was raised from the dead by the glory of the Father, so we too might walk in newness of life." Hence the Pauline addition (as I assume it is, on the basis of Mack's argument) of "was buried" to the "tradition" in 1 Cor 15:3–5 may be less a function of apocalypticism[52] than a reflection of the ways in which Paul imagines the effect of Christ's death and resurrection on the members of Paul's clubs, particularly insofar as what I continue to see as an initiatory rite (i.e., baptism) is made to reproduce Christ's mythological journey from death to life.

And this, in turn, suggests a whole other line of inquiry. For Paul does, quite clearly, speak of baptism as an actual physical act of initiation (as per 1 Cor 1:13–17; cf. also possibly Gal 3:27). But he actually does not refer to baptism all that often in the genuine corpus, and when he does it sometimes has a metaphoric sense, rather than a literal one: a synecdoche for fusion of identity. Indeed, aside from the three central passages just mentioned (Rom 6:3–4; 1 Cor 1:13–17; Gal 3:27) and the reference to baptizing for the dead in 1 Cor 15:29, Paul refers to baptism only twice, both instances of identity language compressed into the symbol of baptism. In 1 Cor 10:2 he refers to the Israelites being "baptized into Moses," and in 1 Cor 12:13 he states that "in the one spirit we were all baptized into one body—Jews and Greeks, slaves or free—and we were all made to drink one spirit." As with the passage from Gal 3:27, "baptism" is here a hallmark, symbol, or synecdoche for unified group identity (and the reconfiguration of identity); it is strongly linked in these passages to being heirs of Abraham (as per Gal 3:29) and to receiving the spirit (as per 1 Cor 12:13). All of this, finally, suggests to me that possession of or by the spirit (whatever this actually means, and however it actually is imagined to occur) is a major factor in Paul's mythologizing activity and may be the glue he

---

Babylon to Jonestown [CSHJ; Chicago: University of Chicago Press, 1982], 94), allows us to use both of these terms typologically, I think, and it is in this sense that I apply them here. See, in particular, Smith's comments in "Here, There, and Anywhere," 33 n. 39; repr. in *Relating Religion*, 339 n. 39: "I have persistently maintained that rather than thinking of 'gnosticism' as a separate religious entity, it should be viewed as a structural possibility within religious traditions, analogous to categories such as mysticism or asceticism, and needs to be seen in relation to exegetical, reinterpretative practices. The wrong king/wrong god element discussed above should be compared to M. A. Williams's category of 'biblical demiurgical' in his important work, *Rethinking 'Gnosticism.'*"

52. Not to deny that Paul is familiar with such schemata and may use their images from time to time, but he deploys those images to his own purposes.

uses to link the Jesus cluster of mythemes to the Abraham cluster of mythemes.[53] The collective representations of Abraham and Jesus both work symbolically and in much the same way; but in Paul's mind they also work literally, and this time, because of different factors. Abraham serves as the collective representation of the "original" Israel because of lineal descent, a factor that Paul emphasizes as important in various places. The Gentiles in turn may be adopted into that lineage because they are "in Christ," and Christ can serve as their collective representation, literally, because of spirit possession. It is in this way that the Gentiles are "grafted on" to Israel. Paul basically says as much in Rom 8:9–17. This matter of spirit possession, therefore, needs to be looked at very carefully, as perhaps the catalyst that allows Paul to fuse Christ and Abraham myths (its sources and its place in Paul's thought also remain questions that beg for investigation). In any case, I would insist that our group deliberations have vastly underestimated the role of this practice, concept, or claim. Certainly the notion of spirit possession is not restricted to the Corinthians, and to whatever extent "enthusiasm" has been a Christian trope, spirit possession does seem to be a cross-cultural phenomenon.

IV. Attractions, Connections, and Unanswered Questions

To return, then, to the primary matter—my issues with the supposed extreme "disjunction" between Paul and his interlocutors—it seems to me that the questions that most animate Paul, and that drive him to do such extravagant things with the Jesus story, are precisely the same questions that animated and inspired the ethnically mixed Corinthian group hypothesized (correctly, I think) by Smith. Their questions are Paul's, and their situation is Paul's (unlike the prior Jesus people from whom Paul gets some of his concepts, whose questions are not Paul's). To assume otherwise is to fall into the traditional trap of making too much of the Jew–Gentile split, rather than seeing "Jewish" identity as just one of many dislocated *ethnē* in the Roman Empire. Paul's questions about being a Jew in a Greco-Roman world are not substantively different from the kinds of questions we might expect from, say, Tyrians in Italy, Egyptians in Antioch, or Italians in Asia Minor, as well as those ethnically diverse and uprooted people, whoever they may be, who made up the club in Corinth to which Paul offered his "gospel." Why give Paul a hearing at all? Because he was offering answers to their questions. The answer, in his case, is offered from his own Jewish perspective, of course, and so may have been more convincing for some auditors than others: it is the answer comprised by his "call" to undertake a "mission" to the nations. But because that answer was a real answer ("you do have an identity, you are now Israel, and you should behave and

---

53. Cf. also Paul's argumentation in Rom 8:2–5. Unlike "baptism," "Abraham," "buried," and even "cross," the word "spirit" occurs in all seven of Paul's genuine letters, appearing approximately 120 times.

view yourselves accordingly") and because it also involved an appeal to a concept or practice that the Corinthians were already attracted to and experimenting with (namely, spirit possession), Paul's notion of *ekklēsia*, his gospel, or however we might conceptualize his main agendum, would have effectively addressed precisely the prior concerns that drew this Corinthian club together in the first place. And so, it is not particularly hard for me to imagine these people as being quite excited by and interested in Paul's message. Paul need not be "implausible." Paul's conceptions, which scholars tend too often to think of exclusively in Jewish and theological terms, mesh exceptionally well with the putative concerns of these uprooted Corinthians. Paul sees himself as an apostle to the Gentiles (*ethnē*); the Corinthians are concerned with being an uprooted cluster of nations (*ethnē*). Paul proposes a new ethnic identity as grafted-on Jews under the rubric of the *ekklēsia*, the assembly of Israel (as per the LXX). His converts find new identities as urban citizens, members of the *ekklēsia* (the citizen assembly) of Thessalonica, Corinth, Philippi, and so on. Belonging in this way must have been attractive to some people (if not all, of course), precisely because it answered, in both an intellectual and a practical way, questions of identity (especially conceived in ethnic terms) that were already pressing, and because it created a bridge between what must have seemed a clear and meaningful ethnic identity and the practicalities of day-to-day life in Greco-Roman cities. I am put in mind of white suburban teens today aping "gangsta" styles, lingo, and music, a phenomenon that itself deserves careful investigation.[54] I would think that such an inherent attractiveness also helps us understand some of Paul's more frivolous arguments in such letters as Galatians. If we imagine a group with essentially intellectual concerns, treating Paul with suspicion and examining his ideas closely with an eye to consistency and logic, then we must certainly conclude that many of the arguments he offers would have certainly been repulsive and elicited little but scorn (the "seed" argument in Gal 3:16, as Mack has noted elsewhere, is rather less than convincing).[55] On the other hand, if we imagine that (even in Corinth) Paul's answer to an already extant question would have been extremely attractive, not so much for its logic as for what it accomplished—so much so, in fact, that some of his adherents went a step further and took on circumcision in order to become "real" Jews (as per Galatians)—then simply hearing (and I stress hearing, not reading: Paul's auditors were not analyzing his letters the way we do exegetically) that Paul could make an argument, any argument, in support of this or that problematic notion may have been sufficiently reassuring as to quell any serious doubts, at least among most people. I think,

---

54. I recognize that my argument here is running entirely counter not only to Smith's discussion of the Corinthians but also to Mack's observations in *Who Wrote the New Testament?* 110: "What if joining the Christ cult exacerbated the problem instead of solving it?" It is my hope that the "gangsta" example at least suggests the possibility that the deliberate adoption of a subaltern identity may have functional rewards.

55. Ibid., 116–17.

therefore, that the question of the disjunction between Paul and his interlocutors, in Corinth and elsewhere, might be profitably revisited.

I note, finally, that even the identification of the problematic behind the activities of both Paul and the preexisting Corinthian association as a fundamentally ethnic one, while in my view wholly correct, should be further elaborated. There are a variety of reasons not to stop with this characterization of ethnicity as a fundamental issue. One is that the outline of Paul's core myth of Christ, especially as it relates to social characteristics of those who have adopted it, may reveal a great deal more about its attractiveness and its functionality than simply its provision of some stable identity. Here comparison is useful. One example, culled unsurprisingly from Smith's work, involves the myth of Hainuwele, or "coconut girl."[56] Among the many fascinating features of this story is its symbolic reconfiguration of a concrete social reality: the presence of Europeans among the Pacific islands and particularly the excessive and overabundant consumer goods that mark their special status. Hainuwele is presented as producing such goods by defecation. The image stands as a striking condemnation of this alien superabundant wealth (such wealth is shit), suggesting as well a sense of befuddlement and disapproval as to its origins (it is not produced by work or growth, but essentially springs forth magically and *ex nihilo*). The decision of the other women to kill coconut girl also expresses disapproval of "unnatural" wealth, and at the same time attempts to assimilate commercial wealth to the natives' own, traditional understanding of wealth as food: Hainuwele is not simply killed, but afterwards, as tubers arise from her dismembered body, becomes a source of a new and—from the native perspective—better kind of wealth. Overarchingly, the narrative may be imagined to suggest also an inversionary restoration: by the end of the story, excrement has been transformed into food, rather than, as is the usual state of affairs, food becoming excrement.

Now, one of the many striking features of 1 Corinthians is its rather excessive language of inversion, and more specifically, its inversionary characterization of the transformation of the adherents of the *ekklēsia* from lowly to lofty standing:

> Consider your own call, brothers: not many of you were wise according to the flesh, not many were powerful, not many were of noble birth. But God chose what is foolish in the world to shame the wise; God chose what is weak in the world to shame the strong; God chose what is low and despised in the world, things that are not, to reduce to nothing things that are, so that no flesh might boast in the presence of God. (1 Cor 1:26–29)

This is applied also to Paul's own message:

---

56. See Smith, "Pearl of Great Price." The interpretation of the Hainuwele story that follows is entirely either a reiteration of, or an extrapolation from, points made by Smith in this article.

God decided, through the foolishness of our proclamation, to save those who believe. For Jews demand signs and Greeks desire wisdom, but we proclaim Christ crucified, a stumbling block to Jews and foolishness to Gentiles, but to those who are called, both Jews and Greeks, Christ the power of God and the wisdom of God. For God's foolishness is wiser than human wisdom, and God's weakness is stronger than human strength. (1 Cor 1:21–25)

And in fact this sort of imagery, applied by Paul both to himself and to his adherents, coheres very well with one of the fundamental Pauline myths, that of Christ's death and resurrection. That story traces out a movement from worthlessness, physical and social degradation (execution as a criminal), and indeed the non-being (τὰ μὴ ὄντα) of death, to infinite value, exaltation, and new life, an inversion that also, of course, closely corresponds to Paul's use of Christ to effect a transition from ethnic non-being to quasi-Israelite identity among his Gentile auditors. The Christ myth and the social self-perceptions of Paul are evidently parallel to each other.

What is striking here is how excellent an analogy this Pauline Christ myth makes to the story of Hainuwele, especially when the former is coordinated with Paul's description of the supposed "social" transformation it effects on its adherents. Both are accounts of a kind of rectifying inversion; an imaginary transformation that benefits the tradents of the respective stories by restoring to them some highly prized item that is currently elusive—appropriate wealth in the case of Hainuwele; appropriate status, perhaps, or belonging, in the case of Christ. Both stories revolve around contradictory juxtapositions of value with debasement: wealth with excrement; or what is "low and despised," or "foolish" and "weak," with wisdom and power. We might say that in the Hainuwele story, wealth is shit, while in the Christ story, shit is wealth, that is, what is degraded in the world is exalted in the eyes of God. The Hainuwele story can be and has been understood as an effort to assimilate or make sense of alien, incomprehensible, and detrimental social changes, changes that can be identified with some specificity.[57] Can we understand the Christ myth analogously? Might we infer similar social processes at work? Can we construct a phenomenology of anticolonialism? Can we make sense of, or learn something from, the differences between the stories? Might the identification of a "foreign" object of derision in the Hainuwele story (in contrast to the general failure of the Christ myth to do likewise) tell us something about how the social formations behind these two myths differed in their constitution and agenda? In any case, more discussion is needed of the concrete social characteristics—including considerations of gender, an inexcusable lacuna[58]—of Paul's auditors and the intellectual or conceptual problems these circumstances might have generated.

---

57. Actually, Smith's major point in his discussion of this story, in keeping with his own theoretical interests, is that it is an effort to assimilate an intellectual contradiction made pressing by social circumstance, rather than an effort to rectify that social circumstance itself.

58. Especially in light of the extensive intersection of gender ideologies with issues of descent,

Another reason to push at the boundaries of the characterization of the social logic of Paul's Christ myth as an ethnic one revolves around ethnicity itself, its status as a category, and its tangible referents. The category appears, at least superficially, itself to constitute a bridge between mythmaking and social formation, since it seems to refer group identity to some form of prior, concrete social reality, such as nation, cultural commonality, or even "race." But to understand ethnicity in such a fashion is to fail to recognize its own socially creative and frankly mythic functions. By contrast, our approach to the trope of ethnicity in ancient Christianity should recognize its discursive character:

> Current research tends to grant at least an intersubjective reality to ethnic identity, though it differs from pre-war scholarship on a number of important points. Firstly, it stresses that the ethnic group is not a biological group but a social group, distinguished from other collectivities by its subscription to a putative myth of shared descent and kinship and by its association with a 'primordial' territory. Secondly, it rejects the nineteenth-century view of ethnic groups as static, monolithic categories with impermeable boundaries for a less restrictive model which recognizes the dynamic, negotiable and situationally constructed nature of ethnicity. Finally, it questions the notion that ethnic identity is primarily constituted by either genetic traits, language, religion or even common cultural forms. While all of these attributes may act as important symbols of ethnic identity, they really only serve to bolster an identity that is ultimately constructed through written and spoken discourse.[59]

In other words, all ethnicity is essentially "fictive" ethnicity.[60] Attempting to relate the Christ myth to an ethnic social identity, or to issues generated by ethnic phenomena, simply defers the problem. One might ask instead: on what actual social basis have the ethnic identities (or the absence thereof) in question been founded? To put this as clearly as I possibly can, if ethnicity is itself a mythic rationalization for social formation, understanding the Christ myth in terms of an extension of Israelite ethnicity, or in terms of a deracination of local Gentile ethnicities, is

---

which is, of course, the symbolic basis of ethnicity (i.e., ethnic identity is identity based on the assertion of common ancestry) and the mechanism (specifically patrilineal descent, with all of the difficulties and ramifications problematized by this construct) by which Paul is able to use Christ and Abraham to draw Gentiles into Israel. Various sophisticated efforts exist to explore the relationship between gender and ideologies of descent and lineage, both generally (e.g., Nancy B. Jay, *Throughout Your Generations Forever: Sacrifice, Religion, and Paternity* [Chicago: University of Chicago Press, 1992]), and more specifically with respect to Paul (e.g., Johnson Hodge, *If Sons, Then Heirs*; Pamela Eisenbaum, "A Remedy for Having Been Born of Woman: Jesus, Gentiles, and Genealogy in Romans," *JBL* 123 [2004]: 671–702).

59. Jonathan M. Hall, *Ethnic Identity in Greek Antiquity* (Cambridge: Cambridge University Press, 1997), 2.

60. Nicola Denzey, "The Limits of Ethnic Categories," in *Handbook of Early Christianity: Social Science Approaches* (ed. Anthony J. Blasi et al.; Walnut Creek, Calif.: AltaMira, 2002), 489–507.

simply to explain one myth in terms of another. This is not in itself unreasonable, but we should not confuse such a procedure with the grounding of a mythic framework in an actual social formation. The question remains to be answered: what concrete social formations express themselves in terms of ethnicity, and why?

Given the limitations (I do not say "problems") involved in linking Paul's Christ myth to ethnic conceptions, it would probably be valuable to explore the linkages that may exist between Paul's formulation of the Christ myth and either household or political identities.[61] As Mack's paper notes, if Paul himself added to the tradition in 1 Cor 15:3–5 the specification that Jesus was crucified, then Paul himself has added an overtly political identification of the tyrant (Rome) to a tradition which lacked that specification. Interestingly, and in support of Mack's reconstruction of this Pauline change, the noun "cross" (σταυρός) and the verb "to crucify" (σταυροῦν) are entirely lacking in 1 Thessalonians (Paul's most apocalyptic letter) and essentially lacking in Romans (Paul's most careful and conciliatory letter).[62] We might speculate that at the very early stage at which 1 Thessalonians was composed, Paul had not yet introduced this personal innovation, and that a great deal of the political heft of the emphasis on crucifixion as such was taken up by the more overt apocalyptic language in this letter and its occasional direct polemic against imperial claims (e.g., 1 Thess 5:3). In the case of Romans, Paul does his best to avoid crucifixion language (slipping up, however, in Rom 6:6), precisely because he wishes to underplay his own innovations to the traditions (thus supporting Mack's conjecture that this specification is a Pauline innovation), but also because he is careful in this letter to avoid any implication of subversive political agenda (see especially Rom 13:1–7). This last point then suggests that Paul is wholly aware of the political implications of characterizing Jesus' death as a result of crucifixion.

In any case, the language of both of the base social institutions of Roman antiquity—state and household—appears copiously in Paul's letters, and both of these formations are concrete and lived "givens" prior to and independent of any activity on Paul's part. How does Paul's Christ myth, for instance, establish Jesus as *kyrios*, and what are the social implications of this designation? In what ways do this title and concept serve to reinforce group boundaries, and what does it imply about the group's constitution? Does it refer, metaphorically or otherwise, to political sovereignty or to a household relationship? Similar questions can be asked, mutatis mutandis, about the linkage between the Christ myth and the social constitution of the Pauline associations implied by other political or household metaphors, such as "church," "brothers," and so on. It may be that attention to this

---

61. The recent work done by Richard A. Horsley on Paul and politics strikes me as immensely promising and offers an important new redescription of the Pauline groups. See especially his edited volumes: *Paul and Politics*; and *Paul and Empire: Religion and Power in Roman Imperial Society* (Harrisburg, Pa.: Trinity Press International, 1997).

62. The exception is Rom 6:6: "we know that our old self was crucified with him."

terminology—both as it is implied by Paul's version of the Christ myth and as it is used to express the social reality of Paul's associations—will reveal some social basis in addition to ethnicity resting at the core of the Pauline "mission." It may be, for instance, that Paul's Christ myth was applied to vertically stratified household units, and functioned to present those units as organic entities, promoting unity in the face of divisions established by class, gender, prior conceptions of ethnicity, and other social forces. Paul does, after all, refer to house churches, and his Christ myth and Christian associations appealing to this myth may represent an intervention into the tensions and strains already present in the first-century urban *oikia*. Or it may be that the myth was applied at a political level, filling a social lacuna for "freedpeople and urban poor isolated from any horizontal supportive social network,"[63] an alternative to vertical patronage relations. Paul does, after all, identify churches as the *ekklēsiai* of their respective *poleis*. Or both factors may be at work, or neither. But the question deserves our attention, and should not be ruled out of consideration as a consequence of satisfaction with too narrow an ethnic construction of the issues.

---

63. Richard A. Horsley, "1 Corinthians: A Case Study of Paul's Assembly as an Alternative Society," in idem, *Paul and Empire*, 243.

Kinds of Myth, Meals, and Power: Paul and the Corinthians

Stanley K. Stowers

Jonathan Z. Smith's comparison of the Corinthians known from Paul's letters and the Atbalmin of Papua New Guinea provides a remarkable opportunity for scholars of early Christianity.[1] The study of the New Testament has understandably been dominated by the internal perspectives of Christian theology. This means that approaches to Paul's letters continually reinscribe an incomparable uniqueness and irresistible relevance. Privileged meta-narratives ensure that the ways scholars imagine Paul and the Corinthians elide many of the human social and cognitive processes that students of a contemporary culture or a scholar in a department of history would assume as requirements for construing the people in question as human. Smith's bold comparison breaks through these constraints that have dominated the field and creates an opening for imagining Paul and the Corinthians in ways that are quite normal in the humanities and the social sciences.[2] Thus, Smith's comparative operation is only bold in view of the norms of New Testament studies and quite familiar as a way of understanding human groups in the wider university.

In this essay, I want to take advantage of the opening created by Smith's paper to raise some questions about certain social and cognitive processes that are usually hidden in traditional approaches. In a more comprehensive study, I would theoretically develop the concepts of *doxai*, interests, recognition, and attraction that I believe need to be added to Smith's concepts of incorporation and resistance.[3] I

---

1. Jonathan Z. Smith, "Re: Corinthians" (in this volume).
2. For the sake of simplicity, I will refer to those people whom Paul depicts and addresses in his letters to the Corinthians as "in Christ" or believers or members of the *ekklēsia* in Corinth as "the Corinthians."
3. Smith, "Re: Corinthians," 28. As will become clear in what follows, the greatest influence on my use of these concepts is Pierre Bourdieu. That said, I do not use them in just Bourdieu's way(s) and in fact would admit debts also to Max Weber, Marshall Sahlins, and others, were I to attempt a genealogy.

understand all of these as attendant on the processes of ongoing mythic formations that Smith's paper allows us to imagine for the Atbalmin, as well as for Paul and the Corinthians. For the purposes of this article, I will stipulate the following. A *doxa* is a body of taken-for-granted beliefs, practical skills, assumptions, and understandings that the researcher through historical investigation imagines that the people in question brought to a social situation.[4] Interests are the most basic and important projects and ends that motivated the people in question. "Most basic" should be a matter of debate and corrigible for scholars. Recognition is the process of someone taking someone else (or another group) to be someone of a certain type or identity (or certain types and identities). Recognition is not all or nothing, but a matter of making more or less sense. It often entails some degree, or lack, of legitimacy or social capital.[5] Attraction is the process of recognizing some sort of mutuality of interests that can be the basis for individuals or groups engaging in common practices or entertaining the possibility. In the latter, it is to be assumed that individual participation is differential and that individuals do not bring exactly the same skills, understandings, and so on, to practices in common with others, even while they share certain common practical understandings with all those who participate in a particular practice.[6] I will not so much explicate these concepts in what follows as presuppose them, as I first engage some facets of Smith's paper and then use Paul's discussion of the Lord's supper as a case to explore how one might imagine the mythmaking and ritualization of Paul and the Corinthians as dynamic social activities. At the end of the paper, I will return to Smith's construal of the incommensurability that he sees between the religion of Paul and the Corinthians and suggest another interpretation. I will preface the discussion by noting some key ways that what I want to do differs from typical approaches.

The dominant approach to Paul and the Corinthian letters I characterize as academic Christian theological modernism.[7] The approach has made enormous contributions to the study of the New Testament and contributes substantially

---

4. I borrow the concept from Bourdieu as used by him throughout his career, beginning with his much cited early work, *An Outline of a Theory of Practice* (trans. Richard Nice; Cambridge Studies in Social and Cultural Anthropology 16; Cambridge: Cambridge University Press, 1977).

5. I borrow social capital from Bourdieu. In crafting this concept, Bourdieu drew upon Weber's concept of legitimation.

6. For practical understanding, see Theodore R. Schatzki, *Social Practices: A Wittgensteinian Approach to Human Activity and the Social* (New York: Cambridge University Press, 1996); idem, *The Site of the Social: A Philosophical Account of the Constitution of Social Life and Change* (University Park: Pennsylvania State University Press, 2002). I agree with Schatzki over against Bourdieu on the role of practical understanding in practices.

7. So, e.g., this would be the scholarship documented by Werner Georg Kümmel in *The New Testament: The History of the Investigation of Its Problems* (trans. S. McLean Gilmour and Howard C. Kee; Nashville: Abingdon, 1972).

to this essay, but its limitations are, I think, clear.[8] The tradition is thoroughly grounded in the situation developing from the aftermath of the Protestant Reformation, but took form as a part of the crystallization of European modernity in the nineteenth century and the institutionalization of confessional faculties in the universities. The approach trades centrally on the dualisms of material/spiritual and orthodox/heretical. With regard to science and cosmology, the ancients and the early Christians are other in a rather absolute sense, but with regard to religion, morals, sociality, and subjectivity, the early Christians are the same as us. They are the same people in different clothes, with a different "science." The early Christians are not only generally the same as modern Europeans, but also the same as the professors and Christian scholars who study them in their focus on specialized intellectual interests, that is, doctrines, theology, and ideas.

The basic moves of the approach are familiar. One first reads the letter for Paul's explicit criticisms of the audience encoded in the rhetoric of the letter. Second, and much more important, one reads passages with irony, sarcasm, and where Paul seems to oppose something or seems defensive as reflections of an opposing point of view, often with supposed behavioral manifestations. Two moves, mirror-reading and asserting that Paul uses the language of his opponents—though, of course, he doesn't really mean what he says in such cases—prove central to the enterprise. With these methods, one constructs opponents and reaches the goal of outlining the theological or ideological positions of these opponents or deficient Corinthians. Typically, the scholar will identify this false teaching with some intellectual position in Greco-Roman or Jewish culture, often represented in the most extreme caricature. Then, in a second major move, the academic theological modernist reads Paul's rhetoric, and the theology supposedly behind the rhetoric, over against and as a response to the ideology of the opponents. Inevitably, the opponents turn out to be suspiciously similar to contemporary religious opponents of the scholar—for example, pietist enthusiasts, evangelical or fundamentalist spiritualists, ascetic world renouncers, sacramentalists, worldly philosophers, libertine intellectuals, and so on.

The central pattern here is the model of orthodoxy and heresy. Religion is a matter of right and wrong depending on what doctrines one holds, right belief and wrong belief. Doctrines are formalized or semiformalized teachings. People consciously adopt beliefs and are conscious of their beliefs/positions as beliefs/positions. Thus, a historian could, on this view, without anachronism ask, What was Paul's or his opponents' position on, say, justification by faith or ecclesiology? To provide perspective on these assumptions, I would argue that it would be

---

8. A very important spinoff from this tradition, but remaining within it, in my view, is the movement to do social history and work inspired by the social sciences pioneered by such figures as John Gager, Wayne A. Meeks, Gerd Theissen, and Bruce Malina. Some feminist interpretation amounts to another line of important work. Owing to limitations of space I cannot treat these here in addition to the dominant stream of the tradition.

highly misleading to ask this question of, for instance, a typical Roman, Greek, or Jew. Greeks ordinarily did not have positions on the doctrine of Zeus or the gods, and neither did Judeans on Yahweh or the nature of belief. There are social conditions for this kind of religion supposed as natural and universal in much scholarship. Rather, I will admit below that Paul does have some interest in religion with a certain focus on right and wrong positions, but one can explain his interest only within the social conditions of a field of intellectualist competition.

A key assumption in most theological modernist interpretation is that the people whom Paul addresses and whom he represents as the church at Corinth form a community. The idea of a community is the idea of a highly integrated social group based on a common ethos, practices, and beliefs. Paul preached the gospel, people converted, and Paul welded them into a community. With this assumption, Paul's words in 1 Cor 1:10 become the basis for asking the question, How did the Corinthian community become divided? What false doctrine from inside the community, or infiltrating from the outside, corrupted the community or seduced a portion of it? Usually the corrupting ideas have an external ideological or theological source, often false beliefs "left over" from "the pre-Christian environment." In positing a community, one is also assuming fully developed Christian subjects—these have to look like Christians that the scholars know from Europe or America, shaped by Christian cultures and centuries of developed Christian institutions. Something cannot derive from nothing, including persons or subjects. The concept of community and communities has been enormously constraining for scholarship on ancient Christianity. Community is a highly ideal and ideological concept. There are a very many kinds of social formations that are not communities.

The approach that I am characterizing simply assumes not only Christian community and Christian subjects, but also that the pre-Christian religious interests and formations would have to a substantial degree coincided with Paul's interests and formation. The Corinthians were looking for the truth about salvation, say, and Paul provided the true beliefs. But are all people just naturally looking for salvation? The approach overlooks the fact, long established from ethnography and the history of religions, that the vast majority of religious people have "practical" religious interests focused on the household and family rather than specialized intellectual interests, such as explaining the nature of the cosmos and human destiny, the true doctrine of God, right worship, the true interpretation of authoritative texts, and the nature of the ideal human community. In fact, it takes a massive cultural-institutional structure, say with something like bishops, textually oriented religious education, the massive production and religious use of texts, and so on, in order to reproduce religions that focus on intellectual practices and doctrines of need and salvation.[9] Greek and Roman religion and the religion of

---

9. Many scholars have worked long and hard over the last two centuries to construct a Judaism at the time of Christian beginnings that is a shadow of Christianity and a preparation for the gospel. In

the Judean temple were not such religions. It is unlikely that Paul's formation and interests substantially overlapped with those of most of the Corinthians.

On the modernist reading, Paul's first contact with the Corinthians must have been somewhat as follows. Paul knocks on a door in Corinth. Gaius comes to the door. Paul says, "Jesus Christ has died for your sins and you have been justified by God." Gaius joyously proclaims, "Thank God I am saved!" Now this may be an exaggeration of what is naively unexamined, but only a small one. The theological modernist approach fails to address the sociological questions of recognition— what are the conditions for someone recognizing someone else as a particular someone representing something?—and similarly, the questions of the coincidence of interests, attraction, practical participation, negotiations of individual self-understanding (identity or subjectivity?), and social formation.[10] All of these remain unasked as the scholar posits Christian subjects and community.

In my view, two things are very clear from the evidence of the Corinthian letters: first, Paul very much wanted the people to whom he wrote to be a community, and he held a theory saying that God had miraculously made them into a community "in Christ"; second, the Corinthians never did sociologically form a community and only partly and differentially shared Paul's interests and formation. In my estimation, it is very unlikely that "the Corinthians" ever had any more social organization than households that may have had previous ties with other households and, after Paul, a roughly shared knowledge that Paul wanted them to be an *ekklēsia* in Christ and that he kept telling them that God had transformed them into one.[11] But Paul's relation with a fraction of the Corinthians that we know

---

my view, this has resulted in a massive distortion of what the religion of Jews/Judeans was like for the sake of a construction of Christianity. The Corinthian letters, unlike Acts, give no hint of the existence of a Jewish community, synagogues, so-called god-fearers, or converted Jews. It is not impossible that there were non-Jews among the Corinthians who had had an interest in things Jewish, but there is little or no evidence for it in the letters except for the coming of Paul and other Jewish teachers. Furthermore, the Corinthian letters may be placed in contrast to Romans and Galatians in which the relation to Judaism looms large.

10. Eva Ebel's *Die Attraktivität früher christlicher Gemeinden: Die Gemeinde von Korinth im Spiegel griechisch-römischer Vereine* (WUNT 2/178; Tübingen: Mohr Siebeck, 2004) provides an analysis of much important material regarding associations and possible parallels with the situation at Corinth, but she does not critically theorize attraction and to a large extent follows the modernist approach. Supposedly universal commonsense categories like the "openness" of early Christianity, the sense of belonging, and "brotherhood" tend to beg the question and ignore the senses of the various modes of religion.

11. Thus I do not find the assumption prevalent in the seminar that the Corinthians formed an association, either before or after Paul, likely for a host of reasons. Paul's language (e.g., 11:18, 19–33; 14:26–38; and places throughout the letters) suggests meetings of households and fractions thereof partly at Paul's encouragement aided by elites and partly for ad hoc reasons according to strategic interests of fractions, for example, perhaps communicating with the dead, baptism for the dead, and so on. Again, a group of elites and others formed a closer association with Paul and each other (e.g., Stephanas and others in 16:15).

included some elites, in the sense of being heads of households and potential heads, was different and more cohesive.

That the primary social formations Paul encountered were households does not mean that there were not many other social formations that either cut across households or that involved individuals and subpopulations within households. The possibilities are numerous: for example, circles of friends, trading networks, cultic associations, neighborhoods, and ethnic identifications. One of which we have firm evidence is a field of intellectualist competition and cultural production that I will discuss below. Because, in spite of our romantic notions, even households might not be communities, individuals associated with Paul might not have ever belonged to any community. I follow contemporary social thought in holding that community or even "groupness" more broadly is something to be demonstrated and not assumed.[12] Community and groupness—that the category *x* (e.g., Jews, Christ followers, Corinthians, local aristocrats, a particular clan) actually constituted a group—should not be axioms of analysis. Holding to this approach typically yields two results: a separation of social ideology from social practice, and the discovery that individuals participate in numerous social formations.

In addition, I want to insist that individuals under specific social conditions produce and interpret myths, not communities. One cannot simply identify the interests of the mythmakers and myth interpreters with the collective minds and wills of communities and peoples. A mythmaker is often best thought of as a kind of entrepreneur attempting to produce and shape groupness. Eytan Bercovitch in his analysis of Atbalmin religion, I think, is attempting to encompass some of these distinctions with his concept of "social multiplicity," the idea that "people possess several, often contradictory sets of beliefs and practices."[13] He is explicitly trying to avoid an old-fashioned, now discredited identification of a posited group with its purported culture seen as a whole and notably including its myths. The approach will aid the imagination of the complexities animating Paul's relations to the Corinthians. Thus, I believe, in agreement with the seminar, that providing an account of this difference between Paul's ideals and the recognition, interests, attractions, and formations of the Corinthians is the key to a helpful way of reading the letter. Of course, we can know a great deal about Paul's views, but must be very modest about those of the Corinthians.

Smith's comparison gives permission to the scholarly imagination for construing the social situations reflected in the Corinthian letters in new ways. I want to engage three central aspects of the two situations in which Smith finds similarity and a basis for further comparison: localism, simultaneous experimentation,

---

12. Rogers Brubaker, *Ethnicity without Groups* (Cambridge, Mass.: Harvard University Press, 2004).

13. Eytan Bercovitch, "The Altar of Sin: Social Multiplicity and Christian Conversion among a New Guinea People," in *Religion and Cultural Studies* (ed. Susan L. Mizruchi; Princeton: Princeton University Press, 2001), 212; cf. 219, 225–30.

and changes in a small homogeneous community. The relevant statements from his article are:

> Two major elements stand out in which the New Guinea materials make more plausible our imagination of some early Christian social formations. The first is the ability of a small, relatively homogeneous community to absorb a stunning series of situational changes within a brief span of time through strategies of incorporation and resistance.... The second element is the capacity of a small, relatively homogeneous community to experiment, simultaneously, with multiple modes of religion. (Bercovitch described four.) The Atbalmin have exhibited, within their social and religious history, the dialectical relations of processes of reproduction and transformation that constitute, with particular clarity, what Marshall Sahlins has termed "structures of conjuncture." As a generalization, all of this makes more plausible the presumption of the coexistence of multiple experiments by early "Christian" communities as well as their localism. It alerts us to the presence of sorts of changes not necessarily captured by the historical record.[14]

By localism, I take Smith to mean, in the case of the Corinthians, their practice of the religion of place manifest in their concern for the dead, for spirits, for kinship and ancestry, and for their common meals.[15] The letters clearly give evidence of the Corinthian practice of religion of the household and family and religion of the temple.[16] Thus, interpreters should take these, and especially the first, as expressing the religious interests of the people to whom Paul wrote and think of Paul's religion of "anywhere" as at least novel for most of the Corinthians and perhaps, with Smith, as a problematic intrusion.[17] This then makes explaining mutual interests, recognition of Paul, and attraction—processes that precede Smith's issues of incorporation and resistance—a central task for the scholar. Even a problematic someone is a someone to the other, but always under conditions. In the minds of at least some of the people whom Paul addresses, what authorized Paul as a purveyor of certain cultural products and practices? In order to follow this approach, New Testament scholars will have to denaturalize their understandings of religion and

---

14. Smith, "Re: Corinthians," 27–28, citing Bercovitch, "Altar of Sin," 211–35; and Marshall Sahlins, *Historical Metaphors and Mythical Realities: Structure in the Early History of the Sandwich Islands Kingdom* (Association for Social Anthropology in Oceania 1; Ann Arbor: University of Michigan Press, 1981).

15. Stanley K. Stowers, "Theorizing the Religion of Ancient Households and Families," in *Household and Family Religion in Antiquity* (ed. John Bodel and Saul M. Olyan; The Ancient World: Comparative Histories; Oxford: Blackwell, 2008), 5–19; Jonathan Z. Smith, "Here, There, and Anywhere," in *Prayer, Magic, and the Stars in the Ancient and Late Antique World* (ed. Scott Noegel et al.; Magic in History Series; University Park: Pennsylvania State University Press, 2003), 21–36; repr. in *Relating Religion: Essays in the Study of Religion* (Chicago: University of Chicago Press, 2004), 323–39.

16. See 1 Cor 8:10 and the discussions of meat sacrificed to non-Jewish deities.

17. Smith, "Re: Corinthians," 28–29, 34.

not assume a contextless universal meaningfulness and attraction to "Paul's gospel." It is simply a fact of ethnography and the history of religions that the religious interests of most people focus on the locative religion of household and family.[18] I will argue that Paul's teachings and mythmaking were centrally about kinship and ancestry, even if not in a typically locative way, and integrally connected to his discourse about the "spirit" (a poor translation) or *pneuma*. An implication of this argument is that modes of religion that are distinctive enough to classify as types may not be pure. Tension, inconsistency, and modes of hybridity ought to be taken as the norm.[19] The mode of religion imagined and advocated in Paul's letters embodies tensions. It denies many of the principles and practices of the locative religion of land, temple, and home precisely by thinking, including mythmaking, about family, kinship, and descent. Is Paul simply incomprehensible to many or all of the Corinthians, as Smith and Burton L. Mack suggest, or does the very evidence of creative differential reaction and resistance to Paul on the part of the Corinthians argue for varied degrees of comprehension and creative response in light of that comprehension?

The case of the Atbalmin and their simultaneous experimentation with multiple modes of religion makes the internal early Christian perspective of absolute religious purity and mutually exclusive practice, a perspective generally adopted in New Testament scholarship, seem fantastic. We can conclude with confidence that even if the Corinthians had fully understood what Paul wanted them to do, they would have been selective about what they wanted to do, and could not have given up their religion wholesale, even if they had wanted to do so.[20] This means that there is a very large gap between the idealized descriptions of the Corinthians as "in Christ" and the real situation. The deep failures that Paul sees among the Corinthians are likely the result of their selective and mixed appropriation and outright resistance to Paul.

Smith describes the social formation subject to these changes as "a small, relatively homogeneous community." While this certainly fits the Atbalmin and to some extent fits Paul's Corinthians, I think it helpful to make some further specifications and modifications of the description. Although the case is complicated by the intrusion of Western modernity and the Indonesians in New Guinea, I would argue that the society of Roman Corinth was in important ways more differentiated and certainly more diverse than traditional Atbalmin society, even with the

---

18. See Smith, "Here, There, and Anywhere"; Stowers, "Theorizing the Religion of Ancient Households and Families."

19. I want to beg the pardon of readers for using the overused and misused term hybridity. The trendy umbrella concept needs analysis.

20. I try to give some sense of the radical embeddedness of religion in life in Stanley K. Stowers, "Greeks Who Sacrifice and Those Who Do Not: Toward an Anthropology of Greek Religion," in *The Social World of the First Christians: Essays in Honor of Wayne A. Meeks* (ed. L. Michael White and O. Larry Yarbrough; Minneapolis: Fortress, 1995), 299–320.

intrusions.[21] Slavery, for example, and a multiethnic urban context make a difference, but I want to draw attention to one feature of the culture/social organization of the Roman Empire in particular. Translocal fields of knowledge with specialists who served as producers and distributors and a niche of people socialized as consumers of this culture had long been a feature of the Mediterranean. By field, I mean a space of norms and practices, a game if you will, that had gained a semiautonomy from kings, patrons, and the economy in general.[22] The dominant and broadly legitimized form of this knowledge and practices is well known to us as Greek and Roman *paideia* or, according to the myth, a single *paideia* whose commonality to Greeks and Romans was based on an ancient shared ancestry.[23] The Augustan classicism and the classicism of the so-called Second Sophistic, for instance, both celebrated ancestral cultural heritage. The two major traditions of this *paideia* were found in rhetoric or sophistry and philosophy.[24] But there were clearly other bodies of knowledge with producers, distributors, and interpreters. Most obviously, these appear as ethnic knowledges, for example, the wisdom of the Egyptians, Syrians, and Jews.[25] Forms of these knowledges with their authoritative texts and interpretive practices ceased to be merely local and both competed and overlapped with the dominant *paideia* at points. Translation of key texts into Greek and writing in Greek were conditions that facilitated the participation of ethnic fields or quasi-fields in the dominant field. The myth of the barbarian origins of Greek wisdom grew during the Hellenistic period and became very influential under the early empire.[26]

---

21. See Smith's qualifications and differences, "Re: Corinthians," 27–29.

22. I discuss the notion of fields, especially in relation to Bourdieu and his critics, in Stanley K. Stowers, "Pauline Scholarship and the Third Way in Social Theory" (paper presented at the annual meeting of the Society of Biblical Literature, Toronto, Ontario, November 2002).

23. There is a massive bibliography that is relevant here. Because *paideia* has not been treated—described or explained—sociologically, the literature uses mostly native categories such as Greek and Roman culture, education, rhetoric, sophistic, philosophy, ancient science, and historical traditions (the First and the Second Sophistic, post-Hellenistic philosophy). There are some synthetic works constructed as the history of traditions such as Werner W. Jaeger's *Paideia: The Ideals of Greek Culture*, vol. 1, *Archaic Greece: The Mind of Athens* (2nd ed.; trans. Gilbert Highet; New York: Oxford University Press, 1945), but to my knowledge no one has treated the sociological field(s) that transcended the traditions, although Weber certainly understood and supposed it. A move in the right direction is Simon Swain, *Hellenism and Empire: Language, Classicism, and Power in the Greek World, AD 50–250* (Oxford: Clarendon, 1996).

24. The classic discussion has been Hans von Arnim, *Leben und Werke des Dio von Prusa, mit einer Einleitung: Sophistik, Rhetorik, Philosophie in ihrem Kampf um die Jugendbildung* (Berlin: Weidmann, 1898).

25. The most influential treatment of Greek/non-Greek interaction seems to be Arnaldo Momigliano, *Alien Wisdom: The Limits of Hellenization* (Cambridge: Cambridge University Press, 1975). This work is looking very dated now, both in light of more recent scholarship on particulars and its uncritical use of native categories and ideas of cultural purity and impurity.

26. Ibid.; see also G. R. Boys-Stones, *Post-Hellenistic Philosophy: A Study of its Development from the Stoics to Origen* (Oxford: Oxford University Press, 2001).

The abundant evidence shows that only a relatively small number of people, often but not always elites of some sort, aspired to become producers, distributors, and even dedicated consumers of *paideia*. The key point is this: two modes of religion existed only by way of specific social conditions and in relative autonomy. Autonomy here refers to the larger fields in which participants set and contested their own rules and practices. Autonomy does not mean that the modes for individuals were mutually exclusive. The beliefs and practices of normal Mediterranean religion (e.g., Greek, Lydian, Judean) were *doxai*: they were given; for the most part, taken for granted.[27] This sort of religion was embedded in the everyday life of farm, family, household, and the order of the city, and thus focused on place. The religion promoted among those in the fields in question was different in that contestation for defining what was true about the gods and the cosmos, and what was the true written tradition, created a dynamic struggle to produce intellectual/cultural products to promote the legitimacy of established or challenging specialists and their consumers. In this social space and game, religion is contested, not given. There must always be defenders of the current form of the dominant intellectual tradition and challengers. Greek philosophies once challenged traditional *paideia* and then became part of the dominant legitimized tradition. Dominant Greek *paideia* was challenged, especially in many local arenas, by claims that Greek wisdom derived from more ancient cultures. "Why not go to the original sources," the challenging specialists said. Greek and Roman traditions kept reinventing themselves and facing new challengers. But none of this meant that those outside these games felt that the givenness of their gods, temples, and practices was normally a matter of debate.

At the same time, it would be a mistake to imagine a hard impermeable boundary between the specialized writing and interpretation of the field and normal local culture outside the field. Indeed, if one avoids a more structuralist-like view of cultural or religious types seen as logical wholes, and introduces temporality, a typical process of domestication can come into view. The odd specialized productions of the field often become domesticated to culture outside the field. So, for instance, a generation of French people who found the paintings of the Impressionists shocking and incomprehensible was followed by another that viewed them as challenging and appealing.[28] In typical fashion the field moved on far ahead of the general population. The Impressionists became orthodox and a succession of rebelling movements arose such as Cubists, Dadaists, and Surrealists. Of course, most farmers and workers, for instance, may never have found the

---

27. I owe the sociological conceptions of *doxa*, orthodoxy, and heresy to many works by Bourdieu. One more recent synthesis by Bourdieu is *The Field of Cultural Production: Essays on Art and Literature* (ed. Randal Johnson; European Perspectives; New York: Columbia University Press, 1993), although his first two books on practice contain greater consideration of premodern cultures.

28. See Pierre Bourdieu, *The Rules of Art: Genesis and Structure of the Literary Field* (trans. Susan Emanuel; Cambridge: Polity, 1996).

products of some of these field movements comprehensible, but some did and it was always possible for individuals to be "educated" into the taste for such products by entrepreneurs of art in the field.

A field is a social space that floats free of certain kinds of place, the reference to fixed objects and locations in the world made meaningful by human imagination. A family shrine has a context conditioned by its fixed site, but a text circulates without the context of its creation, although it must have a context of certain practices embodied as skills (e.g., reading) in order to be and remain a text. One does not have to be in any particular place to read or write a book or to debate an idea. Once written, a text might go anywhere and does not need to have an author attached to it. Literates different from and far away from the time and place of a text's writing can modify it. As with markets, intellectual/cultural products circulate and have effects within fields that are mostly unseen by their producers and modifiers. Because producers in fields compete over the true, the good, and the beautiful and because the field cuts across particular places, the products tend toward universalizing knowledge and rhetoric.[29]

Where does Paul fit? His work was to find Greeks, Romans, and other non-Jews whom he could convince that their religious and moral practices were utterly false and evil. The only true and living god was the God of the ancient Jewish writings that recounted the world's nature and beginnings, and the history and fates of all the world's peoples. Christ was a being possessed of God's own *pneuma* and all humans could possess a share of this divine stuff that God had given to Christ. Paul was certainly not a sophist legitimated in the dominant fraction of the field (as some have supposed), but belonged to one of the aspiring, competing illegitimate fractions that were every bit as necessary to the existence of the field as a field of cultural-production-as-contestation.[30]

By way of illustrating one kind of specialist, an instance of whom we know a good deal is Lucian of Samosata, a Syrian whose first language was probably Syriac rather than Greek. He came from a family of stone carvers and yet he describes how *paideia* lifted him into the elite dominant field known via Philostratus as the

---

29. On this tendancy toward universalizing and systematizing, see Andrew Wallace-Hadrill, "*Mutatio morum*: The Idea of a Cultural Revolution," in *The Roman Cultural Revolution* (ed. Thomas Habinek and Alessandro Schiesaro; Cambridge: Cambridge University Press, 1997), 3–22.

30. Thus I find fantastic Bruce W. Winter's attempt to make Paul into a sophist (cf. many recent discussions of 1 Cor 1:18–2:13) in *Philo and Paul among the Sophists: Alexandrian and Corinthian Responses to a Julio-Claudian Movement* (2nd ed.; Grand Rapids: Eerdmans, 2002). For suggestions about locating Paul's rhetoric and education, see Stanley K. Stowers, "Apostrophe, ΠΡΟΣΩΠΟΠΟΙΙΑ and Paul's Rhetorical Education," in *Early Christianity and Classical Culture: Comparative Studies in Honor of Abraham J. Malherbe* (ed. John T. Fitzgerald et al.; NovTSup 110; Leiden: Brill, 2003), 359–61. On how Paul's thought and practice place him in the "unorthodox" sociological fraction originally staked out by philosophy, see idem, "Does Pauline Christianity Resemble a Hellenistic Philosophy?" (in this volume); and in terms of social description, see idem, "Social Status, Public Speaking, and Private Teaching: The Circumstances of Paul's Preaching Activity," *NovT* 26 (1984): 59–82.

Second Sophistic. Even though this was an archaizing movement of Greek linguistic and literary purity, Lucian suggests the potential power of dominated fields by writing about the Syrian goddess of his homeland and, in several writings, by constructing his authorial persona as that of the marginal disinterested educated barbarian who, as an outsider, can critique other specialist producers of cultural products.[31] In his writings, one encounters every sort of cultural specialist, for example, sophists, philosophers, astrologers, prophets, and experts in foreign books, whom Lucian skewers as would-be competitors in the field of *paideia*. One vivid portrait of the specialist consumer's desire for the status brought by *paideia* appears in the aspiring target of *The Ignorant Book-Collector*, another in the form of well-to-do householders who take in cultural specialists of various sorts to bring the status of learning to their homes (e.g., *On Salaried Posts in Great Houses*). It seems to me that even the arrival of Christian missionaries in New Guinea did not create a comparable cultural field.

I also see another relevant difference between the situation of Christianity among the Atbalmin and Paul's coming to the Corinthians. Christian missionaries and teachers in New Guinea, even when they were natives bringing domesticated forms of the religion, carried the background authority of an enormously powerful imperial culture from the West that exerted both attraction and repulsion. Paul, the Diaspora Judean, carried no such background authority. The Corinthian reception of Paul needs explanation.

Although discussing the most important data for the thesis that I have been developing is far beyond the scope of this article, I can express the thesis theoretically. To explain Paul's recognition by, and attraction of, some Corinthians, one needs three elements. The first condition is a field or, perhaps, a set of overlapping fields of knowledges and intellectual practices in which specialists employed their skills to compete and "debate" in the production and interpretation of oral and written texts and discourses that contest the truth and legitimacy of both traditions and novel doctrines. These practices aimed at a niche of consumers who found social distinction in acquiring such *paideia*. Second, one needs to suppose a number of people among the Corinthians who desired an alternative *paideia*. This desire for an alternative esoteric and exotic *paideia* may have had a basis in their minority or mixed ethnic statuses or other status inconsistencies that both alienated them from the dominant legitimate *paideia* and attracted them to an alternative.[32] Beyond this, we know that certain people now and then have been

---

31. Recent opinion favors Lucian's authorship of *The Syrian Goddess*. See C. P. Jones, *Culture and Society in Lucian* (Cambridge, Mass.: Harvard University Press, 1986), 41. For Lucian claiming his barbarian identity, see especially *The Double Indictment*, *The Dream*, and *The Dead Come to Life*.

32. On evidence for many of Paul's "people" being freedmen, see Stanley K. Stowers, *A Rereading of Romans: Justice, Jews, and Gentiles* (New Haven: Yale University Press, 1994), 74–82; Wayne A. Meeks, *The First Urban Christians: The Social World of the Apostle Paul* (New Haven: Yale University Press, 1983), 55–63.

attracted to the esoteric and the exotic because attachment to the different can involve social distinction in the eyes of the adherents and others. Such adherence can also express a person's broader social and cultural sympathies, a kind of "cosmopolitan" outlook beyond one's local and inherited culture. Lucian's ambition to leave stone carving in order to gain fame and see the larger world illustrates this motivation. Third, one must view Paul as a producer and distributor of an alternative esoteric *paideia* different from the dominant sophistic or philosophical kinds, yet still recognizable as a form of the same broader game of specialized literate learning. With these assumptions, it makes sense that some Corinthians would have shared interests with Paul, recognized him as a person with a certain kind of legitimacy, and found an attraction to some of his performances. It remains to show how Paul's mythmaking and other practices might make sense to such people.

If a minority among "Paul's Corinthians" shared various degrees of this attraction to the "intruder," there is every reason to believe that the attraction was not easily shared by the majority. Those who did not aspire to such *paideia* and did not see it as a feature of their roles, statuses, and aspirations would have had interests focused on the religion of household and family. They would likely have understood Paul on their own terms and have exhibited both repulsion and attraction at points related to their strategic concerns. So, for instance, if those who were attracted found interesting Paul's cosmic *pneuma* doctrines and teachings about the nature of the gods and the one true God, and the myth of a heroic martyr who created a mode of access to the most powerful and sublime kind of *pneuma* and to a renowned ancestry, the majority may have reacted differently. As Smith suggests, they may have seen in Paul's talk of ancestors and baptism a pneumatic link to ancestors, an opportunity to experiment with a technique for interacting with their own significant dead.[33] Baptism for the dead may have been seen as a way to improve the status of the recent or untimely dead, a well-documented concern of families.[34] Further, Smith is right that experimentation with ritual must have involved the Corinthians in their own mythmaking, both among those who did not aspire to be specialized consumers of Paul's cultural production and the attracted.

Who were these people attracted to Paul's myths, pneumatic doctrines and performances, and moral-psychological teachings? It has been a temptation of recent scholarship to make Paul into a champion of the underclasses and a critic of the elite. This preaches well, but goes against all of the evidence that Paul was a person of his age and cultures. Likewise, it might be tempting to make Paul

---

33. Smith, "Re: Corinthians," 30–34.

34. There is much evidence for such private concerns, and the public festivals of the Greek Anthesteria and the Roman Parentalia and Lemuria concerned relations between the living and the dead, and bore on the status of the dead. See especially Sarah Iles Johnston, *Restless Dead: Encounters between the Living and the Dead in Ancient Greece* (Berkeley: University of California Press, 1999).

simply a mentor and client of the elite. We do indeed have evidence for this that is more than the rhetoric of Christlike weakness and suffering and moral weakness to which the proponents of Paul-as-liberal-emancipator appeal. The letters name some of these people and provide valuable information about their activities with the "intruder." Paul admits that the Corinthians understood their baptisms in different ways leading to a lack of unity and is glad that he baptized only Gaius, Crispus, and the household of Stephanas (1 Cor 1:10–16). But the choice of these people for baptism by Paul does not appear to be arbitrary (in spite of 1:17), because these are precisely those who are noted as sharers in Paul's specialist activities. At the end of the letter one reads:

> Brothers, you know that the household of Stephanas is the first fruit of Achaia and they have organized themselves for the service of those who are holy. I beg you to subject yourselves to such people and to all those who work and labor with them. I rejoice at the coming of Stephanas and Fortunatus and Achaicus because they have made up for what you haven't done (or: your failings); for they have refreshed both my *pneuma* and yours. Give recognition to such kind of people. (1 Cor 16:15–18, my trans.)

First, Stephanas and his peers and companions whom Paul describes as "such kind of people" (τοιούτους) are participants in Paul's teaching and organizing activities. Second, this gives them a kind of capital and legitimacy in Paul's view so that the Corinthians who are not distinguished in this way ought to be under their authority. Third, Paul compares the valorized specialized activities of these people to the lack of valorized participation on the part of the rest of the Corinthians. When Paul later wrote Romans from Corinth, he sent greetings from one of the other named three that he baptized, Gaius (Rom 16:23). Gaius is Paul's host and host to the whole assembly. Paul also mentions an *oikonomos* of the city who from contemporary evidence is probably something like a city treasurer. Gaius is certainly an elite with a house large enough to host all of Paul's Corinthians and to provide extended hospitality to Paul. Some of these men are heads of households and in that sense elites. Only they could open the door to Paul. There would have been no "Paul and the Corinthians" without these people and their recognition of him and their attraction to his productions.

The basis of this attraction should be clear in the extensive evidence to which I have alluded that elites at various levels often, but certainly not always, strove for the distinction of learning and culture. Dare I cite Petronius's proverbial Trimalchio, the wealthy freedman who invites cultural specialists into his house in order to pose as interested in the distinction of *paideia*? As outrageous as it might first seem to compare Paul's situation to the world of Petronius, there are some important analogies relevant to the issue at hand in this work that was written about the time that Paul composed his letter to the Romans. Certainly Paul employs his ethnicity in a way different from the characters in the *Satyricon*, and the content of his learning is of a different tradition, a dominated wisdom of a people, and not the dominant legitimized *paideia*. Paul also wants to organize people socially in a way that is rather distinctive.[35] But regarding fields of specialized cultural producers and consumers and the attraction of the latter to the former, the analogy is helpful.

According to the influential interpretation of Gian Biagio Conte, the *Satyricon* is a parodic comic novel about *scholastici*, a word for which there is no English equivalent or near equivalent.[36] The word is a term for the primarily amateur devotees of Greek and Latin literature, learning, and oratory.[37] The hero or rather anti-hero Encolpius seems to be some sort of itinerant lecturer. The fragmentary nature of the novel means that we have lost some information about him. His companion, Agamemnon, heads a rhetorical school for older boys and has an assistant, Menelaus. Eumolpus is a poet and poses as a moralist so as to be invited into a prosperous house in Pergamum as a kind of teacher-advisor that the text compares to an old-fashioned philosopher (*Satyr.* 85). Encolpius meets Agamemnon outside of a hall where *scholastici* have been delivering speeches and launches into a learned tirade against the way declamation is taught and practiced and about the general decline of speaking (*Satyr.* 1–2). *Scholastici* were people who took themselves and their enterprise very seriously. This is why Petronius is able so effectively to satirize and parody them. At their meeting, Agamemnon improvises lofty words in Lucilian style—not the style of the Septuagint—about the calling of *scholastici*:

Ambition to fulfil the austere demands of Art,
The mind moving to mighty themes,
Demands discipline, simplicity—
The heart like a mirror.
Disdain the haughty seats of the mighty,
Humiliating invitations to drunken dinners,
The addictions, the low pleasures.... (*Satyr.* 5)[38]

Here he expresses the field ideals of autonomy. The true intellectual does not produce for a patron, or for money, or to please the powerful, but for the sake of truth

---

35. One difference that should not be claimed is that Paul's letters are religious while the *Satyricon* is supposedly secular. Not only are the gods and religious practices prominent in the latter, but the anti-hero's relation to the god Priapus is central to the plot. A genuine and central difference would stress that humor and satire involving the divine are inconceivable in Paul's tradition. Moreover, the Judean God relates to human desires, aspirations, and emotions in a way quite different from Greek and Roman deities.

36. Gian Biagio Conte, *The Hidden Author: An Interpretation of Petronius' Satyricon* (trans. Elaine Fantham; Sather Classical Lectures 60; Berkeley: University of California Press, 1996).

37. George Kennedy, "Encolpius and Agamemnon in Petronius," *AJP* 99 (1978): 171–78.

38. The trans. is by J. P. Sullivan, *Petronius, The Satyricon and Seneca, The Apocolocyntosis* (rev. ed.; Penguin Classics; New York: Penguin, 1986).

or beauty or god. It is precisely these moral and intellectual ideals that the novel subverts as it makes the "heroes" exact opposites of the ideal.

Edward Courtney persuasively argues that the *Satyricon* is overall about educated freedmen and slaves.[39] He shows that Encolpius, Giton, Ascyltos, Agamemnon, Menelaus, and Eumolpus are highly educated former slaves. The *Satyricon* trades on a social phenomenon that is important for understanding Paul and his reception by certain kinds of people. Only a small percentage of people in the empire were truly literate, but slaves were disproportionately represented among the educated.[40] A literate slave was very valuable to a master, and owners often educated them just to increase their value. Because Roman education developed under the influence of Greek education and by the first century C.E. most aristocratic and prosperous families wanted their sons to be educated bilingually, Greek-speaking urban slaves were considered ideal tutors and teachers. Slaves and freedmen, then, in some sense, dominated most areas of learning, but they faced a glass ceiling that kept them from the ranks of the aristocratic dominant culture of people like Virgil, Pliny, and Aelius Aristides. Courtney shows that Petronius is enforcing this glass ceiling. Even though his freedmen characters have a higher education, instead of possessing the virtue and noble character that such education was supposed to bring, they are utterly debased and out of control. They can create poetry, interpret their experience by myths and epics, and produce learned speeches, but Petronius makes these skills opportunities to show that theirs is a pathetic parody of true culture. Courtney also shows that Encolpius and Ascyltos, who are said to make their livings by their educations, are not *scholastici*, but only mistaken for such by being in the company of Agamemnon. Unfortunately, just what cultural specialty characterized their itinerant lives is lost to the fragmentary nature of the text. Looking past Petronius's aristocratic slur of these characters, they represent the most successful of freedmen who aspired to *paideia*. We must imagine many more who never had their own school or were able to make livings through *paideia*, yet possessed it in various forms and degrees.

Good reasons exist, then, for thinking that among freedmen there would be people alienated from the dominant culture who would be attracted to an alternative wisdom and the autonomous pole of the cultural field. One option that

---

39. Edward Courtney, *A Companion to Petronius* (Oxford: Oxford University Press, 2001).

40. Stanley F. Bonner, *Education in Ancient Rome: From the Elder Cato to the Younger Pliny* (Berkeley: University of California Press, 1977), 65–75; Courtney, *Companion to Petronius*, 41. Johannes Christes studied forty-one slaves and freedmen who became famous enough to be remembered in the sources and who bore the titles of either *grammaticus* or *philologus*. See his *Sklaven und Freigelassene als Grammatiker und Philologen im Antiken Rom* (Forschungen zur Antiken Sklaverei 10; Wiesbaden: Steiner, 1979). Ethnic origins should be added to this mix of the cultural aspirations and anxieties that would have characterized many freedmen. One of the constant liabilities of freedmen in the view of Greeks and Romans of good pedigree was genealogical uncertainty. I cannot treat this relevant issue here, but it is instructive that a large proportion of Christes's examples originally came from the Greek East.

illustrates the attraction of the "autonomous cultural pole" and seems to have been followed by growing numbers during the early empire was the life of Cynic philosophy. Lucian, from his perspective of the elite dominant *paideia*, spends many pages depicting such people as charlatans who were inevitably runaway slaves, base freedmen, and, like Paul, of the despised artisan class. If such people got no respect, there is much evidence to think that they often tried for respectability. Trimalchio, of course, is the cliché. He owns a huge twin Latin and Greek library, but cannot read (*Satyr.* 48.4). He invites *scholastici* to his house who turn out to be also of slavish character. Both Trimalchio and Ascyltos pose as members of the equestrian class by wearing gold rings. When one of Trimalchio's freedmen friends finds offense at Ascyltos's pretensions, he says, "You're a Roman knight, are you? Well, my father was a king" (*Satyr.* 57.4). Courtney thinks that the reason so many slaves in this era were mockingly named Malchio, "little king," is that slaves and freedmen (and freedwomen?) had become proverbial for their obsession with ancestry.[41] So either posing as of a higher rank or claiming to have been enslaved though from some noble line was common enough that Petronius could make casual jokes about it. Such freedmen, freedwomen, and slaves would surely have heard Paul's gospel of ancient wisdom, the *pneuma* of God, and Abraham's lineage "in Christ" in a different way than we moderns understand it.

It would be a mistake, however, to think that only elites—in the special sense that I have been using the term—might want to be consumers of Paul's learning and performances. A definitional feature of cultural fields is their semiautonomy from the economy and outside order of sociality and power. They constitute a game that has its own distinctive order of power, of social and symbolic capital, through the skills, productions, and prestige of its practices. Thus, being a head of household might allow one to give hospitality and patronage to a specialist, but that status alone did not confer an aptitude for skillful learning and literate practices. The elite certainly had advantages such as leisure for cultural activity, but anyone who could master the skills and learning could gain the capital that gave one power and place in the game. Admittedly, non-elites who made it into the cultural field usually had the advantage of a relatively prosperous household. In addition to the examples suggested above, one famous example is Epictetus, the slave who became the head of his own philosophical school.

It may be significant that Paul singles out not just Stephanas, the lord of a household, in order to praise him for his participation in activities that Paul promotes, but also praises his household for such activities. They have done what the rest of the Corinthians have not (1 Cor 16:17). Stephanas's household has organized itself (ἔταξαν ἑαυτούς) for serving those who are holy (16:15). They are fellow workers and laborers (16:16), terms that Paul uses for assistants in his specialist activities. Stephanas's companions, Fortunatus and Achaichus, may have

---

41. Courtney, *Companion to Petronius*, 52.

been relatives, freedmen of Stephanas, or trusted slaves. It is easy to imagine a slave whose literacy had been encouraged in order to facilitate management of the household and family business having the ambition to become learned in Paul's wisdom and pneumatic practices. Except for Stephanas's people and some household heads whom Paul singles out, then, he can generalize about the other Corinthians so as to imply by contrast his disappointment in the way that they have received and participated in his practices. I see no reason to posit some uniform ideology or reason for their resistance beyond attachment to their own interests and practices, and certainly not the corrupting outside heresy such as a fantastic "Gnosticism," or "pneumatic enthusiasm," or "realized eschatology" imagined in academic theological modernism.

Thus, I want to insist that, instead of a simple model of myth and community, one imagine the groups as socially and culturally differentiated. All of the Corinthians may have shared a similar *doxa* to a point, but the elites and the non-elites had some different interests, and some of the elites and others strove to be participant consumers in the field, or overlapping fields, of specialized knowledge that might make them cultured.[42] Unlike in New Guinea, specialized book-learning and literary-rhetorical production were an important means for distinguishing a whole class of elites from the masses and for fostering competition for honor among elites. In his letters, Paul almost certainly intellectualized issues for the sake of attracting such people. So, for example, what might have been quite mundane interests in the extended family of ancestors and the dead for the non-elites were addressed by Paul with the culturally ambitious in view as an opportunity to expound on human nature and the science of the cosmos through the Christ-*pneuma* myth in 1 Cor 15. Paul treats issues among the Corinthians about the pros and cons of competing teachers (1:10–16) with a long discussion about the nature of divine and human wisdom. Many of the passages that the Christian church has cherished as theological are less anachronistically described as Paul appealing to the interests of aspirants to *paideia* by "showing his stuff" in intellectualizing issues that were "practical" and strategic for most of the Corinthians.[43] The letter treats issues about prostitutes, marriage, and sacrificial meat that might have been quite local and mundane for most Corinthians as issues about moral freedom and correct worship of the truly conceived deity.

Some recent scholarship argues that Paul's teachings about *pneuma* and about Christ as the link to the lineage of Abraham have not been fully understood in

---

42. The fact that these Corinthian elites were attracted to Paul's Jewish and esoteric *paideia* may have meant that they felt alienated from the mainstream legitimate Greek *paideia* or saw the alternative *paideia* as an opportunity for some distinction in the face of extreme difficulty in getting into the legitimated club.

43. My claims here have been informed by the Brown University dissertation in progress of Dana Chyung on knowledge and knowledge practices in Paul's letters.

scholarship and their centrality to his gospel not recognized.[44] These are also the themes, as we have seen, that in different ways most likely attracted the interest of the people Paul tried to make his audience. I will provide some comments about my understanding of these narratives in a list of components of Paul's mythmaking. The central vehicle for much of his mythmaking is Paul's interpretation of Judean Scripture. His access to books, ability to read and write proficiently, and exegetical practices gave him intellectual skills that few, if any, of the Corinthians were likely to have had. What follows is based on my own work and on an important study by Caroline Johnson Hodge.[45] The components of the myth that Paul formed from Scripture and other sources are fairly clear, but the order and relationship of the components are more difficult and the following could be arranged in a number of ways with emphases in different places:

- Ancient prophecy said that a descendant of Abraham, ancestor of the lineage chosen by the true God of the cosmos, a righteous forebear out of a world of sinful nations, would bring a great blessing to the other peoples someday.
- It was part of the plan of this God that Paul would be appointed to teach the non-Jewish peoples about this promise and its fulfillment.
- This blessing makes non-Judeans into descendants of Abraham by means of their penetration by the divine *pneuma* that God used to refashion Jesus Christ when he raised him from the dead. Divine *pneuma* interacts with ordinary human *pneuma*, but is a vital substance of a vastly superior quality, the highest of all substances in the cosmos.
- Christ is thus the *pneuma*-bearer whose heroic martyrdom became an occasion for God to reconcile the world's peoples to himself and to perfect the human species.
- Since Christ was "in Abraham" as seed and Gentile believers through baptism gain a material connection to Christ, having a part of his *pneuma* (or: participating in his *pneuma*), they have a material contiguity with Abraham back through the lineage of Christ just like any descendant.
- At the end of the current phase ordained for the cosmos, divine *pneuma* will entirely replace flesh (*sarx*) and blood in the constitution of the human

---

44. See Stanley K. Stowers, "What Is 'Pauline Participation in Christ'?" in *Redefining First-Century Jewish and Christian Identities: Essays in Honor of Ed Parish Sanders* (ed. Fabian E. Udoh et al.; Christianity and Judaism in Antiquity 16; Notre Dame: Notre Dame University Press, 2008), 352–71; and especially Caroline Johnson Hodge, *If Sons, Then Heirs: A Study of Kinship and Ethnicity in the Letters of Paul* (New York: Oxford University Press, 2007), who has much bibliography on this point. See further Pamela Eisenbaum, "Paul as the New Abraham," in *Paul and Politics: Ekklesia, Israel, Imperium, Interpretation. Essays in Honor of Krister Stendahl* (ed. Richard A. Horsley; Harrisburg, Pa.: Trinity Press International, 2000), 130–45; eadem, "A Remedy for Having Been Born of Woman: Jesus, Gentiles, and Genealogy in Romans," *JBL* 123 (2004): 671–702.

45. Johnson Hodge, *If Sons, Then Heirs*.

person. Until then, divine *pneuma* only mixes or communicates with human *pneuma*, but gives special powers to such people who are to understand that their true selves are pneumatic and not of flesh.

Someone might reasonably object that there is nothing about Abraham and Gentiles becoming a lineage of Abraham in the Corinthian letters. One must go to other letters for these. This is true, but evidence does exist to show that Paul presupposes the myth and speaks as if the Corinthians know it. First, it is necessary to establish that Paul thinks of the Corinthians to whom he writes as Gentiles. As the seminar has encountered time after time, on this issue as with so many others, scholarship has subordinated the evidence from Paul's letters to the stories in Acts. It is difficult to ignore 1 Cor 12:1–2, however: "Now concerning pneumatic things, brothers, I do not want you to be ignorant. You know that when you were Gentiles [*ethnē*], you were taken and led away by speechless idols." If Paul were writing according to scholarly consensus that follows Acts and dogmatic definitions of the nature of "the church" or "Christianity," he would have written, "Now brothers and sisters, to the portion of the congregation that converted from a Gentile background, I want to say...." The language of 1 Cor 5:1 presupposes the same assumption that the Corinthians are people who used to be Gentiles—of a non-Jewish ethnicity as seen from the perspective of Jews.

But what are they now? The evidence of the letters, I have argued, overwhelmingly militates against Paul having the idea of Christianity as a distinct religion, neither Judean or Gentile.[46] Rather, Paul thinks of Gentiles who are "in Christ" as a new, but distinct, line grafted into the lineage of Abraham, Isaac, and Jacob. Thus, one reads in 1 Cor 10:1–3, as Paul interprets the exodus legends, "I do not want you to be ignorant, brothers, that our fathers were all under the cloud, and all went through the sea, and all were baptized into Moses in the cloud and in the sea, and all ate the same pneumatic food, and all drank the same pneumatic drink." There are many interpretive challenges here, including the assumption that the Israelites were already in some way given the divine *pneuma*.[47] The relevant point for the present argument is that Paul speaks of the Corinthians as former Gentiles who are now descendants of the Israelite patriarchs, but not Jews.

Johnson Hodge has shown that Paul employs a way of thinking well known to the Greco-Roman world: ethnic mythmaking that employs an aggregative strategy.[48] No one thought that contemporary Romans and Greeks constituted the same social, political, or religious entities, but a myth made them related by an ancient

---

46. Stowers, *Rereading of Romans*, 23–25, 133, and passim.
47. In my view, the church in creating itself reversed Paul's story. Israel is not a prototype, a prophetic shadow of the real thing, the church. Rather, the same active powers of God's *pneuma* and the *pneuma*-bearing seed, Christ, go back to the beginning of the chosen lineages and one major latter-day result is the incorporation of Gentile lines into the larger family tree.
48. Johnson Hodge, *If Sons, Then Heirs*.

ancestor.[49] They were distinct, but related in ways thought to give them important privileges and commonalities, including supposedly the same gods and sacrificial practices. Paul is engaged in a complex and highly negotiable practice of making distinctions by ethnic-religious mythmaking. In his rhetoric, the Corinthians are not Gentiles, but were Gentiles who are importantly different from Gentiles and who are now related to Jews, but are importantly different from them. As Smith writes in another essay, especially reflecting on the kinship system of the Hua people, "Meaning is made possible by difference. Yet thought seeks to bring together what thought necessarily takes apart by means of a dynamic process of disassemblage and reassemblage, which results in an object no longer natural but rather social, no longer factual but rather intellectual. Relations are discovered and reconstituted through projects of differentiation."[50] The appropriation of Paul's discourse under the category of theology makes Paul's writing utterly new, *sui generis*, and therefore unique. But the category of mythmaking renders it an ordinary human activity familiar to discourses that refer to gods, ancestors, and other non-obvious beings from cultures all over the world and across history. Moreover, it is a form of speaking-writing-thinking that implicates itself in familiar human ways of making social distinctions involved in social formation and power.

One other point: in both 1 Cor 10:1 and 12:1, Paul employs the expression "brothers, I do not want you to be ignorant." In the latter, this is followed by "*you know* that when you were Gentiles . . . " (12:2). "I do not want you to be ignorant" is the voice of the specialist in esoteric knowledge giving an authoritative interpretation of a discourse or story that the readers or, in reality, some of the readers—the class of those distinguished by consuming such knowledge—know, but "need" interpreted. At least in Paul's rhetoric, the Corinthians know that they are now descendants of Abraham through *pneuma*, by participating in Christ. As I will show, participation in Christ is presupposed by Paul's discussion of the Lord's supper and talk of the social body and the body of Christ.

A further clue to Corinthian interests might be found in their practice of baptism for the dead (1 Cor 15:29). Paul brought baptism to them, but they made their own uses of it, as Smith argues.[51] Paul taught them that they could share in the *pneuma* of the *pneuma*-bringer, Christ, and that the divine *pneuma* would connect them to the renowned ancient ancestor, Abraham. They saw another ritual means for improving the lot of their more immediate ancestors. Baptism for the dead would incorporate those dead into the distinguished lineage and ancestry. Without baptism for the dead, their own baptisms might cut them off from their extended families of the significant dead. This scenario makes sense, if the Corinthians or some of them were people concerned about their own ambiguous and

---

49. Ibid.; see also Stowers, *Rereading of Romans*.
50. Jonathan Z. Smith, "Differential Equations: On Constructing the Other," in idem, *Relating Religion*, 246.
51. Smith, "Re: Corinthians," 29–34.

ignoble ancestry, a point to which Paul alludes politely in 1:26 ("not many of you are of good ancestry"). Smith points out that the resettlement of Corinth in 44 B.C.E. involved importing large numbers of freed slaves from Greece, Syria, Judea, and Egypt.[52] Such people would not only have had the stain of slave origins, but would also have been cut off from ancestral burial grounds.[53]

Imagining Paul and the Corinthians with the aid of Smith's comparison and also with the insistence on the differentiation of interests, recognition, and attraction leads to imagining plausible religiously contextualized interactions. It allows reading the letters from non-Pauline perspectives. Yet that sort of reading provides a richer and more historically plausible sense of what Paul was about and up against because it casts both Paul and the Corinthians in terms of interests, practices, and discourses from their time, instead of in terms of later and contemporary church interests. The Corinthians reacted in different ways to Paul's mythmaking and ritual practice, partly with their own mythmaking and ritual experimentation. Much more could be said about such things as "speaking in tongues," but by way of an example I will focus on the fact that Paul spends much of 1 Cor 8–11 worrying about Corinthian eating practices, his own meal practices, and sacrificial meals. Can we also tease out likely Corinthian responses to Paul's discourse and practices regarding meals and especially what he calls "the Lord's supper"? In what follows, I will attempt an approach toward that end first by analyzing the senses of the practice and then by telling a "just so story" about the strategically differentiated reactions (e.g., interested recognitions, appropriations, resistances, and accommodations) of the Corinthians.

Much scholarly interpretation of the Corinthian letters naturalizes the specialized intellectual interests and intellectual practices concerned with contesting truths, traditions, and practices of the Corinthians rather than demonstrating them, and makes theological ideas the significant essence of the activity imagined of Paul's addressees. At the same time, interpreters misrecognize and vastly underappreciate the power of Paul as a specialist in intellectual practices. An antidote to these approaches begins with imagining the religious interests of the Corinthians as intelligible in a vast web of practices that made up a whole way of life and doing the same for Paul. The second aspect of the approach is to imagine the logic of the practices that were important to these people and to think of their beliefs, ideas, and texts as embedded within these ongoing activities. Talking of practice provides a way of thinking about the social that avoids the individual/social and

---

52. Ibid., 29.
53. I think it only marginally possible that the descendants of these settlers had resisted assimilation and maintained ancestral burial practices for several generations. Indeed, the settlers may already have been partly hellenized in their homelands. The most likely scenario is that the descendants became assimilated to the dominant Greek culture of the region and the gradually increasing patina of Romanization.

thought/action dualisms that have caused so much mischief in our intellectual history.[54]

Most of human life unfolds in kinds of activities based on practical skills that the individual did not invent. As such, practices are the primary unit that a culture or society reproduces over time.[55] On this view, a society or culture is not greater than the sum of its parts. It is rather a large number of practices and practical skills assembled and linked in characteristic ways that actors pass down from generation to generation. Thus, I want to focus on practices rather than beliefs, texts, structures, symbols, or particular actions and events. I say *focus* because beliefs, texts, actions, and events will not disappear from the account. They are components of practices.

Eating a meal is a practice. Mythmaking and numerous other kinds of activities in which agents produce discourses are practices. In taking this perspective on a culture, it becomes clear that the wills of individuals do not control practices, nor are the supposed instruments of minds such as symbols, beliefs, intentions, texts, myths, and theories the meaning or basis of practices. What is the meaning of dinner or of lunch? You would not persuade me if you said that *the* meaning of dinner for participants, the essence to which it reduces, was a determinate set of beliefs, or a foundational myth, or meeting needs for nutrition or fellowship, although all of these might be involved. Practices are so complex that participants are never aware of all the implications, consequences, possible meanings, or effects of their activity in a practice. To take the practice perspective is to become aware of the high degree of indeterminacy both in the participants' own interpretations of their activities, and in the interpretations of participants' activities and interpretations by scholars. But such actors have great intuitive knowledge. They know how to participate, how to play the game. Such practical skill can be the object of analysis and historical imagination.

I will begin the task of locating the Lord's supper as represented by Paul within the range and relation of practices in the cultures in question. To what other practices were meals and mythmaking practices near, distant, comparable to, and differentiated from at that time? How was mythmaking deployed in relation to and as a part of other practices? This move helps the historian to avoid one of the illusions created by focusing on the beliefs, symbols, and texts of particular groups, or on narratives of events. The illusion natural to focusing on these is the essential or nonreciprocal uniqueness of the community in question. If the meaning of the Lord's supper is the words of "institution" that Paul and the Gospels provide, then it might easily seem incomparable. Those words should be situated first of all in

---

54. For a discussion of the thought/action dualism, see Catherine Bell, *Ritual Theory, Ritual Practice* (New York: Oxford University Press, 1992); and for scholarship on practice, see Theodore R. Schatzki et al., *The Practice Turn in Contemporary Theory* (London and New York: Routledge, 2001).

55. For the concept of practices and its role in recent social theory, see Stowers, "Pauline Scholarship and the Third Way in Social Theory"; and nn. 4, 6, and 27 above.

writing practices, not in eating practices. But if I do imagine Paul's writing as representing an eating practice, then I immediately notice that it shares central and numerous similarities with practices common to cultures throughout the Mediterranean. Any person from that world would immediately recognize it as a type of eating practice and already possess many of the skills necessary to participate, even if he or she found a particular intellectual/cultural specialist's interpretation of it implausible, uninteresting, or confusing.

Paul's discussion of the Lord's supper, then, can be seen as one interpretation of a broader practice. But the practice belonged to the culture and was not under his control, as various people participated in that activity employing practical skills that may have involved a huge variety of social abilities, bodily skills, beliefs, symbols, and strategic interests. The key to the question of why the Corinthians gave some recognition to who Paul was, and what he did, and why they had some interests in him, is not that his message of a crucified Christ and the power of Christ's *pneuma* met a universal intrinsic need or was inherently intelligible or attractive.[56] Rather, the Corinthians possessed fine-grained practical understandings, skill intelligibility, if you will, of most of the practices that Paul advocated, albeit differentiated in various ways, for example, by age, gender, free/slave, elite/non-elite. They therefore already had practical dispositions toward the genres of Paul's doings and sayings, but not necessarily toward his particular interpretations of these practices.

The Lord's supper is a meal, one form of people eating together in the Greek East of the early Roman Empire. A meal has much of its potential for meaning to participants and observers simply because it is recognizable within the logical possibilities of eating socially in that culture. The meal practices of that culture existed many centuries before Paul was born and continued long after he was dead. However he might have used, interpreted, and modified the meal practices, they were not his or "the church's" invention; nor did his or "the church's" will control such cultural formations with their "enormous amount of inertia."[57] The question, then, is what sort of eating practices would ancient participants and observers have been likely to compare and contrast with the Lord's supper in order to make sense of it, if they were to reflect on their implicit and instinctive knowledge of it as a practice? Three types of meals seem absolutely basic for locating the possible "meanings" of the Lord's supper: (1) the common meal at home;

---

56. I do not wish to deny that there are structures in the human brain that should bear in important ways on our understanding of human religiosity and that provide a certain kind of fallibilistic scientific conception of a human nature. Much important, but very young work is being done along these lines in evolutionary biology, cognitive science, and related fields. See, e.g., Scott Atran, *In Gods We Trust: The Evolutionary Landscape of Religion* (Evolution and Cognition; Oxford: Oxford University Press, 2002).

57. Hilary Putnam, *Renewing Philosophy* (Cambridge, Mass.: Harvard University Press, 1992), 73.

(2) meals involving animal sacrifice; and (3) memorial meals for the dead.[58] In Paul's time, one can find Greek, Jewish, and Roman versions of all three, although the Greek types were clearly dominant in the world of the Pauline groups.[59] A common idiom of meal practices and symbols transcended the particularity of ethnic practices and provided the possibility for articulating those distinctions.[60] Commonality in practice, in other words, was the condition for the endless elaboration of difference in practical meaning through ritualization or ad hoc strategic activity by individuals and groups.

The ordinary everyday meal and the meal involving the sacrifice of an animal formed the two most important poles for the meaning of meals in virtually all cultures of the ancient Mediterranean. This is not a distinction between secular and religious meals. At its center stood the differentiation of gender: women and slaves managed by women cooked bread or grain porridge at home for everyday meals; men sacrificed animals at home and at other sites for special meals, feasts.[61] The eating of meat constituted the highest form of eating in relation to the gods and involved some form of sharing of the meat with the gods. Food offerings stood in a hierarchy with meat at the top and grain and vegetable products normally below. According to the evidence of 1 Corinthians, the Lord's supper was constituted so as to distinguish itself from both an ordinary meal and a sacrificial meal, but it was markedly closer to the ordinary meal than to the sacrificial meal in featuring bread instead of meat.[62]

If the Lord's supper seems to have some ambiguous status between sacrificial meals and everyday meals, then perhaps one can clarify the way it worked as a practice by comparing it to a practice for which we have much evidence, Greek alimentary animal sacrifice. I will use a number of examples from classical Attica

---

58. I am wary about the term "meanings" because I think that the analogy that likens practices in general to written texts encoded and decoded is ultimately misleading and unhelpful.

59. For Greek and Roman examples, see Stanley K. Stowers, "Elusive Coherence: Ritual and Rhetoric in 1 Corinthians 10–11," in *Reimagining Christian Origins: A Colloquium Honoring Burton L. Mack* (ed. Elizabeth A. Castelli and Hal Taussig; Valley Forge, Pa.: Trinity Press International, 1996), 68–83. Most Jewish animal sacrifice took place in the temple, but the Passover, when celebrated outside the temple, was a domestic sacrifice. On Jewish meals for the dead, see Hans-Joseph Klauck, *Herrenmahl und hellenistischer Kult: Eine religionsgeschichtliche Untersuchung zum ersten Korintherbrief* (2nd ed.; NTAbh Neue Folge 15; Münster: Aschendorff, 1986), 86–88. For everyday Jewish meals, see idem, *Herrenmahl*, 66–67, who must be read with caution since he uses Jewish sources that are too late for his purposes.

60. Dennis E. Smith, "Social Obligation in the Context of Communal Meals: A Study of the Christian Meal in 1 Corinthians in Comparison with Greco-Roman Communal Meals" (Th.D. diss., Harvard Divinity School, 1980), 259; Kathleen E. Corley, *Private Women, Public Meals: Social Conflict in the Synoptic Tradition* (Peabody, Mass.: Hendrickson, 1993), 68–69.

61. Stowers, "Greeks Who Sacrifice and Those Who Do Not," 299–320.

62. Normally all meals had a religious element that included some kind of offering, thanksgiving, or blessing directed toward the gods. The modern distinction between religious and secular meals can be attributed to ancients only at the cost of a misleading anachronism.

because they are so rich and well documented, but every principle to which I point can also be documented in Paul's own time in the Greek East of the empire. My main points here will be analogical and not genetic. Some of the most interesting sources come from the court speeches of the Attic orators.[63] That fact is interesting in itself. Although the Athenians kept deme and other records, they (surprisingly to us moderns) do not appeal to these when arguing cases concerning identity. These cases about identity—for example, citizen status, lineage, status as heir— make up the bulk of the cases in the orators. Instead of appealing to a birth or marriage record, the orators call witnesses who were present at various events, for example, festivals, funerals, weddings, rituals of entry into *oikoi, genē, thiasoi, orgeōnes*, phratries, and demes.[64] All of these events involved *thysia*, animal sacrifice as a meal.

An example from Isaeus 8 (*Kiron*) is interesting because it explicitly draws attention to the physical contact with the meat that was crucial to the way that sacrificial rites indexed groups of people:

> We also have other proofs that we are sons from the daughter of Kiron. For as is natural since we were male children of his own daughter, he never performed any sacrifice [*thysia*] without us, but whether the sacrifices were great or small, we were always present and sacrificed with him [*synethyomen*] ... and we went to all the festivals with him. But when he sacrificed to Zeus Ktesios he was especially serious about the sacrificial rite [*thysia*], and he did not admit any slaves or free men who were not relatives [or: genuine Athenians, i.e., *othneious*] but he performed all of the sacrificial rites himself. We shared in this sacrifice and we together with him handled the sacred meat and we put offerings on the altar with him and performed the other parts of the sacrifice with him. (8.16)

Here, participation in the sacrifice constitutes membership in a certain social formation, the household (*oikos*) or family lineage (*genos*) of Kiron.[65] Zeus Ktesios is god of the household property. The speaker claims that the *kyrios*, his grandfather, was very pious about this sacrifice to one of the gods of his *oikos* and therefore allowed only his close blood relations to participate.[66] He emphasizes the close

---

63. See Stanley K. Stowers, "Truth, Identity and Sacrifice in Classical Athens" (paper presented at the Ancient History Documentary Research Centre, Macquarie University, North Ryde, New South Wales, Australia, June 1996).

64. I follow the common usage of rendering the two Greek terms as the English deme and phratry.

65. The word *genos* clearly had a number of related meanings. Here I mean the "lineage" of Kiron in a sense similar to the expression "*oikos* of so-and-so." In the orators, speakers raise the specter of their *genos* or *oikos* becoming extinct.

66. The speaker claims to be the son of Kiron's daughter, and he is fighting for the estate over against a son of Kiron's brother. The speaker is ignoring Athenian law, which gave priority to the male line, and is trying to give the impression of closer kinship.

participation in the rite, for example, touching meat with his hands, placing the meat on the altar.

The "truth" in such examples from the orators is a truth about the continuity of blood and of flesh from parent to child. This truth is determined through a particular medium, the body of a domestic animal. Like family members and citizens, such animals were members of the community and thus were duly decked out in garlands as they "willingly" gave their bodies as food for gods and men. These were animals bred by the Greeks to produce the best individuals from the best lineages. Greeks in theory sacrificed only the most perfect products of their breeding practices and put these animals through rigorous testings and scrutinies.[67] The ritualized use of the flesh and blood of animals with whom humans had a kind of kinship, precisely because they both were of flesh and blood, offered excellent ways of thinking about social relations deemed to be in some essential way based on flesh-and-blood kinship.

Sacrificial meals involved very complex types of truth practices.[68] The animal had to behave well and give the proper signs of assent before the altar or hearth. Plutarch tells of a prophetess who died when such signs from the gods were ignored (*Def. orac.* 438A-B; cf. signs in 437A-C). Next, the animal was killed, not because the meaning of sacrifice had anything to do with death or ritual violence but because it is very difficult to eat a live animal. Then came the precise division of the animal into portions that would create relations of differentiation and hierarchy among those eating dinner. The higher ranking citizen males of whatever group the dinner represented, for example, household, *genos*, phratry, tribe, deme, or hero association, would gather around the altar and roast the sacred *splanchna*—heart, liver, lungs, kidneys. Before they ate, they placed the god's portion on the altar and the feasting on the sacred *splanchna* coincided with the god's portion ascending in smoke. Any person being tested must be present at the altar, taste, and touch the holy meat. If the individual was not who he claimed to be, the god would give signs and the men's barbecue would be aborted. To proceed would not truly be to have the god's dinner.

The men inspected the *splanchna* for signs. The liver got special attention. Both the animals that Greeks deemed proper to sacrifice and humans shared the same *splanchna*, with each organ given the same name. It makes sense that the *splanchna* were the locus of messages and effects from the gods when one observes that fifth- and fourth-century Athenians spoke of human *splanchna* as organs of

---

67. Inscriptions use the same terms (e.g., *krinein, diakrinein, dokimazein*) for testing these animals to determine if they were perfect enough for sacrifice that the Athenians used for the testings that determined one's purity of lineage and descent from a pure Athenian mother and father. For evidence, see Stowers, "Truth, Identity and Sacrifice."

68. For discussion of the following practices, see ibid.

consciousness and receptivity to the gods.[69] Feeling, mood, desire, emotion, and thought were located not in a nonphysical mind but in the organs that made up the *splanchna*. This was a discourse of intelligent flesh and blood, not body and mind. Attributing thought or emotion to the heart, liver, gall, and so on, was not metaphorical. Greeks in this period and later believed that one's subjectivity arose from the movements and affections of these bodily parts.[70] One feels lust, anger, and fear in the liver. "The liver is an emotional image receptor."[71] Thus, the *splanchna*, both human and animal, are the receptor of communications from the gods.

One first poured blood on the altar, then removed and divided (*diairein*) the *splanchna*. The word for divide can also mean distribute (e.g., as in sacrificial portions), distinguish, decide (e.g., vote), define, and interpret. All of these activities can take place in conjunction with the division, interpretation, and distribution of the *splanchna*. Animals and their *splanchna* are indeed "good to think" with.[72] Plato compares the logical division of dialectic to division in *thysia*: "let us divide by parts as we divide a sacrificial animal" (*Pol.* 287C). Everyone watched closely as the god's portion of tail, fat, and bones burned on the altar. The movements of the tail and the color and motions of the flame were full of signs of the god's disposition toward the particular social group and the testing.[73]

Those celebrating could also establish the truth by touching the *splanchna* while taking an oath. The orators frequently mention such oaths and in various contexts every Athenian took them as a part of feasts of *dokimasia*, of testing. In Paul's time, such sacrificial testing was still important. The future citizens or elites of the Greek cities, for example, sacrificed with testings (*dokimasiai*) as they feasted and took oaths upon graduation from the ephebic training that made them adult citizens.

The feast entered a second stage as the wider group of men and, sometimes, women and children who had watched the episode around the altar or hearth were given portions of boiled meat from the thighs. All then merrily feasted on meat and accompanying dishes. Numerous versions—simpler or more complex—of this procedure for meals with meat took place in settings such as temples, clubs, private parties, and banquets.

---

69. Ruth Padel, *In and Out of the Mind: Greek Images of the Tragic Self* (Princeton: Princeton University Press, 1992), 12–48. The following discussion is based on Padel.

70. A medical writer from the end of the fifth century, without questioning their status as inner parts, polemicizes against the popular view that people think and perceive with their *phrenes*, equate them with the heart, and imagine that they are a kind of receptacle that receives things (Hippocrates, *Morb. sacr.* 20).

71. Padel, *In and Out of the Mind*, 19.

72. On Claude Lévi-Strauss's famous phrase, see Howard Eilberg-Schwartz, *The Savage in Judaism: An Anthropology of Israelite Religion and Ancient Judaism* (Bloomington: Indiana University Press, 1990), 117–18.

73. F. T. Van Straten, *Hiera kala: Images of Animal Sacrifice in Archaic and Classical Greece* (Religions in the Graeco-Roman World 127; Leiden: Brill, 1995), 122–24.

Now what does all of this have to do with understanding the Lord's supper? We can be certain that, for most of the Gentiles who constituted Paul's communities, any special meal—for example, at a birthday, a friend's dinner party, a holiday at home, a wedding, or a public feast—consisted of a version of the practices that I have described. Paul discusses Corinthian participation in sacrificial meals in 1 Cor 8–10. Greeks believed that eating unsacrificed meat was an abomination that would surely be punished by the gods. Paul presents himself as attempting to train these Greeks or hellenized Corinthians in something called the Lord's supper that he relates to his Christ myth and that is also a special meal. Neither the Corinthians nor Paul could have made sense of it without at least implicit comparison with sacrificial meals. Indeed chs. 8–11 are replete with comparisons to *thysia*. Furthermore, even though I cannot tell you what beliefs and interpretations of the Christ myth these people held when they feasted at the Lord's supper, I can describe many of the skills they possessed that allowed them to participate. They already possessed many of these skills merely by inhabiting a culture that centered on *thysia*. I will focus on four sets of these skills: (1) testing and truth-making skills; (2) group formation and social differentiation skills; (3) skills in interpreting signs and symbols; and (4) skills in relating fragments of mythic narratives to the preceding activities.

Paul's interpretation of the Lord's supper shares a basic assumption with sacrificial practice: in both meals, participants make themselves liable to divine judgment, and signs reveal truths about one's identity. In 1 Cor 11:19, there must be factions so that those who are tested might be revealed (οἱ δόκιμοι φανεροὶ γένωνται). An inscription from a cult to Zeus and other gods from late-second- or early-first-century B.C.E. Philadelphia in the house of a certain Dionysius makes an interesting case for comparison.[74] The inscription encourages participants of this extended household cult "who have confidence in themselves" at the monthly and yearly sacrifices to touch the stele near the altar upon which the cult regulations have been written so that "those who obey the ordinances and those who do not may be revealed" (*phaneroi ginetai*). As in Paul's account, it will be dangerous for those who have not passed the test of self-examination to participate.[75]

Paul seems to say (1 Cor 11:27) that the one who eats the bread or drinks the wine in the wrong way is guilty of destroying the Lord's body and blood, as if one of his crucifiers. He is attempting to shape eating practices and testing practices by an interpretation of a kind of martyr myth that ties a specific manner of ritual practice to social loyalty and unity. The individual participant must test himself (δοκιμάζειν) and then eat only if the person's disposition toward the body and

---

74. See Stanley K. Stowers, "A Cult from Philadelphia: Oikos Religion or Cultic Association?" in *The Early Church in Its Context: Essays in Honor of Everett Ferguson* (ed. Abraham J. Malherbe et al.; NovTSup 90; Leiden: Brill, 1998), 287–301.

75. The emphasis on "confidence in oneself" may be a new development different from classical times, but caution is needed in making such assessments of change in the Hellenistic period (see ibid.).

blood of Christ is correct (11:29). The person who does not distinguish the body, that is, perform an action with a certain social and ideological disposition, will bring down the judgment of the God who is present in that ritualized eating environment. Paul explains that many have been weak and sick and some have even died because they ate the bread and drank the cup without this disposition (v. 30). If the individual makes himself an object of self-examination and is able to discover the truth about his loyalty and disposition for ritual action, then that person can decide that it is safe to participate or decline and save himself from God's testing, which might result in illness and a revelation to the community of the person's false disposition (vv. 28–29, 30–32).

In *Against Neaera*, Demosthenes says that when Phrastor attempted to admit his son by a woman not of Athenian citizen blood, his phratry and his *genos* refused and voted against admission. Phrastor then challenged the rejection, but when he was required to swear an oath at the altar on a perfect sacrificial animal, he backed down and refused. The speaker then calls witnesses from the *genos* who saw Phrastor back down from the altar. Phrastor also had to decide about the truth of his disposition toward a body that was to become the body that constituted the social body in the act of eating: for Phrastor it was the body of a sheep to be rendered as food; for Paul's implied actor, it was bread that symbolizes the body involved in a martyrdom on their behalf. Unlike Paul's truth, Phrastor's cannot be located in his own inner disposition by an act of self-examination.[76] Phrastor's truth was not about his loyalties and the correctness of his beliefs.

Strange as it may sound to the modern ear, unlike the flesh-and-blood body of the sheep and of Phrastor and his purported offspring, the body that is in question in the Pauline text is not a flesh-and-blood body. Nor is it a "merely metaphorical body." According to Paul's mythmaking, the body in which the Corinthians share and with which they have the most literal contact is the pneumatic body of Christ that he gained when the *pneuma* from God replaced his soulish (*psychikos*) flesh body at his resurrection. As Paul explains by good physics of his day (1 Cor 15:35–41), in the cosmic hierarchy of being, various earthly creatures have bodies of different qualities of flesh, and higher in the cosmos bodies are made of qualitatively better materials. Christ, the first fruit, died with a soulish flesh body made of dust and was raised with a pneumatic body (15:44–47). First Corinthians 6 develops the argument that, for one who has been baptized into Christ, to be physically joined with a prostitute means joining the prostitute to Christ: "Do you not know that your bodies are members of Christ? . . . the one who joins with a prostitute is one body with her . . . 'the two shall become one flesh' [Gen 2:24] . . . your bodies are temples of the holy *pneuma* that is in you" (6:15–19). Those who are in Christ

---

76. Paul places the self-examination practices in the context of another myth, God's final judgment of the world. Making the self an object for judgment by the self is best, but if God must punish one whose ritual competence is untrue, then that chastening is an educational punishment to save the person from the final and absolute punishment.

feel what he suffered and can thus "participate in the body and blood of Christ" (10:16) because they have a part of him, his divine *pneuma*, in them. Thus, in the cosmic physics/myth by which Paul desires to gain legitimacy from Corinthians, those "in Christ" are physically connected both to Christ and to all other baptized people. There is one body and for one individual to divide from it in any way is an attack on Christ and the entire body. This is a pneumatic body composed of a stuff belonging to a higher order of existence. It cannot be touched and seen in the way that flesh and blood can, but this conception is radically different from the modern so-called Cartesian dualism of material/spiritual for which there is a material world of cause and effect of uniform matter and principles, and a totally discontinuous and other spiritual realm.

The Greek and Christ myths that ancient interpreters used to manipulate and rationalize the skills of actors in ritual practice are different stories, but the Corinthian actors and the citizens of Athens exercised some of the same skills, skills that connected eating to truth practices and social formation.[77] Note that Paul uses exactly the same terms for testing and self-examination that Greeks used for the testings involved in sacrificial practices: to become manifest (φανεροὶ γένωνται), tested (δόκιμοι), to test (δοκιμάζειν), to distinguish (διακρίνειν), and to judge (κρίνειν).[78] Athenian failure to use deme records stemmed not from poor record keeping but from considering identity to be ritually constituted and confirmed. In the Lord's supper and in Greek sacrifice, who is in or outside the community is not simply predetermined in some juridical or definitional way, but is negotiated in the very exercise of the skills of mythmaking, testing, and eating. Phrastor's son did not become a member of his phratry because Phrastor feared that the god would know the truth. Therefore, he would not swear on the animal and allow it to be cooked and distributed so as to form a feasting community. Other court cases show that if the community had eaten with him, then that fact would be compelling evidence about his son's identity and his truthfulness. Those who claimed to be Kiron's kin said (in my words), "We sacrificed with him to his household god, touched, and ate the meat. No one else in the household did that. We are therefore the ones who are truly of his flesh and blood."

Paul assumes that the Corinthians possess similar skills, but he does not like the way that they have used them. What, more precisely, is Paul's complaint? Some of the Corinthians used their skills to form eating groups that excluded others (11:18–22). Was the criterion social rank, family connection, or ethnic origins? I do not know, but most of the possibilities suggest that the rules of the game followed by the Corinthians might have been for meat meals instead of bread meals, the ordinary meals cooked by women that were much less intently focused on social differentiation. Meat meals organized groups on the basis of characteristics

---

77. This should not surprise us, since this combination continued to be important to sacrificial practices in the Greek East of the early empire.
78. Stowers, "Truth, Identity and Sacrifice."

deemed by the ancients to have been based on blood, on ancestry. To add to the confusion, Paul taught a cult myth for baptism in which having fellowship with this new God connected one to a great ancient ancestor and lineage. Paul's account of what the Corinthians were doing attempts to make the ritual focus of the meal the bread and wine, but supposes a more elaborate meal. Perhaps some of the Corinthians, in Paul's view, had allowed the other cuisine, possibly even some meat, to become the focus. Paul contrasts eating with the goal of satiating appetite in everyday meals with the correct manner of the Lord's supper (11:21–22, 33–34). He associates eating meat with passion, desire, idolatry, and sexual immorality in his warnings from the story of Israel in the wilderness (10:1–22).[79]

It seems to me dead wrong to take Paul's account of the supper's "institution" as a script or liturgy for the ritual. If we did not know that the later church had incorporated these words into its liturgy, we would have no clue to even suggest that the words were repeated in worship. Furthermore, we also have no reason to think that Paul recounted the story in the same way with exactly the same words, even if the story was traditional and certain elements had become essential. The account is also an etiological myth, but that observation may lead us to miss the important point, which is the way it functions in Paul's rhetoric.[80] I suggest that the account is the specification of a genre of eating.[81] Paul is saying that they have confused a genre of eating that focuses on the desire for food and drink, and that produces a certain pattern of social differentiation, with the genre of the Lord's supper.

But as I have tried to show, the signals and expectations suggested by the Lord's supper might be read as confusing and contradictory in the context of the codes of eating in Greco-Roman culture. Paul's account of the "institution" unquestionably shares in the genre of mortuary foundations right down to the words "do this as a memorial."[82] This is so even if it is odd for the dead to also be alive and to promise a return as judge of the world. Paul's account yields a very peculiar yet familiar memorial feast for the dead. On the level of practices, whereas one expects a memorial feast for the dead to be a sacrificial feast, the Lord's supper features bread. Where one expects filet mignon, there is white bread. In this light,

---

79. Stowers, "Elusive Coherence," 76–78.

80. The concept of myth often used in the study of religion treats myth as timeless or as a sort of general background knowledge or ideological foundation. I would argue that all of these are misleading. There is no myth without context, but only instances of particular individuals interpreting stories for particular purposes in specific settings.

81. Paul presents the problem of the misapplication of eating skills in 1 Cor 11:17–22 and says that he will not praise such behavior. Then he introduces the account as if it were a demonstration of the reason (γάρ, v. 23) why such eating is not the Lord's supper. He draws the conclusion (ὥστε, v. 27) from it that unworthy eating places those dining among the killers of Christ.

82. Stowers, "Elusive Coherence," 82 n. 49.

one can understand Paul's need to insist that the supper is not an ordinary meal like the one that is eaten at home.[83]

I suggest that Paul's martyr myth by which he attempts genre specifications about ritualized eating practices plays on a disjunction between the flesh-and-blood body and the self. The Greeks and Paul were concerned about group social formation and the identity of those who ate together. For Greeks, that truth was about the identity of one's flesh and blood.[84] The god provided signs about this truth during the skillful cooking, sharing, and eating of meat in honor of the god. The medium for communicating this truth about flesh and blood was the flesh and blood of an animal from the best lineages that Greek animal husbandry could provide. For the kind of Greeks that we meet in the Attic orators, it would be nonsensical or inconceivable to say, "You can kill my body but you cannot touch me."[85] Body and identity are one.

Paul's Christ myth and ritual, on the other hand, work around a disjunction between the truest self and the body. Instead of the community being constituted and tested by eating meat, it exists by eating bread that is a symbol of an absent body that points both to the significance of giving up that body and to the loyalty of the social body toward that symbol. In the martyr myth, the martyr's obedience, will, and benevolent intention triumph over the body. The body symbolizes both what is expendable and the obedient resolve that triumphed. Because of this triumph of will and obedience to God, Christ lives on a new level of existence transcending the old existence of the body, a pneumatic existence.

The social group tests for the truth about the identities of its members not by observing the signs made by flesh and blood but by making the true self an object of self-examination. "Flesh and blood cannot inherit the kingdom of God" (1 Cor 15:50). In testing oneself to see that one can discern the body, the true self consists in being beyond oneself just as the martyr surpassed himself in giving up his body.[86] Discerning the body means both entertaining Paul's Christ-*pneuma* myth and also acting so as to acknowledge the priority of the social body over the desires of one's body. "Because there is one bread, we the many are one body. . . . Consider

---

83. One hundred years later, Justin Martyr (*1 Apol.* 65–67) has to insist on the same point as he tries to describe the meal to outsiders.

84. Did the claimants to Kiron's household share his flesh and blood? Were the ephebic candidates truly of aristocratic or citizen blood?

85. They were concerned about the issue of to whom a body belonged. If you were a complete master of your body, you were a free citizen. If you were a child, a woman, or a slave, you were in varying degrees bodies under the control of others. There is no disjunction between the truth about your body and the self. Classical Greek myth and ritual can be seen as involved in effecting this order of things.

86. The ritual actors inspect their own dispositions toward the eating to make certain that their actions will manifest the meaning of the martyr's death, which is the triumph of the will over the body for the benefit of others.

Israel according to the flesh; are not those who eat of the sacrifices partners in the altar?" (10:17–18).

The self surpassed is the kind of self seen in traditional Greek sacrificial practice that maintains no disjunction with the self as body in the act of constituting the social body. No wonder that Paul contrasts the Lord's supper to meals with meat.[87] Notice, for example, the implicit contrast with merely bodily *thysia* in Rom 12:1–3: "present your bodies as a living and holy sacrifice [*thysia*] acceptable to God, which is your rational cultic practice. Do not be conformed to this age but have your form changed by the renewal of your mind, so that you might test [*dokimazein*] what is the will of God." Here, true *thysia* is the surpassing and mastery of the body by "rational" practice and a mind that has gained the skills to test for the truth. Verses 3–8 employ the metaphor of the body and its parts to explain that this means consciously defining oneself as a part of a differentiated social body.

What is the yield of this analysis? Above all, I think this analysis can suggest a holistic interpretation of two historical moments. The goal of this type of study is the sense of an interpretation thick enough and with enough of our modern analytic contexts (e.g., religious, social, political, economic, and semantic) that we can warrant some degree of success in bridging the gap between a distant culture and our own requirements for understanding. Comparison provides the leverage to dislodge the text from the categories and questions internal to the tradition that appropriated it and to display it in a new way.

The way of life in the ancient Greek polis worked through practices, including ritual and discursive practices, concerning place and the products born from that place.[88] Sacrificial practice was saturated with physical contiguity: altars on the land; meat of animal lineages from the soil; smoke rising from the altar sending the bodies of animals from the land to the god who owns and occupies the land; the differentiated social body united around and touching the altar while ingesting flesh; meat passed from hand to hand; the god testifying to the truths about the continuity of flesh from parent to child.

If, in this ideological construction, meat is the natural product of men according to the patrilineal principle of the seed of the founding ancestor passed on as flesh, then bread is the fabrication of food by art, like spinning wool, the artifice of women and slaves. In Greek sacrifice, the body is present to be touched and eaten. But where is the body in the Lord's supper? It is present in its absence. The bread of human art is the reminder of a body that occupies no place. Christ, who by the art of his obedience and will triumphed through God's power, lives on a new plane of

---

87. Stowers, "Elusive Coherence," 76–79.

88. In their originary myth, Athenians were a lineage born from the very soil of Attica. All truly of the city could trace themselves back to the soil. To own no soil meant to be a non-citizen resident under the power of citizens: a slave; more ambiguously, a woman; an alien. The lineages of animals from Attica were also produce of the soil and had been given by the gods so that gods and humans might feast together.

pneumatic existence where a body that one can touch seems superfluous. Where is the dead and torn merely human body of the martyr? There seems to be a certain fit between a ritual of a body surpassed by the will and the kind of people associated with Pauline Christianity. Many, like Paul himself, were artisans without ties to the land who lived lives characterized by physical mobility. They also represent a new class of people in a polyethnic world with a predilection toward transcending their ascribed local and ethnic places.

Paul is, above all, an expert in a new knowledge and the practices that go with this knowledge. Paul's power is that of an intellectual. He is a purveyor of knowledges and truths in a way that the typical Greek citizen, even the priest of a particular cult, was not. The truths of Pauline Christianity are not common everyday truths about the disposition of one's social group(s) and the signs seen in the cooking and eating of an animal, but they are truths about a person's interior, soul and mind, and the relation of these to the destiny of the cosmos. So instead of the social group watching the body of an animal, each individual looks inside and strives to obtain a newly socialized mind by reflecting on a symbol for an absent body.

But how does this interpretation play out in terms of the historical particularities of the differentiated interactions between Paul and the Corinthians? I am half-facetiously calling what follows a "just so story" to indicate its status as an explanatory proposal. Daniel C. Dennett has stolen the phrase from jaundiced critics of the stories that adaptationist neo-Darwinian biologists tell as hypotheses about evolutionary episodes.[89] By the expression, I do not mean that the account, or such accounts, are just made up, are "merely" interpretations; or that they cannot in principle be justified by evidence and theory; or that they imply postmodern confusions such as there is no truth or falsehood, that we are trapped in a prison house of language; or that meaning is too slippery to pin down. Rather, instead of claiming a justified explanation of the historical situation among Paul and the Corinthians, it is an account to be tested by the refinement and debate over theorization and assessments of the evidence that ought to go on and on. This ought to be a process in which the activity of theorization transparently makes data into evidence. In other words, scholars should be as reflexive and as self-conscious as possible, and should reason not only by homology but also by analogy. In this case, the limitations and kinds of evidence should be clear. New discoveries of the most particular evidence regarding events and persons are unlikely (e.g., Gaius's letter to his wife), if not impossible. Interpretation of the evidence from Paul's letters and genetically related literature (e.g., Acts, Mark?) will, with critical appraisal of proposed explanatory interpretations and new interpretations, make old supposed evidence disappear and new evidence appear from the same data. Broader data

---

89. Daniel C. Dennett, *Darwin's Dangerous Idea: Evolution and the Meanings of Life* (New York: Simon & Schuster, 1995), 242, 245–46, 308–9, 454–56, 461–66, 485.

about life in Corinth and the culture will become available, but it will be challenging to make such data into evidence; and so on. The limits to this format mean that I can only provide a bare-bones sketch of the story.

Paul's message in 1 Corinthians (but not in 2 Corinthians, where he battles with other specialist producers) is unequivocal: the Corinthians have by baptism into Christ and common participation in the *pneuma* of Christ become one body; they remain one body and total unity is required.[90] His caveat in the supper text, however, suggests that there may be unidentified individuals or groups who are not truly of the one body: "When you come together as the assembly I hear that there are divisions among you, and I partly believe it because there must be sects [αἱρέσεις] among you so that those who have been tested and approved can be revealed" (1 Cor 11:18–19). I find four hypotheses or parts to the story.

First, Paul drew elites to participation in the field, and that involvement in the practices of the field had the effect of causing or exacerbating a social distance from the (at least ideal) unity of the locative religion and household organization of the Corinthians, in spite of the baptism of whole households at the behest of their heads and other elites. As discussed above, some of these people are named, such as Gaius, Crispus, and the household of Stephanas, Fortunatus, and Achaicus. These are participants in Paul's missionary, teaching, and organizing activities on whom he tries to bestow special legitimacy that would give them a kind of authority among the rest of the Corinthians.

My second hypothesis is that Paul naturally places the responsibility for unifying the rest of the Corinthians on the elite fellow specialists and for enforcing their "proper" participation in the practices he advocates. Paul addresses the Lord's supper text most directly to the elites: "Do you not have houses in which to eat and drink; or do you ... despise those who have nothing?" (1 Cor 11:22). This cannot be addressed to everyone because in the previous verse Paul has distinguished people who have meal practices or meal participation and who do not get enough to eat and drink from those who feast. The latter have to include, or be, the elites. Moreover, only the elites truly have houses in the sense that they can control who eats and how people eat. I suggest that the rest of the text is primarily for them with the "institution" passage a model for their organization, leadership, and ideological focus. In ch. 12, where Paul outlines a hierarchy of "practical" skills and specializations, the elite specialists are the leading and more important body parts in the metaphor, like the head, and they are urged not to think that the less important, less honorable parts are dispensable. The list that follows places at the top specialists who are cultural producers involving intellectual practices

---

90. For a massive collection of evidence regarding the theme of unity, see Margaret M. Mitchell, *Paul and the Rhetoric of Reconciliation: An Exegetical Investigation of the Language and Composition of 1 Corinthians* (HUT 28; Tübingen: Mohr Siebeck, 1991). My reservation about this important book is that to identify the concord theme solely with the tradition of *homonoia* speech and its context is too narrow. Appeals to unity were ubiquitous in the traditional but complex society of Paul's world.

with recognized identities that he ranks—missionaries, prophets, teachers—and follows with less well-defined and perhaps single skills.

Third, the less or non-elite Corinthians resisted full participation in Paul's practices and reacted by experimenting with their own mythmaking and ritual activities based on their strategic locative interests. Thus, 11:21 contrasts genres of meals that the Corinthians are having with the one true, united Lord's supper. Scholarship agrees that all of chs. 11–14 are about "church worship" or, less anachronistically, ritual activities of the Corinthians. The body metaphor in 12:14–27 suggests that in Paul's view some of the Corinthians are saying or indicating with their actions, "I don't belong to the body." Although the letter does not supply specifics, Paul clearly registers that he does not like the rituals practiced by a number of Corinthians. I think it likely that the women criticized in 1 Cor 11 and 14, as well as the tongue-speakers who, in Paul's view, need interpreters to make their speech intelligible, were non-elite resisters and experimenters whose practices were not necessarily Paul's and did not fit Paul's intellectualist mode. As I have argued, Paul's meal is gendered toward women's practices by lacking meat and featuring grain. The supper seems very domestic both as a grain meal at home and a memorial meal for the dead, recalling the important participation of women in funerals and memorial practices. This might have been read as a signal by women that elicited their own creativity and participation. Paul clearly thought that it went too far. More broadly, since Paul's meal sent mixed messages pointing to various common locative practices, it likely encouraged creative interpretations of just such practices.

Fourth, in addition to placing weight on the elites to weld the non-elites into one body, Paul addresses what he sees as the problem by adding the testing practices that typically are part of sacrificial practices to his meatless meal of the supper. But as I have noted, this not only sent mixed messages but also meant a translation into a new mode of religion that brought the texts and interpretations of specialists to bear on an inner-judging self enunciated by specialists. This religion shaped by the field would become a religion in which a certain kind of self and self-policing would play a central role.

I will summarize some central points of my argument and underline tensions in my proposals that need to be addressed. Paul's esoteric mythmaking and ritualization depend on his claims to be a chosen spokesperson for the deity. But we can imagine social legitimacy attaching to these claims only by virtue of a field or game widely attested in ancient sources in which Paul played a position both recognizable and attractive to some Corinthians. Apart from broad terms of debate within the field such as the nature of the cosmos and its elements, critique of traditional religion and the nature of the gods, ancient epic and ancestry, and the therapy of the passions as a means to self-mastery, the specifics of Paul's discourse were probably unfamiliar and therefore both exotic and esoteric. The core of Paul's legitimacy, and thus his power among some of the Corinthians, derived rather from his skillful display of abilities native to the game or field such as his education in ancient books; his interpretive skills; his reading, writing, and speaking abilities; and his pneumatic demonstrations, whatever those were. I have specifically argued that Paul's message and appeal focused on Christ as the bearer and dispenser of the most perfect stuff in the cosmos, the *pneuma* of God. These ideas were tied to a prophetic genealogical myth regarding Abraham's lineage and the non-Jewish peoples. Pauline ritual of baptism gave initiates a share of the *pneuma* that God had given to Christ, by connecting with his *pneuma*. Being "in Christ" or having Christ in you gave the baptized a physical connection back to Abraham. I also discussed the significance of the Lord's supper as a ritual practice in the context of everyday meals at home, sacrificial meals, and memorial meals for the dead. I concluded that Paul's version of the practice would have sent mixed messages connected with issues of food and gender. His use of the Christ myth in the interpretation of the meal for the Corinthians points to a self marked by a disjunction between its true self and its body and place.

Jonathan Z. Smith's comparison shows how the local interests of the religion of place were likely to have provided the Corinthians with a basis for a limited and differentiated hearing of Paul. His practices became the occasion for creative mythmaking and ritual experimentation among his hearers, shaped both by the encounter itself and by the interests and *doxai* of the Corinthians themselves. But for there to have been a sustained encounter between Paul and the Corinthians at all requires the existence of a group among the Corinthians who were already habituated, not so as to want to be saved or become Christians, but so as to want to become consumers of Paul's foreign *paideia*, a known commodity supported by a dynamic social arena. The five- to six-year period for which we have evidence of a continued relationship between Paul and at least some of those whom I have been calling "the Corinthians" needs this sort of explanation.

In the important contributions of Smith and Mack, Paul just misunderstood the Corinthians and their locative religious interests owing to his utopian understanding. Smith, in scholarship over many years, has developed the idea of locative religion over against utopian religion. He uses the latter with reference to its sense of a-topic, without place. The categories appear especially as part of discussions about historical persistence and change and have proven an enormous advance over the Christianizing idea that all religion is about salvation or about either nature or salvation. Smith describes the two as "world-views."[91] The locative "is concerned primarily with the cosmic and social issues of keeping one's place and reinforcing boundaries. The vision is one of stability and confidence with respect to an essentially fragile cosmos, one that has been reorganized, with effort, out of previous modes of order and one whose 'appropriate order' must be maintained through acts of conscious labour. We may term such locative traditions, religions

---

91. Jonathan Z. Smith, *Drudgery Divine: On the Comparison of Early Christianities and the Religions of Late Antiquity* (Jordan Lectures in Comparative Religion 14; London: School of Oriental and African Studies, University of London; Chicago: University of Chicago Press, 1990), 121.

of sanctification."[92] Purification and healing are two central modes of labor for keeping this order. Corpse pollution is the model for all sorts of impurity. The living belong to the world of the living and the dead to the place of the dead. On this view, Paul's central idea of a resurrection of the dead is utopian and utterly antithetical to the basic premises of the locative worldview. Although in what Smith calls "locative ideology" everyone is responsible for the labor of maintaining and rectifying the boundaries, the thought suggests rigid social stratification.

By contrast, a worldview that finds the patterns and structures of the cosmos to be "fundamentally perverse" and that good and reality are to be found above and beyond this cosmos is utopian.[93] The utopian mode of salvation involves reversal and rebellion. On Smith's and Mack's interpretation, Paul fits the utopian mold. Unsurprisingly, they base this interpretation largely on the Paul of modernist theological New Testament scholarship since Albert Schweitzer, which has constructed Paul's thought as centered on two aeons, the domination and conquest of demonic powers, cosmic sin, personal transcendence, and related familiar themes. The demolition of this Paul, or at least major parts, is already well under way.[94] Smith writes regarding Paul: "Any pretense of remediation, of rectification, of healing and sanctification is absent."[95] I find it interesting that these are precisely what the divine *pneuma* does in the Christ-*pneuma* myth, and the rectifications are psychological, social, and cosmic. But I will not try to argue for a new Paul beyond what I have done earlier and I do not simply want to deny that Paul is in some sense utopian. The latter may depend on how much of x and y it takes to push one into the utopian category. Instead I want to raise some questions about the locative/utopian concepts that I hope will contribute toward what Smith calls "the rectification of categories." I have both criticism and an explanatory proposal.

I believe that the categories are undertheorized. I also have some worries that with minds less brilliant than Smith's, the categories might prove dangerous. "Locative" partly originated as Smith's correction of Mircea Eliade's interpretation of cosmogonic myth and his "patterns of archaic religion." Smith sought to bring Eliade's timeless "archaic" into history and to show evidence of change in both

---

92. Ibid.

93. Jonathan Z. Smith, "Birth Upside Down or Right Side Up?" *HR* 9 (1969–70): 302; repr. in idem, *Map Is Not Territory: Studies in the History of Religions* (SJLA 23; Leiden: Brill, 1978; repr., Chicago: University of Chicago Press, 1993), 170; cf. idem, "When the Chips are Down," in *Relating Religion*, 15.

94. Among the important literature I would cite are Denise Kimber Buell and Caroline Johnson Hodge, "The Politics of Interpretation: The Rhetoric of Race and Ethnicity in Paul," *JBL* 123 (2004): 235–51; Denise Kimber Buell, *Why This New Race: Ethnic Reasoning in Early Christianity* (New York: Columbia University Press, 2005); Johnson Hodge, *If Sons, Then Heirs*. A particularly definitive and groundbreaking contribution to this reassessment of Paul is Emma Wasserman, *The Death of the Soul in Romans 7: Sin, Death, and the Law in Light of Hellenistic Moral Psychology* (WUNT 2/256; Tübingen: Mohr Siebeck, 2008).

95. Smith, *Drudgery Divine*, 142.

directions between locative and utopian types of religion.[96] My first worry is that, without more satisfactory explanations of the two, locative might, against all of Smith's efforts, seem to be primordial, and utopian essentially psychological. After all, locative is the religion that most people and families just had and utopian seems to be an unnatural rebellion against it. But how does locative religion come about? It can easily seem as though it is based on the natural attitude toward the world. By insisting that these are rather like existential attitudes without further social explanation, the two categories could also seem at base to be psychological in origin and essence. According to Smith, then, Paul works out his thought "from a perspective of alienation and *ressentiment*, to a thoroughly utopian understanding."[97] Smith is also admirably aware of the limitations of his suggested explanations. In an earlier note he writes, "I am aware that, in this formulation, I am offering a tentative and, undoubtedly, partial causal explanation for the co-occurrence of the shift to utopian interpretations in the case of the Cybele-Attis cult, and of Paul . . . in terms of alienation and *ressentiment*."[98]

My proposal is that much of what is or seems utopian in Paul and other ancient writers is a field effect. Indeed, utopian thought may be the result of the semiautonomy and disinterestedness produced by the conditions of cultural fields. In Pierre Bourdieu's account of cultural fields, he attributes much of their creative dynamism to their characteristic of possessing opposing dominant heteronomous and dominated autonomous poles. A field, then, is an arena of a certain type of social activity that sets its own norms, requirements, and conditions for participation, but these norms and so on are matters of contestation. As noted above, Greek and Roman rhetorical culture, Greek and Hellenistic philosophy, and intellectual arts such as Greek and Roman medicine and astrology occupied the dominant and heteronomous side of the field. Here we find official legitimation, financial support by patrons, the public honoring and financial support of cities, and the imperial order.

But some philosophy, for example, defined itself as autonomous in opposition to the dominant philosophy and rhetoric and thus occupied the other pole of the field. Both sides of the field claimed to value autonomy, as Agamemnon's speech (*Satyr.* 5) on the ideals of the *scholastici* asserts. But one side defined itself as truly autonomous over against the other side that had sold out. Cultural specialists on the autonomous pole derive their legitimacy and prestige—the ability to attract some—from demonstrating that they and their cultural products are pure and not compromised by the backing of power, money, or conventional legitimacy. Classic figures who modeled the autonomous form of philosophy would include Socrates,

---

96. Smith, "When the Chips are Down," 13–16.
97. Smith, *Drudgery Divine*, 141.
98. Ibid., 134 n. 35, adding: "However, as indicated above, it is my belief that the determination of such matters 'will be the work of a generation'" (ibid.; cf. 113–14).

Diogenes the Cynic, and Zeno the Stoic, all known for their radical rejection of the wealth, honor, prestige, and institutional power sought by other sorts of intellectuals. Their own prestige and power derived from their practices of disinterestedness regarding wealth, power, and honor. Above all, they developed sharp critiques of traditional Greek religious beliefs and practices as attempts to buy the goodwill of gods, gods falsely represented as having humanlike interests and motivations. Diogenes and Zeno banished temples, priests, and offerings altogether from their *Republics*. The right relationship with the divine was not to be one of traditional reciprocity.

Bourdieu's famous example of the field of art well illustrates the autonomous pole. The museums, academic artists, artists supported by patrons and the state, and by the market formed the heteronomous pole. With the development of the idea of pure and true art, art for art's sake, a succession of artistic movements and individuals defined themselves and their work in contrast to the heteronomous who, they claimed, produced for money, conventional approval, and power. The ideal of the poor starving artist arose. The bohemian lifestyle expressed disinterest in conventional values, approval, and material possessions. In the view of the autonomous pole specialist, true art as opposed to mere craft was of unlimited value, beyond economic price. Since the social and symbolic capital of the autonomous pole producer is derived only from comparison with those who are cast as more heteronomous than they are, autonomous producers must continually and competitively define themselves as even more disinterested than others who claim disinterest. Sociologically, perhaps the most striking thing about Paul's letters is the astounding number of competitors—false apostles, evil workers, proponents of false gospels, super-apostles, law binders of Gentiles, "dogs," and so on—that the letters mention. And here is the interesting point: there is almost no discussion of the content of the "false teachings" (which has led to enormous speculation by scholars convinced that theological orthodoxy and heresy must be the problem). Rather, the letters refer to their false motives regarding money and gain and desire for human prestige and approval. I see a fit between such disinterestedness and a religion focused on the myth of a teacher without teachings whose totalizing act was to die faithfully, only for the interests of God, with no interests of his own.

My proposal, then, entails that the attitudes and practices that Smith describes as utopian derive from conditions of specialists whose religion is that of bookish interpretation whose norms are produced by the interactions with other such specialists in various degrees of distance and autonomy from "everyday religion" outside the field. The most utopian would be those competing to outdo other producers of disinterested religion on the autonomous pole. In Smith's *Drudgery Divine*, the central example for comparison to Paul is the Cybele-Attis cult. He shows its locative forms and then later utopian interpretations. The locative evidence is relatively extensive and largely archaeological, but the utopian interpretations come from highly literate intellectuals with known locations in the cultural field.[99] The interpretations of the cult that take a utopian direction use intellectualizing conventions that are specialized skills (e.g., allegory, allusion to philosophical doctrines, and intertextual interpretation). Fortunately, the activity of these largely late Platonic intellectuals has recently been studied in an illuminating way in view of the theory of cultural fields.[100]

None of this means that people who were not players in the cultural fields could not give intellectually sophisticated, creative, and thoughtful practice and interpretation to their religion. It does mean that such people would not be constrained and habituated by the norms and social dynamics of specialists whose intense interactivity produced and even required distinction from the normal, everyday, locative perspective on religion. I think it likely that Corinthians, including especially people who did not aspire to *paideia*, gave locative interpretation to Paul's Christ-*pneuma* myth. When 1 Cor 15:12 refers to some who say that there is no resurrection of the dead and the long discussion that follows vigorously argues on a number of points about the reality of a resurrection of "all those in Christ," or "of all," and not of Christ only, locative logic over against utopian thinking seems the best explanation for Paul's efforts.[101] After all, a hero who had broken the bounds of place and become a heavenly god was a familiar idea in Paul's world. The two best-known examples are, of course, Heracles and Asclepius.

Heracles can help us to think about the resources that the Corinthians might have had for doing their own thinking and mythmaking about Christ.[102] Heracles was enormously popular in extremely complex varieties of myth, cult, and literature. Most often his cult was heroic in form, but he had the unheroic characteristic of possessing no tomb. Heroes normally were intensely local, given cult where they were buried. Sometimes Heracles was worshiped as an Olympian god, who had received apotheosis and ascended to heaven. The apotheosis was widely seen as a reward for his suffering and virtue. Myth and literature dealt with this category-breaking figure in several different ways. Pindar coined the oxymoron "hero god" (*Nem.* 3.22). Rationalizing writers sometimes claimed that there were two different Heracleses. One died and became a hero; the other was a god. Homer has his shade (*eidōlon*) in Hades while he dwells on Olympus with the gods, another unresolved contradiction. About the time that Paul was in Corinth, Seneca wrote

---

99. Ibid., 133. The figures that Smith mentions are Sallustius, Julian, Firmicus Maternus, and Damascius.

100. Arthur Urbano, "Lives in Competition: Biographical Literature and the Struggle for Philosophy in Late Antiquity" (Ph.D. diss., Brown University, 2005).

101. Paul's argument assumes that the same people who deny the more general resurrection had no problem with Christ's resurrection.

102. For what follows, I draw largely on the important article by David E. Aune, "Heracles and Christ: Heracles Imagery in the Christology of Early Christianity," in *Greeks, Romans, and Christians: Essays in Honor of Abraham J. Malherbe* (ed. David L. Balch et al.; Minneapolis: Fortress, 1990), 3–19.

of Heracles, "He has crossed the streams of Tartarus, subdued the gods of the underworld, and has returned" (*Herc. fur.* 889–90 [Miller, LCL]). Here a writer can even have Heracles conquer death, but there is no reason to think that this would have disrupted the normal locative religion. He was treated as a singular figure, and he did not change the normal course of human life and death, as Paul's Christ did. Paul taught that Christ had been rewarded for his faithfulness with a body of divine *pneuma* vastly superior to mortal flesh. By ritual means, others could have some of his *pneuma* and become physically connected to Christ and a distinguished ancient lineage blessed by God. Only the claim that all the dead with this *pneuma* would soon come back from death and that the living would never die would have perhaps been nonsensical and have certainly contradicted the principles of religion.

Most of the Corinthians may have treated Paul's Christ-*pneuma* myth as an interesting and challenging opportunity for thinking about their religion of household, "ethnicity," and city. Christ, like Heracles, embodied opposites and contradictions that might be treated as exceptions and singularities, but also opportunities for thought. Most of the ways that writers, cultural specialists at least, treated Heracles did not eliminate the tensions, but led to novel and creative formulations. In cult apart from the practices of writing and literate fields, a person might be faced with giving heroic cult to Heracles one day and celebrating him as a god the next. Sometimes the cults were as mixed and as ambiguous as the Lord's supper. I would argue that both Heracles myth and cult could provide opportunities for thinking about boundaries, their transgression, and maintenance. So also Christ myth and cult.

What I have been suggesting makes sense only if one sees this thinking with myth and cult as socially useful thinking. In view of my analysis of the Lord's supper, Smith writes, "Some Corinthians may have understood Paul as providing them, in the figure of Christ, with a more proximate and mobile ancestor for their new, non-ethnic 'Christian' *ethnos*."[103] "Non-ethnic *ethnos*" can be taken in various ways. Some of these would obscure rather than clarify the kind of social creativity for which I want to argue. One could follow popular interpretation of Gal 3:27–28 and say that Paul discovered the principle of non-ethnic liberal individual identity. But this ignores, among other things, the argument beginning in Gal 3:6.

---

103. Smith, "Re: Corinthians," 33; cf. 33–34 n. 48. The quotation draws on Burton L. Mack's response to my paper, "On Construing Meals, Myths and Power in the World of Paul" (now partly incorporated into this article), prepared for the Consultation on Ancient Myths and Modern Theories of Christian Origins and presented at the annual meeting of the Society of Biblical Literature, held in New Orleans in 1996. The expression drawn from Mack is: "Christ [is] the first father of a non-ethnic genealogy." I think that Mack's apt formulation here is close to my own conception. But one of Paul's most interesting passages about kinship and genealogy, Rom 8:29 (brilliantly discussed in Johnson Hodge, *If Sons, Then Heirs*, 109–16; see also Stowers, "What Is 'Pauline Participation in Christ'?"), has God foreordaining Christ as the firstborn of many brothers. The *pneuma* unites the baptized to Christ as contemporaries, brothers, of the lineage of Abraham, Isaac, and Jacob.

The gospel is the promise that all the Gentiles will be blessed in Abraham's seed, Christ. The content of the Abrahamic promise, the blessing, is the divine *pneuma* (3:14).[104] The argument culminates with words of 3:29, "If you are of Christ, you are Abraham's seed, heirs according to the promise." "All are one in Christ" is not a (supposedly) liberal erasure of gender, ethnicity, and social status, but the claim that all those in Christ share the same superior ontological status, possession of Christ's *pneuma*, in spite of other differences. Thus, "non-ethnic" should not be given this popular interpretation through 3:27–28.

Another interpretation of "non-ethnic" might make ethnicity fixed, given, primordial, and essential over against Paul's mere ethnic language that is just made up. Here Paul represents the modern voluntaristic conception of religion over against the persistent conception of ethnicity as fixed and primordial.[105] Such an interpretation would mystify both religion and ethnicity and hide the fact that both are the result of human activity and social processes. Much recent scholarship in the social sciences has worked at explaining these activities and processes and critiquing the essential and primordial conceptions of ethnicity. Two points from one of these scholars will be helpful for interpreting "non-ethnic ethnicity." Rogers Brubaker writes, "The genealogical construction of relationality offers possibilities for extension that are obscured by the contemporary scholar's tendency to look for a neat boundary between inside and outside."[106] Further he says, "In almost all societies, kinship concepts serve as symbolic and ideological resources, yet while they shape norms, self-understandings and perceptions of affinity, they do not necessarily produce kinship 'groups.'"[107] These are useful maxims for an area of scholarship that begins with premises about the existence and inherent qualities of groups such as "the Corinthian community," "the Jews," and "the Romans." Brubaker's sentences occur in a discussion of the "Nuer" and the "Dinka" of East Africa, peoples that earlier scholarship had constructed as neatly bounded ethnic groups. A "group" here means a unity of people who interact and mutually recognize one another as belonging inherently inside its boundaries. Recent scholarship, especially that of Sharon E. Hutchinson, has shown that no such ethnic group "the Nuer" ever existed.[108] Rather, practices of creative genealogy, endogamy, and "fictive kinship" allowed varied populations over a huge region to relate in complex and flexible ways. In this light, and that

---

104. This reading depends on what I and others have argued is a better translation of ἐκ πίστεως and related expressions. Paul is not arguing that Abraham and believers are saved by their faith, but that the status of those "in Christ" springs from Abraham's and Christ's faith or faithfulness. On this, see Stowers, "What Is 'Pauline Participation in Christ'?" 358–60.

105. Buell, *Why This New Race*, 5–6, and passim.

106. Brubaker, *Ethnicity without Groups*, 50.

107. Ibid., 51.

108. Sharon E. Hutchinson, *Nuer Dilemmas: Coping with Money, War, and the State* (Berkeley: University of California Press, 1995).

of many such examples, Paul's entrepreneurial activities employing genealogical myth and concepts and practices appealing to kinship may not appear as "pseudo" over against the "real" ethnicity and religion of the Corinthians (or normal Greeks, Romans, or Jews), but as rather ordinary social activity. So also, the varied resistances, appropriations, and negotiations of "the Corinthians" in the face of Paul's efforts seem unexceptional. Group-making and group-resisting are activities with varied actors who employ categories, schemes of classification, organizations, activities of mobilization, cognitive schemas, taken-for-granted practices, expectations regarding patterns of proximity and distance, and so on.[109] The way I read the work of Smith and Mack, "non-ethnic ethnicity" would best be interpreted as pointing to Paul's activity as an attempt at group-making in view of the human constructedness of all social formations, including locative and ethnic. So I would claim that the tension between a Paul focused on genealogical and kinship mythmaking and his interpretation of the Lord's supper and Christ myth with its implications of breaking socioreligious boundaries is not so odd or rebellious and just the kind of tension required by the constructedness of the ethnic and the non-ethnic. I say "not so odd" only with the caveat that we see Paul as someone working from another quite ordinary form of human sociality, the rather more autonomous pole of a field of cultural specialization.

---

109. For detailed discussion of these, see Brubaker, *Ethnicity without Groups*.

Paul's "Apocalypticism" and the Jesus Associations at Thessalonica and Corinth

Richard S. Ascough

Introduction

Although ancient voluntary associations were not formed solely for the purpose of burial of their members,[1] it is clear that death, burial, and memorial figured prominently in the collective lives of association members. In light of this prominence, it is interesting to note, with Jonathan Z. Smith, that questions concerning the status of dead members of the community trigger Paul's most extensive, and earliest, discussions of the resurrection of the dead (1 Thess 4 and 1 Cor 15).[2] In an attempt to explore further the nature of the Christian community at Thessalonica this essay examines the social context of Paul's eschatological description in 1 Thess 4:13–18.[3] Paul's comments to this community, and the social practices

---

An early version of this paper was prepared for the Ancient Myths and Modern Theories of Christian Origins Seminar and presented at the annual meeting of the Society of Biblical Literature, held in Denver in November 2001. It was subsequently much revised and condensed and published as "A Question of Death: Paul's Community-Building Language in 1 Thessalonians 4:13–18," *JBL* 123 (2004): 509–30. For this volume it has been further revised and broadened. I am grateful to all those who gave comments on various versions of the paper, along with research support from Queen's University, the Government of Ontario (Premier's Research Excellence Award), and the Social Sciences and Humanities Research Council of Canada.

1. John S. Kloppenborg, "Collegia and *Thiasoi*: Issues in Function, Taxonomy and Membership," in *Voluntary Associations in the Graeco-Roman World* (ed. John S. Kloppenborg and Stephen G. Wilson; London and New York: Routledge, 1996), 20–23.

2. Jonathan Z. Smith, *Drudgery Divine: On the Comparison of Early Christianities and the Religions of Late Antiquity* (Jordan Lectures in Comparative Religion 14; London: School of Oriental and African Studies, University of London; Chicago: University of Chicago Press, 1990), 131 n. 33.

3. Since this paper was first presented in 2001 various parts have appeared, in a different form, in other publications: Richard S. Ascough, "A Question of Death"; idem, *Paul's Macedonian Associations: The Social Context of Philippians and 1 Thessalonians* (WUNT 2/161; Tübingen: Mohr Siebeck, 2003). I am grateful to the publishers for permission to republish the material here.

that are lurking behind his words, are brought into contact with the larger database of group discourses and practices around the dead as found among voluntary associations. In particular, this paper takes up Burton L. Mack's suggestion that the Thessalonians' question to Paul concerning dead members was not a question about "personal salvation" but a question of "belonging."[4]

The primary focus of this paper is Thessalonica. One might ask why Thessalonica is brought into the discussion when Corinth is ostensibly our interest. To begin with, there are more *realia* from Thessalonica and its environs with respect to the voluntary associations than we find in Corinth. There are very few inscriptions from first-century Corinth that can be identified as arising from voluntary associations, and those that have been identified as such are badly damaged.[5] However, the presence of these damaged inscriptions shows that associations did exist at Corinth,[6] making the analogous use of the Thessalonian context possible. Furthermore, Paul's words on the *parousia* of Jesus seem to have developed between 1 Thessalonians and 1 Corinthians, suggesting that Paul's "mythmaking" process is at an earlier stage in 1 Thessalonians.[7] Therefore, 1 Thessalonians is promising for understanding the context within which Paul begins this particular trajectory of mythmaking for his own communities.

The Thessalonian Christian community was predominantly, if not exclusively, Gentile. I have argued elsewhere that the group was already formed as a professional association and, under Paul's influence, replaced their patron deities with a new deity named Jesus Christ.[8] If this is the case, we cannot assume that the Thessalonian audience was familiar with the apocalyptic worldview prevalent in much of Judaism at that time, although Paul himself would likely have been conversant with Jewish apocalyptic literature and images. Once Paul began the mythmaking process with his letter to the Thessalonians he continues along that track in his letter to the Corinthians. What arose as an answer to a direct question posed by the Thessalonians from their own context was woven into other contexts as part of the complex mythmaking agenda.

---

4. Burton L. Mack, *Who Wrote the New Testament? The Making of the Christian Myth* (San Francisco: HarperSanFrancisco, 1995), 110.

5. Benjamin Dean Meritt, *Corinth*, vol. 8, pt. 1, *Greek Inscriptions, 1896–1927* (Cambridge, Mass.: Harvard University Press, 1931), nos. 1–10; John Harvey Kent, *Corinth*, vol. 8, pt. 3, *The Inscriptions, 1926–1950* (Princeton: American School of Classical Studies at Athens, 1966), nos. 306–10.

6. The connection between voluntary associations and the Corinthian Christian communities has been debated for some time; see John S. Kloppenborg, "Edwin Hatch, Churches and *Collegia*," in *Origins and Method: Towards a New Understanding of Judaism and Christianity. Essays in Honour of John C. Hurd* (ed. Bradley H. McLean; JSNTSup 86; Sheffield: JSOT Press, 1993), 215 n. 12, 219.

7. Mack, *Who Wrote the New Testament?* 111.

8. For details, see Richard S. Ascough, "The Thessalonian Christian Community as a Professional Voluntary Association," *JBL* 119 (2000): 311–28.

In order to wrestle with the issue of Paul's use of "apocalyptic" language in 1 Thessalonians, I propose to take up the method of reimagining Christian origins promoted by Smith and Mack and perform four interrelated operations:[9]

- Description: What does the text say?
- Comparison: What is the sociocultural context?
- Rectification of Categories: What do we call "it"?
- Redescription: How do we (re)construct the situation?

To do so I want to give particular attention to voluntary associations. There is much evidence for voluntary associations in Macedonia, including Thessalonica. The associations provide an important backdrop for discussing attitudes toward death and dying, particularly insofar as they are linked to the cult of the dead and the memorialization of heroes.

Description: What Does the Text Say?

Many commentators recognize that behind 1 Thess 4:13–18 there is an issue troubling the Thessalonian Christians: "That there is a misunderstanding at Thessalonica is obvious but the object of this misconception needs clarification and better focus."[10] There are a number of possibilities as to why the Thessalonians were grieving over those who had died.[11] Some scholars suggest that Paul failed to convey to the Thessalonians that some of their members might die before the *parousia* of Jesus. However, "it is unlikely that Paul had failed to encounter Christians who had experienced the death of fellow believers" during the course of his travels.[12]

Other scholars suggest that "gnostic interlopers" had infiltrated the community, although, as Charles A. Wanamaker points out, such suggestions caricature Gnosticism and do not recognize the absence of anti-Gnostic polemic in the letter.

---

9. See Jonathan Z. Smith, "The 'End' of Comparison: Redescription and Rectification," in *A Magic Still Dwells: Comparative Religion in the Postmodern Age* (ed. Kimberley C. Patton and Benjamim C. Ray; Berkeley and Los Angeles: University of California Press, 2000), 239; Burton L. Mack, "On Redescribing Christian Origins," *MTSR* 8 (1996): 256–59; repr. in idem, *The Christian Myth: Origins, Logic, and Legacy* (New York: Continuum, 2001), 70–74; see also idem, "Social Formation," in *Guide to the Study of Religion* (ed. Willi Braun and Russell T. McCutcheon; London: Cassell, 2000), 294. I have reversed the order of the final two operations in order to highlight better how the process contributes to the project's aim of redescribing Christian origins at Corinth. This change in order is warranted not only by the interrelated nature of the operations but also by their nonsequential nature (see Mack, "Redescribing Christian Origins," 256; repr. in *Christian Myth*, 70).

10. Earl J. Richard, *First and Second Thessalonians* (SP 11; Collegeville, Minn.: Liturgical Press, 1995), 232; cf. Abraham J. Malherbe, *The Letters to the Thessalonians: A New Translation with Introduction and Commentary* (AB 32B; New York: Doubleday, 2000), 264.

11. See Charles A. Wanamaker, *The Epistles to the Thessalonians: A Commentary on the Greek Text* (NIGTC; Grand Rapids: Eerdmans, 1990), 164–66.

12. Ibid., 165.

At the same time, an alternative suggestion that some of the Thessalonians lost confidence in the *parousia* "runs up against the fact that Paul nowhere in the letter seeks to reassure, let alone prove, that the *parousia* would take place."[13] Some scholars suggest that the Thessalonians did not fully understand Paul's view of the *parousia* and believed it to be only for the living, not the dead.[14] However, it is unlikely that the Thessalonians were familiar with details of the *parousia* as Paul lays it out in 4:13–18 prior to Paul's writing them this letter.[15] It is not the *parousia*, the "second coming" of Jesus, that they misunderstand. Rather, as we will seek to show, they are concerned that only the living will escape the "coming wrath" (1:10) on the "day of the Lord" (5:2). The dead have no fear of "wrath," but also no hope for the future. Since those who have died are no longer part of the community, they will not participate in the benefits offered to the living on "that day."[16]

Recently, Abraham J. Malherbe has suggested that Paul was attempting to correct doctrinal misunderstandings as a means to modify the Thessalonians' behavior.[17] Paul was not contrasting Christian and pagan grief;[18] that is, he was not suggesting that the Thessalonians can evidence some type of "Christian" grief. Instead, Paul was making "an absolute prohibition" against grief—but one that must be understood as a direct reply to the question the Thessalonians had addressed to him. It is this question that has proved most elusive for exegetes. While the precise question that the Thessalonians asked might remain a mystery, we hope that an investigation of the wider sociocultural context can shed some light on what sort of issue the Thessalonians were facing and what concerns they were raising.

Mack asks a number of appropriate questions for determining the context of the Thessalonians' queries about those who had died. He places these questions in the context of the Thessalonians' joining a new "family," suggesting that they were struggling with their responsibilities toward those who had died, wrestling with whether the dead members of the family are incorporated into the larger family of God and God's kingdom. As Mack writes, "[T]hey were asking, do our dead still belong to us and we to them? Or have we lost contact with our dead and they with us?"[19] Similarly, Earl J. Richard submits that "careful reading of 4:13–18 suggests that it is not the resurrection of the dead which is at issue, but the status of those who die before the Lord's return," particularly "the status of the Christian dead

---

13. Ibid.
14. This is the case with Colin R. Nicholl, *From Hope to Despair in Thessalonica: Situating 1 and 2 Thessalonians* (SNTSMS 126; Cambridge: Cambridge University Press, 2004), 48.
15. Ibid., 20–22, 35–38. To my mind, Nicholl's argument on this point mitigates his larger argument that the Thessalonians have misunderstood the *parousia*.
16. Cf. ibid., 183, but again avoiding Nicholl's conclusion that the Thessalonians are thinking in terms of the *parousia* rather than simply escape from conflagration.
17. Malherbe, *Thessalonians*, 279.
18. Ibid., 264.
19. Mack, *Who Wrote the New Testament?* 110.

and living vis-à-vis the returning Lord."[20] Malherbe likewise locates the underlying issue of the passage in terms of how living and dead Christians would each participate in the events marking the end of this world and "how their experience would affect their relationship with each other."[21] Mack poses several other important questions, including:

> What if joining the Christ cult exacerbated the problem instead of solving it? What if joining the Christ cult had inadvertently threatened one's sense of belonging to the ancestral traditions lodged in the local cult of the dead? Could that have been the occasion for the question in Thessalonica about those who had died?[22]

For our investigation I want to add another question: What if adherence to the Christ-hero disrupted a pattern of burial practices without offering anything in its stead? Before we address this question, we need first to gain a broad understanding of death, burial, and memorial in Greco-Roman antiquity.

Comparison: What Is the Sociocultural Context?

The Sociocultural Context of Thessalonica

In general, Macedonia evidences the influence of Roman life and culture. Thessalonica itself has a long history, which extends from its founding in Hellenistic times to modern times. The large, flourishing city of modern Thessalonica is built upon the ancient site. Its commercial success, both now and in antiquity, is due to its location "in the most favourable geographical position in Macedonia."[23] The city of Thessalonica is located on the Thermatic Gulf to the west of the Chalcidice peninsula.[24] The Axios River lies to the west and the Strymon River to the east. The city was probably founded near, but not on, the original site of Therme, a Corinthian colony.[25]

---

20. Richard, *Thessalonians*, 231–32.
21. Malherbe, *Thessalonians*, 275.
22. Mack, *Who Wrote the New Testament?* 110.
23. Apostolos P. Vacalopoulos, *A History of Thessaloniki* (ΕΤΑΙΡΕΙΑ ΜΑΚΕΔΟΝΙΚΩΝ ΣΠΟΥΔΩΝ ΙΔΡΥΜΑ ΜΕΛΕΤΩΝ ΧΕΡΣΟΝΗΣΟΥ ΤΟΥ ΑΙΜΟΥ 63; trans. T. F. Carney; Thessalonica: Institute for Balkan Studies, 1963), 3. For an extensive introduction to the city of Thessalonica in the first century C.E., see Christoph vom Brocke, *Thessaloniki—Stadt des Kassander und Gemeinde des Paulus: Eine frühe christliche Gemeinde in ihrer heidnischen Umwelt* (WUNT 2/125; Tübingen: Mohr Siebeck, 2001), 12–101.
24. Thessalonica was about a three-day walk from Philippi, according to ancient patterns of travel; see Jerome Murphy-O'Connor, *Paul: A Critical Life* (Oxford: Clarendon, 1996), 103.
25. Vacalopoulos, *History of Thessaloniki*, 5; Holland L. Hendrix, "Thessalonica," *ABD* 6:523; see Strabo, *Geogr.* 7, frgs. 21, 24. Therme (Θέρμα) means "hot-spring," the site being so named because of the hot springs of salt water there (Alfred Plummer, *A Commentary on St. Paul's First Epistle to the Thessalonians* [London: Roxburghe, 1918], vii).

Thessalonica was surrendered to Rome after the defeat of Perseus at the battle of Pydna (168 B.C.E.). When Macedonia was divided into four districts (μερίδες) Thessalonica was made the capital of the second μερίς, which lay between the Strymon and Axios rivers. The city retained the right to govern itself according to its ancestral laws and to have its own officials.[26] In 146 B.C.E. it became the capital of the reorganized province of Macedonia and the seat of the provincial governor. This brought with it many commercial and civic privileges, including the right to mint its own coins.[27] Thessalonica's location on the Via Egnatia and its secure harbor in the Thermatic Gulf enhanced its commercial success.[28] During the Roman period, many Roman senators and knights of the equestrian order resided in Thessalonica, making the city a "second Rome."[29] Despite such Roman occupation, the city retained its Greek character, and the dominant written and spoken language throughout the Roman period was Greek.[30]

Many of the cults in Macedonia are of Thracian origin and thus are indigenous to the region. At the same time, there is early evidence for most of the chief Greek deities.[31] During the Hellenistic and Roman periods, the new gods took

---

26. Vacalopoulos, *History of Thessaloniki*, 11.

27. Holland L. Hendrix's dissertation ("Thessalonians Honor Romans" [Th.D. diss., Harvard Divinity School, 1984]) on the honors given to Romans by the inhabitants of Thessalonica from the second century B.C.E. to the first century C.E. provides much historical and political background for the study of the Thessalonian church. Epigraphic, literary, sculptural, and numismatic evidence suggests to Hendrix that the Thessalonians actively bestowed honors on those individuals who served as benefactors of the city. The Romans increasingly "became the objects of a distinct system of honors which rewarded positive administrative policies and other philanthropic activity beneficial to the city" (ibid., 336). This system developed in Thessalonica in ways not found in other urban areas. It is beyond the scope of Hendrix's immediate task to deal directly with the Thessalonian church. His study does, however, show the impact of Roman culture on the city of Thessalonica.

28. Strabo, writing in the late first century B.C.E., refers to Thessalonica as "the metropolis of what is now Macedonia" (ἡ μετρόπολις τῆν νῦν Μακεδονίας; Strabo, *Geogr.* 7, frg. 21).

29. Hendrix, "Thessalonians Honor Romans," 524.

30. Vacalopoulos, *History of Thessaloniki*, 15. Despite various urban centers being founded (or refounded) as Roman colonies, Greek culture continued to persist in many of them (David W. J. Gill, "Macedonia," in *The Book of Acts in Its Graeco-Roman Setting* [ed. David W. J. Gill and Conrad Gempf; The Book of Acts in Its First Century Setting 2; Grand Rapids: Eerdmans; Carlisle: Paternoster, 1994], 407; Fanoula Papazoglou, "Quelques aspects de l'histoire de la province de Macédoine," *ANRW* 7.1:334). In a few important cities during the Principate two distinct communities existed, one a Greek polis and the other a Roman colony (Cassandrea, Pella, Dium, and perhaps even Philippi; see Charles Edson, "Double Communities in Roman Macedonia," in *Essays in Memory of Basil Laourdas* [Thessalonica: N.p., 1975], 97–102; cf. Fanoula Papazoglou, "Macedonia under the Romans," in *Macedonia: 4000 Years of Greek History and Civilization* [ed. M. B. Sakellariou; Athens: Ekdotike Athenon, 1983], 198, who notes: "Political Romanization did not affect language and national conscience.... One became a Roman citizen without ceasing to speak Greek and feeling a Macedonian" [202]).

31. Charles Edson, ed., *Inscriptiones Graecae Epiri, Macedoniae, Thraciae, Scythiae*, II, *Inscriptiones Macedoniae*, fasc. 1, *Inscriptiones Thessalonicae et viciniae* (IG X/2; Berlin: de Gruyter, 1972), 634. The primary deities worshiped at Thessalonica were Pythian Apollo, Pallas Athena, and Hercules (Vacalopoulos, *History of Thessaloniki*, 14).

hold in Macedonia, the most popular being Sarapis and Isis.[32] By the first century C.E. the worship of mystery deities was thriving, including the worship of Dionysos, Asclepius, and Demeter. Karl P. Donfried identifies the cult of Cabirus as "the most important religious cult of Thessalonica at the time of Paul," an identification with which Robert Jewett concurs.[33]

Honorifics granted to the emperor are particularly prevalent at Thessalonica,[34] and there is some evidence for the worship of the goddess Roma. Thessalonica was given the title Neokoros under Gordian III in 238–244 C.E., acknowledging its temple of the imperial cult (it was made a colony only under Decius ca. 250 C.E.). The Thessalonians set up many inscriptions to honor Roman patrons and

---

32. R. E. Witt, "The Egyptian Cults in Ancient Macedonia," in *Ancient Macedonia: Papers Read at the First International Symposium held in Thessaloniki, 26-29 August 1968* (ed. Basil Laourdas and Ch. Makaronas; ΕΤΑΙΡΕΙΑ ΜΑΚΕΔΟΝΙΚΩΝ ΣΠΟΥΔΩΝ ΙΔΡΥΜΑ ΜΕΛΕΤΩΝ ΧΕΡΣΟΝΗΣΟΥ ΤΟΥ ΑΙΜΟΥ 122; Thessalonica: Institute for Balkan Studies, 1970), 324–33. A Sarapeum discovered in the 1920s and the subsequent finds of dedicatory objects, inscriptions, and buildings reveal a great interest at Thessalonica in the Egyptian gods; see Karl P. Donfried, "The Cults of Thessalonica and the Thessalonian Correspondence," *NTS* 31 (1985): 337; Witt, "Egyptian Cults," 324–33. The Sarapeum and its surrounding area that were first discovered at Thessalonica in 1917 have proved to be a rich deposit for archaeological information; see Donfried, "Cults of Thessalonica," 337. Unfortunately these remains are no longer visible as they are covered by modern structures (Dioiketerion Street; a private house). The worship of the Egyptian gods may even date to as early as the third century B.C.E. (Vacalopoulos, *History of Thessaloniki*, 8).

33. Donfried, "Cults of Thessalonica," 338; idem, "Theology of 1 Thessalonians," in *The Theology of the Shorter Pauline Epistles* (ed. Karl P. Donfried and I. Howard Marshall; New Testament Theology; Cambridge: Cambridge University Press, 1993), 15; Robert Jewett, *The Thessalonian Correspondence: Pauline Rhetoric and Millenarian Piety* (FF; Philadelphia: Fortress, 1986), 127–32; cf. R. E. Witt, "The Kabeiroi in Ancient Macedonia," in *Ancient Macedonia II: Papers Read at the Second International Symposium held in Thessaloniki, 19-24 August 1973* (ΕΤΑΙΡΕΙΑ ΜΑΚΕΔΟΝΙΚΩΝ ΣΠΟΥΔΩΝ ΙΔΡΥΜΑ ΜΕΛΕΤΩΝ ΧΕΡΣΟΝΗΣΟΥ ΤΟΥ ΑΙΜΟΥ 155; Thessalonica: Institute for Balkan Studies, 1977), 78–79. Cabirus became the patron god of the city and appeared on coins at least as early as the second century B.C.E. At a later date, the worship of the one Cabirus was "transubstantiated, with all its fervour, into the cult of Saint Demetrius, the patron saint and protector of the city" (Vacalopoulos, *History of Thessaloniki*, 14; but see Christopher Walter, "The Thracian Horseman: Ancestor of the Warrior Saints," *ByzF* 14 [1989]: 657–73). Elsewhere it was the cult of the (two) Cabiri, but at Thessalonica there is evidence for only one Cabirus in the cult (Donfried, "Cults of Thessalonica," 338). Although there is some evidence that in the Greco-Roman world the cult of the Cabiri was conflated with the cult of the Dioscuri, this is not the case at Thessalonica, where the cult of the one Cabirus seems to be different from the cult of the Dioscuri (Donfried, "Cults of Thessalonica," 338–39; *pace* Charles Edson, "Cults of Thessalonica [Macedonica III]," *HTR* 41 [1948]: 192). The Dioscuri are attested at Thessalonica from 40 B.C.E.; see Hendrix, "Thessalonians Honor Romans," 148–50; and the summary in John S. Kloppenborg, "ΦΙΛΑΔΕΛΦΙΑ, ΘΕΟΔΙΔΑΚΤΟΣ and the Dioscuri: Rhetorical Engagement in 1 Thessalonians 4.9–12," *NTS* 39 (1993): 286. Of the mystery deities, only the Cabiri are not referred to in voluntary association inscriptions from Thessalonica, although they are probably the deities indicated in the dedication to "the Great Gods in Samothrace" in *SIG*[3] 1140 from Amphipolis, since Samothrace was the center of the worship of the Cabiri.

34. The system was developed "to attract and sustain influential Romans' commitments and favors" (Hendrix, "Thessalonians Honor Romans," 253).

Roman client rulers who had served as benefactors of the city. A cult even grew around these benefactors, including a special priesthood, the "Priest of Rome and of Roman Benefactors."[35] There was a clear recognition of "a hierarchy of benefaction extending from the gods to the emperor and Roman patrons to the citizens of Thessalonica."[36] Romans received honors at Thessalonica not because of who they were but rather because of what they did.[37]

The city of Thessalonica provides the richest evidence for voluntary associations in Macedonia, with at least forty-four Greek inscriptions dating from the first to the third century C.E. showing a diversity of associations and deities worshiped.[38] Most of the evidence attests to Dionysos associations and professional associations, although there is evidence for other types of associations. It is to these associations that we now turn our attention. Given the tri-cultural identity of Thessalonica—Greek, Roman, Macedonian—we will draw upon a range of data from associations from all three spheres in order to provide a context for understanding Paul's letter to the Thessalonians. We are particularly interested in the activities of associations around death, burial, and memorial.

---

35. Vacalopoulos, *History of Thessaloniki*, 14 (emphasis omitted); Papazoglou, "Macedonia," 540 n. 110; *IG* X/2 31, 32, 133, 226. Holland L. Hendrix notes that at Thessalonica "[t]he title 'benefactor' and '*soter*' (savior) became personalized and regularized epithets of an increasingly divinized Hellenistic royalty (as, for example, with Ptolemy Savior or Eumenes Benefactor)" and that by "95 BCE, Roman benefactors had already become conventionally associated with the civic cult of 'the gods' as honorands of gymnasium activities" ("Benefactor/Patron Networks in the Urban Environment: Evidence from Thessalonica," *Semeia* 56 [1992]: 42, 50; cf. *IG* X/2 4). For a detailed study, see idem, "Thessalonians Honor Romans." On the Emperor cult at Thessalonica, see also Robert M. Evans, "Eschatology and Ethics: A Study of Thessalonica and Paul's Letters to the Thessalonians" (Th.D. diss., Basel University, 1967).

36. Holland L. Hendrix, "Beyond 'Imperial Cult' and 'Cult of Magistrates,'" in *Society of Biblical Literature 1986 Seminar Papers* (SBLSP 25; Atlanta: Scholars Press, 1986), 308; idem, "Thessalonians Honor Romans," 336–37.

37. Hendrix, "Thessalonians Honor Romans," 330, 332. Hendrix shows that, with perhaps the exception of Julius *Theos*, Augustus, and Trajan (and later Fulvus), the inscriptional evidence from Thessalonica does not indicate that the Thessalonians acknowledged the deification of the emperor (see "Thessalonians Honor Romans," some of the pertinent information of which is summarized in idem, "Beyond 'Imperial Cult,'" 300–308; against Papazoglou, "Macedonia," 206–7). In this respect, Thessalonica was different from many of the cities in the empire, especially in Asia Minor.

38. See Richard S. Ascough, "Voluntary Associations and Community Formation: Paul's Macedonian Christian Communities in Context" (Ph.D. diss., University of St. Michael's College, Toronto School of Theology, 1997), 297–307; cf. idem, *Paul's Macedonian Associations*, passim. Appendix I of the dissertation includes the texts and translations of seventy-five Macedonian inscriptions that are associated with voluntary associations. A recent work by Pantelis Mel. Nigdelis (*ΕΠΙΓΡΑΦΙΚΑ ΘΕΣΣΑΛΟΝΙΚΕΙΑ: ΣΥΜΒΟΛΗ ΕΤΗΝ ΠΟΛΙΤΙΚΗ ΚΑΙ ΚΟΙΝΩΝΙΚΗ ΙΣΤΟΡΙΑ ΤΗΣ ΑΡΧΑΙΑΣ ΘΕΣΣΑΛΟΝΙΚΗΣ* [Thessalonica: University Studio Press, 2006], 101–216) adds another thirteen association inscriptions from Thessalonica to the data. See also vom Brocke, *Thessaloniki*, 124–29.

Voluntary Associations and Their Dead

Many ancient tombstones from across the Roman Empire attest to the fact that death was simply the cessation of life:[39] "If you want to know who I am, the answer is ash and burnt embers . . ." (*CIL* IX 1837). Or again,

> We are nothing.
> See, reader, how quickly
> we mortals return
> from nothing to nothing. (*CIL* VI 26003)

There is the more perfunctory "I didn't exist, I existed, I don't exist, I don't care" (*CIL* V 2283).[40] Others offer practical advice from beyond the grave:

> Friends, who read this, listen to my advice: mix wine, tie the garlands around your head, drink deep. And do not deny pretty girls the sweets of love. When death comes, earth and fire consume everything. (*CIL* VI 17985a)

However, not all polytheists had "no hope," though the percentage is not high.[41] For example, a father expresses grief for his nine-year-old daughter along with hope of reunion in the afterlife:

> The cruel Fates have left me a sad old age. I shall always be searching for you, my darling Asiatica. Sadly shall I often imagine your face to comfort myself. My consolation will be that soon I shall see you, when my own life is done, and my shadow is joined with yours. (*CIL* XI 3711)

---

39. Translations of these Latin epitaphs are found in Keith Hopkins, *Death and Renewal* (Sociological Studies in Roman History 2; New York and Cambridge: Cambridge University Press, 1983), 227–30. For the Greeks, outside the mystery religions, afterlife expectation "was probably, at best, a static and rather dull existence and, at worst, one of retribution for earthly deeds" (Sarah Iles Johnston, "Death, the Afterlife, and Other Last Things: Greece," in *Religions of the Ancient World: A Guide* [ed. Sarah Iles Johnston; Cambridge, Mass., and London: Harvard University Press, 2004], 487–88). This started to change with the coming of the Romans with their emphasis on the communal nature of death, particularly the integration of the newly dead into the collectivity of the ancestors (John Bodel, "Death, the Afterlife, and Other Last Things: Rome," in Johnston, *Religions of the Ancient World*, 489).

40. Hopkins (*Death and Renewal*, 230) notes that this is so common that it is sometimes expressed simply by the initials *nf f ns nc* (*non fui, fui, non sum, non curo*). For variations, see Hans-Josef Klauck, *The Religious Context of Early Christianity: A Guide to Graeco-Roman Religions* (Minneapolis: Fortress, 2003), 80.

41. Klauck (*Religious Context*, 80) suggests that "it has been estimated that only at most 10 per cent of the funerary epigrams contain even a hint of a hope for an afterlife," but he does not say who has done such estimating and on what basis. See examples of epitaphs that reflect a belief in the future life in Richard Lattimore, *Themes in Greek and Latin Epitaphs* (Illinois Studies in Language and Literature 28; Urbana: University of Illinois Press, 1942), 45–74, 208–9.

Survival after death is indicated in the depiction of meal scenes in funerary monuments[42] and in the many goods that were buried with an individual, which were intended to make more pleasant the person's life after death.[43] In some cases, pipes were built into the tombs so that food and drink could be poured down for the dead.[44] It would be incorrect simply to assume that Paul, in 1 Thess 4:13, is contrasting Jesus believers with *all* nonbelievers in warning against grieving like those with no hope. Some did have hope for reunification with loved ones. Therefore, another explanation must be found.

In antiquity many persons were members of one or more voluntary associations. Ramsay MacMullen places the number of members of associations at about one-third of the urban population of Rome in the second century C.E., a figure that is likely reflected across the empire, perhaps only slightly less at an earlier time.[45] Modern scholarship usually identifies three broad categories of associations: religious associations, professional associations, and funerary associations.[46] The funerary associations (or *collegia tenuiorum*, or *collegia funeraticia*) are described as being organized to ensure the proper burial of their deceased members. In exchange, members paid entrance fees and/or regular dues that would be pooled for the burials. However, associations formed solely for the burial of members did not exist until the second century C.E. (from the time of Hadrian and beyond).[47] In fact, even at that time they were a "legal fiction," a way of gaining legal recognition

---

42. Katherine M. D. Dunbabin, *The Roman Banquet: Images of Conviviality* (Cambridge: Cambridge University Press, 2003), 126.

43. Hopkins, *Death and Renewal*, 229.

44. Ibid., 234; J. M. C. Toynbee, *Death and Burial in the Roman World* (Baltimore and London: Johns Hopkins University Press, 1971), 51–54; Jon Davies, *Death, Burial and Rebirth in the Religions of Antiquity* (Religion in the First Christian Centuries; London and New York: Routledge, 1999), 152; Dunbabin, *Roman Banquet*, 125–27.

45. Ramsay MacMullen, *Enemies of the Roman Order: Treason, Unrest, and Alienation in the Empire* (Cambridge, Mass.: Harvard University Press, 1966; repr., London and New York: Routledge, 1992), 174.

46. Richard S. Ascough, "Associations, Voluntary," *Eerdmans Dictionary of the Bible* (ed. David Noel Freedman; Grand Rapids: Eerdmans, 2000), 117–18.

47. Kloppenborg, "Collegia and *Thiasoi*," 20–22; Frank M. Ausbüttel, *Untersuchungen zu den Vereinen im Westen des römischen Reiches* (Frankfurter althistorische Studien 11; Kallmünz: Lassleben, 1982), 20, 29; Jonathan Scott Perry, *The Roman Collegia: The Modern Evolution of an Ancient Concept* (Mnemosyne Supplements 277; Leiden and Boston: Brill, 2006), 32; cf. idem, "A Death in the *Familia*: The Funerary Colleges of the Roman Empire" (Ph.D. diss., University of North Carolina at Chapel Hill, 1999). See also Erich G. L. Ziebarth (*Das griechische Vereinswesen* [Stuttgart: Hirzel, 1896; repr., Wiesbaden: Sändig, 1969], 17) and Franz Poland (*Geschichte des griechischen Vereinswesens* [Preisschriften gekrönt und herausgegeben von der fürstlich Jablonowskischen Gesellschaft zu Leipzig 38; Leipzig: Teubner, 1909; repr., Leipzig: Zentral-Antiquariat der Deutschen Demokratischen Republik, 1967], 56, 503–4), who note the lack of evidence for the existence of associations devoted exclusively to the burial of members among the Greek associations; so also Peter M. Fraser, *Rhodian Funerary Monuments* (Oxford: Clarendon, 1977), 58–70; see Kloppenborg, "Collegia and *Thiasoi*," 22, 29 nn. 41, 42.

to meet as a group while another purpose (usually social) was the primary interest of the group. The frequent mention of associations in burial contexts is a result of associations constituted for professional or religious reasons taking care of the burial of their own members. In some cases other persons commissioned an association to carry out certain rites at their tomb, although this was not the principal raison d'être of the association.

Nevertheless, the extent to which many associations were involved in activities around death is striking:

> About one third of the total epigraphic production of Roman associations in the eastern provinces records funerary activities of some sort, some inscriptions commemorating the burial of a collegium member by the association, while others mention collegia in recording the funerary arrangements of (wealthy) outsiders. It has been estimated that about one fifth of all known Italian associations were directly involved in the funerals of their members.[48]

Burial of association members included the setting up of inscriptions in memory of the deceased.[49] In this regard, Macedonia is similar to places elsewhere in the empire. The professional association of donkey drivers from Beroea set up a memorial to one of its members,[50] as did the associates of Poseidonios (set up in conjunction with the deceased's wife and son).[51] Purple-dyers in Thessalonica commemorated their deceased in a similar manner (*IG* X/2 291), as did the worshipers of Dionysos (*IG* X/2 503), Herakles (*IG* X/2 288 and 289), the Asiani (*IG* X/2 309 and 480),[52] and a hero cult (*IG* X/2 821). A more elaborate funerary practice is described in the tomb epigram from Amphipolis, where the dances of the Bacchants are detailed.[53] Some associations may have been involved in the actual burial of these members, as is the case with *SEG* XXXVII 559 (Kassandreia) and *CIG* 2000f (Hagios Mamas). The extensive evidence for the connections between associations and the deceased in Philippi (and Macedonia more generally) led

---

48. Onno M. van Nijf, *The Civic World of Professional Associations in the Roman East* (Dutch Monographs on Ancient History and Archaeology 17; Amsterdam: Gieben, 1997), 31.

49. Kloppenborg, "Collegia and *Thiasoi*," 21. For regulations pertaining to the actual rites associated with burial see *LSCG* 77 (Delphi; fourth century B.C.E.) and *IG* XII/5 593.

50. A. M. Woodward, "Inscriptions from Beroea in Macedonia," *Annual of the British School at Athens* 18 (1911–12): 155 no. 22.

51. G. H. R. Horsley, *New Documents Illustrating Early Christianity: A Review of the Greek Inscriptions and Papyri Published in 1979* (NewDocs 4; North Ryde, N.S.W.: Ancient History Documentary Research Centre, Macquarie University, 1987), 215 no. 19.

52. See also Emmanuel Voutiras, "Berufs- und Kultverein: Ein ΔΟΥΜΟΣ in Thessalonike," *ZPE* 90 (1992): 87–96.

53. William R. Paton, ed. and trans., *The Greek Anthology* (5 vols.; LCL; Cambridge, Mass.: Harvard University Press; London: Heinemann, 1916–18), 2:264–65.

Francis W. Beare to conclude that, "[w]hen Paul came to Philippi, he would find ready hearers for a gospel of resurrection from the dead, and life eternal."[54]

Finances were closely connected to the provision of burials and memorials. Dues collected could be designated for burial. *IG* II² 1278, for example, notes the payment of a "prescribed funeral fee." The bylaws of an association from Lanuvium, Italy, prescribes a small monthly fee of five *asses* (about one-third of a denarius) and, perhaps more interestingly, cites a clause from the *Senatus consultum* which allows that "those who desire to make monthly contributions for funerals may assemble" and form an association (*CIL* XIV 2112; 136 C.E.). In some cases, fundraising was employed to cover, among other things, the costs of funerals.[55] An association inscription from masons from mid-first century C.E. Rough Cilicia lists the names of a number of unrelated men[56] who have joint shares in a tomb that belongs to a κοινόν (*IKilikiaBM* 2 201). Their regulations stipulate:

> If any brother [ἀδελφός] should wish to sell his share, the remaining brothers shall buy it. If the brothers [οἱ ἀδελφοί] do not wish to buy the share, then let them take the aforementioned cash, and let them (all) withdraw from the association.[57]

It is clear that the promise of burial plays a major part in this particular association. In the case of some associations, members could be fined and/or banished from the rituals for a set period of time if they failed to attend the funeral of a member or failed to follow the etiquette of the funeral procedures.[58] For example, the Iobacchi of second-century Athens stipulate that "if one of the Iobacchi dies, let him be crowned up to the cost of 5 drachmae, and let a single jar of wine be set before those who attend the funeral, but let not anyone who has not attended the funeral have any wine" (*IG* II² 1368). In the case of an association from first-century B.C.E. Rhodes, failure to follow the regulations of bestowing honors upon

---

54. Francis W. Beare, *A Commentary on the Epistle to the Philippians* (Black's New Testament Commentaries; London: Black, 1959), 9. Beare calls these associations "burial-clubs" as does Paul Perdrizet, who points out that it is interesting to note the large number of funerary associations at Philippi, the first European city in which Christianity took root ("Inscriptions de Philippes: Les Rosalies," *BCH* 24 [1900]: 318). In both cases they seem to indicate that the associations at Philippi are similar to the Roman *collegia funeriticia*.

55. Livy 2.33.11; Pliny, *Nat.* 21.10; 33.138; Valerius Maximus 4.4.2; 5.2.3; 5.6.8; Nicholas K. Rauh, *The Sacred Bonds of Commerce: Religion, Economy, and Trade Society at Hellenistic Roman Delos, 166–87 B.C.* (Amsterdam: Gieben, 1993), 273 with n. 66.

56. The exceptions are two of the ten who are named as sons of the same father.

57. The men named earlier in the inscription are not the entire κοινόν, just those who have a share in one particular tomb of the κοινόν. The regulation suggests that, should one of these men withdraw, the others must "buy out" his share unless a replacement can be found. If they do not, they must withdraw (as a group) from the larger κοινόν, each receiving the stated amount of cash. However, the tomb remains the property of the κοινόν, which is not disbanded.

58. See *IG* II² 1275; *PCairoDem* 30605, 30606; *PMichTebt* 243, 244.

benefactors at their burial will result in a fine of one hundred drachmae (*IG* XII/1 155).

The commitment of an association to the burial of its deceased members went beyond informal agreement. In a number of cases the records show that the arrangement was formalized and binding, and grievances were subject to the proceedings of a court of law. An inscription from Lanuvium shows that, when the burial of a member took place in a different town, the documents pertaining to the reimbursement of funeral arrangements required the seals of seven Roman citizens (*CIL* XIV 2112). In the case of suicide, the Lanuvium inscription stipulates that the right to burial has been forfeited. In a papyrus find from Egypt, we have a letter from a woman appealing to the King Ptolemaios on behalf of her dead brother:

> I, Krateia, from Alexandrou Nesos, have been wronged by Philip and Dionysius in the following way. My brother Apolodotos was a fellow member of the association with them.... When my brother died, not only did they not provide a funeral for him or accompany him to the burial site, in violation of the association's rule, but they did not reimburse me for the expenses for his funeral. (*PEnteuxeis* 20; 221 B.C.E.)

Written on the papyrus in a different handwriting is this response: "After examining the association's rule, compel them to make good and if they contest, send them to me." In another instance, a man files a similar complaint on behalf of his sister, whose family was not reimbursed for the funeral expenses, even though she was a member and a priestess of the association (*PEnteuxeis* 21; 218 B.C.E.). In each case, despite the deceased's being a member of an association, the association did not pay for the funeral. In the eyes of the complainant this represented a breach of contract.

Another significant aspect of the connection between associations and funerary practices is evidenced in a number of associations that patrons founded or endowed for the purpose of commemorating the anniversary of his or her death at the family tomb. Often association membership not only included the guarantee of a decent burial but also the possibility of the annual commemoration of one's death.[59] A significant number of association inscriptions indicate funerary practices of some sort, particularly memorials for the deceased in the form of banquets.[60] Often an already existing association was endowed with a bequest of money or property (e.g., vineyards or land), the income of which was to be used

---

59. Cf. Ernest Renan, *The Apostles: Including the Period from the Death of Jesus until the Greater Mission of Paul* (New York: Carleton, 1866), 285–86.

60. From her examination of funerary art, Dunbabin concludes that from the Hellenistic period on "the interrelationship of dining and death has become a cliché of funerary art" (*Roman Banquet*, 139).

for a memorial at the tomb of the deceased. The remainder of the income, however, went to the association for its own use, probably for social gatherings like banquets (see *IG* X/2 259). Occasionally an association was formed in order to keep an annual memorial for the deceased, as is the case with *CIL* III 656. A number of tombs include dining facilities (triclinia and sometimes hearths) in order to facilitate the memorial banquets of family or association members.[61]

Many of the Macedonian association inscriptions with funerary contexts indicate that the association was involved in a festival known as the *Rosalia*:[62] from Philippi and its surrounding area we have *CIL* III 703, 704, 707; *IMakedD* 920; *IPhilippi* 133, 029/1. Many *viciani* (associations formed of members of a particular village) participated in the celebration of the *Rosalia* or *Parentalia* at the tomb of the deceased.[63] The *Rosalia* is mentioned in a Thessalonian inscription: in *IG* X/2 260 where a priestess of a θίασος bequeaths two plethra of grapevines to ensure that festivities involving rose crowns are conducted.[64]

In Italy the rose played a significant role in the funeral cult—the Italians called their feasts of the dead the *Rosalia*, or "day of roses."[65] The *Rosalia* had two aspects to it: one was the commemoration of the deceased; the other was the joyous celebration of the return of spring and summer with an emphasis on banqueting and fun.[66] Since there is little evidence that the connection between roses and funerary practices was indigenous to Macedonia or Thrace before the coming of the Romans, it is probable that when the Italian colonists came to Macedonia they brought many of their own practices and beliefs with them, including the *Rosalia*.

---

61. Ibid., 127–30.

62. On the *Rosalia*, see Perdrizet, "Inscriptions de Philippes," 299–333; Poland, *Geschichte des griechischen Vereinswesens*, 511–13; Paul Collart, *Philippes, ville de Macédoine depuis ses origines jusqu'à la fin de l'époque romaine* (École française d'Athènes, travaux et mémoires 5; Paris: Boccard, 1937), 474–85; A. S. Hoey, "Rosaliae Signorum," *HTR* 30 (1937): 22–30; Charles Picard and Charles Avezou, "Le Testament de la prêtresse Thessalonicienne," *BCH* 38 (1914): 53–62. The festival was popular throughout the Roman Empire (C. Robert Phillips, "Rosalia or Rosaria," *OCD* [3rd ed.; 1996], 1335), as well as among associations (Toynbee, *Death and Burial*, 63–64). Poland notes that the evidence for associations involved with the *Rosalia* comes primarily from Bithynia in Asia Minor and around Thessalonica and Philippi "in Thrace" [sic] (*Geschichte des griechischen Vereinswesens*, 511).

63. The *Parentalia* occurred for nine days in February (Feb. 13–21). Temples were closed and marriages did not take place. The days were taken up with private celebrations for the family dead. The final day was a public ceremony called the *Feralia*, in which a household made offerings at the graves of its deceased members (see further Herbert Jennings Rose, "Feralia," *OCD* [2nd ed.; 1970], 434; idem, "Parentalia," *OCD* [2nd ed.; 1970], 781; Davies, *Death, Burial and Rebirth*, 145–46). For benefaction that ensures that guild members hold a banquet at a tomb of a deceased member on the day of the *Parentalia*, see *CIL* XI 5047. An example of the *Parentalia* in Macedonia is found in *CIL* III 656 from Selian; see also Collart, *Philippes*, 474–75 n. 3 no. 7, 479–80.

64. Perdrizet ("Inscriptions de Philippes," 323) points to a large sarcophagus from Thessalonica (now in the Louvre) on the lid of which a man and wife are shown in repose. The wife holds in her hand a crown of roses. See further bibliography in ibid., 323 nn. 1–2.

65. The roses symbolized the return of *"la belle saison,"* when the earth seems to burst into life.

66. Hoey, "Rosaliae," 22.

Since Macedonia was famous for its roses,[67] it is no surprise that Italian settlers imported the *Rosalia*.[68] It seems that "self-commemorators who introduced *Rosalia* into their funerary arrangements were thus making a deliberate statement of (assumed) Roman cultural identity."[69]

A number of voluntary associations celebrated the *Rosalia* festival.[70] However, some Macedonian inscriptions suggest that the deceased was not a member of the association involved in the *Rosalia*.[71] In order to pay for the festival the deceased left an association a plot of land, a vineyard, or a bequest of money to be invested. The revenues from a bequest provided the necessary funds for the *Rosalia* to be carried out.[72] Presumably the unused portions of the interest from the endowment went to further the social practices of the association (cf. *IG* X/2 260). To ensure that the wishes were carried out after the testator's death, the bequest was made public through an inscription, and occasionally alternative recipients of the bequest were designated. For example, the testamentary inscription of Euphronsyne, a priestess of Dionysos at Thessalonica, stipulates that if the designated θίασος of Dionysos does not properly fulfill her wishes, then the bequest is to be transferred to a different θίασος of Dionysos (*IG* X/2 260). The rival group is sure to be watching the first carefully in order to ensure that the *Rosalia* is performed and to look for some flaw in the execution of the ceremonies. The inscription concludes, "if the other *thiasos* does not carry out the terms of the bequest, then the vineyard is to become the property of the city." Likewise, the association of the god Souregethes at Philippi would be sure to carry out the request of Valeria Mantana lest they be fined, with the monies going to the association at the shrine of the hero (*IPhilippi* 133).

In antiquity an endowment could be made in order to ensure that certain rites be performed in memory of an individual and his or her family.[73] There were

---

67. Edson, "Cults of Thessalonica," 169; Picard and Avezou, "Testament de la prêtresse," 53–54. On the making of rose crowns in Macedonia, see Theophrastus, *Caus. plant.* 1.13.11 (Dion); *Hist. plant.* 6.6.4 (the region around Philippi); and Herodotus, *Hist.* 8.138.1 (below the eastern slopes of the Bermion range).

68. However, it is interesting to note that although the Italian *Rosalia* is celebrated, the Thracian Horseman often decorates the tombstones in Macedonian villages (Perdrizet, "Inscriptions de Philippes," 320), obviously suggesting synchronistic funerary practices (see *IPhilippi* 029/1; *IMakedD* 920; and *CIL* III 704).

69. Van Nijf, *Professional Associations*, 64.

70. See Paul R. Trebilco (*Jewish Communities in Asia Minor* [SNTSMS 69; Cambridge: Cambridge University Press, 1991], 80), who mentions only the involvement of professional associations and suggests that these had constituted themselves as funerary associations.

71. *CIL* III 703, 704, 707; *IPhilippi* 133, 029/1. In some of the Macedonian cases, the testator may have been a member; these inscriptions leave his membership unclear.

72. Trebilco, *Jewish Communities*, 80.

73. For a comprehensive collection of such texts, see Bernhard Laum, *Stiftungen in der griechischen und römischen Antike: Ein Beitrag zur antiken Kulturgeschichte* (Leipzig: Teubner, 1914); cf.

two primary types of "foundations": private and public.[74] The latter foundations established a link between the civic magistrates and the deceased. In exchange for a significant bequest, a perpetual memorial was established, with attendant priests and sacrifices. Of more interest for our purposes is the private or "familial" foundation whereby an association was formed (or an existing one endowed) in order to establish a memorial at the family tomb.[75] An example is found in a third-century B.C.E. inscription from the island of Thera, in which a woman bequeaths a large sum in order to begin a private association to honor the memory of her husband, her sons, and herself (*IG* XII/3 330).[76] It provides a social setting for the members to meet and eat together for three days every year. The will aims to create an association of all male relatives of the founder, those living and those to be born. A list of twenty-five names is included, with the son-in-law and the adoptive brother at the head. Wives of the members, their daughters, and a number of specific women are also admitted.

Foundations set up through the benefaction of an association brought honor not only to the person(s) memorialized but also to the association: "Collegia entrusted with tasks which might ideally have gone to such organizations as the *boule* or the *gerousia* had to be regarded as trustworthy and respectable organizations."[77] They represented a claim on the part of the association of belonging to the polis and functioned as a means of establishing status in the hierarchical order of the polis, regardless of whether those outside the association noticed.[78] That is, they were a method of showing where one belonged in the larger social order.

Anneliese Mannzmann, *Griechische Stiftungsurkunden: Studie zu Inhalt und Rechtsform* (Fontes et Commentationes 2; Münster: Aschendorff, 1962), 136–47.

74. Pauline Schmitt-Pantel, "Évergétisme et mémoire du mort: À propos des fondations de banquets publics dans les cités grecques à l'époque hellénistique et romaine," in *La Mort, les morts dans les sociétés anciennes* (ed. Gherardo Gnoli and Jean-Pierre Vernant; Cambridge: Cambridge University Press, 1982), 177; C. P. Jones, "A Deed of Foundation from the Territory of Ephesos," *JRS* 73 (1983): 116–17.

75. See the discussion of Jones, "Deed of Foundation," 116–25. An interesting example of a foundation that benefits extant private associations and the city (*IEphesos* 3803) is discussed by Thomas Drew-Bear, "An Act of Foundation from Hypaipa," *Chiron* 10 (1980): 509–36. A private citizen of Hypaipa serves as benefactor of the wool sellers and the linen weavers with a sum of money and gives to these two guilds and four others the use of a vineyard which he donates to the city (515–16).

76. Jones calls this a "perfectly preserved example" of the establishing of a private memorial association ("Deed of Foundation," 116). A similar inscription can be found in *SIG*³ 1106, the Foundation of Diomedon of Cos. The original deed of Diomedon is not included, but there are extant four columns, each being part of separate documents, "engraved at different, but not very distant times" (William R. Paton and Edward L. Hicks, *The Inscriptions of Cos* [Oxford: Clarendon, 1891], 74). For text and commentary, see *ICos* 36. See also *IG* XII/7 515 (Aigiale; late second century B.C.E.); *IGR* IV 661; *IEphesos* 3214. Cf. *SEG* III 674, which is a document of a funerary κοινόν, although not the foundational document.

77. Van Nijf, *Professional Associations*, 66.
78. Ibid.

Clearly, we see a wide range of practices concerning the dead within associations, from carrying out the funeral of a member or paying the expenses for a family funeral to setting up epitaphs and maintaining tombs, burial grounds, and *columbaria* (collective tombs made up of niches for individual urns). In many associations a major part of the commitment of the association to its membership would include the provision of burial and/or memorial or at least a contribution toward the expenses of burial. Members of some associations were expected to bequeath property to the association.[79]

The Social Impact of Burial within Associations

At this point we need to examine why the burial aspect of associations was so pervasive in the Greco-Roman period, particularly from the first century C.E. It is without doubt linked to the larger social context of the time. A number of studies have investigated why associations took on the tasks of burial and memorial. For the most part, the explanation offered asserts the need of the destitute for an assurance of burial.[80] This is then linked to mortality rates and population distribution in the empire that, it is suggested, led to persons dying without any member of the family surviving to perform the requisite burial rites. This event required reliance on an association to perform traditional funerary rites.[81] While this analysis has some merit, it does not represent the full picture. The expense of association dues would have kept the really destitute outside the membership. Burial by an association was a "relatively expensive privilege." The breakdown of family connections is not a satisfactory explanation, because associations in small, relatively stable villages were just as likely to bury members as those in the city. Thus, Onno M. van Nijf points out, "being buried by a collegium was less a necessity than a conscious choice."[82] There must be other reasons that contribute to the choice to be buried by an association and the emphasis given to the deceased's membership in an association.

Van Nijf's investigation of the social context of association burial practices is instructive.[83] Monuments to the dead were the first things a visitor to Rome would

---

79. Rauh, *Sacred Bonds*, 255, citing *CIL* XIV 2112; and Jean-Pierre Waltzing, *Étude historique sur les corporations professionnelles chez les Romains depuis les origines jusqu'à la chute de l'Empire d'Occident* (4 vols.; Mémoire couronne par l'Academie royale des Sciences, des Lettres et des Beaux-Arts de Belgique; Louvain: Peeters, 1895–1900), 4:440–44.

80. E.g., Hopkins, *Death and Renewal*, 214.

81. For descriptions of these positions, see van Nijf, *Professional Associations*, 33. Hopkins (*Death and Renewal*, 210) describes the problems surrounding the disposal of a large number of bodies every year and cites a first-century B.C.E. boundary stone that stipulates: "No burning of corpses beyond this marker in the direction of the city. No dumping of ordure or of corpses." Underneath is written in red letters: "Take shit further on, if you want to avoid trouble" (*CIL* VI 31615).

82. Van Nijf, *Professional Associations*, 33.

83. The following is summarized from ibid., 34–38.

see.[84] The presence of burial places around the outskirts of a city, and the intermingling of these with roads, garden plots, sanctuaries, workshops, and homes, reveal a mixing of the living and the dead: "The city of the dead was in many ways an extension of the city of the living, and the 'publicity' provided by a tomb and its inscription was intended for a wider purpose than merely mortuary use; that is, it was intended to have an effect upon the wider community of citizens."[85] It is for this reason that the display of inscriptions, tombs, and monuments became an extension of the "zeal for honor" evidenced among the living in the Greco-Roman world. Burial places were the locus for continued affirmation of one's wealth, social status, and identity; indeed, given the proclivity to elaboration, one's identity, and that of one's compatriots, might even be somewhat enhanced with one's death.[86] As van Nijf so nicely summarizes, "Elites can use conspicuous consumption in death as a source of symbolic capital," although the potential for social status "was also recognized by individuals lower down the social scale."[87]

Funerary monuments, including inscriptions, "seem to speak the language of belonging."[88] Funerary practices reflect a "strategy of social differentiation" insofar as the type and extravagance of one's memorial reflect one's status. They are also a means of "cultural integration" since they function as symbols that one has a place within the larger social context. Mausolea, tombs, and gravestones are examples of "conspicuous consumption in death."[89] During the imperial period, a marked increase in funerary epithets that identified the occupation of the deceased suggests

> some change in the sense of community which made it more socially acceptable to construct one's identity primarily in terms of occupation. Indications of collegium membership suggest that this was not just a matter for the individual: it helped to locate the deceased within a wider community of men who, like him, defined themselves in terms of shared occupation.[90]

---

84. Hopkins, *Death and Renewal*, 205. In some Greek cities some heroes and important individuals were buried in front of public buildings; see Robert Garland, *The Greek Way of Death* (London: Duckworth, 1985), 88.

85. Van Nijf, *Professional Associations*, 35; cf. Sandra R. Joshel, *Work, Identity, and Legal Status at Rome: A Study of the Occupational Inscriptions* (Oklahoma Series in Classical Culture 11; Norman: University of Oklahoma Press, 1992), 7–8. Epitaphs also allow the dead to speak to the living from beyond the grave; see Davies, *Death, Burial and Rebirth*, 153–54.

86. See van Nijf, *Professional Associations*, 35–36; E. A. Meyer, "Explaining the Epigraphic Habit in the Roman Empire: The Evidence of Epitaphs," *JRS* 80 (1990): 74–96.

87. Van Nijf, *Professional Associations*, 36–37.

88. Ibid., 38.

89. Richard Gordon, Mary Beard, Joyce Reynolds, and C. Roueché, "Roman Inscriptions 1986–90," *JRS* 83 (1993): 151.

90. Van Nijf, *Professional Associations*, 42.

The evidence takes us beyond the individual, allowing us to see that associations could use monuments "to assert a group identity in the face of others."[91]

As an illustration of the social sense of belonging that arises through funerary practices, van Nijf points to an association inscription from Thessalonica, *IG* X/2 824, in which there seems to be competition over whose remains would occupy a particular niche in the association's *columbarium*. The epitaph reads, in part:

> For Tyche. I have made this niche in commemoration of my own partner out of joint efforts. If one of my brothers dares to open this niche, he shall pay. . . .[92]

It is suggestive of a practice in which desirable places within the *columbarium* might be opened in order to replace the remains of the one interred there. The more general prohibition among association inscriptions against disturbing tombs may be directed to other association members rather than outsiders.[93]

Other studies support the contention that burial and group belonging cannot be separated. In describing the associations Nicholas K. Rauh notes that "by providing opportunities for men with common interests or backgrounds to join together in festival and camaraderie, and to share with one another peak moments of human experience (i.e., births, marriages, festivals, and funerals), they allowed for the development of commonly shared values, friendship, and familial bonds essential to the formation of ancient trade."[94] From his analysis of the burial and commemoration practices of voluntary associations on Rhodes, Peter M. Fraser notes that the "commemorative reunions at the tomb were certainly not only calculated to keep alive the memory of the departed 'friend' or 'brother,' but also in general to cement the bonds which linked the members of the *koinon* to each other."[95]

It seems, then, that there was an interconnection among the cultic, social, and burial aspects of associations.[96] The role that associations played in the burial and memorialization of their members cannot be separated from their sense of

---

91. Ibid., 49.

92. Translation in ibid., 46. I follow van Nijf here in taking ἀδελφός as a reference to a guild member rather than an actual familial relationship (46 n. 73).

93. Ibid., 46. For the more general prohibition, see *IKilikiaBM* 2 197 and 201. For the more general regulations around association responsibility for a tomb and fines for desecration going to an association, see *IEphesos* 2212 (silversmiths); *IHierapJ* 227 (purple-dyers); and F. A. Pennacchietti, "Nuove iscrizion i di Hierapolis Frigia," *Atti della Accademia delle Scienze de Torino* 101 (1966): 287–328, no. 07 (water mill owners and operators) and no. 25 (gardeners).

94. Rauh, *Sacred Bonds*, 40–41, citing Waltzing, *Étude historique sur les corporations professionnelles*, 1:322.

95. Fraser, *Rhodian Funerary Monuments*, 63. This should not overlook the importance placed on the desire to have oneself remembered by others; see Davies, *Death, Burial and Rebirth*, 140.

96. Philip A. Harland, *Associations, Synagogues, and Congregations: Claiming a Place in Ancient Mediterranean Society* (Minneapolis: Fortress, 2003), 55–87.

group identity nor from the sense of identity that individuals would gain within the group. This can be seen in the honors given to a treasurer of an association in Piraeus for, among other things, paying for some members' tombs from his own pocket "so that even though they have died they might remain noble" (*IG* II² 1327). Again, van Nijf nicely summarizes the point: "Craftsmen and traders, just like other groups in society, used funerary epigraphy to make statements about their own identity and about their acquired or desired status in civic life."[97]

This information links well with numerous studies that have suggested that the first century C.E. was a time of social disruption. The burgeoning merchant class and the need of artisans across the empire caused many to migrate to new places in order best to employ their skills. It is, to use Smith's words, a time of "a new geography."[98] As a result, the usual expressions and experiences of religion have been detached from their roots in domestic religion, since "the extended family, the homeplace, as well as the burial place of the honored dead, are no longer coextensive *topoi*." Smith goes on to suggest that, in order to overcome this situation, the domestic religion must be transmuted. An association becomes the "socially constructed replacement for the family"[99] that is overlaid with a new myth in which a true home is imagined "above," one that replaces the longed-for home "down here." Through such mythmaking the religion of the domestic sphere becomes the religion of any sphere, transportable to new locales precisely because a person's true connection is "on high" (think of Paul's claim that the Philippians' πολίτευμα is "in heaven," Phil 3:20). Smith states, "Locale, having been dis-placed, is now re-placed."[100]

Burial becomes an important aspect of this social construction. For example, in imperial Rome patrons would often "construct a large tomb complex to house the remains not only of their natural families, but also of their household slaves, ex-slaves and *their* families."[101] John R. Patterson attributes the central place of the *collegia* in the burial practices in imperial Rome to the association's "humanizing" the city by providing opportunities for social interaction as "a remedy against the anonymity of life in a city of a million people."[102] More interesting for our study is

---

97. Van Nijf, *Professional Associations*, 68.

98. Jonathan Z. Smith, "Here, There, and Anywhere," in *Prayer, Magic, and the Stars in the Ancient and Late Antique World* (ed. Scott Noegel et al.; Magic in History Series; University Park: Pennsylvania State University Press, 2003), 30; repr. in idem, *Relating Religion: Essays in the Study of Religion* (Chicago: University of Chicago Press, 2004), 330.

99. Smith, "Here, There, and Anywhere," 31; repr. in *Relating Religion*, 330.

100. Smith, "Here, There, and Anywhere," 31; repr. in *Relating Religion*, 331; cf. idem, *Map Is Not Territory: Studies in the History of Religions* (SJLA 23; Leiden: Brill, 1978; repr., Chicago: University of Chicago Press, 1993), xii-xv.

101. John R. Patterson, "Patronage, *Collegia*, and Burial in Imperial Rome," in *Death in Towns: Urban Responses to the Dying and the Dead, 100–1600* (ed. Steven Bassett; Leicester: Leicester University Press, 1992), 18 (emphasis original).

102. Ibid., 22–23.

his analysis of the burial of individuals in which cooperation is exhibited between an association and the deceased's family members. This cooperation was worked out in both financial and social terms:

> The clubs therefore provided a double form of insurance. If a member died without leaving a family, he would be buried by the club and saved from the ignominy and anonymity of a pauper's burial. If on the other hand an heir did exist at the time of his death, the club would provide a sum of money for the heir to pay for the funeral (which would otherwise be the first charge on the estate) or perhaps in some cases a niche in the club's *columbarium*. The clubs provided an institution which could in normal circumstances be relied upon to provide a cash sum to pay for a funeral without (much) danger of misappropriation or loss.[103]

We see that the associations become part and parcel of familial funerary duties within the social fabric of the time.[104]

Certainly voluntary associations are implicated in the social construction of fictive kinship. Fictive kin language such as that of "brotherhood" can be found in associations. For example, a monument from Sinope, Pontus, refers to οἱ ἀδελφοὶ εὐξάμενοι[105] and another in Tanais refers to itself as ἰσοποιητοὶ ἀδελφοὶ σεβόμενοι θεὸν ὕψιστον ("the adopted brothers worshiping god Hypsistos").[106] Associations in Rome "tended to have a *columbarium* together with a portico or garden where funeral feasts could be eaten."[107] Such associative practices replace the more traditional practice of having a family meal. Outside Rome, associations often had a field or enclosure that they used as a burial ground and a place for the communal meal. Such communal post-funerary meals serve "to reunite all the surviving members of the group with each other, and sometimes also with the deceased, in the same way that a chain which has been broken by the disappearance of one of its links must be rejoined."[108] Thus, the holding of banquets at gravesides was not simply commemorative but had a social role, one that can be understood within such fictive kinship constructions. "The act of bringing food to the dead had its roots in relationships that had prevailed among living members of

---

103. Ibid., 23.
104. Cf. Davies, *Death, Burial and Rebirth*, 142.
105. G. Doublet, "Inscriptions de Paphlagonie," *BCH* 13 (1889): 303–4 no. 7.
106. *IPontEux* II 449–52, 456; third century c.e.; Harland, *Associations, Synagogues, and Congregations*, 32. See further Ascough, *Paul's Macedonian Associations*, 76–77; idem, "Voluntary Associations and Community Formation," 324–25; S. Scott Bartchy, "Undermining Ancient Patriarchy: The Apostle Paul's Vision of a Society of Siblings," *BTB* 29 (1999): 68–71.
107. Patterson, "Patronage, *Collegia*, and Burial," 21. On the *columbaria*, see Toynbee, *Death and Burial*, 113–16.
108. Arnold van Gennep, *The Rites of Passage* (trans. Monika B. Vizedom and Gabrielle L. Caffee; London: Routledge and Kegan Paul; Chicago: University of Chicago Press, 1960), 164–65, quoted in Garland, *Greek Way of Death*, 39.

the kinship group. The cult of the dead had the effect of preserving those relationships even beyond the boundary of death."[109]

If we take re-placement of kinship as a "necessary condition" for cosmological mythmaking, then we are well disposed to examine 1 Thessalonians. During the first century, Thessalonica was a place full of persons displaced from their homeland. The inscriptional record gives evidence of the presence of associations through the Roman period (a description that would be equally true for Corinth). Thus, we turn our attention again to 1 Thessalonians.

Rectification of Categories: What Do We Call "It"?

One consistently finds that studies of 1 Thess 4:13–18 focus attention on the background of *Paul's* thinking. For example, in his survey of views on the origins of the *parousia*, final judgment, and the day of the Lord in Paul's writings, Larry J. Kreitzer emphasizes the Hebrew Bible and Jewish pseudepigrapha as the originating point for Paul's views but does not discuss how the respective audiences would have received Paul's letters.[110] Similarly, after a detailed study of "echoes" of LXX texts in the words of Paul, particularly the text of Ps 46 (LXX), Craig A. Evans asserts that "it is clear that Paul has pulled together a variety of traditions in forming 1 Thess. 4.13–5.11." He then goes on to suggest that the material had taken shape before Paul's usage; "it is not necessary, therefore, to suppose that Paul was conscious of the precise biblical origin of each tradition." Evans concludes that Paul "may or may not have been conscious" of the inherited biblical material."[111] This being so, one might then ask, what difference does it make to know the precise origin of the texts (the "echoes")? It is more informative to examine how the text functions in its context for the intended audience.

Mack, citing Smith, points out that "the terms we use to name and describe things are important, and that the traditional terms we use are not innocent with respect to parochial connotations."[112] In our investigation we are interested in the term "apocalyptic" as it is applied to Paul's writing in 1 Thessalonians. We observed above that the frequent location for the "source" of Paul's apocalyptic thought is the Jewish writings. The comparative process shows, to the mind of many, the genealogical connections with the Hebrew Bible and the Jewish

---

109. Byron R. McCane, *Roll Back the Stone: Death and Burial in the World of Jesus* (Harrisburg, Pa.: Trinity Press International, 2003), 52.

110. Larry J. Kreitzer, *Jesus and God in Paul's Eschatology* (JSNTSup 19; Sheffield: JSOT Press, 1987), 93–129; see also Martinus C. de Boer, *The Defeat of Death: Apocalyptic Eschatology in 1 Corinthians 15 and Romans 5* (JSNTSup 22; Sheffield: JSOT Press, 1988), 181–83.

111. Craig A. Evans, "Ascending and Descending with a Shout: Psalm 47.6 and 1 Thessalonians 4.16," in *Paul and the Scriptures of Israel* (ed. Craig A. Evans and James A. Sanders; JSNTSup 83; Sheffield: JSOT Press, 1993), 251.

112. Mack, "Redescribing Christian Origins," 259; repr. in *Christian Myth*, 73.

pseudepigrapha.[113] However, in order for this connection to work at Thessalonica one needs to assume that the Gentile Thessalonians were familiar with Jewish apocalyptic or, as is sometimes argued, were thoroughly taught it by Paul. Yet if we were to put aside the question of genealogy and ask the question of social formation, we would need to examine how the Thessalonians might have heard the so-called apocalyptic language when Paul undertook his mythmaking. Again we turn to the wider social context of the Greco-Roman world. John S. Kloppenborg has framed well the context for us:

> much of the conceptual apparatus employed in the description of Pauline communities derives either from Acts, according to which Pauline groups are offshoots of synagogues, or from Paul's own rhetoric, according to which Paul "founded" churches and claimed responsibility for their organization and orientation. This is to confuse rhetorical statement and its persuasive goals with a description of Pauline communities and assumes, implausibly, that peoples in the cities of the Empire, who had been organizing themselves as *thiasotai, eranistai, orgeones, collegia*, and *sussitoi* for more than four centuries, were somehow at a loss when it came to organizing a cult group devoted to Christ.[114]

Despite common claims to the contrary, eschatological and apocalyptic ideas were not limited to Jews in the first century C.E. As Hubert Cancik documents, "eschatological ideas appear in various forms and genres" not only in Judaism but also "in the fine literature of the Greeks—their epics, their wisdom, and their natural philosophy."[115] Nevertheless, as F. Gerald Downing notes, "[d]iscussions of Jewish and then Christian cosmic, universal eschatology have mostly ignored contemporary 'pagan' ideas, or mentioned them only in contrast."[116] This needs rectification.

---

113. While it is true that Christianity and its myths have much in common with the Hebrew Bible and other Jewish writings, Smith has adequately documented the extent to which this reality is used to insulate Christianity from its polytheistic surroundings (*Drudgery Divine*). Nevertheless, many scholars still maintain that all things Christian originate in things Jewish. For example, Martin Hengel has argued recently that "Christianity grew *entirely* out of Jewish soil" and that "whatever pagan influences have been suspected in the origins of Christianity were mediated without exception by Judaism," even in the Diaspora ("Early Christianity as a Jewish-Messianic, Universalistic Movement," in idem and C. K. Barrett, *Conflicts and Challenges in Early Christianity* [ed. Donald A. Hagner; Harrisburg, Pa.: Trinity Press International, 1999], 1, 2–3 [emphasis original]).

114. John S. Kloppenborg, "Critical Histories and Theories of Religion: A Response to Ron Cameron and Burton Mack," *MTSR* 8 (1996): 282–83.

115. Hubert Cancik, "The End of the World, of History, and of the Individual in Greek and Roman Antiquity," in *The Encyclopedia of Apocalypticism* (ed. Bernard McGinn, John J. Collins, and Stephen J. Stein; 3 vols; New York: Continuum, 1998), vol. 1, *The Origins of Apocalypticism in Judaism and Christianity* (ed. John J. Collins), 84, 85.

116. F. Gerald Downing, "Common Strands in Pagan, Jewish and Christian Eschatologies in the First Christian Centuries," in *Making Sense in (and of) the First Christian Century* (ed. F. Gerald Downing; JSNTSup 197; Sheffield: Sheffield Academic Press, 2000), 170.

In some philosophical traditions, particularly that of the Epicureans and the Stoics, there was a belief that this world would come to an end.[117] Downing suggests that Pliny the Elder is echoing an Epicurean commonplace in writing, "You can almost see that the stature of the whole human race is decreasing daily, with few men taller than their fathers, as the crucial conflagration which our age is approaching exhausts the fertility of human semen" (*Nat.* 7.16.73). A similar idea is found in Lucretius: "Even now, indeed, the power of life is broken, and earth, exhausted, scarce produces tiny creatures, she who once produced all kinds, and gave birth to the huge bodies of wild beasts" (*De rerum natura* 2.1150–52). Such sentiments reflect not only their belief in the decline of the natural world but also an expectation of a cataclysmic ending. Other writers of the time such as Pliny the Younger and Seneca have similar notions.[118] Downing points out the similarities between the notions found in Pseudo-Seneca's *Octavia* 391–94 and Mark 13:24:

> Pseudo-Seneca: This sky is growing old, doomed wholly once more to fall into blind nothingness. Then for the universe is that last day at hand which shall crush sinful humankind beneath heaven's ruin....
>
> Mark 13:24: In those days, after that tribulation, the sun will be darkened, and the moon will not give its light, and the stars will be falling from heaven, and the powers in the heavens will be shaken ... heaven and earth will pass away....

Downing correctly refuses to make any genealogical connections between the two passages, but does note that in the Markan passage there is nothing "that would appear unusual to those used to popular Stoic teaching or even aware of Epicurean science."[119] Indeed, this is true for other Christian passages from Revelation and 2 Peter.

Downing concludes, "The way the end, the final destruction, is pictured, seems very similar in various pagan, Jewish and Christian writings."[120] More to the point, "Much of the same range of views as were available to Jews in Palestine were readily available and current and certainly comprehensible in the Greco-Roman world cultural context—where a fair number of them probably originated, anyway."[121] In the face of such an ending, the gods were not marginalized. Cancik notes that

> [t]he proliferation of signs of misfortune gives rise to fear that "eternal night" will darken the world and the hope for a savior: "do not prevent this young man from coming to the aid of the overthrown world" (Virgil, *Georgica* 1.500f., 468ff., 493).

---

117. Ibid., 174.
118. See further Lattimore, *Greek and Latin Epitaphs*, 44–48.
119. Downing, "Common Strands," 177. Downing points out that not all Stoic and Epicurean "eschatologies" were cyclical; some were linear.
120. Ibid., 180; cf. 185.
121. Ibid., 185.

In the schema of question and answer and with an instruction discourse, Apollo answers the question whether the soul endures after death or is dissolved. The visionary women of Dodona, as the first women, say: "Zeus was, Zeus is, Zeus will be, O great Zeus!" (Pausanias, *Descr.* 10.12.10).[122]

An inscription from Tralles records an oracle of a foundation of a cult of Poseidon in Tralles: "Gentle Earth-shaker, enwreathed by a seawater altar, set us free from the wrath [μήνιμα] of Father Zeus for one thousand years" (*ITralleis* 1; second or third century C.E.). It seems that there was an earthquake that the city escaped. Since Poseidon himself was given the epithet of "earth-shaker" (σεισίχθων), he was given thanks for protecting the city from the wrath of Zeus, which was manifested in the earthquake. In polytheist eschatology, the world, or parts of it, come under threat, even threat of annihilation, and it is the gods who can either provoke it or prevent it. Neither Jewish nor Christian apocalyptic thinking influenced the philosophers and inscribers of stone who discuss eschatology. This is not to say that Paul was not influenced by Jewish apocalyptic—it is likely that he was. The point is that the Thessalonians need not have been aware of Jewish apocalyptic thought for Paul's words to make sense.

Mack correctly notes that Paul's preaching was not originally "apocalyptic" in arising out of an already formed group that felt isolated and oppressed.[123] Yet in order to convince the Thessalonians to "turn" from their gods, Paul would need *some* rhetorical device to convince them of their need. I do not think it was the sheer attraction of "monotheism" or the attraction of "Judaism *sans* circumcision," which are the usual suggestions, bolstered by the Acts account. Rather, Paul would need to convince the Thessalonians of the superiority of his god. How better to instill superiority than to threaten destruction? When one announces a coming cataclysmic destruction and then promises "deliverance" only to those who would align themselves with this god, and this god alone, it plays well in a community already used to such discussions. This does not make them "apocalyptic" or millenarian, just scared of destruction. No matter where Paul derived the seeds of this fledgling myth (e.g., Jewish apocalypticism), it plays in a somewhat distinctive way for his Thessalonian audience.

Perhaps more important, however, and more germane to the rise of the Thessalonians' question about the dead, is the pervasiveness of the cult of the dead among the Romans. During the middle of the second century B.C.E. the Romans began to conceive of the spirits of deceased ancestors as more than a collective, divine entity, and we see the emergence of the concept of personal *manes* and an increase "in epitaphs dedicated 'to the divine spirits [D.M. = *Dis Manibus*]' of

---

122. Cancik, "End of the World," 91.
123. Mack, *Who Wrote the New Testament?* 109; against Todd D. Still, *Conflict at Thessalonica: A Pauline Church and Its Neighbors* (JSNTSup 183; Sheffield: Sheffield Academic Press, 1999).

individuals." Banquets, festivals (such as the *Rosalia* and *Parentalia*), and grave offerings were intended to cultivate a relationship with the individual dead. "In general, the increasingly turbulent ideological winds swirling around the core Roman beliefs about death carried the gratifying prospect that the soul of the individual survived and that, for the good or the saved, the world beyond was a happier, more godlike place than that on earth."[124] It is at least plausible that, given the Romanization in Thessalonica, one of the "idols" against which Paul preached and from which the Thessalonian Jesus association turned to serve the "living God" (1 Thess 1:9) was the cult of the ancestors. However, confusion over the inclusion of those who have died would result when members of the newly configured association begin to pass away. Alive they were included in the benefits promised through Jesus, but their death might signal that they are no longer to be included (since one did not continue to honor those of the past, according to Paul). This gives rise, I suggest, to the question the Thessalonians ask Paul concerning the "dead in Christ." It is not a question of judgment (Who, in the end, gets in?) but a question of belonging (Are the dead still in?).

The polytheistic context provides enough evidence that belief in an afterlife and fear of a divinely mandated cataclysm were widely known. Thus, there is no need to posit with Malherbe that "the Greek Thessalonians found it difficult to bring the apocalyptic expectations of resurrection and *Parousia* together into a systematic whole."[125] The labeling of 1 Thess 4:13–18 as "apocalyptic" serves to thrust the Thessalonian Jesus association into the world of Jewish apocalyptic discourse and serves to bolster the modern Christian myth that the community itself had its origins in a predominantly Jewish setting (based on Acts 17:1–8).[126] To my mind, this is not a helpful process in the scholarly project of understanding Christian origins. For this reason, in the next section I will attempt to (re)describe what Paul writes in 1 Thessalonians in a way that is consistent with how it would function within the Thessalonian association,[127] emphasizing their reaction to Paul's

---

124. Bodel, "Death, the Afterlife, and Other Last Things: Rome," 492.

125. Malherbe, *Thessalonians*, 284. He suggests that although both concepts are Jewish apocalyptic ideas that were present in pre-Pauline Christianity, "they were brought together for the first time in 1 Thess 4:13–18" (ibid.). Wayne A. Meeks seems to link Paul's use of "apocalyptic" to moral admonition for the overall health of the community by pointing to the paraenetic section of 1 Thess 5:13–22. However, this latter section takes up a new issue within the letter and thus need not be linked. It is not clear how Meeks thinks "internal discipline" and "obedience of leaders" can be linked to questions about those who have died ("Social Functions of Apocalyptic Language in Pauline Christianity," in *Apocalypticism in the Mediterranean World and the Near East: Proceedings of the International Colloquium on Apocalypticism, Uppsala, August 12–17, 1979* [ed. David Hellholm; Tübingen: Mohr Siebeck, 1983], 694).

126. See Ron Cameron, "The Anatomy of a Discourse: On 'Eschatology' as a Category for Explaining Christian Origins," *MTSR* 8 (1996): 231–45.

127. We need not decide whether Paul's so-called apocalyptic language appealed to the Thessalonians or somehow merged with their already existing beliefs as part of a process of syncretism. Rather, we might better think of it in terms of the analogy of the jigsaw puzzle versus the Chinese boxes

limitations on the cult of the dead and the social (rather than theological) questions such limitations raise for them. I will then suggest a few implications of this redescription for our understanding of the Corinthian context, albeit recognizing that the two community situations remain different.[128]

REDESCRIPTION: HOW DO WE (RE)CONSTRUCT THE SITUATION?

In his study of death in antiquity, Byron R. McCane suggests that Christianity emerged from a sect within Judaism that distinguished itself by "going public with its cult of the dead" by "linking their own distinctive religious beliefs with Greek and Roman cultural mores."[129] This process developed "slowly and gradually," with Jewish and Christian distinctions not fully emerging until the fourth century, "when attitudes toward, and beliefs about, dead bodies became a matter of mutual self-definition."[130] In making such claims, McCane is following the scholarly tradition of protecting early Jesus associations from the corrupting influences of paganism by keeping it embedded within Judaism.[131] Thus, it is not until this later period, when Christianity "emerge[s]" with a public cult of the dead, that we find "a distinctively Christian relationship between the living and the dead, a relationship in which the Jewish boundary between life and death was redrawn along Christian parameters."[132]

Although in his study McCane is focused on the context of Roman Palestine, his claims suggest a monolithic development of Christian burial practices, since there is increasing conformity among the diverse Christian groups already toward the end of the second century. Thus, for McCane the Palestinian situation is "normative" for early Christianities, seemingly because it is the "earliest" location for

---

suggested by Peter Brown with respect to Manichaeism and taken up by Jonathan Z. Smith with respect to wisdom and apocalyptic ("Wisdom and Apocalyptic," in *Religious Syncretism in Antiquity: Essays in Conversation with Geo Widengren* [ed. Birger A. Pearson; Series on Formative Contemporary Thinkers 1; Missoula, Mont.: Scholars Press, 1975], 155–56; repr. in idem, *Map Is Not Territory*, 87, citing Peter Brown, *Religion and Society in the Age of Saint Augustine* [New York: Harper & Row, 1972], 108). Our scholarly enterprise is not one of dismantling a jigsaw puzzle to see the original shape of each individual piece. Rather, we are attempting to see how the Thessalonians' allegiance to one another under the auspices of Jesus was working itself out in practical terms vis-à-vis understanding themselves in relation to "others," in this case, those members who have died.

128. John M. G. Barclay is correct to warn of generalizing about "Pauline Christians" and to take care "not to subscribe to the false assumption that all Paul's churches were of the same stamp" ("Thessalonica and Corinth: Social Contrasts in Pauline Christianity," *JSNT* 47 [1992]: 72–73; cf. Richard S. Ascough, *What Are They Saying about the Formation of Pauline Churches?* [New York: Paulist, 1998], 95–99).

129. McCane, *Roll Back the Stone*, 16.

130. Ibid., 16, 110.

131. See Smith, *Drudgery Divine*, 54–84, for a description and critique of this tendency to insulate early Christian groups from their non-Jewish surroundings.

132. McCane, *Roll Back the Stone*, 16.

concerns for the dead owing to its direct association with the life, and death, of Jesus. Our own reconstruction of the situation at Thessalonica, and the developments Paul introduces in writing to the Corinthians, suggest that if there was an understanding of a separation between the living and the dead, it was short-lived. Paul quickly moves to dispel the notion that the deceased Christians are no longer part of the community. He affirms what would have been the practice of the pre-Christian association of Thessalonian workers—the commemoration and inclusion of the dead in the social configuration of the association of the living.

In light of the pervasiveness of death in the community building of the living members of associations, we want to explore what this might mean for the question that the Thessalonian association asked Paul. All of our evidence suggests that death is not simply a matter of "not living," nor is it the case that the primary concern around death within an associative community was the personal salvation of the individual. Death was indeed inevitable but provided the opportunity for community definition. Death was not the point at which one ceased to be a member of a given association. Rather, death was the point at which that association would celebrate a person's membership. From among the many members the individual would be isolated and celebrated as a member of the community.

Mack points out that Paul has learned about two questions under discussion among the Thessalonians, a question of "proper conduct for Christians" (4:1–12) and a question about "those who had died" (4:13). Mack goes on to suggest that "the exhortation to a life of holiness was Paul's answer to the question about proper conduct. The apocalyptic instruction was his answer to the question about those who had died."[133] However, Paul is providing something more than a theological answer. All four units of 1 Thess 4:1–5:11 (4:1–8, 9–12, 13–18; 5:1–11) not only provide the Thessalonians with indications for their life of faith but also serve as opportunities for Paul to prove what he states earlier, that their faithfulness in the life of faith will be the source of *his* honor at Jesus' *parousia*. Thus, Paul links questions of faith and (un)belief to his own status in the community, and the translation of that status to something greater at a future, divine event. It is not a matter of his credibility but one of his honor as founder and (spiritual) representative of the community. At the same time, Paul uses eschatology as the basis for hope that determines the nature of corporate life for those who worship Jesus. That is to say, the apocalyptic instruction is as much a part of community building as is the exhortation to a life of holiness.

Mack errs in his analysis in thinking that the central issue around 1 Thess 4:13–18 is social formation in terms of what was "attractive" about the congregations of Christ.[134] As I have argued elsewhere, there is evidence that the Thessalonians' turning to God from idols (1:9) was a collective experience.[135] If I am

---

133. Mack, *Who Wrote the New Testament?* 108.
134. Cf. Mack, "Redescribing Christian Origins," 255; repr. in *Christian Myth*, 69.
135. Ascough, "Thessalonian Christian Community," 322–24.

correct, then it is not a question of what was attractive about already existing groups ("we want to be part of one too"). It is a matter of how an already existing group would redefine itself through its alliance with this new patron deity named Jesus Christ.[136]

Mack is correct, however, to suggest that "we can almost see Paul working it out on the spot, desperately trying to find a way to answer the question about those who had died."[137] At the same time, by posing it as a tension between "a Jewish notion of resurrection and the Greek idea of immortality," Mack is maintaining the mythmaking at a theological, or at least a philosophical level.[138] I think, rather, that it is grounded in social practices. Indeed, the question over the dead members may be linked to practices that the Thessalonians thought could be suspended, namely, burial and memorial. When Paul first began speaking with those living and working in Thessalonica, he probably brought them a message that defined death as the "enemy" of the living. We know from 1 Cor 15:21–22 that Paul linked death to the result of sin, brought into this world through Adam. It is death that will be overcome in the triumphal return of Jesus (1 Cor 15:54–55). Death is the last enemy to be destroyed (1 Cor 15:26) in the conflagration that is the coming wrath (1 Thess 1:10; cf. 4:6; Phil 3:20).[139]

Having heard from Paul's preaching about deliverance from coming wrath on a (somewhat vaguely defined) "day of the Lord,"[140] the Thessalonians perhaps

---

136. It would be disingenuous of me to claim that I am engaged in a comparison of the sort argued for so forcefully by Smith. Indeed, whereas Smith would have "the enterprise of comparison, in its strongest form, bring . . . differences together solely within the space of the scholar's mind," my own work suggests that in the case of the Thessalonian Christians and their voluntary associations they are cohabiting as "consenting adults" (to maintain Smith's language, *Drudgery Divine*, 115). Of necessity, then, I do see some "influence" and "derivation." If I am to have any defense it is this: I did not seek to find such and indeed was surprised when my own research took me in this direction.

137. Mack, *Who Wrote the New Testament?* 111.

138. Mack states that "Paul chose to answer their question by spinning out an elaborate scenario that is *clearly apocalyptic*" (ibid. [emphasis added]). It is unclear what he means by this designation in terms of an appropriate background for understanding the text in the Thessalonian context.

139. Cf. Judith L. Hill, "Establishing the Church in Thessalonica" (Ph.D. diss., Duke University, 1990), 177: "While it is unlikely that Paul elaborated greatly on eschatology to unbelievers in Thessalonica, his message to prospective converts did include mention of a coming judgment (1 Thess 1:10; 5:9), a distinct part of apocalyptic writings. The message of impending wrath had to be given by Paul in order to differentiate his God from others and to prepare the Thessalonians to make a commitment to the true and living God who provided a Deliverer (1 Thess 1:9–10). Yet among the Gentile population Paul did not highlight any aspects of apocalypticism that gave predominance to the Jews or that might have had offensive overtones." See Bert Jan Lietaert Peerbolte, "Romans 15:14–29 and Paul's Missionary Agenda," in *Persuasion and Dissuasion in Early Christianity, Ancient Judaism, and Hellenism* (ed. Pieter W. van der Horst et al.; CBET 33; Leuven: Peeters, 2003), 158: "Paul's ministry is as good as incomprehensible without this specific theological meta-structure: Christ as the decisive factor saving people at God's intervention in history."

140. Abraham J. Malherbe, *Paul and the Thessalonians: The Philosophic Tradition of Pastoral Care* (Philadelphia: Fortress, 1987), 30; Barclay, "Thessalonica and Corinth," 50; idem, "Conflict in Thessa-

feel some consternation, even betrayal, that part of their membership have died before that deliverance arrives. Whereas normally they would have ensured not only proper burial but also a pattern of commemoration of some sort, such practices would need no planning in light of the imminent appearance of the deity.[141] The loss of the forum of funerary epigraphy and banquets to make statements about status within a group is clearly an issue of belonging and identity. Underlying the Thessalonians' question to Paul seems to be the issue of whether the dead members can still be considered part of the community. It is not surprising that the giving up of some element of their rituals around death might cause consternation, since these are "typically among the more conservative and stable elements in a society, changing very slowly over generations and centuries."[142] Paul's proclamation of Jesus' death and resurrection and the subsequent (re)formation of an association around this hero have quickly, perhaps too quickly, disrupted the normative rituals of death. They have given up not only their burial rituals but also their normative practice of banqueting with the dead.

In his response, Paul writes that the Christians have not "died," they have "fallen asleep" (κοιμᾶσθαι).[143] Whereas his initial preaching about sin causing death might have led to the conclusion that those who have died are without hope, Paul carefully refers to them as sleeping. Their death does not indicate "sin" and thus a need for the living Christians to dissociate themselves from the dead members. Rather, it is their state of sleeping that requires the Thessalonians to include them in their definition of community, since they are still very much a part of the community. As Wayne A. Meeks puts it, "Paul is not offering any general theodicy, any general 'solution' to the problem of death. It is not the problem of death as a universal phenomenon that is addressed here, but just the power of death to shatter the unique bonds of intimate new community."[144] The Thessalonian Christian community can continue to include their dead members, who, according to Paul, not only are still considered members of the association but will hold a privileged position at the *parousia* of Jesus.

---

lonica," *CBQ* 55 (1993): 516; Charles A. Wanamaker, "'Like a Father Treats His Own Children': Paul and the Conversion of the Thessalonians," *JTSA* 92 (1995): 52.

141. Pushing the historical imagination further, it may also be that they have ceased their practice of collecting regular dues that go into the common chest in order to pay for burial. Indeed, perhaps the funds were even diverted to Paul, since he acknowledges the financial support of the Macedonians (2 Cor 8:1–3, although I think he is thinking specifically of the Philippians). Perhaps the grumbling over his hasty departure with these funds is behind his self-defense in 1 Thess 2:1–12.

142. McCane, *Roll Back the Stone*, 9–10.

143. Indeed, it is in contexts of Christians who have died that Paul uses the verb κοιμᾶσθαι (1 Cor 7:39; 11:30; 15:6, 18, 20, 51; 1 Thess 4:13, 14, 15). Paul uses θανατοῦν in contexts where death is metaphorical (Rom 7:4; 8:13, 36; 2 Cor 6:9) and "the dead" (νεκροί) include Christians and non-Christians. (I am not suggesting that Paul coins this metaphor, since the word κοιμᾶσθαι could be used for death, simply that his choice is interesting.)

144. Meeks, "Social Functions of Apocalyptic Language," 693.

McCane draws a distinction between two different portraits of postmortem paradise in Christian understandings of death and burial, distinctions he notes prevail through the fourth century.[145] One portrait he describes as funerary and is found within burial niches and reflects the domestic sphere insofar as the deceased is represented among family and friends, often around a meal. The other is apocalyptic and is found in textual evidence such as the *Apocalypse of Paul* and its emphasis on the heavenly sphere. Since these two portraits reflect different social locations, they do not come together. Comparing the apocalyptic to a battlefield motif and the funerary to an infirmary, McCane concludes, "The social energies that produced an apocalypse (anonymity and disprivelege) were so different from those that inspired funerary symbolism (dislocation and grief), that a combination of the two—that is, an apocalyptic sarcophagus relief—would have been as out of place as a bugler in an intensive care unit."[146] It seems to me, however, that with Paul this is precisely what we have—bugles blowing *in* an intensive care unit! Paul allows the inclusion of the dead among the living through funerary rites while introducing the apocalyptic arrival of the deity. While the Thessalonians think that the dead are divorced from the Jesus association, Paul uses apocalyptic images from his own tradition to show how the opposite is the case—they are still full members, albeit "sleepers."

The Thessalonians' concern for their dead represents a critical moment "of mythmaking and social formation that make[s] a difference in our understanding of the emergence of Christianities."[147] It begins a trajectory in Paul's thinking that he brings with him in his initial contacts with the Corinthians and subsequently develops in light of the social relationships and questions among the Corinthian Jesus associations. Based on the Thessalonians' concern, when he is in Corinth Paul anticipates the issue of those who have died after having joined the Jesus association. For this reason, during his time among them Paul has introduced a more elaborate means of recognizing the importance of the dead among them. In so doing, Paul has more deliberately founded an association around the cult of a hero.[148]

Theodor H. Gaster defines "hero" as "a person who possesses powers superior to those of ordinary men and who displays them courageously, at the risk of his own life but to the advantage and benefit of others."[149] Yet the term "hero" often

---

145. McCane, *Roll Back the Stone*, 127–40.
146. Ibid., 138.
147. Ron Cameron and Merrill P. Miller, "Introduction: Ancient Myths and Modern Theories of Christian Origins," in *Redescribing Christian Origins* (ed. Ron Cameron and Merrill P. Miller; SBLSymS 28; Atlanta: Society of Biblical Literature; Leiden and Boston: Brill, 2004), 21.
148. I am grateful to Burton L. Mack, whose paper "Rereading the Christ Myth: Paul's Gospel and the Christ Cult Question" (in this volume) has inspired me to define more clearly my own view of the development of the Pauline hero myth.
149. Theodor H. Gaster, "Heroes," *ER* 6:302.

meant "minor deity" and not a "man who lived and died and subsequently received veneration."[150] Such heroes were not necessarily well-known figures and often were local deities with little "national or universal significance."[151] Arthur Darby Nock points out that, although a person might become a god, "no one *became* a hero, except in the sense of being recognized as such."[152] In the case of Jesus the connections with the heroic archetype are clear.[153]

In the recognition of a person's heroic status, there arose opportunities for participation in a banquet honoring the dead hero.[154] Indeed, there is little evidence, according to Nock, that ancient ideas about sacrifice created "an intrinsic antipathy to participation in victims offered to the gods of the underworld and to heroes."[155] That is, the posthumous sacrifices for the hero were shared by the devotees in a banquet setting. Examples abound, but what is more interesting are instances where associations are established around a hero or heroes. While the mythic heroes often received veneration, other, more ordinary persons could take on the qualities of "hero" in the establishing of a group who would honor their memory. One such example I mentioned earlier—the inscription of Epicteta, who founded an association on Thera to provide sacrifices to the Muses and to the heroes, the latter being her dead husband, two dead sons, and herself (*IG* XII/3 330; 210–193 B.C.E.; note, too, the example of the *Rosalia*, discussed above).

As we also noted earlier, it is well attested throughout the eastern Roman Empire that tombs served as the location for funerary banquets eaten in honor of the dead. In the Roman East this practice was a continuation of the classical and Hellenistic customs, although it is marked by "an increasing emphasis on heroization of the deceased." Although most of the evidence comes from the practices of the monumental tombs of the elite, there is evidence that offerings and banquets "extended to small-scale monuments as well."[156] The practice of holding a funerary banquet in honor or memory of the deceased clearly continued in Christian circles in the second century and beyond, as can be seen in the evidence from the catacombs of Rome.

---

150. Arthur Darby Nock, "The Cult of Heroes," *HTR* 37 (1944): 162; repr. in idem, *Essays on Religion and the Ancient World* (ed. Zeph Stewart; 2 vols.; Oxford: Clarendon, 1972), 2:593.

151. Nock, "Cult of Heroes," 162–63; repr. in *Essays on Religion and the Ancient World*, 2:594.

152. Nock, "Cult of Heroes," 143 (emphasis original); repr. in *Essays on Religion and the Ancient World*, 2:577.

153. See Alan Dundes, "The Hero Pattern and the Life of Jesus," in Otto Rank et al., *In Quest of the Hero* (Princeton: Princeton University Press, 1990), 179–223.

154. Nock, "Cult of Heroes," 147–48; repr. in *Essays on Religion and the Ancient World*, 2:581–82.

155. Nock, "Cult of Heroes," 156; repr. in *Essays on Religion and the Ancient World*, 2:588.

156. Sarah Cormack, "Funerary Monuments and Mortuary Practice in Roman Asia Minor," in *The Early Roman Empire in the East* (ed. Susan E. Alcock; Oxbow Monograph 95; Oxford: Oxbow Books, 1997), 151.

The missing piece, it seems to me, is Christian evidence from the first century. And it is to be found, I think, in the traditions of the funerary meal among the Jesus-followers. This practice not only developed into the more formal ritual of the Eucharist but also provided the legitimation for the continuation of the (pagan) funerary banquet tradition among Christians. I would suggest that Paul builds on fairly early traditions of memorializing Jesus—similar to other funerary foundations and reflected in the traditions behind 1 Cor 11:23–25.[157] For Paul the heroic "task" of Jesus is understood as his death on the cross.[158] If I were to become more speculative, I would suggest that one possible explanation for the development of the early tradition of the "raising" of Jesus is the lack of a monumental tomb to the hero (who, presumably, was buried in a nondescript and quickly forgotten grave outside Jerusalem). Whereas the celebration of the funerary banquet (reflected in the traditions behind 1 Cor 11:23–25) is normally held at the site of the tomb of the hero, this is neither possible nor necessary for a hero who has been raised by God and sighted among the living.

Originally, there was no need for a "vindication" of Jesus—it was enough to claim divine intervention in the life of the hero. This, in fact, is the point of heroization. Like so many before him, it is only in death that the hero is raised to be with the immortals. What is distinctive, then, in the pre-Pauline formulation is the claim that this divinized hero has actually (re)appeared to a group composed to honor him at a funerary banquet. Indeed, as Mack points out, this postmortem appearance would not be glorious but "shocking" to auditors of the formula.[159]

So, while I would agree with Mack that we should read the Christ myth in terms of Paul's elaborations concerning his own gospel, I would posit a hero myth, rather than a martyr myth, as the original context of the formulations. The claims of death–burial–rising–appearing make sense in this context, as does the formulaic banquet language of remembrance. I would suggest that the earliest Jesus associations honored the memory of their now divinized human hero. It is from this apotheosis that Jesus Christ increasingly becomes, in Paul's mythmaking, the

---

157. Here I diverge from Mack in suggesting that the practice reflects the founding of the association, rather than the myth of origins grounding a preexisting practice ("Rereading the Christ Myth," 54–58, esp. 56). Nevertheless, I do think that soon after the establishing of the group and the death of the hero, the apotheosis of Jesus became integrated into the traditions. Thus, Jesus was recognized first as a hero and then later began to be recognized as possessing divine qualities. It is at this stage that the practice starts to develop into a fuller myth of origins.

158. Without necessarily positing a dependence on Paul, I would suggest that this too is the understanding of Mark, and subsequently Luke—Jesus "takes up his cross" and marches off to his task. As an aside, it is interesting to note, with Nock, that "the second libation at a symposion was 'of the heroes': you associated them, just as you did Zeus, with the cup of kindness" ("Cult of Heroes," 157; repr. in *Essays on Religion and the Ancient World*, 2:589). I wonder whether this has implications for understanding Luke's inclusion of a second cup in his account of Jesus' final table fellowship (mixed, of course, with Passover traditions).

159. Mack, "Rereading the Christ Myth," 45, 46, 47, 50.

"cosmic sovereign and eschatological judge,"[160] in large part in response to the Thessalonians' question about the fate of the other dead among them. Thus, Paul's statement to the Corinthians that if the dead are not raised it is best to "eat and drink, for tomorrow we die" (1 Cor 15:32) reflects that without this pivotal event Paul sees no difference between members of the Jesus associations and "those who have no hope."[161] That is, without the myth he has elaborated in response to the Thessalonians, the Thessalonians were correct all along—there is no hope.

For the Corinthians, the situation—the membership of dead members—is the same as for the Thessalonians. Their response, however, is different. Whereas the Thessalonians grieved and worried, the Corinthians had a more proactive solution. The dead members were not considered "lost" but were still to be included in the larger associative community. This belief works itself out in the practice of the Corinthians' being baptized on behalf of the dead (1 Cor 15:29). Since at least some of the Corinthians reflect a philosophy that would later become manifest in "Gnosticism," they were able to incorporate the recently departed into their larger mythic framework. Paul's *response* to the Corinthians, on the other hand, represents an alternative process of mythmaking, one that builds on a process already employed in addressing the situation at Thessalonica. He asserts a bodily resurrection of the dead Christians as a means to affirm their continued inclusion in the Corinthian association.

Conclusion

In 1 Thessalonians and 1 Corinthians we see the reflection of two related situations concerning the question of the status of dead members. It is most likely that the questions arose from a similar sociocultural milieu. Although each community raised a somewhat different issue, Paul's own response is consistent but develops as part of his own mythmaking for each community.[162] In light of the death of some of their associates, the members of the Thessalonian Jesus association have concluded—based on Paul's initial preaching against idolatry, including the cult of the dead—that the dead are excluded from the living community and thus will not participate in the good things that the hero will bring when he returns. In order to address this question, Paul introduces eschatological language that functions as mythmaking for this particular "social experiment" of forming Jesus associations.[163] When dealing with the Corinthian Jesus association he anticipates this same issue and thus encourages from the beginning the memorial meal for the dead, building on some earlier traditions in other Jesus associations. The Corinthians, however,

---

160. Ibid., 61.
161. Cf. Klauck, *Religious Context*, 80.
162. Other studies have identified the shifts in Paul's eschatological understanding, and it has not been my intention to rehearse them here, other than to state my agreement with those that see 1 Cor 15:51–57 as having developed from 1 Thess 4:13–18.
163. On the language of early Christian groups as diverse social experiments, see the summary in Cameron and Miller, "Ancient Myths and Modern Theories of Christian Origins," 20–21, 29.

also have questions about the future, but of a different sort (the nature of the resurrection body). In order to address these questions, Paul expands the myth he has introduced to the Thessalonians to provide a somewhat more detailed picture of the return of the hero. By examining Paul's comments on the *parousia* of Jesus in 1 Thessalonians and 1 Corinthians in light of the burial practices of antique voluntary associations, we catch a glimpse of early Christian social formation and mythmaking occurring simultaneously.[164]

Inscriptional and Papyrological Abbreviations

CIG	August Boeckh, ed., *Corpus inscriptionum graecarum* (4 vols.; Berlin: Reimer, 1828–77).
CIL III	Theodor Mommsen et al., eds., *Inscriptiones Asiae, provinciarum Europae Graecarum, Illyrici Latinae* (Berlin: Reimer, 1873–1902).
CIL V	Theodor Mommsen, ed., *Inscriptiones Galliae Cisalpinae Latinae* (2 vols.; Berlin: Reimer, 1872–77).
CIL VI	Wilhelm Henzen and Johannes Baptista de Rossi, eds., *Inscriptiones Urbis Romae Latinae* (Berlin: Reimer, 1876–1902).
CIL IX	Theodor Mommsen, ed., *Inscriptiones Calabriae Apuliae Samnii Sabinorum Piceni Latinae* (Berlin: Reimer, 1883).
CIL XI	Eugene Bormann, ed., *Inscriptiones Aemiliae Umbriae Latinae* (2 vols.; Berlin: Reimer, 1888–1926).
CIL XIV	Hermann Dessau, ed., *Inscriptiones Latii veteris Latinae* (2 vols.; Berlin: Reimer, 1887).
ICos	William R. Paton and Edward L. Hicks, eds., *The Inscriptions of Cos* (Oxford: Clarendon, 1891).
IEphesos	Helmut Engelmann et al., eds., *Die Inschriften von Ephesos* (8 vols.; Inschriften griechischer Städte aus Kleinasien 11–17; Bonn: Habelt, 1979–84).
IG II^2	Johannes E. Kirchner and Friedrich F. Hiller von Gaertringen, eds., *Inscriptiones Graecae (Editio Minor). Inscriptiones Atticae* (Berlin: de Gruyter, 1913–40).
IG X/2	Charles Edson, ed., *Inscriptiones Graecae Epiri, Macedoniae, Thraciae, Scythiae*, II, *Inscriptiones Macedoniae*, fasc. 1, *Inscriptiones Thessalonicae et viciniae* (Berlin: de Gruyter, 1972).
IG XII/1	Friedrich F. Hiller von Gaertringen, ed., *Inscriptiones Rhodi, Chalces, Carpathi cum Saro, Casi* (Berlin: de Gruyter, 1895).
IG XII/3	Friedrich F. Hiller von Gaertringen, ed., *Inscriptiones Symes, Teutlussae, Teli, Nisyri, Astypalaeae, Anaphes, Therae et Therasiae, Pholegandri, Meli, Cimoli* (Berlin: de Gruyter, 1898).

---

164. Cf. Mack, "Redescribing Christian Origins," 254–56; repr. in *Christian Myth*, 67–70.

IG XII/5	Friedrich F. Hiller von Gaertringen, ed., *Inscriptiones Cycladum*, part 1, *Inscriptiones Cycladum praeter Tenum* (Berlin: de Gruyter, 1903); part 2, *Inscriptiones Teni insulae* (Berlin: de Gruyter, 1909).
IG XII/7	Jules Delamarre and Friedrich Hiller von Gaertringen, eds., *Inscriptiones Amorgi et insularum vicinarum* (Berlin: de Gruyter, 1908).
IGR	Rene L. Cagnat, Jules F. Toutain, Victor Henry, and Georges L. Lafaye, eds., *Inscriptiones Graecae ad res Romanas pertinentes* (4 vols.; Paris: Leroux, 1927).
IHierapJ	Carl Humann, "Inschriften," in *Altertümer von Hierapolis* (ed. Carl Humann, Conrad Cichorius, Walther Judeich, and Franz Winter; Jahrbuch des kaiserlich deutschen archäologischen Instituts, Ergänzungsheft 4; Berlin: Reimer, 1898), 67–202.
IKilikiaBM 2	George Ewart Bean and Terence Bruce Mitford, eds., *Journeys in Rough Cilicia 1964–1968* (Österreichische Akademie der Wissenschaften, philosophisch-historische Klasse, Denkschriften 102; Vienna: Böhlaus, 1970).
IMakedD	M. G. Dimitsas, ed., *Sylloge inscriptionum graecarum et latinarum Macedoniae* (1896; 2 vols.; Chicago: Ares, 1980).
IPhilippi	Peter Pilhofer, *Philippi*, vol. 2, *Katalog der Inschriften von Philippi* (WUNT 119; Tübingen: Mohr Siebeck, 2001).
IPontEux	Basillius Latyšev, ed., *Inscriptiones antiquae orae septentrionalis Ponti Euxini Graecae et Latinae* (1885–1901; 3 vols.; Hildesheim: Olms, 1965).
ITralleis	Fjodor B. Poljakov, ed., *Die Inschriften von Tralleis und Nysa*, vol. 1, *Die Inschriften von Tralleis* (Inschriften griechischer Städte aus Kleinasien 36/1; Bonn: Habelt, 1989).
LSCG	Franciszek Sokolowski, *Lois sacrées de cités grecques* (École française d'Athènes, travaux et mémoires 18; Paris: Boccard, 1969).
PCairoDem	W. Spiegelberg, *Die demotischen Papyrus* (Strassburg: Schlesier and Schweikhardt, 1908).
PEnteuxeis	O. Guéraud, *ΕΝΤΕΥΞΕΙΣ: Requêtes et plaints addressées au Roi d'Egypte au IIIe siècle avant J.-C.* (Cairo: Imprimerie de l'Institut français d'archéologie orientale, 1931).
PMichTebt	Alan E. R. Boak, ed., *Papyri from Tebtunis* (University of Michigan Studies Humanistic Series 28; Ann Arbor: University of Michigan Press, 1933).
SEG	J. J. E. Hondius et al., eds., *Supplementum epigraphicum graecum* (Amsterdam: Gieben, 1923–).
*SIG*³	Wilhelm Dittenberger, ed., *Sylloge inscriptionum graecarum* (3rd ed.; 4 vols.; Leipzig: Hirzel, 1915–24).

Greco-Roman *Thiasoi*, the *Ekklēsia* at Corinth, and Conflict Management

John S. Kloppenborg

It is now a commonplace in the academic study of the early Jesus movement that its intellectual and social forms did not arise *ex nihilo* but were formed in the context of the intellectual and social forms of the ancient Mediterranean world. In the study of early Christian *beliefs,* it has been standard practice for decades to relate these to a series of analogies drawn from the Tanak, the literature of Second Temple Judaism, and Hellenistic writers as a means of locating Christian beliefs, assessing their novelty and conventionality, and ascertaining their appeal.

The parallel exploration of the *social forms* adopted by the early Jesus movement has had a more checkered history. Significant attention was devoted to social aspects of early Christianity in the 1870s and 1880s, but this investigation languished for nearly a century thereafter. Only in the 1970s did scholars of Christian origins again make a concerted attempt to find models that might account for the particular social forms and practices adopted by the Jesus movement. Informing this newly found interest in social history is the supposition that beliefs have social implications and that the forms of life adopted by groups of persons have bearing on the beliefs that they embrace. This is not necessarily to make ideas into functions of social arrangements or vice versa, but it acknowledges the reciprocal and complex relationship between practices and beliefs.

Apologetic instincts have at times been close to the surface in the discussion of models. In the first part of the last century, the explicit assertion (or the implicit assumption) that early Christian associative forms lacked significant analogies in their host cultures seems to have masked an ideological commitment that the beliefs and forms of life "created" by the Jesus movement were *nova* and *sui generis.* This historical conclusion was the concomitant of the view of revelation espoused by neo-orthodox theology. The paralyzing effects of neo-orthodoxy can be seen in the 1920s and 1930s when form critics, laboring under a neo-orthodox spell, could declare the "literary" forms of the Jesus movement to be without significant parallels in contemporary Near Eastern and Hellenistic literature.[1] Under such a theological regime, the search for apposite models of early Christian associative practices became fruitful only in the second and following centuries, when (*ex hypothesi*) Christian forms underwent a kind of theological degeneration and accommodation to pagan culture that resulted in "early catholicism," with an attendant loss of "eschatological enthusiasm" and the routinization of "charisma" in ecclesial offices.

A more complex and subtle form of this approach is to argue that the Jesus movement simply extended the associative practices of Diaspora synagogues. Acts gives encouragement to this view. But as several scholars have pointed out, the account of Acts has its own apologetic interests, on the one hand, and, on the other, a comparison of Diaspora synagogues with Pauline groups yields as many differences as it does similarities. From an ideological perspective, however, the view that the Jesus movement was an extension of Diaspora synagogues served the function of "deriving" Christianity from "Judaism" (thereby insulating the former from other "influences"). To regard early Christian forms simply as the natural extension of Jewish forms served the interests of biblical theology, which asserted basic continuities and coherences between the Hebrew Bible and the New Testament, often over against the surrounding culture. This approach naturally provided an easy purchase for supersessionist rhetoric of transformation and transcendence.[2] Again, the Jesus movement could be treated, historically and theologically, as a *novum*.

I do not wish to imply that there is some sort of objective position from which to engage in making comparisons. The task of comparison is always "interested," selecting items for comparison on the basis of their potential relevance to larger theoretical or theological issues.[3] I confess to deep suspicions of the historiographic spillage from neo-orthodox theology since, in the long run, it seems profoundly antihistorical and obscurantist. Nor do I have any attachment to a doctrine of monogenesis in Christian origins,[4] still less to a doctrine of manifest destiny: that

---

1. See Karl Ludwig Schmidt, "Die Stellung der Evangelien in der allgemeinen Literaturgeschichte," in *EYXAPIΣTHPION: Studien zur Religion und Literatur des Alten und Neuen Testaments. Hermann Gunkel zum 60. Geburtstage, dem 23. Mai 1922 dargebracht von seinen Schülern und Freunden* (ed. Hans Schmidt; FRLANT 36/2; Göttingen: Vandenhoeck & Ruprecht, 1923), 134; cf. 76; ET: *The Place of the Gospels in the General History of Literature* (trans. Byron R. McCane; Columbia: University of South Carolina Press, 2002), 86; cf. 27; Rudolf Bultmann, "Evangelien, gattungsgeschichtlich (formgeschichtlich)," *RGG* (2nd ed.; 1928), 2:419: "Thus [the gospels] are a unique phenomenon in the history of literature and at the same time are symbolic of the distinctive nature of the Christian religion as such."

2. See Jonathan Z. Smith, *Drudgery Divine: On the Comparison of Early Christianities and the Religions of Late Antiquity* (Jordan Lectures in Comparative Religion 14; London: School of Oriental and African Studies, University of London; Chicago: University of Chicago Press, 1990).

3. Ibid., 52.

4. I borrow this term from Willi Braun, "Smoke Signals from the North: A Reply to Burton

the Jesus movement unfolded, by a subtle and ineluctable internal logic, into the triumphs of the fourth (or sixteenth, or twentieth) century. Were it not for the pure happenstance of a meteorite striking the earth sixty-five million years ago, *Homo sapiens* might have found itself rather differently situated in relation to its saurian cousins. Had the First or Second Revolts not occurred, or had they come out differently, the Jesus movement might have looked very different, or perhaps not existed at all. On the other hand, I have no particular interest in refuting either the neo-orthodox view of things or versions of the Big Bang theory of Christian origins (although I remain interested in understanding the conditions under which such views became appealing as accounts and for whom they were appealing).

My interests instead have to do with the process by which humans discover or create loci of meaning and the conditions under which various loci fail or perdure. This is inevitably a social process and one that includes both discursive practices and social arrangements bundled together. Such an interest makes comparison crucial, for the very act of assembling differences and similarities between groups with quite different origins, appearances, and fates helps to problematize particular aspects of the group under study, and to raise questions about what in the complex chemistry of social practice and belief helps to account for the success of one group and the failure of another. This interest also accounts for why I have no special concern to connect the dots between Jesus groups in the Galilee and Jesus groups in Achaia or Corinthia. Genetic relationships, even if they existed, are not likely to be as important to issues of survival, success, and failure as synchronic comparisons. In another theoretical framework, of course, thinking about how the dots might be connected could be an obvious and useful activity.

In making comparisons of the Corinthian *ekklēsia* with other models of association, I wish to avoid two extremes. The first is to use stipulative definitions of associative models that are so restrictive that comparison is derailed from the beginning. Minute differences between the Jesus groups and other associations are given decisive significance. This is a strategy that has been employed in many pseudo-efforts at comparison, but it seems preprogrammed to achieve no useful results. On the contrary, its main function would seem to be to permit declarations to the effect that forms of the Jesus movement were indeed *sui generis*. The other extreme is to make the rule of comparison so vague than any similarity will do. Such an approach simply does not take difference seriously enough. Preliminary analysis of the available models makes it unlikely that any one will commend itself fully; there are simply too many loose ends that will not fit. Hence, rather than engaging in rhetorical overstatement and claiming, for example, that the Corinthian *ekklēsia was* a *philosophia*, or *was* a cult association, it is far more useful to compare particular aspects of Christian, Jewish, and pagan associative practices.[5]

Mack's 'Backbay Jazz and Blues,'" in *Redescribing Christian Origins* (ed. Ron Cameron and Merrill P. Miller; SBLSymS 28; Atlanta: Society of Biblical Literature; Leiden and Boston: Brill, 2004), 438–39.

5. I take this to be one of the significant virtues of Stanley K. Stowers's paper, "Does Pauline

This, inevitably, will result in a highly complex picture (the Corinthian *ekklēsia* was like *x* with respect to *a* but not *b*, and like *y* with respect to *c* but not *d*). But such attention to particulars will likely provide a more nuanced picture and one that is better able to account for the breadth of features of the Jesus movement.

The types of social groupings with which the Corinthian *ekklēsia* has been compared are well known: Diaspora synagogues, *collegia* or *thiasoi, philosophiae*, the mysteries, and the household. Already in 1960, E. A. Judge suggested that the organization and practices of early Christian groups bore similarities both to philosophical schools[6] and to associations or *collegia*.[7] The analogy between *ekklēsiai* and *philosophiae* was elaborated first by Robert L. Wilken and then by Abraham J. Malherbe, who focused particular attention on the church at Thessalonica and Paul's psychagogic practices.[8] Others, including Jean Gagé, Wilken, and Hans-Josef Klauck, adduced similarities between Paul's churches as burial societies, which typically met monthly for social and cultic purposes and gathered funds that supplied the needs of their members, including the provision of funerals for deceased members.[9] But it was not until the 1980s that these somewhat

---

Christianity Resemble a Hellenistic Philosophy?" (in this volume). Stowers argues that similarities between Pauline Christianity at Corinth and philosophies are stronger than with Judean communities (synagogues) or voluntary associations (though he does not claim that Pauline Christianity *was* a philosophy). Stowers's convincing analysis focuses, however, on quite particular aspects of the phenomena: Paul's representation of the group rather than the Corinthian group itself. Stowers emphasizes the totalizing claims of Paul's gospel, ascetic tendencies, the importance of conversion or dramatic reorientation, and Paul's focus on technologies of the self and on the mind—features that are not obviously part of other associative models. This type of comparison helpfully illuminates an important aspect of Pauline Christianity, but obviously does not pretend to provide a comprehensive account of its associative practices.

6. See E. A. Judge, "The Early Christians as a Scholastic Community," *JRH* 1 (1960–61): 4–15, 125–37.

7. E. A. Judge, *The Social Pattern of the Christian Groups in the First Century: Some Prolegomena to the Study of New Testament Ideas of Social Obligation* (London: Tyndale, 1960), 40–48; idem, "'Antike und Christentum': Towards a Definition of the Field. A Bibliographical Survey," *ANRW* 23.1:3–58. Judge's suggestions on the parallels between churches and associations were anticipated by almost a decade in the work of Bo I. Reicke, *Diakonie, Festfreude und Zelos in Verbindung mit der altchristlichen Agapenfeier* (UUA 5; Uppsala: Lundequistiska Bokhandeln; Wiesbaden: Harrassowitz, 1951), 310–11, 320–28.

8. Robert L. Wilken, "Collegia, Philosophical Schools, and Theology," in *The Catacombs and the Colosseum: The Roman Empire as the Setting of Primitive Christianity* (ed. Stephen Benko and John J. O'Rourke; Valley Forge, Pa.: Judson, 1971), 268–91; Abraham J. Malherbe, *Social Aspects of Early Christianity* (2nd ed.; Philadelphia: Fortress, 1983); idem, *Paul and the Thessalonians: The Philosophic Tradition of Pastoral Care* (Philadelphia: Fortress, 1987); idem, *Paul and the Popular Philosophers* (Minneapolis: Fortress, 1989). See also Clarence E. Glad, *Paul and Philodemus: Adaptability in Epicurean and Early Christian Psychagogy* (NovTSup 81; Leiden: Brill, 1995); Loveday Alexander, "Paul and the Hellenistic Schools: The Evidence of Galen," in *Paul in His Hellenistic Context* (ed. Troels Engberg-Pedersen; Minneapolis: Fortress, 1995), 60–83.

9. Jean Gagé, *Les classes sociales dans l'Empire romain* (2nd ed.; Bibliothèque historique; Paris: Payot, 1971), 308: Christian groups "offre, à première vue, une resemblance étonnante avec une espèce

preliminary efforts to outline models of associative behavior were summarized and analyzed in Wayne A. Meeks's monographic study, *The First Urban Christians*.[10]

MODELS OF THE *EKKLĒSIA*

Meeks considered four basic models: the household; the voluntary association[11] or *collegium*; the Diaspora synagogue; and the philosophical or rhetorical school. Each of these associative models enlightens some aspects of Christian *ekklēsiai*, but none of the models is for Meeks fully adequate. In this survey, I will comment on only the first three, leaving aside philosophical schools.

The Household

The analogy of the household illumines a number of features of Pauline and post-Pauline *ekklēsiai*: the recurrent phrase ἡ κατ' οἶκον ἐκκλησία (Rom 16:5; 1 Cor 16:19; Col 4:15; Phlm 2) and other references to households (Rom 16:10-11;

---

d'assocation confraternelle qui avait fleuri depuis le IIe siècle, dans le cadre du paganisme et avec une très ouverte tolérance des pouvoirs, des municipaux comme de l'impérial: les *collegia funeraticia*, ou 'collèges funéraires.'" Similarly, Wilken, "Collegia, Philosophical Schools, and Theology," 279-86, who observed that *collegia* and philosophical clubs provided analogies for Christian groups, since these two type of organizations in fact overlapped in several important ways, sharing some of the same terminology (*secta*, σύνοδος, θίασος), often having a cultic dimension, and usually meeting for common meals. In his 1984 volume, Wilken devoted a chapter to "Christianity as a Burial Society" (*The Christians as the Romans Saw Them* [New Haven: Yale University Press, 1984], 31-47), where he concluded: "To the casual observer, the Christian communities in the cities of the Roman Empire appeared remarkably similar to religious associations such as the one described above [i.e., *IG* II[2] 1368] or to a burial society such as the one at Lanuvium [*CIL* XIV 2112]. Like these other associations, the Christian society met regularly for a common meal; it had its own ritual of initiation, rules, and standards for members; when the group came together, the members heard speeches and celebrated a religious rite involving offerings of wine, prayers, and hymns; and certain members of the group were elected to serve as officers and administrators of the association's affairs. It also had a common chest drawn from the contributions of members, looked out for the needs of its members, provided for a decent burial, and in some cities had its own burial grounds. Like the followers of Heracles who were called Heraclists, the devotees of Asclepius called Asclepiasts, or the followers of Isis called Isiacs, the Christians were called *Christianoi*" (44). For other discussions of associations, see L. William Countryman, "Patrons and Officers in Club and Church," in *Society of Biblical Literature 1977 Seminar Papers* (SBLSP 11; Missoula, Mont.: Scholars Press, 1977), 135-43; Hans-Joseph Klauck, *Hausgemeinde und Hauskirche im frühen Christentum* (SBS 103; Stuttgart: Katholisches Bibelwerk, 1981), 11.

10. Wayne A. Meeks, *The First Urban Christians: The Social World of the Apostle Paul* (New Haven: Yale University Press, 1983).

11. Although the term "voluntary" is often used in connection with associations, the adjective is not appropriate in many instances, in particular *collegia domestica*, phratry associations, and even professional associations, where membership, though perhaps not compulsory, was a natural outcome of living on the street in which a particular trade was carried on. On the connection of "voluntary" associations and modern democratic ideals and pluralism, see S. G. Wilson, "Voluntary Associations: An Overview," in *Voluntary Associations in the Graeco-Roman World* (ed. John S. Kloppenborg and Stephen G. Wilson; London and New York: Routledge, 1996), 2.

1 Cor 1:16; 16:15) suggest that some Christian groups were connected with households, probably meeting in those houses. The presence of persons of diverse legal statuses (freeborn, freed, and slaves), both genders, and various social statuses finds a ready explanation if at least some of the *ekklēsiai* were large households that included clients, slaves, and free(d) dependents, all obligated to a patron or patroness such as Phoebe (Rom 16:1–2), Gaius (Rom 16:23; 1 Cor 1:14), or Crispus (1 Cor 1:14). Finally, the metaphor of the "household of God" encountered in post-Pauline literature (1 Tim 3:5; 1 Pet 4:17) and the appearance of household codes in early Christian literature are intelligible if the Christian groups began as household groups.

The model of the household does not account for everything, as Meeks recognizes. First, neither one of the two key rituals of the Jesus movement, an initiatory baptism and a weekly or monthly ritual meal, was a standard part of household practice.

Second, Paul's letters refer not only to house-churches but also to ἡ ἐκκλησία [sing.] τοῦ θεοῦ in a particular city,[12] or collectively to αἱ ἐκκλησίαι (τοῦ θεοῦ) in a larger geographical area.[13] This implies that Paul thinks of the *ekklēsia* as larger than individual households. The same is implied by his comments in 1 Cor 11:18 where, apparently, many households "come together ἐν ἐκκλησίᾳ," but in doing so create σχίσματα. Ekkehard W. and Wolfgang Stegemann observe, rightly I think, that the usage of *ekklēsia* in 1 Thessalonians, with the name of the people in the genitive (τῇ ἐκκλησίᾳ Θεσσαλονικέων, 1:1), creates a parallel with the citizen assembly of the polis of Thessalonica, composed of the heads of all of the citizens of the city.[14] Meeks adds that the model of the household has no place for the authority exercised by Paul and his co-workers, who were not household heads.[15]

There is a rhetorical caveat to be observed here, however. It is important to take seriously Paul's intent in composing 1 Corinthians and to observe how Paul's description of the situation serves the solution he proposes, namely, to live as parts of a single "body." Factionalism is clearly a problem at Corinth, as it was later at Ephesus.[16] Under those circumstances it would be to Paul's advantage

---

12. See Rom 16:1; 1 Cor 1:2; 10:32; 11:22; 2 Cor 1:1; 1 Thess 1:1.

13. See Rom 16:4, 6; 1 Cor 7:17; 11:16; 14:33; 16:1, 19; 2 Cor 8:1, 18; 11:8, 28; 12:13; Gal 1:2, 22; 1 Thess 2:14; 2 Thess 1:1.

14. Ekkehard W. Stegemann and Wolfgang Stegemann, *The Jesus Movement: A Social History of Its First Century* (trans. O. C. Dean, Jr.; Minneapolis: Fortress, 1999), 263–64; similarly, Hans-Joseph Klauck, "Volk Gottes und Leid Christi, oder: Von der kommunikativen Kraft der Bilder," in *Alte Welt und Neuer Glaube: Beiträge zur Religionsgeschichte, Forschungsgeschichte und Theologie des Neuen Testaments* (NTOA 29; Göttingen: Vandenhoeck & Ruprecht, 1994), 290.

15. Meeks, *First Urban Christians*, 77. Additionally, 1 Cor 14:34, which may be an interpolation into 1 Corinthians, distinguishes between the οἶκος and the ἐκκλησία.

16. See Paul R. Trebilco, "Jews, Christians and The Associations in Ephesos: A Comparative Study of Group Structures," in *100 Jahre Österreichische Forschungen in Ephesos: Akten des Symposions Wien*

from a rhetorical perspective to speak of the Corinthian group as a single *ekklēsia*, whether it was or not, rather than playing to his opponents and conceding that the basic unit of organization was the autonomous household.

It should be noted, moreover, that the model of the household partially overlaps others of Meeks's models. Archaeological evidence in Delos, Rome, and Stobi (Macedonia) indicates that some synagogues began as private houses, eventually adapted for nondomestic use.[17] And one of the major subtypes of association was the *collegium domesticum*, composed of the dependents belonging to large Roman households.[18]

1995, vol. 1, *Textband* (ed. H. Friesinger and F. Krinzinger; 3 vols.; Denkschriften der Österreichische Akademie der Wissenschaften, Philosophisch-historische Klasse, 260; Archäologische Forschung 1; Vienna: Österreichischen Akademie der Wissenschaften, 1999), 325–28.

17. See especially L. Michael White, *Building God's House in the Roman World: Architectural Adaptation among Pagans, Jews, and Christians* (ASOR Library of Biblical and Near Eastern Archaeology; Baltimore: Johns Hopkins University Press, 1990); idem, *The Social Origins of Christian Architecture*, vol. 2, *Texts and Monuments for the Christian Domus Ecclesiae in Its Environment* (HTS 42; Valley Forge, Pa.: Trinity Press International, 1997).

18. E.g., *CIL* VI 26032 (first century B.C.E. or first century C.E.), a funerary monument from a domestic association: "Ex domo Scriboniae Caesar(is) libertorum libertar(umque) et qui in hoc monument(um) contulerunt." Several inscriptions refer to the "collegium quod est in domo Sergiae L(uci) f(iliae) Paullinae": *CIL* VI 9148–49; 10260–64. On this, see Jean Pierre Waltzing, *Étude historique sur les corporations professionnelles chez les Romains depuis les origines jusqu'à la chute de l'Empire d'Occident* (4 vols.; Mémoire couronne par l'Academie royale des Sciences, des Lettres et des Beaux-Arts de Belgique; Louvain: Peeters, 1895–1900; repr., Hildesheim: Olms, 1970), 3:253, 274–75; John S. Kloppenborg, "Collegia and *Thiasoi*: Issues in Function, Taxonomy and Membership," in Kloppenborg and Wilson, *Voluntary Associations*, 23; Philip A. Harland, *Associations, Synagogues, and Congregations: Claiming a Place in Ancient Mediterranean Society* (Minneapolis: Fortress, 2003), 30–33; Andrew D. Clarke, *Serve the Community of the Church: Christians as Leaders and Ministers* (Grand Rapids: Eerdmans, 2000), 64. The most impressive example of a domestic *collegium* is the Bacchic society associated with the household of Pompeia Agrippinilla from the Roman Campagna in the mid-second century C.E., consisting of 402 members (*IGUR* 160). On this, see Achille Vogliano, "La grande iscrizione bacchica del Metropolitan Museum," *AJA* 37 (1933): 215–31, with plates 27–29; John Scheid, "Le thiase du Metropolitan Museum (IGUR I, 160)," in *L'association dionysiaque dans les sociétés anciennes: Actes de la table ronde oranisée par l'Ecole française de Rome (Rome 24–25 mai 1984)* (Collection de l'Ecole française de Rome 89; Paris: Boccard, 1986), 275–90; Bradley H. McLean, "The Agrippinilla Inscription: Religious Associations and Early Church Formation," in *Origins and Method: Towards a New Understanding of Judaism and Christianity. Essays in Honour of John C. Hurd* (ed. Bradley H. McLean; JSNTSup 86; Sheffield: JSOT Press, 1993), 239–70. Another example is the cult association of Zeus Eumenes and Agdistis from second-century B.C.E. Lydia, which met in the house of Dionysios, the founder of the household association (*SIG*³ 985). See Otto Weinreich, *Stiftung und Kultsatzungen eines Privatheiligtums in Philadelphia in Lydien* (Sitzungsberichte der Heidelberger Akademie der Wissenschaften, Philosophisch-historische Klasse 1919, 16; Heidelberg: Winter, 1919); Stephen Barton and G. H. R. Horsley, "A Hellenistic Cult Group and the New Testament Churches," *JAC* 24 (1981): 7–41. Independently, both Stanley K. Stowers ("A Cult from Philadelphia: Oikos Religion or Cultic Association?" in *The Early Church in Its Context: Essays in Honor of Everett Ferguson* [ed. Abraham J. Malherbe et al.; NovTSup 90; Leiden: Brill, 1998], 287–301) and Harland (*Associations, Synagogues, and Congregations*, 30–31) have argued that this association ought to be considered a household-centered group rather than a cult-group with a more general membership.

Thiasoi and Collegia

Pagan associations offer a partial analogy to the associative practices of the Jesus movement. *Thiasoi* or *collegia* were small, face-to-face groups; while many were formed around a common cult, trade, neighborhood, or ethnicity, they often included members of diverse legal statuses and genders; most had at least a common meal; and cultic associations sometimes observed other rituals as well. It was common for domestic associations, associations of resident aliens, and professional associations to provide burial for members, and many associations offered other forms of relief to members.[19]

For Meeks and others, however, the differences between *collegia* and *ekklēsiai* are decisive. First, Christian groups were "exclusivistic and totalistic in a way that no club nor even any pagan cultic association was."[20] The motivation for membership went beyond mere fellowship and conviviality to "'salvation' in a comprehensive sense."[21] Second, Meeks thinks that Pauline groups were more inclusive in their membership, embracing a greater range of social and legal statuses.[22] Thomas Schmeller underscores this point by observing that, despite the fact that some associations had elite patrons, the patron was often no more than an honorary president who did not participate in the activities of the group.[23] The point is a bit

---

19. Meeks, *First Urban Christians*, 78. Meeks rightly observes that, while we have no direct evidence of Pauline churches providing for burials, "we can hardly doubt, in the face of the sort of sentiment expressed in, say, 1 Thess. 4:13–5:11 or the enigmatic reference to 'baptism for the dead' in 1 Cor. 15:29, that these groups made appropriate provision for the burial of deceased Christians" (ibid.).

20. Ibid.; similarly, Stegemann and Stegemann, *Jesus Movement*, 281.

21. Meeks, *First Urban Christians*, 79.

22. Ibid.; similarly, Stegemann and Stegemann, *Jesus Movement*, 281. Judge makes the opposite point about membership: "[*ekklēsiai*] were probably also abnormal in the broad constituency from which their members were drawn. This might also be deemed undesirable. There are great difficulties in determining their legal status, but there need be no doubt that whatever it was they were not distinguished in the public's mind from the general run of unofficial associations." Nevertheless, Judge notes that the Corinthians seem to have on balance a *higher* social status than most associations: "Far from being a socially depressed group, then, if the Corinthians are at all typical, the Christians were dominated by a socially pretentious section of the population of the big cities. Beyond that they seem to have drawn on a broad constituency, probably representing the household dependents of the leading members.... The interests brought together in this way probably marked the Christians off from the other unofficial associations, which were generally socially and economically as homogeneous as possible. Certainly the phenomenon led to constant differences among the Christians themselves, and helps to explain the persistent stress on not using membership in the association of equals to justify breaking down the conventional hierarchy of the household (e.g. 1 Cor. vii. 20–24). The interest of the owner and patron class is obvious in this. It was they who sponsored Christianity to their dependents" (*Social Pattern*, 44, 60).

23. Thomas Schmeller, *Hierarchie und Egalität: Eine sozialgeschichtliche Untersuchung paulinischer Gemeinden und griechisch-römischer Vereine* (SBS 162; Stuttgart: Katholisches Bibelwerk, 1995), 35, citing *ILS* II/2 7259 (Narbonne), where the association asks Sextus Fadius Secundus to become its patron, promising to have a special celebration of his birthday, evidently in his absence. But

overstated: while this is true of some associations, from the Hellenistic period on we can also cite instances of benefactors who were simultaneously officers of the association, and of associations, such as the Iobacchoi of Athens (*IG* II² 1368; 178 C.E.), whose patron, Herodes Atticus, was also its priest, or the association of *IG* II² 1369 (Liopesi, Attica; imperial period), whose patron (*prostates*) was intimately involved in the affairs of the associations.[24]

Pagan writers make clear that they regarded *ekklēsiai* as examples of associations and, as Meeks acknowledges, Tertullian and Eusebius referred also to Christian groups as *factiones, corpora,* and θιασῶται.[25] But for Meeks the slight terminological overlap between associations' self-designations and Paul's own description of his churches makes it unlikely that churches modeled themselves on associations. Instead, terms such as *ekklēsia* were mediated by the LXX.[26] He

---

Schmeller acknowledges that in domestic associations the patron perhaps functioned as a real member. The same is the case with the Iobacchoi group (*IG* II² 1368), where Herodes Atticus functioned as the patron and priest, as it is with the domestic association of Zeus Eumenes (*SIG*³ 985), where the patron/host is also a participant, and in the Agrippinilla group (*IGUR* 160).

24. Similarly, *AE* (1940) 75 = Monika Hörig and Elmar Schwertheim, *Corpus cultus Iovis Dolicheni (CCID)* (EPRO 106; Leiden: Brill, 1987), no. 373 (third century C.E.), lists the patrons/priests of an association of Jupiter Dolichenus, along with candidates sponsored by each patron, who include slaves.

25. The list of early authors could be expanded. Pliny the Younger, Lucian of Samosata, and Celsus treated Christian groups as instances of associations. Pliny (*Ep.* 10.96) clearly thought of Christians as constituting a *hetaeria*, one of the terms commonly used for *collegia* (cf. *Ep.* 10.34, of an association of fire-fighters). Lucian (*Peregr.* 11) calls Christianity a new mystery (καινὴ τελετή) and refers to the leaders with the terms προφήτης, θιασάρχης, ξυναγωγεύς, νομοθέτης, and προστάτης. Celsus (Origen, *Cels.* 1.1) claims that "Christians formed secret societies [συνθήκας κρύβδην] with each other, contrary to the law," and that these were "secret and forbidden societies" (ἀφανοῦς καὶ ἀπορρήτου κοινωνίας, 8.17); in 3.23 he calls the disciples θιασῶται Ἰησοῦ. In the late second century, Tertullian (*Apol.* 39), wishing to distinguish Christian groups sharply from "illegal societies" (*illicitae factiones*), described Christians as a "body" (*corpus*) and "congregation" (*coetus Christianorum*), gathered only for prayer, the reading of Scriptures, and a modest banquet. He noted that they kept a common chest (*arca*) for monthly contributions (*strips*), used not for feasting but for support of the poor and burial of the indigent (*egenis alendis huandisque*), and to aid orphans, aged persons, shipwrecks, and prisoners. Cf. Eusebius (*Hist. eccl.* 1.3.12) who refers to Christians as θιασῶται.

26. Meeks (*First Urban Christians*, 79, 222 n. 24) observes that ἐκκλησία does not occur as the *title* of clubs but is used (if rarely) of the business meetings of clubs. He cites two or three inscriptions mentioned by Franz Poland, *Geschichte des griechischen Vereinswesens* (Preisschriften gekrönt und herausgegeben von der fürstlich Jablonowskischen Gesellschaft zu Leipzig 38; Leipzig: Teubner, 1909; repr., Leipzig: Zentral-Antiquariat der Deutschen Demokratischen Republik, 1967), 332 (*CIG* 2271 = *IDelos* 1519 [Delos; 153/152 B.C.E.]; *BCH* 59 [1935]: 476–77, no. 2; *CIG* 3421), but overlooks *LBW* 1381–82 (Aspendus, Pamphylia), cited by Edwin Hatch, *The Organization of the Early Christian Churches: Eight Lectures* (Bampton Lectures, 1880; London: Rivingtons, 1881), 30 n. 11. Meeks's point is dubitable; it is true that ἐκκλησία is not normally the *name* of an association; but in 1 Thess 1:1 neither is ἐκκλησία used as a name of the group. Rather, it appears to mean "the assembly [of Thessalonians in God]." On association terminology on Delos, see now Bradley H. McLean, "Hierarchically Organised Associations on Delos," in *XI Congresso Internazionale di Epigrafia Greca e Latina, Roma, 18–24*

further acknowledges that, while ἐπίσκοπος may have been taken over from associations, "it has scarcely begun to make its appearance in Christian terminology in Paul's time"[27]—a somewhat puzzling comment in view of the fact that along with διάκονος,[28] ἐπίσκοπος is the *only* unambiguous title attested in any of the Pauline churches.[29] Finally, Meeks observes that Pauline churches quickly developed extra-local links in a way that neither professional *collegia* nor cult associations did. But as Richard S. Ascough has shown, some associations did in fact have extra-local links.[30]

From a methodological point of view, there seems little to be gained by arguing on the basis of an idealized description of associations either that *ekklēsiai* were associations or that they were not associations because they fail to conform precisely to that idealization. The examination of the several thousand association inscriptions from fourth-century B.C.E. Athens to fourth-century C.E. Italy or Gaul shows rich variation in nomenclature, membership profile, leadership patterns, and principal functions. Despite this wide variation, ancient observers had no hesitation in identifying these sometimes diversely organized groups under general headings such as *thiasoi* or *collegia*. And, as the second- and third-century evidence cited above suggests, neither did pagan authors think that the designation was inappropriate for *ekklēsiai*. This seems a good instance of *ekklēsiai* displaying a "family resemblance" to associations. Whether *ekklēsiai* were or were not associations is less relevant than whether associative behavior in *collegia* might help us discover something about associative patterns in early churches.

---

settembre 1997 (2 vols.; Rome: Quasar, 1999), 1:361–70; on ἐκκλησία in classical sources, see C. G. Brandis, "Ἐκκλησία," *PW* 5 (1905): 2163–2200.

27. Meeks, *First Urban Christians*, 80; similarly, Stegemann and Stegemann, *Jesus Movement*, 281.

28. Meeks (*First Urban Christians*, 79–80, 222 n. 29) suggests that when διάκονος appears in the inscriptions of associations, it refers to persons waiting on tables. Yet Poland (*Geschichte des griechischen Vereinswesens*, 391–92), to whom Meeks refers, states: "Der διάκονος tritt *als einzelner Beamter* in Troizen ... , Thyrrheion ... und Palairos ... auf; fünf διάκονοι hat ein Kolleg von Metereverehrern in Kyzikos ... und mindestens neun einschließlich eines Priesters ein κοινὸν τῶν διακόνων von Ambrakia, das ägyptische Götter verehrte.... Die Funktionen des Diakonos können wohl sehr verschiedenartig gewesen sein, immerhin läßt die weite Verbreitung dieser Bezeichnung für den Priestergehilfen im staatlichen und privaten Kult es nicht unmöglich erscheinen, daß der christliche Diakonentitel aus dem heidnischen hervorgegangen ist" (emphasis added).

29. I take the occurrences of προφήτης and διδάσκαλος in 1 Cor 12:28–30 (and the corresponding προφητεία, ὁ διδάσκων, ὁ παρακαλῶν, etc., in Rom 12:6–8) to be functional descriptions rather than titles. In both 1 Cor 12:28–30 and Rom 12:6–8 the list of activities in the *ekklēsia* begins with terms that could be titular, but trails off into clearly functional terms: ὁ μεταδιδούς, ὁ προϊστάμενος, δυνάμεις, χαρίσματα ἰαμάτων, ἀντιλήμψεις, κυβερνήσεις, γένη γλωσσῶν.

30. Richard S. Ascough, "Translocal Relationships among Voluntary Associations and Early Christianity," *JECS* 5 (1997): 223–41.

Synagōgai

Meeks's third model is the Diaspora synagogue, appealing because it shares both household and collegial features and because its members presumably had a consciousness of "belonging to a larger entity: Israel, the People of God, concretely represented by the land of Israel and the Temple in Jerusalem."[31]

Further similarities exist: *ekklēsia* presupposes, in Meeks's view, Septuagintal usage; Judeans,[32] like members of the Jesus movement, probably met in private houses (assuming that the houses at Delos, Dura-Europas, and Stobi were used for meeting purposes *prior* to their adaptations as synagogues);[33] the activities at weekly assemblies included Scripture reading, prayers, and common meals; both the Jewish community (as a πολίτευμα) and the Christian group took responsibility for the adjudication of disputes; and, most importantly, both groups employed the Scriptures of Israel.[34]

There is much to be said for the analogy of synagogues. To read the account of church founding given in Acts, one would conclude quite naturally that the *ekklēsiai* formed by Paul and his associates were extensions of Diaspora synagogues. The repetitive pattern of Acts is well known: Paul, upon entering a town, visits the local synagogue (or a place where he supposes that Jews might assemble); then, having attracted some believers and having aroused the hostility of others, he turns to pagans, among whom he wins additional believers.[35] He is especially successful among a class of "god-fearers" (οἱ φοβούμενοι τὸν θεόν)—persons already half-removed from paganism and adhering in some fashion to synagogues.[36]

---

31. In 1983 Meeks argued that the Diaspora synagogue offered "the nearest and most natural model" for urban Christian groups (*First Urban Christians*, 80). In 1985, however, Meeks altered his assessment. Paying more attention to the Pauline letters rather than Acts, he concluded: "the Pauline groups were never a sect of Judaism. They organized their lives independently from the Jewish associations of the cities where they were founded, and apparently, so far as the evidence reveals, they had little or no interaction with the Jews" ("Breaking Away: Three New Testament Pictures of Christianity's Separation from the Jewish Communities," in *"To See Ourselves as Others See Us": Christians, Jews, "Others" in Late Antiquity* [ed. Jacob Neusner and Ernest Frerichs; Scholars Press Studies in the Humanities; Chico, Calif.: Scholars Press, 1985], 106).

32. I use "Judean" to render Ἰουδαῖος in order to retain the geographical sense of the term.

33. See Martin Hengel, "Die Synagoginschrift von Stobi," *ZNW* 57 (1966): 160–64.

34. Meeks, *First Urban Christians*, 80–81.

35. Acts 13:5–12 (Salamis: a synagogue first, then Sergius Paulus); 13:5–42 (Pisidian Antioch: a synagogue first, then pagans); 14:1 (Iconium: summarizing comment that both Jews and pagans believed); 16:11–40 (Philippi: no mention of pagans); 17:1–9 (Thessalonica: a synagogue first, then "devout Greeks"); 17:10–15 (Beroea: synagogue first, then pagans); 18:1–8 (Corinth: synagogue first, then pagans).

36. Acts 10:2, 22, 35; 13:16, 26, 43, 50; 16:14; 17:4, 17; 18:7. The problems with this category are well known. See the discussion inaugurated by A. Thomas Kraabel, "The Disappearance of the God-Fearers," *Numen* 28 (1981): 113–26; idem and Robert S. MacLennan, "The God-Fearers—A Literary and Theological Invention," in *Diaspora Jews and Judaism: Essays in Honor of, and in Dialogue with, A. Thomas Kraabel* (ed. J. Andrew Overman and Robert S. MacLennan; South Florida Studies in the

The reader is left to assume that the groups formed thereby were indebted to the structure of Diaspora synagogues, although Luke provides no details of just how synagogue believers and pagan believers actually combined into a new association.

The connections with the synagogue are strongly implied in the case of Corinth, where Acts states that Paul's first host in Corinth, Titius Justus, lived next door to the synagogue and that Crispus, the ἀρχισυνάγωγος, became a believer (Acts 18:7–8). Luke's implicit characterization of the internal structure of the *ekklēsia* also points toward a synagogue structure: not only is Crispus, the ἀρχισυνάγωγος, a member of the Corinthian congregation, but the *ekklēsiai* founded by Paul in Antioch (Acts 11:30; 15:23), south Galatia (Acts 14:23), and Ephesus (20:17), as well as the Jerusalem church (15:2, 4, 22; 16:4), are also said to have πρεσβύτεροι—a term found frequently in synagogue inscriptions, especially in Syria, Cyprus, Asia, eastern Europe, and western locales outside Rome.[37] The impression that a presbyterial system of governance was imposed on the early *ekklēsiai* is reinforced by the comment of Acts 14:23 that Paul and Barnabas appointed (παρατιθέναι) presbyters in each of the *ekklēsiai* of Derbe, Lystra, and Iconium.[38]

The Lukan model of church origins has in fact been advocated since the seventeenth century[39] and has a respectable following today.[40] James Tunstead

---

History of Judaism 41; Atlanta: Scholars Press, 1992), 131–43; Irina A. Levinskaya, "The Inscription from Aphrodisias and the Problem of the God-Fearers," *TynBul* 41 (1990): 312–18; Bernd Wander, *Gottesfürchtige und Sympathisanten: Studien zum heidnischen Umfeld von Diasporasynagogen* (WUNT 2/104; Tübingen: Mohr Siebeck, 1998).

37. See Baruch Lifshitz, *Donateurs et fondateurs dans les synagogues juives: Répertoire des dédicaces grecques relatives à la construction et à la réfection des synagogues* (CahRB 7; Paris: Gabalda, 1967), 90, for instances of πρεσβύτερος in donative inscriptions for synagogues. For an even more complete list, see now David Noy et al., eds., *Inscriptiones Judaicae Orientis I: Eastern Europe* (TSAJ 101; Tübingen: Mohr Siebeck, 2004), 385; Walter Ameling, ed., *Inscriptiones Judaicae Orientis II: Kleinasien* (TSAJ 99; Tübingen: Mohr Siebeck, 2004), 621; David Noy and Hanswulf Bloedhorn, eds., *Inscriptiones Judaicae Orientis III: Syria and Cyprus* (TSAJ 102; Tübingen: Mohr Siebeck, 2004), 275; David Noy, ed., *Jewish Inscriptions of Western Europe*, vol. 1, *Italy (Excluding the City of Rome), Spain and Gaul* (Cambridge: Cambridge University Press, 1993), 329.

38. The notion of "appointment" of elders is echoed by Titus 1:5: Τούτου χάριν ἀπέλιπόν σε ἐν Κρήτῃ, ἵνα τὰ λείποντα ἐπιδιορθώσῃ καὶ καταστήσῃς κατὰ πόλιν πρεσβυτέρους, ὡς ἐγώ σοι διεταξάμην.

39. See Campegius Vitringa, *De synagoga vetere libri tres: quibus tum de nominibus structura origine praefectis ministris et sacris synagogarum agitur, tum praecipue formam regiminis et ministerii earum in ecclesiam Christianam translatam esse demonstratur: cum prolegomenis* (Leucopetrae: Apud Io. Frid. Wehrmannum, 1696); ET: *The Synagogue and the Church: Being an Attempt to Show, That the Government, Ministers, and Services of the Church, Were Derived from Those of the Synagogue* (London: Fellowes, 1842).

40. See John G. Gager, *Kingdom and Community: The Social World of Early Christianity* (Prentice-Hall Studies in Religion; Englewood Cliffs, N.J.: Prentice-Hall, 1975), 126–27, 135–40; James Tunstead Burtchaell, *From Synagogue to Church: Public Services and Offices in the Earliest Christian Communities* (Cambridge: Cambridge University Press, 1992), 274–357; Judith Lieu, "Do God-Fearers Make Good Christians?" in *Crossing the Boundaries: Essays in Biblical Interpretation in Honour of Michael D. Goulder* (ed. Stanley E. Porter et al.; BibInt 8; Leiden: Brill, 1994), 329–45.

Burtchaell provides the most detailed and compelling defense of this view. His larger interest is to challenge the model, current in much scholarship today, of an initial informal, unstructured, and charismatic (non)organization, which in the second century succumbed to clericalization and hierarchization. Burtchaell assumes that, since the earliest stages of the Jesus movement were exclusively Jewish, it would have organized itself on "the familiar and conventional ways of the synagogue."[41] But then in order to differentiate itself from Diaspora synagogues, the Jesus movement adopted nomenclature that disguised its Jewish roots.[42] Thus, while designations such as ταῖς δώδεκα φυλαῖς ταῖς ἐν τῇ διασπορᾷ (Jas 1:1; cf. 1 Pet 1:1) and συναγωγή (Jas 2:2) are attested, ἐκκλησία quickly became dominant, replacing συναγωγή, a transformation that reflected the developing consciousness of separateness from Judaism. Burtchaell even conjectures that the community chiefs were originally called ἀρχισυνάγωγοι and that the system of ecclesial governance was collegial. The same process of differentiation, he claims, led to the adoption of ἐπίσκοπος, chosen to avoid any identification with synagogues and pagan associations that used the same title.[43] "Elders," moreover, quickly assumed duties that were more individual than collegial.[44] Rather than using the term ὑπηρέτης (= *hazzan*), Christians used an alternate title διάκονος. Thus, for Burtchaell, the indebtedness of *ekklēsiai* to the synagogue is shown both in general structural similarities and in the ways in which *ekklēsiai* employed alternate terminology in order to distinguish themselves from synagogues.

Burtchaell's thesis is consistent with certain evidence from 1 Corinthians. Some connection with a Corinthian synagogue is indicated if the Crispus of 1 Cor 1:14 is the ἀρχισυνάγωγος of Acts 18:8. And although Paul never uses the term πρεσβύτερος in the undisputed letters—a fact that might encourage the thesis that it is Luke, rather than Paul, who thinks of the Corinthian group as synagogue-like—half a century later Clement of Rome, writing to the Corinthians, chastises them for unseating some of their πρεσβύτεροι (*1 Clem.* 44.5; 47.6; cf. 57.1).[45]

---

41. Burtchaell, *From Synagogue to Church*, 274.

42. Ibid., 281: "[T]he tendentious rejection of *synagoge* and adoption of *ekklesia* (which was the harbinger of a general avoidance of the standard Jewish vocabulary for offices, activities and functions even when hardly changed from the tradition) signaled a threshold of self-awareness that their communities were now going to stand by themselves while consciously claiming continuity with the past."

43. On the use of ἀρχισυνάγωγος, see Tessa Rajak and David Noy, "*Archisynagogoi*: Office, Title and Social Status in the Greco-Jewish Synagogue," *JRS* 83 (1993): 75–93; G. H. R. Horsley and John A. L. Lee, "A Lexicon of the New Testament with Documentary Parallels: Some Interim Entries, 1," *Filologia neotestamentaria* 10 (1997): 66–68, 79–80. The titles πρεσβύτερος and ἀρχισυνάγωγος are attested among Jewish Christian groups reported by Epiphanius (*Pan.* 30.18): πρεσβυτέρους γὰρ οὗτοι ἔξουσι καὶ ἀρχισυναγώγους, συναγωγὴν δὲ καλοῦσι τὴν ἑαυτῶν ἐκκλησίαν καὶ οὐχὶ ἐκκλησίαν (GCS 357; cf. *Pan.* 30.11).

44. Burtchaell, *From Synagogue to Church*, 283, 296.

45. Clement also uses the more general term οἱ ἡγούμενοι (*1 Clem.* 1.3; 37.2).

Moreover, in 1 Cor 16:2 Paul instructs the Corinthians to set aside money for the collection for Jerusalem κατὰ μίαν σαββάτου. This not only seems to indicate that the Corinthians chose the day after the Sabbath as their meeting day,[46] but also that they reckoned time in relation to "Jewish time."[47] It is not clear why the day after the Sabbath was chosen.[48] But whatever the case, meeting on a seven-day cycle is more typical of Jewish than pagan associations, which tended to have monthly meetings (supplemented, in some cases, with meetings connected to festivals or the birthdays of patrons).[49] It should be added, however, that it is not entirely certain that Diaspora Jews met in synagogues on the Sabbath at all; Heather A. McKay has recently argued that there is no evidence before 200 C.E. that the Sabbath was a day for communal liturgical gatherings.[50] Nevertheless, Luke assumes that this was the case (Acts 13:14, 44; 16:13), and there seems no good reason to doubt that Luke is reporting a current practice of Jews, at least in his area.

There are difficulties with Burtchaell's thesis, however. First, as Ascough has observed, Burtchaell's argument turns as much on the differences between synagogues and *ekklēsiai* as on their similarities. Burtchaell *assumes* continuity between synagogues and *ekklēsiai* and then seeks to account for differences in terminology; but he fails to demonstrate his initial premise.[51] Burtchaell has anticipated this

---

46. See Hans Lietzmann, *An die Korinther I/II* (rev. Werner Georg Kümmel; 5th ed.; HNT 9; Tübingen: Mohr Siebeck, 1969), 89; C. K. Barrett, *A Commentary on the First Epistle to the Corinthians* (HNTC; New York: Harper & Row, 1968), 387. Hans Conzelmann concludes, "even if the collection is not made during the community meeting, it may be concluded from this statement of date that ... Sunday is already the day of meeting" (*1 Corinthians: A Commentary on the First Epistle to the Corinthians* [Hermeneia; Philadelphia: Fortress, 1975], 296).

47. In Hellenistic and early imperial times, the seven-day week was not a commonly used means of time reckoning, except among Jews. The planetary week (of seven days, ἑβδομάς) became important only in the third century C.E. In Italy, there was a system of periodic market days, once every eight days (*nundinae*), which defined a "week." But this eight-day week never achieved a special calendrical significance. See F. H. Colson, *The Week: An Essay on the Origin and Development of the Seven-Day Cycle* (Cambridge: Cambridge University Press, 1926).

48. Acts 20:7 (ἐν δὲ τῇ μιᾷ τῶν σαββάτων συνηγμένων ἡμῶν κλάσαι ἄρτον) reflects the same practice. From a slightly later period, the *Didache* refers to the "Lord's day" (14.1: κατὰ κυριακὴν δὲ κυρίου συναχθέντες κλάσατε ἄρτον καὶ εὐχαριστήσατε), presumably the day after the Sabbath. *Barnabas* (15.9) provides a rationale: διὸ καὶ ἄγομεν τὴν ἡμέραν τὴν ὀγδόην εἰς εὐφροσύνην, ἐν ᾗ καὶ ὁ Ἰησοῦς ἀνέστη ἐκ νεκρῶν καὶ φανερωθεὶς ἀνέβη εἰς οὐρανούς. Justin (*1 Apol.* 67) states that they assemble τῇ τοῦ ἡλίου λεγομένῃ ἡμέρᾳ πάντων κατὰ πόλεις ἢ ἀγροὺς μενόντων ἐπὶ τὸ αὐτὸ συνέλευσις γίνεται, explaining that this day (Sunday) πρώτη ἐστὶν ἡμέρα, ἐν ᾗ ὁ θεὸς τὸ σκότος καὶ τὴν ὕλην τρέψας κόσμον ἐποίησε, καὶ Ἰησοῦς Χριστὸς ὁ ἡμέτερος σωτὴρ τῇ αὐτῇ ἡμέρᾳ ἐκ νεκρῶν ἀνέστη (Johann Karl Theodor von Otto, ed., *Justini philosophi et martyri opera quae feruntur omnia* [3rd ed.; 3 vols. in 5 parts; Corpus Apologetarum Christianorum Saeculi Secundi; Jena: Dufft, 1876–81], 1/1:188).

49. For monthly meetings, see, e.g., *IG* II² 1283 (Piraeus); *IG* II² 1284 (Piraeus); *IG* II² 1361 (Piraeus). For celebration of patrons' birthdays, *CIL* XIV 2112 (Lanuvium; ca. 136 C.E.).

50. Heather A. McKay, *Sabbath and Synagogue: The Question of Sabbath Worship in Ancient Judaism* (Religions in the Graeco-Roman World 122; Leiden: Brill, 1994).

51. Richard S. Ascough, *What Are They Saying about the Formation of Pauline Churches?* (New

objection by insisting that, while Christians differentiated themselves from synagogues, they did so only in nomenclature, not in structure.[52] But this then raises the question, Why were the *ekklēsiai* of the Jesus movement so keen to differentiate themselves terminologically from synagogues, especially in areas where there was no significant Jewish population? As Ascough points out, there is little evidence beyond Acts itself of a Jewish population in Thessalonica, and the analysis of 1 Thessalonians strongly suggests that the group addressed was pagan.[53] This being the case, it is difficult to imagine why the Thessalonian *ekklēsia* (1 Thess 1:1) would want or need to differentiate itself from synagogues.

There are additional difficulties. In the case of James, who uses both the terms συναγωγή and πρεσβύτεροι, one may plausibly argue that the group represented was a synagogue of the Jesus movement, with a structure and identity similar to other first-century synagogues. In Paul's groups, however, neither term appears, nor do any of the other terms associated with synagogues (ἀρχισυνάγωγος, ὑπηρέτης). Burtchaell dismisses this argument as a "commonplace" that "ignores a continuity of which Paul can be seen as the earliest witness";[54] but such a comment only begs the question.

Our knowledge of the structure and functions of Diaspora synagogues in the early imperial period is rather spotty, and hence to explain the organization of *ekklēsiai* by appeal to synagogues is to explain *obscurum per obscuriorem*. Virtually nothing is known of Jews in Achaia or Corinthia. And what we do know of synagogues more generally does not jibe especially well with what can be surmised of Pauline *ekklēsiai*. In Egypt, προσευχαί (buildings) were established under royal patronage, and at least one had the right of asylum.[55] In the early imperial period, Philo notes that there were buildings with shields, crowns, and stelae honoring the emperor (*Legat.* 133). Philo describes Jews in Rome as meeting on the Sabbath to be "trained" in the ancestral philosophy, collecting money for sacred purposes.[56] This undoubtedly also included the reading of the Scriptures, as Philo elsewhere

---

York: Paulist, 1998), 22.

52. Burtchaell, *From Synagogue to Church*, 278.

53. See Richard S. Ascough, "The Thessalonian Christian Community as a Professional Voluntary Association," *JBL* 119 (2000): 311–13. Beyond Acts 18:1–9 there is a generalizing comment in Philo (*Legat.* 281–83) concerning Jewish populations in Roman provinces (including Macedonia). The earliest epigraphical evidence is a sarcophagus (Nigdelis, *ZPE* 102 [1994]: 297–306) and a fragmentary inscription, *IG* X/2 72, restored by Levinskaya in a way that suggests that the inscription is Jewish, but very dubiously. After that, we have a third-century tomb inscription, *SEG* XLIV 556 (Thessalonica; 250–300 C.E.), and a synagogue inscription, *CIJ* I 694 (Stobi; third century C.E.). For a general discussion of the evidence, see Richard S. Ascough, *Paul's Macedonian Associations: The Social Context of Philippians and 1 Thessalonians* (WUNT 2/161; Tübingen: Mohr Siebeck, 2003), 191–212.

54. Burtchaell, *From Synagogue to Church*, 293.

55. *IJudEg* 25 (Nitriai; 140–116 B.C.E.); 125 (unknown provenance; 145–116 and 47–31 B.C.E. [the two dates refer to the original founding of the synagogue, and its subsequent replacement]).

56. Philo, *Legat.* 156: ἠπίστατο [Augustus] οὖν καὶ προσευχὰς ἔχοντας καὶ συνιόντας εἰς αὐτάς, καὶ μάλιστα ταῖς ἱεραῖς ἑβδόμαις, ὅτε δημοσίᾳ τὴν πάτριον παιδεύονται

suggests.[57] Josephus indicates a similar configuration of activities for Jews of Rome and Delos, including the collection of sacred monies and the holding of common meals;[58] similar statements are made apropos of Jews in Asia, in connection with which Josephus expressly mentions sacred books, sacred funds, a Sabbath-house (σαββατεῖον), and a banquet hall (ἀνδρών) (*Ant.* 16.6.2 §164).[59]

There are, of course, similarities between these functions and those of the Corinthian group(s), but none is really decisive. Both had common banquets, but this commonality hardly distinguishes *ekklēsiai* and *synagōgai* from *thiasoi* in general. Given the numerous allusions to the Tanak in 1 and 2 Corinthians, one should conclude that the Corinthian groups—or at least some of them—had knowledge of the Jewish Scriptures. But this does not require the assumption that scriptural reading was a key feature of the *ekklēsia*. We have no indication at all that it was.

As Stanley K. Stowers has rightly stressed, *synagōgai* displayed a strong orientation to the temple and to Jerusalem, epitomized in the collection of sacred funds for the temple and doubtless reinforced by the reading of the Tanak. Although Paul involved the Corinthians in a collection, his instructions in 1 Cor 16:1–4 do not give the impression that the Corinthian *ekklēsia* had been hitherto engaged in the collection for the temple, nor does Paul use the *tĕrûmâ* as an analogy for his collection.

Finally, the description of Diaspora Judean groups provided by Philo and Josephus at Alexandria, Delos, Rome, and the cities of Asia, as well as epigraphical evidence from Egypt, Cyrenaica, and Delos, indicates the central role played by *buildings*, variously called προσευχαί, συναγωγαί, εὐχεῖα, διδασκαλεῖα, and the like, built or adapted for communal purposes.[60] In Egypt, moreover, vocabulary

---

φιλοσοφίαν, ἠπίστατο καὶ χρήματα συνάγοντας ἀπὸ τῶν ἀπαρχῶν ἱερὰ καὶ πέμποντας εἰς Ἱεροσόλυμα διὰ τῶν τὰς θυσίας ἀναξόντων.

57. Philo, *Mos.* 2.216: ἀφ' οὗ καὶ εἰσέτι νῦν φιλοσοφοῦσι ταῖς ἑβδόμαις Ἰουδαῖοι τὴν πάτριον φιλοσοφίαν τὸν χρόνον ἐκεῖνον ἀναθέντες ἐπιστήμῃ καὶ θεωρίᾳ τῶν περὶ φύσιν· τὰ γὰρ κατὰ πόλεις προσευκτήρια τί ἕτερόν ἐστιν ἢ διδασκαλεῖα φρονήσεως καὶ ἀνδρείας καὶ σωφροσύνης καὶ δικαιοσύνης εὐσεβείας τε καὶ ὁσιότητος καὶ συμπάσης ἀρετῆς, ᾗ κατανοεῖται καὶ κατορθοῦται τά τε ἀνθρώπεια καὶ θεῖα.

58. Josephus, *Ant.* 14.10.8 §§213–14: ἐνέτυχόν μοι οἱ Ἰουδαῖοι ἐν Δήλῳ καί τινες τῶν παροίκων Ἰουδαίων παρόντων καὶ τῶν ὑμετέρων πρέσβεων καὶ ἐνεφάνισαν, ὡς ὑμεῖς ψηφίσματι κωλύετε αὐτοὺς τοῖς πατρίοις ἔθεσι καὶ ἱεροῖς χρῆσθαι. ἐμοὶ τοίνυν οὐκ ἀρέσκει κατὰ τῶν ἡμετέρων φίλων καὶ συμμάχων τοιαῦτα γίνεσθαι ψηφίσματα καὶ κωλύεσθαι αὐτοὺς ζῆν κατὰ τὰ αὐτῶν ἔθη καὶ χρήματα εἰς σύνδειπνα καὶ τὰ ἱερὰ εἰσφέρειν, τοῦτο ποιεῖν αὐτοὺς μηδ' ἐν Ῥώμῃ κεκωλυμένων (on the violation of Jewish rights in Delos); cf. 14.10.8 §215: καὶ γὰρ Γάιος Καῖσαρ ὁ ἡμέτερος στρατηγὸς [καὶ] ὕπατος ἐν τῷ διατάγματι κωλύων θιάσους συνάγεσθαι κατὰ πόλιν μόνους τούτους οὐκ ἐκώλυσεν οὔτε χρήματα συνεισφέρειν οὔτε σύνδειπνα ποιεῖν (of Jews in Rome).

59. See the lucid analysis of pre-70 Diaspora synagogues in Lee I. Levine, *The Ancient Synagogue: The First Thousand Years* (New Haven: Yale University Press, 2000), 74–123.

60. That there were buildings called συναγωγαί prior to the second or third century C.E. has

associated with temples is found in connection with these prayer houses: τέμενος, ἱερὸν περίβολον, and the designations ἅγιος τόπος or ἱερὸς τόπος.[61]

It does not seem likely that the Corinthian *ekklēsia* had such a communal meeting space; on the contrary, Rom 16:23 suggests that the entire *ekklēsia* met in the house of Gaius, also Paul's host. This lack of dedicated meeting space might be simply a function of the fact that the group was only a few years old at the time 1 and 2 Corinthians were written. Such a conclusion is not, however, self-evident. Other new associations sometimes sought to build sanctuaries and meeting spaces in relatively short order. The Kitian merchants of *IG* II[2] 337 (Piraeus; 333/332 B.C.E.), apparently newly arrived from Kition (Cyprus), obtained permission to build a sanctuary to Aphrodite Ourania in the Piraeus. They cited the precedent of a similar concession made to devotees of Isis, whose cult was established sometime earlier in the fourth century B.C.E.[62] A century earlier, immigrants from Thrace were permitted to establish a sanctuary to Bendis (*IG* II[2] 1283.4–7), probably in 431/430 or 430/429 B.C.E.[63] On Delos, Tyrian merchants, with the assistance of a patron (a member of the association), successfully petitioned the

---

been disputed by Howard Clark Kee, "The Transformation of the Synagogue after 70 CE: Its Import for Early Christianity," *NTS* 36 (1990): 1–24; idem, "Early Christianity in the Galilee: Reassessing the Evidence from the Gospels," in *The Galilee in Late Antiquity* (ed. Lee I. Levine; New York: Jewish Theological Seminary of America, 1992), 3–22; idem, "The Changing Meaning of Synagogue: A Response to Richard Oster," *NTS* 40 (1994): 281–83; idem, "Defining the First Century CE Synagogue: Problems and Progress," *NTS* 41 (1995): 481–500 (reprinted essentially unchanged as "Defining the First-Century C.E. Synagogue: Problems and Progress," in *Evolution of the Synagogue: Problems and Progress* [ed. Howard Clark Kee and Lynn H. Cohick; Harrisburg, Pa.: Trinity Press International, 1999], 7–26, in spite of the serious challenge by Richard Oster, "Supposed Anachronism in Luke-Acts' Use of συναγωγή: A Rejoinder to H. C. Kee," *NTS* 39 [1993]: 178–208). Kee's denial of earlier buildings called *synagōgai* runs afoul of *CJZC* 72 (Benghazi; 55/56 C.E.), which uses συναγωγή of a Jewish building, and *CIJ* II 1404, which can now be dated on paleographical grounds prior to 70 C.E. See John S. Kloppenborg, "Dating Theodotos (CIJ II 1404)," *JJS* 51 (2000): 243–80.

61. ἅγιος τόπος: *IJudEg* 16 (?); 17; 127 (?); ἱεροὶ τόποι: Philo, *Prob.* 81; ἱερὸς περίβολος: *IJudEg* 9; τέμενος: *IJudEg* 129.

62. Just how much earlier is the matter of debate. U. Köhler ("Studien zu den attischen Psephismen, XI-XVI," *Hermes* 5 [1871]: 328–53, esp. 352) suggested that the orator responsible for the decree, Lycourgos, was only carrying on the philo-Egyptian policies of his grandfather and namesake, nicknamed "Ibis" by Aristophanes (*Birds* 1296), who, Köhler suggests, first proposed a grant of *enktesis* to the Egyptian metics. There is no evidence to support this conjecture. It is just as likely that the precedent to which Lycourgos referred was his own. On this, see Sterling Dow, "The Egyptian Cults in Athens," *HTR* 30 (1937): 184–85; Jan Pečírka, *The Formula for the Grant of Enktesis in Attic Inscriptions* (Acta universitatis Carolinae; Philosophica et historica monographia 15; Prague: Universita Karlova 1966), 61.

63. *IG* I[3] 383 (Athens; 429/428 B.C.E.); *IG* I[3] 136 (Athens; 431–411 B.C.E.). See Paul Foucart, "Le culte de Bendis en Attique," in *Mélanges Perrot: Recueil de mémoires concernant l'archéologie classique dédié à Georges Perrot* (Paris: Ancienne libraire Thorin et fils, 1902), 95–102; Martin P. Nilsson, "Bendis in Athen," in *From the Collections of the Ny Carlsberg Glyptothek* (3 vols.; Copenhagen: Munksgaard, 1942), 3:169–88.

Athenian *demos* for permission to build a sanctuary to Melkart-Herakles (*IDelos* 1519; Delos; 153/152 B.C.E.).

What was decisive in the establishing of a cultic building is not how long a group has existed at a particular locale, but the social connections required to finance the building and to support such an establishment in the face of opposition from other groups. In the case of the Kitian and Egyptian merchants in the Piraeus, their support came from the influential Athenian finance minister, Lykourgos. In the late first century, a synagogue (called an οἶκος) could be built in Akmonia (Phrygia) because of the support of Julia Severa, one of the Severii, an influential family in the city connected with the imperial family (*MAMA* VI 264).[64] The same principle likely applies in the case of portions of a synagogue built by Tation, daughter of Straton in third-century C.E. Phokaia (*IKyme* 45; Phokaia, Ionia).[65]

It is worth wondering why, despite the fact that the Corinthian *ekklēsia* had (apparently) elite members in Gaius, Erastus, and probably Crispus, no attempt was made to secure a communal meeting space, as seemed to have been the norm with groups of the Judean Diaspora and with other groups of metics resident. Had the Corinthian *ekklēsia* been composed largely of Judean metics, one might have expected the locus of their activities to be in specially built, adapted, or rented quarters. But if the *ekklēsia* had looked more like a *collegium domesticum*—like the Bacchic association of Pompeia Agrippinilla (*IGUR* 160) or the domestic cult of Zeus in Philadelphia (*SIG*[3] 985)—meeting space would have been supplied by the patron of the association, presumably in her or his home. Such a location would also account for the features of *ekklēsiai* that Meeks associated with the household: the presence of persons of various legal statuses, and both genders.

Although the Corinthian *ekklēsia* bears some similarities with Judean *synagōgai*, the differences are such as to cast doubt on the simple thesis that *ekklēsiai* were extensions of Diaspora synagogues.

The brief survey of problems in securing convincing models for the associative practices of the *ekklēsiai* of the Jesus movement in Corinthia underscores the point made earlier, that none of the basic general models displays a happy fit. But rather than declaring at this point that the Corinthian *ekklēsia* was *sui generis*, it may be useful first to compare some of its practices with those of other groups on various particulars. Many topics could be chosen—finances, relation to the polis,

---

64. Now published as *IJO* II 168 (Ameling, ed., *Inscriptiones Judaicae Orientis II*, 348–55).

65. *IJO* II 36 (Ameling, ed., *Inscriptiones Judaicae Orientis II*, 162–67). An intriguing example of a cult that did not manage to establish a cultic site immediately is *IG* XI/4 1299, which relates the introduction of the cult of Sarapis to Delos by a priest, Apollonios. But it was not until his grandson's tenure as priest (ca. 220 B.C.E.) that a Sarapeion was built on disused land that had served as a garbage dump. The building of the sanctuary was immediately opposed by "evil men" who brought a suit. The suit, however, was decided in favor of the grandson, Apollonios II, probably a sign that he had in the meantime secured Delian defenders.

frequency of meetings, demographics, and so forth—but one obvious topic germane to the Corinthian group is the phenomenon of conflict. Conflict is present, of course, in most types of groups and was no doubt part of the life of families, synagogues, *collegia*, and philosophical groups. What makes the study of *collegia* particularly interesting is, first, that the available documentation discloses much more about social conflict than what remains of the other types of associations and, second, that various forms of conflict appear to have been endemic in *collegia* and that many *collegia* developed mechanisms by which to manage conflict, both internal and external.

Managing Conflict at Corinth

It is clear from the Corinthian correspondence that conflict existed at various levels among Corinthian Christians. Rivalries (ἔριδες) and divisions (σχίσματα) are mentioned at the beginning of 1 Corinthians (1:10–17); σχίσματα and αἱρέσεις (factions) are reported at the communal meal (1 Cor 11:17–19); there are tensions evident in 1 Cor 7, regarding one member litigating against another, and in 1 Cor 8–10 in regard to the participation of some Corinthian Christians in meals in pagan temples or, possibly, the meetings of private cultic associations; 2 Cor 10–13 reflects a deep conflict between Paul and those he calls false apostles (2 Cor 11:13) and others (?) that he calls "superapostles" (2 Cor 11:5); and some forty years later, Clement of Rome complains that the Corinthians have unseated their presbyters in favor of others (*1 Clem.* 47).

The Nature of Conflict at Corinth

There is a rich scholarship on the nature of the conflicts at Corinth, with some taking the view that it was primarily theological or ideological, and others suggesting that the conflict was more a matter of personal rivalries. For both, the divisions mentioned in 1 Cor 1:12 are important.

The first approach attempts to give an account of the divisions that coordinates the figures named in 1 Cor 1:12 (and later in 3:4–5; 3:22; and 4:6) with discrete theological positions that are reflected and/or combated elsewhere in the letter. The fact that Apollos, an Alexandrian Jew, is called by Acts 18:24 an ἀνὴρ λόγιος has encouraged the view that the "Apollos party" was characterized by the pursuit of wisdom and eloquence. C. K. Barrett, one of the ablest defenders of the theological approach to the Corinthian divisions, argues that the Apollos group placed a high premium on the constellation of γνῶσις, λόγος, and σοφία, the topics addressed predominantly in 1 Cor 1–4. The Cephas group, he suggested, had adopted a "nomistic" attitude, which entailed the complete rejection of eating meat sacrificed to idols, a view of litigation that forbade appeal to secular courts,[66]

---

66. C. K. Barrett ("Cephas and Corinth," in *Essays on Paul* [Philadelphia: Westminster, 1982], 33)

and the application of *kašrût* considerations to the Lord's supper.⁶⁷ This set of attitudes did not precipitate a rupture within the Corinthian group but was at least serious enough to raise the specter of a rupture.

Barrett's approach has the effect of parcelling out the topics in 1 Corinthians among the rival factions: Apollos's partisans are addressed in 1 Cor 1–4, which concerns *sophia* both as eloquence and as saving wisdom. Paul's willingness to describe himself and Apollos as fellow builders in 3:1–9, however, suggests to Barrett that the divisions between Paul and Apollos were not deep. But there is another unnamed "builder" in view in 3:10–17, whose work, Paul implies, might not stand the test of the coming judgment. This builder is Cephas, the alleged boulder of Matt 16:18 and the pillar of Gal 2. Much of 1 Cor 5–16 is assigned to problems raised by Cephas and his partisans. First Corinthians 6:1–8 (on litigation) was prompted by Cephas's sensibilities that Jewish conflicts should be settled within the ethnic *politeuma* rather than secular courts and, correspondingly, if the church was to be regarded on the analogy of Diaspora *politeumata*, the church itself should adjudicate disputes. The issue of idol meat in 1 Cor 8–10 had been raised by Cephas's group, concerned to comply with the apostolic decree, which according to Acts 15 (though not Gal 2) forbade the consumption of idol meat. Finally, divisions at the Lord's supper had been precipitated by the criticism that this was not a kosher table—Barrett here cites Gal 2:12–13, where Cephas at Antioch also separated himself from Gentiles after the arrival there of partisans of James.

For Barrett, the views of the Christ group can be identified by a process of elimination: once the views of the Apollos and Cephas groups were bracketed, what was left was a theology that, like the Apollos group, privileged wisdom, but was more extreme. The Christ group, perhaps reacting to the Cephas group, developed a theology that insisted on the primacy of "freedom." The slogans of the Christ group can be seen in 1 Cor 6:13, which implicitly rejects *kašrût*; in 1 Cor 7:1, which expresses an indifferent view of sexual relationships; and especially in the slogans in 1 Cor 8–10, which underscore "freedom" as a value.⁶⁸

There are some problems with the ideological approach. The so-called Christ party presents a special problem since, as John Coolidge Hurd, Jr., has pointed out, not only is an allusion to this supposed party absent from the subsequent references to division in 3:4–5 (Paul, Apollos), 3:22 (Paul, Apollos, Cephas), and 4:6 (Paul, Apollos), but the argument made in 1 Cor 1:13—that Christ is not divided, that Paul was not crucified, that no one was baptized into Paul, and that Paul baptized very few Corinthians—would have given a hypothetical "Christ party" an enormous rhetorical advantage over their competitors, something that Paul hardly

---

argues, following T. W. Manson (*Studies in the Gospels and Epistles* [ed. Matthew Black; Manchester: Manchester University Press, 1962], 198), that the Cephas group insisted that Jewish disputes not be transferred to pagan courts, but kept within the jurisdiction of the *ekklēsia*.

67. Barrett, "Cephas and Corinth," 4.
68. Ibid., 12–13.

wished to do.[69] Better to regard ἐγὼ δὲ Χριστοῦ with John Chrysostom as Paul's own gloss on the divisions.[70]

This still leaves the possibility of identifying the Apollos and Cephas parties with specific doctrinal positions, but, as Hurd again notes, this process is rendered difficult by the fact that elsewhere in the letter where the parties are named, the description of their respective positions is vague, and where Paul expressly criticizes behavior (1 Cor 5:1–13 [incest] ; 6:1–11 [civil litigation]; 6:12–20 [immorality]; 11:17–34 [divisions at the meal]), no parties are named. Much of the appeal of Barrett's argument depends, moreover, on assuming information that is not in fact evidenced: that it was primarily a privilege of Diaspora Jews to adjudicate their own legal disputes (more on this below); that those who advocated the consumption of idol meat were Gentiles (1 Cor 8:7 implies otherwise); and that the divisions at the Lord's supper were caused by some withdrawing from the meal (on this, the text is silent).

A second approach to the problem of divisions at Corinth avoids the temptation to identify specific ideological positions and instead understands the divisions in terms of social alignments. Over sixty years ago, Floyd V. Filson suggested that the divisions mirrored the existence of rival house-churches in Corinth,[71] a view that has been adapted in more recent discussions that focus on issues of wealth, status, and benefaction.

Citing Filson's essay, Gerd Theissen pointed out that the persons expressly named in 1 Corinthians and apparently associated with Paul—Crispus, Gaius, Stephanas (one could add Phoebe in Cenchreae)—were all wealthy householders. Theissen surmises that other wealthy householders played hosts to Apollos and Cephas and then became their partisans. Thus, the conflict in Corinth had to do with conflicts among persons of higher social status and their dependents.[72]

More recently, John K. Chow and Andrew D. Clarke have also downplayed the role of ideology in the conflict, insisting instead on personal attachments. Clarke points out that personal loyalties were part and parcel of the mechanisms of three different types of social exchange, each having parallels with the Corinthian

---

69. John Coolidge Hurd, Jr., *The Origin of I Corinthians* (London: SPCK, 1965), 104–5.

70. John Chrysostom, *Homilies on the Epistles of Paul to the Corinthians* (NPNF 12:12): "This was not [Paul's] charge, that they called themselves by the name of Christ, but that they did not all call themselves by that name alone. And I think that he added this of himself, wishing to make the accusation more grievous, and to point out that by this rule Christ must be considered as belonging to one party only, although they were not so using the name themselves." Similarly, Conzelmann, *1 Corinthians*, 34. Georg Heinrici (*Der erste Brief an die Korinther* [8th ed.; KEK 5; Göttingen: Vandenhoeck & Ruprecht, 1896], 56–58) and Johannes Weiss (*Der erste Korintherbrief* [9th ed.; KEK 5; Göttingen: Vandenhoeck & Ruprecht, 1910], xxxvi–xxxviii) treated the phrase as a scribal gloss.

71. Floyd V. Filson, "The Significance of the Early House Churches," *JBL* 58 (1939): 109–12.

72. Gerd Theissen, "Legitimation and Subsistence: An Essay on the Sociology of Early Christian Missionaries," in idem, *The Social Setting of Pauline Christianity: Essays on Corinth* (ed. and trans. John H. Schütz; Philadelphia: Fortress, 1982), 54–57.

situation. The institution of patronage produced groups of dependents or clients, each owing personal allegiance to the patron, and each deriving personal benefits from his or her attachment. Sophists and rhetors likewise cultivated groups of loyal students. And in the context of civic politics, interest groups formed on the basis of personal attachments rather than articulated ideologies were at the heart of political discord. The Corinthian Christians, argues Clarke, exhibited the marks of personal attachment to patrons, the valorization of proficiency in public speaking, and a preoccupation with wrangling that is redolent of civic politics.[73] The factions manifested what Clarke calls "secular leadership" based on high social standing and eloquence, and it is this model of leadership that Paul wished to oppose.

Chow focuses his attention on patron–client relationships, arguing that competition among patrons was at the heart of the conflict in Corinth. Some wealthy patrons opposed Paul or sought to absorb him into their own client network, something that Chow argues had already happened with Apollos.[74] He finds concrete evidence of such powerful patrons at several locations in 1 Corinthians. The matter of litigation in 1 Cor 6 reflects the resort to secular courts by members seeking to gain advantage over fellow members. Since access to the courts was in practice, though perhaps not in theory, the privilege of the wealthy, Chow concludes that the litigants were people of property. If Paul's question in 1 Cor 6:5 ("can it be that there is no one among you who is wise enough to judge between his brother?") is ironic, the litigants are probably among the "wise" identified earlier in the letter.[75] Both Chow and Clarke think that the incestuous man of 1 Cor 5:1–13 was a powerful patron whose social standing also gave him immunity from criticism.[76] And those who had the most to lose by abstaining from the consumption of idol meat were the wealthy, whose social position depended on social connections with other elite, who naturally consumed meat at banquets.

---

73. Andrew D. Clarke, *Secular and Christian Leadership in Corinth: A Socio-Historical and Exegetical Study of 1 Corinthians 1–6* (AGJU 18; Leiden: Brill, 1993), 89–95, cf. idem, *Serve the Community*, 176–81. Particularly influential on Clarke's position are works by L. L. Welborn, "On the Discord in Corinth: 1 Corinthians 1–4 and Ancient Politics," *JBL* 106 (1987): 85–111 (on ancient politics); and Bruce W. Winter, *Philo and Paul among the Sophists* (SNTSMS 96; Cambridge: Cambridge University Press, 1997) (on the relation of sophists and their students). Welborn concludes: "It is no longer necessary to argue against the position that the conflict which evoked 1 Corinthians 1–4 was essentially theological in character. The attempt to identify the parties with the views and practices condemned elsewhere in the epistle, as if the parties represented different positions in a dogmatic controversy, has collapsed under its own weight" ("On the Discord in Corinth," 88).

74. John K. Chow (*Patronage and Power: A Study of Social Networks in Corinth* [JSNTSup 75; Sheffield: JSOT Press, 1992], 106) thinks that Titus 3:13, where the letter writer asks that Apollos be assisted so that he lacks nothing, preserves the memory that Apollos was dependent on others for subsistence.

75. Ibid., 123–30.

76. Ibid., 131–40; Clarke, *Serve the Community*, 181–82.

Clarke and Chow contribute to the understanding of conflict at Corinth by supplying a social context in which Paul's contrapuntal rhetoric seems to make good sense. Chow's quest for powerful patrons seems, however, overdone. There are no good indications that the incestuous man of 1 Cor 5 is powerful; had he been a patron (whose house had been made available to Christian groups), it would make little sense to insist, as Paul does, on "driving out the wicked among you" (1 Cor 5:13). His advice, rather, would be to leave the wicked to himself. And while it is true that the regular consumption of meat was more common among the elite than the non-elite, the slogans in 1 Cor 8–10 which defend the consumption of idol meat appear to derive from Hellenistic Judaism.[77] This in turn suggests that the defenders of eating idol meat were not necessarily wealthy patrons, but others who aspired to the social connections enjoyed by the wealthy.

The organizational model that seems best to fit the scenarios described by Clarke and Chow is not that of a simple household dominated by a *paterfamilias*, but that of a network of *collegia domestica* (each with a patron) or a small private cult that was subscribed to by members of several families (and their dependents). In order to make sense of the description of conflict in 1 Cor 1:12 and 11:18, it is necessary to imagine a context in which factionalism and conflict become *public*—that is, a context in which various subgroups appear together.

An Associative Context for Conflict

One of the better-documented settings where one finds persons of several distinct families assembling for the purposes of sharing a common meal and participating in a common cult is the *thiasos* or *collegium*. Most of these associations seemed to have at least a common meal, and cultic associations observed other rituals as well. Moreover, it was common for domestic associations, associations of resident aliens, and professional associations to provide burial for members, and many associations offered other forms of relief to members.

What is interesting for our purposes is the fact that conflict in various forms was common and that many of these groups seem to have developed mechanisms for managing conflict. Some provide useful analogies for imaging how conflict was managed in Pauline churches.

It is not at all new to suggest that ancient *thiasoi* and *collegia* may offer some analogies to the associative practices of the earliest Jesus movement. In the late nineteenth century Georg Heinrici and Edwin Hatch both suggested that *ekklēsiai* were modeled on associations.[78] Although Heinrici and Hatch attracted some

---

77. Jerome Murphy-O'Connor, "Freedom or the Ghetto?" *RB* 85 (1978): 543–74.

78. Georg Heinrici, "Die Christengemeinden Korinths und die religiösen Genossenschaften der Griechen," *ZWT* 19 (1876): 465–526; idem, "Zur Geschichte der Anfänge paulinischer Gemeinden," *ZWT* 20 (1877): 89–130; Hatch, *Organization of the Early Christian Churches*.

following for their views,[79] their thesis languished for the better part of a century[80] until it was revived by Judge and others. Heinrici's 1876 essay on Corinth broached the issue of conflict by suggesting that an Athenian inscription published by Paul Foucart provided an instance of a religious association that, like the church at Corinth, contained several distinct *thiasoi*, each identified by a proper name.[81] The inscription in question, *IG* II 986 = *IG* II² 2345, was discovered in Athens on the road leading to Phaleron, and has ninety-one inscribed lines listing the names of approximately ninety males, subdivided into probably six *thiasoi*, each designated by a proper name (e.g., Ἀγνοθέο θίασος). Heinrici suggested this as an analogy for the subdivision of the Corinthian group into factions, each identified by the name of its founder or most prominent figure. He surmised that these subdivisions were produced as the association grew. But more recent study of this inscription, and the discovery of other inscriptions having a similar form (e.g., *IG* II² 2343), indicate that *IG* II² 2345 is the membership role of an Athenian phratry or brotherhood. These were citizen associations of the legitimate males of interrelated families;[82] and, though they probably engaged in cultic activities (*IG* II² 2343 is inscribed on a cult table),[83] these phratry groups do not offer a very close analogy to the constitution of the Corinthian *ekklēsia*.

---

79. For earlier advocates, see Theodor Mommsen, *De Collegiis et Sodaliciis Romanorum: Accedit Inscriptio Lanuvina* (Kiliae: Libraria Schwersiana, 1843); Giovanni Battista De Rossi, *La Roma sotteranea cristiana* (Rome: Cromo-litografia Pontificia, 1864–77); Ernest Renan, *Les apôtres* (Histoire des origines du christianisme 2; Paris: Levy, 1866), 351–53; ET: *The Apostles* (Origins of Christianity 2; London: Trübner, 1869), 278–79. See also Hermann Weingarten, "Die Umwandlung der ursprünglichen christlichen Gemeindeorganisation zur katholischen Kirche," *Historische Zeitschrift* 9 (1881): 441–67; Ernest George Hardy, *Studies in Roman History* (London: Sonnenschein, 1906), 129–50; Max Radin, *The Legislation of the Greeks and Romans on Corporations* (New York: Tuttle, Morehouse and Taylor, 1910), 126–28; Thomas Wilson, *St. Paul and Paganism* (Gunning Lectures, 1926; Edinburgh: T&T Clark, 1927), 120–35.

80. In 1951, Reicke (*Diakonie, Festfreude und Zelos*, 320–21) observed, "Forscher einer älteren Generation haben bisweilen die antiken Korporationen als Analogien der christlichen Gemeinden studiert; dabei wurden nicht gerade die Unsitten dieser Korporationen zur Erklärung der das Urchristentum bedrohenden Unsitten herangezogen, was tatsächlich ergiebiger als das Studium der positiven Beziehungen gewesen wäre. Heutzutage sind die antiken Korporationen wenigstens den Theologen nicht mehr so bekannt. Es dürfte sich deswegen lohnen, über die politische und soziale Agitation im Rahmen dieser Korporationen einiges darzutun."

81. Heinrici, "Die Christengemeinden Korinths und die religiösen Genossenschaften der Griechen," 505, citing Paul Foucart, *Des associations religieuses chez les Grecs: thiases, éranes, orgéons, avec le texte des inscriptions rélatives à ces associations* (Paris: Klincksieck, 1873; repr., New York: Arno, 1975) (incorrectly cited as Foucart no. 32). The text is now published as *IG* II² 2345.

82. See William Scott Ferguson, "The Athenian Phratries," *CP* 5 (1910): 257–84; S. D. Lambert, *The Phratries of Attica* (Michigan Monographs in Classical Antiquity; Ann Arbor: University of Michigan Press, 1993).

83. See David H. Gill, *Greek Cult Tables* (Harvard Dissertations in Classics; New York: Garland, 1991).

Associations, nonetheless, provide numerous instances of factionalism and rivalry. Rivalry typically manifested itself at meals, where seating arrangements and the amount of food and drink received served as indicators of status. A guild ordinance of a cult association of Zeus (*PLond* VII 2193; Philadelphia [Fayûm]; 69–58 B.C.E.) enjoins members to obey the president (ὁ ἡγούμενος) and his assistant (ὑπηρέτης); requires them to be present at all meetings (συναγωγαί); and prohibits members from causing divisions (σχίσματα), calumniating other members or abusing them at the banquet, or bringing fellow members to law.[84] Thus, we have an ordinance that discusses four of the topics with which Paul was also concerned in 1 Corinthians: factions, etiquette at communal banquets, lawsuits, and respect for leadership.

Another association from the time of Tiberius (*PMich* V 243) requires members to be present at all meetings and fines those who take the seats of others at the banquet, or who prosecute fellow members in the courts, or who speak ill of fellow members.[85] This papyrus is of further relevance because it contains a membership role: sixteen members (all male), representing nine families. Hence it is possible to imagine that some of the conflict anticipated by the *nomos* is interfamilial conflict.

Disturbances at the communal meal are mentioned in the bylaws of a benevolent association from Lanuvium, south of Rome from the time of Hadrian (*CIL* XIV 2112). The bylaws forbid members from causing disturbances by moving from one place to another at the banquet, or from using abusive language. A few decades later, the Iobacchoi inscription (*IG* II² 1368; Athens; 178 C.E.) prohibits unauthorized singing, speech making, seat stealing, and abuse of fellows at the banquets, and it appoints a set of bouncers (called *hippoi*) to maintain order. Like *PLond* VII 2193, it prohibits resort to the secular courts, instead requiring the members to bring their disputes to the priest, who will decide the case.

Some of the disorderly conduct of which these ordinances speak was no doubt spontaneous. But the regularity with which the topics of seat stealing, litigation against fellows, verbal abuse, and nonattendance at banquets are mentioned suggests that such phenomena were structural problems within associations. The common denominator in these practices has to do with status: the assertion of status at the expense of others; attacks on the status of fellows, either in court or in public settings; and the withholding of status recognition from others to whom it is due.

---

84. *PLond* inv. 2710 VII 2193; published by Colin Roberts, Theodore C. Skeat, and Arthur Darby Nock, "The Gild of Zeus Hypsistos," *HTR* 29 (1936): 39–88; repr. in Arthur Darby Nock, *Essays on Religion and the Ancient World* (ed. Zeph Stewart; 2 vols.; Oxford: Clarendon, 1972), 1:414–43; later published as *PLond* VII 2193 in T. C. Skeat, *The Zenon Archive* (Greek Papyri in the British Museum 7; London: British Museum, 1974).

85. The fragmentary state of the papyrus leaves it unclear whether the association is a cultic group or a professional guild—there is mention of celebrations on the occasion of a member purchasing a flock of sheep or herd of cattle.

Seating arrangements at banquets are, of course, visible markers of social standing. Within a family setting, seating arrangements were no doubt fixed and uncontroversial. But as soon as one entered a social space where unrelated persons were present or in which multiple family groups took part, both personal interests and the interests to promote one's own group manifested themselves. For this reason, it was standard practice of associations to try to preserve fixed seating arrangements—although we do not know on what basis seating was assigned—and to discourage members from displacing others from their seats. In some associations, such as the Lanuvium society, officers and former officers who had conducted themselves fittingly not only enjoyed good seats but also received an enhanced portion (double or one and one-half times) of the normal distributions of food and drink (*CIL* XIV 2112). This mechanism enforced status distinctions within the group, but since leadership apparently rotated, it also provided incentive for members to seek leadership, despite the fact that leadership also brought with it the *leitourgia* of providing dinner for the members.

An examination of the conflict found in the associations cited above provides an opportunity to make some adjustments in the model proposed by Chow and Clarke. One does not have to posit a set of powerful patrons struggling with one another for advantage in order to account for what is observed in 1 Corinthians. In the Iobacchoi inscription, there is only one patron, Herodes Atticus, but plenty of signs of factionalism among the membership. The same is the case with the Lanuvium inscription; the patron is named (L. Caesennius Rufus) but there is no indication that he had rivals of the same social status. The bylaws, however, anticipate factionalism among the general membership. In the case of the two Egyptian rules, there is no indication of the presence of patronal figures at all; and many of the members bear Egyptian rather than Greek names, probably an indication of the low status of their members. Rivalry, factionalism, and litigation are nonetheless imagined as possible outcomes to be anticipated and avoided.

Of course, it does not follow from these data that the Corinthian *ekklēsia* did not have rival patrons. Gaius, Crispus, and probably Stephanas were all persons of means, though Paul's favorable mention of each of them probably indicates that he did not see them as among the disruptive forces. The analogy of other associations suggests, however, that internal conflict did not necessarily come from patrons; it could just as easily arise from the general membership.

This is the point where we might usefully distinguish between patronage and benefaction, that is, between the relation of elite persons and their dependents, on the one hand, and peer benefaction, on the other. Patrons had much to provide: they might offer meeting space or large donations of money sufficient to build a meeting hall, or regular disbursements of *sportulae*. Some were active, officiating members of their associations; others were individuals who patronized associations but who seldom if ever darkened their doors. But there was another sort of benefactor, the peer/member who contributed to the operation of the association through lesser administrative functions. Conflict within this sector was just as common as conflict higher up the status ladder.

Conflict Production and Conflict Management

In Attica, where our documentation is the best, non-elite members regularly served as officers and thereby found themselves in roles where they might act as benefactors, acquiring honor. Honorific inscriptions typically record the decision of the *koinon* to confer honors on a supervisor (*epimelētēs, episkopos*) or a treasurer or secretary who has executed his office well, or a priestess who has performed her duties in exemplary fashion. Such inscriptions are in fact just as common as those honoring elite benefactors. But many such inscriptions also include a codicil warning the member officers of the current year that if they do not inscribe and erect the stele, or make the required announcements of the honors or bestow the appropriate wreaths, they will be fined.

The best way to make sense of these codicils is to suppose that rivalry between officers and their predecessors might easily tempt one to withhold the honors and recognition due to one's fellows. The injunctions laid upon members to attend all meetings should be interpreted similarly: the temptation to stay away from a meeting might be strong if one's rival, or members of rival families, were to receive honors at that month's meeting. Persistent nonattendance at meetings amounted to the formation of factions, which, in the long run, could only injure the interests of the society. These rulings underscore just how significant a role the association's general meeting played, and how it could become an occasion for conflict, if members were not honored appropriately, or for insult, if attendance was poor.

It is sometimes argued that Pauline churches were unlike associations insofar as they did not award honors to their benefactors, a practice that may have caused patrons to feel slighted.[86] This possibility is surely worth considering, though we have no clear evidence of slighted persons. But it might also be noted that the structure of 1 Cor 11 is governed by a contrasting commendation (ἐπαινῶ δὲ ὑμᾶς, 11:2) and refusal to commend (οὐκ ἐπαινῶ, 11:17, 22), where Paul uses the verb that is stereotypical in Attic honorific decrees praising association members and patrons for their service and benefactions. Paul seems at least aware of the mechanisms of commendation, takes for granted that his addressees also understand them, and invokes the vocabulary of commendation precisely at a point where association-like activities—conduct of meetings, and conduct of the communal meal—are at issue.

A similar case might be made apropos of 1 Cor 3:10–17, where Paul alludes to the various "builders" active among the Corinthians, but warns that only those efforts which withstand testing will receive a reward (μισθός, v. 14); those whose work does not survive the test will "suffer damage" (RSV). The translation of the

---

86. Countryman, "Patrons and Officers"; followed by Meeks, *First Urban Christians*, 78.

term ζημιοῦσθαι has troubled commentators, who rightly note that the rendering "he will be punished" does not go well with the next, contrasting statement, "but he himself will be saved, though only as one passing through fire" (αὐτὸς δὲ σωθήσεται, οὕτως δὲ ὡς διὰ πυρός, v. 15).[87] The verb ζημιοῦσθαι, however, appears often in connection with the disciplinary fining of association members who misconduct themselves.[88] Such fines, or fines of officials who fail to enact the association's honorific decrees, do not amount to exclusion from the society. They instead serve as disciplinary punishment.

I do not wish to insist that the Corinthian group engaged in the rewarding and fining of members; but Paul appears to know and invoke a scenario of reward and fining that was fairly typical of the behavior of associations.

The texts cited so far illustrate how associations attempted to control potentially divisive and destructive behavior. But it is also the case that associations employed mechanisms that in fact created and cultivated rivalry. In several Attic inscriptions, members are encouraged to become benefactors and thus to rise through a kind of *cursus honorum*. Two inscriptions from third–second-century B.C.E. Attica (*IG* II² 1297; *IG* II² 1327) vote honors to members who have benefacted the groups, adding that this was done

> so that there might be a rivalry among the rest who aspire to honors, knowing that they too will receive rewards befitting those who are benefactors of the *koinon* of *orgeones*. (*IG* II² 1327.30–32)

Rivalry for honors clearly benefited the association; but it was precisely the type of behavior that could also easily lead to officers refusing to cooperate in honoring their predecessors, or partisans staying home from assemblies, or otherwise creating factions.

Thus, associations both cultivated a degree of rivalry and had to devise means by which such rivalry could be limited and contained. Fines for disorderly conduct at meals, injunctions prohibiting members from taking other members to court, and the insistence on settling all disputes among members within the association—all served as means by which an association sought to prevent internal conflict from reaching divisive proportions.

A final case illustrates efforts taken by an association to overcome rivalry. Sometime about 430 B.C.E. a cult of the Thacian goddess Bendis was founded in the Piraeus. For the Athenian *demos* to permit a foreign cult in Piraeus is somewhat unusual, but it is explicable on the supposition that Athens, in need of allies during the Peloponnesian War, sought good relations with Thrace and hence was

---

87. Barrett, *First Corinthians*, 89.
88. *IG* II² 1328.12 (fining of a priestess); *IG* II² 1330.42 (fining of members); *IG* II² 1369.42 (fining of members for fighting); *IDelta* 889.29 (fining of members).

eager to comply with the request of Thracian merchants resident in the Piraeus.[89] By the next century, there was not only a Bendis cult in the Piraeus, but also one in the Asty (i.e., Athens), and a procession, beginning in Athens near the Prytaneion and proceeding to the Bendis temple in the Piraeus, a procession mentioned at the beginning of Plato's *Republic*. A decree dated 261/260 B.C.E. (*IG* II² 1283) seeks to ensure that harmonious relations be established and maintained between the two Thracian groups and mandates that the officers of the Piraean association supply sponges, cups of water, wreaths, and a meal in the sanctuary to the Athenian group, when they arrive, and that prayers be said specifically for them when the priest and priestess offer their sacrifices for the Piraean *cultores*. The expectation is

> that when these events take place and the entire *ethnos* lives in harmony, the sacrifices shall be made to the gods, and the other rites shall be offered in accordance both with the ancestral customs of the Thracians and the laws of the city and ... that it will go well and piously for the entire *ethnos* in matters concerning the gods. (*IG* II² 1283.32–36)

Whether the expectations of the decree were met, we do not know. Evidence of Bendis associations in the Piraeus and Athens disappears after 260 (although there is a Thracian group in Salamis). What is noteworthy for our purposes is the use of a common ritual, a joint procession followed by a common meal, prayers, and sacrifices, all performed in the interests of establishing and maintaining *homonoia* between two related groups which, given the competitive nature of public life, might easily become bitter rivals. The decree's insistence on hospitality and equality between the two groups seems a conscious anticipation of conflict and a concerted attempt to mitigate divisions.

Paul evidently expects the Corinthian Lord's supper to be a similar demonstration of harmony and mutual hospitality (11:33: ὥστε, ἀδελφοί μου, συνερχόμενοι εἰς τὸ φαγεῖν ἀλλήλους ἐκδέχεσθε). He recommends, like the Piraean *cultores* of Bendis, that consumption at the public meal be equal, and be seen to be equal, so that the common ritual cannot become an occasion for the exhibiting of status differences. Stowers, without expressly referring to associations, has recently made the helpful suggestion that the preference for bread and wine over meat as ritual substances had real if unanticipated social consequences. The act of sacrificing within the home was normally a gendered activity—males conducted the sacrifices. The consumption of meat was an activity fraught with social consequences, since meat was ordinarily accessible only to the elite and their dependents. Stowers suggests that the adoption by the Jesus movement of a ritual based on substances less implicated in gender and social ranking may have had the effect of creating

---

89. See Nilsson, "Bendis in Athen."

a new order in which gender and status ranking were somewhat less pronounced than in other groups.[90]

The Corinthian *ekklēsia* was not up to something totally new and unprecedented. To the ancient observer, the Corinthian Jesus people would probably appear as *thiasotai* in a club that resembled domestic *collegia* or small cult associations more than groups of immigrant metics who met to preserve their ancestral customs. The phenomenon of conflict within the Christian group and Paul's strategies for conflict management fall within the spectrum of conflict managment seen in other *collegia*. There are, of course, noteworthy features of the Corinthian *ekklēsia* too. A significant Judean component seems to be indicated by the choice of meeting time, and the use of the Tanak within the association; yet its conduct and geopolitical orientation do not appear typical of Diaspora synagogues. There are some similarities with domestic *collegia*, though the *ekklēsia* seems to have experimented with transfamilial assemblies too, a practice that offered the occasion for serious conflict. And though the group displayed some similarities with cultic *collegia* and may even have adopted some form of recognition of benefactors, Paul's efforts were directed to a certain leveling of status differences and a concerted effort at the maintenance of *homonoia*.

Epigraphical and Papyrological Abbreviations

AE	*L'Année épigraphique* (Paris: Presses Universitaires de France, 1888–).
BCH	*Bulletin de correspondance hellénique*
CIG	August Boeckh et al., eds., *Corpus inscriptionum graecarum* (4 vols.; Berlin: Reimer, 1828–77). Vol. I., ed. August Boeckh (1828); vol. II, ed. August Boeckh (1843); vol. III, ed. Johannes Franz (1853); vol. IV, ed. Ernst Curtius and Adolph Kirchhoff (1877).
CIJ	Jean-Baptiste Frey, ed., *Corpus inscriptionum iudaicarum: Recueil des inscriptions juives qui vont du IIIe siècle avant J.-C.* (2 vols.; Sussidi allo studio delle antichità cristiane; Rome: Pontificio Istituto di archeologia cristiana, 1936–52). Vol. I, *Europe* (1936), nos. 1–734; vol. II, *Asie-Afrique* (1952), nos. 735–1539.
CIL	*Corpus inscriptionum latinarum: Consilio et auctoritate Academiae litterarum Regiae Borussicae editum* (17 vols.; Berlin: Reimer, 1863–1989).

---

90. Stanley K. Stowers, "Greeks Who Sacrifice and Those Who Do Not: Toward an Anthropology of Greek Religion," in *The Social World of the First Christians: Essays in Honor of Wayne A. Meeks* (ed. L. Michael White and O. Larry Yarbrough; Minneapolis: Fortress, 1995), 299–320; idem, "Elusive Coherence: Ritual and Rhetoric in 1 Corinthians 10–11," in *Reimagining Christian Origins: A Colloquium Honoring Burton L. Mack* (ed. Elizabeth A. Castelli and Hal Taussig; Valley Forge, Pa.: Trinity Press International, 1996), 68–83.

CJZC	Gerd Lüderitz, ed., *Corpus jüdischer Zeugnisse aus der Cyrenaika* (Wiesbaden: Reichert, 1983).
IDelos	Félix Durrbach, Pierre Roussel, Marcel Launey, André Plassart, and Jacques Coupry, eds., *Inscriptions de Délos* (7 vols.; Paris: Champion and Boccard, 1926-73). Vol. I, *Comptes des hiéropes*, ed. André Plassart (1926), nos. 290-371; vol. II, *Comptes des hiéropes: Lois ou règlements, contrats d'enterprises et devis*, ed. Jacques Coupry (1929), nos. 372-498, 499-509; vol. III, *Actes des fonctionnaires athéniens préposés à l'administration des sanctuaires après 166 av. J.-C. Fragments d'actes divers*, ed. Félix Durrbach and Pierre Roussel (1935), nos. 1400-1479, 1480-96; vol. IV, *Décrets postérieurs à 166 av. J.-C. Dédicaces postérieures à 166 av. J.-C.*, ed. Pierre Roussel and Marcel Launey (1937), nos. 1497-1524, 1525-2219; vol. V, *Dédicaces postérieures à 166 av. J.-C. Textes divers, listes et catalogues, fragments divers postérieurs à 166 av. J.-C.*, ed. Pierre Roussel and Marcel Launey (1937), nos. 2220-2528, 2529-2879; vol. VI, *Période de l'amphictyonie ionienne et de l'amphictyonie attico-délienne. Dédicaces et textes divers écrits dans les alphabets cycladiques. Dédicaces, bornes, règlements, d'alphabet ionien classique. Décrets déliens. Ordonnance lacédémonienne. Décrets athéniens*, ed. André Plassart (1950), nos. 1-35, 36-70, 71-88; vol. VII, *Période de l'amphictyonie attico-délienne. Actes administratifs*, ed. Jacques Coupry (1972), nos. 89-104.
IDelta	André Bernand, ed., *Le Delta égyptien d'après les textes grecs, 1, Les Confins libyques* (3 vols.; Cairo: Institut français d'archéologie orientale, 1970-).
IG	Adolf Kirchhoff, Friedrich Hiller von Gaertringen, Ulrich Koehler, and Wilhelm Dittenberger, eds., *Inscriptiones Graecae: Consilio et auctoritate Academiae litterarum Regiae Borussicae editae* (14+ vols.; Berlin: Reimer, 1873-; Berlin: de Gruyter, 1924-).
IG I³	David Lewis and Lilian Jeffery, eds., *Inscriptiones Graecae* (3rd ed.; Berlin and New York: de Gruyter, 1981-).
IG II²	*Inscriptiones Atticae Euclidis anno posteriores.* In *Inscriptiones Graecae II* (4 vols.; Berlin: de Gruyter, 1913-40).
IG X/2	Charles Edson, ed., *Inscriptiones Graecae Epiri, Macedoniae, Thraciae, Scythiae*, II, *Inscriptiones Macedoniae*, fasc. 1, *Inscriptiones Thessalonicae et viciniae* (Berlin: de Gruyter, 1972).
IG XI/4	Pierre Roussel, ed., *Inscriptiones Deli: Consilio et auctoritate Academiae inscriptionum et humaniorum litterarum francogallicae editae* (Berlin: Reimer, 1914).
IGSK	*Inschriften griechischer Städte aus Kleinasien* (Bonn: Habelt, 1972-).

IGUR	Luigi Moretti, ed., *Inscriptiones Graecae urbis Romae* (4 vols.; Rome: Istituto Italiano per la storia antica, 1968–90).
IJO	*Inscriptiones Judaicae Orientis* (3 vols.; Tübingen: Mohr Siebeck, 2004). Vol. I, *Eastern Europe*, ed. David Noy, Alexander Panayotov, and Hanswulf Bloedhorn (Texts and Studies in Ancient Judaism 101); vol. II, *Kleinasien*, ed. Walter Ameling (Texts and Studies in Ancient Judaism 99); vol. 3, *Syria and Cyprus*, ed. David Noy and Hanswulf Bloedhorn (Texts and Studies in Ancient Judaism 102).
IJudEg	William Horbury and David Noy, eds., *Jewish Inscriptions of Graeco-Roman Egypt, with an Index of Jewish Inscriptions of Egypt and Cyrenaica* (Cambridge: Cambridge University Press, 1992).
IJudEur	David Noy, ed., *Jewish Inscriptions of Western Europe* (2 vols.; Cambridge: Cambridge University Press, 1993–95).
IKyme	Helmut Engelmann, ed., *Die Inschriften von Kyme* (IGSK 5; Bonn: Habelt, 1976).
ILS	Hermann Dessau, ed., *Inscriptiones latinae selectae* (3 vols.; Berlin: Weidmann, 1892–1916; repr., Berlin: Weidmann, 1962).
ISmyrna	Georg Petzl, ed., *Die Inschriften von Smyrna* (IGSK 23–24/1–2; Bonn: Habelt, 1982–90).
LBW	Philippe Le Bas and William Henry Waddington, eds., *Inscriptions grecques et latines recueillies en Asie Mineure*, I, *Textes en majuscules*; II, *Textes en minuscules et explications* (2 vols.; Paris: Firmin-Didot, 1870; repr., Hildesheim: Olms, 1972).
MAMA	William M. Calder, Ernst Herzfeld, Samuel Guyer, and C. W. M. Cox, eds., *Monumenta Asiae Minoris antiqua* (10 vols.; Publications of the American Society for Archaeological Research in Asia Minor 1–8; Journal of Roman Studies Monographs 4, 7; Manchester: Manchester University Press, 1928–93).
PLond VII	*Greek Papyri in the British Museum*, VII, *The Zenon Archive*, ed. T. C. Skeat (London: British Museum, 1974), nos. 1930–2193.
PMich V	*Michigan Papyri*, V, *Papyri from Tebtunis*, part 2, ed. Elinor Mullett Husselman, Arthur E. R. Boak, and William F. Edgerton (Ann Arbor: University of Michigan Press, 1944), nos. 226–356.
SEG	Jacobus Johannes Ewoud Hondius, A. Geoffrey Woodhead, and Gerhard Pfohl, eds., *Supplementum epigraphicum graecum* (Leiden: Sijthoff and Brill, 1923–).
*SIG*³	Wilhelm Dittenberger, ed., *Sylloge inscriptionum graecarum* (3rd ed.; 4 vols.; Leipzig: Hirzel, 1915–24).

Does Pauline Christianity Resemble a Hellenistic Philosophy?

Stanley K. Stowers

Introduction

Scholars have rightly judged that in order properly to describe early Christian groups they must compare these groups to other social formations in the environment of the early Christians.[1] But to which group or groups are the Christians best compared? The most frequently appearing candidates are synagogues, voluntary associations, mystery religions, and philosophical schools.[2] Scholars are apt to point out that all of these groups had a religious or cultic element, requirements for membership, meetings, common meals, and a mode of organization and leadership.[3] A moment of reflection, however, ought to give us pause about

---

This paper was presented at the annual meeting of the Society of Biblical Literature, held in Nashville in 2000, and first published in Troels Engberg-Pedersen, ed., *Paul Beyond the Judaism/Hellenism Divide* (Louisville: Westminster John Knox, 2001), 81–102, 276–83. It is reprinted here with permission.

1. On the necessity of comparison and failures resulting from lack of comparison, see Jonathan Z. Smith, *Drudgery Divine: On the Comparison of Early Christianities and the Religions of Late Antiquity* (Jordan Lectures in Comparative Religion 14; London: School of Oriental and African Studies, University of London; Chicago: University of Chicago Press, 1990); Luther H. Martin, "Comparison," in *Guide to the Study of Religion* (ed. Willi Braun and Russell T. McCutcheon; London: Cassell, 2000), 45–56.

2. Richard S. Ascough, *What Are They Saying about the Formation of the Pauline Churches?* (New York: Paulist, 1998). Ascough's helpful book selects these models and reviews scholarship that has compared them with Pauline communities. I have not treated mystery religions as a separate topic in what follows because most of what I say about "voluntary cults" also applies to them. They were not distinct religions, but elaborations of polytheism. The modern concept of mystery religions places a highly heterogeneous collection of entities into a category shaped to match up with Christianity and nineteenth-century interests in religious experience. See Walter Burkert, *Ancient Mystery Cults* (Carl Newell Jackson Lectures; Cambridge, Mass.: Harvard University Press, 1987).

3. Scholars mention many other points of comparison, but these seem to be the most frequent and broadest, that is, divisible into all the models. For examples of these categories of comparison, see Robert L. Wilken, *The Christians as the Romans Saw Them* (New Haven: Yale University Press, 1984),

basing comparisons on these characteristics, especially when abstracted from the particular web of beliefs and practices of the groups. The Senate of the United States, a Hasidic community in Brooklyn, Bob and Shirley's trucking company dedicated to Jesus, and the New Age-oriented Bristol Bird Watching Club all can be said to have a religious element, requirements for membership, meetings, common meals, and a mode of organization and leadership. Comparisons made on this basis do not indicate which practices are most important to the particular groups and what goods the members of the groups consider to be internal to those practices rather than external or incidental.

Part of the instinct, I suggest, that impels scholars toward this set of features for comparison derives from a twentieth-century Western notion that religious groups are naturally voluntary associations. Definitions of a Greco-Roman voluntary association given by scholars in 1936 and 1993, respectively, are "a group which a man joins of his own free will, and which accept him of its free will, and this mutual acceptance creates certain obligations on both parties" and "a coherent group, which could be recognized as such by outsiders, with its own rules for membership, leadership, and association with one another."[4] Such definitions express the modern Western conception of social contract. In groups of this sort, free individuals are said to consciously and freely enter into rationally articulated modes of association with other individuals for the pursuit of a limited and specified set of purposes which the individuals agree to pursue jointly. In the early nineteenth century, Alexis de Tocqueville was amazed at how characteristic such groups and an attendant ideology had become in the young United States.[5] For de Tocqueville, these groups were precisely what distinguished the new nation from old Europe with its, in his description, organic solidarity based on family and an interdependent hierarchy of social ranks.[6] The definitions of a voluntary association given above rather naively lack one half of the equation for understanding the phenomenon historically, a certain conception of the person that does not fit

---

44; S. G. Wilson, "Voluntary Associations: An Overview," in *Voluntary Associations in the Graeco-Roman World* (ed. John S. Kloppenborg and Stephen G. Wilson; London and New York: Routledge, 1996), 9–13. Wilson is more nuanced than most and is aware of some of the problems connected with the category of voluntary (see esp. 1–2).

4. Colin Roberts, Theodore C. Skeat, and Arthur Darby Nock, "The Gild of Zeus Hypsistos," *HTR* 29 (1936): 75; Lloyd Gaston, "Pharisaic Problems," in *Approaches to Ancient Judaism, New Series*, vol. 3, *Historical and Literary Studies* (ed. Jacob Neusner; South Florida Studies in the History of Judaism 56; Atlanta: Scholars Press, 1993), 85. These are cited in Ascough, *Formation*, 74.

5. Alexis de Tocqueville, *Democracy in America* (ed. J. P. Mayer; trans. George Lawrence; 2 vols. in 1; New York: Doubleday, 1969).

6. Note how, like many who have written on ancient associations in the Hellenistic age, de Tocqueville associates forming groups "to his taste" (i.e., choice) with individualism; for example, "'Individualism' is a word recently coined to express a new idea. Our fathers only knew about egoism. . . . Individualism is a calm and considered feeling which disposes each citizen to isolate himself from the mass of his fellows and withdraw into a circle of family and friends; with this little society formed to his taste, he gladly leaves the greater society to look after itself" (ibid., 506).

antiquity. An influential version of this modernist conception was articulated in the philosophy of Immanuel Kant. The person is an autonomous self-legislating and universalizing agent whose identity and activity are based on fully conscious choice. I would argue that the ancient association members were more like de Tocqueville's romanticized medieval people than the Kantian individual.

An important recent collection of essays places various Greek and Roman religious and trade groups, Jewish synagogues, philosophical schools, and Christian groups all in the category of voluntary associations.[7] I want to challenge the appropriateness of the criteria of comparison implied in the conception of voluntary associations and propose another approach.[8] In order to illustrate the approach, I will first do some ground clearing with remarks on synagogues and Greek and Roman groups and then focus on philosophical schools. Because there were many different early Christian groups that seem to have differed rather widely in character, I will choose one for which we do have some evidence, the assemblies of Paul's letters. In this case, it is important to remind ourselves that we have only Paul's representation of these groups.[9] I am skeptical about inferring much concerning

---

7. Kloppenborg and Wilson, *Voluntary Associations*. In spite of my critique of categories and mode of comparison, I nevertheless view this as a significant and pioneering volume on a long-neglected topic.

8. The approach is one broadly informed by theories of practice. I believe, however, that all of the current theories have major problems that hinder a more explicit theorization in such studies as this one. Pierre Bourdieu wants to make background understanding explicit, even though on his own theory and in philosophy in general, "the background" is by definition what cannot be articulated. He also collapses the organization of practices into practical understanding (see Theodore R. Schatzki, *Social Practices: A Wittgensteinian Approach to Human Activity and the Social* [New York: Cambridge University Press, 1996], 150–51). Anthony Giddens's theory also yields a similar collapse of organization into practical understanding to be described by the scholar or social scientist in terms of rule-following. I believe that Ludwig Wittgenstein's critique of using rule-following to explain such regularities is persuasive. In my estimation, Schatzki's theory has many advantages over the others. I adopt, with some modifications to be noted, his conceptions of practice, sociality, expressions, reactions, dispersed and integrative practices, nexuses, spaces, and signifying, among others. Social formations are constituted of bundled practices. Unfortunately, the benefits of Schatzki's theory are greatly limited because he follows the kind of use theory of meaning found in Wittgenstein, Martin Heidegger, and W. V. Quine. I follow Robert B. Brandom (*Making It Explicit: Reasoning, Representing, and Discursive Commitment* [Cambridge, Mass.: Harvard University Press, 1994]) in seeing inference (rather than "use" or representation) as central to discursive practice and discursive practice as making explicit what is implicit in our nondiscursive doings, for example, asserting and changing commitments and entitlements. Thus, I am still working on solving some quite basic problems in practice theory at this point, but I have a definite orientation and some useful tools. For a helpful discussion of a key term, see Burton L. Mack, "Social Formation," in Braun and McCutcheon, *Guide to the Study of Religion*, 283–96. I use social formation in the way that *soziales Gebilde* is commonly used by German social theorists. I call a practice or social formation religious if it involves (imagined) reciprocity with, or with reference to, a god or objects and practices associated with gods.

9. Thus, in what follows, I will be drawing on Paul's representation of what life in Christ was and ought to be, and not making inferences about how members of the groups received and reacted to Paul's conceptions.

the Pauline groups themselves and thus will focus on Paul's conceptions in the letters.

Toward Reassessing "Synagogues" and Associations

Many New Testament scholars have held that the Pauline groups were modeled on "the Jewish synagogue."[10] A host of highly complex and hotly debated issues surround the definition of and evidence for synagogues in the period before 70 C.E. and after.[11] Everyone agrees that the term "synagogue" can refer to some sort of meeting or assembly of Jews or even to institutionalized, if not locally uniform, meeting practices. But when did the term designate a building for specific meeting practices? In the fifth century and later, synagogues look like institutions and buildings that are comparable to and, in my opinion, clearly influenced by churches. But, of course, in the fifth century as compared to the period before 70, the situation of Judaism had changed dramatically and we ought to expect a different type of institution.[12] With the decisive redating of important synagogues and challenge to the traditional typology by Jodi Magness and the critique of the picture dominant in New Testament studies by Howard Clark Kee, one can only characterize scholarly opinion as in transition.[13] I will not enter directly into this debate about evidence for synagogues. Instead, I want to refocus the issue of comparison.

In basing comparison on categories such as meeting places, meetings, membership, and organization, I suggest that our modern instincts about religious institutions keep us from contextualizing synagogues and from selecting the practices that were most important to the ancient Jews in question. We must remember that first-century Jews were Judeans. Interpreters should not, in principle, segregate Judeans from Greeks, Romans, Egyptians, and so on by creating something

---

10. Ascough, *Formation*, 11–28.

11. Dan Urman and Paul V. M. Flesher, eds., *Ancient Synagogues: Historical Analysis and Archeological Discovery* (2 vols.; StPB 47/1–2; Leiden: Brill, 1995); Ascough, *Formation*, 11–28.

12. L. Michael White, *The Social Origins of Christian Architecture*, vol. 1 (2 vols.; HTS 42; Valley Forge, Pa.: Trinity Press International, 1990), 60–101.

13. Jodi Magness, "The Question of the Synagogue: The Problem of Typology," in *Judaism in Late Antiquity*, part 3, *Where We Stand: Issues and Debates in Ancient Judaism*, vol. 4, *The Special Problem of the Synagogue* (ed. Alan J. Avery-Peck and Jacob Neusner; HO 55; Leiden: Brill, 2001), 1–48; eadem, "Synagogue Typology and Earthquake Chronology at Khirbet Shema' in Israel," *Journal of Field Archeology* 24 (1997): 211–20; eadem, "The Dating of the Black Ceramic Bowl with a Depiction of the Torah Shrine from Nabratein," *Levant* 26 (1994): 199–206; Howard Clark Kee, "The Transformation of the Synagogue after 70 C.E.: Its Import for Early Christianity," *NTS* 36 (1990): 1–24; idem, "The Changing Meaning of Synagogue: A Response to Richard Oster," *NTS* 40 (1994): 281–83; idem, "Defining the First-Century CE Synagogue: Problems and Progress," *NTS* 41 (1995): 481–500. It should be noted that my arguments about the links of synagogues or Jewish communities to the temple apply not only to synagogues in the Diaspora, but even to those in Palestine with some modifications for communities close to Jerusalem.

suspiciously like a modern religion called Judaism.[14] Even Jews who lived permanently in Rome or Alexandria were Judeans living outside their traditional homeland and therefore similar to Syrians, Greeks, or Egyptians who lived abroad. A synagogue is a meeting place or meeting practices of Judeans. In our language, Judeans were an ethnic people. Unfortunately the idea of "the synagogue" as the Jewish church still haunts much scholarship.

Instead of the criteria of rules of membership, meetings, and so on that are instinctive for moderns who think of religions as associations of individuals, I want to ask what these Judeans considered to be their most important religious practices. On the basis of their discourses, their articulated conceptions, and the social organization of their practices, which religious activities ranked highest in the hierarchy of practices? The best answer, I believe, is the practices of the temple in Jerusalem and practices that related Judeans to the temple.[15] The religious practices of synagogues or of communities of Judeans were to a large extent activities that oriented those Judeans, no matter where they lived, toward the temple. I can only suggest an outline for this case here, but let me note that the claim goes against much of traditional interest in the synagogue by New Testament scholars. The synagogue has appealed to scholars precisely because it has been understood as a religious institution that is independent of the temple and the temple's cultus and locative ethnic nature, a preparation for Christianity. I want to argue that orientation toward the temple was central in the period before 70 C.E.

Evidence exists for the celebration of the great temple festivals in the Diaspora.[16] These celebrations suggest that Jews in the Diaspora were attempting to participate from a distance in festivals of the temple that had a strong agricultural and local orientation.[17] The connection between the gifts of land and lineage and rituals of reciprocity with God was not lost on Judeans of the Diaspora. Temple time with its agriculturally oriented calendar shaped the calendar of Jews in general. Pilgrimage to Jerusalem for the festivals and sacrifices was a major feature

---

14. I do not mean to suggest that modern forms of Judaism do not to various degrees have an ethnic element, but that forms of modern Judaism are often conceived of as religions in the modern sense, especially by Christians.

15. "Most important" does not mean that practices such as circumcision, Sabbath observance, and prayer, which were not necessarily tied to the temple, were unimportant, but Jews did not generally consider these either a substitute for the temple or the center of their interactions with divine. If I were to press my case, I would argue that the way that Philo and Josephus, for example, discuss the temple and cult makes this absolutely clear. Furthermore those practices were not tied to an institution called the synagogue.

16. For the evidence, see Margaret Williams, *The Jews among the Greeks and Romans: A Diasporan Sourcebook* (Baltimore: Johns Hopkins University Press, 1998), 59–64.

17. I would expect this sense of the relationship between God and land/place/blessings to shape concretely the Diaspora Judean's life where he or she lived, and not just to be an attitude toward a distant place.

of the period.[18] Many Judeans of the Diaspora directly participated in the temple cultus sometime during their lives. The temple tax that supported the daily sacrifices in the temple and the first fruit offerings that signified the ancient pattern of reciprocity and divine giving of productivity were among the major yearly efforts of Diaspora communities.[19] Rome recognized these collections to be so significant for Judeans that they made a major and economically risky exception to the prohibition on exporting large quantities of money from one province to another.[20] When Philo wants to argue (*Legat.* 156) that the emperor supported Judean rights, his illustration falls into two parts, Judean philosophy and Judean religion. Let me urge the usefulness of taking seriously Philo's typical Greek and Roman distinction between intellectual activity (e.g., philosophers, philological and rhetorical teachers, and scholars)—even if the gods sometimes might also be discussed by philosophers—and religious practice. First, Philo says that the emperor allowed the Judeans to meet on the Sabbath in houses of prayer for instruction in "their ancestral philosophy." Second, the emperor knew with approval that "they collected sacred dedications from first fruits and sent them to Jerusalem by those who would offer the sacrifices [*tas thysias*]." Evidence shows that prayer, which could take place almost anywhere and was not tied to an institution called the synagogue or house of prayer, was sometimes said facing Jerusalem and often timed to coincide with the offering of the *tāmîd* in the temple.[21] Some evidence exists for the practice of sacrificing the Passover lamb in homes rather than only in the temple or Jerusalem as Deut 16:1–8 directs.[22] If widespread, this would have been a very important extension and linking of sacrificial religion.

Experts on synagogues seem to agree that study or reading of Scripture was important. The Torah, Prophets, and Psalms are, in my view, absolutely dominated by the centrality of the temple, priesthood, and cult. The epics and myths of Judeans were about land, people, and socioeconomic reciprocity with God and other Judeans. Even in the extreme case of the Judean philosopher Philo, he still reads Scripture in terms of temple, people, land, and reciprocity, but finds additionally stories about the soul and the nature of the cosmos. For Judeans, unlike for Christians, to study Scripture was to be oriented toward an actual temple, a place where reciprocity with the divine was enacted in the imagined exchange of produce from the land and shop, womb and market. Although a culture of imagination, it at the same time involved the exchange of economic and social goods.

---

18. Williams, *Diasporan Sourcebook*, 67–68.

19. Ibid., 68–71.

20. Here one might note that Gentile interference with and resentment toward these Diaspora offerings were a major source of violence between Jews and their neighbors (see ibid.).

21. For scriptural bases for these temple-oriented prayer practices, see, e.g., Dan 6:11; Ezra 9:4–5; and compare Jdt 9:1; Luke 1:10; Acts 3:1.

22. E. P. Sanders, *Judaism: Practice and Belief, 63 BCE–66 CE* (London: SCM; Philadelphia: Trinity Press International, 1992), 133–34.

The resulting cultus of the imagination was so powerful that the framers of later Judaism would write with attention to the minutest detail of its operation as if the temple still existed centuries after its demise.[23] These and other practices, I would argue, allowed Judeans living outside Judea to participate in the practices of the temple cult.

Christianity of the fourth and fifth centuries re-created itself by imagining that it, and not the Jews, was carrying on the true cult of the temple and its priesthood, but in a "spiritual" way. Earlier Christian myth and ritual were bizarre by ancient Mediterranean standards in not explicitly relating the practitioners to land, lineage, and economy.

What more concretely, then, were the practices in the temple to which the local activities of Jews both in Judea and elsewhere linked? The dominant activities of the temple were sacrificial offerings of grain and animal products. These were practices that Judeans shared with Greeks, Romans, and most peoples of the Mediterranean world. Josephus proudly proclaims that Judeans share the practices of sacrificing domestic animals with "all the rest of humanity" (*Ag. Ap.* 2.137). I have elsewhere argued that sacrificial practices were central to the constructions of ethnic peoplehood in the ancient Mediterranean cultures.[24] At the heart of my thesis lies the claim that through sacrificial practices the productivity of the land was interpreted in terms of reciprocity with god or the gods. Productivity included not only the products of agriculture and—by extension down a hierarchy of gifts—even the products of artisans but, above all, the offspring of animal and human lineages. Ethnic peoples are groups that understand themselves to be organized by kinship and descent from common ancestors and to have traditional homelands. As if mirroring the principle of descent, the finest specimens of animal lineages were the highest in the hierarchy of gifts from God or the gods that humans returned as offerings. The great range of offerings, cleansings, and strategic circumstances for offerings produced a highly complex and life-encompassing order of reciprocity with the divine and within the social order that had a marked local character.[25] Judeans living at a distance from the temple ranked these practices

---

23. This, of course, begins with the Mishnah.

24. Stanley K. Stowers, "Greeks Who Sacrifice and Those Who Do Not: Toward an Anthropology of Greek Religion," in *The Social World of the First Christians: Essays in Honor of Wayne A. Meeks* (ed. L. Michael White and O. Larry Yarbrough; Minneapolis: Fortress, 1995), 299–320; idem, "Truth, Identity and Sacrifice in Classical Athens" (paper presented at the Ancient History Documentary Research Centre, Macquarie University, North Ryde, New South Wales, Australia, June 1996); idem, "A Cult from Philadelphia: Oikos Religion or Cultic Association?" in *The Early Church in Its Context: Essays in Honor of Everett Ferguson* (ed. Abraham J. Malherbe et al.; NovTSup 90; Leiden: Brill, 1998), 287–301; idem, "On the Comparison of Blood in Greek and Israelite Ritual," in *HESED VE-EMET: Essays in Honor of Ernest S. Frerichs* (ed. Jodi Magness and Seymour Gitin; BJS 320; Atlanta: Scholars Press, 1998), 179–94.

25. Thus, for instance, I would expect that Judeans living in the Diaspora before 70 C.E. widely recognized and dealt with birth and death pollution because they were Judeans who had contact with

connected with the temple and practices involving social/economic/religious reciprocity with the divine—no matter where they lived—as their most important.

Jews in the Diaspora also developed a whole range of local religious practices, from rites described as magical that Judeans practiced in common with other groups to very specific local festivals like those celebrated in Alexandria. But I would make two points. First, most of these would have had a local and ethnic character fitting the larger patterns of sacrificial religion. Second, insofar as the practitioners maintained an identity as Judeans, they would have ranked higher the core of practices linking them with the sacrificial cultus of the temple. My case would thus not be an argument for uniformity or systematic coherence of practices, but a case for loose and variable networks of activities with a hierarchy that ranked some practices as most important.

Known early Christian groups did not look very much like religious groups because they were almost entirely missing this whole set of practices related to sacrifice, intergenerational continuity, and productivity. In Pauline Christianity, there are no temples on the land, no ties to or concern for the land, no animal or other types of sacrifice, and no agricultural festivals or festivals of other types of productivity. For the ethnic peoples, ritual activities and settings for sacrificial rituals that relate to intergenerational continuity were absolutely essential. Ritual and other practices related to intergenerational continuity have no place in the Pauline groups. Paul's representation of these groups lacks rituals of birth and death and sacrificial practices for purification from birth and death pollution. Without sacred spaces on the land—that is, altars—purity and pollution became moral metaphors. One finds nothing like circumcision or the sacrificial initiation of the ephebes and no Christian marriage rituals.[26] Indeed, Paul does not even encourage marriage except as a remedy for passionate desire.[27] All that is missing here constituted the heart of ancient religion. Paul has no altar to Hephaestus in his shop and he does not belong to an association of leather workers with a calendar of sacrificial feasts. He does not tell myths about how God or the gods gave to humans crafts, land, and agricultural skills so that they could possess the goods of human life. Nor does he instruct members of his churches to collect first fruits and tithes for the temple in Jerusalem. He tells those who have business dealings to act as if they were of no importance (1 Cor 7:30–31).[28] He sees his work not as

---

people who traveled to the temple, and, more importantly, just because they in principle could sacrifice in the temple.

26. Animal sacrifice played an important part in Greek and Roman weddings.

27. David Fredrickson, "Passionless Sex in Paul's Epistles" (paper presented at the annual meeting of the Society of Biblical Literature, San Francisco, California, November 1997); Dale B. Martin, *The Corinthian Body* (New Haven: Yale University Press, 1995), 214–17.

28. It is not a sufficient historical explanation to say that Paul gave such advice because he believed that the "eschaton" was imminent. First, although scholars talk about the end of the world, I think it more accurate to say that he looked for a changed world that would have substantial continuities as well as differences. Second, whatever Paul believed, he and his churches were still social groups

a source of goods for supporting a valued way of life organized as a household, but as an instrument to aid his work in teaching others the Christ myth (1 Cor 9:1–27; 4:11–13; 1 Thess 2:9). The Christians did not develop their own versions or replacements for such practices until centuries later. When they did, a landowning Christian elite appeared along with holy places and attendant festivals scattered across the landscape of the empire.

Whatever kind of community center or assembly the synagogue was for Judeans, it must have supported these practices. In regard to these activities, Judeans differed most from Greeks and others in that the transport of first fruits, tithes, and other offerings was a long-distance project, and that orientation by imagination played a large role. But, in principle, the religion of a Judean who lived five hundred miles from Jerusalem did not differ radically from one who lived twenty miles away. The comparison reads differently when one understands that the synagogue was an instrument of the practices that constituted the ethnicity of the Judeans. Framed in this way, the synagogue does not seem to be the best model for Pauline groups. The contrast, it should be emphasized, is not between the supposedly primordial natural ties of families or ethnic groups and opposing consciously human-made and chosen groups (as in Weberian theory and some folk belief).[29] Rather, I will draw a contrast between different sorts of practices that hang together in patterns of social formations that cannot be reduced to the inherited/chosen dichotomy.

Scholars who argue that Greek and Roman voluntary associations that were organized by common trade, a particular deity, or by household are the best model for comparison also often fail to focus on the practices most central to these groups, and show how these activities tie into larger ways of life.[30] Joining a *thiasos* of Dionysus or a *collegium* of the wool workers was not like a Methodist becoming a Baptist or converting to Buddhism. The deities were deities that—in principle, even if not necessarily in practice—had always belonged to the devotee's religious universe. This would be true even for a foreign deity like Isis who had characteristics that made it possible for Greeks and Romans to place her somewhere in the family of gods. Scholars who emphasize that a person, when joining an association dedicated to a particular deity, "chose devotion to that deity" simply fail to understand the way that Greek and Roman religion worked. Such language seems to echo the modern idea that what is important about a religious act or choice is

---

both organizing themselves in ways that they understood and also being shaped by social forces that were beyond their awareness. Eschatology should not be used as a slogan to limit social analysis.

29. On this tendency among Weberians, see Stanley B. Greenberg, *Race and State in Capitalist Development: Comparative Perspectives* (New Haven: Yale University Press, 1980), 13–16.

30. There is a long-standing tendency to treat these groups in isolation from the rest of Greek and Roman religion and to fail to see how intimately religious practices are tied to the economic and social productivity of the people involved. See Stowers, "Cult from Philadelphia," for a domestic cult's relation to the order of the household.

that one chose it for oneself. Dionysus of the association and Athena of the wool workers make no sense as objects of devotion isolated from the family of gods. In Greek and Roman conceptions, the basic unit of the religion was not the cult of a particular god but primarily the gods and rites of a particular city and secondarily of the corresponding ethnic people. On the other hand, unlike what some have thought, Greek or Roman polytheism was not a massive body of systematic beliefs upon which one consciously drew in order to act.[31] Rather, although practices could involve prior conscious reflective thinking, more basically situations—environments and the contexts of events—evoked what Ludwig Wittgenstein called reactions (*Reaktion*).[32] Reciprocity with the gods was embedded in the practical skills for coping with life that were evoked by the situations and contexts that these ancient polytheists encountered. The family of gods, therefore, had to be as complex, multivalent, and locally particular as the web of lived lives. Whether offering a libation to Zeus or the Good Daimon of a household, placating Poseidon before travel, merchants sealing a contract with an oath by sacrifice, the pageantry of celebrating the city's gods, the creation of divine comradeship and mutual honors in an association, or countless other contexts, the responses drew on the practical know-how for dealing with everyday life.

A Greek was someone who had Greek parents and whose life was shaped by patterns of reciprocity with other Greeks and with Greek gods. An aristocracy of elites defined the religion and politics of the Greek city and was defined as elite precisely by the ownership of enough land to support the surfeit of animals required for the city's sacrificial victims. As with Judeans, a host of ritual practices helped to construct Greek ethnicity, including patterns of intergenerational continuity, and wove religion into areas that moderns cordon off as economic, political, and social.

A way of summarizing a number of these observations is to say that the goods of traditional Mediterranean religion, including Judean religion, were the varied, complex, and conflicting goods of the traditional ethnic peoples. The network of religious practices helped to maintain a complex balance of potentially conflicting goods by giving each good its own bounded place. The proverbial exuberant sociality of Dionysus and the cool deliberation of Apollo each had a place along with numerous other oppositions. Judeans, I believe, maintained a similar complexity through the intricacy and interplay of cult, festival, rites of orientation toward the temple, and legal interpretation. Precisely on this point the Hellenistic philosophies and the groups advocated by Paul organized themselves differently than the ethnic peoples. Both, of course, worked from a context of ethnic heritage,

---

31. In particular, for all of the great contributions of the so-called French structuralists and their followers elsewhere, they have the tendency to make beliefs and motifs in literature, myth, and rites into one great text in which they find a systematic order of fundamental ideas that lie behind everything in the culture.

32. For a useful discussion of some of the issues involved here, see G. E. M. Anscombe, *Intention* (Ithaca, N.Y.: Cornell University Press, 1957).

but reduced and reordered the complexity of traditional goods by creating ways of life that focused on a somewhat different and more limited range of goods.

TOWARD COMPARING PAUL AND HELLENISTIC PHILOSOPHY

I have identified at least seven closely connected areas in which the Hellenistic philosophies and Pauline Christianity possessed similar features. I want to be clear about what I mean by "similar features."[33] First, I am not making claims about origins, that is, genetic relations. The question of how the similarities seen in the Pauline groups came about is a different and more difficult question. Second, similarity is not sameness. I do not think that Pauline Christianity was a philosophy, and differences are as important as similarities. Third, the similarities with the philosophies are not exclusive of similarities with other social formations. I do, in fact, think that it is worth comparing the Christian groups to Judean communities and to so-called voluntary associations.[34] Similarities do exist, but, for the reasons given above, overall I judge differences to be greater than the similarities. Comparison is thus a complex, multitaxonomic activity.[35]

First, the Hellenistic philosophies conceived of themselves as distinct and mutually exclusive *haireseis*, choices, or sects.[36] The schools developed conceptions of the good characterized by a unitary focus on a central value. A. A. Long has pointed out that our English words "cynical," "stoical," "skeptical," and "epicurean" reflect the nature of the Hellenistic philosophies as mutually exclusive attitudes toward life.[37] By contrast, "Aristotelian" has no such connotation because

---

33. I am using the loose language of areas and features to indicate the possibility of the detailed description and complex comparison of practices and social formations. Features are thus roughly social practices and social formations. Areas are sites where dispersed and integrative social practices are "bundled" into social formations and social formations are linked to produce more complex formations.

34. With the kind of comparison (or perhaps taxonomic distinctions) that I advocate in this essay, one could compare such activities as meals—say, Judean, Christian, and pagan—in a way that would more adequately allow for the analysis of differences.

35. See Jonathan Z. Smith, "Fences and Neighbors: Some Contours of Early Judaism," in *Approaches to Ancient Judaism*, vol. 2 (ed. William Scott Green; BJS 9; Chico, Calif.: Scholars Press, 1980), 1–25; repr. in idem, *Imagining Religion: From Babylon to Jonestown* (CSHJ; Chicago: University of Chicago Press, 1982), 1–18, 135–39.

36. A. A. Long, "Hellenistic Ethics and Philosophical Power," in *Hellenistic History and Culture* (ed. Peter Green; Hellenistic Culture and Society 9; Berkeley: University of California Press, 1993), 138–56, esp. 138–42. When I speak of choice in connection with someone adopting a Hellenistic philosophy, I do not mean to imply the idea frequently found in modern thought that what is important about the choice is that it is "mine." On another point, one unfortunately still sometimes encounters the idea that the schools had by Paul's era melded into an eclectic or syncretistic Hellenistic philosophy in which the schools could hardly be distinguished. The last thirty years of intensive work on Hellenistic philosophy should have destroyed this myth that was promoted by Eduard Zeller and others near the turn of the century.

37. Ibid., 138.

his philosophy rejected the idea of a unitary good and accepted what I have characterized above as the traditional ethnic view that the good consisted of a balanced accommodation of different and often conflicting values. For a Stoic, virtue is the only good. This focus on a single good means that traditional goods like marriage, family, ethnic heritage, possessions, and everyday pleasures have only a relative and, in some circumstances, quite dispensable value. This way of thinking often tends to put concrete relations into opposition with abstract ideals. Epictetus says, "For this reason, the good must be preferred above every relation of kinship. My father is nothing to me, but only the good" (*Diatr.* 3.3.5). Epicureans made freedom from pain and friendship the focusing goods, and so on with the other schools. Because of the focus on different unitary goods, the schools were mutually exclusive and tended to define themselves over against other alternatives in a way that made totalizing claims on their adherents.

Paul also constructs life in Christ as a distinct and mutually exclusive choice with a unitary good. In 1 Cor 7, Paul counsels "undistracted devotion to the Lord" (7:35) instead of marriage. He gives no indication that marriage, procreation, and running a household are central goods in their own right. He does not want the divided interests that marriage entails (7:32–34). In light of the approaching day of the Lord, wives, possessions, and business dealings have no intrinsic significance (7:32–35). Members of the group who make up the audience of this advice are those who have called upon the name of the Lord (1:2). Christ is the only foundation for the group (3:11) and there is only one God, not the many of Greco-Roman religion (8:1–6). Although the beliefs about the one God, mutually exclusive loyalty to the one God, and apocalyptic intensification of these beliefs are Judean in origin, they function differently in Paul's letters, where they are freed from the ethnic, cultic, and legal contexts that instantiate a range of human goods. Paul's difficulties in relating the law to his Gentile churches reflect this shift of context. In 1 Cor 7:19, where he relativizes matters of ethnicity and status, he writes, "circumcision is nothing and uncircumcision is nothing, but only keeping the commandments of God matters." The reduction of goods becomes evident when one realizes that circumcision *is* a commandment of God for Judeans according to the Scriptures, which Paul holds as authoritative. Indeed, it is a central ritual of intergenerational continuity, procreative promise, and ethnic identity. For Paul, the teaching about Christ's faithfulness meant that even earlier commandments of God were relativized and refocused on the new good, at least for Gentiles. Thus, although one sees a very different content to the sense in which Pauline groups were choices, there remains a structural similarity with the Hellenistic philosophies.

Second, the choices of the Hellenistic philosophies were paradoxes in the sense going back to the pre-Socratics of being *para doxa*—that is, contrary to conventional thinking.[38] They asserted that the happy life could not be founded on

---

38. Ibid., 152.

ordinary civic virtue.[39] The modified beliefs created by critical reflection changed one's motivations, desires, and needs, resulting in a tension between conventional life and postreflective life. I have discussed possible implications of such a change above in terms of departures from the complex goods of ethnic peoples. I believe it no accident that the founders of the Hellenistic schools were not married and that Jesus and Paul were also not married. Ancient Christianity thus interpreted Paul primarily as the great ascetic and shared a strong ascetic impulse with the Hellenistic philosophies.[40] The ascetic impulses of both stem from a reduction and focusing of more conventional goods and goals. The positive side of this feature is the seventh characteristic discussed below, a tendency toward radical social formations.

Pauline Christianity claimed to oppose itself to traditional thinking on moral matters and regarding religious belief and practices. For Gentiles, at least, Paul conceived an ethical field that corresponded neither to the traditional norms of Greek or other Gentile cultures nor to the traditional norms of Judean culture.[41] Paul sets God's wisdom in opposition to the wisdom of the world, both Greek and Judean (1 Cor 1:22–25). Again, the structural similarities with the philosophies are obvious.

Third, the change to the new life might be described as a conversion in the sense of a dramatic reorientation of the self. Scholars speak of conversion to Judaism, but important distinctions tend to be lost. How is it that we speak of conversion to being a Judean, but not for becoming a Greek, Roman, or Egyptian? An Egyptian who became a citizen of a Greek polis changed religious practices and adopted a whole range of cultural and social relations, but we do not call this conversion. I judge it fruitless to look for some essence in the way that scholars have employed the concept of conversion. For my purposes it is helpful merely to point out that the letters of Paul share a very specific tradition of describing the process of conversion, a rhetoric of conversion.[42] Admittedly, there has been much oversimplification of conversion in Hellenistic philosophy, including A. D. Nock's famous discussion.[43] The Stoics, for example, emphasized that the attainment of

---

39. E.g., A. A. Long and D. N. Sedley, *The Hellenistic Philosophers* (2 vols.; Cambridge: Cambridge University Press, 1987), 1:18–22, 154–57, 377–86.

40. There is now a vast literature on the topic of anti-family and ascetic tendencies in early Christianity. For a recent contribution with excellent bibliography, see Andrew S. Jacobs, "A Family Affair: Marriage, Class, and Ethics in the Apocryphal Acts of the Apostles," *JECS* 7 (1999): 105–38.

41. Gentiles are not to become Judeans, that is, to keep the law, but the Gentile cultures are morally and religiously debased (e.g., Rom 1:18–32) and must be rejected.

42. Abraham J. Malherbe, "Conversion to Paul's Gospel," in idem et al., *The Early Church in Its Context*, 230–44. Malherbe does not speak of a "rhetoric of conversion," but I think that such language is necessary seeing that the philosophies had no theory of conversion and that it never functioned as a normative conception. It is best to think of it as a literary and discursive tradition made possible by my characteristics 1, 2, and 4.

43. A. D. Nock, *Conversion: The Old and New in Religion from Alexander the Great to Augustine of Hippo* (Oxford: Oxford University Press, 1933).

virtue was grounded in one's nature and the conventional goodness habituated by participation in ordinary social life. If one were very bad, then, transition to virtue would be impossible or extremely unlikely. The acquisition of virtue—in the Stoic sense of virtue (dispositions to perform proper functions perfectly)—they claimed was instantaneous and might not even be noticed by the person undergoing the change.[44] Epicureans and Platonists ridiculed these teachings and said that coming to virtue was ordinarily a process of progress in intermediate steps of relative virtuousness.[45] Scholars have suggested conceptions of conversion that range from repentance of past life and the beginning of moral progress, to a commitment to a particular school, or even to the acquisition of virtue and wisdom. I would also argue that Christian conversion contains an element largely unparalleled in the philosophies in making submission to a divine being part of conversion.[46] In spite of these problems, there is a literary tradition that becomes most prominent in the early empire, in which writers give vivid descriptions of the turmoil and changes in the soul of those who convert to philosophy. Paul uses exactly the same language for conversion to the gospel.

Conversion relates closely to the fourth mark of the Hellenistic schools, namely, that this choice made possible and required a new technology of the self. Socrates is the first to have detailed the notion that one could reconstitute the self on a new basis and that the self could have an authority and power to take complete charge of life and its goals by mastering passions and desires.[47] The Hellenistic schools presented differing technologies for asserting this new self formed around its sharply focused goals. The schools agreed that people had unhealthy desires owing to false beliefs about the nature of the world. True beliefs would reorder the soul, turn it from vice to virtue. Epicureans, for example, asserted that the primary impediments to moral health were fear of death and fear of the gods. Eradicating these false beliefs and destructive desires might begin with a dramatic reorientation, but typically also required a sustained and conscious process of rehabituation with the help of fellow Epicureans.[48] The early empire seems to have been a time that saw an increasing specification of techniques for self-care and self-scrutiny.[49]

---

44. Long and Sedley, *Hellenistic Philosophers*, 368 (virtue), 385–86 (the possibility of attaining virtue and instantaneous change).

45. E.g., Plutarch, *Stoic. abs.* 4 (1058B-C).

46. E.g., Phil 2:10–11; 1 Cor 15:24–28. Even this difference should not be exaggerated in light of conceptions such as those attributed to Demetrius in the prayer of Seneca, *Prov.* 1.5.5, and Seneca's treatise in general.

47. Long, "Hellenistic Ethics," 142–45.

48. Martha C. Nussbaum, *The Therapy of Desire: Theory and Practice in Hellenistic Ethics* (Princeton: Princeton University Press, 1994); Clarence E. Glad, *Paul and Philodemus: Adaptability in Epicurean and Early Christian Psychagogy* (NovTSup 81; Leiden: Brill, 1995). Note Glad's important corrections (152–60) of points on the nature of Epicurean communities in Nussbaum's excellent study.

49. Michel Foucault, *The History of Sexuality*, vol. 3, *The Care of the Self* (trans. Robert Hurley; New York: Pantheon, 1986); Pierre Hadot, *Exercices spirituels et philosophie antique* (2nd rev. ed.; Paris:

Paul's basic teaching began with the call to turn from idols to a true God and included the idea that worship of the false gods entailed bondage to passions and desire (1 Thess 1:10, cf. 4:1–5; Rom 1:18–32). Turning to the true God meant a dramatic reorientation and mastery of passions and desire, but also a continuing struggle for self-mastery. In 1 Cor 9:24–27, Paul presents himself as a model for the Corinthians: "Do you not know that all those in a race compete but only one receives the prize? So run that you might win! Everyone who is an athlete exercises self-mastery in all things. They do it to win a perishable wreath, but we for one imperishable. So then I pummel my body and subject it to slavery, lest after preaching to others I myself not meet the test." Self-mastery allows him to order his life around the unitary *telos*: "I do it all for the sake of the gospel, so that I might share in its blessings" (9:23). The important work of Abraham J. Malherbe and of Clarence E. Glad on Pauline psychagogy concerns Paul's technology of the self.[50]

Fifth, the Hellenistic philosophies developed the notion of the wise man.[51] The wise man was someone like Socrates who stood against conventional society and exhibited a redefined paradigm of human excellence seen in his unitary focus and extraordinary self-mastery. Similarly, the authority of the founders of Pyrrhonism, Stoicism, Epicureanism, and Cynicism was seen to stem not only from their teachings, but also from their exemplary focus and self-mastery. Such founders and sages of the past might become the subject of mythmaking and exemplary anecdote by schools. Diogenes Laertius (7:27) tells us that a proverbial saying arose, "more self-controlled than the philosopher Zeno." He was known for his extreme frugality and poverty, toughness and independence from social convention.[52] The paradigms of Pyrrho, Epicurus, and Diogenes the Cynic are well known. Again Aristotle makes a useful contrast. His philosophy has no place for a wise man since his model of excellence is the Athenian gentleman. Because ideal wise men, founders of school traditions, and devoted followers must exhibit their unconventional choice of life, one sees a certain theatricality among members of

---

Études Augustiniennes, 1987); Catherine Edwards, "Self-Scrutiny and Self-Transformation in Seneca's Letters," *GR* 44 (1997): 21–38.

50. Abraham J. Malherbe, *Paul and the Thessalonians* (Philadelphia: Fortress, 1987), 34–94; idem, *Paul and the Popular Philosophers* (Minneapolis: Fortress, 1989), 67–77; Glad, *Paul and Philodemus*.

51. Already noted by Nock, *Conversion*, 175–76; Abraham J. Malherbe, "Hellenistic Moralists and the New Testament," *ANRW* 26.1:293–301.

52. On the figures of Zeno and Epicurus, see Fernanda Decleva Caizzi, "The Porch and the Garden: Early Hellenistic Images of the Philosophical Life," in *Images and Ideologies: Self-Definition in the Hellenistic World* (ed. Anthony Bulloch et al.; Hellenistic Culture and Society 12; Berkeley: University of California Press, 1993), 303–29. Zeno is one extreme among Stoics for whom the wise man would generally lead a fairly conventional life unless circumstances arose where preferred "indifferents" like wealth conflicted with virtue. Seneca, *Ep.* 14.14 is perhaps the other extreme that reflects the tenor of middle and Roman Stoicism. Thus, the degree of contrast between the wise man and convention varied by school, historical period, and circumstances. The Cynic wise man is certainly the most extreme.

the Hellenistic schools.[53] Both Stoics and Epicureans said that the wise man would remain happy and tranquil under torture on the rack.[54] Aristotle had pronounced this idea absurd (*Eth. nic.* 7.1153b19). One could make a great list of the dramatic episodes of philosophers from Socrates' trial and death, to the Cynic Proteus, who burned himself, and many less destructive but equally showy acts. How would the story of Jesus' attack on the money changers at the temple and his death have seemed to Hellenistic audiences? Surely Paul's long lists of sufferings fall into the same genre.[55] Paul writes, "Be imitators of me, as I am of Christ" (1 Cor 11:1).

Sixth, encompassing the previous five characteristics, the central practices of the Hellenistic schools and of Pauline Christianity were intellectual practices and practices that made reference to mind. The most basic move in creating a technology of the self is articulating a self. Of what functions, faculties, and parts does a person consist? What is the proper ordering and functioning of these parts? What part of the person is the true self? Traditional Greek, Roman, and Jewish religion got along quite well without articulating a human psychology, but the philosophies and Pauline Christianity made discourse about the self central. Moreover, the chief practices of both emphasized types of speaking, writing, and interpretation. Both were centrally concerned with the reading, writing, transmission, and interpretation of texts: on the one hand, the writings of the chief authorities of the particular philosophical school and, on the other hand, the Greek translation of the Judean sacred writings.[56] Teaching, learning, and moral training were also central to both. Whatever else they were, Jesus and Paul were teachers. The existence of Pauline social groups depended on his textual interpretive skills, his expertise in forms of esoteric knowledge, and his teaching abilities.[57] In this regard, Paul resembled the teacher of a philosophical school.

The centrality of mind and self becomes apparent when one compares the major rituals of Pauline Christianity to the sacrificial rituals of the Greeks, Romans, and Jews. In animal sacrifice, there might be nothing said at all; no speech and no text.[58] There was interpretation, but not interpretation of the soul or of texts. The animal's body was divided, distributed, manipulated, and interpreted. Did its

---

53. Long, "Hellenistic Ethics," 153.

54. Long and Sedley, *Hellenistic Philosophers*, 133, 138–39.

55. John T. Fitzgerald, *Cracks in an Earthen Vessel: An Examination of the Catalogues of Hardships in the Corinthian Correspondence* (SBLDS 99; Atlanta: Scholars Press, 1988).

56. Harlow G. Snyder, "Teachers, Texts and Students: Textual Performance and Patterns of Authority in Greco-Roman Schools" (Ph.D. diss., Yale University, 1998).

57. Dana Chyung is currently writing a dissertation at Brown University on Paul's presentation of himself as a producer of knowledge and a teacher in 1 and 2 Corinthians.

58. On animal sacrifice and for bibliography on this complex practice, see n. 24 above. Although myths were certainly associated with specific cults, it is misleading to think of sacrificial cults as the expression of myths or the representation of beliefs. For a discussion of this problem in the study of ritual, see Catherine Bell, *Ritual Theory, Ritual Practice* (New York: Oxford University Press, 1992). Telling and writing stories about the gods are practices themselves that can play a part in rituals, but

opened body give signs of the god's disposition? Had the deity received the burned gift? If so, some designated group of participants might share in the occasion by making a festive meal from a portion of the animal's flesh. In the Lord's supper according to 1 Cor 11, the meal recalls a foundational myth of the group and certain words and actions in the ritual make reference to that story. Participants are to examine their motivations and attitudes toward the community in light of the story and of God's knowledge of their inner condition. Unlike the first ritual, the second requires speaking, interpretive, textual practices, and an articulated technology of the self. Romans 12:1–2 nicely illustrates the point with its reinterpretation of sacrifice as a metaphor that concerns the care of the self: "present your bodies as a living and holy sacrifice [*thysia*] acceptable to God, which is your rational worship. Do not be conformed to this age but have your form changed by the renewal of your mind so that you might test what is the will of God."

Seventh, the goals and practices of the Hellenistic philosophies and Paul's "Christianity" might give rise to nontraditional and radical social formations. This characteristic is a tendency and not an invariant feature of the two groups. For Epicureans, one sees this feature in their ideal of the garden, a return to a simpler, earlier phase of human social evolution based on friendship rather than the patriarchal family and city that, in their view, had led to conflict and empty competition by overly concentrating power and wealth. The radical proposals of Zeno's *Politeia* are well known. Malcolm Schofield has done much work to clarify the nature of this writing as anti-utopian.[59] Zeno wanted to contrast his attainable society of friends characterized by wisdom and virtue to Plato's unrealizable ideal society. Some scholars have found evidence that early Stoics fomented revolts and advised politicians in attempts to implement Stoic social and political ideals.[60] Sphaerus, for instance, a student of Zeno and Cleanthes, may have been the thinker behind the Spartan revolution of 220 B.C.E., in which land was redistributed according to egalitarian principles, the wider population was enfranchised with citizenship, and a common citizen's mess was instituted. Zeno's state had no slavery, marriage, or traditional families. Men and women performed the same occupations, wore the same clothes, exercised naked together, and had sex and children in common. Zeno abolished temples and large public buildings, traditional Greek education, and money. There would be common meals and the glue that held the city together would be rational *erōs* and friendship. The second-century Christian Epiphanes,

---

rituals should not be reduced to representations of them. Animal sacrifice could take place without any reference to myth beyond the belief that the offering was being given to a deity.

59. Malcolm Schofield, *Saving the City: Philosopher-Kings and Other Classical Paradigms* (London: Routledge, 1999), 51–68. See also idem, *The Stoic Idea of the City* (Cambridge: Cambridge University Press, 1991).

60. Andrew Erskine, *The Hellenistic Stoa: Political Thought and Action* (Ithaca, N.Y.: Cornell University Press, 1990). Erskine provides much evidence for Stoics' political and social activity as reformers. Schofield (*Stoic Idea*, 42 n. 37) doubts that Sphaerus's influence was as strong as Erskine thinks.

who tried to institute a community similar to Zeno's, believed that he was following Paul.[61] Later Stoicism shifted to the idea of a world society that transcended cities and might be interpreted in either a conservative or a radical way. Philo and Josephus cast the Essenes and Therapeutae as radical philosophical communities.[62] I labor these examples to illustrate that the focus on a single good and mind/character/intellectual practices of the Hellenistic philosophies tended to give rise to experimental and alternative social formations. All of these groups share the principle that economic and other "ordinary" practices must be demoted and serve only purposes that are instrumental to the virtue, friendship, and intellectual practices upon which the group is to focus. One might interpret what I describe below as "the Pauline household" along these lines.

These seven features are not just incidental, but relate closely to what the philosophers and Paul himself understood to be the goods internal to their central practices. Nock was correct in arguing that early Christian groups would have typically appeared more like philosophies than cults. But in my view, Nock based his conclusions on an analysis that did not take seriously the goods of the practices that the participants valued. He also sent scholarship down the wrong road with his description of cults, philosophies, and Christianities in terms of the psychological needs that the groups supposedly met. For Nock, external similarities clothed incommensurable essential contents.[63]

I have come to a different conclusion. Pauline Christianity and probably other kinds of Christianity did resemble Hellenistic philosophies, but not necessarily because they derived from philosophies or directly borrowed much. Troels Engberg-Pedersen has recently argued impressively that Pauline thought owes some central features to Stoicism.[64] I have sympathies with that claim, but my major point is different, although also compatible with Engberg-Pedersen's conclusions: aside from the question of borrowings, the network of practices that Paul conceived as assemblies of Christ had structural similarities to the Hellenistic philosophies because both organized themselves by similar practices and goals.[65] First, the central practices of both were intellectual practices and practices relating to mind and

---

61. For Epiphanes and his work *On Justice*, see Morton Smith, *Clement of Alexandria and a Secret Gospel of Mark* (Cambridge, Mass.: Harvard University Press, 1973), 46, 266-67, 273. On the similarities to Zeno, see Erskine, *Hellenistic Stoa*, 112-13.

62. On the latter, see Troels Engberg-Pedersen, "Philo's *DE VITA CONTEMPLATIVA* as a Philosopher's Dream," *JSJ* 30 (1999): 40-64.

63. I am, of course, also rejecting any fixed form/content scheme that implies essentialism. Form/content is a trope of our own analyses in virtue of specific contexts, purposes, and practices.

64. This paper was written before Troels Engberg-Pedersen's *Paul and the Stoics* (Louisville: Westminster John Knox, 2000) appeared. Otherwise the paper would have been in conversation with his important book. See also idem, "Stoicism in Philippians," in *Paul in His Hellenistic Context* (ed. Troels Engberg-Pedersen; Minneapolis: Fortress, 1995), 256-90.

65. There is now a large bibliography on these similarities. On the similarities and bibliography on the subject, see Malherbe, *Paul and the Popular Philosophers*; Ascough, *Formation*, 29-49.

self or soul. But this first similarity alone would not have made earliest Christianity like a Hellenistic philosophy. Ancient rhetorical and legal schools, for instance, also focused on intellectual practices, but they did not much resemble Hellenistic philosophies because they lacked the second feature, namely, that the practices were ordered by a tightly focused and totalizing understanding of a unitary good. These two structural features of Pauline Christianity together made it resemble a Hellenistic philosophy. Formulated from another perspective, the structure produced a life that resembled a philosophical life, especially for Christian teachers.

In order to understand the unitary good in Paul, however, one must attend to the fifth characteristic, Jesus Christ as a model of human excellence. Even early Christian sources attest that whatever Jesus and his students were about, it concerned the way of life and future of the Judeans and must be understood in the context of Judean culture and politics. In Paul's letters, however, probably in virtue of reinterpreting Jesus for Gentiles, whatever vision Jesus had for Judeans gets displaced by mythmaking about Jesus as the Christ who died and rose to rule from above and serves as a model for imitation. Paul ignores Jesus' teachings and focuses on the paradigmatic character of Christ, especially as exhibited in his death.[66] In dying, Jesus exhibited self-mastery, trusting loyalty or faithfulness (*pistis*) to God, and mercy toward both Judeans and non-Judeans.[67] Jesus showed that character and mind oriented toward God are invulnerable, while ordinary products of human activity fail. You can kill the teacher and forget his teachings, but the idea of the martyr and his virtues lives on. Paul thus makes Jesus into a model of human excellence that is characterized by self-mastery, trusting loyalty, mercy, and invulnerability. The goods of Pauline Christianity focus intently upon these and loyalty to the continuing mission of the risen Christ who is a pioneer of the ideal life to come.[68] In this way, Paul interprets the unitary good in terms of certain virtues or excellencies, as do the Hellenistic philosophies.

Josephus was able to represent (*Ant.* 13.5.9 §§171–73; 18.1.3–5 §§12–20; *War* 2.8.2–14 §§119–66) Essenes, Pharisees, and Sadducees as Jewish schools of philosophy by attributing the two major structural features to them. According to

---

66. He also, of course, most emphasizes what Jesus' actions have objectively effected.

67. See Stanley K. Stowers, *A Rereading of Romans: Justice, Jews, and Gentiles* (New Haven: Yale University Press, 1994), 194–226.

68. In light of gross distortions of Greek conceptions of virtue or excellence in Christian apologetics going back to Augustine, I would emphasize that virtues and, of course, Pauline virtues are social virtues. Put in theological terms, character is to a large extent constitutive of ecclesiology, the community. For an example of the apologetic distortion of Greek conceptions of virtue, see Wolfgang Schrage, *The Ethics of the New Testament* (trans. David E. Green; Philadelphia: Fortress, 1988), 217–18. Such misrepresentations seem to combine Augustine's and Luther's charge that pagan virtue was motivated by pride and the projection of a Kantian ethics and individualism onto the Greeks. On endurance and related virtues in Paul, see Themistocles Adamopoulo, "Endurance, Greek and Early Christian: The Moral Transformation of the Greek Idea of Heroic Endurance from Homer to the Apostle Paul" (Ph.D. diss., Brown University, 1995).

Josephus, they were all occupied with intellectual practices relating to the sacred texts and the teaching and promotion of certain doctrines. Second, the schools like Hellenistic philosophies distinguished themselves as mutually exclusive choices by centering on particular doctrines. The Pharisees resembled dogmatic Stoics attributing everything to fate and providence; the Sadducees, like skeptical Epicureans, made humans free and removed God from dealings with the world (*War* 2.8.14 §§162–66). Not only do Josephus and Philo (*Prob.* 75–88; *Hypoth.* 11.1–18) in this way construct certain groups as Jewish philosophers, but they also tend to present Jews and Judaism in general as philosophical.[69] This has made them wonderful sources for Christian readers, writers, and theologians, but makes their depiction of Judaism and Judeans highly unrepresentative.[70]

The oddity of Pauline ritualization and mythmaking in comparison to ancient Mediterranean religion is to be explained by the different practices and relations to types of production of each. The typical sacrificial religion of the Greco-Roman world was closely intertwined with economic production and made no sense apart from that production. This holds true of associations, the Judean temple, and the religious practices of dispersed Judean communities. The ideal economic production in this Mediterranean religion is the fruit of the land, but artisanal, trade, and other sorts of economic production were also included in the structuration effected by the linking of shared practices. Even the potter and the shoemaker made offerings at the workshop shrine and at meetings of associations of fellow workers from plants and animals received from landowners. The potter, of course, did not see that in honoring the gods with the products deemed most natural to the gods, he was reproducing—among other forms of sociality—an order that gave power to the landowners and ranked artisans with slaves. Paul may have been a leather worker, but he had no workshop altar and was alienated from local communities of Judeans who made a great corporate effort of collecting and delivering to the temple in Jerusalem first fruit offerings gleaned from trades such as leather working. Pauline offerings were not translated into the plant and animal products

---

69. This was made especially clear by the discovery of the Qumran literature. Philo and Josephus portray the Essenes as having an asceticism based on a limited good whereas the Dead Sea Scrolls show purity concerns that order life in certain ways, but do not necessarily require a limited good. The purity concerns are generated by the priestly community's obsession with the temple and not principles about the good being based on the soul or virtue rather than the body. In fact, their practices concern people, temple, and land. It is their specialization as intellectuals (textual interpretative experts) that gives them a focus and discipline.

70. One can certainly use them as sources for understanding ancient Judaism, but they must be read very critically in view of the biases of their cultural and social strata and power interests. Reading them only in light of their "Jewish apologetic" bias has often worked against a recognition of the extent to which they are unrepresentative. The philosophical bias connects with apologetic in the way they construct Jews, and especially Jewish heroes, as fanatically strict, preferring adherence to central principle and practice above all else. Unfortunately, scholars have often accepted this picture of "strict Judaism" uncritically.

of Judean landowners. Paul describes the proper offering to God as a disciplined body and a renewed mind (Rom 12:1–2) with virtues productive of a certain ideal sociality (Rom 12:3–21). Paul, like the model Cynic Simon the Shoemaker, probably used his workshop as a place for teaching, the activity that he ranked as important.[71]

The Christ followers rejected offerings from the land and cultivated other activities. The cultural production, including mythmaking and ritualization, of Paul's Christ groups hid or even explicitly renounced connections with economic production. Christ, unlike Dionysus, Diana, or Demeter, was not "worshiped" with the return of products (e.g., of land, of workshop) given by him to Paul and his followers as producers. The foundational myth of a teacher who "died for us" and traveled to heaven for a temporary stay does not open a space for reflection on the relation between economics and sociality. No matter what else Greek and Roman myths did, they dwelt on that relation. The Judean epic is about a land flowing with milk and honey given to a certain people by a God who dwells in that land.

I have already spoken of ritual, but let me add that what is entirely missing from early Christianity in comparison with ancient religion is huge in terms of cultural space. One example is the aesthetics of produce and production that are so massively important to sacrificial religion. Greeks customarily summed up what a successful sacrifice meant with the expression *ta hiera kala*, "the holy things are beautiful." The Roman attitude was the same. The most beautiful animals decked out in ribbons and garlands, perfect fruits and grains, finely formed loaves of bread, sacred groves of olive trees, temples of marble and bright colors, processions of beautiful youths in the best clothes carrying flasks of oil, jars of honey, baskets of golden wheat, sumptuous tables for joyous feasts shared with the gods, and so on suggest the aesthetics of ancient religion. The Hebrew Bible waxes eloquent about the beauty of the temple and the sacrifices, and the sweet smell that God enjoys. Philosophers were known more for their ragged dirty clothes and their foul smell than an aesthetic. If one wants to call it an aesthetic, then theirs was one of dialogue, books, self-mastery, and endurance in suffering. Even the kinds of philosophers who valued the ordinary goods ranked the latter higher.

Not only is the meat missing from the Lord's supper, but Paul says that the event is not even about eating. If the Corinthians want food and feast, they have their own homes (1 Cor 11:20–22, 34). The food in the supper is not important as food, but as something that symbolizes and points to something else. There is virtually no place in ancient Mediterranean religion for putting enjoyment of the food of meals into opposition to devotion to god. Such practices as the following constitute the proper activities of the Lord's "meal": reflecting on the suffering of

---

71. Ronald F. Hock, *The Social Context of Paul's Ministry: Tentmaking and Apostleship* (Philadelphia: Fortress, 1980), esp. 37–42.

a martyr (11:24–26), examining oneself (11:29), practicing living in view of God's judgment (11:30–32), cultivating virtues of sociality with an egalitarian strain, or perhaps more precisely, an emphasis on solidarity (11:18–22, 29), reflecting on the ideal of the community brought into existence by the teacher's words (11:17–26, 29). How different were the sacrificial feasts and drinking parties of associations! Both groups had food on the table, but the activities that counted for Paul's people were to be exercises of mind and character distinguished from and made more important than ordinary practical activities like feasting and the exchange of goods and honors, for example, thinking something, reflecting on a text, examining, discerning, judging, acting with solidarity. The Lord's supper does not even have an offering or an offerer. In the foundational story, Jesus does give thanks for the food, but no food is given back. Words and thoughts are enough. Philosophers knew that the gods did not need food. Pure mind does not need flesh. In sacrificial religion there is always an offerer and the offering indicates something about the wealth of the offerer. The fine cattle or the dove is his and was given to him by the god. The same principle holds true for collective offerings made by groups. But just as the Lord's supper is not about food or eating, it is also not about anyone's wealth made natural by the gods.

When Paul mentions reciprocity that involves wealth, it is not of material for material, but material for spiritual (Rom 15:25–28).[72] Work, for Paul, is not an activity through which God provides the goods for a valued way of life, but a form of suffering for a higher purpose (1 Cor 4:11–13). In 1 Cor 7:30–31 he tells his audience to focus only on Christ and not to give any value to their buying, selling, and economic activities.[73] In 1 Cor 9 he treats his work not as productive of its own goods that belong to a way of life, but as an instrument for the preaching of the gospel. The ancient household was the locus for almost all of the economic production in Greco-Roman antiquity. The *kyrios* ruled his household and participated in civic and cultural activities because of the leisure opened up for him by the labor of wives, children, slaves, and other dependents. The ethos inside the household was, ideally at least, to be one of family affection and a sharing of goods according to the roles given by nature and fate. Outside the household, the *kyrios* forged friendships with male peers. What we might reasonably call the Pauline household had no wife to manage the labor of the children and slaves. There were no children and probably no slaves. He wishes that all Christ people were unmarried like him, free for important activities. Paul probably lived with friends and fellow workers for the gospel, who on occasion might also happen to share his trade.

---

72. I use material and spiritual in an ancient and not a Cartesian sense.
73. I do not think that calling this attitude eschatological changes anything. I say this with two points of view in mind. From the perspective of social formation, the actual human sociality is constituted as such whatever the beliefs. From the perspective internal to Paul's thought, I see no indication that the sole focus on Christ as a good would be lost in the age to come or that the ordinary human goods would be reintroduced.

The economic engine is missing from the Pauline household. The only labor and goods that he values are those related to his teaching, assembly building, and leading activities. Paul's social formations resembled those of Hellenistic philosophers because they were productive of "mind goods" in a way that subordinated other goods. In sum, Paul's groups were constituted by social formations that "exalted" discursive practices over nondiscursive practices and that tended to treat nondiscursive practices and affects as valuable to the extent that agents could attribute discursiveness to them (e.g., eating bread *symbolizes* x; one's sufferings *indicate* that Christ will soon return).

Conclusions

My conclusion, I hope, will help explain an important feature of ancient Christianity. From at least early in the second century there appear Christians like Justin and Athenagoras who with all seriousness style themselves philosophers and Christianity a philosophy. This identification became a major characteristic of ancient Christianity. I would argue that this claim made sense to many people because as early as Paul, certain types of Christianity focused on intellectual practices and ordered these around a totalizing unitary vision of the good. Even though Christianity did not derive from philosophy in any direct way, but from Judaism, it shared the structural features that made it philosophy-like. Eventually the church would solve the problem by dividing Christian life into two types: those who lived the compromised conventional life and those who lived lives as monks and ascetics focused only on the ultimate good. The hierarchy of the two ways reflected the powerful new arrangement that the Hellenistic philosophies pioneered in making life a choice focused on a limited good or set of goods produced by intellectual practices.

Three caveats are in order. First, Pauline Christianity was not a neat package, fully integrated and consistent. A major tension seen most clearly in his letter to the Romans reveals him continuing to accept and to understand himself as working within Judaism even as, being the apostle to the Gentiles, he adapts himself to the life of a Gentile who is in Christ.[74] While Christ and the new age of the Spirit certainly modify traditional forms of Judaism in some ways, the change for Gentile culture is much more radical. In Paul's thought, Gentiles in Christ must undergo a radical modification of the self because they have been fundamentally and consistently shaped by idolatry and *porneia*. They do not, like Judeans, merely get a "messiah" and a new moment in history. Rather, the culture of the Greek, Roman, Egyptian, and so on must be largely abandoned and reread in terms of a new version of the master narrative of the Judeans (although Gentiles are not to adopt Judean religious practices that relate to the temple) and a re-created self. The

---

74. See Stowers, *Rereading of Romans*, 219, 222, 266–68, 292–93.

resemblance to a Hellenistic philosophy would thus apply most clearly to Paul's Gentile groups and presumably less so or not at all, for instance, to Judean Jesus people in Jerusalem. The future of Christianity, of course, would lie in Paul's direction.

Second, Hellenistic philosophers tend to associate as friends. In Pauline Christianity, however, one finds the language of fictive kinship.[75] Since the kinship is fictive and not "real," it in many ways resembles friendship and draws on the language of friendship.[76] Paul also writes about Gentile adoption into the lineage of Abraham through Christ.[77] The dominant metaphor of a family, albeit an oxymoronic family not founded on marriage, descent, and property, might be counted as a dissimilarity from the Hellenistic philosophies, but needs to be better understood.[78] No matter how often one utters the word "brother" or "father," using the language of family is not the same thing as the practices of a family, which include much more than the language. Some later Christian writers made an easy move from speaking of Christianity as a "brotherhood" to Christianity as the third ethnicity, a *genos* or *ethnos* that is neither Greek/Roman nor barbarian/Judean.

Third, specific rituals play an intrinsic role in Pauline Christianity that they do not for the Hellenistic philosophies, except possibly for Epicureans. Again, let me emphasize that the philosophies assume to various degrees that the practices, institutions, and virtues of the Greek city are a basis that the philosophy modifies and rectifies by critical reflection. Thus, a Stoic does not throw out traditional religion and ritual of the city but obtains a modified critical understanding of it that is less local. But only the Epicureans developed their own rituals.[79] Evidence also exists for ritual among later Pythagoreans and Platonists, which needs study.[80] To diminish even further the force of the caveat, one should remember that the Christian rituals dispensed with animal sacrifice and almost all of the other practices central to ancient ritual, except for public prayer and ritual washing. But in traditional religion, the latter only had its sense in relation to temples and sacred places where purity had to be maintained in order to sacrifice. Christian ritual in

---

75. On the character of Greek and Roman friendship with attention to philosophers and ancient Christianity, see David Konstan, *Friendship in the Classical World* (Key Themes in Ancient History; Cambridge: Cambridge University Press, 1997).

76. See John T. Fitzgerald, ed., *Friendship, Flattery, and Frankness of Speech: Studies in Friendship in the New Testament World* (NovTSup 82; Leiden: Brill, 1996); idem, ed., *Greco-Roman Perspectives on Friendship* (Resources for Biblical Study 34; Leiden: Brill, 1997).

77. Stowers, *Rereading of Romans*, 227–53; Caroline Johnson Hodge, *If Sons, Then Heirs: A Study of Kinship and Ethnicity in the Letters of Paul* (New York: Oxford University Press, 2007).

78. The language of fictive kinship may have been at home among later Platonists and Pythagoreans. This phenomenon also deserves study.

79. Glad, *Paul and Philodemus*, 8–9 and n.14; Richard A. Wright, "Christians, Epicureans, and the Critique of Greco-Roman Religion" (Ph.D. diss., Brown University, 1994), 83–95.

80. I am following scholarly convention in not classifying Platonism and Pythagoreanism as Hellenistic philosophies since they began before the Hellenistic age.

the first two hundred years was an odd sort of ritual by ancient standards. Its form decisively broke the link with land and lineages of peoples that was intrinsic to traditional Mediterranean ritual.

Finally, let me very briefly suggest a context in ancient Mediterranean cultural history for this phenomenon of a religion that looked in many ways like a philosophy.[81] The traditional religion and wider cultures of Greeks, Judeans, Romans, and so on were based on the local knowledges of face-to-face communities led by aristocrats who administered the lore and practices, for example, how to sacrifice an animal, calculate when to have a festival, and read events for signs from the gods of the place. Led by the so-called Greek enlightenment, the centuries before the Common Era saw a massive growth in the specialization of knowledge that was no longer local. Greek philosophy led this trend for many areas of knowledge. The particular character of the Hellenistic philosophies derived from creating specialized knowledge and practices about the soul or "how to live an entire life." In place of the local morals of peoples, they claimed a universal expertise regarding character and mind. Judean scribes and scholars also attained a similar authority as specialists in knowledges that were becoming increasingly important to Judean culture. The shift in knowledge practices also meant a shift in authority toward the specialists and away from the local knowledges of the aristocrats, who now had to employ specialists themselves. Christianity was a new form of religion based on the new shape of knowledge that depended on expert interpreters and teachers like Paul.[82] It is not surprising, then, that Pauline Christianity might in many respects have more in common with the Hellenistic philosophies than with the traditional religions based in the landed aristocracies of Rome, Greece, and Judea.

---

81. For what follows, see my suggestions in "Kinds of Myth, Meals, and Power: Paul and the Corinthians" (in this volume); idem, "Elusive Coherence: Ritual and Rhetoric in 1 Corinthians 10–11," in *Reimagining Christian Origins: A Colloquium Honoring Burton L. Mack* (ed. Elizabeth A. Castelli and Hal Taussig; Valley Forge, Pa.: Trinity Press International, 1996), esp. 78–79; idem, *Rereading of Romans*, 328–29, especially in light of my discussion in ch. 2; and now the important article by Andrew Wallace-Hadrill, "*Mutatio morum*: The Idea of a Cultural Revolution," in *The Roman Cultural Revolution* (ed. Thomas Habinek and Alessandro Schiesaro; Cambridge: Cambridge University Press, 1997), 3–22.

82. I do not mean "new" here in the sense of unique, unrecognizable, or not fitting the social context. Rather, Pauline Christianity capitalized on tendencies that had been in formation for centuries by creating a religion dependent on specialized knowledge that claimed universal validity at the same time that it broke the links with land, ethnic people, and the landed aristocracy.

Redescribing Paul and the Corinthians

Ron Cameron and Merrill P. Miller

"Some Corinthians"

In order to engage the work of the seminar and the papers in this volume, we adopt the strategy of referring to some part of the real audience of 1 Corinthians as "some Corinthians," in deliberate distinction from the holistic and Pauline "*ekklēsia* of Corinth," and even from the more generalized "Corinthian association." There are a number of advantages in using this vague and partial designation. The recent renewal of interest in comparing Pauline churches to Greco-Roman associations, to which some members of this seminar have made important contributions,[1] has neither aimed at, nor succeeded in, establishing the identity of Pauline churches with some particular type of association. As John S. Kloppenborg notes, "Preliminary analysis of the available models makes it unlikely that any one will commend itself fully. . . . Hence, rather than engaging in rhetorical overstatement and claiming, for example, that the Corinthian *ekklēsia was* a *philosophia*, or *was* a cult association, it is far more useful to compare particular aspects of Christian, Jewish, and pagan associative practices."[2] Similarly, to refer to the Corinthians as the *ekklēsia* of Corinth or the *ekklēsia* of Christ may acknowledge the addressees of Paul's Corinthian correspondence, but it identifies the implied audience in too facile a way with the real audience of 1 Corinthians. Inevitably, such an identification tends to set limits in advance on the range and scope of differences between Paul's rhetorical aims and behavioral ideals, between his convictions about his own identity and authority, and Corinthian practices, identities, and recognition

---

1. See John S. Kloppenborg and Stephen G. Wilson, eds., *Voluntary Associations in the Graeco-Roman World* (London and New York: Routledge, 1996); Richard S. Ascough, *What Are They Saying about the Formation of Pauline Churches?* (New York: Paulist, 1998); idem, *Paul's Macedonian Associations: The Social Context of Philippians and 1 Thessalonians* (WUNT 2/161; Tübingen: Mohr Siebeck, 2003).

2. John S. Kloppenborg, "Greco-Roman *Thiasoi*, the *Ekklēsia* at Corinth, and Conflict Management," 189 (in this volume [emphasis original]).

of authority. By referring to "some Corinthians," we are also keeping in view the differences of social status that have been the focus of so much recent study.[3] Most

---

3. The view of Pauline communities as socially stratified has sometimes been referred to as a "new consensus" (so Abraham J. Malherbe, *Social Aspects of Early Christianity* [2nd ed.; Philadelphia: Fortress, 1983], 31), in contrast to an earlier view, influenced especially by the work of Adolf Deissmann early in the twentieth century, that saw the early Christians mainly situated in the lowest strata of society (*Paul: A Study in Social and Religious History* [2nd ed.; trans. William E. Wilson; New York: Harper & Brothers, 1927]). E. A. Judge set Paul and his co-workers in the upper strata of the Mediterranean cities (*The Social Pattern of the Christian Groups in the First Century: Some Prolegomena to the Study of New Testament Ideas of Social Obligation* [London: Tyndale, 1960]). In studies conducted in the 1970s, Gerd Theissen drew attention to the named individuals in Paul's letters and developed criteria for distinguishing people of higher social strata, associating references to the "strong" and the "weak" with persons from higher and lower social strata, respectively (*The Social Setting of Pauline Christianity: Essays on Corinth* [ed. and trans. John H. Schütz; Philadelphia: Fortress, 1982]). Wayne A. Meeks pointed to the phenomenon of status inconsistency to account in part for the attraction of Pauline Christianity (*The First Urban Christians: The Social World of the Apostle Paul* [New Haven: Yale University Press, 1983]). For other contributions to the new consensus, emphasizing in particular the effect of patronal networks and leadership exercised by the more wealthy and socially powerful on the divisions in the church at Corinth, see John K. Chow, *Patronage and Power: A Study of Social Networks in Corinth* (JSNTSup 75; Sheffield: JSOT Press, 1992); Andrew D. Clarke, *Secular and Christian Leadership in Corinth: A Socio-Historical and Exegetical Study of 1 Corinthians 1–6* (AGJU 18; Leiden: Brill, 1993); Bruce W. Winter, *Seek the Welfare of the City: Early Christians as Benefactors and Citizens* (First-Century Christians in the Graeco-Roman World; Grand Rapids: Eerdmans; Carlisle: Paternoster, 1994); idem, *After Paul Left Corinth: The Influence of Secular Ethics and Social Change* (Grand Rapids: Eerdmans, 2001); see also Philip A. Harland, "Connections with Elites in the World of the Early Christians," in *Handbook of Early Christianity: Social Science Approaches* (ed. Anthony J. Blasi et al.; Walnut Creek, Calif.: AltaMira, 2002), 385–408. For dissenters from the consensus, see Ekkhard W. Stegemann and Wolfgang Stegemann, *The Jesus Movement: A Social History of Its First Century* (trans. O. C. Dean, Jr.; Minneapolis: Fortress, 1999); Justin J. Meggitt, *Paul, Poverty and Survival* (Studies of the New Testament and Its World; Edinburgh: T&T Clark, 1998). Meggitt argues that the distinctions of status in the Greco-Roman world have depended almost exclusively on elite sources. In his view, almost all of the population of the empire, beyond the imperial and city elites, belonged to the poor in the sense that the overriding concern was the daily struggle to survive. Meggitt, Theissen, and Dale B. Martin have debated some of the issues raised by Meggitt's book in an issue of the *Journal for the Study of the New Testament* (84 [2001]): see Dale B. Martin, "Review Essay: Justin J. Meggitt, *Paul, Poverty and Survival*," 51–64; Gerd Theissen, "The Social Structure of the Pauline Communities: Some Critical Remarks on J. J. Meggitt, *Paul, Poverty and Survival*," 65–84. While maintaining his position on social stratification and its significance for understanding the factions in the church at Corinth, Theissen rejects the view that there has been any new consensus. Rather, in his view, Meggitt's book continues an old debate from the nineteenth century. What has occurred in recent decades, Theissen says, is "a renewed socio-historical interest with different results" (66). See Meggitt's "Response to Martin and Theissen," 85–94; Gerd Theissen, "Social Conflicts in the Corinthian Community: Further Remarks on J. J. Meggitt, *Paul, Poverty and Survival*," *JSNT* 25 (2003): 371–91. Steven J. Friesen has recently presented a more extensive comparison of Deissmann and the new consensus in "Poverty in Pauline Studies: Beyond the So-Called New Consensus," *JSNT* 26 (2004): 323–61. In a subsequent article, Friesen argues that economic factors have not been given sufficient weight in New Testament studies of social stratigraphy. His conclusions are close to those of Meggitt, though based on a more gradated scale of poverty. He also points out that our evidence for the demography of Pauline assemblies is skewed by two other factors: (1) almost all the evidence comes from Corinth and Rom 16; and (2) we know more

of all, the reference to "some Corinthians" highlights an important feature of the papers: they are not all focused on the same Corinthians, or at least they may not be the same Corinthians. And the Corinthians brought into focus may operate in certain respects with conflicting interests. By being deliberately vague, we accept the likelihood of plural identities and fluid boundaries, which contrast so dramatically with, yet also help to account for, Paul's counterstrategies of linking group concord with stronger boundary markers, and behavioral ideals of self-control with recognition of the primacy of his authority in establishing and maintaining group cohesion as the *ekklēsia* of Christ.

The "parting of the ways" can be stated as a general observation on the different focus of the papers by Jonathan Z. Smith and Burton L. Mack, and William E. Arnal and Stanley K. Stowers ("Kinds of Myth, Meals, and Power: Paul and the Corinthians"). For Smith and Mack, "some Corinthians" are those for whom Paul's Christ myth would have remained largely opaque and "implausible."[4] For Arnal and Stowers, "some Corinthians" are those for whom Paul's Christ myth would have been attractive on the basis of shared interests. The disjunction (between and among the papers) is related to the continuing discussion and debate among members of the seminar. However, it should not be overlooked that Arnal and Stowers also find "some Corinthians" as presented by Smith and Mack to be highly instructive, though limited, in representing the situation in Corinth. Stowers accepts Smith's view of a largely domestic setting for some, even most, Corinthians, presupposing the sort of religious interests generally appropriate to households.[5] Arnal also acknowledges Smith's "some Corinthians" as those who would have resisted Paul's intrusion and recognizes a dialectical situation of creative "misunderstandings."[6]

---

about traveling missionaries who were mostly Jewish and the local leaders of assemblies, than about local residents in the assemblies, about whom we know almost nothing (Steven J. Friesen, "Prospects for a Demography of the Pauline Mission: Corinth among the Churches," in *Urban Religion in Roman Corinth: Interdisciplinary Approaches* [ed. Daniel N. Schowalter and Steven J. Friesen; HTS 53; Cambridge, Mass.: Harvard Divinity School, 2005], 351–70).

4. Jonathan Z. Smith, "Re: Corinthians," 31 (in this volume): "I raise these matters as having relevance to my assigned topic: Paul's Christ myth at Corinth. If what I have redescribed is at all plausible, then Paul is implausible." Burton L. Mack expands on this judgment in his paper, "Rereading the Christ Myth: Paul's Gospel and the Christ Cult Question," 62–65 (in this volume).

5. Stanley K. Stowers, "Kinds of Myth, Meals, and Power: Paul and the Corinthians," 111 (in this volume): "By localism, I take Smith to mean, in the case of the Corinthians, their practice of the religion of place manifest in their concern for the dead, for spirits, for kinship and ancestry, and for their common meals. The letters clearly give evidence of the Corinthian practice of religion of the household and family and religion of the temple. Thus, interpreters should take these, and especially the first, as expressing the religious interests of the people to whom Paul wrote and think of Paul's religion of 'anywhere' as at least novel for most of the Corinthians and perhaps, with Smith, as a problematic intrusion."

6. William E. Arnal, "Bringing Paul and the Corinthians Together? A Rejoinder and Some Proposals on Redescription and Theory," 89 (in this volume): "We can indeed assume that significant

From the other side of this disjunction, Smith and Mack recognize that there must have been some shared interests. Smith calls attention to the potential interest of "some Corinthians" in what they may have understood Paul to be providing in the figure of Christ: "a more proximate and mobile ancestor for their new, non-ethnic 'Christian' *ethnos*."[7] Moreover, though he does not elaborate on the observation, Smith suggests that one might explore "the attraction of the promise of participation in an enlarged Christian landscape for a relatively small group, as described for the Atbalmin, and as suggested in 1 Corinthians with its multiple references to an extended Christian 'family,' present in other locales but bound together by a communications network of letters, travels, and gifts."[8] However, Smith does not have to posit some other group of Corinthians in order to imagine mutual interests between Paul and the Corinthians, in part because the same people will have a variety of interests related to the wider milieu, however differentially these interests may be ranked, and in part because the mutuality is constructed dialectically in the process of exchange, in efforts of "translation."[9] Mack also supposes that the common Diaspora situation could have predisposed the Corinthians and

---

disjunctions exist between Paul's agenda and ideas, on the one hand, and the bulk of the original group, which has remained unpersuaded by his 'gospel.'" He also states, "I am convinced that they [Smith and Mack] are correct in describing a Paul who creatively (and deliberately?) 'misunderstands' the extant practices of a Corinthian association in order to attempt to swerve those practices in a direction more congenial to his *euangelion*. My reservations concern the assumption and argument that this remodeling could have held no attraction for the group in question" (81). On cultural production as dialectical and mutually transformative, referring to Smith's citations of Marshall Sahlins and Claude Lévi-Strauss and their implicit critique of the notion of a linear progression of ideas that is self-generating, see ibid., 79, citing Smith, "Re: Corinthians," 28; idem, "Differential Equations: On Constructing the Other," in idem, *Relating Religion: Essays in the Study of Religion* (Chicago: University of Chicago Press, 2004), 246. Note also the similar pattern to which Arnal appeals in suggesting a correlation between Smith's "some Corinthians" and Arnal's own *Fight Club* analogy: "an informal movement among porous group boundaries themselves in a state of flux" ("Paul and the Corinthians," 85 n. 23).

7. Smith, "Re: Corinthians," 33, adding: "Certainly, celestial figures often have a mobile advantage over chthonic ones, who are more readily bound to a place. Perhaps some Corinthians found support for a new sort of ancestor in Paul's first/last Adam language in 1 Cor 15 (esp. v. 45), but this is vitiated by its context as part of a defense of resurrection.... Perhaps some Corinthians found support for a new sort of ancestor in the complex set of registers played by Paul on *sōma*, with the body of Christ understood in a corporate sense (1 Cor 12:12–14, 27) as a new collective ancestor.... However, none of this will do without a major effort in non-Pauline mythmaking by some Corinthians" (33–34; cf. 33–34 n. 48). Smith's choice of collective expression, referring to "their new, non-ethnic 'Christian' *ethnos*" (33), may also have important implications. Is the designation intended to refer only to Paul's notion of fictive kinship and corporate belonging, or does it signify what might also be the collective understanding of "some Corinthians" when they assemble? See Stowers's discussion of "non-ethnic ethnicity" as Paul's "attempt at group-making in view of the human constructedness of all social formations" ("Kinds of Myth," 149).

8. Smith, "Re: Corinthians," 34.

9. "The Corinthian situation may well be defined as the efforts at translations between these understandings and misunderstandings" (ibid.). This last sentence of Smith's paper should be taken seriously. Thus, Stowers's characterization of the position of Smith and Mack as saying that "Paul just

Paul to think "they had much in common."[10] And though he maintains that the gap between Paul "with his resurrected, heavenly Christ, and they with their dead and properly buried ancestors"[11] could not be bridged, he sees that they were nevertheless comparing notes,[12] working on "translations," and "talking past one another"[13] (and evidently keeping at it)—all of which also suggests some level of shared interest and mutual attraction accounting for the exchange of letters, the receiving of reports, and the visits over a protracted period of time.[14]

The papers differ principally in identifying the generative problematic for a redescription of the data. This accounts for the different subject position held by "some Corinthians" in the papers of Smith and Mack, on one side, and the papers of Arnal and Stowers, on the other. For Smith, what is puzzling is the "oddness" of Paul's responses to matters of practice and issues in dispute that appear to be local and domestic affairs. Since Paul refers to households in 1 Corinthians, it seems likely that they constitute a significant portion of those addressed in the letter. Other oddities are noticed. Talk about *pneuma* and practices related to it, or

---

misunderstood the Corinthians and their locative religious interests owing to his utopian understanding" is a bit too flat, leaving out the efforts at translations ("Kinds of Myth," 142).

10. Mack, "Rereading the Christ Myth," 65, adding: "And since Paul appeared as a teacher from afar, the Corinthians may have received him just as they would have any wandering philosopher" (ibid.).

11. Ibid.

12. "They may well have wanted to compare notes with a traveling teacher talking about the spirit of a martyred folk hero at a distance from his tomb, and about how Gentiles were really heirs of Abraham now that God had made that clear at the end of history" (ibid., 64).

13. Ibid., 65.

14. Mack turns to Jonathan Z. Smith's essay, "Here, There, and Anywhere," in *Prayer, Magic, and the Stars in the Ancient and Late Antique World* (ed. Scott Noegel et al.; Magic in History Series; University Park: Pennsylvania State University Press, 2003), 21–36; repr. in *Relating Religion*, 323–39), to explain the impasse: "The Corinthians were apparently working with the problems of 'translating' their homeland 'domestic' cults in a place away from home. Paul was working with the 'translation' of a 'polis-based' cult in a city of the Diaspora. Features of each of these two types of ancient religious practice could be dislodged in the Hellenistic period and translated in the practice of religion 'anywhere,' that is, within an association. But the concerns, practices, 'spirits,' deities, social models, and social notions were still quite different. In the case of Paul's Christ, there was no tomb, whether 'here' or 'there,' to provide the 'locative' anchor for re-placement in the 'anywhere' of the present social system. And his Christ was not a likely candidate for representing or substituting for patriarchal ancestors" ("Rereading the Christ Myth," 65). Compare Richard S. Ascough's explanation for the appeal of Paul's "apocalypticism," drawing on the same essay of Smith: "Smith goes on to suggest that, in order to overcome this situation [of displacement], the domestic religion must be transmuted. An association becomes the 'socially constructed replacement for the family' that is overlaid with a new myth in which a true home is imagined 'above,' one that replaces the longed-for home 'down here.' Through such mythmaking the religion of the domestic sphere becomes the religion of any sphere, transportable to new locales precisely because a person's true connection is 'on high.' . . . Smith states, 'Locale, having been dis-placed, is now re-placed'" ("Paul's 'Apocalypticism' and the Jesus Associations at Thessalonica and Corinth," 170 [in this volume], citing Smith, "Here, There, and Anywhere," 31; repr. in *Relating Religion*, 330, 331). See above, n. 7.

demonstrations of it, are more prominent in the letter than explicit elaborations of Christ's death and resurrection, despite the place in his preaching that Paul claims for the *kērygma* at the beginning of the letter and in ch. 15.[15] And even 1 Cor 15 turns out to be more a disquisition on spirit and different kinds of substance or bodies, and the contrasting powers, aeons, and ancestors (Adam and Christ) to which they properly belong, than a defense of the resurrection, whose reality or necessity some Corinthians have apparently denied. That there is some interest in, or concern for, the dead and their spirits is suggested by Paul's presentation of the Lord's meal as a kind of mortuary foundation in ch. 11 and his reference to the Corinthian practice of baptism for the dead in ch. 15.[16] However, it is the analogy from New Guinea that makes it possible to see a pattern in many of the practices that come up in Paul's letter. Thus, sexual conduct, kinship, eating, and "idolatry" are arenas of dispute among the Atbalmin of New Guinea and also topics addressed in 1 Corinthians, and in both cases the issues relate to tensions between indigenous practices and the behaviors regarded as appropriate for Christians, or, in Paul's letter, the behaviors appropriate for those who are members of the body of Christ and have his spirit. But it is especially the way in which cultic relations with the ancestors in dislocation and with the more proximate dead inform the relation between *pneuma* and *gnōsis*, between *pneuma* and "sin(s)," and the sources of oracular authority and moral guidance, that has suggested to Smith a different biblical genealogy of *pneuma* and *pneumata* and their (mis)translation in Tok Pidgin "Holy Spirit" and in Paul's differently formed concept of "the Spirit":

> Thus, I think, Paul would have understood one thing, some groups of Corinthians another, when *pneuma* is associated with *gnōsis*; when Paul claims to have authority for guiding present behavior because he "has the spirit of God" . . . or when he himself can be present "in spirit" . . . at the occasion of a communal moral dilemma; when they meet together for a meal for/with the dead . . . to which a Lord's supper has apparently been added; or when they are concerned about baptism for the dead.[17]

---

15. Smith, "Re: Corinthians," 31–32: "the [Christ] myth is rarely elaborated in 1 Corinthians. It appears to play a role chiefly in those instances where Paul is palpably in difficulty: his shift on 'idols' from being meaningless to meaningful . . . ; the polemic against Corinthian meal practice . . . where his strongest argument, finally, is not mythmaking but rather the threat of supernatural sanction . . . ; and the discourse on resurrection."

16. Cf. the reference to the Israelite fathers who were all "baptized into Moses in the cloud and in the sea" (1 Cor 10:2). In context, Paul's use of this as a warning and object lesson makes most sense if one supposes that baptism is thought of in this passage as an apotropaic ritual. Paul warns that it failed in that respect; neither baptism nor eating the same spiritual food and drinking the same spiritual drink offered protection from the wrath of God.

17. Smith, "Re: Corinthians," 31.

The redescription of the Corinthians is bold, hardly a paraphrase or merely a mirror reading of 1 Corinthians. In Mack's brief formulation, the Corinthian "association" is "no longer a 'church' converted by Paul's preaching of 'Christ crucified,' but a grouping of displaced peoples working on the 'translations' called for by separations from their homelands."[18]

In Stowers's paper, the generative problematic is directly related to the success of Smith's comparison in creating a plausible social context rooted in typical domestic interests governing religious practices for both contemporary Atbalmin and ancient Corinthians; in denaturalizing the attraction of Paul's message of salvation in Christ;[19] and in making simultaneous experimentation with multiple modes of religion documented for the Atbalmin even more likely in the more diverse, multiethnic context of Roman Corinth.[20] But the success of Smith's comparison, which makes a differentiated response to Paul likely, also leaves the sustained encounter between Paul and the Corinthians without adequate explanation, in Stowers's estimation.

In order to address both differentiated responses and sustained encounter, Stowers has introduced the concepts of *doxai*, interests, recognition, and attraction "as attendant on the processes of ongoing mythic formations."[21] It is the concept of recognition,[22] in particular, that is central to the development of his thesis, because it establishes several crucial differences between contemporary New Guinea and Roman Corinth. The latter was more differentiated and diverse than traditional Atbalmin society. "Unlike in New Guinea, specialized book-learning and literary-rhetorical production were an important means for distinguishing a whole class of elites from the masses and for fostering competition for honor among elites."[23] This is crucial for understanding the reception of Paul. He is recognized as a producer and distributor of an esoteric *paideia*.[24] The practices of

---

18. Mack, "Rereading the Christ Myth," 63.

19. "New Testament scholars will have to denaturalize their understandings of religion and not assume a contextless universal meaningfulness and attraction to 'Paul's gospel'" (Stowers, "Kinds of Myth," 111–12).

20. "The case of the Atbalmin and their simultaneous experimentation with multiple modes of religion makes the internal early Christian perspective of absolute religious purity and mutually exclusive practice ... seem fantastic.... This means that there is a very large gap between the idealized descriptions of the Corinthians as 'in Christ' and the real situation" (ibid., 112).

21. Ibid., 106.

22. For Stowers's definition of the concept of recognition, see ibid.

23. Ibid., 122, adding: "In his letters, Paul almost certainly intellectualized issues for the sake of attracting such people. So, for example, what might have been quite mundane interests in the extended family of ancestors and the dead for the non-elites were addressed by Paul with the culturally ambitious in view as an opportunity to expound on human nature and the science of the cosmos through the Christ-*pneuma* myth in 1 Cor 15.... The letter treats issues about prostitutes, marriage, and sacrificial meat that might have been quite local and mundane for most Corinthians as issues about moral freedom and correct worship of the truly conceived deity" (ibid.).

24. "One must view Paul as a producer and distributor of an alternative esoteric *paideia* different

specialized literate learning were "aimed at a niche of consumers who found social distinction in acquiring such *paideia*," perhaps because of "minority or mixed ethnic statuses or other status inconsistencies." Others, probably the majority, "would likely have understood Paul on their own terms and have exhibited both repulsion and attraction at points related to their strategic concerns."[25] In sum:

> Smith's comparison shows how the local interests of the religion of place were likely to have provided the Corinthians with a basis for a limited and differentiated hearing of Paul.... But for there to have been a sustained encounter between Paul and the Corinthians at all requires the existence of a group among the Corinthians who were already habituated, not so as to want to be saved or become Christians, but so as to want to become consumers of Paul's foreign *paideia*.[26]

Arnal makes a similar, though less qualified point in his paper, expanding on the ramifications:

> Mack and Smith have constructed what is, in my view, too great a disjunction between Paul and the folks to whom he is writing.... [W]e are required to assume an extended communicative incompetence among members of the same (urban, Greco-Roman) culture, and among people and groups whose social circumstances appear to be more or less identical.... [A]nd so we are left without any way to understand the preservation of Paul's letters, the later influence of Pauline-style ideology, [and] Pauline *ekklēsiai*.[27]

In this light, the generative problematic is bringing Paul and the Corinthians together by exploring a basis for shared interests and mutual attraction, but without falling back on the familiar narrative pattern of the place of Paul in the unfolding Christian story.[28] Like Stowers, Arnal looks for the conditions that could account for mutual attraction, but he looks in a different direction. Rather than pointing to the existence of a field of specialized knowledge and a class of producers, distributors, and consumers increasingly competing with traditional forms and sources of knowledge in the period of the early Roman Principate, he calls attention to the commonality of the social situation of ethnically uprooted and ethnically mixed people living in a Roman colony such as Corinth and states with emphasis that "*this characterization applies to Paul too*."[29] Drawing on Smith's notion of situational

---

from the dominant sophistic or philosophical kinds, yet still recognizable as a form of the same broader game of specialized literate learning" (ibid., 117).

25. Ibid., 116, 117.
26. Ibid., 142.
27. Arnal, "Paul and the Corinthians," 80, 81.
28. See Arnal's introductory discussion (ibid., 75–77).
29. Ibid., 80 (emphasis original).

incongruity as a social ground for shared interests in rectification,[30] Arnal suggests a scenario in which Paul's intrusion creates a Pauline faction among Corinthians who are already associated and with whom Paul has come into contact. The initial attraction for Paul is the mixed constituency of the group(s) and a shared experience of deracination. For "some Corinthians," that is, those (Arnal suggests) who come to constitute a Pauline faction, the attraction is Paul's gospel, inasmuch as it offers a meaningful resolution of problematic identities:[31]

> Paul's questions about being a Jew in a Greco-Roman world are not substantively different from the kinds of questions we might expect from, say, Tyrians in Italy, Egyptians in Antioch, or Italians in Asia Minor, as well as those ethnically diverse and uprooted people ... who made up the club in Corinth to which Paul offered his "gospel." ... Paul's conceptions ... mesh exceptionally well with the putative concerns of these uprooted Corinthians. Paul sees himself as an apostle to the Gentiles (*ethnē*); the Corinthians are concerned with being an uprooted cluster of nations (*ethnē*). Paul proposes a new ethnic identity as grafted-on Jews under the rubric of the *ekklēsia*, the assembly of Israel (as per the LXX). ... Belonging in this way must have been attractive to some people (if not all, of course), precisely because it answered, in both an intellectual and a practical way, questions of identity (especially conceived in ethnic terms) that were already pressing.[32]

Arnal's effort to construct a plausible context for bringing Paul and "some Corinthians" together raises several important issues that require comment and extended discussion at this point. First, Arnal reads Smith's reference to the Roman resettlement of Corinth in 44 B.C.E., resulting in a "relatively recent displacement and re-placement," from the perspective of a deracinated population open to the construction of new identities. However, it is more in keeping with Smith's description of "some Corinthians" to view them from the perspective of ongoing interest in preserving and adapting the native practices of the homeland, especially with reference to cultic contact with ancestors and interest in the land of the dead. Smith is influenced here by the analogy of the West Papuans in New Guinea. The analogy of the Atbalmin in New Guinea does not depend on geographical dislocation. With the Atbalmin, Smith highlights ongoing local domestic practices under

---

30. See especially Jonathan Z. Smith, "A Pearl of Great Price and a Cargo of Yams: A Study in Situational Incongruity," *HR* 16 (1976): 1–19; repr. in idem, *Imagining Religion: From Babylon to Jonestown* (CSHJ; Chicago: University of Chicago Press, 1982), 90–101, 156–62.

31. Arnal, "Paul and the Corinthians," 83–89. If the Pauline faction that Arnal has in mind is related to the divisions and quarreling of 1 Cor 1:10–17, it leads to the observation that Paul remonstrates with the Corinthians for the divisions that his intrusion has created. He grudgingly mentions those whom he baptized and recalls as if parenthetically that he baptized the household of Stephanas (1:14–16; cf. 16:15–16). This bit of exculpation may also have something to do with Paul's judgment on the necessity of factions in 1 Cor 11:18–19. See Stowers's discussion of the role of Stephanas and his household ("Kinds of Myth," 109 n. 11, 118, 121–22, 140).

32. Arnal, "Paul and the Corinthians," 98, 99.

a variety of changing conditions resulting in complex negotiations, but continuing relations with ancestors and the more proximate dead as relations of crucial importance.[33] Domestic practices with respect to the dead that presuppose significant ongoing relations with native traditions are not matters entertained in Arnal's paper, we suspect, because he has constructed situational incongruity and shared social interests around a more extreme, or at least a more thoroughgoing, view of ethnic deracination.[34]

There is an important issue here concerning the population of Corinth in its initial refounding as a Roman colony and with the arrival of immigrants in later periods. Arnal and Stowers both refer to slaves in Corinth, and both take Smith's reference to the refounding of Corinth not only as an indication of the multiethnic character of its population but also as a reason to suppose that Paul's Abraham myth would appeal to slaves and to those whose family and ethnic origins were in some ways seen as problematic.[35] The issue is not simply having to take

---

33. Smith, "Re: Corinthians," 29, 30.

34. As an example, we refer to Arnal's description of "the problem of a national identity for people—various ethnically mixed Jews and Gentiles living in nonancestral cities—who have no nation" ("Paul and the Corinthians," 92). This is not to say that Arnal is unaware of the distinction between Smith's "some Corinthians" and his own Pauline faction or subgroup, for he notes: "While one might claim that Paul's offer of inclusion in the Israelite *ethnos* by virtue of a creative redescription of its boundaries might not appeal to persons more interested in reviving contact with overseas touchstones, it may indeed have spoken quite poignantly to those lacking ancestors altogether," that is, slaves (90 n. 33). But this distinction makes no difference with respect to a redescription of the data of 1 Corinthians, if we suppose on the basis of Arnal's scenario that Paul is addressing only his own faction in the letter. In that case, those interested in continuing contact with overseas touchstones do not belong to the faction. This makes the question of the actual audience addressed in 1 Corinthians, which is raised but not resolved in Arnal's paper (89 n. 32), a crucial issue with respect to the redescription of the data of 1 Corinthians, since if Paul is writing only to his own faction, we do not have to suppose that the "various less-fundamental disjunctions [namely, those very issues addressed by Paul in 1 Corinthians that] persist even between Paul and those who have essentially become convinced by his message" have anything to do with the "significant disjunctions [that] exist between Paul's agenda . . . and the bulk of the original group, which has remained unpersuaded by his 'gospel'" (89).

35. According to Arnal, "If Corinthian colonists face the problem of interrupted contact with the ancestral graves or spirits, how much more so do slaves, who may not, in some instances, even have ancestors or an *ethnos*" (ibid., 89–90 n. 33). And as Stowers observes, "Baptism for the dead would incorporate those dead into the distinguished lineage and ancestry [of Abraham]. Without baptism for the dead, their own baptisms might cut them off from their extended families of the significant dead. This scenario makes sense, if the Corinthians or some of them were people concerned about their own ambiguous and ignoble ancestry, a point to which Paul alludes politely in 1:26. . . . Such people would not only have had the stain of slave origins, but would also have been cut off from ancestral burial grounds" ("Kinds of Myth," 125–26; cf. 120 with n. 40, 121, 126 n. 53). An earlier example suggested by Stowers would not have the same implication: "Baptism for the dead may have been seen as a way to improve the status of the recent or untimely dead, a well-documented concern of families" (117). Ascough cites Smith's work to similar effect: "The burgeoning merchant class and the need of artisans across the empire caused many to migrate to new places in order best to employ their skills. It is, to use Smith's words, a time of 'a new geography.' As a result, the usual expressions and experiences of religion have been detached from their roots in domestic religion, since 'the extended family, the homeplace, as

account of how long most of those whom Paul addresses have lived in Corinth. It concerns the situations from which they have come. Since many of the colonists who refounded Corinth were freedmen and -women,[36] and since it is likely that some, and perhaps a considerable portion, of the Corinthian population occupied that status in Paul's time, it is with respect to that population in particular that questions about the continuation of practices aimed at contact with the more distant and powerful ancestors of the homelands become especially pressing.[37] At the same time, it should be noted that these considerations regarding the relationship of slaves and freed persons to original homelands would not have the same bearing on cultic practices aimed at relations with the proximate and recent dead.[38]

---

well as the burial place of the honored dead, are no longer coextensive *topoi*'" (Ascough, "Paul's 'Apocalypticism,'" 170, citing Smith, "Here, There, and Anywhere," 30, 31; repr. in *Relating Religion*, 330).

36. Strabo, *Geog.* 8.6.23; cf. Appian, *Hist. rom.* 8.136.

37. Note that it is the relationship of slave and freed to which Paul refers in 1 Cor 7:22. Corinth was a major urban center of the slave trade in Paul's time. In her article on the nationality of Roman slaves, Mary L. Gordon points out that freedmen were the most deracinated elements of the population on account of the experience of slavery itself ("The Nationality of Slaves under the Early Roman Empire," *JRS* 14 [1924]: 93–111), concluding: "The slave had no *patria*, but emancipation gave him not only a city but a home; as a freedman, he could contract a legal marriage, his children were citizens, and he could found a Romanised and respectable family. How eagerly this privilege was accepted, how much affection and hope surrounded the children so born, and how tragic was their loss, is revealed even in the abbreviated and laconic grief of ancient grave-stones" (111). For calculations of the high percentage of slaves to freeborn based on the evidence of Rom 16, see Peter Lampe, "The Roman Christians of Romans 16," in *The Romans Debate* (ed. Karl P. Donfried; rev. and exp. ed.; Peabody, Mass.: Hendrickson, 1991), 227–29; for more detailed information, see idem, *From Paul to Valentinus: Christians at Rome in the First Two Centuries* (ed. Marshall D. Johnson; trans. Michael Steinhauser; Minneapolis: Fortress, 2003), 170–83. For major studies of slavery in the Roman Empire and in early Christianity, see Moses I. Finley, *Ancient Slavery and Modern Ideology* (ed. Brent D. Shaw; exp. ed.; Princeton: Wiener, 1998); Orlando Patterson, *Slavery and Social Death: A Comparative Study* (Cambridge, Mass.: Harvard University Press, 1982); K. R. Bradley, *Slaves and Masters in the Roman Empire: A Study in Social Control* (Revue d'étude latines 185; Brussels: Latomus, 1984; repr., New York: Oxford University Press, 1987); Dale B. Martin, *Slavery as Salvation: The Metaphor of Slavery in Pauline Christianity* (New Haven: Yale University Press, 1990); J. Albert Harrill, *The Manumission of Slaves in Early Christianity* (HUT 32; Tübingen: Mohr Siebeck, 1995); Jennifer A. Glancy, *Slavery in Early Christianity* (New York: Oxford University Press, 2002); and *Semeia* 83–84 (1998), edited by Allen Dwight Callahan, Richard A. Horsley, and Abraham Smith and titled *Slavery in Text and Interpretation*.

38. On funerary evidence from Asia Minor for slave families, see Dale B. Martin, "Slave Families and Slaves in Families," in *Early Christian Families in Context: An Interdisciplinary Dialogue* (ed. David L. Balch and Carolyn Osiek; Religion, Marriage and Family; Grand Rapids: Eerdmans, 2003), 207–30, who concludes: "Though the evidence I have presented is admittedly sparse and anecdotal, it does allow us to form an impression of the variety of family structures and experiences that must have been possible for at least some slaves in Asia Minor in the early Roman Empire" (230). See also Martin's questioning of the nuclear/extended family dichotomy based on tombstone inscriptions in Asia Minor in idem, "The Construction of the Ancient Family: Methodological Considerations," *JRS* 86 (1996): 57: "The varied configurations of relationships that emerge from my study suggest that family structures could have a much greater variety of boundaries and *kinds* of boundaries than can be encompassed by the nuclear versus extended categories" (emphasis original).

Moreover, while dislodgement from homeland challenges the conditions under which native practices involving cultic contact with the powerful dead buried in the homeland can be maintained, it does not necessarily dislodge interest in and ritual experiments aimed at maintaining these touchstones, especially in the case of recent immigrants who were freeborn. Nevertheless, if it is the case that households composed of persons originating from different homelands were already associated before Paul arrived, we think it unlikely that the motivations for such assembling and the practices engaged would have remained only those intended to preserve or adapt the customs of the homelands in a distant setting. Alternatively, Paul's intrusion may have contributed to assembling on a larger scale (Rom 16:23; 1 Cor 11:18; 14:26).[39]

A second issue is the almost opposite estimate of the place of intellectual practices in Paul's appeal to the Corinthians. This disagreement is significant in the papers of Arnal and Stowers, because it bears directly on identifying the subjects of Paul's appeal and accounting for mutual attraction. What Arnal views as overestimated in the papers of Mack and Smith, Stowers sees as generally underestimated in Pauline scholarship. Thus, while Arnal acknowledges that Paul is an intellectual "by any definition of the term," he thinks that Mack, following Smith, "exaggerates the intellectual dimension of Paul's motivations and mental production." Paul's mythmaking should not be seen as "taking place at a kind of intellectual remove from the Corinthians." The logical inconsistencies of Paul's arguments would have been a problem only for "a group with essentially intellectual concerns."[40] Stowers, on the contrary, thinks that "in his letters, Paul almost certainly intellectualized issues for the sake of attracting ... [elites]." In Stowers's opinion, "interpreters misrecognize and vastly underappreciate the power of Paul as a specialist in intellectual practices." But in fact, "the core of Paul's legitimacy, and thus his power among some of the Corinthians, derived rather from his skillful display of abilities native to the game or field such as his education in ancient books; his interpretive skills; his reading, writing, and speaking abilities; and his pneumatic demonstrations."[41]

Arnal's effort to explore ways of imagining how we might bring Paul and the Corinthians together has the consequence of reducing discord among those in his Pauline faction and between Paul and the faction, a consequence that runs counter to the tendencies of much recent scholarship. This is a third issue of importance. It is true that Arnal never denies that those who constitute his Pauline subgroup have issues with Paul or that mutual and creative "misunderstandings" are present

---

39. Cf. Kloppenborg, "Greco-Roman *Thiasoi*," 216: "To the ancient observer, the Corinthian Jesus people would probably appear as *thiasotai* in a club that resembled domestic *collegia* or small cult associations more than groups of immigrant metics who met to preserve their ancestral customs.... There are some similarities with domestic *collegia*, though the *ekklēsia* seems to have experimented with transfamilial assemblies too, a practice that offered the occasion for serious conflict."

40. Arnal, "Paul and the Corinthians," 84, 87, 99.

41. Stowers, "Kinds of Myth," 122, 126, 141–42.

in the process of their continuing communications. But it is not what Arnal refers to as the "less-fundamental disjunctions" that he explores, but the larger conjunctions between Paul and the Corinthians. Consequently, compared to the much less concordant picture of Paul's Corinthians in scholarship that is focused on evidence of social stratification and its relation to Paul–Corinthian disjunctions, Arnal has described the Corinthians as "people and groups whose social circumstances appear to be more or less identical."[42] This impression of concord would be qualified in a significant way, if we do *not* assume that a Pauline faction has split from a larger, original group, and therefore, if Paul's actual audience includes the more heterogeneous interests and makeup of the original group(s).[43] This would bring the data of 1 Corinthians back into consideration as data bearing on "significant disjunctions . . . between Paul's agenda and ideas . . . and the bulk of the original group, which has remained unpersuaded by his 'gospel.'" Moreover, this picture fits better with Arnal's description of the correlation between Smith's "some Corinthians" and Arnal's own *Fight Club* analogy: "an informal movement among porous group boundaries themselves in a state of flux."[44]

Finally, we must take note of an issue that bears on the central categories and strategies of our redescription project. Arnal has stated that the failure to find a plausible way of understanding the attraction of Paul's project for "some Corinthians" makes the site uninteresting for testing our categories of mythmaking and social interests, and for exploring their nexus. The identification of junctures of mythmaking and social formation is, indeed, a strategy and goal of the seminar's redescription project.[45] But questioning the formative place of Paul's gospel in responding to social interests and generating social formation at Corinth is not to say that Paul's "intrusion" has no effect on how we might imagine a nexus of mythmaking and social interests among the Corinthians. If we acknowledge the capacity for experimentation with multiple modes of religion, we should expect that one of the forms that Corinthian response to Paul would take would be their own experiments in mythmaking and ritual related to their own differentiated social interests.[46]

---

42. Arnal, "Paul and the Corinthians," 89, 81. This strategy of exploring the larger conjunctions of the situation of Paul and the Corinthians continues in the last section of his paper, where Arnal suggests that we explore Paul's *ekklēsia* as an alternative society to "vertically stratified household units" and to "vertical patronage relations" (104).

43. See above, n. 34.

44. Arnal, "Paul and the Corinthians," 89, 85 n. 23; and see above, n. 6.

45. See Ron Cameron and Merrill P. Miller, eds., *Redescribing Christian Origins* (SBLSymS 28; Atlanta: Society of Biblical Literature; Leiden and Boston: Brill, 2004), 17–18, 21–22, 511–16. Arnal appears to have the testing of these categories in view when he concludes that what is "especially damaging for our project" is that we are left "without any way to understand the attraction of Paul's project. . . . If this is so, then Corinth is a uniquely bad site for our inquiries" ("Paul and the Corinthians," 81).

46. This is a point that Stowers makes in his paper, with several examples ("Kinds of Myth," 125–26, 140–41).

The Christ Myth and Paul's Gospel

Paul's claim in 1 Corinthians that he preached Christ crucified and resurrected is not only taken at face value in modern scholarship; it is also regarded as the core of Paul's gospel and the basis of everything else that he teaches, even though, as Mack points out, the mechanisms by which death–resurrection becomes a pervasive metaphor have been debated without end.[47] As we have already noted, the papers in this volume that take up Paul's gospel for redescription agree that the single *kērygma* assumption cannot account for Paul's "mission" to the Gentiles or his self-identification as the one whom God has called and set aside for this apostleship.[48] The papers also agree that Paul's reading of Scripture, especially his reading of the promise to Abraham, and the way in which he has merged several myths are of more central significance in the construction of his gospel:

> The problem that scholars have had trying to explain everything in Paul's program from the "Christ crucified" gospel he claims was basic, is that it will not work, that most of his program was rooted in the other gospel [referring to Gal 3:6–9 and the promise to Abraham].... All of the terms customarily thought to be Pauline coins derived from the meaning of the *kērygma* ... are instead found to be the product of very clever moves in the interstices between the Christ myth and the scriptural accounts of the promise to Abraham.[49]

> Paul has, in essence, fused two independent mythic considerations: the cluster of martyrological ideas inherited from Jesus/*christos* people before him, and the cluster of ideas associated with the righteousness/faithfulness of Abraham as the ethnic progenitor of Israel, as well as ... the one through whom the nations (Gentiles) will be blessed.... Paul (apparently) places these concepts [death and vindication] at the center of his *kērygma*—but in fact they are logically secondary to the much more pressing issue of ethnic identity and place in the world.[50]

I will argue that Paul's teachings and mythmaking were centrally about kinship and ancestry, even if not in a typically locative way, and integrally connected to his discourse about the "spirit" (a poor translation) or *pneuma*.[51]

---

47. Mack, "Rereading the Christ Myth," 58–59.
48. See Ron Cameron and Merrill P. Miller, "Introducing Paul and the Corinthians," 4–6 with nn. 10, 12 (in this volume).
49. Mack, "Rereading the Christ Myth," 60.
50. Arnal, "Paul and the Corinthians," 93.
51. Stowers, "Kinds of Myth," 112. For the connection between animal sacrifice and patrilineal descent in the construction of ethnicity and gender in the ancient world, see especially Nancy Jay, *Throughout Your Generations Forever: Sacrifice, Religion, and Paternity* (Chicago: University of Chicago Press, 1992); and, for Greek religion, Stanley K. Stowers, "Greeks Who Sacrifice and Those Who Do Not: Toward an Anthropology of Greek Religion," in *The Social World of the First Christians: Essays in Honor of Wayne A. Meeks* (ed. L. Michael White and O. Larry Yarbrough; Minneapolis: Fortress, 1995), 293–333. The emphasis on Paul's ethnic mythmaking is found especially in idem, *A Rereading of Romans: Justice, Jews, and Gentiles* (New Haven: Yale University Press, 1994); and, more recently, Caro-

While these agreements contribute in a fundamental way to a redescription of Paul's gospel, important differences remain among the papers in the significance attributed to Paul's Christ myth, its place in Paul's gospel, and its relationship to his ethnic and spirit myths. These differences can be generalized by noting Mack's treatment of Paul's apocalyptic orientation,[52] Arnal's construction of Paul's situational incongruity and its relation to a reconfiguring of Israel's epic,[53] and Stowers's reference to Paul's "Christ-*pneuma*" myth and its implications for discerning the true self, constituting of the social body, and perfecting the human species.[54] These generalizations are admittedly oversimplifications, since none of the writers would deny a Pauline apocalyptic orientation, insofar as its presence is evident in particular Pauline tropes, topoi, and mythemes, or his reading of Scripture with a view to the revision of biblical epic, or the presence of a Pauline ethic of self-mastery and harmony of the social body. The differences, then, are matters of emphasis.

A major conclusion of Mack's analysis of the Christ traditions in 1 Corinthians and the construction of Paul's gospel is the difference between the social logic of a martyr myth for Jesus schools and *christos* associations and the logic of Paul's elaborated Christ myth. The figure of Christ is inserted by Paul "as the mechanism by which the promise [to Abraham and his descendants] became a message," but it can serve that function only because Paul conceives of Christ's death and resurrection "as an event of cosmic restructuring and apocalyptic inauguration.... [I]t was Paul's apocalyptic mentality that drove his mythmaking":

> And it was this apocalyptic persuasion, not the Christ myth, that informed the ways in which he understood the legacy and promise of "Israel"; the state of the world on its way to final judgment; the threat to the traditions of the fathers that he saw in the Jesus movements; his precipitous conversion, intellectual about-face, and tumble into the *christos* associations; his obsession with thoughts of the sovereignty, power, and agency of God; and his vision of a universal kindom of God calling for mission to the Gentiles and the restoration of Israel.[55]

Thus, it is the resurrection of Christ as an event of apocalyptic inauguration that turns a martyr myth into "the message of great changes occurring in history, cosmos, and divine plans for the eschaton."[56] In Mack's paper, it is this apocalypticized Christ myth that also accounts for the disjunction he sees between Paul and the

---

line Johnson Hodge, *If Sons, Then Heirs: A Study of Kinship and Ethnicity in the Letters of Paul* (New York: Oxford University Press, 2007); see also Denise Kimber Buell and Caroline Johnson Hodge, "The Politics of Interpretation: The Rhetoric of Race and Ethnicity in Paul," *JBL* 123 (2004): 235–51; and, more broadly, Denise Kimber Buell, *Why This New Race: Ethnic Reasoning in Early Christianity* (New York: Columbia University Press, 2005).

52. Mack, "Rereading the Christ Myth," 61–62.
53. Arnal, "Paul and the Corinthians," 89–91.
54. Stowers, "Kinds of Myth," 123–24, 134–35.
55. Mack, "Rereading the Christ Myth," 60, 62.
56. Ibid., 63.

Corinthians on communication about or with spirit(s)/Spirit, which very likely had surfaced as the most sustaining topic of mutual interest. The disjunction is explained along the lines of Smith's proposal. "The Corinthians were working with standard, age-old funereal conceptions of memorials for their special dead as ancestors. Paul was proposing a proleptically eschatological crucifixion and resurrection as an image of transformation."[57]

Arnal relies largely on Stowers's reading of Romans to propose a situational incongruity that not only has important features of commonality for Paul and his Corinthian audience, but which is also specific to Paul's "focus on righteousness, ethnicity, and collective identities as considerations driving Paul's comments in Romans and, perhaps, his gospel as a whole."[58] However, the departure from Stowers's reading to which Arnal refers[59] is no minor matter for understanding Paul's gospel and the role of the Christ myth in it. Indeed, it is the difference that generates Arnal's own proposal for bringing Paul and the Corinthians together. In Stowers's reading of Romans, the problem addressed by Paul is consistently the status of Gentiles before the righteousness of the God of Israel, not the status of Israel. In the interest of constructing a plausible social context for the emergence of Paul's gospel, Arnal proposes that it is the state of Israel's condition in the world and the failure of Israel to achieve righteousness ("by Paul's exacting standards") that occasions a situational incongruity for Paul.[60] If this is the case, the rectification of this situational incongruity is the vindication of the martyr because it announces God's approval for righteousness. The Christ myth thereby provides the crucial resolution of the problem of Israel's status with respect to righteousness, even if it is "not the substance or motive of Paul's work, but a lever that he uses to accomplish his real agenda, a mission to the Gentiles and, thereby, a reconstitution of Israel."[61]

> This is a commonplace enough notion for a martyr, and so we hardly need imagine any earth-shattering *novum* to account for it prior to Paul. For Paul himself, however, struggling, as it were, with the "anti-vindication" of Israel's scattered

---

57. Ibid., 64–65, adding: "Even if the Corinthians may have been interested in 'belonging to Israel,' some apparently balked at the acceptance of the Christ myth as the means. And it apparently was not clear, even to those who may have been willing to entertain the Christ myth, how it might affect their relation to their own recent and special dead, how they were to live differently in the world, and why the new spirits (of Christ and the Lord) wanted to cancel out their relations with (and 'knowledge' of) the old familiar ones" (65).

58. Arnal, "Paul and the Corinthians," 90.

59. Ibid., 90–91.

60. Ibid., 91. Arnal has stated the difference in relation to the reading of the specific passage in Rom 2:17–24, but the different reading there has implications for Stowers's general thesis. For his part, Arnal has sought to avoid misunderstanding of his position and carefully specifies what he means by the crisis of identity and failure of Israel to achieve thoroughgoing righteousness (90–91).

61. Ibid., 92.

existence, as a result of its identity-confounding lack of perfect righteousness, such an action on God's part assumes enormous consequentiality.... By combining this rather prosaic idea with the larger problem of Israel's identity, function in the world . . . , and the need for divine rectification . . . , the idea of Jesus' death and vindication suddenly assumes cosmic importance.[62]

Apparently, the difference between Mack and Arnal on the significance of the Christ myth in Paul's gospel turns on the former's appeal to Paul's apocalyptic persuasion and the latter's appeal to the problematic status of Israel for Paul. But this is misleading in two ways and overlooks points of greater consequence. First, Mack is not attempting to *explain* Paul's project or self-identification; he does not think that Paul's attraction to a martyr myth can account for either of these.[63] Mack's appeal to Paul's apocalyptic thinking is instead an attempt to account for Paul's use of the Christ myth in the interest of giving his project both urgency and worldwide, world-historical significance.[64] This emphasis on the way in which Paul uses the Christ myth may actually make the notion of a Pauline apocalyptic myth itself misleading, as though such a myth were somehow prior to and independent of Paul's use of the Christ myth for his gospel. For Mack, apocalyptic themes, topoi, images, and scenarios are varied, but are always to be seen as secondary to other social interests which they serve. On Mack's analysis, Paul's Christ myth does not explain Paul's Gentile mission or Corinthian social formation in any singular way. That does not mean that Mack thinks no significant interaction between Paul and the Corinthians was taking place, including social formation and mythmaking. But it is precisely the role of the Christ myth as an *explanation* of Paul's own formation and of social formation among the Corinthians that Arnal wants to show, by attributing to this discursive formation significance as a meaningful response to a situational incongruity shared by Paul and those to whom he writes in 1 Corinthians.

Second, Arnal sees the martyr myth in Pauline usage, and especially the element of vindication, as the resolution of an "apocalyptic situation," a situation, defined by Smith, as the perception of a world out of order because of the loss

---

62. Ibid., 93, adding: "Jesus' death is an act of obedience on par, as an etiological founding gesture, with Abraham's call by God; and his 'resurrection,' an act of divine intervention as consequential as God's 'gift' of the land of Canaan to his people" (ibid.).

63. Mack, "Rereading the Christ Myth," 59: "All we have to do is recognize that Paul was a Jew much interested in this question [of Gentile attraction to Judean institutions in Diaspora], and that he thought he had found a way to use the Jesus-*christos* associations and their martyr myth to invite and enable Gentiles to become 'Israel' without having strictly to become Jews. How and why he came to think that are questions that have never really been asked, much less answered, for all we have in his writings are arguments for his mission drawn from the many myths he had put together as his rationalization for the conviction."

64. Ibid., 61: "The event of 'Christ crucified and raised' had become the point in recent history where God or God's son touched down for a moment to let those open to a revelation of its significance know that the human situation that pertained since 'times past' had changed."

of native kingship.[65] This perception that the wrong king rules becomes increasingly widespread in the post-Alexandrian period of worldwide empires. In spite of Arnal's view that Mack has exaggerated Paul's apocalypticism,[66] Arnal's identification of Paul's problem with the status and righteousness of Israel and with the status of other native peoples under imperial conditions reflects an apocalyptic situation requiring divine rectification of cosmic importance.[67] This construction

---

65. "Apocalyptic situation" is the label used by Smith to describe the social and intellectual conditions that give rise to the production of an apocalyptic literary genre, though responses to the perception of an apocalyptic situation are by no means limited to the literary genre *apocalypse*. "In the Near Eastern context, two elements are crucial: scribalism and kingship. The *situation* of apocalypticism seems to me to be the cessation of native kingship; the *literature* of apocalypticism appears to me to be the expression of archaic, scribal wisdom as it comes to lack a royal patron" (Smith, "Pearl of Great Price and a Cargo of Yams," 7 [emphasis original]; repr. in *Imagining Religion*, 94).

66. "In general," Arnal writes, "I think that the apocalypticism of Paul and its salience for understanding his project have been greatly exaggerated, both in standard scholarship and in Mack's redescription of Paul" ("Paul and the Corinthians," 96).

67. See above, 260–61 with n. 62. Arnal's critique of Mack on the significance of Paul's apocalypticism is especially the problem of equating the use of apocalyptic tropes and mythemes with a utopian worldview, whereas a typological characterization of worldviews along the lines of Smith's distinction between an "apocalyptic situation" and a "Gnostic situation" would lead to a characterization of Paul's thought, if utopian, as tending toward the Gnostic end of the typological spectrum (ibid., 95–97; and see Arnal's comparison of the myth of Hainuwele and Paul's inversionary language in 1 Cor 1:21–29 [100–101]). Arnal's observation about the essentially locative orientation of apocalyptic in Smith's work is correct; however, a utopian type worldview is not *limited* by Smith to the Gnostic pattern characterized by the perception that the wrong god is on the throne. See the discussion of the long history of reinterpretation of the Egyptian *Potter's Oracle* in Jonathan Z. Smith, "Wisdom and Apocalyptic," in *Religious Syncretism in Antiquity: Essays in Conversation with Geo Widengren* (ed. Birger A. Pearson; Series on Formative Contemporary Thinkers 1; Missoula, Mont.: Scholars Press, 1975), 145–54; repr. in idem, *Map Is Not Territory: Studies in the History of Religions* (SJLA 23; Leiden: Brill, 1978; repr., Chicago: University of Chicago Press, 1993), 78–85.

In any case, both Smith and Mack regard Paul's Christ myth as an example of a utopian worldview. It is the utopian worldview of Paul in particular that Stowers has argued is undertheorized in Smith's work, proposing a rectification of the category in terms of the conditions and effects of a semiautonomous cultural field: "My proposal, then, entails that the attitudes and practices that Smith describes as utopian derive from conditions of specialists whose religion is that of bookish interpretation whose norms are produced by the interactions with other such specialists in various degrees of distance and autonomy from 'everyday religion'" ("Kinds of Myth," 145). This is a useful proposal, particularly in showing the connection between the intellectualizing practices of Paul and those of later interpreters of the Cybele-Attis cult, and it certainly has an advantage as an explanation over Smith's limited appeal to "alienation and *ressentiment*" (Jonathan Z. Smith, *Drudgery Divine: On the Comparison of Early Christianities and the Religions of Late Antiquity* [Jordan Lectures in Comparative Religion 14; London: School of Oriental and African Studies, University of London; Chicago: University of Chicago Press, 1990], 134 n. 35, 141). But the question is whether Stowers's proposal is itself too limited in suggesting the attitudes and practices of a counterculture of disaffected intellectuals, even when this is theorized as the conditions that make a particular cultural field possible. Smith has stressed that locative and utopian worldviews are "coeval existential possibilities," so that locative should not

is important for understanding the appeal of the Christ myth, according to Arnal, even though at the same time he wants to move away from Mack's emphasis on apocalyptic schemata, particularly with respect to the significance of burial (1 Cor 15:4) as a Pauline addition to the *kērygma*, seeing the emphasis for Paul to fall on unified group identity in baptism and the reception of the spirit.[68] Finally, since

---

be equated with primordial and archaic (Jonathan Z. Smith, "The Wobbling Pivot," *JR* 52 [1972]: 147; repr. in *Map Is Not Territory*, 101; cf. idem, "When the Chips are Down," in *Relating Religion*, 16). Moreover, when he has identified the dominance, or seeming dominance, of one over the other in a particular time and place, Smith has related this to political and social conditions of very wide scope, affecting also the attitudes, practices, and vested interests of intellectuals. Some of the perspectives of Paul's intellectual activity may be described appropriately as the effect of the autonomy of a field of cultural practices. But it is questionable whether such a "field effect" (Stowers, "Kinds of Myth," 144) can be disengaged from what Stowers agrees is the utopian thinking of a collective resurrection from the dead. Rectification and sanctification in Paul are ancillary to a deliverance from the wrath to come when Christ destroys every rule, authority, power, and finally death, the last enemy to be destroyed (1 Thess 1:10; 1 Cor 15:24, 26). One may legitimately appeal to the broader contemporary Greco-Roman descriptions of an age of decline, death, and renewal and justifiably call into question the scholarly construction of a two-aeon eschatology. But it remains quite clear that divine deliverance for Paul is inextricably linked to a collective resurrection from the dead, and thus also to a Christ who is the first fruits (1 Cor 15:20).

Taking into consideration that locative and utopian worldviews are found in the world on a continuum, and taking note of the *aspectual* feature in Smith's comparative methodology, there will be borderline phenomena and phenomena that fall into both categories. For an example of this in the interpretation of the archaeological data of early Christian burial, see Byron R. McCane, *Roll Back the Stone: Death and Burial in the World of Jesus* (Harrisburg, Pa.: Trinity Press International, 2003), 109–25, esp. 121–23; for an example applied to a study of the *Chaldean Oracles*, see Sarah Iles Johnston, "Working Overtime in the Afterlife; or, No Rest for the Virtuous," in *Heavenly Realms and Earthly Realities in Late Antique Religions* (ed. Ra'anan S. Boustan and Annette Yoshiko Reed; Cambridge: Cambridge University Press, 2004), 85–100, esp. 98–100. Arnal ("Paul and the Corinthians," 96–97 n. 51) also suggests that the terms "apocalyptic" and "apocalypticism" should be submitted to the same sort of critique to which "Gnosticism" recently has been subjected in the work of Michael Allen Williams (*Rethinking "Gnosticism": An Argument for Dismantling a Dubious Category* [Princeton: Princeton University Press, 1996]) and Karen L. King (*What Is Gnosticism?* [Cambridge, Mass.: Belknap Press of Harvard University Press, 2003]). For a critique of the use of "apocalyptic" and "apocalypticism" as synthetic theological categories in twentieth-century Pauline scholarship, see R. Barry Matlock, *Unveiling the Apocalyptic Paul: Paul's Interpreters and the Rhetoric of Criticism* [JSNTSup 127; Sheffield: Sheffield Academic Press, 1996]). The category of "biblical demiurgical traditions" suggested by Williams as a replacement for "Gnosticism" does not appear to fit Paul's thought or, for that matter, to offer comparison with the Corinthians. For an application of Williams's study to 1 Corinthians, see Todd E. Klutz, "Re-Reading 1 Corinthians after *Rethinking 'Gnosticism,'" JSNT* 26 (2003): 193–216. Klutz draws analogies between "the strong" of 1 Corinthians and the implied author of the *Gospel of Philip*, correlating high social status with intensified intragroup conflict, on the one hand, and with stronger intergroup harmony, that is, harmony with the wider society, on the other.

68. Arnal relies especially on Rom 6:3–4 to make the connection ("Paul and the Corinthians," 97).

"spirit possession" appears to have something to do with discourse and practices for both Paul and the Corinthians, Arnal concludes that "possession of or by the spirit (whatever this actually means, and however it actually is imagined to occur) is a major factor in Paul's mythologizing activity and may be the glue he uses to link the Jesus cluster of mythemes to the Abraham cluster of mythemes."[69]

Arnal's case for the place of the Christ myth in Paul's gospel is part of an argument intended to establish a link between Paul's mythmaking and the social interests and formation at Corinth. In making the argument, he has taken up the central analytical categories of our project and sought to demonstrate their nexus at a particular site. In response to his contribution, we would pose several questions. (1) Since Smith regards apocalyptic as an essentially scribal phenomenon characteristic of intellectual elites of native homelands,[70] is it helpful to extend perception of an apocalyptic situation to Diaspora populations in general, even to those more recently dislocated from their homelands? Imperial domination had existed in the Mediterranean world for centuries prior to the early Principate, and many different arrangements for dealing with this had developed, including the flourishing of native cultures in local temple centers, the existence of client kings and kingdoms, and the production of discursive formations that view diasporas as colonies of a homeland based on an imperial model—all of which suggest that the overriding political factor of imperial domination cannot be translated simply into cultural hegemony and the loss of traditional identities. Given these factors of long duration, is it likely that most people living in non-ancestral cities would have seen the status of their homelands as problematic and themselves as people "who have no nation"?[71] (2) Even if we assume that "burial" was triggered by baptism,

---

69. Ibid., 97–98. The importance of "spirit talk" as an index of matters of mutual interest for Paul and the Corinthians has been recognized in seminar discussions. The problem is that "spirit possession" has been made to cover many different kinds of practices and ignores the issue of reference to many different kinds of spirit. See Smith, "Re: Corinthians," 24–25 n. 24; and the reference there to the work of Raymond Firth (*Tikopia Ritual and Belief* [Boston: Beacon, 1967]).

70. Smith, "Wisdom and Apocalyptic," 154; repr. in *Map Is Not Territory*, 85: "In this paper I have suggested that Wisdom and Apocalyptic are interrelated in that both are essentially scribal phenomena. They both depend on the relentless quest for paradigms, the problematics of applying these paradigms to new situations and the *Listenwissenschaft* which are the characteristic activities of the Near Eastern scribe."

71. Arnal, "Paul and the Corinthians," 92; cf. 89–90, which we suggest is too narrow a construction of the sources of discontent and too broad an equation of the existence of empires with the problematic status of homelands. Nevertheless, Arnal's case for the appeal of Paul's ethnic mythmaking in the context of Roman imperial subjugation of nations could draw on the analogy of the West Papuans. While Smith's focus on the West Papuans concerns their recent uprooting and distance from ancestral gravesites, he also cites reports of their response to colonial expansion in the form of a native cargo movement. Some Corinthians may have seen in Paul's "more … mobile ancestor" and expanded Israel, his "non-ethnic 'Christian' *ethnos*" (Smith, "Re: Corinthians," 33), an expression of nativism, that is, a new traditionalism. Arnal has drawn on Smith's study of the myth of Hainuwele, a myth that according to Smith reflects "a *cargo situation* without a cargo cult," comparing it with Paul's rhetoric of inversion in 1 Cor 1 (Smith, "Pearl of Great Price and a Cargo of Yams," 15 [emphasis original]; repr.

does baptism as a rite of initiation explain Paul's insistence on the reality of the resurrection of Christ? (3) If righteousness and the status of Israel are the central factors that form Paul's situational incongruity, why does Paul at several points in his letters seem to be the opposite of one who had been deeply troubled by the adequacy of his own righteousness under the law or by the status of his Judean heritage in the world (Phil 3:3–6; 2 Cor 11:22; Rom 4:4–5)? (4) If the vindication of the martyr was seen by Paul to address the problem of righteousness with respect to the identity of Israel, how would this account for Paul's project, self-identity, and a preoccupation so intensely focused on Gentiles? Would the mixed constituency of the Jesus groups he encountered be sufficient to account for this? While raising these questions, we acknowledge that it is unlikely that Paul's self-identification and the scope of his entrepreneurial activities can be adequately accounted for apart from some sort of shared perception of situational incongruity.

The first part of Stowers's paper shows how Paul has constructed an identity for his audience as "former Gentiles who are now [to regard themselves as] descendants of the Israelite patriarchs, but not Jews." In so doing, Paul exhibits an "ethnic mythmaking that employs an aggregative strategy," a strategy and way of thinking that were common in the Greco-Roman world.[72] The occasion and the means of establishing a common ancestor of Judeans and former Gentiles are expressed in Paul's Christ myth. Jesus' heroic martyrdom is the occasion for realizing God's plan to bless the Gentiles. His resurrection shows that the promised blessing is about life that is lived in a condition transformed by God's *pneuma*, which is the most powerful and sublime material substance of the cosmos. Christ is the seed of Abraham by birth and the *pneuma*-bearer by his resurrection from the dead. Gentiles have come to share in this most powerful and sublime substance by baptism. Thus, Stowers suggests that, for Paul, the Christ myth is about noble ancestry and cosmic physics.[73] Both Arnal and Stowers see Paul's use of the Christ myth as essentially the construction of an ethnic and cosmic myth, but whereas for Arnal the context of significance is the imperial subjugation and dislocation of native peoples, for Stowers the historical context of significance is

---

in *Imagining Religion*, 98; cf. Arnal, "Paul and the Corinthians," 100–101). For a formulation very similar to Arnal's, making use of Roman visual representation, see Davina C. Lopez, "Paul, Gentiles, and Gender Paradigms," *USQR* 59/3–4 (2005): 101, 103: "Consideration of the imperial cult as the primary religio-political system in Paul's context must take its gendered expression, including but not limited to the depiction of conquered nations as women's bodies, seriously. . . . Judaea, then, is but *one* of *many* defeated nations. Could Paul have finally realized this and suggested not division but solidarity among the defeated, Jew and Greek alike?" (emphasis original). For a different characterization of Diaspora and its relationship to homeland for Judeans, see Erich S. Gruen, *Diaspora: Jews Amidst Greeks and Romans* (Cambridge, Mass.: Harvard University Press, 2002), 232–52.

72. Stowers, "Kinds of Myth," 124, citing Johnson Hodge, *If Sons, Then Heirs*. Stowers counters the objection that this ethnic construction is not present in 1 Corinthians by pointing to the evidence of 1 Cor 5:1; 10:1–3; 12:1–2 ("Kinds of Myth," 124–25).

73. Stowers, "Kinds of Myth," 122–26, 134–35.

the increasing production of specialized knowledge and the types of authority and practices associated with it among a class of producers, distributors, and consumers. And so, Stowers, more than Arnal, stresses a differentiated interest and reception of Paul's mythmaking related to social status concerns. Stowers is not offering an explanation of Paul's mission to the Gentiles, but is attempting to show how the audience of Paul's letters is constructed, and how his mission is legitimated. It is only in the second part of Stowers's paper that the death of Christ comes into focus as emblematic of a social ethos. Paul adapts a version of the martyr myth to construct a genre of eating practice, a peculiar mortuary foundation, which may have been construed by some as giving mixed and confusing signals, but which was also capable of revealing a genre error in Corinthian eating practices by appealing to practical skills known to his audience, "skills that connected eating to truth practices and social formation."[74] The absent body of the martyr is emblematic of a self that triumphs over the body of flesh and blood, entailing an ethic of self-mastery over personal desire and loyalty to the social body. Accordingly, just as the true self that is revealed in the benevolent will of the martyr exists in disjunction with the self of flesh and blood, so the tests of truth in eating are those of self-examination and a transformed mind, rather than signs discerned in the body of the sacrificed animal.[75]

There are several interesting tensions that are best seen in Stowers's account of Paul's Christ myth. First of all, there is what might be seen as a tension between the martyr and the *pneuma*-bearer. Do they reflect the same ethos? How is the ethic of self-mastery and communal loyalty achieved? By a struggle of the will and by right thinking similar to that of the martyr, or by an endowment of supernatural

---

74. Ibid., 135; cf. 133–34, 135–38. In agreement with Mack, Stowers strongly rejects taking Paul's words in this context "as a script or liturgy for the ritual," adding: "The account is also an etiological myth, but that observation may lead us to miss the important point, which is the way it functions in Paul's rhetoric. I suggest that the account is the specification of a genre of eating. Paul is saying that they have confused a genre of eating that focuses on the desire for food and drink, and that produces a certain pattern of social differentiation, with the genre of the Lord's supper" (136). In his article discussing poverty in the Pauline assembly, Friesen complains that scholars such as Theissen and Meeks, in analyzing 1 Cor 11:17–22, see that the situation described by Paul is about relative wealth and relative poverty, but end by focusing on differences of social status with the result that the poor referred to in the text disappear ("Prospects for a Demography of the Pauline Mission," 363–64). However, if it is for some a situation of poverty below the subsistence level, they also seem to disappear from Paul's sight. Stowers is right when he recognizes that the Lord's meal for Paul is not about eating. "If the Corinthians want food and feast, they have their own homes.... The food in the supper is not important as food, but as something that symbolizes and points to something else." Waiting for others rather than going ahead with one's own meal, and sharing the food, are important because they demonstrate the virtue of solidarity, and evidently not because they allow everybody to have enough food. The latter may indeed have been a pressing concern to some of the Corinthians; but it does not seem to be what is important to Paul (Stanley K. Stowers, "Does Pauline Christianity Resemble a Hellenistic Philosophy?" 239 [in this volume]). For a contrary view, see Suzanne Watts Henderson, "'If Anyone Hungers...': An Integrated Reading of 1 Cor 11:17–34," *NTS* 48 (2002): 195–208.

75. Stowers, "Kinds of Myth," 137–38.

substance by being physically connected with Christ the *pneuma*-bearer?[76] There is also a tension between Paul's ethnic mythmaking, which requires the principle of patrilineal lineage, and Paul's discourse on the Lord's meal, which rejects that principle, and from which it must be generically distinguished as a meal practice. Similarly, in his paper "Does Pauline Christianity Resemble a Hellenistic Philosophy?" Stowers contrasts the religious practices of "ethnic peoples" with Pauline practices that bear a closer resemblance to the practices of philosophy. Responding to those who emphasize Paul's familial language over the philosophical relationship of friendship, Stowers counters, "No matter how often one utters the word 'brother' or 'father,' using the language of family is not the same thing as the practices of a family, which include much more than the language." Yet, for Stowers, Paul's ethnic mythmaking is a discursive practice that intends to establish a substantive ethnic identity.[77]

There certainly are oddities in Paul's taking up the myth of a martyr and his vindication in order to construct an ethnic identity for Gentiles. On the one hand, the figure of Christ seems to be inserted into the construction. It would not be needed, if the issue were simply the status of Gentiles as full members of Diaspora synagogues, without becoming fully practicing Jews.[78] The same aggregative strategy and distinction between Judeans and full-member former Gentiles could apply on the basis of Abraham's faithfulness and God's promise. On the other hand, Christ is a descendant of Abraham by birth and one who, like Abraham, is faithful, though not by having a child, but by being handed over and put to death. Nevertheless, as the progenitor of a new Abrahamic lineage, the role of Christ would make sense in ancestral terms. But his place in this new lineage is not that of father but that of eldest sibling, despite the fact that the formula "in Christ," Paul's ubiquitous expression of belonging and identity, is far more appropriate for expressing the relationship of ancestor and descendants than the relationship of contemporaries, of brothers and sisters.[79] There is also considerable strain on

---

76. Ibid., 123–24, 125, 134–35. In addition to Stowers's treatment of self-mastery in *Rereading of Romans*, see idem, "Paul and Self-Mastery," in *Paul in the Greco-Roman World: A Handbook* (ed. J. Paul Sampley; Harrisburg, Pa.: Trinity Press International, 2003), 524–50. On Paul's picture of himself in 1 Cor 9:24–27, Stowers comments: "This passage confirms my reading of Romans in which the defeat of *akrasia* and the attainment of self-mastery is *one* central goal of the gospel. The surprise is that Paul represents himself as still violently struggling rather than having reached the calm victory of the wise man." According to Stowers, the "surprise" (from a Stoic perspective) can be accounted for by recognizing that "Paul posits an inherently irrational tendency to the body that can only be fully eliminated by a substantive change caused by the divine *pneuma*" (540 [emphasis original]). If this is the case, it implies that those who are in Christ do not achieve this self-mastery in the same way that Jesus achieved it.

77. Stowers, "Pauline Christianity," 242. This is not meant to ignore Stowers's discussion of the tensions in Paul's mythmaking nor Stowers's account of how they make sense ("Kinds of Myth," 112, 141–42). But for the moment we wish to present our own formulation of these tensions.

78. Cf. Mack, "Rereading the Christ Myth," 59–60.

79. Mack explains this oddity by reference to the function of Christ's death and resurrection

the use of an aggregative ethnic strategy. While the asymmetry of such constructions is quite usual, in this case the asymmetry is pronounced, if not jarring, and an obvious reason for resistance to Paul's message. As Caroline Johnson Hodge remarks, "Paul never says . . . that the *Ioudaioi* have to give up any portion of their ethnic and religious identity. Their God, their practices, their scriptures are all intact. The gentiles, by contrast, must give up goods that are central to their identity: their gods, religious practices, myths of origin, epic stories of their ancestors and origins."[80]

It is difficult to avoid the conclusion that Paul's interest falls especially on the vindication of the martyr as an event of transformation, of divine approval of righteousness, and of apocalyptic inauguration expressed as the sharing of the divine *pneuma* that raised Christ from the dead. Those who are "in Christ" have received the power of a transformed moral and material existence and are now enabled to live on a pneumatic level different from that of most of the children of Abraham, a level of existence that might already be thought of as more appropriate for another world. In the formulation of Johnson Hodge: although "we might understand Paul as fostering a common habitus for the assemblies"—a set of "shared experiences, practical skills, and ways of viewing the world"—we must acknowledge that these assemblies did not look like other ethnic groups. For

> Paul does not develop a language of peoplehood for the established communities of Christ followers. . . . Paul is also unconcerned with intergenerational continuity among the assemblies. . . . Perhaps both of these characteristics make sense given Paul's own apocalyptic expectation. Paul constructs kinship ties to give gentiles a new heritage, but he is not interested in their descendants. Indeed, intergenerational continuity is irrelevant for those awaiting the imminent end of the world and an age to come. . . . For Paul, the logic of ethnicity and kinship offers a solution to the problem of how Jews and the non-Jewish peoples can be reconciled on Jewish terms at the end of the age.[81]

But surely this reconciliation is also ironic, since it is achieved by means of a construction of ethnic identity that eliminates the very concerns, practices, and interactions that such constructions are normally designed to rationalize. The oddity of

---

in Paul's gospel "as an event of cosmic restructuring and apocalyptic inauguration," bringing together his Abraham myth and his apocalyptic myth "in such a way as to imagine the turn of the aeons in the grand plan of Israel's God, and so commission as urgent his own mission to the Gentiles" (ibid., 62).

80. Johnson Hodge, *If Sons, Then Heirs*, 140–41; cf. Stowers, "Pauline Christianity," 241.

81. Johnson Hodge, *If Sons, Then Heirs*, 150, 151, citing G. Carter Bentley, "Ethnicity and Practice," *Journal for the Comparative Study of Society and History* 29 (1987): 24–55; Pierre Bourdieu, *Outline of a Theory of Practice* (trans. Richard Nice; Cambridge Studies in Social and Cultural Anthropology 16; Cambridge: Cambridge University Press, 1977).

Christian ritual for the first two hundred years, to which Stowers refers,[82] is clearly related to the oddity of Paul's ethnic thinking and his figure of Christ at the meal. As Stowers himself has noted, though almost parenthetically, "Paul's teachings and mythmaking were centrally about kinship and ancestry, *even if not in a typically locative way.*" The Lord's meal belongs to "the genre of mortuary foundations. . . . This is so *even if it is odd for the dead to also be alive and to promise a return as judge of the world.*"[83] What Stowers describes as untypical and odd are the very matters that Smith and Mack appeal to as evidence that Paul and the Corinthians were talking past one another.[84] Nevertheless, these tensions do not argue against Stowers's main point: Pauline mythmaking and practice must be seen as the production and distribution of a specialized knowledge whose direct appeal would be to a limited niche of consumers.

---

82. Stowers, "Pauline Christianity," 242–43: "Christian ritual in the first two hundred years was an odd sort of ritual by ancient standards."

83. Stowers, "Kinds of Myth," 112, 136 (emphasis added).

84. Although it would be likely and unsurprising that "talking past one another" was also in the mix of communication between Paul and the Corinthians, this should not discount or diminish the significance of "varied resistances, appropriations, and negotiations" (ibid., 149). However, we are not persuaded that the tension in Paul's case of "non-ethnic" and "ethnic" is accounted for as a quite ordinary example of ethnic construction joined to a myth and ritual that breaks socioreligious boundaries. The issue is not resolved by recognizing that ethnicity is constructed even when it is appealed to as primordial. Paul's construction of ethnicity for Gentiles in Christ entails a radical abandonment, or at least a severe devaluing, of any kind of previously constructed sociocultural or socioreligious identity. This can be attributed only in part to philosophical critique of traditional cultural practices, including relations with the gods, because it requires acknowledging the God of one of the recognized ethnic peoples, the Judeans, and, as Stowers notes, "a new version of the master narrative of the Judeans" ("Pauline Christianity," 241). What Paul's ethnic construction might entail for relating in complex and flexible ways to the varied populations of Corinth or to branches of the Abrahamic family outside Christ is less than clear in Paul's writings, which are deeply concerned with erecting boundaries. Nor does it seem that, for *Paul*, Christ is a boundary-crossing figure in the sense of Herakles or other dual-aspect figures, both dead hero and god. Christ is a boundary-breaking figure because of his resurrection from the dead, the first fruits of those who sleep, not because he continues to be both dead hero and sovereign Lord. And while it is possible, perhaps even likely, that a figure like Herakles might come to mind for Corinthians attempting to understand Paul's Christ, it would perhaps have been closer to home for Corinthians to think of such dual figures who were honored as heroes with certain rites at their tombs and with other rites when worshiped as gods (see below, n. 124). It is true that "Paul's argument [in 1 Cor 15] assumes that the same people who deny the more general resurrection had no problem with Christ's resurrection" (Stowers, "Kinds of Myth," 146 n. 101). But this is no more indicative of Corinthian understanding or acceptance of that teaching than Paul's argumentative use of their practice of baptism for the dead is indicative of why it made sense to them to engage in the practice. Stowers seems closer to accounting for the tension when he recognizes that Paul continues "to understand himself as working within Judaism" ("Pauline Christianity," 241) and sees that "even if the Corinthians had fully understood what Paul wanted them to do, they would have been selective about what they wanted to do, and could not have given up their religion wholesale, even if they had wanted to do so" ("Kinds of Myth," 112).

Burial, Memorials, and Cults of the Dead

Richard S. Ascough's survey clearly demonstrates the close relationship between burial practices and the display of social status.[85] Most important for the argument of his paper are the clear involvement of associations in the familial duties of burial and memorial and the establishment of fictive kinship among association members.[86] "An association becomes the 'socially constructed replacement for the family.'"[87] It follows from this that burial, memorials, and graveside banquets in association settings can be viewed as a new context for the display of social status, the maintenance of collective identity, and the concerns of generational continuity found in kinship groups.[88] The flourishing of associations in the early Roman

---

85. Ascough, "Paul's 'Apocalypticism,'" 155–72. Similarly, Joseph Lee Rife has stressed social differentiation from the archaeological evidence of burial in Corinth. The variation in design of monumental tombs in the Corinthia "reflects a subtle differentiation into many layers of status among the highest elite and the somewhat lower social strata." Individual burials also varied in the type, value, and quantity of burial goods. "This diversity is an important index of the microcosmic variation in individual identity that operated below the highest class, a variability that is absent from the contemporary literature. It reflects a complex society in which status was determined by a network of factors and on numerous levels in reference to a clearly delineated elite model" ("Death, Ritual, and Memory in Greek Society During the Early and Middle Roman Empire" [2 vols.; Ph.D. diss., University of Michigan, 1999], 1:257, 327). This picture of variation in burial related to status makes a different impression, however, if one compares the changes that occur with the introduction of the Roman practice of cremation in Roman Corinth and Asian Ephesos. In both cities the practice was introduced by Roman settlers. "At Ephesos, however, the introduction of cremation led to the opposite of what one finds at Corinth. Instead of a stable collection of modest receptacles, cremation at Ephesos led to a cycle of increasing ostentation in burial containers, a 'style war' between the Roman settlers and the provincials. Thus, the same burial practice shows diametrically opposite patterns of use at Corinth and at Ephesos" (Christine M. Thomas, "Placing the Dead: Funerary Practice and Social Stratification in the Early Roman Period at Corinth and Ephesos," in Schowalter and Friesen, *Urban Religion in Roman Corinth*, 293). Thomas explains that the Roman freedmen in Corinth held Roman citizenship and did not have to confront a powerful and wealthy Greek provincial elite that did not have Roman citizenship. But this was the case for Roman freedmen and citizens in Ephesos, who sought to distinguish themselves from a provincial elite—guardians of a Greek cultural heritage, wealthy, but without Roman citizenship, and emulating Roman burial practices in the new situation—by a show of greater ostentation in the design of their ash chests (292–99).

86. Ascough, "Paul's 'Apocalypticism,'" 169–72.

87. Ibid., 170, citing Smith, "Here, There, and Anywhere," 31; repr. in *Relating Religion*, 330.

88. Ascough relates the matter of replacement to associations in Rome with their *columbarium* and gardens for funeral feasts. "Such associative practices replace the more traditional practice of having a family meal" ("Paul's 'Apocalypticism,'" 171). The notion of replacement is made even more emphatic because Ascough cites passages from the work of Arnold van Gennep (*The Rites of Passage* [trans. Monika B. Vizedom and Gabrielle L. Caffee; London: Routledge and Kegan Paul; Chicago: University of Chicago Press, 1960], 164–65) on rites of passage and from McCane (*Roll Back the Stone*, 52) on death and burial in first-century Palestine, which are concerned with explaining the import of graveside meals for maintaining generational continuity among family members. Ascough applies these statements to the practices of associations and the relations of fictive kin ("Paul's 'Apocalypticism,'" 171–72 with nn. 108–9). In fact, McCane (*Roll Back the Stone*, 49–52) is emphasizing the strictly

Empire is related to the high level of social disruption. The first century C.E. was a time of a "new geography" and Thessalonica in this period "was a place full of persons displaced from their homeland." Corresponding to social formations located "anywhere" are mythmaking strategies transferring the locus of home from "down here" to a home that is "on high."[89] What Ascough is bringing into view is the appropriate sociocultural setting for understanding both the question raised by the Thessalonians and the response given by Paul in his "apocalyptic" scenario.

Ascough presents a strong case for locating "the social practices that are lurking behind [Paul's] words" in 1 Thess 4:13–18.[90] The Thessalonians are asking about their relation to their dead and Paul's response is that those who have died in Christ not only continue to belong to the association but will "hold a privileged position at the *parousia* of Jesus."[91] Questions about belonging and group boundaries prove to be pertinent and are likely to have arisen inevitably with respect to the dead in view of Paul's preaching of Christ. Equally pertinent is the question that Ascough adds to the mix: "What if adherence to the Christ-hero disrupted a pattern of burial practices without offering anything in its stead?"[92] But surely we may press further on precisely this question and ask, What does Paul's response offer in its stead? It would seem to be the expectation of a cataclysmic event, in which the living and the dead of the community are collectively saved from the wrath of God (1 Thess 5:9–10). While we agree that Paul clearly has the question of belonging in view as the goal of the *parousia* of Christ ("and so we shall always be with the Lord," 1 Thess 4:17b), this affirmation is made in the context of a collective deliverance (1 Thess 1:10; 5:9). The question about the status of the dead in 1 Thessalonians is not treated apart from the issue of escaping the wrath of God. We must therefore continue to ask how this apocalyptic scenario relates to the typical concerns of burial, memorials, and cults of the dead in the practices of associations surveyed in the paper.[93]

---

private context of this practice, which was deeply rooted for centuries among Jews in Palestine, despite the public recognition of the impurity of corpses and graves and the biblical injunctions that sought to forbid or discourage such practices.

89. Ascough, "Paul's 'Apocalypticism,'" 170, 172 with nn. 98–100, drawing on the description in Smith, "Here, There, and Anywhere," 30, 31; repr. in *Relating Religion*, 330–31.

90. Ascough, "Paul's 'Apocalypticism,'" 151–52.

91. Ibid., 180.

92. Ibid., 155.

93. In our judgment, McCane's observation about the social locations and social energies differentiating funerary from apocalyptic representations of paradise retains its significance, even though we do not agree with the way he dissolves the tension in 1 Thess 4:13–18. "At first glance it might seem that 1 Thess 4:13–18 forms an exception to this assertion, since both funerary and apocalyptic content appear to be present in that text, but as a matter of fact the subject matter is entirely apocalyptic" (*Roll Back the Stone*, 139 n. 13). Ascough does not dispute the general validity of McCane's differentiation, only the validity of its application to Paul in 1 Thessalonians ("Paul's 'Apocalypticism,'" 181). Yet, in fact, Ascough does not take the different contexts seriously. He joins the evidence of Greco-Roman eschatological beliefs with the evidence of Roman funerary banquets and beliefs in an afterlife as the

It is not clear from Ascough's account how we are to imagine a move by Paul from a situation in which his preaching turned them away from "idols," including the cult of the ancestors, to serve the living God ("since one did not continue to honor those of the past, according to Paul"), to a situation in which he "affirms what would have been the practice of the pre-Christian association of Thessalonian workers" and "allows the inclusion of the dead among the living through funerary rites while introducing the apocalyptic arrival of the deity."[94] As Ascough presents it, this move seems far too facile.[95] Is it not more likely that Paul addresses the issue of the relation of the dead and the living in the context of the *parousia* of Christ precisely because he recognizes the importance of the status of the dead for establishing group cohesion and boundary formation, while intending at the same time to "wean" the association from the very sorts of practices that bound them to their "idolatrous" past? This dual aim can be compared with Paul's treatment of another matter of widespread practice and social bonding, the eating of sacrificial meat (εἰδωλόθυτος) in 1 Cor 8–10. Whatever concessions Paul is ready to make on the issue of "idol" food, because what one eats is a matter of indifference, his primary concern is to establish unity by strengthening the social boundaries of those who would follow his instructions and avoid inviting continued competing loyalties.[96] Moreover, the exclusivity of the Jerusalem sanctuary space can work as

---

appropriate background for the Thessalonian reception of Paul's scenario, without any indication that the eschatology and the funerary practices may apply to very different contexts: "The polytheistic context provides enough evidence that belief in an afterlife and fear of a divinely mandated cataclysm were widely known" (176).

94. Ascough, "Paul's 'Apocalypticism,'" 176, 178, 181.

95. If Ascough is correct that Paul's initial preaching would necessarily have been directed also against cults of the dead and that the Thessalonians "have given up not only their burial rituals but also their normative practice of banqueting with the dead" (ibid., 180), one has to ask quite pointedly what is meant by interpreting Paul's response in 1 Thess 4:13–18 as an affirmation of the practice of their pre-Christian association of "commemoration and inclusion of the dead in the social configuration of the association of the living" (178). Would Paul now be approving the practice of banqueting with the dead? Although Ascough and McCane presuppose a different question being asked by the Thessalonians, what is common to their treatment of 1 Thess 4:13–18 is that they both dissolve the tension between the question asked and the response given by Paul.

96. See Stanley K. Stowers, "Elusive Coherence: Ritual and Rhetoric in 1 Corinthians 10–11," in *Reimagining Christian Origins: A Colloquium Honoring Burton L. Mack* (ed. Elizabeth A. Castelli and Hal Taussig; Valley Forge, Pa: Trinity Press International, 1996), 76–79, on the deep tension that runs through Paul's discourse in chs. 8–10, oscillating between a "calculus of differing goods for different people in the community" and an opposition of epic proportions "of loyalty to the true self, morality, God and the people of God versus unbounded desire, sin against self, kin, and nature, rejection of God and one's people for service to demons and false gods[.] The two discourses are so out of proportion that they fracture the unity of the rhetoric" (78). On the problematic for Paul of all other social identities and loyalties outside Christ, see Alistair Scott May, '*The Body for the Lord': Sex and Identity in 1 Corinthians 5–7* (JSNTSup 278; London: T&T Clark, 2004), 267. May notes that Paul's desire to preserve existing marriages overcomes his objection to exogamy (1 Cor 7:14), but he also observes that the logic of this position is not maintained. "If the sanctification of the unbelieving spouse is the result

a heuristic model for the way in which Paul represents *ekklēsia* space with obvious implications for cultic meals outside the *ekklēsia*.[97] On this heuristic model, the implications would be similar for participation in ancestral cults. Indeed, Paul's exhortation to the Corinthians to shun the worship of idols (1 Cor 10:14) may well include cults of the dead, if εἰδωλόθυτος can also refer to meals and offerings to the dead.[98]

---

of (marital) union with a believer, then what objection can there be to a believer marrying one who is not 'in the Lord'?" (230, in reference to 1 Cor 7:39).

97. For the influence of Jerusalem sanctuary space as a discursive model for the construction of *ekklēsia* space, see Jorunn Økland, *Women in Their Place: Paul and the Corinthian Discourse of Gender and Sanctuary Space* (JSNTSup 269; London: T&T Clark, 2004). Økland refers to the unusual degree of cultic references in 1 Corinthians demonstrated in the work of John R. Lanci, "Building a Temple of God: Paul's Metaphor of the Community as a Temple in its Roman Corinthian Context" (Ph.D. diss., Harvard University, 1992); idem, *A New Temple for Corinth: Rhetorical and Archaeological Approaches to Pauline Imagery* (Studies in Biblical Literature 1; New York: Lang, 1997). In ch. 5 of her book, Økland focuses on 1 Cor 11–14 dealing with ritual gatherings. Here she highlights the tensions of communication between discursive formations based on the representation of household space and Paul's representation of the *ekklēsia* as sanctuary space, as well as the tensions resulting from differing conceptions of sanctuary space (*Women in Their Place*, 131–67). In ch.7, she addresses the relationship between ritual, cosmology, and hierarchy, drawing on Jonathan Z. Smith's observations on Ezekiel (*To Take Place: Toward Theory in Ritual* [CSHJ; Chicago: University of Chicago Press, 1987], 73), and observing that Paul may be shaped by the same sanctuary discourse: "Because the ideal sanctuary space that Paul outlines has a firm boundary between holiness and pollution, as well as an ordered hierarchy, it could be decentered. In his ordering of the ritual gatherings [in] chs. 11–14, Paul 'maps' the internal space of the *ekklēsia* as a systemic hierarchy, defining where men are in relation to Christ and to women, where women are in relation to men and angels, where prophets are in relation to apostles, teachers and tongue speakers, and so on" (*Women in Their Place*, 229). Concluding on matters of intercultural translation, she observes, "Paul . . . seems to presuppose that as a micro-cosmos the *ekklesia* must claim exclusivity like the Jerusalem sanctuary and not become just another sanctuary in the Graeco-Roman civic cult system. This view also colours his understanding (or lack thereof) of what is going on in Corinth's various rituals and sanctuaries. . . . The associations that his notions and terminology . . . produced in his readers may not have been at all what he intended when he brought one spatial discourse (Jerusalem) into another one (Corinth)" (230). Martin has noted Økland's argument and concurs "that Paul's rhetoric in 1 Corinthians represents an attempt to configure the meetings of the gathered ἐκκλη-σία as 'sanctuary space' instead of 'household space'" ("Slave Families and Slaves in Families," 207 n. 1).

98. For this view, see Charles A. Kennedy, "The Cult of the Dead in Corinth," in *Love and Death in the Ancient Near East: Essays in Honor of Marvin H. Pope* (ed. John H. Marks and Robert M. Good; Guilford, Conn.: Four Quarters, 1987), 227–36. Derek Newton, *Deity and Diet: The Dilemma of Sacrificial Food at Corinth* (JSNTSup 169; Sheffield: Sheffield Academic Press, 1998), 102 n. 109, suggests that "the cult of the dead may well be one, rather than the only, ingredient of a variety of cultic backgrounds to 1 Cor. 8–10." The curse tablets found at the Demeter site in Roman Corinth also attest the role of the dead with the living (139–40); cf. Richard E. DeMaris, "Demeter in Roman Corinth: Local Development in a Mediterranean Religion," *Numen* 42 (1995): 105–17, esp. 108. Graydon F. Snyder is more emphatic in connecting the term with the dead in *Inculturation of the Jesus Tradition: The Impact of Jesus on Jewish and Roman Cultures* (Harrisburg, Pa.: Trinity Press International, 1999), 170: "The term εἴδωλον did not mean false gods and goddesses to the Gentiles. It referred positively to the presence or images of the special dead. There is no reason to exclude this meaning, that is, for the special dead,

Ascough's reference to the "practice of the pre-Christian association of Thessalonian workers"[99] raises another point. Is it likely that loyalty to a new patron deity of the association actually brought an end to all other existing loyalties, Paul's initial preaching and representation of the matter notwithstanding? Much of Ascough's discussion presupposes that their question about relations with the dead pertains only to the status of those who have died as members of the *ekklēsia*. True, these are the dead Paul has in mind when he refers to "those who are asleep" (1 Thess 4:13), but the questions raised by Mack, which Ascough is addressing in the course of his paper, are not limited to members of the *ekklēsia*.[100] The sense of belonging to the ancestral traditions lodged in the cult of the dead is concerned especially with the continuity of the generations.[101] Without discounting Ascough's view that the Thessalonians collectively "switched" their patron deity,[102] are we not still too wedded to Paul's imagination of the *ekklēsiai* of God as strongly bounded, cohesive alternative societies to be able to appreciate the complexity, tenacity, and extent of the concerns and practices impinging on the relations of the living and the dead? If the membership of the *ekklēsia* of the Thessalonians was constituted from an earlier professional association, these mostly male members did not cease to have families and are likely to have participated in other social networks.[103] We should recognize both the possibility for associations to take on familial duties in respect of the dead and the potential for associations to come into conflict with these duties.[104] What does not seem likely is for Paul to be encouraging the very

---

from the term εἰδωλόθυτος as Paul used it. To the contrary, the discussion of the table of δαιμονίων in 1 Cor. 10:14–22 requires it."

99. Ascough, "Paul's 'Apocalypticism,'" 178.

100. Mack includes the following questions: "What about genealogy? Have we as Christians lost our rootedness in the people to which we belonged, in our land and our ancestral lineage? Do the old traditional rites take our dead away from us? What about those who have died? What does belonging to the kingdom of God mean for us who still have our dead to consider? And what about Christians who die?" (Burton L. Mack, *Who Wrote the New Testament? The Making of the Christian Myth* [San Francisco: HarperSanFrancisco, 1995], 110).

101. Mack notes that this concern about generational continuity marked a widespread and deeper dis-ease in the Greco-Roman age because of the scale of dislocation from homelands and thus from traditional burial grounds. This is the context in which he asks, "What if joining the Christ cult exacerbated the problem instead of solving it?" (ibid.). If we assume that most of the recipients of Paul's letter are first- and second-generation residents of Thessalonica, it is likely that for some, especially those not carrying the burden of slave backgrounds, the ties to homeland are still important. But even those whose ties have been largely dissolved would have confronted matters of burial and commemoration of their dead since the time of residency in Thessalonica.

102. Richard S. Ascough, "The Thessalonian Christian Community as a Professional Voluntary Association," *JBL* 119 (2000): 322–24.

103. Ibid., 324–27.

104. Smith notes that "associations have the potential of working at cross purposes to the older conceptualizations of family in the religions of 'here,' as when differing memberships divide genealogical siblings while at the same time establishing new, intimate relations and loyalties among their socially created fellow 'brothers' and 'sisters'" ("Here, There, and Anywhere," 35; repr. in *Relating Reli-*

practices he had preached against,[105] or for his intervention in an earlier association, however successful in his view, to have constituted a dramatic "before" and "after" with respect to who counted as "their dead."[106]

Paul is writing to a predominantly, if not exclusively, Gentile audience.[107] The sections of Ascough's paper on category rectification and redescription are thematically joined by demonstrating the relevance of Greco-Roman eschatological beliefs and funerary practices against "the scholarly tradition of protecting early Jesus associations from the corrupting influences of paganism by keeping it embedded within Judaism."[108] Ascough has identified the appropriate cultural context for Thessalonian reception of Paul's apocalyptic scenario and shown the fundamentally social rather than theological issues addressed in 1 Thess 4:13–18. However, the demonstration of Greco-Roman eschatological beliefs similar to those of Jewish apocalyptic is not in itself a rectification of "apocalyptic" as a descriptive category. The terms we use make a difference when they are not simply another way of saying the same thing. The recognition of similar eschatological ideas found in Greek and Roman writers does indeed help to clarify how a Gentile audience is likely to "hear" Paul's mythmaking. But does it rectify the category, or simply call attention to the range of data belonging to the category? What seems to make the difference in Ascough's discussion is the flexibility of Paul's discourse in terms of its function. Paul can use it to threaten destruction and demonstrate the power of his God alone to deliver from the approaching cataclysm. He can also use it to address questions of status and group boundaries regarding "those who have fallen asleep."

The widespread currency of eschatological discourse in the early Roman Principate may be better described as a variety of expressions of a narrative genre concerned with the decline of civilization and the present age of sin.[109] In his commentary on Romans, Stowers summarizes the themes of this genre for his reading of Rom 1:18–2:16:

---

gion, 333). These cross-purposes may account in part for the "affliction" suffered by the Thessalonians (1 Thess 1:6; 2:14).

105. Ascough, "Paul's 'Apocalypticism,'" 176: "It is at least plausible that, given the Romanization in Thessalonica, one of the 'idols' against which Paul preached and from which the Thessalonian Jesus association turned to serve the 'living God' . . . was the cult of ancestors."

106. In his paper in this volume, Smith ("Re: Corinthians") has drawn specific analogies between the contemporary Atbalmin of Papua New Guinea and "some Corinthians." The intense preoccupation with relations to the dead among millions of converts to Christianity in the modern colonial and postcolonial era has a general relevance in this regard. For a recent postcolonial response, see Steven J. Friesen, ed., *Ancestors in Post-Contact Religion: Roots, Ruptures, and Modernity's Memory* (Religions of the World; Cambridge, Mass.: Center for the Study of World Religions, Harvard Divinity School, 2001).

107. Ascough, "Paul's 'Apocalypticism,'" 152.

108. Ibid., 177, a tradition extensively documented in Smith, *Drudgery Divine*.

109. Some of these expressions are cited by Ascough ("Paul's 'Apocalypticism,'" 173–75).

By the end of Augustus's reign, the themes of primeval degeneration, the sinful age, and the wrath of God had become established together with expectations of a return to the golden age.... Part of the historical meaning of Romans comes from imagining how readers in Paul's day would have received his pronouncement of God's judgment with hope of salvation and his account of the sinful degeneration of the Greeks and other nations. The revolution that created the Roman empire witnessed a developing ideology of sin, God's wrath, and hopes of a golden age. These ideas transcended ethnic boundaries of Jewish, Greek, and Roman. The labor of so much New Testament scholarship of attributing to Paul a pure Jewish pedigree falsifies history and is itself an ideological construct. Part of the power in Romans' discourse would have come not from the novelty of the message but from the way in which it played on politically and culturally charged themes that readers met daily on the images of coins, in public monuments, and in everyday discouse.[110]

Stowers and Ascough are making the same point about how Paul's readers would have received his pronouncements of God's judgment. In the Augustan age eschatological discourse is preeminently an imperial discourse, though of course it is also prominent in condemning and countering imperial agendas and propaganda.[111] However, it is not the term "apocalyptic" that is rectified in Stowers's wider discussion of the genre as much as the classical Western doctrine of "sin" as a universal demonic power or as the bondage of the will thought to be found especially in Romans. "Paul's language about the times being sinful ... fits within that broad and varied Jewish discourse known as apocalyptic."[112] While it is important to recognize overlapping cultural codes in the early Roman Empire for assessing the function of apocalyptic language in 1 Thessalonians, we would also maintain that there are differences of interests, agendas, and cultural codes operating in the question of the Thessalonians and the response of Paul to be taken into account, and thus a necessary labor of translation between them.

We have departed from Ascough's evaluation of the significance of 1 Thess 4:13–18 in seeing Paul's apocalyptic scenario not only as an assurance that the dead in Christ are included within the boundaries of the *ekklēsia* but also as a strategy for discouraging participation in rituals of mourning, memorial, and meals

---

110. Stowers, *Rereading of Romans*, 124.

111. On the Roman cultural revolution, see Andrew Wallace-Hadrill, "*Mutatio morum*: The Idea of a Cultural Revolution," in *The Roman Cultural Revolution* (ed. Thomas Habinek and Alessandro Schiesaro; Cambridge: Cambridge University Press, 1997), 3–22, who concludes: "Augustus' achievement was not just the establishment of a new political order, but also of a new cultural order" (22). The social expression of this new order was the use of specialist authority over traditional local elites; the mythic expression was what Mack has aptly characterized as "epic revision" (Mack, *Who Wrote the New Testament?* 35–38).

112. Stowers, *Rereading of Romans*, 185; see also Mack, "Rereading the Christ Myth," 42. Cf. Stowers's proposals for rectification of the categories "locative" and "utopian" ("Kinds of Myth," 142–46); and see above, n. 67.

with/for the dead, and especially, we would add, to discourage associating these practices with the status of the dead in Christ. As discussed above, this seems to be consistent with Paul's approach in 1 Corinthians to banqueting in other cultic contexts and with his tendency to represent "house churches" not as household space but as sanctuary space, especially on the model of an exclusive sanctuary space.[113] Thus, it would also be appropriate to suppose that if death in an apocalyptic context is the last enemy to be destroyed (1 Cor 15:26) in an age of decline and death, Paul's associations with death in a funerary context might be dominated by conceptions of the impurity of corpses and the danger of graves, precisely in a setting conceived of as sanctuary space. If this is correct, it would not necessarily have entailed a direct condemnation by Paul of participation in small family gatherings at gravesides on the part of those addressed in the letter, though we strongly suspect that Paul would not have been pleased to see such gatherings identified with what it meant to belong to Christ in the *ekklēsia*.[114] Paul's reference to "those

---

113. See above, 271–73 with nn. 96–97.

114. This would also be consistent with the broad range of evidence found among Jews for the public presumption of corpse impurity and the impurity of tombs in the placement and marking of graves in Roman Palestine, on the one hand, and the practice of eating meals with/for the dead among family members even in the vicinity of Jerusalem, on the other. Summarizing the archaeological evidence for early Roman Palestine, McCane states, "The funerary ritual of Jews in early Roman Palestine gave symbolic prominence to two cultural life values: kinship and ritual purity. As an expression of Jewish ethnicity, burial practices in this region and period were laden with symbolic representations of family and piety. Kinship relations were celebrated in the rituals of primary burial, mourning, and secondary burial, as well as in the persistence of a private cult of the dead" (*Roll Back the Stone*, 56). McCane reminds his readers that cooking pots are one of the most common finds in Jewish tombs from Roman Palestine. "Clearly [Jews in early Roman Palestine] were not obsessed with—or compulsive about—purity, since they did not hesitate to enter tombs for primary burial and secondary burial, and they also occasionally brought food to their dead. In this region and period, corpse impurity was a conventional boundary, not an inviolable barrier" (ibid.). Our view of the relevance of McCane's observations on Roman Palestine for Paul is based not on prioritizing a Palestinian Jewish environment in the background of Paul, but on what seems to be the larger discursive formation at work in 1 Corinthians in Paul's imagination of *ekklēsia* space. Furthermore, pollution resulting from death is hardly a notion limited to Jews in the Greco-Roman world. Diaspora Jews probably had about the same conceptions of pollution resulting from death as Greeks and Romans. For example, you would not bury the dead within the city walls. On Roman Corinth, Mary E. Hoskins Walbank writes, "To avoid pollution, the urban cemeteries had to be outside the *pomerium*, the legal and religious boundary of the city. This prohibition against burial within the city held until at least the mid-fourth century C.E., when it began to crumble under the impact of Christianity and the preference of Christians for burying near their place of worship" ("Unquiet Graves: Burial Practices of the Roman Corinthians," in Schowalter and Friesen, *Urban Religion in Roman Corinth*, 250). Our point is simply that, while Paul would have had a strong interest in distinguishing the *ekklēsia* in which the living and the dead await the *parousia* of Christ from those "who have no hope" (1 Thess 4:13), he would have been sufficiently familiar with the widespread practices of relations with the dead in the Greco-Roman world, including among Jews in Palestine and the Diaspora, to know that he could not require avoidance of all ritual relations with the dead in family contexts, any more than he could require Corinthians to avoid all dinner invitations outside the *ekklēsia*, or prohibit associations with "the immoral of this world" (1 Cor 5:10).

who are asleep" may be a euphemism, but in the context of 1 Thess 4:13-18 it is likely to have more significance. If Paul uses the expression to signify that the dead in Christ are not really dead but in some interim state, or if some of the recipients of the letter understood it that way, there are two very different conclusions that could be drawn: (1) the dead in Christ do not require and cannot benefit from meals with/for the dead; or (2) proximity to the dead in Christ does not convey impurity. We have suggested that it is the first that Paul intends for the *ekklēsia*; it is the second that was drawn in later Christian banquets for the dead.[115]

Ascough's position that 1 Thess 4:13-18 dispels any notion of a separation between the living and the dead does not clarify how relations between the living and the dead are maintained, or the relevance of Paul's response for the practices associated with burial, memorials, and cults of the dead.[116] His view of the significance of Paul's response is intended, at least in part, to counter the notion of a monolithic development of Christian burial practices, which he associates with Byron R. McCane's account of the later, Byzantine period of separation of Jewish and Christian burial practices in Palestine.[117] If Ascough is suggesting that 1 Thess

---

115. McCane cites the explicit repudiation of Jewish observances of corpse impurity as well as other Jewish practices in the third-century *Didascalia Apostolorum* and the fourth-century *Apostolic Constitutions* from Syria. These texts refer to the dead as those who sleep in the Lord and are at rest. This state of sleep is held to be the grounds for holding public worship in the cemeteries of the Christian dead (*Roll Back the Stone*, 115-16, citing *Did. Apost.* 6.22; *Apost. Const.* 6.30). McCane's judgment about the social significance of these texts may be correct: "[They] openly and aggressively advocate for change, and the energy with which they call for Christians to renounce Jewish ritual practices strongly suggests that their view was probably not the social norm. The implied reader of these documents, in fact, is a Jewish-Christian who still observes a number of customs from the 'Second Legislation'" (116-17).

116. Nor should it be forgotten that separation of the dead from the living is a normal part of death rituals not only with respect to the corpse but also with respect to the social persona. Indeed, there is as much of a need to maintain a boundary between the living and the dead as there is to maintain interactivity. Negotiating these conflicting needs in the interest of generational well-being and continuity can invite many occasions for thought, as Jonathan Z. Smith noted in an informal conversation with the editors. Cf. Sarah Iles Johnston, *Restless Dead: Encounters between the Living and the Dead in Ancient Greece* (Berkeley and Los Angeles: University of California Press, 1999), 286, 287: "Gods, dead, *goētes*: it is to the extraordinary figure that one looks for extraordinary help and the extraordinary, by definition, cannot dwell too comfortably among us. If the dead refrain from molesting us and agree to accommodate our desires, it is because the *goēs* understands what makes them extraordinary.... Like the diffracted images of a Picasso painting, the dead offer views of our own world that challenge our presumptions about it, but like such a painting, too, they also reward us with insights that we could not obtain from a simple photographic reflection."

117. Ascough, "Paul's 'Apocalypticism,'" 177, referring to McCane, *Roll Back the Stone*, 109-25. Ascough sees McCane's account as another instance of protecting Christianity from pagan influences by embedding the origins of Christianity in Judaism and allowing pagan influences only in subsequent periods with the implication that the later development is evidence of corruption and decline from pristine origins. This judgment of McCane's work is hardly justified by Ascough. The particular trajectory that McCane traces with respect to where the dead are buried is just as much an innovation in the fourth and fifth centuries among Greeks and Romans as among Jews in Palestine (see the reference to

4:13–18 provides us with mid-first-century data for burial and memorial practices that enter the archaeological record only at the end of the second century, the noneschatological character of the third-century findings has been presented in the work of Graydon F. Snyder:

> At death each person was remembered in the meal for the dead. Inscriptions often carried the information for that celebration. In any case, the prayers and acclamations, such as "In Peace, In Christ, In God," reflect the faith that the same peace that marked the faith community in life also marked the faith community with its extended family (in death). There is no sign of a more sophisticated immortality, nor does resurrection, at least as revivification or resuscitation, play any role. One must assume then that the popular story of Lazarus, and perhaps even Jonah, refers to the Christian peace (Orante) in the face of death.[118]

Although it seems unlikely that Paul's response was intended to encourage or condone cultic relations with the dead in Christ, his reference to those who are asleep and their privileged place at the *parousia* may have led some recipients of the letter to engage in their own mythmaking regarding the efficacy of the dead. This is not to suppose that all recipients of the letter understood 4:13–18 one particular way or responded in the same way. Why not suppose instead that this part of the letter as well as other parts occasioned a lively debate? Some may have been interested in the fate of the dead exclusively at the *parousia*, others may have advocated maintaining relations with the dead in the setting of their extended

---

Walbank, "Unquiet Graves," 250, cited above, n. 114). Moreover, Ascough's case can be sustained only if he could demonstrate that McCane is protecting Judaism from pagan influences in Roman Palestine. McCane also has a complaint about a scholarly tradition: "A generation ago, studies of early Judaism and Christianity drew heavily—*too* heavily—from early Christian literature, and generally concluded that Judaism and Christianity had effectively separated from each other by the end of the first century C.E.... The old notion of an early 'split' may still have its defenders, but social differentiation between Jews and Christians now appears to have been neither early nor abrupt, and may not have become pronounced in the region of Palestine until as late as the fourth century" (*Roll Back the Stone*, 109 [emphasis original]). The so-called parting of the ways has been addressed in some recent works and shown to be problematic, not least because it often equates ways in which Jews and Christians could be distinguished with the differentiation of Judaism and Christianity as bounded religions, mutually exclusive, and disembedded from social and political environments. See Adam H. Becker and Annette Yoshiko Reed, eds., *The Ways That Never Parted: Jews and Christians in Late Antiquity and the Early Middle Ages* (TSAJ 95; Tübingen: Mohr Siebeck, 2003); Daniel Boyarin, *Dying for God: Martyrdom and the Making of Christianity and Judaism* (Figurae: Reading Medieval Culture; Stanford: Stanford University Press, 1999); idem, *Border Lines: The Partition of Judaeo-Christianity* (Divinations: Rereading Late Ancient Religion; Philadelphia: University of Pennsylvania Press, 2004). On Christian influence on Judaism in Palestine from ca. 350 to 640, see Seth Schwartz, *Imperialism and Jewish Society, 200 B.C.E. to 640 C.E.* (Jews, Christians, and Muslims from the Ancient to the Modern World; Princeton: Princeton University Press, 2001), 179–202.

118. Graydon F. Snyder, *Ante Pacem: Archaeological Evidence of Church Life before Constantine* (Macon, Ga.: Mercer University Press, 1985), 167. This passage and others are cited by Smith (*Drudgery Divine*, 130–32) in support of a strictly locative model of Christian meals for the dead.

family traditions, while others may have taken Paul's references to the privileged dead in Christ as an indication of a special dead of powerful efficacy. Perhaps it was just the way in which the *ekklēsia* of the Thessalonians served as a forum for conversation and debate—as well as for ritual experimentation occasioned by the knowledge of a powerful patron—on such varied concerns as deliverance in an age of crisis, an enlarged sense of place in a multicultural city, and continuing responsibility to their dead that enhanced the attraction of what was formerly a group meeting on occasions of more limited horizon with fellow handworkers. While these interests are probably incompatible and do not correspond to a coherent set of practices, the same people may have maintained the tension of different landscapes, and even of incompatible practices, as long as each was important in some context. They may have fully intended to maintain older touchstones *and* also to be delivered by Jesus Christ from the impending wrath of God, without being able to bring these together either conceptually or in terms of a single, coherent identity. The Atbalmin of Papua New Guinea also participated in the Revival which would fill them with the Holy Spirit in anticipation of the return of Christ, if only they would destroy the temples of the indigenous religion, which they did not do. At the same time, most participated in a rival indigenous millenarian movement. There was much interest, debate, changing of sides, and innovating of new understandings. On the whole, however, they continued to live in the tension of competing landscapes that they themselves recognized to be incompatible. The ancient Thessalonian recipients of Paul's letter were even more recent *ekklēsia* people than the contemporary Atbalmin.[119]

Turning to 1 Corinthians in the last part of his paper, Ascough sees Paul engaged in a more deliberate founding of "an association around the cult of a hero."[120] Accordingly, he proposes that the Lord's meal text (1 Cor 11:23–25) and the Christ myth (1 Cor 15:3–5) point to a funerary foundation for some early, pre-Pauline Jesus association and that Paul's use and application of these traditions show that he has anticipated with the Corinthians the issue that arose among the Thessalonians "and thus encourages from the beginning the memorial meal for the dead."[121] Stowers has also commented on the similarity of Paul's description in 1 Cor 11 to a funerary meal. However, in noting the similarity Stowers calls attention to the mixed signals given by Paul's account, which differs from a typical mortuary foundation by featuring bread instead of the meat expected for a sacrificial feast.[122] If Ascough's proposal is correct that in coming to Corinth Paul made a point of emphasizing the funerary context of the meal eaten to honor the hero,

---

119. See Eytan Bercovitch, "The Altar of Sin: Social Multiplicity and Christian Conversion among a New Guinea People," in *Religion and Cultural Studies* (ed. Susan L. Mizruchi; Princeton: Princeton University Press, 2001), 211–35, esp. 221–30.
120. Ascough, "Paul's 'Apocalypticism,'" 181.
121. Ibid., 184.
122. Stowers, "Kinds of Myth," 135–37.

Paul's teaching may have contributed to the eating groups he finds so objectionable, since they are readily understood as arising from social status issues associated with family connections in groups that appear to be largely family based. Some Corinthians seem to have understood the meal to be for the special dead, which they associate with the display of social status and probably with benefits for the recently deceased. Whatever Paul initially taught about meal practice, it is his disapproval of the Corinthian practice that drives his discussion of the meal. On this basis, we can suggest that there is a connection between his "correction" of the Thessalonians and his "correction" of the Corinthians. Just as Paul assures the Thessalonians that the boundaries of the *ekklēsia* include the dead in Christ in order to "wean" them from "idolatrous" cults, so Paul stresses to the Corinthians that the meal is a memorial of the Lord's death "until he comes" in order to distinguish it not only from ordinary meals eaten at home but also from meals eaten with/for the special dead.

Ascough agrees with Mack that we must distinguish carefully between Paul's use of traditions in 1 Cor 11 and 15 and the pre-Pauline contexts, but posits a hero myth rather than a martyr myth as the original context. He proposes that the Lord's meal reflects the origins of an early Jesus association on the basis of a memorial foundation, rather than a myth of origins arising from an already existing meal practice of a Jesus-*christos* group, as Mack argued.[123] There are two major difficulties with Ascough's alternative proposal. The first is whether it is at all likely that a hero memorial would arise in the first place without a tomb. Since it would have been a local phenomenon to begin with, it is very difficult to think of analogies. Reference to burial (1 Cor 15:4a) would only call attention to the anomaly. Moreover, the death of the hero need not be a noble death since, as Ascough states, "it is only in death that the hero is raised to be with the immortals."[124] This points

---

123. Ascough, "Paul's 'Apocalypticism,'" 183 with n. 157.

124. Ibid., 183. The apotheosis of the hero does not resolve the anomaly, even if one takes ἐγή-γερται (1 Cor 15:4) as a statement of apotheosis, though that is certainly not the usual term to express the transformation to divine status, as Mack has noted ("Rereading the Christ Myth," 45–46). If one supposes that the tradition referred to a noneschatological sequel expressing transposition to a transcendent state, this sequel could as easily be joined to a martyr myth (47). The connection between the funerary meal and the apotheosis of the hero is also strange. Even in the case of figures of dual aspect, both human hero and god, the rites appropriate to each aspect seem to have been maintained, or at least to have been discussed (see Elizabeth R. Gebhard, "Rites for Melikertes-Palaimon in the Early Roman Corinthia," in Schowalter and Friesen, *Urban Religion in Roman Corinth*, 165–203, esp. 173, 179–81, 193–94). Gebhard believes that the Roman colonists continued the specifically chthonic rites of the hero cult for the hero-god Melikertes-Palaimon when the Isthmian games were returned to Corinth ca. 40 B.C.E. The oddity is even more pronounced in Paul's meal text because the meal, which is like a mortuary foundation, is the *kyriakon deipnon* and is described with reference to *kyrios Iēsous*, who lives in a transcendent realm as cosmic Lord and is coming as eschatological judge. Not only is this no ordinary meal to satiate appetite; it is hardly a mortuary foundation either, because it is not intended (by Paul) to mourn or to celebrate a dead hero who remains in one aspect of his persona still within the world of the dead, much less to invite the presence of the dead Jesus to participate. Ascough seems

to a second problem. The statements of the meal text, identifying the bread and wine with the body and blood of Jesus, are surely martyrological statements represented as being spoken in advance of his death on the night in which he was handed over, intimating that it is those gathered for whom he is to be put to death. On the proposal presented in Ascough's paper, we would have to suppose that Jesus as martyr is a tradition invented by Paul.[125]

As Ascough notes at the end of his discussion, compared to the Thessalonians, the response of the Corinthians to the status of dead members of the community is more proactive, which is demonstrated in their rite of baptism on behalf of the dead (1 Cor 15:29). Paul's response appeals to the resurrection of Christ as the basis for their continued inclusion, developing the scenario found in 1 Thess 4:13–18, with a view to addressing in particular the issues found in 1 Cor 15:12, 35.[126] Paul's reference to those who are baptized on behalf of the dead is formulated as a rhetorical question (1 Cor 15:29) and indicates that he understands the practice, or at least that he wants to use it, to help him make his case for the reality of the resurrection. But the difference between the Corinthian practice and Paul's rhetorical reference to it is not between some kind of Corinthian proto-Gnostic enthusiasm and Pauline eschatological reservation. Nor would baptism for the dead appear to be concerned with the continued inclusion of the dead of the *ekklēsia*. If Paul introduced baptism as an initiation ritual and the baptism being practiced is on behalf of dead members, we should assume that it is carried out on behalf of those who had already received baptism as a rite of entry. Why should the same ritual of initiation be done vicariously in order to guarantee that death has not cut them off from the community? It seems more likely that baptism for the dead was seen by some as "another ritual means for improving the lot of their more immediate ancestors" by incorporating them into the distinguished lineage and ancestry of the fathers of Israel.[127] Or, from a somewhat different direction, it could have served to benefit the dead by easing the passage from the world of the living to the world of the dead. What normally functioned as a ritual of initiation served the Corinthians equally well as a rite of passage between life and death. "The practice

---

to move from the attribution of divine status to Jesus to Paul's cosmic Lord and eschatological judge, as though these are stages that follow some inevitable progression from the memorializing of a local hero. In fact, the sequence of death, burial, resurrection, and appearance is as problematic as a narrative sequence on the model of a hero myth as it is on the model of a martyr myth. And while a divinized hero might (re)appear in dreams, that will not help to explain the "appearances" in 1 Cor 15:5–8.

125. One of the major points of Mack's analysis of Paul's use of the Christ myth is to show that the social logic of a martyr myth was not central to his own mythmaking, though Paul was able to make use of the myth for his mission to the Gentiles. And while Mack proposes that the ὑπέρ phrase as it appears in 1 Cor 15:3 is a Pauline construction, he has not eliminated from the pre-Pauline tradition a prepositional phrase expressing the cause for which the martyr dies ("Rereading the Christ Myth," 40–45).

126. Ascough, "Paul's 'Apocalypticism,'" 184–85.

127. Stowers, "Kinds of Myth," 125; and see above, n. 35.

confirmed the movement of the deceased from an uncertain, liminal status into the world of the dead and thereby signaled that life could begin anew for the surviving community with no anxiety about the departed."[128]

---

128. Richard E. DeMaris, "Corinthian Religion and Baptism for the Dead (1 Corinthians 15:29): Insights from Archaeology and Anthropology," *JBL* 114 (1995): 679. From this perspective, the vicarious practice would have obviously been intended for the recent dead. Citing Smith on the difference between locative and utopian soteriologies—"what is soteriological [from a locative perspective] is for the dead to remain dead" (*Drudgery Divine*, 124)—DeMaris concludes, "The Corinthian Christians evidently understood baptism for the dead as a means of maintaining or restoring boundaries" ("Corinthian Religion and Baptism for the Dead," 679 n. 79). DeMaris explains why the practice arose among the Corinthians and appears to have been limited to the *ekklēsia* of that city on the basis of archaeological evidence for the chthonic orientation of religious practices in Corinth and its environs. Even if not all of the evidence presented by DeMaris for the chthonic orientation of Corinthian cult holds up or proves adequate to account for the practice and its limitation to Corinth, there is abundant evidence to which he points of Greek and Roman death rituals intended to benefit the dead in making the transition from the world of the living to the world of the dead. We should not be surprised that we do not find the particular practice more generally in Greco-Roman society (though that is not to say that we do not find analogies). It was probably Paul who introduced a water ritual to the Corinthians as a rite of initiation. Nor is it surprising that it is among the Corinthians that the ritual was adapted for the benefit of the dead, since Paul's other references to baptism in 1 Corinthians suggest that the Corinthians took a special interest in baptism (1:10–17; 10:1–13; cf. 12:13). DeMaris thinks that Paul would have been highly ambivalent about baptism for the dead, not because of its vicarious action (Paul urged the view that family members could act vicariously for each other [1 Cor 7:14]), but because it may have strengthened the position of women in the group of whom Paul disapproved, since funerary rituals were largely in their hands, and because some Corinthians obviously saw no necessary connection between baptism to benefit the dead and resurrection. However, the practice was evidently not a source of contention among the Corinthians, so rather than disapprove, as we might have expected, Paul translated a ritual of benefit for the dead—whether or not he himself was completely clear about the practice—into a ritual of benefit conceived for the dead in the only way Paul could imagine that would benefit the dead: the resurrection of the dead (677–81). Stowers has made a similar point about the way in which the Lord's meal would have encouraged the creativity and participation of the women ("Kinds of Myth," 141). DeMaris concludes his article by suggesting that the Corinthian practice was provocative for further Pauline mythmaking: "What likelier source is there for the burial imagery in Romans 6 than vicarious baptism, a funerary ritual of the Corinthian Christians? Inspired by them to connect baptism and burial, Paul appears to explore in Rom 6:1–11 what he implied in 1 Cor 15:29. . . . Baptism joins the believer to the death and resurrection of Christ. Perhaps Paul's christological anchoring of baptism was his way of hinting at a deficiency in the Corinthians' understanding of baptism for the dead, for language of dying and rising with Christ to new life represents a reversal of the journey from life to death. . . . Paul did not confront the Corinthians; he simply, deftly turned their theory on its head" ("Corinthian Religion and Baptism for the Dead," 682). Cf. Norman R. Petersen, "Pauline Baptism and 'Secondary Burial,'" *HTR* 79 (1986): 217–26, who also relates Rom 6 to funerary practices.

In a recent study, Michael F. Hull (*Baptism on Account of the Dead (1 Cor 15:29): An Act of Faith in the Resurrection* [SBL Academia Biblica 22; Atlanta: Society of Biblical Literature, 2005]) rejects what has been the dominant view that the passage refers to vicarious baptism. He does so on the grounds that such a practice is completely isolated in early Christianity and not found elsewhere in the Greco-Roman world. The argument is based on the requirement of having both incontrovertible evidence of vicarious baptism at Corinth and of being able to trace references to the practice in Origen, Tertullian, John Chrysostom, Epiphanius, and Ambrosiaster directly back

284   REDESCRIBING PAUL AND THE CORINTHIANS

Earlier, we cited Snyder on the noneschatological setting of later Christian meals for the dead as evidence of the problematic of moving from an affirmation of the place of the dead in Paul's *parousia* scenario to funerary practices. In a broader temporal reflection, Ascough points to the funerary meal among the followers of Jesus as "the missing piece . . . [of] evidence from the first century" to account for "the more formal ritual of the Eucharist" and to provide "the legitimation for the continuation of the (pagan) funerary banquet tradition among Christians."[129] In responding to what we see as problematic in this trajectory, we turn again to Snyder's work, on the *Inculturation of the Jesus Tradition*:

---

to Paul and Corinth in a genealogical fashion, despite the fact that these references are in any case mired in the polemics of "orthodoxy" and "heresy." A clear example of this approach is seen in his treatment (39–43, 166–67) of the study of DeMaris to which we have just referred ("Corinthian Religion and Baptism for the Dead"). Granted that 1 Cor 15:29 is difficult in its immediate literary context—although that context is the main reason for the archive of studies and proposals on the passage that exist in modern scholarship—that we have no direct literary evidence of the burial practices of those in Corinth addressed in Paul's letter, and that the passage constitutes a *crux interpretum*, we find the dismissal of analogical comparison for establishing plausible proposals completely unsatisfactory in historical work. Hull opts for a much less characteristic causal use of the preposition and translates the passage, "Otherwise what are they to do, who have themselves baptized on account of the dead? If the dead are not really raised, why are they baptized on account of them?" (*Baptism on Account of the Dead*, 230–31). By itself this translation does not eliminate the possibility of a vicarious ritual. Even a paraphrase required for Hull's interpretation, "have themselves baptized on account of (their faith in the resurrection of) the dead," does not have to rule out a vicarious ritual, for example, a rite undertaken by the living on account of the dead (who died without being baptized) in order that they might participate in the resurrection of the dead. What Hull's translation signifies is that those now entering the group through baptism as a rite of initiation constitute a Pauline faction (the βαπτιζόμενοι of 15:29), for their entry into the community at the same time serves as an example of complete faith in Paul's teaching of the resurrection of the dead and as a witness against those who say there is no resurrection. Thus, we might suppose that Paul's rhetorical reference in 15:29 is an "in your face" demonstration of the truth of his message. Whereas DeMaris thinks that one of the reasons Paul did not oppose baptism for the dead was that he knew that it did not constitute an occasion for factionalism, Hull sees Paul drawing to his side a Pauline faction precisely through baptism as a rite of entry, the very thing Paul seems to have opposed in 1 Cor 1. The implication would be that those who have been baptized but who say there is no resurrection of the dead do not belong to the community. Of course, Hull will have none of this. Paul does not want to establish one group over another. Rather, the example of the βαπτιζόμενοι in 1 Cor 15:29 is intended as an *"aide memoire."* The Corinthians who say there is no resurrection of the dead once knew the truth and were strong in their faith in the resurrection, but somehow they have gone wrong, have lost their earlier enthusiasm, are responsible for factionalism, and are in danger of falling away. They need the reminder and correction of Paul and the βαπτιζόμενοι (235 [emphasis original]). A familiar reading of 1 Corinthians indeed!

129. Ascough, "Paul's 'Apocalypticism,'" 183.

[Paul] offers in place of the δαιμόνιον [1 Cor 10:20-21] a resurrected special dead, Jesus Christ, who cannot be localized. Paul countered the effectiveness of the Corinthian cult of the dead by joining the Christian κοινωνία meal, the Agape [reflected in 10:16-17, in distinction from the ἀνάμνησις meal], with the Christian memorial of the universal special dead, Jesus Christ. Like his Jewish ancestors before him, he tried to develop local kinship community on an ideological basis [the Passover in place of local cults of the dead]. Paul failed. There remained in early Christianity two celebrative meals, the ἀνάμνησις Eucharist and the Agape.... The Agape was the kinship meal of early Christianity. Eventually it did not compete with the table of δαιμόνια; it became the table of δαιμόνια, not of pagan heroes, but of Christian saints and martyrs.... The evidence is unmistakable. However much patristic literature may reflect on the meaning and practice of the ἀνάμνησις meal, the art and architecture of early Christianity portray more often the agape meal with the dead, with its bread, fish, wine, and baskets. It was Augustine and Ambrose who finally succeeded where Paul failed; they brought together in one meal the ἀνάμνησις Eucharist of the universal church and the Agape with its δαιμόνιον of the martyr.[130]

Without adopting Snyder's identification of two distinctive Christian meals in 1 Corinthians or the origins of the Agape and the Eucharist with meals of the historical Jesus and his "Last supper," respectively, it is clear that Paul's meal text is at odds not only with ordinary daily meals but also with ordinary funerary foundations, precisely on the grounds of the local significance of the latter. Snyder is emphatic that the later Christian Eucharist and the meal for the dead do not arise from the same funerary meal practice of a hero cult. But if Paul failed to counter a Corinthian cult of the dead with the nonlocalized, universal special dead, the resurrected Christ, we are certainly permitted to imagine that the continuing communication between Paul and the Corinthians must have entailed some shared interests as well as the mutual labor of translation of cultural codes. Moreover, if Paul and many of the recipients of 1 Thessalonians and 1 Corinthians share the experience of recent dislocation from the homelands of conquered peoples, resulting in a shared eagerness for social experimentation and mythmaking in the context of Roman imperialism, if they gather in social situations that bear a resemblance to associations, and if, following Smith's religious topography, the variety of associations is characteristic of the religions of "anywhere," it is especially important for our considerations to underline that religions of "anywhere" sometimes draw more closely on domestic models and, at other times, on polis-based or district-based temple models. Associations "may be understood primarily as re-placements of the religion of 'here' [home]," in part, however, "by adapting elements more characteristic of the religions of 'there' [temple]."[131] In this connection, it seems appropriate to suggest that Paul and the Corinthians may be working

---

130. Snyder, *Inculturation of the Jesus Tradition*, 171; and see above, n. 98.
131. Smith, "Here, There, and Anywhere," 34; cf. 30; repr. in *Relating Religion*, 332; cf. 329-30.

on similar transpositions of social models and mythmaking for the "anywhere" of their current gatherings, but that Paul brings to the tasks of transposition and translation a more imperial (royal, transcendentalized) language characteristic of the religions of "there," whereas some Corinthians are bringing to these tasks the domestic codes and practices characteristic of the religions of "here."[132]

Associations and Philosophical Schools

The papers by Kloppenborg and Stowers ("Pauline Christianity") draw on different models for analogical comparison with Paul and the Corinthians, highlighting for comparison particular features of *collegia* and philosophies, respectively, without identifying Paul's *ekklēsia* at Corinth as a particular kind of association or philosophical school. Both writers have also acknowledged the usefulness of comparing a variety of models with aspects of our data. However, merely to call attention to the different features selected for comparison and to acknowledge the value of each selection misses the more critical difference of criteria for making the selection and the results of comparison when setting Paul's practices in a larger context.

Stowers has made explicit the criterion he adopts in selecting certain features for comparison. It is based on his calculation of "which practices are most important to the particular groups and what goods the members of the groups consider to be internal to those practices rather than external or incidental."[133] In this respect it is somewhat beside the point when Kloppenborg agrees that Stowers's analysis is convincing, but not comprehensive, since selectivity and partiality are characteristics of any comparison. The question is whether Stowers's judgment about the practices and goods most central to Pauline Christianity is correct.[134] In considering the question, the distinction between Paul's representation of his addressees and the Corinthians themselves must be methodologically maintained. But one cannot use the distinction to cordon off completely the Corinthians from Paul's representation of them, since to do so would ignore the fact that 1 Corinthians belongs to a context of interaction with others and would be subject to the judgment that Pauline Christianity is a purely idiosyncratic construct. The difference is crucial for the conclusions Stowers has reached in his paper on "Kinds of Myth," where the goods and practices internal to the groups addressed by Paul in 1 Corinthians are seen to be related to the Corinthians' own differentiated responses.

In identifying a structural feature endemic to *collegia*, whereby competition for honors and rivalry among members are both encouraged and contained,

---

132. See Mack's expanded description in "Rereading the Christ Myth," 65.
133. Stowers, "Pauline Christianity," 220.
134. Stowers has clearly stated the issue of comparison of practices as one of determining which activities rank "highest in the hierarchy of practices" (ibid., 223), discussing the orientation of Judean religious practices toward the temple throughout the Greco-Roman world prior to 70 C.E. (223–26).

anticipated and managed, Kloppenborg is not merely selecting a different set of features to compare from those highlighted by Stowers but making a different assessment of the practices and goods internal to Paul and the *ekklēsia* in Corinth.[135] The many examples drawn by Kloppenborg from *collegia* to establish a set of analogies to Paul and the Corinthians of the rivalries that typically arise and the ways in which they are managed all presuppose the kinds of goods characterized by Stowers as "the varied, complex, and conflicting goods of the traditional ethnic peoples."[136] For Stowers, these goods are internal to the practices of sacrificial religions to which associations are also linked in their cultic practices.[137] This is to be seen in sharp contrast to the structural similarity of Pauline Christianity and Hellenistic philosophies, which are organized around intellectual practices and "ordered by a tightly focused and totalizing understanding of a unitary good."[138] While Kloppenborg acknowledges Paul's leveling of status and gender differences in distinguishing the Lord's meal from θυσία feasts,[139] he concludes

---

135. Kloppenborg, "Greco-Roman *Thiasoi*," 205: "What makes the study of *collegia* particularly interesting is, first, that the available documentation discloses much more about social conflict than what remains of the other types of associations and, second, that various forms of conflict appear to have been endemic in *collegia* and that many *collegia* developed mechanisms by which to manage conflict, both internal and external." Summarizing his findings from the data of *collegia*, Kloppenborg concludes, "Thus, associations both cultivated a degree of rivalry and had to devise means by which such rivalry could be limited and contained. Fines for disorderly conduct at meals, injunctions prohibiting members from taking other members to court, and the insistence on settling all disputes among members within the association—all served as means by which an association sought to prevent internal conflict from reaching divisive proportions" (214; for the data from associations on which Kloppenborg's summary is based, see 211–14, and for his final case of efforts to overcome rivalry between two cults of the Thracian goddess Bendis, see 214–15).

136. Stowers, "Pauline Christianity," 228.

137. Ibid., 227–29, for a description of associations as a kind of extension of the sacrificial religion of ethnic peoples. Summarizing, Stowers concludes, "The typical sacrificial religion of the Greco-Roman world was closely intertwined with economic production and made no sense apart from that production. This holds true of associations, the Judean temple, and the religious practices of dispersed Judean communities. The ideal economic production in this Mediterranean religion is the fruit of the land, but artisanal, trade, and other sorts of economic production were also included in the structuration effected by the linking of shared practices" (238). The kinds of social rivalries highlighted in Kloppenborg's association materials as analogous to the factionalism in Corinth and to Paul's management of behaviors would seem to point to relationships embedded inevitably in the linkage of economic production and sociality described by Stowers as characteristic of the sacrificial religions of Mediterranean peoples.

138. Ibid., 237, adding in order to highlight the oddity of the Pauline "household": "The ancient household was the locus for almost all of the economic production in Greco-Roman antiquity. . . . The economic engine is missing from the Pauline household. The only labor and goods that he values are those related to his teaching, assembly building, and leading activities. Paul's social formations resembled those of Hellenistic philosophers because they were productive of 'mind goods' in a way that subordinated other goods" (240, 241).

139. Kloppenborg, "Greco-Roman *Thiasoi*," 215–16 with n. 90, referring to Stowers's discussion in "Greeks Who Sacrifice and Those Who Do Not," 299–320.

that "the phenomenon of conflict within the Christian group and Paul's strategies for conflict management fall within the spectrum of conflict management seen in other *collegia*."[140] Similarly, in the comparative perspective of Kloppenborg's discussion, the social and political value of *homonoia* is not as much an expression of the philosophical virtue of self-mastery, though the latter is understood as a social virtue, as it is an expression of the containment of rivalries occasioned by typical concerns for status, honor, and commendation that become public in "a context in which various subgroups appear together."[141] Finally, it is instructive, though not surprising, when Stowers and Kloppenborg set their comparative projects in a broader context, that the former highlights "the oddity of Pauline ritualization and mythmaking in comparison to ancient Mediterranean religion,"[142] while the latter concludes that the Corinthians were not so odd: "The Corinthian *ekklēsia* was not up to something totally new and unprecedented."[143] The difference should not be effaced despite the necessary qualifications.[144] The outsider would see something

---

140. Kloppenborg, "Greco-Roman *Thiasoi*," 216.

141. Ibid., 209, referring to the Corinthian *ekklēsia* as "a network of *collegia domestica* (each with a patron) or a small private cult that was subscribed to by members of several families (and their dependents)" (ibid.). Kloppenborg compares the use of ritual meals to demonstrate harmony and mutual hospitality. His discussion notes Stowers's analysis of the Lord's meal, referring to the "real if unanticipated social consequences" of "preference for bread and wine over meat as ritual substances." But the analogy focuses not on the cultivation of self-mastery leading to the practice of solidarity, but on the need to anticipate and contain the conflicts of normal social life. Discussing the Bendis associations in the Piraeus and Athens, Kloppenborg concludes, "What is noteworthy for our purposes is the use of a common ritual, a joint procession followed by a common meal, prayers, and sacrifices, all performed in the interests of establishing and maintaining *homonoia* between two related groups which, given the competitive nature of public life, might easily become bitter rivals. The decree's insistence on hospitality and equality between the two groups seems a conscious anticipation of conflict and a concerted attempt to mitigate divisions" (215). Compare Stowers's references to the exhibition of self-mastery in connection with techniques for self-care and self-scrutiny, the ordering of life around a unitary *telos*, and in reflection on what Jesus exhibited in his death ("Pauline Christianity," 232–33, 237, 239–40). To be sure, Stowers recognizes other contexts for promoting the virtue of self-mastery, especially the Augustan reform and the hierarchical assumptions of ethnicity and gender to which this virtue is closely tied, and which also constrain Paul's discourse ("Paul and Self-Mastery," 529–46). In his paper under discussion here, however, it is clearly the philosophical context of a totalizing good that is seen to be operative.

142. Stowers, "Pauline Christianity," 238.

143. Kloppenborg, "Greco-Roman *Thiasoi*," 216.

144. For example, Kloppenborg's acknowledgment of the effect of a ritual less implicated in gender and status rankings (see above, 286–88 with nn. 139, 141). Compare Stowers's remark, "Christianity was a new form of religion based on the new shape of knowledge that depended on expert interpreters and teachers like Paul" ("Pauline Christianity," 243), and its qualification: "I do not mean 'new' here in the sense of unique. . . . Rather, Pauline Christianity capitalized on tendencies that had been in formation for centuries by creating a religion dependent on specialized knowledge that claimed universal validity at the same time that it broke the links with land, ethnic people, and the landed aristocracy" (243 n. 82). The difference should not be neutralized even in light of Stowers's concluding statement, in "Kinds of Myth," that Paul's mythmaking efforts are "not so odd." Naturally, the question is, "Odd

closer to domestic *collegia* or to philosophical schools not because Kloppenborg and Stowers have randomly selected different features to highlight, but because they have made different judgments about the features that deserve priority.

To read the two papers together, and in some tension with each other in their comparative strategies, is to be able to see more clearly how little Pauline Christianity described by Stowers fits the goods and practices internal to associations, and yet how closely the kinds of "problems" addressed by Paul in 1 Corinthians resemble the rivalries, and the practices that encourage and contain them, typically found in associations. What this shows is not the problem of determining the degree of fit/no fit with associations and schools, only to fall back on some notion of the uniqueness of a Pauline *ekklēsia*.[145] Rather, it highlights in the case of Paul and the Corinthians the oddity of Paul's responses to matters that appear to be largely local and domestic concerns. Focusing on this oddity and its significance for problematizing the assumption of the Corinthians as a group formed by Paul's Christ myth and ritual is at the heart of Smith's paper in this volume. The dissonance is also registered strongly by Stowers in "Kinds of Myth," and relates to his challenge to resist thinking of the Corinthians as a Christian community and to focus instead on fields constituted in bundles of practices producing social formations rooted in differentiated responses.[146]

Conclusion

The strategy of the editors in reading all of the papers in this volume as a set of proposals for redescription has been to call attention to Paul and the Corinthians as a site under construction, not at all identical to the new building of Christ that Paul constructs in the interest of defining and authorizing his own place and leadership (1 Cor 3:10–15; 4:14–21). Nor is it the site of a new age the Corinthians have entered only to find themselves in danger of falling back, or the site of dramatic oppositions between Paul's resistance to, and the Corinthians' accommodation of, the vertical structures of family, city, and empire. Instead, we have in view a site that is not constructed from the ground up but that makes use of and refashions older structures, a site that is also built with materials taken from different environments, a site in which the builders have not yet agreed on the arrangement of

---

with respect to what? However, we are not as persuaded as Stowers that Paul's ethnic mythmaking and his Christ myth and Lord's meal are not so odd, especially when they are brought together. While agreeing with Stowers that Paul can be recognized as participating in the "more autonomous pole of a field of cultural specialization" ("Kinds of Myth," 149; cf. 113–14, 116–17, 121, 144–45), Paul does not operate only in that field, and his apocalyptic perspective of imminent worldwide judgment linked to the resurrection of the dead cannot be set aside as if it were not fundamental for all the transformations he imagines (see above, nn. 67, 84).

145. Cf. Smith, "*Dayyeinu*," 485 n. 5; and see Cameron and Miller, "Introducing Paul and the Corinthians," 9 with nn. 26–27.

146. Stowers, "Kinds of Myth," 108, 122.

structures or on the symbolic significance of proposed arrangements and styles. Nevertheless, the site is being built while it remains a contested space. In "reading" the construction of this site, we have learned that we cannot always infer social formations from the evidence of mythmaking, as though there were some simple way to specify the nexus that links them. But we have also become more aware that the site for redescription does not have to constitute a single social formation, as though it consisted in some firmly bounded corporate identity. Paul and the Corinthians must include more than only Paul's mythmaking, and more than a group bonded only by reference to Paul's Christ myth and ritual. We have urged that the site be viewed as intercultural with implications for communication but without excluding shared interests or the shared experience of deracination, and that the factors impinging on group formations be seen as interactive: local interests and identities as well as local and imperial forms of social cohesion and domination, intrusions or interventions and differentiated responses, perceived incongruities of expectation and situation, consequences of translation and (mis)understanding, conditions for attracting forums of lively debate, ritual experimentation, and myths of rectification.

For heuristic purposes, we propose our own version of a "just so story," modifying somewhat Stowers's proposal in "Kinds of Myth."[147] Paul's social formations are rooted in intellectual, social, and cultic practices engaged by those persons who follow his teachings and practices, mostly patrons, companions, and co-workers, but including some of the addressees of 1 Corinthians, who are attracted for various reasons to his foreign *paideia*.[148] Paul's self-understanding as the apostle to the Gentiles does not exclude his being recognized and credited primarily as a teacher by those who receive his teaching as a benefaction.[149] Paul is obviously distressed

---

147. Ibid., 126, 139–42, citing Daniel C. Dennett, *Darwin's Dangerous Idea: Evolution and the Meanings of Life* (New York: Simon & Schuster, 1995), 242, 245–46, 308–9, 454–56, 461–66, 485. Admittedly, we are doing this more as a tentative taxonomy than a narrative.

148. We follow Stowers in accounting for these reasons ("Kinds of Myth," 116–19).

149. We refer to "benefaction" in this context intentionally and with particular reference to the recent study by Zeba A. Crook, *Reconceptualising Conversion: Patronage, Loyalty, and Conversion in the Religions of the Ancient Mediterranean* (BZNW 130; Berlin and New York: de Gruyter, 2004). In this study, Crook compares the rhetoric and expectations of behavior in relations between humans and the gods and finds that they are governed by the system of patronage and benefaction operating in so many of the relations between humans in the ancient Mediterranean. "Whether one was a client of a human elite, a philosopher or a god, the expectations of conduct and the rhetoric employed alongside it were largely the same. The necessary conclusion is that for all intents and purposes there are very few meaningful distinctions to be drawn between human and divine patronage and benefaction" (92). The intent of Crook's study is to show that conversion, both philosophical and cultic, including Paul's conversion, is expressed in terms of normal expectations of human relations and relations with the divine. It is a matter of "the relationship between two parties" and not about "the internal measure of emotional tumult" (244). "For Paul, as for his ancient peers and predecessors, the language of cult and philosophy and thus the language of conversion is the language of ancient human and divine patronage and benefaction" (196). Of course there are differences in the kinds of benefactions, or goods, received

in 2 Corinthians by the failure of the Corinthians to recognize and honor him appropriately for the benefactions they have received (2 Cor 12:11–13). That Paul seeks to establish and maintain a relationship of dependency on the grounds of his preaching of the gospel, and expects loyalty to the teaching and the honoring of the teacher, should not be sublimated by theological rationales or overridden by rhetoric or practices of mutuality identified in his letters.[150] Paul's assumptions about gender and ethnicity make it clear that mutuality and solidarity were conceivable for Paul and the world to which he belonged not as matters of equality but as consequences of interdependent hierarchy. Resistance to the structures of domination of an empire rooted in the vertical relationships created by the concentration of wealth in a landed aristocracy is largely the unintended consequence of Paul's work habits and ascetic practices.[151] The picture of the Corinthians as a

---

from cult and from philosophy, and philosophy makes use of persuasive rhetoric for its benefactions to be received and generally requires a more exclusive loyalty to the teacher or school (100–106). "In his travelling and teaching, in his attempts to benefit humanity with a share in the divine benefactions to which he was himself party, Paul would have looked every bit the part of the philosopher patron" (192).

150. Neither do we think it can be ruled out by Paul's appeal to disinterestedness. In the context of his own circle of competitors, his repeated accusations of false motives are part of the game (see Stowers, "Kinds of Myth," 145). They do not bring an end to constructing and maintaining relationships of dependency. To think that they do runs the risk of removing Paul from his world. Philosophical critique of traditional reciprocity with the divine is also strained if directly applied to Paul. How else could Paul have thought of sharing the most sublime substance in the cosmos except as a recipient of a supreme divine benefaction?

151. We are drawing here directly on the comments of Stanley K. Stowers, "Paul and Slavery: A Response," *Semeia* 83–84 (1998): 295–311, written primarily as a reply to Richard A. Horsley, "Paul and Slavery: A Critical Alternative to Recent Readings," *Semeia* 83–84 (1998): 153–200, in a volume of papers entitled *Slavery in Text and Interpretation* (see above, n. 37). Stowers observes that "appeal to interdependent hierarchy is the ubiquitous ancient Mediterranean and Medieval European way of conceiving any sort of social unity. Unity in antiquity almost never implied equality" ("Paul and Slavery," 303–4). Moreover, "Paul's attack on slavery and the abuse of women and children came not through any doctrine of social equality or program of liberation or any intentional plan, but through refusing to marry and thus form a traditional household and by insisting on living by his own labor" (309). The collection for the poor in Jerusalem is the most obvious candidate for arguing that the "economic engine" is not entirely absent from Paul's practices but represents a different economic practice. The collection cannot be *limited* to the notion of reciprocity in which material goods are exchanged for spiritual (against Stowers, "Pauline Christianity," 240–41). Second Corinthians 8:14 refers to an equality achieved in mutual exchanges of material gifts. This appears to be an expression of an exchange of gifts among equals (at least potentially, since the exchange depends on the circumstance of material need), rather than a benefaction and the dependency it entails. But we must also look at the constraints that may be operating in the situation. Paul may not want to depend on the benefactions of patrons, when it comes to a matter so closely tied to the success of his mission, or, alternatively, there may not be enough wealth from such sources to carry through the collection. Depending mostly on his own labor surely has something to do with the desire to remain free of such dependencies. Moreover, 2 Cor 8–9; 11:7–11; 12:16 show that Paul's financial practices were controversial; evidently it required a great deal of persuasion to complete the collection, and we should not simply assume that all families or individuals participated. Finally, the collection is hardly free of ambiguities, including the intention to demonstrate through the collection the greater success, and thus the priority, of the Gentile mission

Christ-identified religious community and of Paul as a founder and builder of religious communities is as dependent on Paul's own mythmaking, and on contemporary scholarly desires, as the view of Paul as the innovator of a program of social and political reform:

> Paul is opposed to the order of the current age including the political and social order, but his letters do not provide a clear social and political critique and a plan for a new order except in terms that are too mythic to be practical for the reform of human social and political communities. An apocalyptic mythology makes the current order doomed and provides hope for a band of true believers. It does not reform society.[152]

---

in God's present plans, implying that in fact the collection is intended to be received as a benefaction requiring acknowledgment of Paul's mission and the honoring of it in Jerusalem (see Merrill P. Miller, "Antioch, Paul, and Jerusalem: Diaspora Myths of Origins in the Homeland," in Cameron and Miller, *Redescribing Christian Origins*, 227).

At the same time we acknowledge the importance of the work of the SBL "Paul and Politics Group" in insisting on the embeddedness of religious practices in the institutions of family and politics and in exploring the relationship of Pauline Christianity to these institutions and practices in a number of volumes edited by Richard A. Horsley: *Paul and Empire: Religion and Power in Roman Imperial Society* (Harrisburg, Pa.: Trinity Press International, 1997); *Paul and Politics: Ekklesia, Israel, Imperium, Interpretation. Essays in Honor of Krister Stendahl* (Harrisburg, Pa.: Trinity Press International, 2000); *Paul and the Roman Imperial Order* (Harrisburg, Pa.: Trinity Press International, 2004); *Hidden Transcripts and the Arts of Resistance: Applying the Work of James C. Scott to Jesus and Paul* (SemeiaSt 48; Atlanta: Society of Biblical Literature, 2004). The simple alternatives of accommodation/emulation or resistance must be avoided. Not only have colonial studies taught us the complexity of structures of power, but much recent work on responses to Roman domination among the peoples of the Mediterranean has stressed the differences of response as well as the interactive and dialogical character of responses in both their material and their symbolic dimensions. See, e.g., D. J. Mattingly, ed., *Dialogues in Roman Imperialism: Power, Discourse, and Discrepant Experience in the Roman Empire* (Journal of Roman Archaeology Supplementary Series 23; Portsmouth, R.I.: Journal of Roman Archaeology, 1997). For Greek responses to Roman imperialism, see Susan E. Alcock, *Graecia Capta: The Landscapes of Roman Greece* (Cambridge: Cambridge University Press, 1993); eadem, "Greece: A Landscape of Resistance?" in *Dialogues in Roman Imperialism*, 103–15; Greg Woolf, "Becoming Roman, Staying Greek: Culture, Identity and the Civilizing Process in the Roman East," in *Proceedings of the Cambridge Philological Society* NS 40 (1994): 116–43; Simon Goldhill, ed., *Being Greek under Rome: Cultural Identity, the Second Sophistic and the Development of Empire* (Cambridge: Cambridge University Press, 2001). For the relationship of Roman imperialism and Greek cultural identity in Roman Corinth and its possible bearing on Paul and the Corinthians, see Richard E. DeMaris, "Cults and the Imperial Cult in Early Roman Corinth: Literary Versus Material Record," in *Zwischen den Reichen: Neues Testament und Römische Herrschaft* (ed. Michael Labahn and Jürgen Zangenberg; Texte und Arbeiten zum neutestamentlichen Zeitalter 36; Tübingen: Francke, 2002), 73–91.

152. Stowers, "Paul and Slavery," 308. On Paul's political discourse as an expression of "earliest Christianity's intrinsic will to rule," see Leif E. Vaage, "Why Christianity Succeeded (in) the Roman Empire," in *Religious Rivalries in the Early Roman Empire and the Rise of Christianity* (ed. Leif E. Vaage;

It seems far more likely that what Paul actually achieved at Corinth was not the establishment of an alternative community founded on the Christ myth and unified through Paul's moral and ritual instructions but the attraction of a certain cadre of followers. Paul's legacy in the first and second centuries consists of schools of thought rooted in contrary claims about the traditions he established and the practices he followed. Therefore, caution should also be exercised in the way we think about Pauline ritual constituting a "new form" or mode of religion that has broken decisively with land and lineages.[153] The break with land and lineages in Paul's meal practice and the limiting of offering to the service of the mind are also constrained by his gospel for the Gentiles. Offerings from land and labor were not an option, since they would have meant either approval of pagan sacrificial practices or becoming Judeans.[154] More important, reference to a new form of religion arising from Paul's practice should not be identified with a religious community. Such a community is present in Paul's mythmaking, but not as a social fact. Paul's success in establishing a following can be viewed as an instance of social formation. But we should be careful that this does not shift in connotation to a conception of religious community as a primary category of identity. Such a shift confuses a mode of religious practice in the context of the production and cultivation of a foreign *paideia*, with religion as an independent and disembedded source of identity. Such a view would be anachronistic and runs the danger of reversing Stowers's careful statement locating "a group among the Corinthians who were already habituated, not so as to want to be saved or become Christians, but so as to want to become consumers of Paul's foreign *paideia*, a known commodity supported by a dynamic social arena."[155] Stowers himself has shown the sort of institutional development and structure entailed for the establishment and maintenance of religious communities rooted in intellectual practices.[156] Thus, we think that what he has written in "Kinds of Myth" is an appropriate formulation of the matter. "Social fractions" are what create the myths for reasons of interests related to power, rather than their being an expression of the collective creativity of communities;[157] it is these same "social fractions" that by adopting Paul's practices constitute a Pauline social formation.

There are other social fractions among the addressees of 1 Corinthians. One of these would correspond to Stowers's non-elite, though we would not characterize them in particular as resisters who do not see themselves as belonging to the

---

Studies in Christianity and Judaism 18; Waterloo, Ont.: Wilfrid Laurier University Press, 2006), 278; cf. 270–77.

153. See above, n. 144.

154. See Jonathan Klawans, *Purity, Sacrifice, and the Temple: Symbolism and Supersessionism in the Study of Ancient Judaism* (Oxford: Oxford University Press, 2006), 219–21.

155. Stowers, "Kinds of Myth," 142.

156. Ibid., 108.

157. Ibid., 109–10, 115, 140–42.

collection of families when they meet together. However, they would have little interest in adopting Paul's celestial Christ, and so Paul's talk of the Spirit and the Body of Christ is likely to be referred to the collective spirit of their special dead and the souls of the recent dead. Their orientation is thoroughly chthonic. They may be descendants of an older Greek population of the Corinthia pushed to the margins in the founding of the Roman colony.[158] Several of these families may have met together initially out of interest in comparing local genealogies,[159] and then were joined by a few Greek families that had migrated from other parts of Achaia or from other provinces of the empire. Comparing genealogies could also interest more recent immigrants of other ethnic groups, including Judeans, as an effort directed toward integration in the new environment that would not be inconsistent with sensibilities arising from continued ties to a homeland. Among these families there would also be slaves and freedmen and -women proverbially obsessed with matters of ancestry.[160] If one can imagine the interests of some Corinthians attracted to Paul's practices and teachings on analogy with major ascetic streams of second- and third-century Christians who appealed to Paul's example and authority, one can also think of the local and chthonic interests of some Corinthians on analogy with the thousands of ordinary Christians who would eat meals with their Christian dead and seek sources of well-being at the graves of the martyrs and saints.[161]

A third social fraction could be thought of in some ways as resisters, and therefore not those whom Paul commends, but whose resistance is not the consequence

---

158. Following the suggestion of DeMaris, "Cults and the Imperial Cult," 80–84, though we think that Paul's preaching of the crucified Jesus and the mortuary setting of the meal would have evoked interest among those seeking to maintain chthonic hero cults and cults of the dead largely as a consequence of their own efforts of translation and (mis)understanding. For DeMaris's effort to establish an intensified interest in chthonic aspects of Greek cults in Roman Corinth, see idem, "Demeter in Roman Corinth"; for a demurral, see Nancy Bookidis and Ronald S. Stroud, *The Sanctuary of Demeter and Kore: Topography and Architecture* (Corinth 18/3; Princeton: American School of Classical Studies at Athens, 1997), 434 n. 67; and see above, n. 128. On the chthonic aspects of the rites for Melikertes-Palaimon in Isthmia, see Gebhard, "Rites for Melikertes-Palaimon," 165–203.

159. We thank Jonathan Z. Smith for this suggestion.

160. See Stowers, "Kinds of Myth," 120–21. This description is not meant to suggest that when these households and other individuals met they had the appearance of immigrant metics preserving ancestral customs. The intention is to create a plausibility structure for imagining Paul's coming to Corinth as an intrusion or intervention in family groups already meeting for a purpose, without thinking of these groups as necessarily constituting an association that must have agreed already on qualifications for membership, on the intervals or conduct of a common meal, or the divinities to be recognized and honored in common. An interest in comparing genealogies, however, does suggest an opening for Paul to talk about the noble family of the ancestors of Israel.

161. Assuredly, these projections are intended as analogies in the interest of a plausible, if not yet justified, account of the Corinthian *ekklēsia*, an account that is consciously distanced from Paul's representations without denying an impact and consequence resulting from his intervention and continuing interaction. These projections are not genealogies, as if the addressees of 1 Corinthians could be imagined as the actual historical beginnings of the many formations of Christians of later centuries.

in particular of local and chthonic orientations that inhibited direct assimilation of Paul's Christ myth. Instead, they might be seen as those who value Paul as a producer of specialized knowledge and value his Christ myth as a source of identity and power that carries enhanced social prestige. What they resist is Paul's insistence on Christ as the source of a single exclusive unitary good that relativizes all other goods as matters of indifference and pronounces judgment on other landscapes of their lives. They know perfectly well that Paul's gospel requires them to abandon features of these landscapes, but they are unwilling and incapable of doing so, because their lives are lived not in the field of Paul's exclusive good but in the continuing negotiation of multiple goods and in the tension of living in plural landscapes. It is this social fraction, especially, who will recognize Paul's competitors as those who share Paul's field of practices and excel in discourses about Moses and Christ. And they will make their own comparative judgments of the power produced by these teachers and the bearing of their teachings on the negotiation of multiple goods. The distant analogy for this social fraction are the Atbalmin of Papua New Guinea.[162] Eytan Bercovitch introduces the concept of *social multiplicity* as a way of giving emphasis to the continuing tension experienced by the Atbalmin because of their capacity to absorb a series of situational changes in

---

162. We should make several clarifications at this point. First, the description of the Atbalmin in Smith's paper ("Re: Corinthians"), which draws especially on an anthropological essay by Bercovitch ("Altar of Sin"), makes clear not only the various and changing physical landscapes of the Atbalmin but also the emergence of different sources of knowledge integral to the landscape of government and business, when compared with native sources of knowledge. While we agree with Stowers that these knowledges are not yet the distinguishing mark of a whole class of native elite ("Kinds of Myth," 122), they belong to landscapes the Atbalmin increasingly inhabit. Moreover, Christianity does constitute for the Atbalmin a field of specialized knowledge and a greatly enlarged landscape, and native missionaries do fit the role of an emerging native elite, though on the point about recognition Stowers is certainly correct to emphasize that Paul as a Diaspora Judean would not have carried the background authority of an imperial culture (116). Second, we are not suggesting that the *ekklēsia* in Corinth is a distinctive Christian landscape in the same way that Bercovitch views Christianity as one of a number of landscapes impinging upon the lives of the Atbalmin. To do so would undermine the purpose of constructing a tentative taxonomy of social fractions as a contribution to the redescription of Paul and the Corinthians. We are interested in the analogy for the way it calls attention to the blurring of the boundaries of identity and symbolic worlds and highlights the capacity for affirming and negotiating incompatible goods. Third, in distinguishing this third social fraction from the second, we are acknowledging that typical local religious concerns for appropriate relations with the dead, concerns largely overlooked in scholarship on Paul and the Corinthians but clearly documented for associations in the paper by Ascough, are nevertheless not a single encompassing framework for elucidating the various issues and behaviors Paul addresses in 1 Corinthians. While these concerns seem to us to be of major significance in accounting for both resistance and continuing interaction between Paul and the Corinthians on the sources of wisdom and *gnōsis*, the identification of *pneuma/pneumata*, meal practices and baptism for the dead, and the plausibility of resurrection, we have not been concerned to reduce the quarreling and factions, the range of behavioral issues, or the differences of social status and competition for honor to some common denominator, reductions in any case that have failed to win a consensus. As a more associative context emerges, Kloppenborg's assessment of rivalries and their containment is an appropriate way to account for some of these phenomena.

a short period of time.¹⁶³ As an analytical category, social multiplicity is intended to highlight the stress of living in multiple landscapes, rather than their integration or accommodation.¹⁶⁴ It is this stress, Bercovitch suggests, that explains in part the continuing impact of Christianity in the colonial context, because it provides a meaning and offers a resolution of the conflicts it helps to create, but at a cost that is unacceptable, and guarantees at the same time Atbalmin experimentation and innovation in being Christian and not Christian, alternative positions depending on situation, and alternative ways of conceiving of personhood, depending on context.¹⁶⁵ The capacity to live in different discursive and social worlds is occasioned by the fact that they are not integrated or bounded wholes.¹⁶⁶ So some Corinthians, those imagined as constituting a third social fraction, might have appeared to Paul and his closest followers to be those most resistant to his authority and to the practices he authorized for establishing the boundaries and unity of the *ekklēsia*; but they would not have been those uninterested in being consumers of his foreign *paideia*.¹⁶⁷ For a temporally closer analogy, we might imagine those Corinthians reprimanded by Clement of Rome for removing their presbyters and exhorted to bring sedition and schisms to an end and be at peace with their presbyters (*1 Clem.* 44–54). Or, contrariwise, we might project them as the Pauline schools capable of accommodating the culture of household, city, and empire, while domesticating an esoteric *paideia* and institutionalizing products of Christian intellectual practices in conjunction with monarchical government.

By entering into a conversation with all of the papers in this volume, the editors have sought to justify the working assumptions of the seminar in approaching this site and to support and elaborate the conclusions announced in our introduction.¹⁶⁸ In response to the papers, we have taken account of contested issues, formulated our own views, and raised questions for further debate. Paul's representation of

---

163. Bercovitch, "Altar of Sin," 212–13: "I use this term to refer to a situation where people possess several, often contradictory sets of beliefs and practices.... The concept of social multiplicity draws on long-standing concepts framed to account for conditions of coexisting cultural practices: social change, acculturation, pluralism, syncretism, and compartmentalization. However, while many of these concepts suggest an untroubled coexistence or synthesis, social multiplicity stresses the conflicted character of life when people live with a number of very different sets of social and economic forms and forces." He adds, drawing on the language of Michel Foucault (*The History of Sexuality*, vol. 1, *An Introduction* [trans. Robert Hurley; New York: Pantheon, 1978]), that "the Atbalmin lived with what might be called several quite different regimes of knowledge/power" ("Altar of Sin," 219).

164. "Rather than choosing one context, people tried to maintain ties to several. In this way, they sought to keep their footing in a world that was always made up of multiple landscapes, landscapes which embodied, but also were embodied in, partially distinct sets of powers and meanings, fears and desires" (Bercovitch, "Altar of Sin," 221).

165. This is a capsule summary for our purposes of a longer discussion in ibid., 218–30.

166. Ibid., 225; and see Stowers's critique of the concept of *symbolic universe* in "Paul and Slavery," 300–302.

167. For the perspective we intend in drawing on Bercovitch's analytical framework, see the second clarification presented above, n. 162.

168. See Cameron and Miller, "Introducing Paul and the Corinthians," 4–5.

the Corinthians is an expression of his gospel, a production of his mythmaking. Only in limited and specific senses can some Corinthians be thought of as Pauline "Christians," though this is not to say that our findings are unimportant for the redescription of Christian beginnings.[169] Paul's addressing the Corinthians as "the *ekklēsia* of God which is at Corinth ... sanctified in Christ Jesus, called to be a holy people together with all those who in every place call on the name of our Lord Jesus Christ" (1 Cor 1:2), should not be taken as evidence of a social charter or collective identity of a Pauline Christian community. The papers have used a variety of comparative strategies to call into question the common assumption that the addressees of 1 Corinthians are, in fact, all converts to Paul's Christ myth, but are "behaviorally challenged" because of lingering "pagan" and "secular" involvements in Roman Corinth. On the contrary, we have found reason to suppose that families were already getting together around some common interests and that some found the esoteric features of Paul's gospel to be implausible. Others knew the "deeper" meaning of Paul's Christ, of baptism and meal practice. They were not passive recipients, but engaged in their own mythmaking and ritual experiments related to a different estimate of their situation and interests. The hunch is that some of the family groups to whom Paul brought his gospel were more interested in finding their place in the emerging civic identity of the Roman colony of Corinth than in finding their place in the cosmos or in some holy *politeia* outside the city.[170] An

---

169. We have in mind especially the valorizing of specialized knowledge claimed by teachers and their followers to have universal validity at the expense of the authority and power of traditional aristocracies. In the Augustan age, the broader political context of this valorizing of specialized expertise claiming universal validity was the aggrandizement of imperial authority and power. A foreign *paideia*, such as Paul's, claiming universal validity while encompassed by the imperial practice, necessarily ran counter to the validity of its claims. The change of the locus of authority has been described as the Roman cultural revolution; see Wallace-Hadrill, "*Mutatio morum*." On the relationship between disinterest and ideology in the Roman sacerdotal system, utilizing the concept of "symbolic capital," see Richard Gordon, "From Republic to Principate: Priesthood, Religion and Ideology," in *Pagan Priests: Religion and Power in the Ancient World* (ed. Mary Beard and John North; Ithaca, N.Y.: Cornell University Press, 1990), 193, 194: "The attention devoted to formal ritual should be understood as exemplary of a much more extensively operative social good in Roman society, action inspired by pure respect for the customs and conventions recognized by the social group.... Religious action, and above all sacrifice, could be made into aesthetic action, action for itself, free of self interest. In other words, formulaic religious action represented the pure accumulation of 'symbolic capital.' ... The sacerdotal colleges of Rome can be seen as the guardians of the alchemical transmutation of base wealth into inexhaustible prestige, through the insistence upon the minutely exact performance of forms; and part of the ideological value of the religious system to the élite can be seen as its being the purest case of this 'disinterested' action." The empire also accrued this symbolic capital by representing the emperor as the supreme example of the system, at the same time weakening the position of traditional Roman elites to compete for the same symbolic capital; see idem, "The Veil of Power: Emperors, Sacrificers and Benefactors," in *Pagan Priests*, 201–31.

170. On the changing civic-religious identity of Roman Corinth in the first century C.E. and its possible effect of reducing pressure for conformity of private associations to the official cults of the city, see James Walters, "Civic Identity in Roman Corinth and Its Impact on Early Christians," in Schowalter and Friesen, *Urban Religion in Roman Corinth*, 397–418. In contrast to the situation in Thessa-

important conclusion about Paul's Christ myth as a component of his gospel also emerges from the papers. It cannot be understood simply as an elaboration of "the *kērygma*," the latter itself having been deconstructed in the papers by Mack and Ascough, though with different results. Nor does Paul's Christ myth depend on the social logic of a martyr myth. Despite his statement about preaching Christ crucified, the Christ myth is not the definitive component of his gospel, but serves Paul's interest in dramatizing the scope and urgency of his message, and in constructing an ethnic myth for Gentiles and a Spirit myth, the latter having less to do with ecstatic religious experience than with the cosmic "science" of his day.[171]

The common perception of the Corinthians as a worshiping community formed by Paul's preaching of the gospel and his instructions for the formation of Christian liturgy is a thoroughly anachronistic picture. In his paper, Mack gives three reasons for dispensing with the label *Christ cult* not only for the pre-Pauline groups we have redescribed as *christos* associations but also for our current site. His third reason is that "the term easily shifts in connotation from 'ritual practices' to 'veneration,' and we have not been able to document any 'veneration' (presumably of Jesus as a divine figure and presence) in our redescription of the *christos* associations, or in the logics of the 'Christ myth' and 'supper text,' or in our investigations of Paul and the Corinthians."[172] The seminar has strongly supported Mack's conclusion to drop the term *Christ cult*, and "veneration" and "worship" of Christ

---

Ionica, Walters suggests that the absence of conflict with outsiders in Corinth, occasioned in part by the absence of a traditional native elite in the early history of the colony, had the effect of increasing internal conflict within the *ekklēsia* (416). On the changing civic-religious identity of Roman Corinth, the ensuing wider dialogue and debate, and the maintenance and blurring of boundaries of Roman and Greek, see Antony J. S. Spawforth, "Corinth, Argos, and the Imperial Cult," *Hesperia* 63 (1994): 211–32; idem, "Roman Corinth: The Formation of a Colonial Elite," in *Roman Onomastics in the Greek East: Social and Political Aspects* (ed. A. D. Rizakis; Μελετήματα 21; Athens: Research Centre for Greek and Roman Antiquity, National Hellenic Research Foundation; Paris: Boccard, 1996), 167–82; Onno M. van Nijf, "Local Heroes: Athletics, Festivals and Elite Self-Fashioning in the Roman East," in Goldhill, *Being Greek under Rome*, 306–34, esp. 334; Rebecca Preston, "Roman Questions, Greek Answers: Plutarch and the Construction of Identity," in *Being Greek under Rome*, 86–119, esp. 91; Alcock, "Greece: A Landscape of Resistance," 110. For recent discussions of imperialism, indigenization, and eclecticism attending cultural and cultic continuity and change in the Roman colony of Corinth, see Betsey A. Robinson, "Fountains and the Formation of Cultural Identity at Roman Corinth," in Schowalter and Friesen, *Urban Religion in Roman Corinth*, 111–40; and, in the same volume, Nancy Bookidis, "Religion in Corinth: 146 B.C.E. to 100 C.E.," 141–64; Gebhard, "Rites for Melikertes-Palaimon," 165–203; see also C. K. Williams II, "The Refounding of Corinth: Some Roman Religious Attitudes," in *Roman Architecture in the Greek World* (ed. Sarah Macready and F. H. Thompson; Society of Antiquaries of London Occasional Papers NS 10; London: Society of Antiquaries of London, 1987), 26–37; Mary E. Hoskins Walbank, "Evidence for the Imperial Cult in Julio-Claudian Corinth," in *Subject and Ruler: The Cult of the Ruling Power in Classical Antiquity* (ed. Alastair Small; Journal of Roman Archaeology Supplementary Series 17; Ann Arbor: University of Michigan Press, 1996), 201–13; DeMaris, "Demeter in Roman Corinth"; idem, "Cults and the Imperial Cult."

171. Stowers, "Kinds of Myth," 134–35.
172. Mack, "Rereading the Christ Myth," 68.

as a divine figure never surfaced in seminar discussions as a way of characterizing social formation at this site. Nevertheless, we think it is important to give this matter closer scrutiny.

Cultic activities were not peripheral practices in associations. They had an integral place in the sociality that formed in associations.[173] Stowers has made the point emphatically: "There is virtually no place in ancient Mediterranean religion for putting enjoyment of the food of meals into opposition to devotion to god."[174] While associations participated in the system of human patronage and benefaction, they also participated in a theodicy of good fortune, acknowledging the goods of divine protection and blessing by honoring the divine benefactors in an appropriate manner, or, in some cases, by honoring the local heroes and ancestors. A range of cultic activities is typically found in associations, including hymns, dancing, thanksgivings, vows, and votive offerings, with sacrifice as the most significant form of divine–human reciprocity. To be sure, as we have already indicated, the embeddedness of cultic activity in kinship and politics is a far cry from the worship of Christ in a religious community conceived of as a distinct category of social identity disembedded from kinship and politics. But acknowledging the gods was embedded in an array of institutions in a normal ancient Mediterranean city. As Paula Fredriksen writes, "Since ancient cities were religious institutions, participation in civic life was itself a form of worship."[175]

Despite cautions about the implications of Paul's meal ritual as a new form of religion,[176] Stowers's description of the oddity of Paul's specification of a meal genre is no exaggeration. To imagine a mortuary meal with no offering and no offerer is peculiar indeed! Waiting for one another and eating and drinking together, in

---

173. See especially Philip A. Harland, *Associations, Synagogues, and Congregations: Claiming a Place in Ancient Mediterranean Society* (Minneapolis: Fortress, 2003), 55–87. Harland has documented the central place of cultic activities in all types of associations. Contrary to an older tradition that saw an overwhelming interest in "partying," he has argued that conviviality, status, solidarity, and security were not concerns separable from those of appropriate acknowledgment of the gods in ritual activity. Harland's analysis of the evidence suggests that associations were more concerned with their place in the city and with participation in civic and imperial cults, than they were in imitating civic life and occupying a niche between family and civic institutions, or in engaging in activities subversive of these institutions. He includes synagogues in these aims, short of offering sacrifice, and also argues that most of the churches of Roman Asia at the end of the first century and early second century, including those to whom the author of the Apocalypse writes, would fit the description of "finding a place." Thus, he has challenged the largely sectarian picture of Christian groups in Roman Asia in this period.

174. Stowers, "Pauline Christianity," 239.

175. Paula Fredriksen, "What 'Parting of the Ways'? Jews, Gentiles, and the Ancient Mediterranean City," in Becker and Reed, *The Ways That Never Parted*, 44, adding: "There is no good word for characterizing the Jewish presence in such majority-culture activities. 'Worship' underscores the intrinsically religious nature of these activities, but it too readily (and naturally) conjures the term and religious practice that it customarily translates, *latreia*: Worship *as* sacrifice was precisely where ancient Jews generally seem to have—and were thought to have—drawn the line" (44 n. 29 [emphasis original]).

176. See above, 288 with n. 144, 292–93.

themselves, hardly constitute a ritual. And if eating and drinking, together with self-examination and meditation on the absent body of the martyr, proclaim the death of Jesus as a memorial, these practices could more easily be imagined as school-like activity intended to honor a martyred founder-teacher than veneration of the Lord "until he comes" (1 Cor 11:26). Some may have imagined with Paul that the Christ honored in the meal had become a divine figure of sovereignty, but we can think of other more easily imagined alternatives: an agent of the benefactions of God, that is, a broker in the system of divine patronage and benefaction;[177] an agent of mediation between the living and the dead; the collective spirit of the ancestors; an apotheosized hero; a founder-teacher.

It is often remarked that 1 Cor 12 and 14 give us a glimpse of early Christian "worship." Yet, if we adopt the perspective of the human client's expressions of gratitude in reciprocation for receiving divine benefactions and the client's prayers of supplication in the hope of receiving benefactions, these chapters are striking for how little evidence of "worship" they actually offer.[178] There is of course some evidence. First Corinthians 14:14-17 refers to singing, prayer, blessing, and thanksgiving,[179] but even here what Paul is emphasizing (v. 17) is the underlying theme of these chapters: the proper use, evaluation, and arrangement of God's various benefactions, which in this context are all manifestations of the same Spirit, or workings of the same Spirit, distributed to each for the common good (12:7, 11). Honoring the patron who has given these benefactions is certainly to be expected, but when Paul actually mentions "bow[ing] down before God and worship[ing] him" (14:25) his concerns have to do with the effect of prophecy on an outsider (vv. 24-25). Even vv. 26-33 do not signify coming together for the worship of God (excepting possibly the reference to a hymn, v. 26), and nothing in these chapters refers to acts of worship or veneration of Christ. The proper use of these benefactions and their goal are edification (v. 26), "so that all may learn and

---

177. See most recently Crook, *Reconceptualising Conversion*, 195-96.

178. The intent here is to acknowledge that what are usually referred to as gifts of the Spirit and thought to belong to a Pauline theology of grace are more appropriately understood as expressions of a system of patronage and benefaction in which the *charismata* are not gifts that can be reciprocated in an exchange of equal value, but benefactions given by a person of higher status to dependents (clients) who reciprocate by appropriate acts of honoring and demonstrating gratitude. Crook has argued that the χάρ- root belongs to the semantic domain of Possess, Transfer, Exchange in close association with the εὐεργ- root (ibid., 139-40 n. 86). Although Paul never uses the εὐεργ- terminology, "he has simply replaced the εὐεργ- root words with an equally explicit range of patronage and benefaction words, those of the χάρ- root: χάρις, χαρίζομαι, χάρισμα" (145). See also the book-length study on this by James R. Harrison, *Paul's Language of Grace in Its Graeco-Roman Context* (WUNT 2/172; Tübingen: Mohr Siebeck, 2003).

179. "As a rule, Greek and Roman cultic practices—offerings, sacrifices, vows, prayers, hymns, incantations, erecting temples, statues and inscriptions—were each of them designed to acknowledge, to express gratitude towards, and to honour the gods, as well as to secure the future favour of the gods. . . . Not only were the gods understood to be patrons and benefactors, but humans participating in this religious system reflect all the expected behaviour of clients in a relationship with a patron or benefactor" (Crook, *Reconceptualising Conversion*, 148-49).

all be encouraged" (v. 31). Clearly, Paul wants to orchestrate something closer to a philosophical symposium than to establish a Christian worship service, though with emphasis on the divine source of the various kinds of utterances and demonstrations.[180] One might also wonder whether Paul could have known in advance what content might be conveyed in a hymn, a lesson, a revelation, or an interpretation of a tongue, or what different participants would learn from these utterances or might think was the common good.

The major advantage in viewing cultic practices in the context of a system of divine patronage and benefaction is that it situates these practices squarely in the Greco-Roman world, making it unnecessary to construct a genealogy from Jesus the teacher to Christ the Lord, or to require elaborate explanations for the ritualization of the meal[181] or for the creation of acclamations, doxologies, and hymns addressed to Christ.[182] We have stressed the school-like features of 1 Cor 11, 12, and 14. But a school-like setting could also accommodate teachings about devotion to the true God and contribute, along with influences from Judaic practice, to a recognition of an exclusive, single divine patron. In the system of divine patronage, the recognition of Jesus as broker requires only that he be regarded in some sense as an agent of God's benefactions. The benefactions would not have to be ranked in the same way, nor would Christ as agent-broker have to occupy a particular rank in the order of beings, excepting subordination to God.[183] These are differences that would relate to particular constellations of myth addressing particular situations in the interest of particular agendas.[184]

The elimination of the term *Christ cult* as a foil for distinguishing Jesus movements and as a placeholder "for all of those 'churches' traditionally imagined to be visible through the windows of the Pauline corpus" does have important implications "for the large-scale map of Christian beginnings that we have been sketching for the first century."[185] It is now more difficult to find labels to distinguish the social formations of Christian beginnings. References to schools and associations are found repeatedly in the papers, but these are intended as analogies, not identities.

---

180. Cf. Dennis E. Smith, *From Symposium to Eucharist: The Banquet in the Early Christian World* (Minneapolis: Fortress, 2003), 200–214.

181. See Mack's observations, "Rereading the Christ Myth," 51–58.

182. See Burton L. Mack, *A Myth of Innocence: Mark and Christian Origins* (Philadelphia: Fortress, 1988; repr., Minneapolis: Fortress, 2006), 100 n. 2.

183. As an example, Crook writes concerning Paul: "Jesus as broker is always subordinate to God as divine patron. The confusion of the two for one is a later theological development that, from the perspective of patronage and benefaction, would have appeared foreign to Paul. Paul is consistent on this: Jesus *must* be honoured—as God's broker his benefactions are utterly indispensable to Paul—but he is the broker and not therefore to be confused with the divine patron. Indeed, such a confusion would have been quite insulting to the patron. Imagine somebody worshipping the priest (or broker) of Asclepius rather than Asclepius and what this would have communicated to the god" (*Reconceptualising Conversion*, 195–96 [emphasis original]).

184. Mack, "Rereading the Christ Myth," 68–71.

185. Ibid., 68.

And even though the redescription of this site would not have been possible without drawing on these analogies and distinguishing them in some ways, there seems little point in using "school" and "association" as labels to distinguish groups cultivating teachings of Jesus from groups that also cultivated a martyr myth, and to distinguish both of these from the redescription of Paul and the Corinthians. But this may actually point to a more significant issue for thinking about the beginnings of Christianity in the first century. It is not the labels themselves, but their use to distinguish what we perhaps still imagine inappropriately as Jesus- or Christ-identified groups that are clearly marked off from settings and constituencies that are not Jesus- or Christ-identified. Such an imagination is exactly what the seminar's work on this site has called into question. It is usually thought that even the earliest literature is addressed to Jesus-identified "communities." But inasmuch as these texts in their written form are the production of intellectuals, they are likely to have been patronized by individuals and often produced in and for settings and constituencies identified largely in other ways: by gender, household, civic and ethnic identity, by status, particular agendas, intellectual interests, and cultural fields. *Social formation* throughout most of the century may point less to bonded groups of Jesus people, kingdom of God people, or Christ people than to forums of discourse and debate about authority and rule, to settings for the display of wisdom and the cultivation of virtue, and to places for constructing social charters to guide responses to changed circumstances and imagine alternative forms of social cohesion. In such forums, settings, and places the teachings of Jesus (or of Jesus-*christos*), the works of Jesus, the wisdom of Jesus, and the faith, person, and destiny of Jesus could be found to be of interest among still largely other-identified groups. To the extent that traditional forms of authority and social cohesion were in retreat, those who brought Jesus or Jesus-*christos* or Christ "traditions" may often have had an advantage in the greater malleability and flexibility of invented traditions of recent vintage. Such an advantage could also carry the cost of being annoying, and maybe even threatening, seeming to play a recognizable game, but with the wrong equipment. Although these considerations may appear to inhibit sketching a new map of Christian beginnings, they are intended to address what is probably the major challenge of constructing any map of beginnings: the labor of imagination required to avoid anachronism in a temporal frame in which it is most tempting to cheat. Such labor is quite a challenge. As a "theoretically informed practice,"[186] historiography is a critical method of selection and classification, construction and redescription, explanation and interpretation, and making comparative judgments. The labor of such an imagination is thus a work of argumentation, of making matters consequential, of making them complicated—for "the historian's task is to complicate."[187]

---

186. Luther H. Martin, "History, Historiography, and Christian Origins: The Jerusalem Community," in Cameron and Miller, *Redescribing Christian Origins*, 264.

187. Jonathan Z. Smith, "The Influence of Symbols upon Social Change: A Place on Which to Stand," *Worship* 44 (1970): 457; repr. in *Map Is Not Territory*, 129; and, in the same volume, idem, "Map Is Not Territory," 290.

Selected Bibliography

Adams, Edward, and David G. Horrell, eds. *Christianity at Corinth: The Quest for the Pauline Church*. Louisville: Westminster John Knox, 2004.
Ascough, Richard S. *Paul's Macedonian Associations: The Social Context of Philippians and 1 Thessalonians*. WUNT 2/161. Tübingen: Mohr Siebeck, 2003.
———. "The Thessalonian Christian Community as a Professional Voluntary Association." *JBL* 119 (2000): 311–28.
———. "Translocal Relationships among Voluntary Associations and Early Christianity." *JECS* 5 (1997): 223–41.
———. *What Are They Saying about the Formation of Pauline Churches?* New York: Paulist, 1998.
Aune, David E. "Heracles and Christ: Heracles Imagery in the Christology of Early Christianity." Pages 3–19 in *Greeks, Romans, and Christians: Essays in Honor of Abraham J. Malherbe*. Edited by David L. Balch, Everett Ferguson, and Wayne A. Meeks. Minneapolis: Fortress, 1990.
Barclay, John M. G. "Thessalonica and Corinth: Social Contrasts in Pauline Christianity." *JSNT* 47 (1992): 49–74.
Becker, Adam H., and Annette Yoshiko Reed, eds. *The Ways That Never Parted: Jews and Christians in Late Antiquity and the Early Middle Ages*. TSAJ 95. Tübingen: Mohr Siebeck, 2003.
Bercovitch, Eytan. "The Altar of Sin: Social Multiplicity and Christian Conversion among a New Guinea People." Pages 211–35 in *Religion and Cultural Studies*. Edited by Susan L. Mizruchi. Princeton: Princeton University Press, 2001.
Bourdieu, Pierre. *An Outline of a Theory of Practice*. Translated by Richard Nice. Cambridge Studies in Social and Cultural Anthropology 16. Cambridge: Cambridge University Press, 1977.
Brandom, Robert B. *Making It Explicit: Reasoning, Representing, and Discursive Commitment*. Cambridge, Mass.: Harvard University Press, 1994.
Brubaker, Rogers. *Ethnicity without Groups*. Cambridge, Mass.: Harvard University Press, 2004.
Buell, Denise Kimber. *Why This New Race: Ethnic Reasoning in Early Christianity*. New York: Columbia University Press, 2005.
Bultmann, Rudolf. *Theology of the New Testament*. Translated by Kendrick Grobel. 2 vols. London: SCM, 1952–55.
Burtchaell, James Tunstead. *From Synagogue to Church: Public Services and Offices in the Earliest Christian Communities*. Cambridge: Cambridge University Press, 1992.
Cameron, Ron, and Merrill P. Miller, eds. *Redescribing Christian Origins*. SBLSymS 28. Atlanta: Society of Biblical Literature; Leiden and Boston: Brill, 2004.

Chow, John K. *Patronage and Power: A Study of Social Networks in Corinth*. JSNTSup 75. Sheffield: JSOT Press, 1992.

Clarke, Andrew D. *Secular and Christian Leadership in Corinth: A Socio-Historical and Exegetical Study of 1 Corinthians 1–6*. AGJU 18. Leiden: Brill, 1993.

Conte, Gian Biagio. *The Hidden Author: An Interpretation of Petronius' Satyricon*. Translated by Elaine Fantham. Sather Classical Lectures 60. Berkeley: University of California Press, 1996.

Courtney, Edward. *A Companion to Petronius*. Oxford: Oxford University Press, 2001.

Crook, Zeba A. *Reconceptualising Conversion: Patronage, Loyalty, and Conversion in the Religions of the Ancient Mediterranean*. BZNW 130. Berlin and New York: de Gruyter, 2004.

Davies, Jon. *Death, Burial and Rebirth in the Religions of Antiquity*. Religion in the First Christian Centuries. London and New York: Routledge, 1999.

DeMaris, Richard E. "Corinthian Religion and Baptism for the Dead (1 Corinthians 15:29): Insights from Archaeology and Anthropology." *JBL* 114 (1995): 661–82.

———. "Cults and the Imperial Cult in Early Roman Corinth: Literary Versus Material Record." Pages 73–91 in *Zwischen den Reichen: Neues Testament und Römische Herrschaft*. Edited by Michael Labahn and Jürgen Zangenberg. Texte und Arbeiten zum neutestamentlichen Zeitalter 36. Tübingen: Francke, 2002.

Donfried, Karl P. "The Cults of Thessalonica and the Thessalonian Correspondence." *NTS* 31 (1985): 336–56.

Downing, F. Gerald, ed. *Making Sense in (and of) the First Christian Century*. JSNTSup 197. Sheffield: Sheffield Academic Press, 2000.

Eisenbaum, Pamela. "A Remedy for Having Been Born of Woman: Jesus, Gentiles, and Genealogy in Romans." *JBL* 123 (2004): 671–702.

Engberg-Pedersen, Troels, ed. *Paul Beyond the Judaism/Hellenism Divide*. Louisville: Westminster John Knox, 2001.

Glad, Clarence E. *Paul and Philodemus: Adaptability in Epicurean and Early Christian Psychagogy*. NovTSup 81. Leiden: Brill, 1995.

Hall, Jonathan M. *Ethnic Identity in Greek Antiquity*. Cambridge: Cambridge University Press, 1997.

Harland, Philip A. *Associations, Synagogues, and Congregations: Claiming a Place in Ancient Mediterranean Society*. Minneapolis: Fortress, 2003.

Hendrix, Holland L. "Thessalonians Honor Romans." Th.D. diss., Harvard Divinity School, 1984.

Hopkins, Keith. *Death and Renewal*. Sociological Studies in Roman History 2. New York and Cambridge: Cambridge University Press, 1983.

Horsley, Richard A., ed. *Paul and Empire: Religion and Power in Roman Imperial Society*. Harrisburg, Pa.: Trinity Press International, 1997.

———, ed. *Paul and Politics: Ekklesia, Israel, Imperium, Interpretation*. Essays in Honor of Krister Stendahl. Harrisburg, Pa.: Trinity Press International, 2000.

Hurd, John Coolidge, Jr. *The Origin of I Corinthians*. London: SPCK, 1965.

Johnson Hodge, Caroline. *If Sons, Then Heirs: A Study of Kinship and Ethnicity in the Letters of Paul*. New York: Oxford University Press, 2007.

Johnston, Sarah Iles, ed. *Religions of the Ancient World: A Guide*. Cambridge, Mass., and London: Harvard University Press, 2004.

———. *Restless Dead: Encounters between the Living and the Dead in Ancient Greece*. Berkeley: University of California Press, 1999.

Judge, E. A. "The Early Christians as a Scholastic Community." *JRH* 1 (1960-61): 4-15, 125-37.
———. *The Social Pattern of the Christian Groups in the First Century: Some Prolegomena to the Study of New Testament Ideas of Social Obligation*. London: Tyndale, 1960.
Keane, Webb. "Materialism, Missionaries, and Modern Subjects in Colonial Indonesia." Pages 137-70 in *Conversion to Modernities: The Globalization of Christianity*. Edited by Peter van der Veer. Zones of Religion. New York: Routledge, 1996.
Kloppenborg, John S. "Edwin Hatch, Churches and *Collegia*." Pages 212-38 in *Origins and Method: Towards a New Understanding of Judaism and Christianity. Essays in Honour of John C. Hurd*. Edited by Bradley H. McLean. JSNTSup 86. Sheffield: JSOT Press, 1993.
Kloppenborg, John S., and Stephen G. Wilson, eds. *Voluntary Associations in the Graeco-Roman World*. London and New York: Routledge, 1996.
Long, A. A. "Hellenistic Ethics and Philosophical Power." Pages 138-56 in *Hellenistic History and Culture*. Edited by Peter Green. Hellenistic Culture and Society 9. Berkeley: University of California Press, 1993.
Long, A. A., and D. N. Sedley. *The Hellenistic Philosophers*. 2 vols. Cambridge: Cambridge University Press, 1987.
Mack, Burton L. *The Christian Myth: Origins, Logic, and Legacy*. New York: Continuum, 2001.
———. *A Myth of Innocence: Mark and Christian Origins*. Philadelphia: Fortress, 1988. Repr., Minneapolis: Fortress, 2006.
———. "Social Formation." Pages 283-96 in *Guide to the Study of Religion*. Edited by Willi Braun and Russell T. McCutcheon. London: Cassell, 2000.
———. *Who Wrote the New Testament? The Making of the Christian Myth*. San Francisco: HarperSanFrancisco, 1995.
Malherbe, Abraham J. *Paul and the Popular Philosophers*. Minneapolis: Fortress, 1989.
Martin, Dale B. *The Corinthian Body*. New Haven: Yale University Press, 1995.
———. "Slave Families and Slaves in Families." Pages 207-30 in *Early Christian Families in Context: An Interdisciplinary Dialogue*. Edited by David L. Balch and Carolyn Osiek. Religion, Marriage and Family. Grand Rapids: Eerdmans, 2003.
McCane, Byron R. *Roll Back the Stone: Death and Burial in the World of Jesus*. Harrisburg, Pa.: Trinity Press International, 2003.
Meeks, Wayne A. *The First Urban Christians: The Social World of the Apostle Paul*. New Haven: Yale University Press, 1983.
Meggitt, Justin J. *Paul, Poverty and Survival*. Studies of the New Testament and Its World. Edinburgh: T&T Clark, 1998.
Mitchell, Margaret M. *Paul and the Rhetoric of Reconciliation: An Exegetical Investigation of the Language and Composition of 1 Corinthians*. HUT 28. Tübingen: Mohr Siebeck, 1991.
Murphy-O'Connor, Jerome. *St. Paul's Corinth: Texts and Archaeology*. GNS 6. Wilmington, Del.: Glazier, 1983.
Nock, Arthur Darby. *Essays on Religion and the Ancient World*. Edited by Zeph Stewart. 2 vols. Oxford: Clarendon, 1972.
Økland, Jorunn. *Women in Their Place: Paul and the Corinthian Discourse of Gender and Sanctuary Space*. JSNTSup 269. London: T&T Clark, 2004.
Padel, Ruth. *In and Out of the Mind: Greek Images of the Tragic Self*. Princeton: Princeton University Press, 1992.

Poland, Franz. *Geschichte des griechischen Vereinswesens*. Preisschriften gekrönt und herausgegeben von der fürstlich Jablonowskischen Gesellschaft zu Leipzig 38. Leipzig: Teubner, 1909. Repr., Leipzig: Zentral-Antiquariat der Deutschen Demokratischen Republik, 1967.

Rafael, Vicente L. *Contracting Colonialism: Translation and Christian Conversion in Tagalog Society under Early Spanish Rule*. Ithaca, N.Y.: Cornell University Press, 1988. Repr., Durham, N.C.: Duke University Press, 1993.

Sahlins, Marshall. *Historical Metaphors and Mythical Realities: Structure in the Early History of the Sandwich Islands Kingdom*. Association for Social Anthropology in Oceania 1. Ann Arbor: University of Michigan Press, 1981.

Sanders, E. P. *Paul and Palestinian Judaism: A Comparison of Patterns of Religion*. Philadelphia: Fortress, 1977.

Schatzki, Theodore R. *The Site of the Social: A Philosophical Account of the Constitution of Social Life and Change*. University Park: Pennsylvania State University Press, 2002.

———. *Social Practices: A Wittgensteinian Approach to Human Activity and the Social*. New York: Cambridge University Press, 1996.

Schatzki, Theodore R., Karin Knorr Cetina, and Eike von Savigny, eds. *The Practice Turn in Contemporary Theory*. London and New York: Routledge, 2001.

Schowalter, Daniel N., and Steven J. Friesen, eds. *Urban Religion in Roman Corinth: Interdisciplinary Approaches*. HTS 53. Cambridge, Mass.: Harvard Divinity School, 2005.

Smith, Dennis E. *From Symposium to Eucharist: The Banquet in the Early Christian World*. Minneapolis: Fortress, 2003.

Smith, Jonathan Z. *Drudgery Divine: On the Comparison of Early Christianities and the Religions of Late Antiquity*. Jordan Lectures in Comparative Religion 14. London: School of Oriental and African Studies, University of London; Chicago: University of Chicago Press, 1990.

———. "The 'End' of Comparison: Redescription and Rectification." Pages 237–41 in *A Magic Still Dwells: Comparative Religion in the Postmodern Age*. Edited by Kimberley C. Patton and Benjamin C. Ray. Berkeley and Los Angeles: University of California Press, 2000.

———. *Imagining Religion: From Babylon to Jonestown*. CSHJ. Chicago: University of Chicago Press, 1982.

———. *Map Is Not Territory: Studies in the History of Religions*. SJLA 23. Leiden: Brill, 1978. Repr., Chicago: University of Chicago Press, 1993.

———. *Relating Religion: Essays in the Study of Religion*. Chicago: University of Chicago Press, 2004.

———. "Too Much Kingdom, Too Little Community." *Zygon* 13 (1978): 123–30.

Snyder, Graydon F. *Inculturation of the Jesus Tradition: The Impact of Jesus on Jewish and Roman Cultures*. Harrisburg, Pa.: Trinity Press International, 1999.

Stowers, Stanley K. "Apostrophe, ΠΡΟΣΩΠΟΠΟΙΙΑ and Paul's Rhetorical Education." Pages 351–69 in *Early Christianity and Classical Culture: Comparative Studies in Honor of Abraham J. Malherbe*. Edited by John T. Fitzgerald, Thomas H. Olbricht, and L. Michael White. NovTSup 110. Leiden: Brill, 2003.

———. "A Cult from Philadelphia: Oikos Religion or Cultic Association?" Pages 287–301 in *The Early Church in Its Context: Essays in Honor of Everett Ferguson*. Edited by Abraham J. Malherbe, Frederick W. Norris, and James W. Thompson. NovTSup 90. Leiden: Brill, 1998.

---. "Elusive Coherence: Ritual and Rhetoric in 1 Corinthians 10–11." Pages 68–83 in *Reimagining Christian Origins: A Colloquium Honoring Burton L. Mack*. Edited by Elizabeth A. Castelli and Hal Taussig. Valley Forge, Pa.: Trinity Press International, 1996.

---. "Greeks Who Sacrifice and Those Who Do Not: Toward an Anthropology of Greek Religion." Pages 293–333 in *The Social World of the First Christians: Essays in Honor of Wayne A. Meeks*. Edited by L. Michael White and O. Larry Yarbrough. Minneapolis: Fortress, 1995.

---. "Paul and Self-Mastery." Pages 524–50 in *Paul and the Greco-Roman World: A Handbook*. Edited by J. Paul Sampley. Harrisburg, Pa.: Trinity Press International, 2003.

---. "Paul and Slavery: A Response." *Semeia* 83–84 (1998): 295–311.

---. *A Rereading of Romans: Justice, Jews, and Gentiles*. New Haven: Yale University Press, 1994.

---. "Social Status, Public Speaking, and Private Teaching: The Circumstances of Paul's Preaching Activity." *NovT* 26 (1984): 59–82.

---. "Theorizing the Religion of Ancient Households and Families." Pages 5–19 in *Household and Family Religion in Antiquity*. Edited by John Bodel and Saul M. Olyan. The Ancient World: Comparative Histories. Oxford: Blackwell, 2008.

---. "What Is 'Pauline Participation in Christ'?" Pages 352–71 in *Redefining First-Century Jewish and Christian Identities: Essays in Honor of Ed Parish Sanders*. Edited by Fabian E. Udoh, with Susannah Heschel, Mark Chancey, and Gregory Tatum. Christianity and Judaism in Antiquity Series 16. Notre Dame: Notre Dame University Press, 2008.

Theissen, Gerd. *The Social Setting of Pauline Christianity: Essays on Corinth*. Edited and translated by John H. Schütz. Philadelphia: Fortress, 1982.

Tropper, J. "Spirit of the Dead." Pages 1524–30 in *Dictionary of Deities and Demons in the Bible (DDD)*. Edited by Karel van der Toorn, Bob Becking, and Pieter W. van der Horst. Leiden: Brill, 1995.

Van Nijf, Onno M. *The Civic World of Professional Associations in the Roman East*. Dutch Monographs on Ancient History and Archaeology 17. Amsterdam: Gieben, 1997.

Wallace-Hadrill, Andrew. "*Mutatio morum*: The Idea of a Cultural Revolution." Pages 3–22 in *The Roman Cultural Revolution*. Edited by Thomas Habinek and Alessandro Schiesaro. Cambridge: Cambridge University Press, 1997.

Waltzing, Jean Pierre. *Étude historique sur les corporations professionnelles chez les Romains depuis les origines jusqu'à la chute de l'Empire d'Occident*. 4 vols. Mémoire couronne par l'Academie royale des Sciences, des Lettres et des Beaux-Arts de Belgique. Louvain: Peeters, 1895–1900. Repr., Hildesheim: Olms, 1970.

Wasserman, Emma. *The Death of the Soul in Romans 7: Sin, Death, and the Law in Light of Hellenistic Moral Psychology*. WUNT 2/256. Tübingen: Mohr Siebeck, 2008.

Williams, Margaret. *The Jews among the Greeks and Romans: A Diasporan Sourcebook*. Baltimore: Johns Hopkins University Press, 1998.

Williams, Sam K. *Jesus' Death as Saving Event: The Background and Origin of a Concept*. HDR 2. Missoula, Mont.: Scholars Press, 1975.

Index of Ancient Texts

Hebrew Bible

Genesis
2:24	134
5:24	46
12:2–3	60
15:6	60
18:18	60

Leviticus
19:31	30
20:5–6	30
20:27	30

Deuteronomy
16:1-8	224

1 Samuel
28:13	30

2 Samuel
14:16	30

Ezra
9:4–5	224

Psalms
46	172

Isaiah
8:19	30

Daniel
6:11	224

Micah
3:7	30

Jewish Apocrypha and Pseudepigrapha

4 Ezra
3:35–36	91

Judith
9:1	224

Wisdom of Solomon
3:1-9	46

New Testament

Matthew
16:18	206

Mark
13:24	174

Luke
1:10	224
24:37	29
24:39	29

Acts
2:4	31
3:1	224
10:2	197
10:22	197
10:35	197
11:30	198
13:5–12	197
13:5–42	197
13:14	200
13:16	197
13:26	197

Acts (*continued*)
13:43	197
13:44	200
13:50	197
14:1	197, 200
14:23	198
15	206
15:2	198
15:4	198
15:22	198
15:23	198
16:4	198
16:11-40	197
16:13	200
16:14	197
16:18-19	75
17:1-8	176
17:1-9	197
17:4	197
17:10–15	197
17:17	197
18:1-8	197
18:1-9	201
18:7	197
18:7-8	198
18:8	199
18:24	205
18:24–25	82
19:24–29	75
20:7	200
20:17	198

Romans
1:13	94
1:16–4:25	90
1:18-32	231, 233
1:18-2:16	275
1:18-2:29	91
2:9-10	95
2:17–24	90, 260
2:21-23	91
2:24	91
3:9	95
3:21-26	41, 42
4:4–5	265
5:12–17	92
5:17	95

6:3–4	97, 263
6:6	94, 103
6:23	118
7:4	180
8:2–5	98
8:9-17	98
8:13	180
8:29	147
8:36	180
11:1-32	91
12:1-2	235, 239
12:1-3	138
12:3–8	138
12:3–21	239
12:6–8	196
13:1-7	103
15:25–27	88
15:25–28	240
15:33	94
16	94, 246, 255
16:1	94, 192
16:1-2	192
16:4	94, 192
16:5	94, 191
16:6	192
16:10–11	191
16:16	94
16:23	94, 192, 203, 256

1 Corinthians
1	264, 284
1-4	205, 206, 208
1:2	192, 230, 297
1:4–7	4
1:10	3, 108
1:10–16	118, 122
1:10–17	205, 253, 283
1:11	4, 87
1:12	88, 205, 209
1:12–13	82
1:13	206
1:13–17	97
1:14	192, 199
1:14–16	88, 253
1:16	192
1:17	3, 118
1:18–2:13	115

1:21–25	101	7:27	233
1:21–29	262	7:30–31	226, 240
1:23	3	7:32–34	230
1:26	126, 254	7:32–35	230
1:26–29	100	7:35	230
2:2	3, 4, 36	7:39	180, 273
3:1	4	7:40	31
3:1–9	206	8–10	133, 205, 206, 209, 272, 273
3:4	88		
3:4–5	205, 206	8–11	126, 133
3:5–15	88	8:1–6	230
3:10–11	4	8:7	207
3:10–15	289	8:10	111
3:10–17	206, 213	9	240
3:11	230	9:1–27	227
3:14	213	9:23	233
3:15	214	9:24–27	233, 267
3:22	205, 206	10:1	125
4:6	205, 206	10:2	250
4:11–13	227, 240	10:1–3	124, 265
4:14–21	289	10:1–13	283
4:15	3, 4	10:1–22	136
4:18–21	4	10:2	97
5	209	10:14	273
5–16	206	10:14–22	274
5:1	124, 265	10:14–30	31
5:1–13	207, 208	10:16	135
5:3–4	31	10:16–17	285
5:3–5	4	10:17	34
5:9	4, 87	10:17–18	138
5:10	277	10:20–21	285
5:13	209	10:32	192
6	134, 208	11	6, 7, 37, 51, 56, 141, 213, 235, 250, 280, 281, 301
6:1–8	206		
6:1–11	207		
6:5	208	11–14	141, 273
6:12–20	207	11:1	234
6:13	206	11:2	4, 213
6:15–19	134	11:16	4, 192
7	87, 205, 230	11:17	213
7:1	4, 87, 206	11:17–19	205
7:14	272, 283	11:17–22	136, 266
7:17	192	11:17–26	240
7:19	230	11:17–34	58, 207
7:20–24	194	11:18	4, 109, 192, 209, 256
7:21	89	11:18–19	140, 253
7:22	255	11:18–22	135, 240

1 Corinthians (*continued*)

11:19	133	14:34	192
11:19–33	109	14:37–38	4
11:20–21	31	15	6, 7, 11, 32, 34, 50, 64, 122, 151, 248, 250, 251, 269, 281
11:20–22	239	15:1–2	4
11:21	141	15:3	282
11:21–22	136	15:3–5	36, 38, 40, 56, 78, 79, 93, 94, 97, 103, 280
11:22	140, 192, 213		
11:23	136	15:4	263, 281
11:23–25	36, 51, 78, 79, 183, 280	15:4a	281
11:23–26	31	15:5–8	282
11:24–26	240	15:6	180
11:27	133, 136	15:12	146, 282
11:26	300	15:13	47, 95
11:28–29	134	15:18	180
11:29	134, 240	15:20	47, 180, 263
11:30	134, 180	15:21–22	179
11:30–32	134, 240	15:22–23	4
11:31–32	32	15:24	263
11:33	215	15:24–28	232
11:33–34	136	15:26	179, 263, 277
11:34	239	15:29	31, 34, 97, 125, 184, 194, 282, 283, 284
12	140, 300, 301		
12:1	125	15:32	184
12:1–2	124, 265	15:35	282
12:2	125	15:35–41	134
12:7	300	15:44–47	134
12:11	300	15:45	34, 64, 248
12:12–13	4	15:50	137
12:12–14	34, 248	15:51	180
12:13	97, 283	15:51–57	184
12:14–27	141	15:52	46
12:27	4, 34, 248	15:54–55	179
12:28	4	16:1	192
12:28–30	196	16:1–4	4, 202
14	141, 300, 301	16:2	200
14:14–17	300	16:5–7	4
14:17	300	16:10–11	4
14:24–25	300	16:12	82
14:25	300	16:15	109, 121, 192
14:26	256, 300	16:15–16	253
14:26–33	300	16:15–18	118
14:26–38	109	16:16	121
14:31	301	16:17	121
14:33	192	16:19	191, 192

2 Corinthians	
1:1	192
1:15–16	4
1:23	4
2:1	4
6:9	180
7:6–8	4
8–9	291
8:1	192
8:1–3	180
8:2–4	88
8:6	4
8:14	291
8:16	4
8:18	192
10–13	205
11:5	205
11:7–11	291
11:8	192
11:13	205
11:22	265
11:28	192
12:11–13	291
12:13	192
12:14	4
12:16	291
13:1–3	4

Galatians	
1:2	192
1:11–12	38
1:15	48
1:17	76
1:18	82
1:22	192
2	206
2:12–13	206
3:6	147
3:6–9	60
3:6–14	90
3:8	38, 59
3:14	148
3:16	92, 99
3:27	97
3:27–28	147, 148
3:29	97, 148
5:3	90

Philippians	
2:6–11	69
2:10–11	232
2:15	90
2:25–26	88
3:3–6	265
3:5	90
3:6	90
3:20	170, 179

Colossians	
4:15	191

1 Thessalonians	
1:1	192, 195, 201
1:6	31, 275
1:9	86, 176, 178
1:9–10	179
1:10	154, 179, 233, 263, 271
2:1–12	180
2:9	227
2:14	192, 275
4	151
4:1–5	233
4:1–8	178
4:1–12	178
4:1–5:11	178
4:6	179
4:9–12	178
4:13	160, 178, 180, 274, 277
4:13–14	95
4:13–18	11, 12, 151, 153, 154, 172, 176, 184, 271, 272, 275, 276, 278, 279, 282
4:13–5:11	172, 194
4:14	180
4:15	180
4:17b	271
5:1–11	178
5:2	154
5:3	103
5:9	179, 271
5:9–10	271
5:13–22	176
5:23	31

2 Thessalonians
1:1	192

1 Timothy
3:5	192

Titus
1:5	198
3:13	208

Philemon
2	191

Hebrews
11:5–6	46
12:23	29

James
1:1	199
2:2	199

1 Peter
1:1	199
3:19	29
4:17	192

EARLY CHRISTIAN LITERATURE

Apostolic Constitutions
6.30	278

Barnabas
15.9	200

1 Clement
1.3	199
37.2	199
44–54	296
44.5	199
47	2, 205
47.6	199
57.1	199

Didache
9–10	56
9.4	56

Didascalia Apostolorum
6.22	278

Epiphanius, *Panarion*
30.11	199
30.18	199

Eusebius, *Historia ecclesiastica*
1.3.12	195

Justin, *1 Apology*
65–67	137
67	200

Origen, *Contra Celsum*
1.1	195
3.23	195
8.17	195

Tertullian, *Apology*
39	195

GREEK AND LATIN TEXTS

Appian, *Historia romana*
8.136	255

Aristophanes, *Birds*
1296	203

Aristotle, *Ethica nichomachea*
7.1153b19	234

Epictetus, *Diatribae*
3.3.5	230

Herodotus, *Historiae*
8.138.1	165

Hippocrates, *De morbo sacro*
20	132

Isaeus
8	130
8.16	130

Josephus, *Against Apion*
2.137   225

Josephus, *Jewish Antiquities*
13.5.9 §§171-73   237
14.10.8 §§213-14 202
14.10.8 §215   202
16.6.2 §164   202
18.1.3-5 §§12-20 237

Josephus, *Jewish War*
2.8.2-14 §§119-66 237
2.8.14 §§162-66   238

Livy
2.33.11   162

Lucian, *De morte Peregrini*
11   195

Lucretius, *De rerum natura*
2.1150-52   174

Pausanias, *Graeciae descriptio*
10.12.10   175

Petronius, *Satyricon*
1-2   119
5   119, 144
48.4   121
57.4   121
85   119

Philo, *De gigantibus*
47-57   46

Philo, *Hypothetica*
11.1-18   238

Philo, *Legatio ad Gaium*
133   201
156   201, 224

Philo, *De vita Mosis*
1.158-59   46
2.216   202
2.288-91   46

Philo, *Quod omnis probus liber sit*
75-88   238
81   203

Philo, *De sacrificiis Abelis et Caini*
8-10   46

Philo, *De virtutibus*
73-79   46

Pindar, *Nemeonikai*
3.22   146

Plato, *Politicus*
287C   132

Pliny the Elder, *Naturalis historia*
7.16.73   174
21.10   162
33.138   162

Pliny the Younger, *Epistulae*
10.34   195
10.96   195

Plutarch, *De defectu oraculorum*
437A-C   131
438A-B   131

Plutarch, *Stoicos absurdiora poetis dicere*
4 (1058B-C)   232

Seneca, *Epistulae morales*
14.14   233

Seneca, *Hercules furens*
889-90   147

Seneca, *De providentia*
1.5.5   232

Pseudo-Seneca, *Octavia*
391-94   174

Strabo, *Geographica*
7, frg. 21   155, 156
7, frg. 24   155
8.6.23   255

316 Index of Ancient Texts

Theophrastus, *De causis plantarum*
1.13.11   165

Theophrastus, *Historia plantarum*
6.64   165

Valerius Maximus
4.4.2   162
5.2.3   162
5.6.8   162

Virgil, *Georgica*
1.468ff., 493, 500f.   174

Inscriptions and Papyri

CIG 2000f	161
CIG 2271	195
CIG 3421	195
CIJ I 694	201
CIJ II 1404	203
CIL III 656	164
CIL III 703	164, 165
CIL III 704	164, 165
CIL III 707	164, 165
CIL V 2283	159
CIL VI 9148–49	193
CIL VI 10260–64	193
CIL VI 17985a	159
CIL VI 26003	159
CIL VI 26032	193
CIL VI 31615	167
CIL IX 1837	159
CIL XI 3711	159
CIL XI 5047	164
CIL XIV 2112	162, 163, 167, 191, 200, 211, 212
CJZC 72	203
ICos 36	166
IDelos 1519	195, 204
IDelta 889.29	214
IEphesos 2212	169
IEphesos 3214	166
IEphesos 3803	166
IG I³ 136	203
IG I³ 383	203
IG II² 337	203
IG II² 1275	162
IG II² 1278	162
IG II² 1283	200
IG II² 1283.4–7	203
IG II² 1283.32–36	215
IG II² 1284	200
IG II² 1297	214
IG II² 1327	170, 214
IG II² 1327.30–32	214
IG II² 1328.12	214
IG II² 1330.42	214
IG II² 1361	200
IG II² 1368	162, 191, 195, 211
IG II² 1369	195
IG II² 1369.42	214
IG II² 2343	210
IG II² 2345	210
IG X/2 4	158
IG X/2 31	158
IG X/2 32	158
IG X/2 72	201
IG X/2 133	158
IG X/2 226	158
IG X/2 259	164
IG X/2 260	164, 165
IG X/2 288	161
IG X/2 289	161
IG X/2 291	161
IG X/2 309	161
IG X/2 480	161
IG X/2 503	161
IG X/2 821	161
IG X/2 824	169
IG XI/4 1299	204
IG XII/1 155	163
IG XII/3 330	166, 182
IG XII/5 593	161
IG XII/7 515	166
IGR IV 661	166
IGUR 160	193, 195, 204
IHierapJ 227	169
IJO II 36	204
IJudEg 9	203
IJudEg 16	203
IJudEg 17	203
IJudEg 25	201
IJudEg 127	203

Index of Ancient Texts

IJudEg 129	203	*PCairoDem* 30605	162
IKilikiaBM 2 197	169	*PCairoDem* 30606	162
IKilikiaBM 2 201	162, 169	*PEnteuxeis* 20	163
IKyme 45	204	*PEnteuxeis* 21	163
ILS II/2 7259	194	*PLond* VII 2193	211
IMakedD 920	164, 165	*PMich* V 243	211
IPhilippi 029/1	164, 165	*PMichTebt* 243	162
IPhilippi 133	164, 165	*PMichTebt* 244	162
IPontEux II 449–52	171	*SEG* III 674	166
IPontEux II 456	171	*SEG* XXXVII 559	161
ITralleis 1	175	*SEG* XLIV 556	201
LBW 1381–82	195	*SIG*³ 985	193, 195, 204
LSCG 77	161	*SIG*³ 1106	166
MAMA VI 264	204	*SIG*³ 1140	157

Select Index of Modern Authors

Adams, Edward, 2, 3
Anderson, Bernhard W., 29–30
Arnal, William E., 5, 247–48, 252–54, 256–58, 260–62, 264
Ascough, Richard S., 86, 249, 254–55, 270–72, 274–75, 280–81, 284

Barclay, John M. G., 3, 177
Beard, Mary, 168
Beare, Francis W., 162
Bercovitch, Eytan, 23–26, 33, 110, 296
Bodel, John, 175–76
Braun, Willi, 7, 8
Brubaker, Rogers, 148
Buck, Peter, 17
Bultmann, Rudolf, 66, 67, 188
Burridge, Kenelm, 26
Burtchaell, James Tunstead, 199, 201

Cameron, Ron, 6, 181
Cancik, Hubert, 173, 174–75
Clarke Andrew D., 208
Conzelmann, Hans, 200
Cormack, Sarah, 182
Crook, Zeba A., 290–91, 300–301

DeMaris, Richard E., 282–83
Donfried, Karl P., 157
Downing, F. Gerald, 173, 174
Dunbabin, Katherine M. D., 163

Evans, Craig A., 172

Firth, Raymond, 25
Fraser, Peter M., 169
Fredriksen, Paula, 299

Gagé, Jean, 190–91
Gager, John G., 96
Gaster, Theodor H., 181
Goody, Jack, 23
Gordon, Mary L., 255
Gordon, Richard, 168, 297
Grant, Robert M., 17

Hall, Jonathan M., 102
Harris, Stephen L., 80–81
Hendrix, Holland L., 156, 157, 158
Hengel, Martin, 173
Hicks, Edward L., 166
Hill, Judith L., 179
Horn, F. W., 29
Horrell, David G., 2, 3
Horsley, Richard A., 104
Hull, Michael F., 283–84

Johnson Hodge, Caroline, 60, 268
Johnston, Sarah Iles, 159, 278
Jones, C. P., 166
Judge, E. A., 194

Keane, Webb, 19–20
Kempf, Wolfgang, 32–33
Klauck, Hans-Josef, 159
Kloppenborg, John S., 5, 13, 14, 173, 245, 256, 287–88

Lawrence, Peter, 32
Lopez, Davina C., 265

MacDonald, Margaret Y., 3
Mack, Burton L., 6–7, 12, 34, 82, 84, 99, 147, 152, 154–55, 172, 178–79, 183–84, 249, 251, 258–61, 268, 274, 276, 298, 301

Malherbe, Abraham J., 155, 176, 246
Martin, Dale B., 255, 273
Martin, Luther H., 302
May, Alistair Scott, 272–73
McCane, Byron R., 47, 171–72, 177, 180, 181, 271, 277–79
Meeks, Wayne A., 176, 180, 194, 196–97
Milgrom, Jacob, 30
Miller, Merrill P., 181

Newton, Derek, 273
Nock, Arthur Darby, 182, 183, 220

Økland, Jorunn, 273

Papazoglou, Fanoula, 156
Paton, William R., 166
Patterson, John R., 170–71
Peerbolte, Bert Jan Lietaert, 179
Poland, Franz, 164, 196
Putnam, Hilary, 128

Rauh, Nicholas K., 169
Reicke, Bo I., 210
Reynolds, Joyce, 168
Richard, Earl J., 153, 154–55
Rife, Joseph Lee, 12, 270
Roberts, Colin, 220
Robertson, C. K., 3
Roueché, C., 168

Sahlins, Marshall, 28, 111
Sanders, E. P., 96
Skeat, Theodore C., 220
Smith, Jonathan Z., 5–6, 8, 9, 10, 11, 27, 36, 47, 65, 71, 76, 79, 85, 88, 97, 111, 125, 142–44, 147, 170, 179, 247–50, 253, 262, 264, 271, 274, 283, 285, 302
Snyder, Graydon F., 273–74, 279, 285
Stowers, Stanley K., 3, 4, 6, 11, 13, 14, 33, 42, 247–49, 251–52, 254, 256, 258, 262–63, 265–67, 269, 272, 276, 282, 286–89, 291–93, 299

Theissen, Gerd, 246
Thomas, Christine M., 270
Tocqueville, Alexis de, 220

Vaage, Leif E., 292
Vacalopoulos, Apostolos P., 155, 157–58
Van Gennep, Arnold, 171
Van Nijf, Onno M., 161, 165, 166, 167, 168, 169, 170

Walbank, Mary E. Hoskins, 12, 277
Wallace-Hadrill, Andrew, 276
Wanamaker, Charles A., 153–54
Welborn, L. L., 208
Wilken, Robert L., 191

Index of Subjects

Abraham myth, 4, 38, 58–60, 62–65, 83, 91–93, 97–98, 102, 121–25, 142, 147–48, 242, 249, 254, 258–59, 261, 264–65, 267–69
ancestor, 18–19, 23, 25, 27, 29–34, 52, 63–65, 71, 81, 84, 89–90, 92, 102, 111–13, 117, 121–23, 125–26, 136, 138, 141, 147, 155–56, 159, 175–76, 215–16, 225, 247–51, 253–56, 258, 260, 264–65, 267–69, 272–75, 282, 285, 294, 299–300
ancestry. *See* ancestor
apocalyptic, 3, 11–12, 14, 18, 40, 46–50, 53, 58–59, 61–63, 69, 79, 84, 93, 95, 96–97, 103, 151–53, 172–73, 175–79, 181, 230, 249, 259, 261–64, 268, 271–72, 275–77, 289, 292
Atbalmin, 22–29, 31, 34, 63, 71–72, 105–6, 110–12, 116, 248, 250–51, 253, 275, 280, 295–96
attraction, 1, 4, 11, 15, 27, 34, 59, 72, 75, 81–82, 86, 89, 98–100, 105–6, 109–12, 116–23, 126, 128, 141, 144, 157, 175, 178–79, 197, 246–49, 251–53, 256–57, 261, 280, 290, 293–94

baptism for the dead, 31, 34, 97, 109, 117, 125, 184, 194, 250, 254, 269, 282–84, 295
benefaction, 76, 156, 158, 163–64, 166, 195, 207, 212–14, 216, 290–92, 299–301

Christ myth, 1, 5–8, 14–15, 26–27, 31–39, 42, 45–51, 53–54, 58–66, 68–69, 83, 93, 101–4, 133, 135, 137, 142, 147, 149, 183, 227, 247, 250, 258–66, 280, 282, 289–90, 293, 295, 297–98

collective identity, 3–5, 12, 15, 52, 63, 72, 84, 90, 92–93, 97, 102, 169–70, 260, 263, 270, 290, 297
collegia, 14, 160–62, 166–68, 170, 173, 190–91, 193–96, 204–5, 209, 216, 227, 256, 286–89
community, 3–6, 9, 11, 13, 15, 23–24, 27–28, 33, 35–38, 41, 51, 53–54, 65–66, 71–72, 108–12, 122, 127, 131, 133–35, 137, 148, 151–54, 156, 168, 173, 175–78, 180, 184, 190–91, 197, 199–200, 219–20, 222–24, 227, 229, 232, 235–38, 240, 243, 246, 268, 271–72, 279, 282, 283–85, 287, 289, 292–93, 297–99, 302
comparison, 1, 3, 9–10, 12–14, 22, 26–27, 29–30, 33–34, 42, 48, 50, 54, 63–64, 67–68, 71, 78, 97, 100, 105, 110, 116, 118–19, 126–29, 132–33, 138, 142, 145, 153, 155, 172, 179, 181, 188–90, 204, 219–22, 227, 229, 234, 238–39, 245–46, 249, 251–52, 257, 262–64, 270, 272, 282, 284, 286–90, 294–95, 297, 302
cults of the dead, 12, 14, 46, 71, 153, 155, 164, 172, 175, 177, 184, 271–74, 277–79, 285, 294
cultural field, 108, 110, 113–16, 119–22, 140–41, 144–47, 149, 231, 252, 256, 262–63, 289, 295, 302

deracination. *See* dislocation
disjunction, 1–2, 6–7, 9, 36, 78–81, 86–87, 89, 98, 100, 137–38, 142, 247–48, 252, 254, 257, 259–60, 266
dislocation, 3–4, 30, 80, 84, 89, 98–99, 102, 181, 250, 252–55, 264–65, 274, 285, 290

321

322 INDEX OF SUBJECTS

ethnic identity, 63, 84, 87, 93, 99, 102, 230, 253, 258, 267–68, 302
ethnic mix, 4, 41–42, 61, 80, 82, 89, 92, 98, 116, 120, 147, 252–54, 265
experimentation, 18, 28, 34, 70, 99, 110–12, 117, 126, 141–42, 184, 216, 236, 251, 256–57, 280, 285, 290, 296–97

factions, 2, 4, 52, 82, 85, 88–89, 133, 192, 195, 205–6, 208–14, 246, 253–54, 256–57, 284, 287, 295
field. *See* cultural field

group identity. *See* collective identity

here, there, and anywhere, 10, 30, 65, 71, 88, 111–12, 170, 247, 249, 254–55, 271, 274, 285–86

intervention. *See* intrusion
intrusion, 5, 9, 11, 28–29, 34, 89, 94, 104, 111–13, 247, 253, 256–57, 275, 290, 294

kērygma, 6, 50, 58–60, 64, 78, 93, 250, 258, 263, 298

locative and utopian, 47, 65, 69, 88, 95–96, 112, 140–47, 149, 233, 249, 258, 262–63, 269, 276, 279, 283

martyr myth, 7–8, 37–50, 53–59, 61–62, 64, 66, 69, 72–73, 93–94, 117, 123, 133–34, 137, 139, 183, 237, 249, 258–61, 265–68, 281–82, 298, 300, 302
meals for the dead, 30–31, 129, 136, 141–42, 163–65, 171, 180, 182, 184, 250, 272–73, 276–81, 284–85, 294–95
misunderstandings, 11, 31, 34, 79–81, 153–54, 156, 247–49, 256, 260
mythmaking, 1, 7–8, 12, 15, 32, 34, 37, 39, 43, 45, 57, 61–62, 64, 70, 77, 87, 102, 106, 112, 117, 123–27, 134–35, 141–42, 146, 149, 152, 170, 172–73, 179, 181, 183–85, 233, 237–39, 248–50, 256–59, 261, 264–67, 269, 271, 275, 279, 282–83, 285–86, 288–90, 292–93, 297

paideia, 113–22, 142, 146, 251–52, 290, 293, 296–97
patronage, 2, 104, 121, 201, 208, 212, 246, 257, 290, 299–301
Paul and the Corinthians, 1–2, 4, 6, 8, 10–12, 14–15, 35–36, 51–52, 62, 68, 80, 105–6, 118, 126, 139, 142, 248, 251–52, 256–57, 260–61, 264, 269, 285–87, 289–90, 292, 295, 298, 302
Paul's gospel, 1–2, 4, 6, 8, 14, 36, 38, 45, 52–53, 57–60, 69–71, 75, 77–78, 80, 83, 89–90, 94, 98–99, 112, 121, 123, 148, 183, 190, 248, 251, 253–54, 257–61, 264, 267–68, 293, 295, 297–98
pneuma, 29–31, 112, 115, 117–18, 121–25, 128, 134–35, 137, 140, 142–43, 146–48, 249–51, 258–59, 265–68, 295
practices, 1–5, 8, 10, 13–14, 18–20, 23–25, 27, 30–32, 36–38, 42, 52, 57–58, 63, 65–71, 77–78, 81–82, 88, 90–91, 97–99, 106, 108, 110–15, 117, 119, 121–22, 125–29, 131, 133–36, 138, 140–42, 145–49, 151–52, 164–65, 167, 178–80, 182–84, 187, 189–90, 192, 200, 204, 208, 211, 213, 216, 220–29, 231, 234–43, 245, 247–51, 253–56, 262–64, 266–72, 274–75, 277–78, 280, 282–83, 286–97, 299–302
associative, 13, 51–52, 56, 73, 171, 188, 190, 194, 204, 209, 211–13, 222–23, 245, 270–71
burial, 12, 14, 50, 126, 141, 155, 161, 163–65, 167–70, 177, 179, 185, 270–72, 275, 277–79, 283–84
discursive, 138, 189, 221, 241, 264
intellectual, 6, 108, 116, 123, 126, 139–40, 234, 236–38, 241, 251–52, 256, 262, 287, 290, 293, 296
meal, 14, 30–34, 36, 44, 51–58, 63, 71–73, 79–81, 86, 111, 126–33, 135–38, 140–42, 160, 163–64, 171, 180–83, 191, 194, 197, 202, 205, 207, 209, 211, 213–15, 219–20, 229, 235, 239, 247, 250, 266–67, 269–72, 276–77, 280–85, 287–89, 293–95, 297, 299–300
memorial, 12, 14, 30, 51–54, 56–57, 64, 71, 129, 136, 141–42, 151, 153, 155,

158, 161–69, 171, 178–80, 183–84, 260, 270–72, 274, 276, 278–82, 285, 300
ritual, 5–7, 12, 15, 18, 20, 23, 28, 32–38, 51, 56–58, 66–68, 73, 117, 125–26, 130–31, 133–39, 141–42, 147, 162, 180, 183, 191–92, 194, 209, 215, 223, 225–26, 228, 230, 234–35, 239, 242–43, 250, 256–57, 266, 269, 272–73, 276–78, 280, 282–84, 288–90, 293, 297–301
sacrificial, 19–20, 34, 52, 71, 88, 111, 122, 125–26, 129–36, 138, 141–42, 166, 182, 205, 215, 223–26, 228, 234–35, 238–40, 242–43, 251, 258, 266, 272, 287–88, 293, 297, 299, 300

rectification, 1, 9–10, 12, 34, 101, 143, 153, 172–73, 253, 260, 262, 275–76, 290
redescription, 1–2, 5–6, 8–10, 12–15, 20, 27, 31, 34–36, 41, 59, 63, 66, 68–71, 73, 75–78, 80–81, 83, 87, 90, 96, 103, 153, 177, 247, 249, 251, 254, 257–59, 262, 275, 289–90, 295, 297–98, 302
resurrection, 4, 11, 32–34, 38–39, 45–50, 52–53, 58, 61–65, 67–69, 79–80, 93, 95, 97, 101, 123, 134, 143, 146, 151, 154, 162, 176, 179–80, 183–85, 248–50, 258–61, 263, 265, 267–69, 279, 281–85, 289, 295

situational incongruity, 11, 57, 61, 83–86, 90–93, 252–54, 259–61, 265, 290

social formation, 1, 4–5, 7–9, 12–13, 15, 27, 37–39, 41, 43–44, 55–57, 61–62, 64, 70, 72–73, 77–78, 83–84, 86, 101–3, 108–12, 125, 130, 135, 137, 149, 173, 178, 181, 185, 219, 221, 227, 229, 231, 235–36, 240–41, 248, 257, 261, 266, 271, 287, 289–90, 293, 299, 301–2
social fractions, 109, 115, 293–96
some Corinthians, 4–5, 29–34, 59, 63–65, 71, 85–86, 88–89, 98–99, 110–11, 116–18, 122, 125, 135–36, 140–42, 146–47, 184, 192, 202, 205, 207–8, 245–50, 253–57, 260, 264, 266, 274–75, 278–79, 281–83, 286, 290, 294, 296–97, 300
specialized knowledge, 4, 113, 116, 122, 125, 139, 234, 243, 252, 266, 269, 288, 295, 297
spirit myth, 4–5, 34, 52, 62–63, 259, 298
spirits of the dead, 25, 29–32, 63–65, 175, 249–50, 294, 300

translation, 1, 10–11, 24–25, 29–34, 42–43, 46, 50, 52, 63–65, 112–13, 141, 148, 178, 213–14, 234, 238, 248–51, 258, 264, 273, 276, 283–86, 290, 294, 299

West Papuans, 22, 25–26, 28–29, 33, 63, 71, 253, 264

Contributors

William E. Arnal
University of Regina
Regina, Saskatchewan

Richard S. Ascough
Queen's School of Religion
Kingston, Ontario

Ron Cameron
Wesleyan University
Middletown, Connecticut

John S. Kloppenborg
University of Toronto
Toronto, Ontario

Burton L. Mack
Claremont Graduate University
Claremont, California

Merrill P. Miller
University of North Carolina at Pembroke
Pembroke, North Carolina

Jonathan Z. Smith
University of Chicago
Chicago, Illinois

Stanley K. Stowers
Brown University
Providence, Rhode Island